THE COLLECTED PAPERS OF FRANCO MODIGLIANI

VOLUME 3

The Theory of Finance and Other Essays

THE COLLECTED PAPERS OF FRANCO MODIGLIANI

Edited by Andrew Abel

Franco Modigliani

The MIT Press
Cambridge, Massachusetts, and London, England

Second printing, 1986
Portrait of Franco Modigliani by Bachrach Photographers of Boston, Massachusetts.

See pages 481–483 for acknowledgments to publishers.

Printed and bound by Edwards Brothers, Inc.
in the United States of America

Library of Congress Cataloging in Publication Data

Modigliani, Franco.
The collected papers of Franco Modigliani.

Includes bibliographical references and indexes.
CONTENTS: v. 1. Essays in macroeconomics.—v. 2. The life cycle hypothesis of saving.—v. 3. Essays in the theory of finance. Stabilization policies. Essays in international finance. The role of expectations and plan in economic behavior. Miscellanea.
1. Economics—Addresses, essays, lectures. I. Abel, Andy.
HB171.M557 330 78-21041
ISBN 0-262-13150-1 (v.1)
ISBN 0-262-13151-X (v. 2)
ISBN 0-262-13152-8 (v. 3)

TO SERENA

CONTENTS

Volume 3 The Theory of Finance and Other Essays

Preface ix

Introduction xi

Part I. Essays in the Theory of Finance

1. "The Cost of Capital, Corporation Finance and the Theory of Investment," (with Merton H. Miller), *American Economic Review* 48 (June 1958): 261–297. 3
2. "Dividend Policy, Growth and the Valuation of Shares," (with Merton H. Miller), *Journal of Business* 34 (October 1961): 411–433. 40
3. "Corporate Income Taxes and the Cost of Capital: A Correction," (with Merton H. Miller), *American Economic Review* (June 1963): 433–443. 63
4. "A Theory and Test of Credit Rationing," (with Dwight M. Jaffee), *American Economic Review* 59 (December 1969): 850–872. 74
5. "Some Economic Implications of the Indexing of Financial Assets with Special Reference to Mortgages," *The New Inflation and Monetary Policy* by Mario Monti, pp. 90–116. London and Basingstoke: Macmillan, 1976. 97

Part II. Stabilization Policies

6. "Inflation, Balance of Payments Deficit and their Cure through Monetary Policy: The Italian Example," (with Giorgio La Malfa), *Banca Nazionale del Lavoro Quarterly Review,* no. 80 (March 1967): 3–47. 127
7. "The 1974 Report of the President's Council of Economic Advisers: A Critique of Past and Prospective Policies," *American Economic Review* 64 (September 1974): 544–557. 172
8. "Monetary Policy for the Coming Quarters: The Conflicting Views," (with Lucas Papademos), *New England Economic Review,* March/April 1976, pp. 2–35. 186

9. *The Management of an Open Economy with "100% Plus" Wage Indexation,* (with Tommaso Padoa-Schioppa), Essays in International Finance, no. 130. International Finance Section, Dept. of Economics, Princeton University, Dec. 1978. 220

Part III. Essays in International Finance

10. "A Suggestion for Solving the International Liquidity Problem," (with Peter Kenen), *Banca Nazionale del Lavoro Quarterly Review,* no. 76 (March 1966): 3–17. 263
11. *The Reform of the International Payments System,* (with Hossein Askari), Essays in International Finance, no. 89, pp. 3–28. International Finance Section, Dept. of Economics, Princeton University, Sept. 1971. 278
12. "International Capital Movements, Fixed Parities, and Monetary and Fiscal Policies," *Development and Planning: Essays in Honor of Paul Rosenstein-Rodan,* edited by Jagdish Bhagwati and Richard S. Eckaus, pp. 239–253. London: George Allen & Unwin, Ltd., 1972. 305
13. "The International Transfer of Capital and the Propagation of Domestic Disturbances Under Alternative Payment Systems," (with Hossein Askari), *Banca Nazionale del Lavoro Quarterly Review,* no. 107 (December 1973): 3–18. 321
14. "Balance of Payments Implications of the Oil Crisis and How to Handle Them through International Cooperation," *1974 Economic Report of the President,* pp. 650–655. Washington, D.C.: U.S. Government Printing Office, 1974. Prepared statement for Hearings before the Joint Economic Committee, Congress of the United States, Ninety-third Congress, Second Session, Part 2, Feb. 19–22, 1974. 338

Part IV. The Role of Expectations and Plans in Economic Behavior

15. "Production Planning over Time and the Nature of the Expectation and Planning Horizon," (with Franz E. Hohn), *Econometrica* 23 (January 1955): 46–66. 347
16. *The Role of Anticipations and Plans in Economic Behavior and Their Use in Economic Analysis and Forecasting,* (with Kalman J. Cohen), Studies in Business Expectations and Planning, no. 4. pp. 9–11, 14–42, 81–96, 158–166. Bureau of Economic and Business Research, University of Illinois, January 1961. 368
17. "Forecasting Uses of Anticipatory Data on Investment and Sales," (with H. M. Weingartner), *Quarterly Journal of Economics* 72 (February 1958): 23–54. 426

Part V. Miscellaneus

18. "The Predictability of Social Events," (with Emile Grunberg), *Journal of Political Economy* 62 (December 1954): 465–478. 461

Contents of Volumes 1 and 2 477

Acknowledgments 481

Name Index 485

PREFACE

The essays collected in these volumes represent a selection of my scientific contribution to economics published over a span of nearly four decades. The volumes do not include more popular writings in newspapers, magazines, and the like.

This collection has been on the drawing board for a good many years. But I kept postponing it on the grounds that there were one or more nearly finished papers whose inclusion in the collection seemed to me essential to elucidate my thinking. As it turned out, those essays took much longer than expected to reach publication. By the time they were ready, there were always some new, almost completed papers to take their place. I have finally been persuaded by many friends not to tarry any longer, especially since I have at long last come to realize that there is no such thing as "the final word."

I wish to express my gratitude to Andy Abel for undertaking the task of editing these volumes. He waded patiently through most of my writings, helped me in the final selection, and also meticulously looked out for needed corrections due to misprints or more serious errors. Such corrections are reported in the errata at the end of each essay. Fortunately, and to my pleasant surprise, Andy's zealous effort has yielded a surprisingly meager crop of errors. All the essays have been reprinted in their original form, with the single exception of an unpublished paper with Richard Brumberg, which appears in volume 2.

Throughout my career I have had the good fortune to be associated with stimulating colleagues. Many of these associations have blossomed into scientific collaborations, as evidenced by the substantial number of joint papers included in this selection. I wish to express my appreciation for permission to reprint these joint papers and extend my thanks to these coauthors for their contribution to these volumes: Albert Ando, Hossein Askari, the late Richard Brumberg, Kalman J. Cohen, J. Phillip Cooper, Jacques Drèze, Emile Grunberg, the late Franz Hohn, Dwight Jaffee, Peter Kenen, Giorgio La Malfa, Merton H. Miller, Tommaso Padoa-Schioppa, Lucas Papademos, Robert Rasche, Robert Shiller, Richard Sutch, Ezio Tarantelli, Stephen J. Turnovsky, H. Martin Weingartner.

My thanks go also to my secretary, Judy Mason, who not only helped with these volumes but patiently typed countless, almost illegible, drafts of many of the essays collected here.

Finally, I want to acknowledge my gratitude to my wife Serena, knowing that words can not adequately accomplish this task. Throughout the forty years of our married life she has given me the encouragement to aim for the stars while trying her best to see that my feet remained planted on the ground.

INTRODUCTION

I have chosen to arrange the papers collected in these three volumes by topic—except when a paper covers more than one topic. Under each topic the order is generally chronological. The major exceptions are the lead papers in volumes 1 and 2. In volume 1 the first paper is one of my most recent contributions, the Presidential Address to the American Economic Association in 1976. I feel that this essay serves as an overview of my present thinking on macroeconomics, the focus of my contribution to economics and of these volumes. Its numerous references to other papers contained in the volumes make it a useful guide to the entire collection.

The topical arrangement helps to bring into relief the basic theme that has dominated my scientific concern, namely that of sorting out the lasting contribution of the Keynesian revolution by (1) integrating the main building blocks of the *General Theory* with the more traditional and established methodology of economics that rest on the basic postulate of rational maximizing behavior on the part of economic agents; (2) testing and estimating the resulting structure by means of empirical data; and (3) applying the results to policy issues, including the issue raised by the monetarist counterrevolution as to whether there is a valid case for active policies.

The first line of endeavor has been pursued from my very first significant scientific contribution in 1944, which appears as the second essay in part I of volume 1. Its main purpose was to examine to what extent the novel results of the *General Theory,* including its explanation of "equilibrium" unemployment, could be traced to the unorthodox assumption of wage rigidity. My conclusion was that the ability of the model set out in the *General Theory* to explain the persistence of unemployment could be traced primarily to the assumption of wage rigidity. The one exception was the so-called liquidity trap, or "Keynesian case." It is logically of undeniable importance, although its empirical relevance appears now very limited, especially once the message of the Keynesian revolution served to innoculate the economy against the repetition of the Great Depression.

The same basic issue, as well as the analysis of the working of monetary and fiscal policies in a system with rigid wages (at least in the short run), was picked up some twenty years later in the third essay, a more polished and rigorous presentation benefiting from later developments, including valuable criticisms of the previous essay. This paper also attacked a new issue, namely how the working of the system is affected if the standard assumption of competitive money and credit markets is replaced by that of systematic credit rationing.

The conclusion of these two essays concerning the monetary mechanism is supported and illustrated in the last two papers of part I, but this time with the benefit of specific estimates of the relevant parameters. The estimates were the result of a lifelong concern with empirically modeling and testing the main behavioral equations of the Keynesian system, a concern that is evidenced by many of the essays collected in these volumes. This endeavor found a synthesis with the construction of the so-called FMP (Federal Reserve-MIT-University of Pennsylvania) Econometric Model of the United States in the second half of the 1960s, in collaboration with Albert Ando—an invaluable lifelong associate in this as well as numerous other undertakings—Frank deLeuw, and many others.

As is well known, the Keynesian system rests on four basic blocks: the consumption function, the investment function, the demand for and supply of money and other deposits, and the mechanisms determining wages and prices. The two essays in part II of volume 1 deal with the derivation and estimation of demand and supply functions for currency and deposits, based on the assumption of (expected) profit maximization on the part of banks and deposit holders, with proper allowances for U.S. institutional features and the cost of adjustment.

The original streamlined Keynesian model assumed that one interest rate controlled both the demand and supply of money and the rate of investment in various types of physical assets. In reality what is determined in the money market is a short-term nominal rate (or a family of closely interrelated short-term rates), whereas investment in physical assets, whose very nature is durability, must respond to long-term real yields of a maturity commensurate to the life of the asset. Furthermore, the yields also must generally reflect the uncertainty of the cash flow generated by physical assets in contrast with the contractual certainty of the return from loan instruments. The three essays in part III are devoted to modeling the relationship between short- and long-term nominal yields on loans. Earlier work had provided a definitive answer to the nature of that relation in a world of certainty; to wit, that the long-term rate depends, in a well-defined fashion, on the path of short-term rates over the life of the long-term instrument. The first essay in part III, written with Richard Sutch—one of the many outstanding graduate students with whom I have been blessed—proposes and tests an extension of this earlier model to a world of uncertainty, dealing with both the formation of expectations of future rates and the effect of their uncertainty. The second essay, also written with Richard Sutch, uses the same framework to test the then-fashionable view that the term structure could be readily and significantly manipulated through changes in the maturity structure of the national debt (''operation twist''); the results were negative. The third essay, the result of collaboration with another outstanding graduate student, Robert Shiller, extends the model to a world characterized by significant and uncertain inflation—an extension inspired by the experience of recent years. It also shows that the hypothesis about the formation of expectations embedded in the model is consistent with rational expectations.

The relationship between the bond yield and the return required to justify an investment in risky physical assets is developed in three essays, the results of a long and productive cooperation with Merton H. Miller. Because the issue examined and the method of attack fall somewhat outside traditional macroeconomics and lie close to the heart of the theory of corporate finance, the essays are grouped under the heading of ''Essays in the Theory of Finance'' in volume 3. Indeed, their greatest impact has been in the field of corporate finance—at least if one is to judge from the efforts devoted to refute them. The basic message that has caused all the furor is that (1) in a world of uncertainty, the maximization of profit criterion is ill defined and must be replaced by the maximization of market value and (2) with well-functioning markets (and neutral taxes) and rational investors, who can ''undo'' the corporate financial structure by holding positive or negative amounts of debt, the market value of the firm—debt plus equity—depends *only* on the income stream generated by its assets. It follows, in particular, that the value of a firm should not be affected by the share of debt in its financial structure or by what will be done with the returns—paid out as dividends or reinvested (profitably). In essence, it will be determined by the capitalization of the expected stream of returns before interest at the rate which differs from the sure loan rate by a risk factor reflecting the risk characteristics of that stream. From the viewpoint of macroeconomics, the main implication of the analysis is that there exists one further slip between monetary policy and the investment component of aggregate demand, namely the risk premium required by the market to induce it to hold equities (or directly physical assets) instead of bonds.

Part IV of volume 1 deals with another major critical building block, investment in physical capital, which the early Keynesians (if not Keynes himself) tended to regard as largely unpredictable and capricious. The essay reproduced in this part—the result of teamwork with three coauthors, Albert Ando, Robert Rasche, and Stephen Turnowsky—endeavors to derive an aggregate investment function from the classical postulates of maximization over the relevant horizon, allowing for both technological progress and the effect of (anticipated) inflation. The function relies on the twin assumptions of a putty-clay technology—whose implications for aggregate investment were developed earlier in a path-breaking contribution by Charles Bischoff—and of oligopolistic pricing behavior as elaborated in the essay, "New Developments on the Oligopoly Front," reproduced in part V. The resulting aggregate investment function appears to account quite well for the behavior of investment in the postwar U.S. economy.

The concluding part V of volume 1 contains my main published contributions to the analysis of the mechanism determining wages and prices. I must acknowledge that the models of wage determination proposed and tested in these papers—aside from the analysis of the dynamics of the flows through the labor market inspired by the work of Charles Holt—remain, in good part, in the old Keynesian tradition of empirical generalization and are not supported by a rigorous analysis based on maximizing behavior. But then I do not believe that anyone else has yet provided a convincing analysis satisfying this requirement while accounting for the distressing slowness with which wages and prices appear to respond to unutilized labor and plant capacity. Indeed, the modeling of wage behavior remains to this day the Achilles heel of macroeconomic analysis.

The remaining basic building block of the Keynesian system, the consumption or saving function, is the one to which I have unquestionably dedicated the greatest attention, and it in turn has provided me with the greatest reward. Volume 2 is entirely devoted to twelve essays dealing with this subject.

The second contribution offers a recent overview of the life cycle hypothesis of saving (LCH), the empirical support for it that has been built over the years, and some major implications of both an analytical type and a policy type, providing appropriate references to other papers collected in volume 2. It first reviews the foundations of the model, as laid out in the early 1950s, by relying on the classical postulates of utility maximization applied to a decision horizon consisting of the household's life cycle. It then shows that this framework, once supplemented by some plausible assumptions about the nature of tastes and combined with well-established regularities about the profile of the life cycle of earnings, can provide a unified explanation for many well-known, but sometimes puzzling, empirical regularities in saving behavior. These include such disparate phenomena as the short-run cyclical variability and the long-run stability of the saving ratio; the long-run tendency for the proportion of income saved by a family at any given level of real income to decline as an economy develops; the evidence that family net worth tends to rise with age through much of life but tends to fall beyond dome point; or the finding that black families tend to save more than white families at any given level of income. At the same time, the model has yielded a number of implications, sometimes counterintuitive, that were not known at the time the model was proposed and have since been largely confirmed. Among these implications one might cite the apparent lack of significant association of the aggregate (private) saving rate with the economic well being of the country as measured by per capita real income or with the retention policies of corporate enterprises, and the very striking association of the saving rate with the rate of growth of per capita income and the age structure of the population.

Part II of volume 2 covers the basic LCH theory. The first two essays, which are the result of collaboration with a young graduate student, Richard Brumberg, lay the foundation for what has become known as the Life Cycle Hypothesis. The first contribution is well known, but the second was never published, as Richard Brumberg's untimely death sapped my will to undertake the revisions and tightening that would no doubt have been required to make the paper acceptable to one of the standard professional journals. Much of the content of the second essay has since become known through other papers and even through some limited private circulation. But some portions are still novel, notably the analysis of the implications of the LCH for the working of the so-called Pigou effect. It is shown that this effect is transient rather than permanent, as is usually supposed, and that it can maintain full employment equilibrium through time only on condition of a constant rate of deflation. As I see it now, this result has one further interesting "general equilibrium" implication that I intend to pursue at some future time. Once the nominal interest rate has been reduced to its institutional minimum, a steady (and hence fully anticipated) rate of deflation implies a real rate of interest at least as high as the rate of price decline. Accordingly, while steady deflation would reduce the rate of saving, it would (at least under neo-classical assumptions) also reduce the rate of investment. To establish that the Pigou effect can maintain full-employment equilibrium, one must, therefore, consider whether and under what conditions steady deflation can be expected to reduce saving more than investment.

The third essay of part II, the result of a collaboration initiated with Jacques Drèze when he too was a graduate student, examines the implications of uncertainty for saving within the general framework of the life cycle. Among the many results reported, one that is of particular interest for macroeconomics is the derivation of the rather restrictive sufficient conditions that allow for the saving decision to be independent of portfolio composition decisions—an independence that is usually taken for granted in macroeconomic models.

Part III focuses on the empirical verification of LCH. The first essay is the abstract of a much longer monograph, written with Albert Ando, devoted to cross-sectional verification. It also deals with clarifying the relationship between the LCH and its contemporary, the Permanent Income Hypothesis of Milton Friedman, which shares with LCH the postulate of utility maximizing over time as well as the powerful intellectual influence of Margaret Reid's work and teachings. The second and third essays, coauthored respectively with Albert Ando and Ezio Tarantelli, are devoted primarily to time series tests, one for the United States and the other for a developing country like Italy. The second essay also explores the implications of LCH with respect to the short- and long-run propensity to consume out of labor and property income, respectively. It is shown that these propensities will in general be different, a result qualitatively consistent with Kaldor's model of two castes—parsimonious capitalists and spendthrift laborers. However, according to the LCH, the long-run propensity to consume out of property income could very well exceed that out of labor income and, in fact, could exceed unity. These quantitative implications, shown to be consistent with the empirical evidence, are altogether irreconcilable with the Kaldorian paradigm and the many applications thereof.

The fourth essay examines and tests the implications of LCH with respect to the short- and long-run relationship between wealth and income, including inferences about the effect of the national debt on the stock of private wealth and private tangible wealth developed in the first essay of part 4. Finally, the last essay applies the LCH to the explanation of intercountry differences in the long-run saving rate, confirming the insignificant role of per capita income and the dominant role of the rate of growth of per capita income predicted by the model.

The two contributions in part IV apply the LCH to policy issues. In the first essay, the conceptual framework is used to throw new light on the classical issue of the burden of the national debt. It implies that the burden can be attributed to the public debt "crowding out" productive private capital with a resulting loss of income. To a first approximation, this loss is commensurate with the future flow of debt service, although it might be somewhat smaller or larger, depending on a variety of circumstances such as tax laws and the responsiveness of the demand for wealth to the rate of interest. The second essay shows that the LCH implies a novel channel by which monetary policy affects consumption, namely through the market value of wealth responding to changes in the capitalization rate of property income induced by changes in market interest rates. Furthermore, simulation experiments with empirically estimated parameters suggest that this mechanism could play a major role in the working of monetary policy, since the response to consumption is not only appreciable but also fast relative to other channels. However, these results must be regarded as tentative until a number of remaining conceptual issues have been clarified.

Volume 3 includes the balance of my selected works in macroeconomics and closely related areas, as well as a selection of papers in other areas. The first three essays in part I—"The Theory of Finance"—were discussed earlier in the introduction. The remaining two contributions examine the impact of inflation on financial markets and investment decisions, with special reference to the disruptive effects of inflation on the mortgage and housing markets. They also explore the role and consequences of the introduction of indexed loan contracts and summarize some results of a larger monograph on "Mortgage Designs for an Inflationary Environment," written by a research team at the Massachusetts Institute of Technology.

Part II brings together a number of contributions in which the view of the macroeconomic system set forth in all the preceding essays is brought to bear on various issues of policy. The lead essay, coauthored with Giorgio LaMalfa, analyzes the first Italian endeavor at dealing with a nominal wage explosion in 1963–64 still in a world of fixed parities. The second essay criticizes the U.S. economic policy in 1973 and warns that the Federal Reserve's announced policy of adhering strictly to a no-more-than 6 percent growth rate of the money supply would lead to a serious contraction—as it did. The main relevance of the third contribution, coauthored with Lucas Papademos, is found not in the policy recommendations as such but in its analysis of the reasons for the sharp differences in policies prescribed by different schools for dealing with the great stagflation beginning in 1974–75. It attempts to sort out the role of different views of the monetary mechanism, different estimates of the relevant parameters in contrast with different valuations of the cost of tolerating inflation and unemployment, and different assessments of the risks of entrusting government with discretionary powers. It concludes that analytical differences play a minor role compared to value judgments and even political philosophy. In other words, contrary to the popular stereotype, economists do not really disagree on policy as economists—they disagree as men.

The last essay in part II, coauthored with an Italian colleague, Tommaso Padoa-Schioppa, was again inspired by the recent Italian experience. It examines the nearly hopeless task confronting stabilization authorities in an economy in which, with the help of 100 percent indexation, powerful unions are able to fix the real wage rate arbitrarily. In a closed, and even more clearly in an open, economy the authorities are confronted with a Phillips-curve type trade-off between permanent inflation and unemployment that is worse the higher the real wage, and which cannot be improved by conventional demand policies. It is shown, in particular, that the inflation does not significantly depend on the size of the government deficit (within limits) and that, in fact, an endeavor to reduce the deficit by measures such as raising indirect taxes or reducing government employment is likely to increase rather than decrease inflation. Other means of improving the trade-off are explored, with disappointingly meager results.

Part III of volume 3 brings together a number of essays in international economics. This is an area to which I first devoted major attention in the second half of the 1940s while working on the book *National Income and International Trade* in collaboration with Hans Neisser. This collaboration proved to be of great educational value to me.

The first of the essays in part III marks my return to international economics fifteen years later. This contribution, as well as the second essay, represents an endeavor—not very successful—to improve the tottering Bretton Woods system by attacking some of the major shortcomings of the day. The first paper, coauthored with Peter Kenen, was written at a time when the U.S. balance of payment deficit was the main source of international liquidity, and yet the rest of the world was deeply troubled by the size and persistence of that deficit. We proposed as a solution the creation of a new international fiat money—the Medium for International Transactions, or MIT. Its quantity was to be regulated by the agreed upon reserve targets of the participating countries, thus solving the troublesome problem of the potential instability in the demand for reserves. At the same time, the adjustment mechanism was to be improved by symmetrical penalties on the deviations of reserves from the target in either direction, and through more flexibility in changing parities. A mechanism was even suggested for stabilizing the purchasing power of the new money. An international money was later created—though with the much less colorful name of Special Drawing Rights (SDR)—but the other more novel suggestions had no visible impact.

The second essay, written with Hossein Askari, came five years later, by which time an even larger U.S. balance of payment deficit, compounded by a deteriorating current account balance, had brought the Bretton Woods System to the verge of collapse. Now the major difficulty was arising from the inability of the United States to devalue its currency relative to other currencies and from the threat of mass demands for conversion of foreign official dollar claims into gold or an equivalent. The two demands made on the United States—that it should make the dollar freely convertible while forsaking the right of changing parity unilaterally—were clearly inconsistent. The inconsistency would be resolved by the United States giving up control over its exchange rate, which would be entrusted to the other countries, but at the same time making the dollar inconvertible de jure. In addition, holders of dollar reserves would be given an option of exchange rate guarantees in terms of the SDR, which was to be turned into a stable purchasing power money by letting the rate of exchange between the dollar and the SDR vary inversely with an index of the purchasing power of the dollar. As it turned out, by the time the proposal came out in print, the Bretton Woods system had already received its death blow through the unilateral suspension of convertibility of the dollar.

The third essay takes issue with the then-popular view that fixed parities could be made consistent with full employment and freedom of capital movements even in the presence of price rigidities, provided fiscal policy was used to offset the gap between full-employment saving and the sum of investment at the world interest rates and whatever current account balance might result from the given exchange rate and domestic price level. The essay shows that, in fact, this approach is highly wasteful because it is inconsistent with capital flowing from countries with a potential surplus of saving to those with a potential deficit. In the absence of price flexibility, the flow can be achieved only via adjustment in exchange rates. The purported solution, instead of preserving freedom of capital movement so that capital would move, relied, in effect, on fiscal policy to control the movement of capital for the sake of preserving freedom of capital movement.

The next essay in part III, written in cooperation with Hossein Askari, endeavors to analyze the effectiveness of alternative exchange regimes, ranging from fixed parities through crawling pegs to free floating rates, in terms of the twin criteria of allowing long-term capital movements and minimizing the international transmission of internal disturbances. The analysis points to the crawling peg as the most promising solution, with floating rates as a second best.

The last essay is one sample of my many testimonies offered over the years to congressional committees. It was given in the spring of 1974, but is based on two articles written in January 1974 for the Italian newspaper, "Il Corriere della Sera," at the height of the oil crisis. It provides an analysis of the problems created for the world economy by the rise in the price of oil and how they should have been handled to minimize the negative consequences, which, I feel, still makes good reading.

From 1949 to 1952, I was in charge of a research project on "Expectations and Business Fluctuations" financed on a generous scale (for the time) by the Merrill Foundation for the Advancement of Financial Knowledge. Part IV of volume 3 contains two contributions that have come out of the project. Both deal with the role of expectations and plans in economic behavior and with the nature of the relevant expectation and planning horizon. Although limitations of space have made it possible to include only a token representation of the outcome of the project, I want to stress that the impact of that research on my professional development goes well beyond what one might infer from the relative allotment of space. For instance, as is pointed out in the first note of each of the joint papers with Richard Brumberg, the Life Cycle Model was partly inspired by the analysis, undertaken in the course of that project, of the role of inventories in permitting smoothing of the production schedule, with attendant cost advantages, in the face of variability—predictable and unpredictable—of sales. Another fallout from that project is reflected in my contribution to the book *Planning Production, Inventories, and Work Force,* coauthored with C. C. Holt, H. Simon and J. Muth.

The single essay in the concluding part V was written with Emil Grunberg while we were colleagues at the then-Carnegie Institute of Technology. It was originally conceived as a clever essay in methodology but has since acquired a new interest. The problem posed in the essay, whether it is possible to make correct public forecasts given that those whose behavior is forecasted respond to the forecast was answered by means of Brower's fixed point theorem. But that problem is formally the same as the one posed by the analysis of the working of an economic system in which agents form rational expectations in the Muthian sense. These expectations must be correct on the average after allowing for the fact that the future realization depends on these expectations.

PART I
Essays in the Theory of Finance

The American Economic Review

VOLUME XLVIII JUNE 1958 NUMBER THREE

THE COST OF CAPITAL, CORPORATION FINANCE AND THE THEORY OF INVESTMENT

By FRANCO MODIGLIANI AND MERTON H. MILLER*

What is the "cost of capital" to a firm in a world in which funds are used to acquire assets whose yields are uncertain; and in which capital can be obtained by many different media, ranging from pure debt instruments, representing money-fixed claims, to pure equity issues, giving holders only the right to a pro-rata share in the uncertain venture? This question has vexed at least three classes of economists: (1) the corporation finance specialist concerned with the techniques of financing firms so as to ensure their survival and growth; (2) the managerial economist concerned with capital budgeting; and (3) the economic theorist concerned with explaining investment behavior at both the micro and macro levels.[1]

In much of his formal analysis, the economic theorist at least has tended to side-step the essence of this cost-of-capital problem by proceeding as though physical assets—like bonds—could be regarded as yielding known, sure streams. Given this assumption, the theorist has concluded that the cost of capital to the owners of a firm is simply the rate of interest on bonds; and has derived the familiar proposition that the firm, acting rationally, will tend to push investment to the point

* The authors are, respectively, professor and associate professor of economics in the Graduate School of Industrial Administration, Carnegie Institute of Technology. This article is a revised version of a paper delivered at the annual meeting of the Econometric Society, December 1956. The authors express thanks for the comments and suggestions made at that time by the discussants of the paper, Evsey Domar, Robert Eisner and John Lintner, and subsequently by James Duesenberry. They are also greatly indebted to many of their present and former colleagues and students at Carnegie Tech who served so often and with such remarkable patience as a critical forum for the ideas here presented.

[1] The literature bearing on the cost-of-capital problem is far too extensive for listing here. Numerous references to it will be found throughout the paper though we make no claim to completeness. One phase of the problem which we do not consider explicitly, but which has a considerable literature of its own is the relation between the cost of capital and public utility rates. For a recent summary of the "cost-of-capital theory" of rate regulation and a brief discussion of some of its implications, the reader may refer to H. M. Somers [20].

where the marginal yield on physical assets is equal to the market rate of interest.[2] This proposition can be shown to follow from either of two criteria of rational decision-making which are equivalent under certainty, namely (1) the maximization of profits and (2) the maximization of market value.

According to the first criterion, a physical asset is worth acquiring if it will increase the net profit of the owners of the firm. But net profit will increase only if the expected rate of return, or yield, of the asset exceeds the rate of interest. According to the second criterion, an asset is worth acquiring if it increases the value of the owners' equity, *i.e.*, if it adds more to the market value of the firm than the costs of acquisition. But what the asset adds is given by capitalizing the stream it generates at the market rate of interest, and this capitalized value will exceed its cost if and only if the yield of the asset exceeds the rate of interest. Note that, under either formulation, the cost of capital is equal to the rate of interest on bonds, regardless of whether the funds are acquired through debt instruments or through new issues of common stock. Indeed, in a world of sure returns, the distinction between debt and equity funds reduces largely to one of terminology.

It must be acknowledged that some attempt is usually made in this type of analysis to allow for the existence of uncertainty. This attempt typically takes the form of superimposing on the results of the certainty analysis the notion of a "risk discount" to be subtracted from the expected yield (or a "risk premium" to be added to the market rate of interest). Investment decisions are then supposed to be based on a comparison of this "risk adjusted" or "certainty equivalent" yield with the market rate of interest.[3] No satisfactory explanation has yet been provided, however, as to what determines the size of the risk discount and how it varies in response to changes in other variables.

Considered as a convenient approximation, the model of the firm constructed via this certainty—or certainty-equivalent—approach has admittedly been useful in dealing with some of the grosser aspects of the processes of capital accumulation and economic fluctuations. Such a model underlies, for example, the familiar Keynesian aggregate investment function in which aggregate investment is written as a function of the rate of interest—the same riskless rate of interest which appears later in the system in the liquidity-preference equation. Yet few would maintain that this approximation is adequate. At the macroeconomic level there are ample grounds for doubting that the rate of interest has

[2] Or, more accurately, to the marginal cost of borrowed funds since it is customary, at least in advanced analysis, to draw the supply curve of borrowed funds to the firm as a rising one. For an advanced treatment of the certainty case, see F. and V. Lutz [13].

[3] The classic examples of the certainty-equivalent approach are found in J. R. Hicks [8] and O. Lange [11].

as large and as direct an influence on the rate of investment as this analysis would lead us to believe. At the microeconomic level the certainty model has little descriptive value and provides no real guidance to the finance specialist or managerial economist whose main problems cannot be treated in a framework which deals so cavalierly with uncertainty and ignores all forms of financing other than debt issues.[4]

Only recently have economists begun to face up seriously to the problem of the cost of capital *cum* risk. In the process they have found their interests and endeavors merging with those of the finance specialist and the managerial economist who have lived with the problem longer and more intimately. In this joint search to establish the principles which govern rational investment and financial policy in a world of uncertainty two main lines of attack can be discerned. These lines represent, in effect, attempts to extrapolate to the world of uncertainty each of the two criteria—profit maximization and market value maximization—which were seen to have equivalent implications in the special case of certainty. With the recognition of uncertainty this equivalence vanishes. In fact, the profit maximization criterion is no longer even well defined. Under uncertainty there corresponds to each decision of the firm not a unique profit outcome, but a plurality of mutually exclusive outcomes which can at best be described by a subjective probability distribution. The profit outcome, in short, has become a random variable and as such its maximization no longer has an operational meaning. Nor can this difficulty generally be disposed of by using the mathematical expectation of profits as the variable to be maximized. For decisions which affect the expected value will also tend to affect the dispersion and other characteristics of the distribution of outcomes. In particular, the use of debt rather than equity funds to finance a given venture may well increase the expected return to the owners, but only at the cost of increased dispersion of the outcomes.

Under these conditions the profit outcomes of alternative investment and financing decisions can be compared and ranked only in terms of a *subjective* "utility function" of the owners which weighs the expected yield against other characteristics of the distribution. Accordingly, the extrapolation of the profit maximization criterion of the certainty model has tended to evolve into utility maximization, sometimes explicitly, more frequently in a qualitative and heuristic form.[5]

The utility approach undoubtedly represents an advance over the certainty or certainty-equivalent approach. It does at least permit us

[4] Those who have taken a "case-method" course in finance in recent years will recall in this connection the famous Liquigas case of Hunt and Williams, [9, pp. 193–96] a case which is often used to introduce the student to the cost-of-capital problem and to poke a bit of fun at the economist's certainty-model.

[5] For an attempt at a rigorous explicit development of this line of attack, see F. Modigliani and M. Zeman [14].

to explore (within limits) some of the implications of different financing arrangements, and it does give some meaning to the "cost" of different types of funds. However, because the cost of capital has become an essentially subjective concept, the utility approach has serious drawbacks for normative as well as analytical purposes. How, for example, is management to ascertain the risk preferences of its stockholders and to compromise among their tastes? And how can the economist build a meaningful investment function in the face of the fact that any given investment opportunity might or might not be worth exploiting depending on precisely who happen to be the owners of the firm at the moment?

Fortunately, these questions do not have to be answered; for the alternative approach, based on market value maximization, can provide the basis for an operational definition of the cost of capital and a workable theory of investment. Under this approach any investment project and its concomitant financing plan must pass only the following test: Will the project, as financed, raise the market value of the firm's shares? If so, it is worth undertaking; if not, its return is less than the marginal cost of capital to the firm. Note that such a test is entirely independent of the tastes of the current owners, since market prices will reflect not only their preferences but those of all potential owners as well. If any current stockholder disagrees with management and the market over the valuation of the project, he is free to sell out and reinvest elsewhere, but will still benefit from the capital appreciation resulting from management's decision.

The potential advantages of the market-value approach have long been appreciated; yet analytical results have been meager. What appears to be keeping this line of development from achieving its promise is largely the lack of an adequate theory of the effect of financial structure on market valuations, and of how these effects can be inferred from objective market data. It is with the development of such a theory and of its implications for the cost-of-capital problem that we shall be concerned in this paper.

Our procedure will be to develop in Section I the basic theory itself and to give some brief account of its empirical relevance. In Section II, we show how the theory can be used to answer the cost-of-capital question and how it permits us to develop a theory of investment of the firm under conditions of uncertainty. Throughout these sections the approach is essentially a partial-equilibrium one focusing on the firm and "industry." Accordingly, the "prices" of certain income streams will be treated as constant and given from outside the model, just as in the standard Marshallian analysis of the firm and industry the prices of all inputs and of all other products are taken as given. We have chosen to focus at this level rather than on the economy as a whole because it is at the level of the firm and the industry that the interests of the various specialists concerned with the cost-of-capital problem come most closely together. Although the emphasis has thus been placed on partial-equilibrium analysis, the results obtained also provide the essential building blocks for a general equilibrium model which shows how those prices which are here taken as given, are themselves determined. For reasons of space, however, and because the material is of interest in its own right, the presentation of the general equilibrium model which rounds out the analysis must be deferred to a subsequent paper.

I. *The Valuation of Securities, Leverage, and the Cost of Capital*

A. *The Capitalization Rate for Uncertain Streams*

As a starting point, consider an economy in which all physical assets are owned by corporations. For the moment, assume that these corporations can finance their assets by issuing common stock only; the introduction of bond issues, or their equivalent, as a source of corporate funds is postponed until the next part of this section.

The physical assets held by each firm will yield to the owners of the firm—its stockholders—a stream of "profits" over time; but the elements of this series need not be constant and in any event are uncertain. This stream of income, and hence the stream accruing to any share of common stock, will be regarded as extending indefinitely into the future. We assume, however, that the mean value of the stream over time, or average profit per unit of time, is finite and represents a random variable subject to a (subjective) probability distribution. We shall refer to the average value over time of the stream accruing to a given share as the return of that share; and to the mathematical expectation of this average as the expected return of the share.[6] Although individual investors may have different views as to the shape of the probability distri-

[6] These propositions can be restated analytically as follows: The assets of the ith firm generate a stream:

$$X_i(1),\ X_i(2) \cdots X_i(T)$$

whose elements are random variables subject to the joint probability distribution:

$$\chi_i[X_i(1),\ X_i(2) \cdots X_i(t)].$$

The return to the ith firm is defined as:

$$X_i = \lim_{T\to\infty} \frac{1}{T} \sum_{t=1}^{T} X_i(t).$$

X_i is itself a random variable with a probability distribution $\Phi_i(X_i)$ whose form is determined uniquely by χ_i. The expected return $\bar{X}_i$ is defined as $\bar{X}_i = E(X_i) = \int_{X_i} X_i \Phi_i(X_i) dX_i$. If N_i is the number of shares outstanding, the return of the ith share is $x_i = (1/N) X_i$ with probability distribution $\phi_i(x_i) dx_i = \Phi_i(Nx_i) d(Nx_i)$ and expected value $\bar{x}_i = (1/N)\bar{X}_i$.

bution of the return of any share, we shall assume for simplicity that they are at least in agreement as to the expected return.[7]

This way of characterizing uncertain streams merits brief comment. Notice first that the stream is a stream of profits, not dividends. As will become clear later, as long as management is presumed to be acting in the best interests of the stockholders, retained earnings can be regarded as equivalent to a fully subscribed, pre-emptive issue of common stock. Hence, for present purposes, the division of the stream between cash dividends and retained earnings in any period is a mere detail. Notice also that the uncertainty attaches to the mean value over time of the stream of profits and should not be confused with variability over time of the successive elements of the stream. That variability and uncertainty are two totally different concepts should be clear from the fact that the elements of a stream can be variable even though known with certainty. It can be shown, furthermore, that whether the elements of a stream are sure or uncertain, the effect of variability per se on the valuation of the stream is at best a second-order one which can safely be neglected for our purposes (and indeed most others too).[8]

The next assumption plays a strategic role in the rest of the analysis. We shall assume that firms can be divided into "equivalent return" classes such that the return on the shares issued by any firm in any given class is proportional to (and hence perfectly correlated with) the return on the shares issued by any other firm in the same class. This assumption implies that the various shares within the same class differ, at most, by a "scale factor." Accordingly, if we adjust for the difference in scale, by taking the *ratio* of the return to the expected return, the probability distribution of that ratio is identical for all shares in the class. It follows that all relevant properties of a share are uniquely characterized by specifying (1) the class to which it belongs and (2) its expected return.

The significance of this assumption is that it permits us to classify firms into groups within which the shares of different firms are "homogeneous," that is, perfect substitutes for one another. We have, thus, an analogue to the familiar concept of the industry in which it is the commodity produced by the firms that is taken as homogeneous. To complete this analogy with Marshallian price theory, we shall assume in the

[7] To deal adequately with refinements such as differences among investors in estimates of expected returns would require extensive discussion of the theory of portfolio selection. Brief references to these and related topics will be made in the succeeding article on the general equilibrium model.

[8] The reader may convince himself of this by asking how much he would be willing to rebate to his employer for the privilege of receiving his annual salary in equal monthly installments rather than in irregular amounts over the year. See also J. M. Keynes [10, esp. pp. 53–54].

analysis to follow that the shares concerned are traded in perfect markets under conditions of atomistic competition.[9]

From our definition of homogeneous classes of stock it follows that in equilibrium in a perfect capital market the price per dollar's worth of expected return must be the same for all shares of any given class. Or, equivalently, in any given class the price of every share must be proportional to its expected return. Let us denote this factor of proportionality for any class, say the kth class, by $1/\rho_k$. Then if p_j denotes the price and $\bar{x}_j$ is the expected return per share of the jth firm in class k, we must have:

$$p_j = \frac{1}{\rho_k}\bar{x}_j; \tag{1}$$

or, equivalently,

$$\frac{\bar{x}_j}{p_j} = \rho_k \text{ a constant for all firms } j \text{ in class } k. \tag{2}$$

The constants ρ_k (one for each of the k classes) can be given several economic interpretations: (a) From (2) we see that each ρ_k is the expected rate of return of any share in class k. (b) From (1) $1/\rho_k$ is the price which an investor has to pay for a dollar's worth of expected return in the class k. (c) Again from (1), by analogy with the terminology for perpetual bonds, ρ_k can be regarded as the market rate of capitalization for the expected value of the uncertain streams of the kind generated by the kth class of firms.[10]

B. *Debt Financing and Its Effects on Security Prices*

Having developed an apparatus for dealing with uncertain streams we can now approach the heart of the cost-of-capital problem by dropping the assumption that firms cannot issue bonds. The introduction of debt-financing changes the market for shares in a very fundamental way. Because firms may have different proportions of debt in their capi-

[9] Just what our classes of stocks contain and how the different classes can be identified by outside observers are empirical questions to which we shall return later. For the present, it is sufficient to observe: (1) Our concept of a class, while not identical to that of the industry is at least closely related to it. Certainly the basic characteristics of the probability distributions of the returns on assets will depend to a significant extent on the product sold and the technology used. (2) What are the appropriate class boundaries will depend on the particular problem being studied. An economist concerned with general tendencies in the market, for example, might well be prepared to work with far wider classes than would be appropriate for an investor planning his portfolio, or a firm planning its financial strategy.

[10] We cannot, on the basis of the assumptions so far, make any statements about the relationship or spread between the various ρ's or capitalization rates. Before we could do so we would have to make further specific assumptions about the way investors believe the probability distributions vary from class to class, as well as assumptions about investors' preferences as between the characteristics of different distributions.

tal structure, shares of different companies, even in the same class, can give rise to different probability distributions of returns. In the language of finance, the shares will be subject to different degrees of financial risk or "leverage" and hence they will no longer be perfect substitutes for one another.

To exhibit the mechanism determining the relative prices of shares under these conditions, we make the following two assumptions about the nature of bonds and the bond market, though they are actually stronger than is necessary and will be relaxed later: (1) All bonds (including any debts issued by households for the purpose of carrying shares) are assumed to yield a constant income per unit of time, and this income is regarded as certain by all traders regardless of the issuer. (2) Bonds, like stocks, are traded in a perfect market, where the term perfect is to be taken in its usual sense as implying that any two commodities which are perfect substitutes for each other must sell, in equilibrium, at the same price. It follows from assumption (1) that all bonds are in fact perfect substitutes up to a scale factor. It follows from assumption (2) that they must all sell at the same price per dollar's worth of return, or what amounts to the same thing must yield the same rate of return. This rate of return will be denoted by r and referred to as the rate of interest or, equivalently, as the capitalization rate for sure streams. We now can derive the following two basic propositions with respect to the valuation of securities in companies with different capital structures:

Proposition I. Consider any company j and let $\overline{X}_j$ stand as before for the expected return on the assets owned by the company (that is, its expected profit before deduction of interest). Denote by D_j the market value of the debts of the company; by S_j the market value of its common shares; and by $V_j \equiv S_j + D_j$ the market value of all its securities or, as we shall say, the market value of the firm. Then, our Proposition I asserts that we must have in equilibrium:

$$V_j \equiv (S_j + D_j) = \overline{X}_j/\rho_k, \text{ for any firm } j \text{ in class } k. \tag{3}$$

That is, the *market value of any firm is independent of its capital structure and is given by capitalizing its expected return at the rate ρ_k appropriate to its class.*

This proposition can be stated in an equivalent way in terms of the firm's "average cost of capital," $\overline{X}_j/V_j$, which is the ratio of its expected return to the market value of all its securities. Our proposition then is:

$$\frac{\overline{X}_j}{(S_j + D_j)} \equiv \frac{\overline{X}_j}{V_j} = \rho_k, \text{ for any firm } j, \text{ in class } k. \tag{4}$$

That is, *the average cost of capital to any firm is completely independent of its capital structure and is equal to the capitalization rate of a pure equity stream of its class.*

To establish Proposition I we will show that as long as the relations (3) or (4) do not hold between any pair of firms in a class, arbitrage will take place and restore the stated equalities. We use the term arbitrage advisedly. For if Proposition I did not hold, an investor could buy and sell stocks and bonds in such a way as to exchange one income stream for another stream, identical in all relevant respects but selling at a lower price. The exchange would therefore be advantageous to the investor quite independently of his attitudes toward risk.[11] As investors exploit these arbitrage opportunities, the value of the overpriced shares will fall and that of the underpriced shares will rise, thereby tending to eliminate the discrepancy between the market values of the firms.

By way of proof, consider two firms in the same class and assume for simplicity only, that the expected return, $\bar{X}$, is the same for both firms. Let company 1 be financed entirely with common stock while company 2 has some debt in its capital structure. Suppose first the value of the levered firm, V_2, to be larger than that of the unlevered one, V_1. Consider an investor holding s_2 dollars' worth of the shares of company 2, representing a fraction α of the total outstanding stock, S_2. The return from this portfolio, denoted by Y_2, will be a fraction α of the income available for the stockholders of company 2, which is equal to the total return X_2 less the interest charge, rD_2. Since under our assumption of homogeneity, the anticipated total return of company 2, X_2, is, under all circumstances, the same as the anticipated total return to company 1, X_1, we can hereafter replace X_2 and X_1 by a common symbol X. Hence, the return from the initial portfolio can be written as:

$$Y_2 = \alpha(X - rD_2). \tag{5}$$

Now suppose the investor sold his αS_2 worth of company 2 shares and acquired instead an amount $s_1 = \alpha(S_2 + D_2)$ of the shares of company 1. He could do so by utilizing the amount αS_2 realized from the sale of his initial holding and borrowing an additional amount αD_2 on his own credit, pledging his new holdings in company 1 as a collateral. He would thus secure for himself a fraction $s_1/S_1 = \alpha(S_2 + D_2)/S_1$ of the shares and earnings of company 1. Making proper allowance for the interest payments on his personal debt αD_2, the return from the new portfolio, Y_1, is given by:

[11] In the language of the theory of choice, the exchanges are movements from inefficient points in the interior to efficient points on the boundary of the investor's opportunity set; and not movements between efficient points along the boundary. Hence for this part of the analysis nothing is involved in the way of specific assumptions about investor attitudes or behavior other than that investors behave consistently and prefer more income to less income, *ceteris paribus*.

$$Y_1 = \frac{\alpha(S_2 + D_2)}{S_1} X - r\alpha D_2 = \alpha \frac{V_2}{V_1} X - r\alpha D_2. \tag{6}$$

Comparing (5) with (6) we see that as long as $V_2 > V_1$ we must have $Y_1 > Y_2$, so that it pays owners of company 2's shares to sell their holdings, thereby depressing S_2 and hence V_2; and to acquire shares of company 1, thereby raising S_1 and thus V_1. We conclude therefore that levered companies cannot command a premium over unlevered companies because investors have the opportunity of putting the equivalent leverage into their portfolio directly by borrowing on personal account.

Consider now the other possibility, namely that the market value of the levered company V_2 is less than V_1. Suppose an investor holds initially an amount s_1 of shares of company 1, representing a fraction α of the total outstanding stock, S_1. His return from this holding is:

$$Y_1 = \frac{s_1}{S_1} X = \alpha X.$$

Suppose he were to exchange this initial holding for another portfolio, also worth s_1, but consisting of s_2 dollars of stock of company 2 and of d dollars of bonds, where s_2 and d are given by:

$$s_2 = \frac{S_2}{V_2} s_1, \qquad d = \frac{D_2}{V_2} s_1. \tag{7}$$

In other words the new portfolio is to consist of stock of company 2 and of bonds in the proportions S_2/V_2 and D_2/V_2, respectively. The return from the stock in the new portfolio will be a fraction s_2/S_2 of the total return to stockholders of company 2, which is $(X - rD_2)$, and the return from the bonds will be rd. Making use of (7), the total return from the portfolio, Y_2, can be expressed as follows:

$$Y_2 = \frac{s_2}{S_2}(X - rD_2) + rd = \frac{s_1}{V_2}(X - rD_2) + r\frac{D_2}{V_2} s_1 = \frac{s_1}{V_2} X = \alpha \frac{S_1}{V_2} X$$

(since $s_1 = \alpha S_1$). Comparing Y_2 with Y_1 we see that, if $V_2 < S_1 \equiv V_1$, then Y_2 will exceed Y_1. Hence it pays the holders of company 1's shares to sell these holdings and replace them with a mixed portfolio containing an appropriate fraction of the shares of company 2.

The acquisition of a mixed portfolio of stock of a levered company j and of bonds in the proportion S_j/V_j and D_j/V_j respectively, may be regarded as an operation which "undoes" the leverage, giving access to an appropriate fraction of the unlevered return X_j. It is this possibility of undoing leverage which prevents the value of levered firms from being consistently less than those of unlevered firms, or more generally prevents the average cost of capital $\overline{X}_j/V_j$ from being systematically higher for levered than for nonlevered companies in the same class.

Since we have already shown that arbitrage will also prevent V_2 from being larger than V_1, we can conclude that in equilibrium we must have $V_2 = V_1$, as stated in Proposition I.

Proposition II. From Proposition I we can derive the following proposition concerning the rate of return on common stock in companies whose capital structure includes some debt: the expected rate of return or yield, i, on the stock of any company j belonging to the kth class is a linear function of leverage as follows:

$$i_j = \rho_k + (\rho_k - r)D_j/S_j. \tag{8}$$

That is, *the expected yield of a share of stock is equal to the appropriate capitalization rate* ρ_k *for a pure equity stream in the class, plus a premium related to financial risk equal to the debt-to-equity ratio times the spread between* ρ_k *and* r. Or equivalently, the market price of any share of stock is given by capitalizing its expected return at the continuously variable rate i_j of (8).[12]

A number of writers have stated close equivalents of our Proposition I although by appealing to intuition rather than by attempting a proof and only to insist immediately that the results were not applicable to the actual capital markets.[13] Proposition II, however, so far as we have been able to discover is new.[14] To establish it we first note that, by definition, the expected rate of return, i, is given by:

$$i_j \equiv \frac{\bar{X}_j - rD_j}{S_j}. \tag{9}$$

From Proposition I, equation (3), we know that:

$$\bar{X}_j = \rho_k(S_j + D_j).$$

Substituting in (9) and simplifying, we obtain equation (8).

[12] To illustrate, suppose $\bar{X} = 1000$, $D = 4000$, $r = 5$ per cent and $\rho_k = 10$ per cent. These values imply that $V = 10{,}000$ and $S = 6000$ by virtue of Proposition I. The expected yield or rate of return per share is then:

$$i = \frac{1000 - 200}{6000} = .1 + (.1 - .05)\frac{4000}{6000} = 13\tfrac{1}{3} \text{ per cent.}$$

[13] See, for example, J. B. Williams [21, esp. pp. 72–73]; David Durand [3]; and W. A. Morton [15]. None of these writers describe in any detail the mechanism which is supposed to keep the average cost of capital constant under changes in capital structure. They seem, however, to be visualizing the equilibrating mechanism in terms of switches by investors between stocks and bonds as the yields of each get out of line with their "riskiness." This is an argument quite different from the pure arbitrage mechanism underlying our proof, and the difference is crucial. Regarding Proposition I as resting on investors' attitudes toward risk leads inevitably to a misunderstanding of many factors influencing relative yields such as, for example, limitations on the portfolio composition of financial institutions. See below, esp. Section I.D.

[14] Morton does make reference to a linear yield function but only " . . . for the sake of simplicity and because the particular function used makes no essential difference in my conclusions" [15, p. 443, note 2].

C. *Some Qualifications and Extensions of the Basic Propositions*

The methods and results developed so far can be extended in a number of useful directions, of which we shall consider here only three: (1) allowing for a corporate profits tax under which interest payments are deductible; (2) recognizing the existence of a multiplicity of bonds and interest rates; and (3) acknowledging the presence of market imperfections which might interfere with the process of arbitrage. The first two will be examined briefly in this section with some further attention given to the tax problem in Section II. Market imperfections will be discussed in Part D of this section in the course of a comparison of our results with those of received doctrines in the field of finance.

Effects of the Present Method of Taxing Corporations. The deduction of interest in computing taxable corporate profits will prevent the arbitrage process from making the value of all firms in a given class proportional to the expected returns generated by their physical assets. Instead, it can be shown (by the same type of proof used for the original version of Proposition I) that the market values of firms in each class must be proportional in equilibrium to their expected return net of taxes (that is, to the sum of the interest paid and expected net stockholder income). This means we must replace each $\bar{X}_j$ in the original versions of Propositions I and II with a new variable $\bar{X}_j^\tau$ representing the total income net of taxes generated by the firm:

$$\bar{X}_j^\tau \equiv (\bar{X}_j - rD_j)(1 - \tau) + rD_j \equiv \bar{\pi}_j^\tau + rD_j, \tag{10}$$

where $\bar{\pi}_j^\tau$ represents the expected net income accruing to the common stockholders and τ stands for the average rate of corporate income tax.[15]

After making these substitutions, the propositions, when adjusted for taxes, continue to have the same form as their originals. That is, Proposition I becomes:

$$\frac{\bar{X}_j^\tau}{V_j} = \rho_k^\tau, \text{ for any firm in class } k, \tag{11}$$

and Proposition II becomes

$$i_j \equiv \frac{\bar{\pi}_j^\tau}{S_j} = \rho_j^\tau + (\rho_k^\tau - r)D_j/S_j \tag{12}$$

where ρ_k^τ is the capitalization rate for income net of taxes in class k.

Although the form of the propositions is unaffected, certain interpretations must be changed. In particular, the after-tax capitalization rate

[15] For simplicity, we shall ignore throughout the tiny element of progression in our present corporate tax and treat τ as a constant independent of $(X_j - rD_j)$.

ρ_k^τ can no longer be identified with the "average cost of capital" which is $\rho_k = \overline{X}_j/V_j$. The difference between ρ_k^τ and the "true" average cost of capital, as we shall see, is a matter of some relevance in connection with investment planning within the firm (Section II). For the description of market behavior, however, which is our immediate concern here, the distinction is not essential. To simplify presentation, therefore, and to preserve continuity with the terminology in the standard literature we shall continue in this section to refer to ρ_k^τ as the average cost of capital, though strictly speaking this identification is correct only in the absence of taxes.

Effects of a Plurality of Bonds and Interest Rates. In existing capital markets we find not one, but a whole family of interest rates varying with maturity, with the technical provisions of the loan and, what is most relevant for present purposes, with the financial condition of the borrower.[16] Economic theory and market experience both suggest that the yields demanded by lenders tend to increase with the debt-equity ratio of the borrowing firm (or individual). If so, and if we can assume as a first approximation that this yield curve, $r = r\,(D/S)$, whatever its precise form, is the same for all borrowers, then we can readily extend our propositions to the case of a rising supply curve for borrowed funds.[17]

Proposition I is actually unaffected in form and interpretation by the fact that the rate of interest may rise with leverage; while the average cost of *borrowed* funds will tend to increase as debt rises, the average cost of funds from *all* sources will still be independent of leverage (apart from the tax effect). This conclusion follows directly from the ability of those who engage in arbitrage to undo the leverage in any financial structure by acquiring an appropriately mixed portfolio of bonds and stocks. Because of this ability, the ratio of earnings (*before* interest charges) to market value—*i.e.*, the average cost of capital from all

[16] We shall not consider here the extension of the analysis to encompass the time structure of interest rates. Although some of the problems posed by the time structure can be handled within our comparative statics framework, an adequate discussion would require a separate paper.

[17] We can also develop a theory of bond valuation along lines essentially parallel to those followed for the case of shares. We conjecture that the curve of bond yields as a function of leverage will turn out to be a nonlinear one in contrast to the linear function of leverage developed for common shares. However, we would also expect that the rate of increase in the yield on new issues would not be substantial in practice. This relatively slow rise would reflect the fact that interest rate increases by themselves can never be completely satisfactory to creditors as compensation for their increased risk. Such increases may simply serve to raise r so high relative to ρ that they become self-defeating by giving rise to a situation in which even normal fluctuations in earnings may force the company into bankruptcy. The difficulty of borrowing more, therefore, tends to show up in the usual case not so much in higher rates as in the form of increasingly stringent restrictions imposed on the company's management and finances by the creditors; and ultimately in a complete inability to obtain new borrowed funds, at least from the institutional investors who normally set the standards in the market for bonds.

sources—must be the same for all firms in a given class.[18] In other words, the increased cost of borrowed funds as leverage increases will tend to be offset by a corresponding reduction in the yield of common stock. This seemingly paradoxical result will be examined more closely below in connection with Proposition II.

A significant modification of Proposition I would be required only if the yield curve $r=r(D/S)$ were different for different borrowers, as might happen if creditors had marked preferences for the securities of a particular class of debtors. If, for example, corporations as a class were able to borrow at lower rates than individuals having equivalent personal leverage, then the average cost of capital to corporations might fall slightly, as leverage increased over some range, in reflection of this differential. In evaluating this possibility, however, remember that the relevant interest rate for our arbitrage operators is the rate on brokers' loans and, historically, that rate has not been noticeably higher than representative corporate rates.[19] The operations of holding companies and investment trusts which can borrow on terms comparable to operating companies represent still another force which could be expected to wipe out any marked or prolonged advantages from holding levered stocks.[20]

Although Proposition I remains unaffected as long as the yield curve is the same for all borrowers, the relation between common stock yields and leverage will no longer be the strictly linear one given by the original Proposition II. If r increases with leverage, the yield i will still tend to

[18] One normally minor qualification might be noted. Once we relax the assumption that all bonds have certain yields, our arbitrage operator faces the danger of something comparable to "gambler's ruin." That is, there is always the possibility that an otherwise sound concern—one whose long-run expected income is greater than its interest liability—might be forced into liquidation as a result of a run of temporary losses. Since reorganization generally involves costs, and because the operation of the firm may be hampered during the period of reorganization with lasting unfavorable effects on earnings prospects, we might perhaps expect heavily levered companies to sell at a slight discount relative to less heavily indebted companies of the same class.

[19] Under normal conditions, moreover, a substantial part of the arbitrage process could be expected to take the form, not of having the arbitrage operators go into debt on personal account to put the required leverage into their portfolios, but simply of having them reduce the amount of corporate bonds they already hold when they acquire underpriced unlevered stock. Margin requirements are also somewhat less of an obstacle to maintaining any desired degree of leverage in a portfolio than might be thought at first glance. Leverage could be largely restored in the face of higher margin requirements by switching to stocks having more leverage at the corporate level.

[20] An extreme form of inequality between borrowing and lending rates occurs, of course, in the case of preferred stocks, which can not be directly issued by individuals on personal account. Here again, however, we would expect that the operations of investment corporations plus the ability of arbitrage operators to sell off their holdings of preferred stocks would act to prevent the emergence of any substantial premiums (for this reason) on capital structures containing preferred stocks. Nor are preferred stocks so far removed from bonds as to make it impossible for arbitrage operators to approximate closely the risk and leverage of a corporate preferred stock by incurring a somewhat smaller debt on personal account.

rise as D/S increases, but at a decreasing rather than a constant rate. Beyond some high level of leverage, depending on the exact form of the interest function, the yield may even start to fall.[21] The relation between i and D/S could conceivably take the form indicated by the curve MD

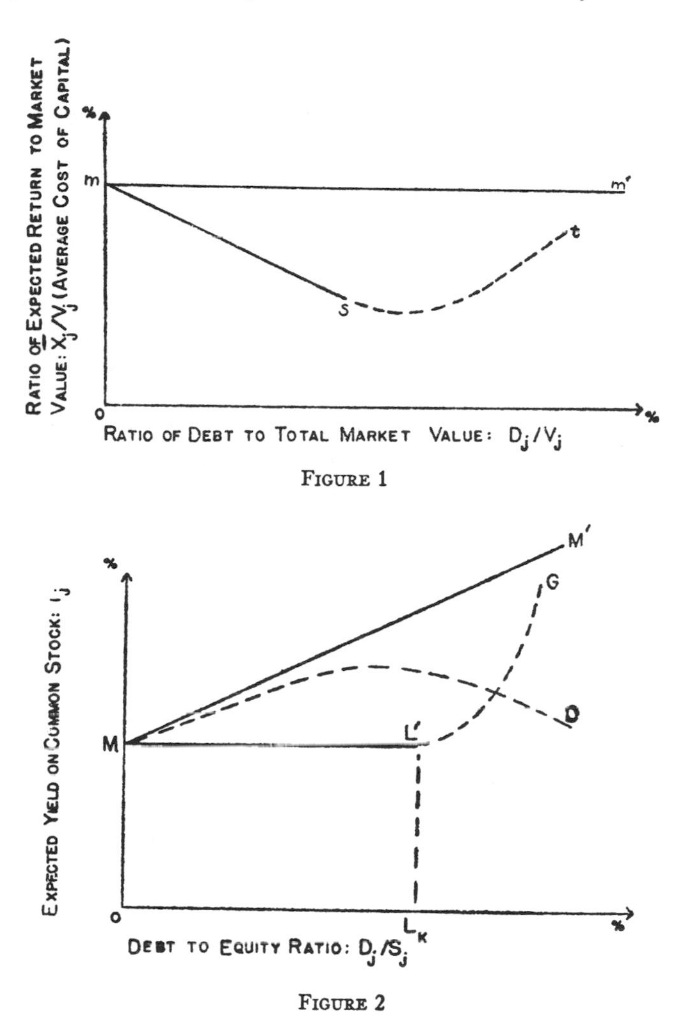

FIGURE 1

FIGURE 2

in Figure 2, although in practice the curvature would be much less pronounced. By contrast, with a constant rate of interest, the relation would be linear throughout as shown by line MM', Figure 2.

The downward sloping part of the curve MD perhaps requires some

[21] Since new lenders are unlikely to permit this much leverage (*cf.* note 17), this range of the curve is likely to be occupied by companies whose earnings prospects have fallen substantially since the time when their debts were issued.

comment since it may be hard to imagine why investors, other than those who like lotteries, would purchase stocks in this range. Remember, however, that the yield curve of Proposition II is a consequence of the more fundamental Proposition I. Should the demand by the risk-lovers prove insufficient to keep the market to the peculiar yield-curve *MD*, this demand would be reinforced by the action of arbitrage operators. The latter would find it profitable to own a pro-rata share of the firm as a whole by holding its stock *and* bonds, the lower yield of the shares being thus offset by the higher return on bonds.

D. *The Relation of Propositions I and II to Current Doctrines*

The propositions we have developed with respect to the valuation of firms and shares appear to be substantially at variance with current doctrines in the field of finance. The main differences between our view and the current view are summarized graphically in Figures 1 and 2. Our Proposition I [equation (4)] asserts that the average cost of capital, $\bar{X}_j^\tau/V_j$, is a constant for all firms j in class k, independently of their financial structure. This implies that, if we were to take a sample of firms in a given class, and if for each firm we were to plot the ratio of expected return to market value against some measure of leverage or financial structure, the points would tend to fall on a horizontal straight line with intercept ρ_k^τ, like the solid line mm' in Figure 1.[22] From Proposition I we derived Proposition II [equation (8)] which, taking the simplest version with r constant, asserts that, for all firms in a class, the relation between the yield on common stock and financial structure, measured by D_j/S_j, will approximate a straight line with slope $(\rho_k^\tau - r)$ and intercept ρ_k^τ. This relationship is shown as the solid line MM' in Figure 2, to which reference has been made earlier.[23]

By contrast, the conventional view among finance specialists appears to start from the proposition that, other things equal, the earnings-price ratio (or its reciprocal, the times-earnings multiplier) of a firm's common stock will normally be only slightly affected by "moderate" amounts of debt in the firm's capital structure.[24] Translated into our no-

[22] In Figure 1 the measure of leverage used is D_j/V_j (the ratio of debt to market value) rather than D_j/S_j (the ratio of debt to equity), the concept used in the analytical development. The D_j/V_j measure is introduced at this point because it simplifies comparison and contrast of our view with the traditional position.

[23] The line MM' in Figure 2 has been drawn with a positive slope on the assumption that $\rho_k^\tau > r$, a condition which will normally obtain. Our Proposition II as given in equation (8) would continue to be valid, of course, even in the unlikely event that $\rho_k^\tau < r$, but the slope of MM' would be negative.

[24] See, *e.g.*, Graham and Dodd [6, pp. 464–66]. Without doing violence to this position, we can bring out its implications more sharply by ignoring the qualification and treating the yield as a virtual constant over the relevant range. See in this connection the discussion in Durand [3, esp. pp. 225–37] of what he calls the "net income method" of valuation.

tation, it asserts that for any firm j in the class k,

$$\frac{\overline{X}_j^\tau - rD_j}{S_j} \equiv \frac{\bar{\pi}_j^\tau}{S_j} = i_k^*, \text{ a constant for } \frac{D_j}{S_j} \leq L_k \tag{13}$$

or, equivalently,

$$S_j = \bar{\pi}_j^\tau / i_k^*. \tag{14}$$

Here i_k^* represents the capitalization rate or earnings-price ratio on the common stock and L_k denotes some amount of leverage regarded as the maximum "reasonable" amount for firms of the class k. This assumed relationship between yield and leverage is the horizontal solid line ML' of Figure 2. Beyond L', the yield will presumably rise sharply as the market discounts "excessive" trading on the equity. This possibility of a rising range for high leverages is indicated by the broken-line segment $L'G$ in the figure.[25]

If the value of shares were really given by (14) then the over-all market value of the firm must be:

$$V_j \equiv S_j + D_j = \frac{\overline{X}_j^\tau - rD_j}{i_k^*} + D_j = \frac{\overline{X}_j^\tau}{i_k^*} + \frac{(i_k^* - r)D_j}{i_k^*}. \tag{16}$$

That is, for any given level of expected total returns after taxes ($\overline{X}_j^\tau$) and assuming, as seems natural, that $i_k^* > r$, the value of the firm must tend to *rise* with debt;[26] whereas our Proposition I asserts that the value of the firm is completely independent of the capital structure. Another way of contrasting our position with the traditional one is in terms of the cost of capital. Solving (16) for $\overline{X}_j^\tau / V_j$ yields:

$$\overline{X}_j^\tau / V_j = i_k^* - (i_k^* - r) D_j / V_j. \tag{17}$$

According to this equation, the average cost of capital is not independent of capital structure as we have argued, but should tend to *fall* with increasing leverage, at least within the relevant range of moderate debt ratios, as shown by the line *ms* in Figure 1. Or to put it in more familiar terms, debt-financing should be "cheaper" than equity-financing if not carried too far.

When we also allow for the possibility of a rising range of stock yields for large values of leverage, we obtain a U-shaped curve like *mst* in

[25] To make it easier to see some of the implications of this hypothesis as well as to prepare the ground for later statistical testing, it will be helpful to assume that the notion of a critical limit on leverage beyond which yields rise rapidly, can be epitomized by a quadratic relation of the form:

$$\bar{\pi}_j^\tau / S_j = i_k^* + \beta(D_j/S_j) + \alpha(D_j/S_j)^2, \qquad \alpha > 0. \tag{15}$$

[26] For a typical discussion of how a promoter can, supposedly, increase the market value of a firm by recourse to debt issues, see W. J. Eiteman [4, esp. pp. 11–13].

Figure 1.[27] That a yield-curve for stocks of the form *ML'G* in Figure 2 implies a U-shaped cost-of-capital curve has, of course, been recognized by many writers. A natural further step has been to suggest that the capital structure corresponding to the trough of the U is an "optimal capital structure" towards which management ought to strive in the best interests of the stockholders.[28] According to our model, by contrast, no such optimal structure exists—all structures being equivalent from the point of view of the cost of capital.

Although the falling, or at least U-shaped, cost-of-capital function is in one form or another the dominant view in the literature, the ultimate rationale of that view is by no means clear. The crucial element in the position—that the expected earnings-price ratio of the stock is largely unaffected by leverage up to some conventional limit—is rarely even regarded as something which requires explanation. It is usually simply taken for granted or it is merely asserted that this is the way the market behaves.[29] To the extent that the constant earnings-price ratio has a rationale at all we suspect that it reflects in most cases the feeling that moderate amounts of debt in "sound" corporations do not really add very much to the "riskiness" of the stock. Since the extra risk is slight, it seems natural to suppose that firms will not have to pay noticeably higher yields in order to induce investors to hold the stock.[30]

A more sophisticated line of argument has been advanced by David Durand [3, pp. 231–33]. He suggests that because insurance companies and certain other important institutional investors are restricted to debt securities, nonfinancial corporations are able to borrow from them at interest rates which are lower than would be required to compensate

[27] The U-shaped nature of the cost-of-capital curve can be exhibited explicitly if the yield curve for shares as a function of leverage can be approximated by equation (15) of footnote 25. From that equation, multiplying both sides by S_j we obtain: $\bar{\pi}_j^\tau = \bar{X}_j^\tau - rD_j = i_k^* S_j + \beta D_j + \alpha D_j^2 / S_j$ or, adding and subtracting $i_k^* D_k$ from the right-hand side and collecting terms,

$$\bar{X}_j^\tau = i_k^*(S_j + D_j) + (\beta + r - i_k^*)D_j + \alpha D^2{}_j/S_j. \tag{18}$$

Dividing (18) by V_j gives an expression for the cost of capital:

$$\bar{X}_j^\tau/V_j = i_k^* - (i_k^* - r - \beta)D_j/V_j + \alpha D_j^2/S_j V_j = i_k^* - (i_k^* - r - \beta)D_j/V_j + \alpha(D_j/V_j)^2/(1 - D_j/V_j) \tag{19}$$

which is clearly U-shaped since α is supposed to be positive.

[28] For a typical statement see S. M. Robbins [16, p. 307]. See also Graham and Dodd [6, pp. 468–74].

[29] See *e.g.*, Graham and Dodd [6, p. 466].

[30] A typical statement is the following by Guthmann and Dougall [7, p. 245]: "Theoretically it might be argued that the increased hazard from using bonds and preferred stocks would counterbalance this additional income and so prevent the common stock from being more attractive than when it had a lower return but fewer prior obligations. In practice, the extra earnings from 'trading on the equity' are often regarded by investors as more than sufficient to serve as a 'premium for risk' when the proportions of the several securities are judiciously mixed."

creditors in a free market. Thus, while he would presumably agree with our conclusions that stockholders could not gain from leverage in an unconstrained market, he concludes that they can gain under present institutional arrangements. This gain would arise by virtue of the "safety superpremium" which lenders are willing to pay corporations for the privilege of lending.[31]

The defective link in both the traditional and the Durand version of the argument lies in the confusion between investors' subjective risk preferences and their objective market opportunities. Our Propositions I and II, as noted earlier, do not depend for their validity on any assumption about individual risk preferences. Nor do they involve any assertion as to what is an adequate compensation to investors for assuming a given degree of risk. They rely merely on the fact that a given commodity cannot consistently sell at more than one price in the market; or more precisely that the price of a commodity representing a "bundle" of two other commodities cannot be consistently different from the weighted average of the prices of the two components (the weights being equal to the proportion of the two commodities in the bundle).

An analogy may he helpful at this point. The relations between $1/\rho_k$, the price per dollar of an unlevered stream in class k; $1/r$, the price per dollar of a sure stream, and $1/i_j$, the price per dollar of a levered stream j, in the kth class, are essentially the same as those between, respectively, the price of whole milk, the price of butter fat, and the price of milk which has been thinned out by skimming off some of the butter fat. Our Proposition I states that a firm cannot reduce the cost of capital—*i.e.*, increase the market value of the stream it generates—by securing part of its capital through the sale of bonds, even though debt money appears to be cheaper. This assertion is equivalent to the proposition that, under perfect markets, a dairy farmer cannot in general earn more for the milk he produces by skimming some of the butter fat and selling it separately, even though butter fat per unit weight, sells for more than whole milk. The advantage from skimming the milk rather than selling whole milk would be purely illusory; for what would be gained from selling the high-priced butter fat would be lost in selling the low-priced residue of thinned milk. Similarly our Proposition II—that the price per dollar of a levered stream falls as leverage increases—is an ex-

[31] Like Durand, Morton [15] contends "that the actual market deviates from [Proposition I] by giving a changing over-all cost of money at different points of the [leverage] scale" (p. 443, note 2, inserts ours), but the basis for this contention is nowhere clearly stated. Judging by the great emphasis given to the lack of mobility of investment funds between stocks and bonds and to the psychological and institutional pressures toward debt portfolios (see pp. 444–51 and especially his discussion of the optimal capital structure on p. 453) he would seem to be taking a position very similar to that of Durand above.

act analogue of the statement that the price per gallon of thinned milk falls continuously as more butter fat is skimmed off.[32]

It is clear that this last assertion is true as long as butter fat is worth more per unit weight than whole milk, and it holds even if, for many consumers, taking a little cream out of the milk (adding a little leverage to the stock) does not detract noticeably from the taste (does not add noticeably to the risk). Furthermore the argument remains valid even in the face of instituional limitations of the type envisaged by Durand. For suppose that a large fraction of the population habitually dines in restaurants which are required by law to serve only cream in lieu of milk (entrust their savings to institutional investors who can only buy bonds). To be sure the price of butter fat will then tend to be higher in relation to that of skimmed milk than in the absence such restrictions (the rate of interest will tend to be lower), and this will benefit people who eat at home and who like skim milk (who manage their own portfolio and are able and willing to take risk). But it will still be the case that a farmer cannot gain by skimming some of the butter fat and selling it separately (firm cannot reduce the cost of capital by recourse to borrowed funds).[33]

Our propositions can be regarded as the extension of the classical theory of markets to the particular case of the capital markets. Those who hold the current view—whether they realize it or not—must as-

[32] Let M denote the quantity of whole milk, B/M the proportion of butter fat in the whole milk, and let p_M, p_B and p_α denote, respectively, the price per unit weight of whole milk, butter fat and thinned milk from which a fraction α of the butter fat has been skimmed off. We then have the fundamental perfect market relation:

$$\text{(a)} \qquad p_\alpha(M - \alpha B) + p_B \alpha B = p_M M, \qquad 0 \leq \alpha \leq 1,$$

stating that total receipts will be the same amount $p_M M$, independently of the amount αB of butter fat that may have been sold separately. Since p_M corresponds to $1/\rho$, p_B to $1/r$, p_α to $1/i$, M to $\bar{X}$ and αB to rD, (a) is equivalent to Proposition I, $S+D=\bar{X}/\rho$. From (a) we derive:

$$\text{(b)} \qquad p_\alpha = p_M \frac{M}{M - \alpha B} - p_B \frac{\alpha B}{M - \alpha B}$$

which gives the price of thinned milk as an explicit function of the proportion of butter fat skimmed off; the function decreasing as long as $p_B > p_M$. From (a) also follows:

$$\text{(c)} \qquad 1/p_\alpha = 1/p_M + (1/p_M - 1/p_B) \frac{p_B \alpha B}{p_\alpha(M - \alpha B)}$$

which is the exact analogue of Proposition II, as given by (8).

[33] The reader who likes parables will find that the analogy with interrelated commodity markets can be pushed a good deal farther than we have done in the text. For instance, the effect of changes in the market rate of interest on the over-all cost of capital is the same as the effect of a change in the price of butter on the price of whole milk. Similarly, just as the relation between the prices of skim milk and butter fat influences the kind of cows that will be reared, so the relation between i and r influences the kind of ventures that will be undertaken. If people like butter we shall have Guernseys; if they are willing to pay a high price for safety, this will encourage ventures which promise smaller but less uncertain streams per dollar of physical assets.

sume not merely that there are lags and frictions in the equilibrating process—a feeling we certainly share,[34] claiming for our propositions only that they describe the central tendency around which observations will scatter—but also that there are large and *systematic* imperfections in the market which permanently bias the outcome. This is an assumption that economists, at any rate, will instinctively eye with some skepticism.

In any event, whether such prolonged, systematic departures from equilibrium really exist or whether our propositions are better descriptions of long-run market behavior can be settled only by empirical research. Before going on to the theory of investment it may be helpful, therefore, to look at the evidence.

E. *Some Preliminary Evidence on the Basic Propositions*

Unfortunately the evidence which has been assembled so far is amazingly skimpy. Indeed, we have been able to locate only two recent studies—and these of rather limited scope—which were designed to throw light on the issue. Pending the results of more comprehensive tests which we hope will soon be available, we shall review briefly such evidence as is provided by the two studies in question: (1) an analysis of the relation between security yields and financial structure for some 43 large electric utilities by F. B. Allen [1], and (2) a parallel (unpublished) study by Robert Smith [19], for 42 oil companies designed to test whether Allen's rather striking results would be found in an industry with very different characteristics.[35] The Allen study is based on average figures for the years 1947 and 1948, while the Smith study relates to the single year 1953.

The Effect of Leverage on the Cost of Capital. According to the received view, as shown in equation (17) the average cost of capital, $\overline{X}^\tau/V$, should decline linearly with leverage as measured by the ratio D/V, at least through most of the relevant range.[36] According to Proposition I, the average cost of capital within a given class k should tend to have the same value ρ_k^τ independently of the degree of leverage. A simple test

[34] Several specific examples of the failure of the arbitrage mechanism can be found in Graham and Dodd [6, *e.g.*, pp. 646–48]. The price discrepancy described on pp. 646–47 is particularly curious since it persists even today despite the fact that a whole generation of security analysts has been brought up on this book!

[35] We wish to express our thanks to both writers for making available to us some of their original worksheets. In addition to these recent studies there is a frequently cited (but apparently seldom read) study by the Federal Communications Commission in 1938 [22] which purports to show the existence of an optimal capital structure or range of structures (in the sense defined above) for public utilities in the 1930's. By current standards for statistical investigations, however, this study cannot be regarded as having any real evidential value for the problem at hand.

[36] We shall simplify our notation in this section by dropping the subscript j used to denote a particular firm wherever this will not lead to confusion.

of the merits of the two alternative hypotheses can thus be carried out by correlating $\overline{X}^{\tau}/V$ with D/V. If the traditional view is correct, the correlation should be significantly negative; if our view represents a better approximation to reality, then the correlation should not be significantly different from zero.

Both studies provide information about the average value of D—the market value of bonds and preferred stock—and of V—the market value of all securities.[37] From these data we can readily compute the ratio D/V and this ratio (expressed as a percentage) is represented by the symbol d in the regression equations below. The measurement of the variable $\overline{X}^{\tau}/V$, however, presents serious difficulties. Strictly speaking, the numerator should measure the expected returns net of taxes, but this is a variable on which no direct information is available. As an approximation, we have followed both authors and used (1) the average value of actual net returns in 1947 and 1948 for Allen's utilities; and (2) actual net returns in 1953 for Smith's oil companies. Net return is defined in both cases as the sum of interest, preferred dividends and stockholders' income net of corporate income taxes. Although this approximation to expected returns is undoubtedly very crude, there is no reason to believe that it will systematically bias the test in so far as the sign of the regression coefficient is concerned. The roughness of the approximation, however, will tend to make for a wide scatter. Also contributing to the scatter is the crudeness of the industrial classification, since especially within the sample of oil companies, the assumption that all the firms belong to the same class in our sense, is at best only approximately valid.

Denoting by x our approximation to $\overline{X}^{\tau}/V$ (expressed, like d, as a percentage), the results of the tests are as follows:

$$\text{Electric Utilities} \quad x = 5.3 + \underset{(\pm .008)}{.006d} \qquad r = .12$$

$$\text{Oil Companies} \quad x = 8.5 + \underset{(\pm .024)}{.006d} \qquad r = .04.$$

The data underlying these equations are also shown in scatter diagram form in Figures 3 and 4.

The results of these tests are clearly favorable to our hypothesis.

[37] Note that for purposes of this test preferred stocks, since they represent an *expected* fixed obligation, are properly classified with bonds even though the tax status of preferred dividends is different from that of interest payments and even though preferred dividends are really fixed only as to their maximum in any year. Some difficulty of classification does arise in the case of convertible preferred stocks (and convertible bonds) selling at a substantial premium, but fortunately very few such issues were involved for the companies included in the two studies. Smith included bank loans and certain other short-term obligations (at book values) in his data on oil company debts and this treatment is perhaps open to some question. However, the amounts involved were relatively small and check computations showed that their elimination would lead to only minor differences in the test results.

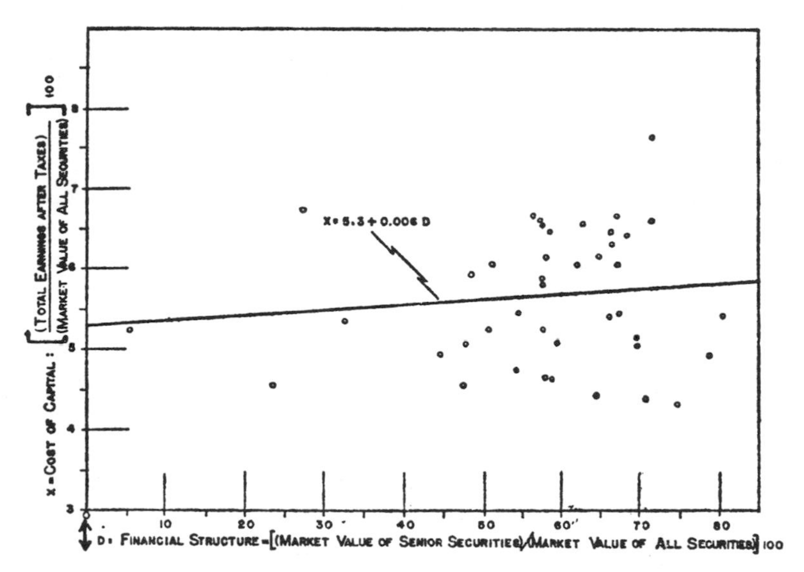

Figure 3. Cost of Capital in Relation to Financial Structure for 43 Electric Utilities, 1947–48

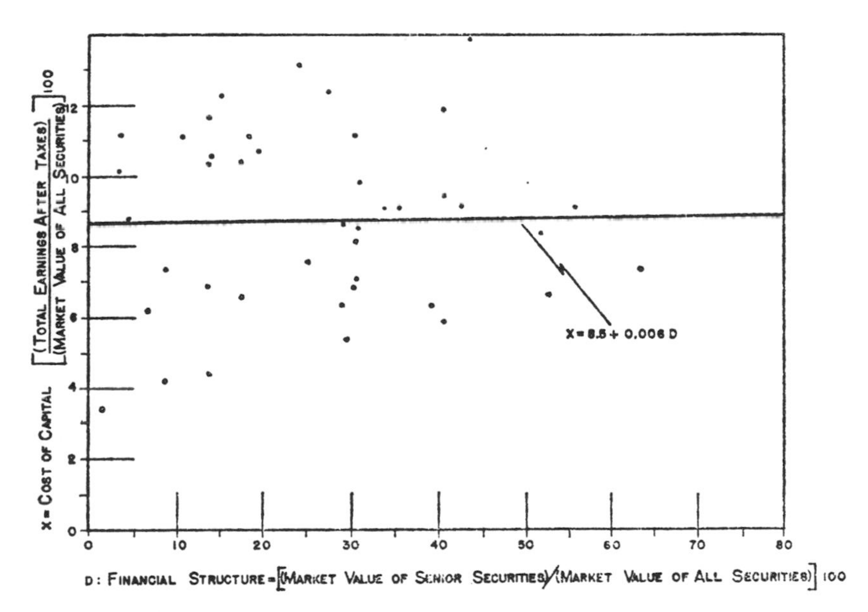

Figure 4. Cost of Capital in Relation to Financial Structure for 42 Oil Companies, 1953

Both correlation coefficients are very close to zero and not statistically significant. Furthermore, the implications of the traditional view fail to be supported even with respect to the sign of the correlation. The data in short provide no evidence of any tendency for the cost of capital to fall as the debt ratio increases.[38]

It should also be apparent from the scatter diagrams that there is no hint of a curvilinear, U-shaped, relation of the kind which is widely believed to hold between the cost of capital and leverage. This graphical impression was confirmed by statistical tests which showed that for both industries the curvature was not significantly different from zero, its sign actually being opposite to that hypothesized.[39]

Note also that according to our model, the constant terms of the regression equations are measures of ρ_k^τ, the capitalization rates for unlevered streams and hence the average cost of capital in the classes in question. The estimates of 8.5 per cent for the oil companies as against 5.3 per cent for electric utilities appear to accord well with a priori expectations, both in absolute value and relative spread.

The Effect of Leverage on Common Stock Yields. According to our Proposition II—see equation 12 and Figure 2—the expected yield on common stock, $\bar{\pi}^\tau/S$, in any given class, should tend to increase with leverage as measured by the ratio D/S. The relation should tend to be linear and with positive slope through most of the relevant range (as in the curve MM' of Figure 2), though it might tend to flatten out if we move

[38] It may be argued that a test of the kind used is biased against the traditional view. The fact that both sides of the regression equation are divided by the variable V which may be subject to random variation might tend to impart a positive bias to the correlation. As a check on the results presented in the text, we have, therefore, carried out a supplementary test based on equation (16). This equation shows that, if the traditional view is correct, the market value of a company should, foı given $\bar{X}^\tau$, increase with debt through most of the relevant range; according to our model the market value should be uncorrelated with D, given $\bar{X}^\tau$. Because of wide variations in the size of the firms included in our samples, all variables must be divided by a suitable scale factor in order to avoid spurious results in carrying out a test of equation (16). The factor we have used is the book value of the firm denoted by A. The hypothesis tested thus takes the specific form:

$$V/A = a + b(\bar{X}^\tau/A) + c(D/A)$$

and the numerator of the ratio X^τ/A is again approximated by actual net returns. The partial correlation between V/A and D/A should now be positive according to the traditional view and zero according to our model. Although division by A should, if anything, bias the results in favor of the traditional hypothesis, the partial correlation turns out to be only .03 for the oil companies and $-.28$ for the electric utilities. Neither of these coefficients is significantly different from zero and the larger one even has the wrong sign.

[39] The tests consisted of fitting to the data the equation (19) of footnote 27. As shown there, it follows from the U-shaped hypothesis that the coefficient α of the variable $(D/V)^2/(1-D/V)$, denoted hereafter by d^*, should be significant and positive. The following regression equations and partials were obtained:

Electric Utilities $x = 5.0 + .017d - .003d^*;\ r_{xd^*.d} = -.15$

Oil Companies $x = 8.0 + .05d - .03d^*;\ r_{xd^*.d} = -.14.$

far enough to the right (as in the curve MD'), to the extent that high leverage tends to drive up the cost of senior capital. According to the conventional view, the yield curve as a function of leverage should be a horizontal straight line (like ML') through most of the relevant range; far enough to the right, the yield may tend to rise at an increasing rate. Here again, a straight-forward correlation—in this case between $\bar{\pi}^\tau/S$ and D/S—can provide a test of the two positions. If our view is correct, the correlation should be significantly positive; if the traditional view is correct, the correlation should be negligible.

Subject to the same qualifications noted above in connection with $\bar{X}^\tau$, we can approximate $\bar{\pi}^\tau$ by actual stockholder net income.[40] Letting z denote in each case the approximation to $\bar{\pi}^\tau/S$ (expressed as a percentage) and letting h denote the ratio D/S (also in percentage terms) the following results are obtained:

$$\text{Electric Utilities} \quad z = 6.6 + .017h \quad r = .53$$
$$(+.004)$$

$$\text{Oil Companies} \quad z = 8.9 + .051h \quad r = .53.$$
$$(\pm .012)$$

These results are shown in scatter diagram form in Figures 5 and 6.

Here again the implications of our analysis seem to be borne out by the data. Both correlation coefficients are positive and highly significant when account is taken of the substantial sample size. Furthermore, the estimates of the coefficients of the equations seem to accord reasonably well with our hypothesis. According to equation (12) the constant term should be the value of $\rho_k{}^\tau$ for the given class while the slope should be $(\rho_k{}^\tau - r)$. From the test of Proposition I we have seen that for the oil companies the mean value of $\rho_k{}^\tau$ could be estimated at around 8.7. Since the average yield of senior capital during the period covered was in the order of $3\frac{1}{2}$ per cent, we should expect a constant term of about 8.7 per cent and a slope of just over 5 per cent. These values closely approximate the regression estimates of 8.9 per cent and 5.1 per cent respectively. For the electric utilities, the yield of senior capital was also on the order of $3\frac{1}{2}$ per cent during the test years, but since the estimate of the mean value of $\rho_k{}^\tau$ from the test of Proposition I was 5.6 per cent,

[40] As indicated earlier, Smith's data were for the single year 1953. Since the use of a single year's profits as a measure of expected profits might be open to objection we collected profit data for 1952 for the same companies and based the computation of $\bar{\pi}^\tau/S$ on the average of the two years. The value of $\bar{\pi}^\tau/S$ was obtained from the formula:

$$\left(\text{net earnings in 1952}\cdot\frac{\text{assets in '53}}{\text{assets in '52}} + \text{net earnings in '1953}\right)\frac{1}{2}$$
$$\div\ (\text{average market value of common stock in '53}).$$

The asset adjustment was introduced as rough allowance for the effects of possible growth in the size of the firm. It might be added that the correlation computed with $\bar{\pi}^\tau/S$ based on net profits in 1953 alone was found to be only slightly smaller, namely .50.

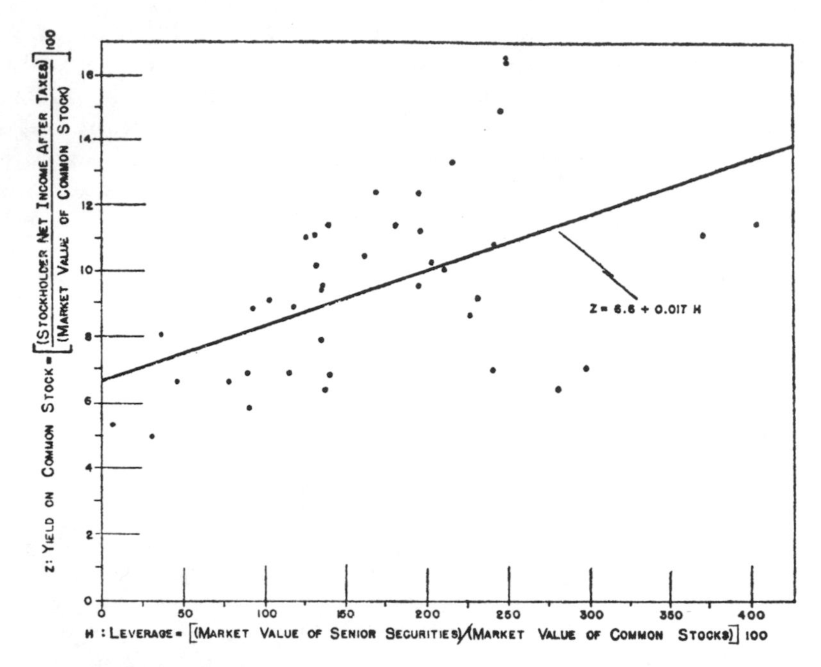

FIGURE 5. YIELD ON COMMON STOCK IN RELATION TO LEVERAGE FOR 43 ELECTRIC UTILITIES, 1947–48

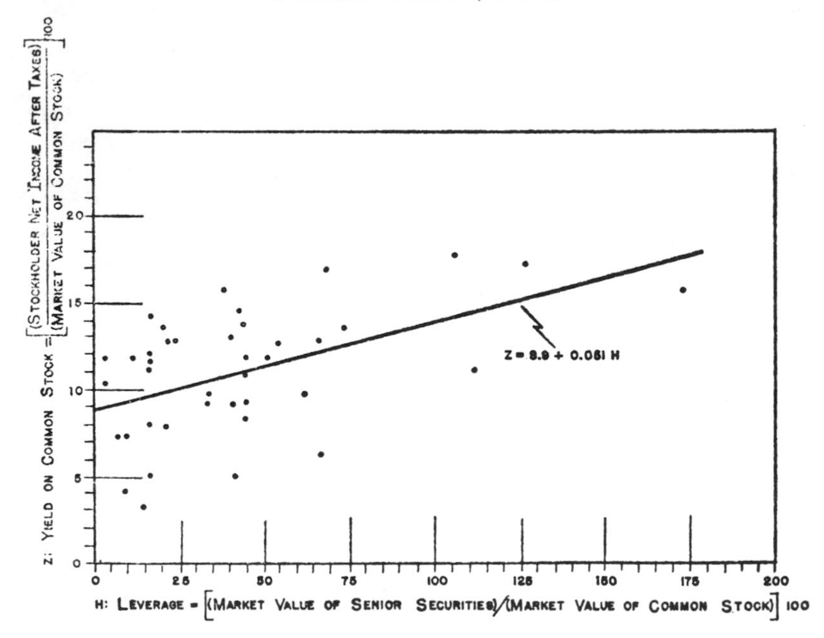

FIGURE 6. YIELD ON COMMON STOCK IN RELATION TO LEVERAGE FOR 42 OIL COMPANIES, 1952–53

the slope should be just above 2 per cent. The actual regression estimate for the slope of 1.7 per cent is thus somewhat low, but still within one standard error of its theoretical value. Because of this underestimate of the slope and because of the large mean value of leverage ($\bar{h}=160$ per cent) the regression estimate of the constant term, 6.6 per cent, is somewhat high, although not significantly different from the value of 5.6 per cent obtained in the test of Proposition I.

When we add a square term to the above equations to test for the presence and direction of curvature we obtain the following estimates:

$$\text{Electric Utilities} \quad z = 4.6 + .004h - .007h^2$$

$$\text{Oil Companies} \quad z = 8.5 + .072h - .016h^2.$$

For both cases the curvature is negative. In fact, for the electric utilities, where the observations cover a wider range of leverage ratios, the negative coefficient of the square term is actually significant at the 5 per cent level. Negative curvature, as we have seen, runs directly counter to the traditional hypothesis, whereas it can be readily accounted for by our model in terms of rising cost of borrowed funds.[41]

In summary, the empirical evidence we have reviewed seems to be broadly consistent with our model and largely inconsistent with traditional views. Needless to say much more extensive testing will be required before we can firmly conclude that our theory describes market behavior. Caution is indicated especially with regard to our test of Proposition II, partly because of possible statistical pitfalls[42] and partly because not all the factors that might have a systematic effect on stock yields have been considered. In particular, no attempt was made to test the possible influence of the dividend pay-out ratio whose role has tended to receive a great deal of attention in current research and thinking. There are two reasons for this omission. First, our main objective has been to assess the prima facie tenability of *our* model, and in this model, based as it is on rational behavior by investors, dividends per se play no role. Second, in a world in which the policy of dividend stabilization is widespread, there is no simple way of disentangling the true effect of dividend payments on stock prices from their apparent effect,

[41] That the yield of senior capital tended to rise for utilities as leverage increased is clearly shown in several of the scatter diagrams presented in the published version of Allen's study. This significant negative curvature between stock yields and leverage for utilities may be partly responsible for the fact, previously noted, that the constant in the linear regression is somewhat higher and the slope somewhat lower than implied by equation (12). Note also in connection with the estimate of ρ_k^τ that the introduction of the quadratic term reduces the constant considerably, pushing it in fact below the a priori expectation of 5.6, though the difference is again not statistically significant.

[42] In our test, *e.g.*, the two variables z and h are both ratios with S appearing in the denominator, which may tend to impart a positive bias to the correlation (*cf.* note 38). Attempts were made to develop alternative tests, but although various possibilities were explored, we have so far been unable to find satisfactory alternatives.

the latter reflecting only the role of dividends as a proxy measure of long-term earning anticipations.[43] The difficulties just mentioned are further compounded by possible interrelations between dividend policy and leverage.[44]

II. *Implications of the Analysis for the Theory of Investment*

A. *Capital Structure and Investment Policy*

On the basis of our propositions with respect to cost of capital and financial structure (and for the moment neglecting taxes), we can derive the following simple rule for optimal investment policy by the firm:

Proposition III. If a firm in class k is acting in the best interest of the stockholders at the time of the decision, it will exploit an investment opportunity if and only if the rate of return on the investment, say ρ^*, is as large as or larger than ρ_k. That is, *the cut-off point for investment in the firm will in all cases be ρ_k and will be completely unaffected by the type of security used to finance the investment.* Equivalently, we may say that regardless of the financing used, the marginal cost of capital to a firm is equal to the average cost of capital, which is in turn equal to the capitalization rate for an unlevered stream in the class to which the firm belongs.[45]

To establish this result we will consider the three major financing alternatives open to the firm—bonds, retained earnings, and common stock issues—and show that in each case an investment is worth undertaking if, and only if, $\rho^* \geqq \rho_k$.[46]

Consider first the case of an investment financed by the sale of bonds. We know from Proposition I that the market value of the firm before the investment was undertaken was:[47]

$$V_0 = \overline{X}_0/\rho_k \tag{20}$$

[43] We suggest that failure to appreciate this difficulty is responsible for many fallacious, or at least unwarranted, conclusions about the role of dividends.

[44] In the sample of electric utilities, there is a substantial negative correlation between yields and pay-out ratios, but also between pay-out ratios and leverage, suggesting that either the association of yields and leverage or of yields and pay-out ratios may be (at least partly) spurious. These difficulties however do not arise in the case of the oil industry sample. A preliminary analysis indicates that there is here no significant relation between leverage and pay-out ratios and also no significant correlation (either gross or partial) between yields and pay-out ratios.

[45] The analysis developed in this paper is essentially a comparative-statics, not a dynamic analysis. This note of caution applies with special force to Proposition III. Such problems as those posed by expected changes in r and in ρ_k over time will not be treated here. Although they are in principle amenable to analysis within the general framework we have laid out, such an undertaking is sufficiently complex to deserve separate treatment. *Cf.* note 17.

[46] The extension of the proof to other types of financing, such as the sale of preferred stock or the issuance of stock rights is straightforward.

[47] Since no confusion is likely to arise, we have again, for simplicity, eliminated the subscripts identifying the firm in the equations to follow. Except for ρ_k, the subscripts now refer to time periods.

and that the value of the common stock was:

$$S_0 = V_0 - D_0. \tag{21}$$

If now the firm borrows I dollars to finance an investment yielding ρ^* its market value will become:

$$V_1 = \frac{\overline{X}_0 + \rho^* I}{\rho_k} = V_0 + \frac{\rho^* I}{\rho_k} \tag{22}$$

and the value of its common stock will be:

$$S_1 = V_1 - (D_0 + I) = V_0 + \frac{\rho^* I}{\rho_k} - D_0 - I \tag{23}$$

or using equation 21,

$$S_1 = S_0 + \frac{\rho^* I}{\rho_k} - I. \tag{24}$$

Hence $S_1 \gtreqless S_0$ as $\rho^* \gtreqless \rho_k$.[48]

To illustrate, suppose the capitalization rate for uncertain streams in the kth class is 10 per cent and the rate of interest is 4 per cent. Then if a given company had an expected income of 1,000 and if it were financed entirely by common stock we know from Proposition I that the market value of its stock would be 10,000. Assume now that the managers of the firm discover an investment opportunity which will require an outlay of 100 and which is expected to yield 8 per cent. At first sight this might appear to be a profitable opportunity since the expected return is double the interest cost. If, however, the management borrows the necessary 100 at 4 per cent, the total expected income of the company rises to 1,008 and the market value of the firm to 10,080. But the firm now will have 100 of bonds in its capital structure so that, paradoxically, the market value of the stock must actually be reduced from 10,000 to 9,980 as a consequence of this apparently profitable investment. Or, to put it another way, the gains from being able to tap cheap, borrowed funds are more than offset for the stockholders by the market's discounting of the stock for the added leverage assumed.

Consider next the case of retained earnings. Suppose that in the course of its operations the firm acquired I dollars of cash (without impairing

[48] In the case of bond-financing the rate of interest on bonds does not enter explicitly into the decision (assuming the firm borrows at the market rate of interest). This is true, moreover, given the conditions outlined in Section I.C, even though interest rates may be an increasing function of debt outstanding. To the extent that the firm borrowed at a rate other than the market rate the two I's in equation (24) would no longer be identical and an additional gain or loss, as the case might be, would accrue to the shareholders. It might also be noted in passing that permitting the two I's in (24) to take on different values provides a simple method for introducing underwriting expenses into the analysis.

the earning power of its assets). If the cash is distributed as a dividend to the stockholders their wealth W_0, after the distribution will be:

$$W_0 = S_0 + I = \frac{\overline{X}_0}{\rho_k} - D_0 + I \tag{25}$$

where $\overline{X}_0$ represents the expected return from the assets exclusive of the amount I in question. If however the funds are retained by the company and used to finance new assets whose expected rate of return is ρ^*, then the stockholders' wealth would become:

$$W_1 = S_1 = \frac{\overline{X}_0 + \rho^* I}{\rho_k} - D_0 = S_0 + \frac{\rho^* I}{\rho_k}. \tag{26}$$

Clearly $W_1 \gtreqless W_0$ as $\rho^* \gtreqless \rho_k$ so that an investment financed by retained earnings raises the net worth of the owners if and only if $\rho^* > \rho_k$.[49]

Consider finally, the case of common-stock financing. Let P_0 denote the current market price per share of stock and assume, for simplicity, that this price reflects currently expected earnings only, that is, it does not reflect any future increase in earnings as a result of the investment under consideration.[50] Then if N is the original number of shares, the price per share is:

$$P_0 = S_0/N \tag{27}$$

and the number of new shares, M, needed to finance an investment of I dollars is given by:

$$M = \frac{I}{P_0}. \tag{28}$$

As a result of the investment the market value of the stock becomes:

$$S_1 = \frac{\overline{X}_0 + \rho^* I}{\rho_k} - D_0 = S_0 + \frac{\rho^* I}{\rho_k} = NP_0 + \frac{\rho^* I}{\rho_k}$$

and the price per share:

$$P_1 = \frac{S_1}{N + M} = \frac{1}{N + M}\left[NP_0 + \frac{\rho^* I}{\rho_k}\right]. \tag{29}$$

[49] The conclusion that ρ_k is the cut-off point for investments financed from internal funds applies not only to undistributed net profits, but to depreciation allowances (and even to the funds represented by the current sale value of any asset or collection of assets). Since the owners can earn ρ_k by investing funds elsewhere in the class, partial or total liquidating distributions should be made whenever the firm cannot achieve a marginal internal rate of return equal to ρ_k.

[50] If we assumed that the market price of the stock did reflect the expected higher future earnings (as would be the case if our original set of assumptions above were strictly followed) the analysis would differ slightly in detail, but not in essentials. The cut-off point for new investment would still be ρ_k, but where $\rho^* > \rho_k$ the gain to the original owners would be larger than if the stock price were based on the pre-investment expectations only.

Since by equation (28), $I = MP_0$, we can add MP_0 and subtract I from the quantity in bracket, obtaining:

$$(30)\quad \begin{aligned} P_1 &= \frac{1}{N+M}\left[(N+M)P_0 + \frac{\rho^* - \rho_k}{\rho_k} I\right] \\ &= P_0 + \frac{1}{N+M}\,\frac{\rho^* - \rho_k}{\rho_k} I > P_0 \text{ if,} \end{aligned}$$

and only if, $\rho^* > \rho_k$.

Thus an investment financed by common stock is advantageous to the current stockholders if and only if its yield exceeds the capitalization rate ρ_k.

Once again a numerical example may help to illustrate the result and make it clear why the relevant cut-off rate is ρ_k and not the current yield on common stock, i. Suppose that ρ_k is 10 per cent, r is 4 per cent, that the original expected income of our company is 1,000 and that management has the opportunity of investing 100 having an expected yield of 12 per cent. If the original capital structure is 50 per cent debt and 50 per cent equity, and 1,000 shares of stock are initially outstanding, then, by Proposition I, the market value of the common stock must be 5,000 or 5 per share. Furthermore, since the interest bill is $.04 \times 5{,}000 = 200$, the yield on common stock is $800/5{,}000 = 16$ per cent. It may then appear that financing the additional investment of 100 by issuing 20 shares to outsiders at 5 per share would dilute the equity of the original owners since the 100 promises to yield 12 per cent whereas the common stock is currently yielding 16 per cent. Actually, however, the income of the company would rise to 1,012; the value of the firm to 10,120; and the value of the common stock to 5,120. Since there are now 1,020 shares, each would be worth 5.02 and the wealth of the original stockholders would thus have been increased. What has happened is that the dilution in expected earnings per share (from .80 to .796) has been more than offset, in its effect upon the market price of the shares, by the decrease in leverage.

Our conclusion is, once again, at variance with conventional views,[51] so much so as to be easily misinterpreted. Read hastily, Proposition III seems to imply that the capital structure of a firm is a matter of indifference; and that, consequently, one of the core problems of corporate finance—the problem of the optimal capital structure for a firm—is no problem at all. It may be helpful, therefore, to clear up such possible misundertandings.

[51] In the matter of investment policy under uncertainty there is no single position which represents "accepted" doctrine. For a sample of current formulations, all very different from ours, see Joel Dean [2, esp. Ch. 3], M. Gordon and E. Shapiro [5], and Harry Roberts [17].

B. *Proposition III and Financial Planning by Firms*

Misinterpretation of the scope of Proposition III can be avoided by remembering that this Proposition tells us only that the type of instrument used to finance an investment is irrelevant to the question of whether or not the investment is worth while. This does not mean that the owners (or the managers) have no grounds whatever for preferring one financing plan to another; or that there are no other policy or technical issues in finance at the level of the firm.

That grounds for preferring one type of financial structure to another will still exist within the framework of our model can readily be seen for the case of common-stock financing. In general, except for something like a widely publicized oil-strike, we would expect the market to place very heavy weight on current and recent past earnings in forming expectations as to future returns. Hence, if the owners of a firm discovered a major investment opportunity which they felt would yield much more than ρ_k, they might well prefer not to finance it via common stock at the then ruling price, because this price may fail to capitalize the new venture. A better course would be a pre-emptive issue of stock (and in this connection it should be remembered that stockholders are free to borrow and buy). Another possibility would be to finance the project initially with debt. Once the project had reflected itself in increased actual earnings, the debt could be retired either with an equity issue at much better prices or through retained earnings. Still another possibility along the same lines might be to combine the two steps by means of a convertible debenture or preferred stock, perhaps with a progressively declining conversion rate. Even such a double-stage financing plan may possibly be regarded as yielding too large a share to outsiders since the new stockholders are, in effect, being given an interest in any similar opportunities the firm may discover in the future. If there is a reasonable prospect that even larger opportunities may arise in the near future and if there is some danger that borrowing now would preclude more borrowing later, the owners might find their interests best protected by splitting off the current opportunity into a separate subsidiary with independent financing. Clearly the problems involved in making the crucial estimates and in planning the optimal financial strategy are by no means trivial, even though they should have no bearing on the basic decision to invest (as long as $\rho^* \geqq \rho_k$).[52]

Another reason why the alternatives in financial plans may not be a matter of indifference arises from the fact that managers are concerned

[52] Nor can we rule out the possibility that the existing owners, if unable to use a financing plan which protects their interest, may actually prefer to pass up an otherwise profitable venture rather than give outsiders an "excessive" share of the business. It is presumably in situations of this kind that we could justifiably speak of a shortage of "equity capital," though this kind of market imperfection is likely to be of significance only for small or new firms.

with more than simply furthering the interest of the owners. Such other objectives of the management—which need not be necessarily in conflict with those of the owners—are much more likely to be served by some types of financing arrangements than others. In many forms of borrowing agreements, for example, creditors are able to stipulate terms which the current management may regard as infringing on its prerogatives or restricting its freedom to maneuver. The creditors might even be able to insist on having a direct voice in the formation of policy.[53] To the extent, therefore, that financial policies have these implications for the management of the firm, something like the utility approach described in the introductory section becomes relevant to financial (as opposed to investment) decision-making. It is, however, the utility functions of the managers per se and not of the owners that are now involved.[54]

In summary, many of the specific considerations which bulk so large in traditional discussions of corporate finance can readily be superimposed on our simple framework without forcing any drastic (and certainly no systematic) alteration of the conclusion which is our principal concern, namely that for investment decisions, the marginal cost of capital is ρ_k.

C. *The Effect of the Corporate Income Tax on Investment Decisions*

In Section I it was shown that when an unintegrated corporate income tax is introduced, the original version of our Proposition I,

$$\overline{X}/V = \rho_k = \text{a constant}$$

must be rewritten as:

$$\frac{(\overline{X} - rD)(1 - \tau) + rD}{V} \equiv \frac{\overline{X}^\tau}{V} = \rho_k^\tau = \text{a constant.} \tag{11}$$

Throughout Section I we found it convenient to refer to $\overline{X}^\tau/V$ as the cost of capital. The appropriate measure of the cost of capital relevant

[53] Similar considerations are involved in the matter of dividend policy. Even though the stockholders may be indifferent as to payout policy as long as investment policy is optimal, the management need not be so. Retained earnings involve far fewer threats to control than any of the alternative sources of funds and, of course, involve no underwriting expense or risk. But against these advantages management must balance the fact that sharp changes in dividend rates, which heavy reliance on retained earnings might imply, may give the impression that a firm's finances are being poorly managed, with consequent threats to the control and professional standing of the management.

[54] In principle, at least, this introduction of management's risk preferences with respect to financing methods would do much to reconcile the apparent conflict between Proposition III and such empirical findings as those of Modigliani and Zeman [14] on the close relation between interest rates and the ratio of new debt to new equity issues; or of John Lintner [12] on the considerable stability in target and actual dividend-payout ratios.

to investment decisions, however, is the ratio of the expected return *before* taxes to the market value, *i.e.*, $\overline{X}/V$. From (11) above we find:

$$\frac{\overline{X}}{V} = \frac{\rho_k^\tau - \tau_r(D/V)}{1-\tau} = \frac{\rho_k^\tau}{1-\tau}\left[1 - \frac{\tau r D}{\rho_k^\tau V}\right], \tag{31}$$

which shows that the cost of capital now depends on the debt ratio, decreasing, as D/V rises, at the constant rate $\tau r/(1-\tau)$.[55] Thus, with a corporate income tax under which interest is a deductible expense, gains can accrue to stockholders from having debt in the capital structure, even when capital markets are perfect. The gains however are small, as can be seen from (31), and as will be shown more explicitly below.

From (31) we can develop the tax-adjusted counterpart of Proposition III by interpreting the term D/V in that equation as the proportion of debt used in any additional financing of V dollars. For example, in the case where the financing is entirely by new common stock, $D=0$ and the required rate of return $\rho_k{}^S$ on a venture so financed becomes:

$$\rho_k{}^S = \frac{\rho_k^\tau}{1-\tau}. \tag{32}$$

For the other extreme of pure debt financing $D=V$ and the required rate of return, $\rho_k{}^D$, becomes:

$$\rho_k{}^D = \frac{\rho_k^\tau}{1-\tau}\left[1 - \tau\frac{r}{\rho_k^\tau}\right] = \rho_k{}^S\left[1 - \tau\frac{r}{\rho_k^\tau}\right] = \rho_k{}^S - \frac{\tau}{1-\tau}r. \tag{33}$$[56]

For investments financed out of retained earnings, the problem of defining the required rate of return is more difficult since it involves a comparison of the tax consequences to the individual stockholder of receiving a dividend versus having a capital gain. Depending on the time of realization, a capital gain produced by retained earnings may be taxed either at ordinary income tax rates, 50 per cent of these rates, 25 per

[55] Equation (31) is amenable, in principle, to statistical tests similar to those described in Section I.E. However we have not made any systematic attempt to carry out such tests so far, because neither the Allen nor the Smith study provides the required information. Actually, Smith's data included a very crude estimate of tax liability, and, using this estimate, we did in fact obtain a negative relation between $\overline{X}/V$ and D/V. However, the correlation ($-.28$) turned out to be significant only at about the 10 per cent level. While this result is not conclusive, it should be remembered that, according to our theory, the slope of the regression equation should be in any event quite small. In fact, with a value of τ in the order of .5, and values of ρ_k^τ and r in the order of 8.5 and 3.5 per cent respectively (*cf.* Section I.E) an increase in D/V from 0 to 60 per cent (which is, approximately, the range of variation of this variable in the sample) should tend to reduce the average cost of capital only from about 17 to about 15 per cent.

[56] This conclusion does not extend to preferred stocks even though they have been classed with debt issues previously. Since preferred dividends except for a portion of those of public utilities are not in general deductible from the corporate tax, the cut-off point for new financing via preferred stock is exactly the same as that for common stock.

cent, or zero, if held till death. The rate on any dividends received in the event of a distribution will also be a variable depending on the amount of other income received by the stockholder, and with the added complications introduced by the current dividend-credit provisions. If we assume that the managers proceed on the basis of reasonable estimates as to the average values of the relevant tax rates for the owners, then the required return for retained earnings ρ_k^R can be shown to be:

$$\rho_k^R = \rho_k^\tau \frac{1}{1-\tau} \frac{1-\tau_d}{1-\tau_g} = \frac{1-\tau_d}{1-\tau_g} \rho_k^* \tag{34}$$

where τ_d is the assumed rate of personal income tax on dividends and τ_g is the assumed rate of tax on capital gains.

A numerical illustration may perhaps be helpful in clarifying the relationship between these required rates of return. If we take the following round numbers as representative order-of-magnitude values under present conditions: an after-tax capitalization rate ρ_k^τ of 10 per cent, a rate of interest on bonds of 4 per cent, a corporate tax rate of 50 per cent, a marginal personal income tax rate on dividends of 40 per cent (corresponding to an income of about $25,000 on a joint return), and a capital gains rate of 20 per cent (one-half the marginal rate on dividends), then the required rates of return would be: (1) 20 per cent for investments financed entirely by issuance of new common shares; (2) 16 per cent for investments financed entirely by new debt; and (3) 15 per cent for investments financed wholly from internal funds.

These results would seem to have considerable significance for current discussions of the effect of the corporate income tax on financial policy and on investment. Although we cannot explore the implications of the results in any detail here, we should at least likc to call attention to the remarkably small difference between the "cost" of equity funds and debt funds. With the numerical values assumed, equity money turned out to be only 25 per cent more expensive than debt money, rather than something on the order of 5 times as expensive as is commonly supposed to be the case.[57] The reason for the wide difference is that the traditional

[57] See *e.g.*, D. T. Smith [18]. It should also be pointed out that our tax system acts in other ways to reduce the gains from debt financing. Heavy reliance on debt in the capital structure, for example, commits a company to paying out a substantial proportion of its income in the form of interest payments taxable to the owners under the personal income tax. A debt-free company, by contrast, can reinvest in the business all of its (smaller) net income and to this extent subject the owners only to the low capital gains rate (or possibly no tax at all by virtue of the loophole at death). Thus, we should expect a high degree of leverage to be of value to the owners, even in the case of closely held corporations, primarily in cases where their firm was not expected to have much need for additional funds to expand assets and earnings in the future. To the extent that opportunities for growth were available, as they presumably would be for most successful corporations, the interest of the stockholders would tend to be better served by a structure which permitted maximum use of retained earnings.

view starts from the position that debt funds are several times cheaper than equity funds even in the absence of taxes, with taxes serving simply to magnify the cost ratio in proportion to the corporate rate. By contrast, in our model in which the repercussions of debt financing on the value of shares are taken into account, the *only* difference in cost is that due to the tax effect, and its magnitude is simply the tax on the "grossed up" interest payment. Not only is this magnitude likely to be small but our analysis yields the further paradoxical implication that the stockholders' gain from, and hence incentive to use, debt financing is actually smaller the lower the rate of interest. In the extreme case where the firm could borrow for practically nothing, the advantage of debt financing would also be practically nothing.

III. *Conclusion*

With the development of Proposition III the main objectives we outlined in our introductory discussion have been reached. We have in our Propositions I and II at least the foundations of a theory of the valuation of firms and shares in a world of uncertainty. We have shown, moreover, how this theory can lead to an operational definition of the cost of capital and how that concept can be used in turn as a basis for rational investment decision-making within the firm. Needless to say, however, much remains to be done before the cost of capital can be put away on the shelf among the solved problems. Our approach has been that of static, partial equilibrium analysis. It has assumed among other things a state of atomistic competition in the capital markets and an ease of access to those markets which only a relatively small (though important) group of firms even come close to possessing. These and other drastic simplifications have been necessary in order to come to grips with the problem at all. Having served their purpose they can now be relaxed in the direction of greater realism and relevance, a task in which we hope others interested in this area will wish to share.

References

1. F. B. Allen, "Does Going into Debt Lower the 'Cost of Capital'?," *Analysts Jour.*, Aug. 1954, *10*, 57–61.
2. J. Dean, *Capital Budgeting*. New York 1951.
3. D. Durand, "Costs of Debt and Equity Funds for Business: Trends and Problems of Measurement" in Nat. Bur. Econ. Research, *Conference on Research in Business Finance*. New York 1952, pp. 215–47.
4. W. J. Eiteman, "Financial Aspects of Promotion," in *Essays on Business Finance* by M. W. Waterford and W. J. Eiteman. Ann Arbor, Mich. 1952, pp. 1–17.
5. M. J. Gordon and E. Shapiro, "Capital Equipment Analysis: The Required Rate of Profit," *Manag. Sci.*, Oct. 1956, *3*, 102–10.

6. B. GRAHAM and L. DODD, *Security Analysis*, 3rd ed. New York 1951.
7. G. GUTHMANN and H. E. DOUGALL, *Corporate Financial Policy*, 3rd ed. New York 1955.
8. J. R. HICKS, *Value and Capital*, 2nd ed. Oxford 1946.
9. P. HUNT and M. WILLIAMS, *Case Problems in Finance*, rev. ed. Homewood, Ill. 1954.
10. J. M. KEYNES, *The General Theory of Employment, Interest and Money*. New York 1936.
11. O. LANGE, *Price Flexibility and Employment*. Bloomington, Ind. 1944.
12. J. LINTNER, "Distribution of Incomes of Corporations among Dividends, Retained Earnings and Taxes," *Am. Econ. Rev.*, May 1956, *46*, 97–113.
13. F. LUTZ and V. LUTZ, *The Theory of Investment of the Firm*. Princeton 1951.
14. F. MODIGLIANI and M. ZEMAN, "The Effect of the Availability of Funds, and the Terms Thereof, on Business Investment" in Nat. Bur. Econ. Research, *Conference on Research in Business Finance*. New York 1952, pp. 263–309.
15. W. A. MORTON, "The Structure of the Capital Market and the Price of Money," *Am. Econ. Rev.*, May 1954, *44*, 440–54.
16. S. M. ROBBINS, *Managing Securities*. Boston 1954.
17. H. V. ROBERTS, "Current Problems in the Economics of Capital Budgeting," *Jour. Bus.*, 1957, *30* (1), 12–16.
18. D. T. SMITH, *Effects of Taxation on Corporate Financial Policy*. Boston 1952.
19. R. SMITH, "Cost of Capital in the Oil Industry," (hectograph). Pittsburgh: Carnegie Inst. Tech. 1955.
20. H. M. SOMERS, " 'Cost of Money' as the Determinant of Public Utility Rates," *Buffalo Law Rev.*, Spring 1955, *4*, 1–28.
21. J. B. WILLIAMS, *The Theory of Investment Value*. Cambridge, Mass. 1938.
22. U. S. Federal Communications Commission, *The Problem of the "Rate of Return" in Public Utility Regulation*. Washington 1938.

Errata

Page 265, footnote 6, line 5: "$\chi_i[X_i(1), X_i(2) \cdots X_i(t)]$ " should read "$\chi_i[X_i(1), X_i(2) \cdots X_i(T)]$."

Page 294: the first equality in equation (31) should read

$$``\frac{X}{V} = \frac{\rho_k^\tau - \tau r(D/V)}{1 - \tau}."$$

DIVIDEND POLICY, GROWTH, AND THE VALUATION OF SHARES*

MERTON H. MILLER† AND FRANCO MODIGLIANI‡

The effect of a firm's dividend policy on the current price of its shares is a matter of considerable importance, not only to the corporate officials who must set the policy, but to investors planning portfolios and to economists seeking to understand and appraise the functioning of the capital markets. Do companies with generous distribution policies consistently sell at a premium over those with niggardly payouts? Is the reverse ever true? If so, under what conditions? Is there an optimum payout ratio or range of ratios that maximizes the current worth of the shares?

Although these questions of fact have been the subject of many empirical studies in recent years no consensus has yet been achieved. One reason appears to be the absence in the literature of a complete and reasonably rigorous statement of those parts of the economic theory of valuation bearing directly on the matter of dividend policy. Lacking such a statement, investigators have not yet been able to frame their tests with sufficient precision to distinguish adequately between the various contending hypotheses. Nor have they been able to give a convincing explanation of what their test results do imply about the underlying process of valuation.

In the hope that it may help to overcome these obstacles to effective empirical testing, this paper will attempt to fill the existing gap in the theoretical literature on valuation. We shall begin, in Section I, by examining the effects of differences in dividend policy on the current price of shares in an ideal economy characterized by perfect capital markets, rational behavior, and perfect certainty. Still within this convenient analytical framework we shall go on in Sections II and III to consider certain closely related issues that appear to have been responsible for considerable misunderstanding of the role of dividend policy. In particular, Section II will focus on the long-standing debate about what investors "really" capitalize when they buy shares; and Section III on the much mooted relations between price, the rate of growth of

* The authors wish to express their thanks to all who read and commented on earlier versions of this paper and especially to Charles C. Holt, now of the University of Wisconsin, whose suggestions led to considerable simplification of a number of the proofs.

† Professor of finance and economics, University of Chicago.

‡ Professor of economics, Northwestern University.

profits, and the rate of growth of dividends per share. Once these fundamentals have been established, we shall proceed in Section IV to drop the assumption of certainty and to see the extent to which the earlier conclusions about dividend policy must be modified. Finally, in Section V, we shall briefly examine the implications for the dividend policy problem of certain kinds of market imperfections.

I. EFFECT OF DIVIDEND POLICY WITH PERFECT MARKETS, RATIONAL BEHAVIOR, AND PERFECT CERTAINTY

The meaning of the basic assumptions.—Although the terms "perfect markets," "rational behavior," and "perfect certainty" are widely used throughout economic theory, it may be helpful to start by spelling out the precise meaning of these assumptions in the present context.

1. In "perfect capital markets," no buyer or seller (or issuer) of securities is large enough for his transactions to have an appreciable impact on the then ruling price. All traders have equal and costless access to information about the ruling price and about all other relevant characteristics of shares (to be detailed specifically later). No brokerage fees, transfer taxes, or other transaction costs are incurred when securities are bought, sold, or issued, and there are no tax differentials either between distributed and undistributed profits or between dividends and capital gains.

2. "Rational behavior" means that investors always prefer more wealth to less and are indifferent as to whether a given increment to their wealth takes the form of cash payments or an increase in the market value of their holdings of shares.

3. "Perfect certainty" implies complete assurance on the part of every investor as to the future investment program and the future profits of every corporation. Because of this assurance, there is, among other things, no need to distinguish between stocks and bonds as sources of funds at this stage of the analysis. We can, therefore, proceed as if there were only a single type of financial instrument which, for convenience, we shall refer to as shares of stock.

The fundamental principle of valuation.—Under these assumptions the valuation of all shares would be governed by the following fundamental principle: the price of each share must be such that the rate of return (dividends plus capital gains per dollar invested) on every share will be the same throughout the market over any given interval of time. That is, if we let

$d_j(t)$ = dividends per share paid by firm j during period t

$p_j(t)$ = the price (ex any dividend in $t-1$) of a share in firm j at the start of period t,

we must have

$$\frac{d_j(t)+p_j(t+1)-p_j(t)}{p_j(t)} = \rho(t) \text{ independent of } j\,; \tag{1}$$

or, equivalently,

$$p_j(t)=\frac{1}{1+\rho(t)}\left[d_j(t)+p_j(t+1)\right] \tag{2}$$

for each j and for all t. Otherwise, holders of low-return (high-priced) shares could increase their terminal wealth by selling these shares and investing the proceeds in shares offering a higher rate of return. This process would tend to drive down the prices of the low-return shares and drive up the prices of high-return shares until the differential in rates of return had been eliminated.

The effect of dividend policy.—The implications of this principle for our problem of dividend policy can be seen somewhat more easily if equation (2) is restated in terms of the value of the enterprise as a whole rather than in terms of the value of an individual share. Dropping the firm subscript j since this will lead to no ambiguity in the present context and letting

$n(t)$ = the number of shares of record at the start of t

$m(t+1)$ = the number of new shares (if any) sold during t at the ex dividend closing price $p(t+1)$, so that

$n(t+1) = n(t) + m(t+1)$

$V(t) = n(t)\,p(t)$ = the total value of the enterprise and

$D(t) = n(t)\,d(t)$ = the total dividends paid during t to holders of record at the start of t,

we can rewrite (2)

$$V(t)=\frac{1}{1+\rho(t)}\,[D(t)+n(t)\,p(t+1)]$$

$$=\frac{1}{1+\rho(t)}\,[D(t)+V(t+1)-m(t+1)\,p(t+1)]. \quad (3)$$

The advantage of restating the fundamental rule in this form is that it brings into sharper focus the three possible routes by which current dividends might affect the current market value of the firm $V(t)$, or equivalently the price of its individual shares, $p(t)$. Current dividends will clearly affect $V(t)$ via the first term in the bracket, $D(t)$. In principle, current dividends might also affect $V(t)$ indirectly via the second term, $V(t+1)$, the new ex dividend market value. Since $V(t+1)$ must depend only on future and not on past events, such could be the case, however, only if both (*a*) $V(t+1)$ were a function of future dividend policy and (*b*) the current distribution $D(t)$ served to convey some otherwise unavailable information as to what that future dividend policy would be. The first possibility being the relevant one from the standpoint of assessing the effects of dividend policy, it will clarify matters to assume, provisionally, that the future dividend policy of the firm is known and given for $t+1$ and all subsequent periods and is independent of the actual dividend decision in t. Then $V(t+1)$ will also be independent of the current dividend decision, though it may very well be affected by $D(t+1)$ and all subsequent distributions. Finally, current dividends can influence $V(t)$ through the third term, $-m(t+1)\,p(t+1)$, the value of new shares sold to outsiders during the period. For the higher the dividend payout in any period the more the new capital that must be raised from external sources to maintain any desired level of investment.

The fact that the dividend decision effects price not in one but in these two conflicting ways—directly via $D(t)$ and inversely via $-m(t)\,p(t+1)$—is, of course, precisely why one speaks of there being a dividend policy *problem.* If the firm raises its dividend in t, given its investment decision, will the increase in the cash payments to the current holders be more or less than enough to offset their lower share of the terminal value? Which is the better strategy for the firm in financing the investment: to reduce dividends and rely on retained earnings or to raise dividends but float more new shares?

In our ideal world at least these and related questions can be simply and immediately answered: the two dividend effects must always exactly cancel out so that the payout policy to be followed in t will have *no* effect on the price at t.

We need only express $m(t+1)\cdot p(t+1)$ in terms of $D(t)$ to show that such must indeed be the case. Specifically, if $I(t)$ is the given level of the firm's investment or increase in its holding of physical assets in t and if $X(t)$ is the firm's total net profit for the period, we know that the amount of outside capital required will be

$$m(t+1)p(t+1) = I(t) - [X(t) - D(t)] . \tag{4}$$

Substituting expression (4) into (3), the $D(t)$ cancel and we obtain for the value of the firm as of the start of t

$$V(t) \equiv n(t)p(t) = \frac{1}{1+\rho(t)}[X(t) - I(t) + V(t+1)] . \tag{5}$$

Since $D(t)$ does not appear directly among the arguments and since $X(t)$, $I(t)$, $V(t+1)$ and $\rho(t)$ are all independent of $D(t)$ (either by their nature or by assumption) it follows that the current value of the firm must be independent of the current dividend decision.

Having established that $V(t)$ is unaffected by the current dividend decision it is easy to go on to show that $V(t)$ must also be unaffected by any future dividend decisions as well. Such future decisions can influence $V(t)$ only via their effect on $V(t+1)$. But we can repeat the reasoning above and show that $V(t+1)$—and hence $V(t)$—is unaffected by dividend policy in $t+1$; that $V(t+2)$—and hence $V(t+1)$ and $V(t)$—is unaffected by dividend policy in $t+2$; and so on for as far into the future as we care to look. Thus, we may conclude that given a firm's investment policy, the dividend payout policy it chooses to follow will affect neither the current price of its shares nor the total return to its shareholders.

Like many other propositions in economics, the irrelevance of dividend policy, given investment policy, is "obvious, once you think of it." It is, after all, merely one more instance of the general principle that there are no "financial illusions" in a rational and perfect economic environment. Values there are determined solely by "real" considerations—in this case the earning power of the firm's assets and its investment policy—and not by how the fruits of the earning power are "packaged" for distribution.

Obvious as the proposition may be, however, one finds few references to it in the extensive literature on the problem.[1] It is true that the literature abounds with statements that in some "theoretical" sense, dividend policy ought not to count; but either that sense is not clearly specified or, more frequently and especially among economists, it is (wrongly) identified with a situation in which the firm's internal rate of return is the same as the external or market rate of return.[2]

A major source of these and related misunderstandings of the role of the dividend policy has been the fruitless concern and controversy over what investors "really" capitalize when they buy shares. We say fruitless because as we shall now proceed to show, it is actually possible to derive from the basic principle of valuation (1) not merely one, but several valuation formulas each starting from one of the "classical" views of what is being capitalized by investors. Though differing somewhat in outward appearance, the various formulas can be shown to be equivalent in all essential respects including, of course, their implication that dividend policy is irrelevant. While the

[1] Apart from the references to it in our earlier papers, especially [16], the closest approximation seems to be that in Bodenborn [1, p. 492], but even his treatment of the role of dividend policy is not completely explicit. (The numbers in brackets refer to references listed below, pp. 432–33).

[2] See below p. 424.

controvery itself thus turns out to be an empty one, the different expressions do have some intrinsic interest since, by highlighting different combinations of variables they provide additional insights into the process of valuation and they open alternative lines of attack on some of the problems of empirical testing.

II. WHAT DOES THE MARKET "REALLY" CAPITALIZE?

In the literature on valuation one can find at least the following four more or less distinct approaches to the valuation of shares: (1) the discounted cash flow approach; (2) the current earnings plus future investment opportunities approach; (3) the stream of dividends approach; and (4) the stream of earnings approach. To demonstrate that these approaches are, in fact, equivalent it will be helpful to begin by first going back to equation (5) and developing from it a valuation formula to serve as a point of reference and comparison. Specifically, if we assume, for simplicity, that the market rate of yield $\rho(t) = \rho$ for all t,[3] then, setting $t = 0$, we can rewrite (5) as

$$V(0) = \frac{1}{1+\rho}[X(0) - I(0)] + \frac{1}{1+\rho} V(1) . \qquad (6)$$

Since (5) holds for all t, setting $t = 1$ permits us to express $V(1)$ in terms of $V(2)$ which in turn can be expressed in terms of $V(3)$ and so on up to any arbitrary terminal period T. Carrying out these substitutions, we obtain

$$V(0) = \sum_{t=0}^{T-1} \frac{1}{(1+\rho)^{t+1}}[X(t) - I(t)] + \frac{1}{(1+\rho)^T} V(T) . \qquad (7)$$

In general, the remainder term $(1+\rho)^{-T} \cdot V(T)$ can be expected to approach zero as T approaches infinity[4] so that (7) can be expressed as

$$V(0) = \lim_{T\to\infty} \sum_{t=0}^{T-1} \frac{1}{(1+\rho)^{t+1}} \times [X(t) - I(t)] , \qquad (8)$$

which we shall further abbreviate to

$$V(0) = \sum_{t=0}^{\infty} \frac{1}{(1+\rho)^{t+1}} [X(t) - I(t)] . \qquad (9)$$

The discounted cash flow approach.—Consider now the so-called discounted cash flow approach familiar in discussions of capital budgeting. There, in valuing any specific machine we discount at the market rate of interest the stream of cash receipts generated by the machine; plus any scrap or terminal value of the machine; and minus the stream of cash outlays for direct labor, materials, repairs, and capital additions. The same approach, of course, can also be applied to the firm as a whole which may be thought of in this context as simply a large, composite machine.[5] This ap-

[3] More general formulas in which $\rho(t)$ is allowed to vary with time can always be derived from those presented here merely by substituting the cumbersome product

$$\prod_{\tau=0}^{t} [1 + \rho(\tau)] \quad \text{for} \quad (1+\rho)^{t+1} .$$

[4] The assumption that the remainder vanishes is introduced for the sake of simplicity of exposition only and is in no way essential to the argument. What is essential, of course, is that $V(0)$, i.e., the sum of the two terms in (7), be finite, but this can always be safely assumed in economic analysis. See below, n. 14.

[5] This is, in fact, the approach to valuation normally taken in economic theory when discussing the value of the *assets* of an enterprise, but much more rarely applied, unfortunately, to the value of the liability side. One of the few to apply the approach to the shares as well as the assets is Bodenhorn in [1], who uses it to derive a formula closely similar to (9) above.

proach amounts to defining the value of the firm as

$$V(0) = \sum_{t=0}^{T-1} \frac{1}{(1+\rho)^{t+1}} \times [\mathcal{R}(t) - \mathcal{O}(t)] + \frac{1}{(1+\rho)^{T}} V(T), \quad (10)$$

where $\mathcal{R}(t)$ represents the stream of cash receipts and $\mathcal{O}(t)$ of cash outlays, or, abbreviating, as above, to

$$V(0) = \sum_{t=0}^{\infty} \frac{1}{(1+\rho)^{t+1}} [\mathcal{R}(t) - \mathcal{O}(t)]. \quad (11)$$

But we also know, by definition, that $[X(t) - I(t)] = [\mathcal{R}(t) - \mathcal{O}(t)]$ since, $X(t)$ differs from $\mathcal{R}(t)$ and $I(t)$ differs from $\mathcal{O}(t)$ merely by the "cost of goods sold" (and also by the depreciation expense if we wish to interpret $X(t)$ and $I(t)$ as net rather than gross profits and investment). Hence (11) is formally equivalent to (9), and the discounted cash flow approach is thus seen to be an implication of the valuation principle for perfect markets given by equation (1).

The investment opportunities approach.—Consider next the approach to valuation which would seem most natural from the standpoint of an investor proposing to buy out and operate some already-going concern. In estimating how much it would be worthwhile to pay for the privilege of operating the firm, the amount of dividends to be paid is clearly not relevant, since the new owner can, within wide limits, make the future dividend stream whatever he pleases. For him the worth of the enterprise, as such, will depend only on: (*a*) the "normal" rate of return he can earn by investing his capital in securities (i.e., the market rate of return); (*b*) the earning power of the physical assets currently held by the firm; and (*c*) the opportunities, if any, that the firm offers for making additional investments in real assets that will yield more than the "normal" (market) rate of return. The latter opportunities, frequently termed the "good will" of the business, may arise, in practice, from any of a number of circumstances (ranging all the way from special locational advantages to patents or other monopolistic advantages).

To see how these opportunities affect the value of the business assume that in some future period t the firm invests $I(t)$ dollars. Suppose, further, for simplicity, that starting in the period immediately following the investment of the funds, the projects produce net profits at a constant rate of $\rho^*(t)$ per cent of $I(t)$ in each period thereafter.[6] Then the present worth as of t of the (perpetual) stream of profits generated will be $I(t)\,\rho^*(t)/\rho$, and the "good will" of the projects (i.e., the difference between worth and cost) will be

$$I(t)\frac{\rho^*(t)}{\rho} - I(t) = I(t)\left[\frac{\rho^*(t) - \rho}{\rho}\right].$$

The present worth as of now of this future "good will" is

$$I(t)\left[\frac{\rho^*(t) - \rho}{\rho}\right](1+\rho)^{-(t+1)},$$

and the present value of all such future opportunities is simply the sum

$$\sum_{t=0}^{\infty} I(t)\frac{\rho^*(t) - \rho}{\rho}(1+\rho)^{-(t+1)}.$$

Adding in the present value of the (uniform perpetual) earnings, $X(0)$, on the as-

[6] The assumption that $I(t)$ yields a uniform perpetuity is not restrictive in the present certainty context since it is always possible by means of simple, present-value calculations to find an equivalent uniform perpetuity for any project, whatever the time shape of its actual returns. Note also that $\rho^*(t)$ is the *average* rate of return. If the managers of the firm are behaving rationally, they will, of course, use ρ as their cut-off criterion (cf. below p. 418). In this event we would have $\rho^*(t) \geq \rho$. The formulas remain valid, however, even where $\rho^*(t) < \rho$.

sets currently held, we get as an expression for the value of the firm

$$V(0) = \frac{X(0)}{\rho} + \sum_{t=0}^{\infty} I(t) \times \frac{\rho^*(t) - \rho}{\rho} (1+\rho)^{-(t+1)}. \tag{12}$$

To show that the same formula can be derived from (9) note first that our definition of $\rho^*(t)$ implies the following relation between the $X(t)$:

$$X(1) = X(0) + \rho^*(0) I(0),$$

$$\cdots\cdots\cdots\cdots\cdots\cdots\cdots$$

$$X(t) = X(t-1) + \rho^*(t-1) I(t-1)$$

and by successive substitution

$$X(t) = X(0) + \sum_{\tau=0}^{t-1} \rho^*(\tau) I(\tau),$$

$$t = 1, 2 \ldots \infty .$$

Substituting the last expression for $X(t)$ in (9) yields

$$V(0) = [X(0) - I(0)] (1+\rho)^{-1} + \sum_{t=1}^{\infty} \left[X(0) + \sum_{\tau=0}^{t-1} \rho^*(\tau) I(\tau) - I(t) \right] (1+\rho)^{-(t+1)}$$

$$= X(0) \sum_{t=1}^{\infty} (1+\rho)^{-t} - I(0)(1+\rho)^{-1} + \sum_{t=1}^{\infty} \left[\sum_{\tau=0}^{t-1} \rho^*(\tau) I(\tau) - I(t) \right] \times (1+\rho)^{-(t+1)}$$

$$= X(0) \sum_{t=1}^{\infty} (1+\rho)^{-t} + \sum_{t=1}^{\infty} \left[\sum_{\tau=0}^{t-1} \rho^*(\tau) I(\tau) - I(t-1) \times (1+\rho) \right] (1+\rho)^{-(t+1)}.$$

The first expression is, of course, simply a geometric progression summing to $X(0)/\rho$, which is the first term of (12). To simplify the second expression note that it can be rewritten as

$$\sum_{t=0}^{\infty} I(t) \left[\rho^*(t) \sum_{\tau=t+2}^{\infty} (1+\rho)^{-\tau} - (1+\rho)^{-(t+1)} \right].$$

Evaluating the summation within the brackets gives

$$\sum_{t=0}^{\infty} I(t) \left[\rho^*(t) \frac{(1+\rho)^{-(t+1)}}{\rho} - (1+\rho)^{-(t+1)} \right]$$

$$= \sum_{t=0}^{\infty} I(t) \left[\frac{\rho^*(t) - \rho}{\rho} \right] (1+\rho)^{-(t+1)},$$

which is precisely the second term of (12).

Formula (12) has a number of revealing features and deserves to be more widely used in discussions of valuation.[7] For one thing, it throws considerable light on the meaning of those much abused terms "growth" and "growth stocks." As can readily be seen from (12), a corporation does not become a "growth stock" with a high price-earnings ratio merely because its assets and earnings are growing over time. To enter the glamor category, it is also necessary that $\rho^*(t) > \rho$. For if $\rho^*(t) = \rho$, then however large the growth in assets may be, the second term in (12) will be zero and the firm's price-earnings ratio would not rise above a humdrum $1/\rho$. The essence of "growth," in short, is not expansion, but the existence of opportunities to invest significant quantities of funds at higher than "normal" rates of return.

[7] A valuation formula analogous to (12) though derived and interpreted in a slightly different way is found in Bodenhorn [1]. Variants of (12) for certain special cases are discussed in Walter [20].

Notice also that if $\rho^*(t) < \rho$, investment in real assets by the firm will actually reduce the current price of the shares. This should help to make clear among other things, why the "cost of capital" to the firm is the same regardless of how the investments are financed or how fast the firm is growing. The function of the cost of capital in capital budgeting is to provide the "cut-off rate" in the sense of the minimum yield that investment projects must promise to be worth undertaking from the point of view of the current owners. Clearly, no proposed project would be in the interest of the current owners if its yield were expected to be less than ρ since investing in such projects would reduce the value of their shares. In the other direction, every project yielding more than ρ is just as clearly worth undertaking since it will necessarily enhance the value of the enterprise. Hence, the cost of capital or cut-off criterion for investment decisions is simply ρ.[8]

Finally, formula (12) serves to emphasize an important deficiency in many recent statistical studies of the effects of dividend policy (such as Walter [19] or Durand [4, 5]). These studies typically involve fitting regression equations in which price is expressed as some function of current earnings and dividends. A finding that the dividend coefficient is significant—as is usually the case—is then interpreted as a rejection of the hypothesis that dividend policy does not affect valuation.

Even without raising questions of bias in the coefficients,[9] it should be apparent that such a conclusion is unwarranted since formula (12) and the analysis underlying it imply only that dividends will not count given current earnings *and growth potential*. No general prediction is made (or can be made) by the theory about what will happen to the dividend coefficient if the crucial growth term is omitted.[10]

The stream of dividends approach.—From the earnings and earnings opportunities approach we turn next to the dividend approach, which has, for some reason, been by far the most popular one in the literature of valuation. This approach too, properly formulated, is an entirely valid one though, of course, not the only valid approach as its more enthusiastic proponents frequently suggest.[11] It does, however, have the disadvantage in contrast with previous approaches of obscuring the role of dividend policy. In particular, uncritical use of the

[8] The same conclusion could also have been reached, of course, by "costing" each particular source of capital funds. That is, since ρ is the going market rate of return on equity any new shares floated to finance investment must be priced to yield ρ; and withholding funds from the stockholders to finance investment would deprive the holders of the chance to earn ρ on these funds by investing their dividends in other shares. The advantage of thinking in terms of the cost of capital as the cut-off criterion is that it minimizes the danger of confusing "costs" with mere "outlays."

[9] The serious bias problem in tests using current reported earnings as a measure of $X(0)$ was discussed briefly by us in [16].

[10] In suggesting that recent statistical studies have not controlled adequately for growth we do not mean to exempt Gordon in [8] or [9]. It is true that his tests contain an explicit "growth" variable, but it is essentially nothing more than the ratio of retained earnings to book value. This ratio would not in general provide an acceptable approximation to the "growth" variable of (12) in any sample in which firms resorted to external financing. Furthermore, even if by some chance a sample was found in which all firms relied entirely on retained earnings, his tests then could not settle the question of dividend policy. For if all firms financed investment internally (or used external financing only in strict proportion to internal financing as Gordon assumes in [8]) then there would be no way to distinguish between the effects of dividend policy and investment policy (see below p. 424).

[11] See, e.g., the classic statement of the position in J. B. Williams [21]. The equivalence of the dividend approach to many of the other standard approaches is noted to our knowledge only in our [16] and, by implication, in Bodenhorn [1].

dividend approach has often led to the unwarranted inference that, since the investor is buying dividends and since dividend policy affects the amount of dividends, then dividend policy must also affect the current price.

Properly formulated, the dividend approach defines the current worth of a share as the discounted value of the stream of dividends to be paid on the share in perpetuity. That is

$$p(t) = \sum_{\tau=0}^{\infty} \frac{d(t+\tau)}{(1+\rho)^{\tau+1}}. \qquad (13)$$

To see the equivalence between this approach and previous ones, let us first restate (13) in terms of total market value as

$$V(t) = \sum_{\tau=0}^{\infty} \frac{D_t(t+\tau)}{(1+\rho)^{\tau+1}}, \qquad (14)$$

where $D_t(t+\tau)$ denotes that portion of the total dividends $D(t+\tau)$ paid during period $t+\tau$, that accrues to the shares of record as of the start of period t (indicated by the subscript). That equation (14) is equivalent to (9) and hence also to (12) is immediately apparent for the special case in which no outside financing is undertaken after period t, for in that case

$$D_t(t+\tau) = D(t+\tau) = X(t+\tau) - I(t+\tau).$$

To allow for outside financing, note that we can rewrite (14) as

$$\begin{aligned} V(t) &= \frac{1}{1+\rho}\left[D_t(t) + \sum_{\tau=1}^{\infty} \frac{D_t(t+\tau)}{(1+\rho)^{\tau}}\right] \\ &= \frac{1}{1+\rho}\left[D(t) + \sum_{\tau=0}^{\infty} \frac{D_t(t+\tau+1)}{(1+\rho)^{\tau+1}}\right]. \end{aligned} \qquad (15)$$

The summation term in the last expression can be written as the difference between the stream of dividends accruing to all the shares of record as of $t+1$ and that portion of the stream that will accrue to the shares newly issued in t, that is,

$$\sum_{\tau=0}^{\infty} \frac{D_t(t+\tau+1)}{(1+\rho)^{\tau+1}} = \left(1 - \frac{m(t+1)}{n(t+1)}\right) \times \sum_{\tau=0}^{\infty} \frac{D_{t+1}(t+\tau+1)}{(1+\rho)^{\tau+1}}. \qquad (16)$$

But from (14) we know that the second summation in (16) is precisely $V(t+1)$ so that (15) can be reduced to

$$\begin{aligned} V(t) &= \frac{1}{1+\rho}\left[D(t) + \left(1 - \frac{m(t+1)p(t+1)}{n(t+1)p(t+1)}\right) \times V(t+1)\right] \\ &= \frac{1}{1+\rho}\left[D(t) + V(t+1) - m(t+1)p(t+1)\right], \end{aligned} \qquad (17)$$

which is (3) and which has already been shown to imply both (9) and (12).[12]

There are, of course, other ways in which the equivalence of the dividend approach to the other approaches might

[12] The statement that equations (9), (12), and (14) are equivalent must be qualified to allow for certain pathological extreme cases, fortunately of no real economic significance. An obvious example of such a case is the legendary company that is expected *never* to pay a dividend. If this were literally true then the value of the firm by (14) would be zero; by (9) it would be zero (or possibly negative since zero dividends rule out $X(t) > I(t)$ but not $X(t) < I(t)$); while by (12) the value might still be positive. What is involved here, of course, is nothing more than a discontinuity at zero since the value under (14) and (9) would be positive and the equivalence of both with (12) would hold if that value were also positive as long as there was some period T, however far in the future, beyond which the firm would pay out $\epsilon > 0$ per cent of its earnings, however small the value of ϵ.

have been established, but the method presented has the advantage perhaps of providing some further insight into the reason for the irrelevance of dividend policy. An increase in current dividends, given the firm's investment policy, must necessarily reduce the terminal value of existing shares because part of the future dividend stream that would otherwise have accrued to the existing shares must be diverted to attract the outside capital from which, in effect, the higher current dividends are paid. Under our basic assumptions, however, ρ must be the same for all investors, new as well as old. Consequently the market value of the dividends diverted to the outsiders, which is both the value of their contribution and the reduction in terminal value of the existing shares, must always be precisely the same as the increase in current dividends.

The stream of earnings approach.—Contrary to widely held views, it is also possible to develop a meaningful and consistent approach to valuation running in terms of the stream of earnings generated by the corporation rather than of the dividend distributions actually made to the shareholders. Unfortunately, it is also extremely easy to mistate or misinterpret the earnings approach as would be the case if the value of the firm were to be defined as simply the discounted sum of future total earnings.[13] The trouble with such a definition is not, as is often suggested, that it overlooks the fact that the corporation is a separate entity and that these profits cannot freely be withdrawn by the shareholders; but rather that it neglects the fact that additional capital must be acquired at some cost to maintain the future earnings stream at its specified level. The capital to be raised in any future period is, of course, $I(t)$ and its opportunity cost, no matter how financed, is ρ per cent per period thereafter. Hence, the current value of the firm under the earnings approach must be stated as

$$V(0)=\sum_{t=0}^{\infty}\frac{1}{(1+\rho)^{t+1}}\times\left[X(t)-\sum_{\tau=0}^{t}\rho I(\tau)\right]. \tag{18}$$

That this version of the earnings approach is indeed consistent with our basic assumptions and equivalent to the previous approaches can be seen by regrouping terms and rewriting equation (18) as

$$\begin{aligned}V(0)&=\sum_{t=0}^{\infty}\frac{1}{(1+\rho)^{t+1}}X(t)-\sum_{t=0}^{\infty}\left(\sum_{\tau=t}^{\infty}\frac{\rho I(t)}{(1+\rho)^{\tau+1}}\right)\\&=\sum_{t=0}^{\infty}\frac{1}{(1+\rho)^{t+1}}X(t)-\sum_{t=0}^{\infty}\frac{1}{(1+\rho)^{t+1}}\times\left(\sum_{\tau=0}^{\infty}\frac{\rho I(t)}{(1+\rho)^{\tau+1}}\right).\end{aligned} \tag{19}$$

Since the last inclosed summation reduces simply to $I(t)$, the expression (19) in turn reduces to simply

$$V(0)=\sum_{t=0}^{\infty}\frac{1}{(1+\rho)^{t+1}}[X(t)-I(t)], \tag{20}$$

[13] In fairness, we should point out that there is no one, to our knowledge, who has seriously advanced this view. It is a view whose main function seems to be to serve as a "straw man" to be demolished by those supporting the dividend view. See, e.g., Gordon [9, esp. pp. 102–3]. Other writers take as the supposed earnings counter-view to the dividend approach not a relation running in terms of the *stream* of earnings but simply the proposition that price is proportional to current earnings, i.e., $V(0) = X(0)/\rho$. The probable origins of this widespread misconception about the earnings approach are discussed further below (p. 424).

which is precisely our earlier equation (9).

Note that the version of the earnings approach presented here does not depend for its validity upon any special assumptions about the time shape of the stream of total profits or the stream of dividends per share. Clearly, however, the time paths of the two streams are closely related to each other (via financial policy) and to the stream of returns derived by holders of the shares. Since these relations are of some interest in their own right and since misunderstandings about them have contributed to the confusion over the role of dividend policy, it may be worthwhile to examine them briefly before moving on to relax the basic assumptions.

III. EARNINGS, DIVIDENDS, AND GROWTH RATES

The convenient case of constant growth rates.—The relation between the stream of earnings of the firm and the stream of dividends and of returns to the stockholders can be brought out most clearly by specializing (12) to the case in which investment opportunities are such as to generate a constant rate of growth of profits in perpetuity. Admittedly, this case has little empirical significance, but it is convenient for illustrative purposes and has received much attention in the literature.

Specifically, suppose that in each period t the firm has the opportunity to invest in real assets a sum $I(t)$ that is k per cent as large as its total earnings for the period; and that this investment produces a perpetual yield of ρ^* beginning with the next period. Then, by definition

$$\begin{aligned} X(t) &= X(t-1) + \rho^* I(t-1) \\ &= X(t-1)[1+k\rho^*] \qquad (21) \\ &= X(0)\,[1+k\rho^*]^t \end{aligned}$$

and $k\rho^*$ is the (constant) rate of growth of total earnings. Substituting from (21) into (12) for $I(t)$ we obtain

$$\begin{aligned} V(0) &= \frac{X(0)}{\rho} + \sum_{t=0}^{\infty}\left(\frac{\rho^*-\rho}{\rho}\right) \times kX(0)[1+k\rho^*]^t \times (1+\rho)^{-(t+1)} \\ &= \frac{X(0)}{\rho}\left[1+\frac{k(\rho^*-\rho)}{1+\rho} \times \sum_{t=0}^{\infty}\left(\frac{1+k\rho^*}{1+\rho}\right)^t\right]. \end{aligned} \qquad (22)$$

Evaluating the infinite sum and simplifying, we finally obtain[14]

$$\begin{aligned} V(0) &= \frac{X(0)}{\rho}\left[1+\frac{k(\rho^*-\rho)}{\rho-k\rho^*}\right] \\ &= \frac{X(0)(1-k)}{\rho-k\rho^*}, \end{aligned} \qquad (23)$$

which expresses the value of the firm as a function of its current earnings, the rate of growth of earnings, the internal rate of return, and the market rate of return.[15]

[14] One advantage of the specialization (23) is that it makes it easy to see what is really involved in the assumption here and throughout the paper that the $V(0)$ given by any of our summation formulas is necessarily finite (cf. above, n. 4). In terms of (23) the condition is clearly $k\rho^* < \rho$, i.e., that the rate of growth of the firm be less than market rate of discount. Although the case of (perpetual) growth rates greater than the discount factor is the much-discussed "growth stock praradox" (e.g. [6]), it has no real economic significance as we pointed out in [16, esp. n. 17, p. 664]. This will be apparent when one recalls that the discount rate ρ, though treated as a constant in partial equilibrium (relative price) analysis of the kind presented here, is actually a variable from the standpoint of the system as a whole. That is, if the assumption of finite value for all shares did not hold, because for some shares $k\rho^*$ was (perpetually) greater than ρ, then ρ would necessarily rise until an over-all equilibrium in the capital markets had been restored.

[15] An interesting and more realistic variant of (22), which also has a number of convenient features from the standpoint of developing empirical tests, can be obtained by assuming that the special invest-

Note that (23) holds not just for period 0, but for every t. Hence if $X(t)$ is growing at the rate $k\rho^*$, it follows that the value of the enterprise, $V(t)$, also grows at that rate.

The growth of dividends and the growth of total profits.—Given that total earnings (and the total value of the firm) are growing at the rate $k\rho^*$ what is the rate of growth of dividends per share and of the price per share? Clearly, the answer will vary depending on whether or not the firm is paying out a high percentage of its earnings and thus relying heavily on outside financing. We can show the nature of this dependence explicitly by making use of the fact that whatever the rate of growth of dividends per share the present value of the firm by the dividend approach must be the same as by the earnings approach. Thus let

g = the rate of growth of dividends per share, or, what amounts to the same thing, the rate of growth of dividends accruing to the shares of the current holders (i.e., $D_0(t) = D_0(0)[1+g]^t$);

k_r = the fraction of total profits retained in each period (so that $D(t) = X(0)[1-k_r]$);

$k_e = k - k_r$ = the amount of external capital raised per period, expressed as a fraction of profits in the period.

Then the present value of the stream of dividends to the original owners will be

$$D_0(0)\sum_{t=0}^{\infty}\frac{(1+g)^t}{(1+\rho)^{t+1}} = \frac{D(0)}{\rho - g} = \frac{X(0)[1-k_r]}{\rho - g}. \tag{24}$$

By virtue of the dividend approach we know that (24) must be equal to $V(0)$. If, therefore, we equate it to the right-hand side of (23), we obtain

$$\frac{X(0)[1-k_r]}{\rho - g} = \frac{X(0)[1-(k_r+k_e)]}{\rho - k\rho^*}$$

from which it follows that the rate of growth of dividends per share and the rate of growth of the price of a share must be[16]

ment opportunities are available not in perpetuity but only over some finite interval of T periods. To exhibit the value of the firm for this case, we need only replace the infinite summation in (22) with a summation running from $t = 0$ to $t = T - 1$. Evaluating the resulting expression, we obtain

$$V(0) = \frac{X(0)}{\rho}\left\{1 + \frac{k(\rho^* - \rho)}{\rho - k\rho^*} \times \left[1 - \left(\frac{1+k\rho^*}{1+\rho}\right)^T\right]\right\}. \tag{22a}$$

Note that (22*a*) holds even if $k\rho^* > \rho$, so that the so-called growth paradox disappears altogether. If, as we should generally expect, $(1+k\rho^*)/(1+\rho)$ is close to one, and if T is not too large, the right hand side of (22*a*) admits of a very convenient approximation. In this case in fact we can write

$$\left[\frac{1+k\rho^*}{1+\rho}\right]^T \cong 1 + T(k\rho^* - \rho)$$

the approximation holding, if, as we should expect, $(1+k\rho^*)$ and $(1+\rho)$ are both close to unity. Substituting this approximation into (22*a*) and simplifying, finally yields

$$V(0) \cong \frac{X(0)}{\rho}\left[1 + \frac{k(\rho^* - \rho)}{\rho - k\rho^*} \times T(\rho - k\rho^*)\right] = \left[\frac{X(0)}{\rho} + kX(0) \times \left(\frac{\rho^* - \rho}{\rho}\right)T\right]. \tag{22b}$$

The common sense of (22*b*) is easy to see. The current value of a firm is given by the value of the earning power of the currently held assets plus the market value of the special earning opportunity multiplied by the number of years for which it is expected to last.

[16] That g is the rate of price increase per share as well as the rate of growth of dividends per share fol-

$$g = k\rho^* \frac{1-k_r}{1-k} - k_e\rho \frac{1}{1-k}. \quad (25)$$

Notice that in the extreme case in which all financing is internal ($k_e = 0$ and $k = k_r$), the second term drops out and the first becomes simply $k\rho^*$. Hence the growth rate of dividends in that special case is exactly the same as that of total profits and total value and is proportional to the rate of retention k_r. In all other cases, g is necessarily less than $k\rho^*$ and may even be negative, despite a positive $k\rho^*$, if $\rho^* < \rho$ and if the firm pays out a large fraction of its income in dividends. In the other direction, we see from (25) that even if a firm is a "growth" corporation ($\rho^* > \rho$) then the stream of dividends and price per share must grow over time even though $k_r = 0$, that is, even though it pays out *all* its earnings in dividends.

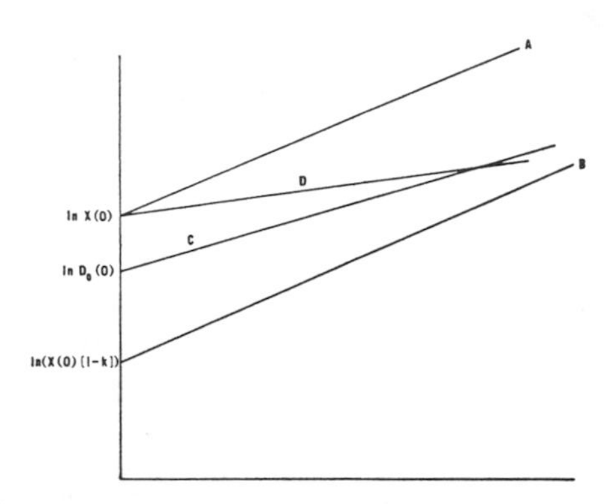

FIG. 1.—Growth of dividends per share in relation to growth in total earnings:
A. Total earnings: $\ln X(t) = \ln X(0) + k\rho^* t$;
B. Total earnings minus capital invested: $\ln [X(t) - I(t)] = \ln X(0) [1 - k] + k\rho^* t$;
Dividends per share (all financing internal): $\ln D_0(t) = \ln D(0) + gt = \ln X(0) [1 - k] + k\rho^* t$;
C. Dividends per share (some financing external): $\ln D_0(t) = \ln D(0) + gt$;
D. Dividends per share (all financing external): $\ln D_0(t) = \ln X(0) + [(k/1 - k) (\rho^* - \rho)]t$.

The relation between the growth rate of the firm and the growth rate of dividends under various dividend policies is illustrated graphically in Figure 1 in which for maximum clarity the natural logarithm of profits and dividends have been plotted against time.[17]

Line *A* shows the total earnings of the firm growing through time at the constant rate $k\rho^*$, the slope of *A*. Line *B* shows the growth of (1) the stream of total earnings minus capital outlays and

lows from the fact that by (13) and the definition of g

$$p(t) = \sum_{\tau=0}^{\infty} \frac{d(t+\tau)}{(1+\rho)^{\tau+1}}$$

$$= \sum_{\tau=0}^{\infty} \frac{d(0)[1+g]^{t+\tau}}{(1+\rho)^{\tau+1}}$$

$$= (1+g)^t \sum_{\tau=0}^{\infty} \frac{d(\tau)}{(1+\rho)^{\tau+1}}$$

$$= p(0)[1+g]^t.$$

[17] That is, we replace each discrete compounding expression such as $X(t) = X(0) [1 + k\rho^*]^t$ with its counterpart under continuous discounting $X(t) = X(0)e^{k\rho^* t}$ which, of course, yields the convenient linear relation $\ln X(t) = \ln X(0) + k\rho^* t$.

(2) the stream of dividends to the original owners (or dividends per share) in the special case in which all financing is internal. The slope of B is, of course, the same as that of A and the (constant) difference between the curves is simply $\ln(1 - k)$, the ratio of dividends to profits. Line C shows the growth of dividends per share when the firm uses both internal and external financing. As compared with the pure retention case, the line starts higher but grows more slowly at the rate g given by (25). The higher the payout policy, the higher the starting position and the slower the growth up to the other limiting case of complete external financing, Line D, which starts at $\ln X(0)$ and grows at a rate of $(k/1 - k) \cdot (\rho^* - \rho)$.

The special case of exclusively internal financing.—As noted above the growth rate of dividends per share is not the same as the growth rate of the firm except in the special case in which all financing is internal. This is merely one of a number of peculiarities of this special case on which, unfortunately, many writers have based their entire analysis. The reason for the preoccupation with this special case is far from clear to us. Certainly no one would suggest that it is the only empirically relevant case. Even if the case were in fact the most common, the theorist would still be under an obligation to consider alternative assumptions. We suspect that in the last analysis, the popularity of the internal financing model will be found to reflect little more than its ease of manipulation combined with the failure to push the analysis far enough to disclose how special and how treacherous a case it really is.

In particular, concentration on this special case appears to be largely responsible for the widely held view that, even under perfect capital markets, there is an optimum dividend policy for the firm that depends on the internal rate of return. Such a conclusion is almost inevitable if one works exclusively with the assumption, explicit or implicit, that funds for investment come *only* from retained earnings. For in that case *dividend policy* is indistinguishable from *investment policy;* and there *is* an optimal investment policy which does in general depend on the rate of return.

Notice also from (23) that if $\rho^* = \rho$ and $k = k_r$, the term $[1 - k_r]$ can be canceled from both the numerator and the denominator. The value of the firm becomes simply $X(0)/\rho$, the capitalized value of current earnings. Lacking a standard model for valuation more general than the retained earnings case it has been all too easy for many to conclude that this dropping out of the payout ratio $[1 - k_r]$ when $\rho^* = \rho$ must be what is meant by the irrelevance of dividend policy and that $V(0) = X(0)/\rho$ must constitute the "earnings" approach.

Still another example of the pitfalls in basing arguments on this special case is provided by the recent and extensive work on valuation by M. Gordon.[18] Gordon argues, in essense, that because of increasing uncertainty the discount rate $\hat{\rho}(t)$ applied by an investor to a future dividend payment will rise with t, where t denotes not a specific date but rather the distance from the period in which the investor performs the discounting.[19]

[18] See esp. [8]. Gordon's views represent the most explicit and sophisticated formulation of what might be called the "bird-in-the-hand" fallacy. For other, less elaborate, statements of essentially the same position see, among others, Graham and Dodd [11, p. 433] and Clendenin and Van Cleave [3].

[19] We use the notation $\hat{\rho}(t)$ to avoid any confusion between Gordon's purely subjective discount rate and the objective, market-given yields $\rho(t)$ in Sec. I above. To attempt to derive valuation formulas under uncertainty from these purely subjective discount factors involves, of course, an error essentially

Hence, when we use a single uniform discount rate ρ as in (22) or (23), this rate should be thought of as really an average of the "true" rates $\hat{\rho}(t)$ each weighted by the size of the expected dividend payment at time t. If the dividend stream is growing exponentially then such a weighted average ρ would, of course, be higher the greater the rate of growth of dividends g since the greater will then be the portion of the dividend stream arising in the distant as opposed to the near future. But if all financing is assumed to be internal, then $g = k_r\rho^*$ so that given ρ^*, the weighted average discount factor ρ will be an increasing function of the rate of retention k_r which would run counter to our conclusion that dividend policy has no effect on the current value of the firm or its cost of capital.

For all its ingenuity, however, and its seeming foundation in uncertainty, the argument clearly suffers fundamentally from the typical confounding of dividend policy with investment policy that so frequently accompanies use of the internal financing model. Had Gordon not confined his attention to this special case (or its equivalent variants), he would have seen that while a change in dividend policy will necessarily affect the size of the expected dividend payment on the share in any future period, it need not, in the general case, affect either the size of the *total* return that the investor expects during that period or the degree of uncertainty attaching to that total return. As should be abundantly clear by now, a change in dividend policy, given investment policy, implies a change only in the distribution of the total return in any period as between dividends and capital gains. If investors behave rationally, such a change cannot affect market valuations. Indeed, if they valued shares according to the Gordon approach and thus paid a premium for higher payout ratios, then holders of the low payout shares would actually realize consistently higher returns on their investment over any stated interval of time.[20]

Corporate earnings and investor returns.—Knowing the relation of g to $k\rho^*$ we can answer a question of considerable interest to economic theorists, namely: What is the precise relation between the earnings of the corporation in any period $X(t)$ and the total return to the owners of the stock during that period?[21] If we let $G_t(t)$ be the capital gains to the owners during t, we know that

$$D_t(t) + G_t(t) = X(t) \times (1 - k_r) + gV(t) \qquad (26)$$

analogous to that of attempting to develop the certainty formulas from "marginal rates of time preference" rather than objective market opportunities.

[20] This is not to deny that growth stocks (in our sense) may well be "riskier" than non-growth stocks. But to the extent that this is true, it will be due to the possibly greater uncertainty attaching to the size and duration of future growth opportunities and hence to the size of the future stream of total returns quite apart from any questions of dividend policy.

[21] Note also that the above analysis enables us to deal very easily with the familiar issue of whether a firm's cost of equity capital is measured by its earnings/price ratio or by its dividend/price ratio. Clearly, the answer is that it is measured by neither, except under very special circumstances. For from (23) we have for the earnings/price ratio

$$\frac{X(0)}{V(0)} = \frac{\rho - k\rho^*}{1 - k},$$

which is equal to the cost of capital ρ, only if the firm has no growth potential (i.e., $\rho^* = \rho$). And from (24) we have for the dividend/price ratio

$$\frac{D(0)}{V(0)} = \rho - g,$$

which is equal to ρ only when $g = 0$; i.e., from (25), either when $k = 0$; or, if $k > 0$, when $\rho^* < \rho$ and the amount of external financing is precisely

$$k_e = \frac{\rho^*}{\rho} k [1 - k_r],$$

so that the gain from the retention of earnings exactly offsets the loss that would otherwise be occasioned by the unprofitable investment.

since the rate of growth of price is the same as that of dividends per share. Using (25) and (26) to substitute for g and $V(t)$ and simplifying, we find that

$$D_t(t)+G_t(t)=X(t)\left[\frac{\rho(1-k)}{\rho-k\rho^*}\right]. \quad (27)$$

The relation between the investors' return and the corporation's profits is thus seen to depend entirely on the relation between ρ^* and ρ. If $\rho^*=\rho$ (i.e., the firm has no special "growth" opportunities), then the expression in brackets becomes 1 and the investor returns are precisely the same as the corporate profits. If $\rho^*<\rho$, however, the investors' return will be less than the corporate earnings; and, in the case of growth corporations the investors' return will actually be greater than the flow of corporate profits over the interval.[22]

Some implications for constructing empirical tests.—Finally the fact that we have two different (though not independent) measures of growth in $k\rho^*$ and g and two corresponding families of valuation formulas means, among other things, that we can proceed by either of two routes in empirical studies of valuation. We can follow the standard practice of the security analyst and think in terms of price per share, dividends per share, and the rate of growth of dividends per share; or we can think in terms of the total value of the enterprise, total earnings, and the rate of growth of total earnings. Our own preference happens to be for the second approach primarily because certain additional variables of interest—such as dividend policy, leverage, and size of firm—can be incorporated more easily and meaningfully into test equations in which the growth term is the growth of total earnings. But this can wait. For present purposes, the thing to be stressed is simply that two approaches, properly carried through, are in no sense *opposing* views of the valuation process; but rather equivalent views, with the choice between them largely a matter of taste and convenience.

IV. THE EFFECTS OF DIVIDEND POLICY UNDER UNCERTAINTY

Uncertainty and the general theory of valuation.—In turning now from the ideal world of certainty to one of uncertainty our first step, alas, must be to jettison the fundamental valuation principle as given, say, in our equation (3)

$$V(t)=\frac{1}{1+\rho(t)}\left[D(t)+n(t)p(t+1)\right]$$

and from which the irrelevance proposition as well as all the subsequent valua-

[22] The above relation between earnings per share and dividends plus capital gains also means that there will be a systematic relation between retained earnings and capital gains. The "marginal" relation is easy to see and is always precisely one for one regardless of growth or financial policy. That is, taking a dollar away from dividends and adding it to retained earnings (all other things equal) means an increase in capital gains of one dollar (or a reduction in capital loss of one dollar). The "average" relation is somewhat more complex. From (26) and (27) we can see that

$$G_t(t)=k_rX(t)+kX(t)\frac{\rho^*-\rho}{\rho-k\rho^*}.$$

Hence, if $\rho^*=\rho$ the total capital gain received will be exactly the same as the total retained earnings per share. For growth corporations, however, the capital gain will always be greater than the retained earnings (and there will be a capital gain of

$$kX(t)\left[\frac{\rho^*-\rho}{\rho-k\rho^*}\right]$$

even when all earnings are paid out). For non-growth corporations the relation between gain and retentions is reversed. Note also that the absolute difference between the total capital gain and the total retained earnings is a constant (given, ρ, k and ρ^*) unaffected by dividend policy. Hence the *ratio* of capital gain to retained earnings will vary directly with the payout ratio for growth corporations (and vice versa for non-growth corporations). This means, among other things, that it is dangerous to attempt to draw inferences about the relative growth potential or relative managerial efficiency of corporations solely on the basis of the ratio of capital gains to retained earnings (cf. Harkavy [12, esp. pp. 289–94]).

tion formulas in Sections II and III were derived. For the terms in the bracket can no longer be regarded as given numbers, but must be recognized as "random variables" from the point of view of the investor as of the start of period t. Nor is it at all clear what meaning can be attached to the discount factor $1/[1 + \rho(t)]$ since what is being discounted is not a given return, but at best only a probability distribution of possible returns. We can, of course, delude ourselves into thinking that we are preserving equation (3) by the simple and popular expedient of drawing a bar over each term and referring to it thereafter as the mathematical expectation of the random variable. But except for the trivial case of universal linear utility functions we know that $V(t)$ would also be affected, and materially so, by the higher order moments of the distribution of returns. Hence there is no reason to believe that the discount factor for expected values, $1/[1 + \rho(t)]$, would in fact be the same for any two firms chosen arbitrarily, not to mention that the expected values themselves may well be different for different investors.

All this is not to say, of course, that there are insuperable difficulties in the way of developing a testable theory of rational market valuation under uncertainty.[23] On the contrary, our investigations of the problem to date have convinced us that it is indeed possible to construct such a theory—though the construction, as can well be imagined, is a fairly complex and space-consuming task. Fortunately, however, this task need not be undertaken in this paper which is concerned primarily with the effects of dividend policy on market valuation. For even without a full-fledged theory of what *does* determine market value under uncertainty we can show that dividend policy at least is *not* one of the determinants. To establish this particular generalization of the previous certainty results we need only invoke a corresponding generalization of the original postulate of rational behavior to allow for the fact that, under uncertainty, choices depend on expectations as well as tastes.

"Imputed rationality" and "symmetric market rationality."—This generalization can be formulated in two steps as follows. First, we shall say that an individual trader "imputes rationality to the market" or satisfies the postulate of "imputed rationality" if, in forming expectations, he assumes that every other trader in the market is (*a*) rational in the previous sense of preferring more wealth to less regardless of the form an increment in wealth may take, and (*b*) imputes rationality to all other traders. Second, we shall say that a market as a whole satisfies the postulate of "symmetric market rationality" if every trader both behaves rationally and imputes rationality to the market.[24]

Notice that this postulate of sym-

[23] Nor does it mean that all the previous certainty analysis has no relevance whatever in the presence of uncertainty. There are many issues, such as those discussed in Sec. I and II, that really relate only to what has been called the pure "futurity" component in valuation. Here, the valuation formulas can still be extremely useful in maintaining the internal consistency of the reasoning and in suggesting (or criticizing) empirical tests of certain classes of hypotheses about valuation, even though the formulas themselves cannot be used to grind out precise numerical values for specific real-world shares.

[24] We offer the term "symmetric market rationality" with considerable diffidence and only after having been assured by game theorists that there is no accepted term for this concept in the literature of that subject even though the postulate itself (or close parallels to it) does appear frequently. In the literature of economics a closely related, but not exact counterpart is Muth's "hypothesis of rational expectations" [18]. Among the more euphonic, though we feel somewhat less revealing, alternatives that have been suggested to us are "putative rationality" (by T. J. Koopmans), "bi-rationality" (by G. L. Thompson), "empathetic rationality" (by Andrea Modigliani), and "panrationality" (by A. Ando).

metric market rationality differs from the usual postulate of rational behavior in several important respects. In the first place, the new postulate covers not only the choice behavior of individuals but also their expectations of the choice behavior of others. Second, the postulate is a statement about the market as a whole and not just about individual behavior. Finally, though by no means least, symmetric market rationality cannot be deduced from individual rational behavior in the usual sense since that sense does not imply imputing rationality to others. It may, in fact, imply a choice behavior inconsistent with imputed rationality unless the individual actually believes the market to be symmetrically rational. For if an ordinarily rational investor had good reason to believe that other investors would not behave rationally, then it might well be rational for him to adopt a strategy he would otherwise have rejected as irrational. Our postulate thus rules out, among other things, the possibility of speculative "bubbles" wherein an individually rational investor buys a security he knows to be overpriced (i.e., too expensive in relation to its expected *long-run* return to be attractive as a permanent addition to his portfolio) in the expectation that he can resell it at a still more inflated price before the bubble bursts.[25]

The irrelevance of dividend policy despite uncertainty.—In Section I we were able to show that, given a firm's investment policy, its dividend policy was irrelevant to its current market valuation. We shall now show that this fundamental conclusion need not be modified merely because of the presence of uncertainty about the future course of profits, investment, or dividends (assuming again, as we have throughout, that investment policy can be regarded as separable from dividend policy). To see that uncertainty about these elements changes nothing essential, consider a case in which current investors believe that the future streams of total earnings and total investment whatever actual values they may assume at different points in time will be identical for two firms, 1 and 2.[26] Suppose further, provisionally, that the same is believed to be true of future total dividend payments from period one on so that the only way in which the two firms differ is possibly with respect to the prospective dividend in the current period, period 0. In terms of previous notation we are thus assuming that

$$\tilde{X}_1(t) = \tilde{X}_2(t) \qquad t = 0 \ldots \infty$$
$$\tilde{I}_1(t) = \tilde{I}_2(t) \qquad t = 0 \ldots \infty$$
$$\tilde{D}_1(t) = \tilde{D}_2(t) \qquad t = 1 \ldots \infty$$

[25] We recognize, of course, that such speculative bubbles have actually arisen in the past (and will probably continue to do so in the future), so that our postulate can certainly not be taken to be of universal applicability. We feel, however, that it is also not of universal inapplicability since from our observation, speculative bubbles, though well publicized when they occur, do not seem to us to be a dominant, or even a fundamental, feature of actual market behavior under uncertainty. That is, we would be prepared to argue that, as a rule and on the average, markets do not behave in ways which do not obviously contradict the postulate so that the postulate may still be useful, at least as a first approximation, for the analysis of long-run tendencies in organized capital markets. Needless to say, whether our confidence in the postulate is justified is something that will have to be determined by empirical tests of its implications (such as, of course, the irrelevance of dividend policy).

[26] The assumption of two identical firms is introduced for convenience of exposition only, since it usually is easier to see the implications of rationality when there is an explicit arbitrage mechanism, in this case, switches between the shares of the two firms. The assumption, however, is not necessary and we can, if we like, think of the two firms as really corresponding to two states of the same firm for an investor performing a series of "mental experiments" on the subject of dividend policy.

the subscripts indicating the firms and the tildes being added to the variables to indicate that these are to be regarded from the standpoint of current period, not as known numbers but as numbers that will be drawn in the future from the appropriate probability distributions. We may now ask: "What will be the return, $\tilde{R}_1(0)$ to the current shareholders in firm 1 during the current period?" Clearly, it will be

$$\tilde{R}_1(0) = \tilde{D}_1(0) + \tilde{V}_1(1) - \tilde{m}_1(1)\,\tilde{p}_1(1)\,. \quad (28)$$

But the relation between $\tilde{D}_1(0)$ and $\tilde{m}_1(1)\,\tilde{p}_1(1)$ is necessarily still given by equation (4) which is merely an accounting identity so that we can write

$$\tilde{m}_1(1)\,\tilde{p}_1(1) = \tilde{I}_1(0) - [\tilde{X}_1(0) - \tilde{D}_1(0)], \quad (29)$$

and, on substituting in (28), we obtain

$$\tilde{R}_1(0) = \tilde{X}_1(0) - \tilde{I}_1(0) + \tilde{V}_1(1) \quad (30)$$

for firm 1. By an exactly parallel process we can obtain an equivalent expression for $\tilde{R}_2(0)$.

Let us now compare $\tilde{R}_1(0)$ with $\tilde{R}_2(0)$. Note first that, by assumption, $\tilde{X}_1(0) = \tilde{X}_2(0)$ and $\tilde{I}_1(0) = \tilde{I}_2(0)$. Furthermore, with symmetric market rationality, the terminal values $\tilde{V}_i(1)$ can depend only on prospective future earnings, investment and dividends from period 1 on and these too, by assumption, are identical for the two companies. Thus symmetric rationality implies that every investor must expect $\tilde{V}_1(1) = \tilde{V}_2(1)$ and hence finally $\tilde{R}_1(0) = \tilde{R}_2(0)$. But if the return to the investors is the same in the two cases, rationality requires that the two firms command the same current value so that $V_1(0)$ must equal $V_2(0)$ regardless of any difference in dividend payments during period 0. Suppose now that we allow dividends to differ not just in period 0 but in period 1 as well, but still retain the assumption of equal $\tilde{X}_i(t)$ and $\tilde{I}_i(t)$ in all periods and of equal $\tilde{D}_i(t)$ in period 2 and beyond. Clearly, the only way differences in dividends in period 1 can effect $\tilde{R}_i(0)$ and hence $V_i(0)$ is via $\tilde{V}_i(1)$. But, by the assumption of symmetric market rationality, current investors know that as of the start of period 1 the then investors will value the two firms rationally and we have already shown that differences in the current dividend do not affect current value. Thus we must have $\tilde{V}_1(1) = \tilde{V}_2(1)$—and hence $V_1(0) = V_2(0)$—regardless of any possible difference in dividend payments during period 1. By an obvious extension of the reasoning to $\tilde{V}_i(2)$, $\tilde{V}_i(3)$, and so on, it must follow that the current valuation is unaffected by differences in dividend payments in *any* future period and thus that dividend policy is irrelevant for the determination of market prices, given investment policy.[27]

Dividend policy and leverage.—A study of the above line of proof will show it to be essentially analogous to the proof for the certainty world, in which as we know, firms can have, in effect, only two alternative sources of investment funds: retained earnings or stock issues. In an uncertain world, however, there is the additional financing possibility of debt issues. The question naturally arises, therefore, as to whether the conclusion about irrelevance remains valid even in the presence of debt financing, particularly since there may very well be inter-

[27] We might note that the assumption of symmetric market rationality is sufficient to derive this conclusion but not strictly necessary if we are willing to weaken the irrelevance proposition to one running in terms of long-run, average tendencies in the market. Individual rationality alone could conceivably bring about the latter, for over the long pull rational investors could enforce this result by buying and holding "undervalued" securities because this would insure them higher long-run returns when eventually the prices became the same. They might, however, have a long, long wait.

actions between debt policy and dividend policy. The answer is that it does, and while a complete demonstration would perhaps be too tedious and repetitious at this point, we can at least readily sketch out the main outlines of how the proof proceeds. We begin, as above, by establishing the conditions from period 1 on that lead to a situation in which $\tilde{V}_1(1)$ must be brought into equality with $\tilde{V}_2(1)$ where the V, following the approach in our earlier paper [17], is now to be interpreted as the total market value of the firm, debt plus equity, not merely equity alone. The return to the original investors taken as a whole—and remember that any individual always has the option of buying a proportional share of both the equity and the debt—must correspondingly be broadened to allow for the interest on the debt. There will also be a corresponding broadening of the accounting identity (4) to allow, on the one hand, for the interest return and, on the other, for any debt funds used to finance the investment in whole or in part. The net result is that both the dividend component and the interest component of total earnings will cancel out making the relevant (total) return, as before, $[\tilde{X}_i(0) - \tilde{I}_i(0) + \tilde{V}_i(1)]$ which is clearly independent of the current dividend. It follows, then, that the value of the firm must also therefore be independent of dividend policy given investment policy.[28]

The informational content of dividends.—To conclude our discussion of dividend policy under uncertainty, we might take note briefly of a common confusion about the meaning of the irrelevance proposition occasioned by the fact that in the real world a change in the dividend rate is often followed by a change in the market price (sometimes spectacularly so). Such a phenomenon would not be incompatible with irelevance to the extent that it was merely a reflection of what might be called the "informational content" of dividends, an attribute of particular dividend payments hitherto excluded by assumption from the discussion and proofs. That is, where a firm has adopted a policy of dividend stabilization with a long-established and generally appreciated "target payout ratio," investors are likely to (and have good reason to) interpret a change in the dividend rate as a change in management's views of future profit prospects for the firm.[29] The dividend change, in other words, provides the occasion for the price change though not its cause, the price still being solely a reflection of future earnings and growth opportunities. In any particular instance, of course, the investors might well be mistaken in placing this interpretation on the dividend change, since the management might really only be changing ing its payout target or possibly even attempting to "manipulate" the price. But this would involve no particular conflict with the irrelevance proposition, unless, of course, the price changes in such cases were not reversed when the unfolding of events had made clear the true nature of the situation.[30]

[28] This same conclusion must also hold for the current market value of all the shares (and hence for the current price per share), which is equal to the total market value minus the given initially outstanding debt. Needless to say, however, the price per share and the value of the equity at *future* points in time will not be independent of dividend and debt policies in the interim.

[29] For evidence on the prevalence of dividend stabilization and target ratios see Lintner [15].

[30] For a further discussion of the subject of the informational content of dividends, including its implications for empirical tests of the irrelevance proposition, see Modigliani and Miller [16, pp. 666–68].

V. DIVIDEND POLICY AND MARKET IMPERFECTIONS

To complete the analysis of dividend policy, the logical next step would presumably be to abandon the assumption of perfect capital markets. This is, however, a good deal easier to say than to do principally because there is no unique set of circumstances that constitutes "imperfection." We can describe not one but a multitude of possible departures from strict perfection, singly and in combinations. Clearly, to attempt to pursue the implications of each of these would only serve to add inordinately to an already overlong discussion. We shall instead, therefore, limit ourselves in this concluding section to a few brief and general observations about imperfect markets that we hope may prove helpful to those taking up the task of extending the theory of valuation in this direction.

First, it is important to keep in mind that from the standpoint of dividend policy, what counts is not imperfection per se but only imperfection that might lead an investor to have a systematic preference as between a dollar of current dividends and a dollar of current capital gains. Where no such systematic preference is produced, we can subsume the imperfection in the (random) error term always carried along when applying propositions derived from ideal models to real-world events.

Second, even where we do find imperfections that bias individual preferences —such as the existence of brokerage fees which tend to make young "accumulators" prefer low-payout shares and retired persons lean toward "income stocks"—such imperfections are at best only necessary but not sufficient conditions for certain payout policies to command a permanent premium in the market. If, for example, the frequency distribution of corporate payout ratios happened to correspond exactly with the distribution of investor preferences for payout ratios, then the existence of these preferences would clearly lead ultimately to a situation whose implications were different in no fundamental respect from the perfect market case. Each corporation would tend to attract to itself a "clientele" consisting of those preferring its particular payout ratio, but one clientele would be entirely as good as another in terms of the valuation it would imply for the firm. Nor, of course, is it necessary for the distributions to match exactly for this result to occur. Even if there were a "shortage" of some particular payout ratio, investors would still normally have the option of achieving their particular saving objectives without paying a premium for the stocks in short supply simply by buying appropriately weighted combinations of the more plentiful payout ratios. In fact, given the great range of corporate payout ratios known to be available, this process would fail to eliminate permanent premiums and discounts only if the distribution of investor preferences were heavily concentrated at either of the extreme ends of the payout scale.[31]

Of all the many market imperfections that might be detailed, the only one that would seem to be even remotely capable of producing such a concentration is the substantial advantage accorded to capital gains as compared with dividends un-

[31] The above discussion should explain why, among other reasons, it would not be possible to draw any valid inference about the relative preponderance of "accumulators" as opposed to "income" buyers or the strength of their preferences merely from the weight attaching to dividends in a simple cross-sectional regression between value and payouts (as is attempted in Clendenin [2, p. 50] or Durand [5, p. 651]).

der the personal income tax. Strong as this tax push toward capital gains may be for high-income individuals, however, it should be remembered that a substantial (and growing) fraction of total shares outstanding is currently held by investors for whom there is either no tax differential (charitable and educational institutions, foundations, pension trusts, and low-income retired individuals) or where the tax advantage is, if anything, in favor of dividends (casualty insurance companies and taxable corporations generally). Hence, again, the "clientele effect" will be at work. Furthermore, except for taxable individuals in the very top brackets, the required difference in before-tax yields to produce equal after-tax yields is not particularly striking, at least for moderate variations in the composition of returns.[32] All this is not to say, of course, that differences in yields (market values) caused by differences in payout policies should be ignored by managements or investors merely because they may be relatively small. But it may help to keep investigators from being too surprised if it turns out to be hard to measure or even to detect any premium for low-payout shares on the basis of standard statistical techniques.

Finally, we may note that since the tax differential in favor of capital gains is undoubtedly the major *systematic* imperfection in the market, one clearly cannot invoke "imperfections" to account for the difference between our irrelevance proposition and the standard view as to the role of dividend policy found in the literature of finance. For the standard view is not that low-payout companies command a premium; but that, in general, they will sell at a discount![33] If such indeed were the case—and we, at least, are not prepared to concede that this has been established—then the analysis presented in this paper suggests there would be only one way to account for it; namely, as the result of systematic irrationality on the part of the investing public.[34]

To say that an observed positive premium on high payouts was due to irrationality would not, of course, make the phenomenon any less real. But it would at least suggest the need for a certain measure of caution by long-range policy-makers. For investors, however naïve they may be when they enter the market, do sometimes learn from experience; and perhaps, occasionally, even from reading articles such as this.

[32] For example, if a taxpayer is subject to a marginal rate of 40 per cent on dividends and half that or 20 per cent on long-term capital gains, then a before-tax yield of 6 per cent consisting of 40 per cent dividends and 60 per cent capital gains produces an after-tax yield of 4.32 per cent. To net the same after-tax yield on a stock with 60 per cent of the return in dividends and only 40 per cent in capital gains would require a before-tax yield of 6.37 per cent. The difference would be somewhat smaller if we allowed for the present dividend credit, though it should also be kept in mind that the tax on capital gains may be avoided entirely under present arrangements if the gains are not realized during the holder's lifetime.

[33] See, among many, many others, Gordon [8, 9], Graham and Dodd [11, esp. chaps. xxxiv and xxxvi], Durand [4, 5], Hunt, Williams, and Donaldson [13, pp. 647–49], Fisher [7], Gordon and Shapiro [10], Harkavy [12], Clendenin [2], Johnson, Shapiro, and O'Meara [14], and Walter [19].

[34] Or, less plausibly, that there is a systematic tendency for external funds to be used more productively than internal funds.

REFERENCES

1. Bodenhorn, Diran. "On the Problem of Capital Budgeting," *Journal of Finance*, XIV (December, 1959), 473–92.
2. Clendenin, John. "What Do Stockholders Like?" *California Management Review*, I (Fall, 1958), 47–55.

3. Clendenin, John, and Van Cleave, M. "Growth and Common Stock Values," *Journal of Finance*, IX (September, 1954), 365–76.
4. Durand, David. *Bank Stock Prices and the Bank Capital Problem.* ("Occasional Paper," No. 54.) New York: National Bureau of Economic Research, 1957.
5. ———. "The Cost of Capital and the Theory of Investment: Comment," *American Economic Review*, XLIX (September, 1959), 639–54.
6. ———. "Growth Stocks and the Petersburg Paradox," *Journal of Finance*, XII (September, 1957), 348–63.
7. Fisher, G. R. "Some Factors Influencing Share Prices," *Economic Journal*, LXXI, No. 281 (March, 1961), 121–41.
8. Gordon, Myron. "Corporate Saving, Investment and Share Prices," *Review of Economics and Statistics* (forthcoming).
9. ———. "Dividends, Earnings and Stock Prices," *ibid.*, XLI, No. 2, Part I (May, 1959), 99–105.
10. Gordon, Myron, and Shapiro, Eli. "Capital Equipment Analysis: The Required Rate of Profit," *Management Science*, III, 1956, 102–10.
11. Graham, Benjamin, and Dodd, David. *Security Analysis.* 3d ed. New York: McGraw-Hill Book Co., 1951.
12. Harkavy, Oscar, "The Relation between Retained Earnings and Common Stock Prices for Large Listed Corporations," *Journal of Finance*, VIII (September, 1953), 283–97.
13. Hunt, Pearson, Williams, Charles, and Donaldson, Gordon. *Basic Business Finance.* Homewood, Ill.: Richard D. Irwin, 1958.
14. Johnson, L. R., Shapiro, Eli, and O'Meara, J. "Valuation of Closely Held Stock for Federal Tax Purposes: Approach to an Objective Method," *University of Pennsylvania Law Review*, C, 166–95.
15. Lintner, John. "Distribution of Incomes of Corporations among Dividends, Retained Earnings and Taxes," *American Economic Review*, XLVI (May, 1956), 97–113.
16. Modigliani, Franco, and Miller, Merton. "'The Cost of Capital, Corporation Finance and the Theory of Investment,': Reply," *American Economic Review*, XLIX (September, 1959), 655–69.
17. ———. "The Cost of Capital, Corporation Finance and the Theory of Investment," *ibid.*, XLVIII (1958), 261–97.
18. Muth, John F. "Rational Expectations and the Theory of Price Movements," *Econometrica* (forthcoming).
19. Walter, James E. "A Discriminant Function for Earnings-Price Ratios of Large Industrial Corporations," *Review of Economics and Statistics*, XLI (February, 1959), 44–52.
20. ———. "Dividend Policies and Common Stock Prices," *Journal of Finance*, XI (March, 1956), 29–41.
21. Williams, John B. *The Theory of Investment Value.* Cambridge, Mass.: Harvard University Press, 1938.

Errata

Page 413, column 2, paragraph 2, line 2: "effects" should read "affects."

Page 420, column 2, 4 lines from the bottom: "inclosed" should read "enclosed."

Page 429, column 1, equation 28: As is clear from equation 28, "return " here means terminal value, not return over cost.

Corporate Income Taxes and the Cost of Capital: A Correction

The purpose of this communication is to correct an error in our paper "The Cost of Capital, Corporation Finance and the Theory of Investment" (this *Review*, June 1958). In our discussion of the effects of the present method of taxing corporations on the valuation of firms, we said (p. 272):

> The deduction of interest in computing taxable corporate profits will prevent the arbitrage process from making the value of all firms in a given class proportional to the expected returns generated by their

physical assets. Instead, it can be shown (by the same type of proof used for the original version of Proposition I) that *the market values of firms in each class must be proportional in equilibrium to their expected returns net of taxes (that is, to the sum of the interest paid and expected net stockholder income).* (Italics added.)

The statement in italics, unfortunately, is wrong. For even though one firm may have an *expected* return after taxes (our $\bar{X}^{\tau}$) twice that of another firm in the same risk-equivalent class, it will not be the case that the *actual* return after taxes (our X^{τ}) of the first firm will always be twice that of the second, if the two firms have different degrees of leverage.[1] And since the distribution of returns after taxes of the two firms will not be proportional, there can be no "arbitrage" process which forces their values to be proportional to their expected after-tax returns.[2] In fact, it can be shown—and this time it really will be shown—that "arbitrage" will make values within any class a function not only of expected after-tax returns, but of the tax rate and the degree of leverage. This means, among other things, that the tax advantages of debt financing are somewhat greater than we originally suggested and, to this extent, the quantitative difference between the valuations implied by our position and by the traditional view is narrowed. It still remains true, however, that under our analysis the tax advantages of debt are the *only* permanent advantages so that the gulf between the two views in matters of interpretation and policy is as wide as ever.

I. *Taxes, Leverage, and the Probability Distribution of After-Tax Returns*

To see how the distribution of after-tax earnings is affected by leverage, let us again denote by the random variable X the (long-run average) earnings before interest and taxes generated by the currently owned assets of a given firm in some stated risk class, k.[3] From our definition of a risk class it follows that X can be expressed in the form $\bar{X}Z$, where $\bar{X}$ is the expected value of X, and the random variable $Z = X/\bar{X}$, having the same value for all firms in class k, is a drawing from a distribution, say $f_k(Z)$. Hence the

[1] With some exceptions, which will be noted when they occur, we shall preserve here both the notation and the terminology of the original paper. A working knowledge of both on the part of the reader will be presumed.

[2] Barring, of course, the trivial case of universal linear utility functions. Note that in deference to Professor Durand (see his Comment on our paper and our reply, this *Review*, Sept. 1959, *49*, 639–69) we here and throughout use quotation marks when referring to arbitrage.

[3] Thus our X corresponds essentially to the familiar EBIT concept of the finance literature. The use of EBIT and related "income" concepts as the basis of valuation is strictly valid only when the underlying real assets are assumed to have perpetual lives. In such a case, of course, EBIT and "cash flow" are one and the same. This was, in effect, the interpretation of X we used in the original paper and we shall retain it here both to preserve continuity and for the considerable simplification it permits in the exposition. We should point out, however, that the perpetuity interpretation is much less restrictive than might appear at first glance. Before-tax cash flow and EBIT can also safely be equated even where assets have finite lives as soon as these assets attain a steady state age distribution in which annual replacements equal annual depreciation. The subject of finite lives of assets will be further discussed in connection with the problem of the cut-off rate for investment decisions.

random variable X^τ, measuring the after-tax return, can be expressed as:

$$(1)\quad X^\tau = (1-\tau)(X-R)+R = (1-\tau)X+\tau R = (1-\tau)\overline{X}Z+\tau R$$

where τ is the marginal corporate income tax rate (assumed equal to the average), and R is the interest bill. Since $E(X^\tau)\equiv\overline{X}^\tau=(1-\tau)\overline{X}+\tau R$ we can substitute $\overline{X}^\tau-\tau R$ for $(1-\tau)\overline{X}$ in (1) to obtain:

$$(2)\qquad X^\tau = (\overline{X}^\tau-\tau R)Z+\tau R = \overline{X}^\tau\left(1-\frac{\tau R}{\overline{X}^\tau}\right)Z+\tau R.$$

Thus, if the tax rate is other than zero, the shape of the distribution of X^τ will depend not only on the "scale" of the stream $\overline{X}^\tau$ and on the distribution of Z, but also on the tax rate and the degree of leverage (one measure of which is $R/\overline{X}^\tau$). For example, if Var $(Z)=\sigma^2$, we have:

$$\text{Var}\,(X^\tau) = \sigma^2(\overline{X}^\tau)^2\left(1-\tau\frac{R}{\overline{X}^\tau}\right)^2$$

implying that for given $\overline{X}^\tau$ the variance of after-tax returns is smaller, the higher τ and the degree of leverage.[4]

II. *The Valuation of After-Tax Returns*

Note from equation (1) that, from the investor's point of view, the long-run average stream of after-tax returns appears as a sum of two components: (1) an uncertain stream $(1-\tau)\overline{X}Z$; and (2) a sure stream τR.[5] This suggests that the equilibrium market value of the combined stream can be found by capitalizing each component separately. More precisely, let ρ^τ be the rate at which the market capitalizes the expected returns net of tax of an unlevered company of size $\overline{X}$ in class k, i.e.,

$$\rho^\tau = \frac{(1-\tau)\overline{X}}{V_U} \quad\text{or}\quad V_U = \frac{(1-\tau)\overline{X}}{\rho^\tau};$$ [6]

[4] It may seem paradoxical at first to say that leverage *reduces* the variability of outcomes, but remember we are here discussing the variability of total returns, interest plus net profits. The variability of stockholder net profits will, of course, be greater in the presence than in the absence of leverage, though relatively less so than in an otherwise comparable world of no taxes. The reasons for this will become clearer after the discussion in the next section.

[5] The statement that τR—the tax saving per period on the interest payments—is a sure stream is subject to two qualifications. First, it must be the case that firms can always obtain the tax benefit of their interest deductions either by offsetting them directly against other taxable income in the year incurred; or, in the event no such income is available in any given year, by carrying them backward or forward against past or future taxable earnings; or, in the extreme case, by merger of the firm with (or its sale to) another firm that can utilize the deduction. Second, it must be assumed that the tax rate will remain the same. To the extent that neither of these conditions holds exactly then some uncertainty attaches even to the tax savings, though, of course, it is of a different kind and order from that attaching to the stream generated by the assets. For simplicity, however, we shall here ignore these possible elements of delay or of uncertainty in the tax saving; but it should be kept in mind that this neglect means that the subsequent valuation formulas overstate, if anything, the value of the tax saving for any given permanent level of debt.

[6] Note that here, as in our original paper, we neglect dividend policy and "growth" in the

and let r be the rate at which the market capitalizes the sure streams generated by debts. For simplicity, assume this rate of interest is a constant independent of the size of the debt so that

$$r = \frac{R}{D} \quad \text{or} \quad D = \frac{R}{r}.$$ [7]

Then we would expect the value of a levered firm of size $\overline{X}$, with a permanent level of debt D_L in its capital structure, to be given by:

$$V_L = \frac{(1-\tau)\overline{X}}{\rho\tau} + \frac{\tau R}{r} = V_U + \tau D_L. \tag{3}$$ [8]

In our original paper we asserted instead that, within a risk class, market value would be proportional to expected after-tax return $\overline{X}^\tau$ (cf. our original equation [11]), which would imply:

$$V_L = \frac{\overline{X}^\tau}{\rho^\tau} = \frac{(1-\tau)\overline{X}}{\rho^\tau} + \frac{\tau R}{\rho^\tau} = V_U + \frac{r}{\rho^\tau}\tau D_L. \tag{4}$$

We will now show that if (3) does not hold, investors can secure a more efficient portfolio by switching from relatively overvalued to relatively undervalued firms. Suppose first that unlevered firms are overvalued or that

$$V_L - \tau D_L < V_U.$$

An investor holding m dollars of stock in the unlevered company has a right to the fraction m/V_U of the eventual outcome, i.e., has the uncertain income

$$Y_U = \left(\frac{m}{V_U}\right)(1-\tau)\overline{X}Z.$$

Consider now an alternative portfolio obtained by investing m dollars as follows: (1) the portion,

$$m\left(\frac{S_L}{S_L + (1-\tau)D_L}\right),$$

is invested in the stock of the levered firm, S_L; and (2) the remaining portion,

$$m\left(\frac{(1-\tau)D_L}{S_L + (1-\tau)D_L}\right),$$

sense of opportunities to invest at a rate of return greater than the market rate of return. These subjects are treated extensively in our paper, "Dividend Policy, Growth and the Valuation of Shares," *Jour. Bus.*, Univ. Chicago, Oct. 1961, 411–33.

[7] Here and throughout, the corresponding formulas when the rate of interest rises with leverage can be obtained merely by substituting $r(L)$ for r, where L is some suitable measure of leverage.

[8] The assumption that the debt is permanent is not necessary for the analysis. It is employed here both to maintain continuity with the original model and because it gives an upper bound on the value of the tax saving. See in this connection footnote 5 and footnote 9.

is invested in its bonds. The stock component entitles the holder to a fraction,

$$\frac{m}{S_L + (1-\tau)D_L},$$

of the net profits of the levered company or

$$\left(\frac{m}{S_L + (1-\tau)D_L}\right)[(1-\tau)(\overline{X}Z - R_L)].$$

The holding of bonds yields

$$\left(\frac{m}{S_L + (1-\tau)D_L}\right)[(1-\tau)R_L].$$

Hence the total outcome is

$$Y_L = \left(\frac{m}{(S_L + (1-\tau)D_L)}\right)[(1-\tau)\overline{X}Z]$$

and this will dominate the uncertain income Y_U if (and only if)

$$S_L + (1-\tau)D_L \equiv S_L + D_L - \tau D_L \equiv V_L - \tau D_L < V_U.$$

Thus, in equilibrium, V_U cannot exceed $V_L - \tau D_L$, for if it did investors would have an incentive to sell shares in the unlevered company and purchase the shares (and bonds) of the levered company.

Suppose now that $V_L - \tau D_L > V_U$. An investment of m dollars in the stock of the levered firm entitles the holder to the outcome

$$\begin{aligned} Y_L &= (m/S_L)[(1-\tau)(\overline{X}Z - R_L)] \\ &= (m/S_L)(1-\tau)\overline{X}Z - (m/S_L)(1-\tau)R_L. \end{aligned}$$

Consider the following alternative portfolio: (1) borrow an amount $(m/S_L)(1-\tau)D_L$ for which the interest cost will be $(m/S_L)(1-\tau)R_L$ (assuming, of course, that individuals and corporations can borrow at the same rate, r); and (2) invest m plus the amount borrowed, i.e.,

$$m + \frac{m(1-\tau)D_L}{S_L} = m\frac{S_L + (1-\tau)D_L}{S_L} = (m/S_L)[V_L - \tau D_L]$$

in the stock of the unlevered firm. The outcome so secured will be

$$(m/S_L)\left(\frac{V_L - \tau D_L}{V_U}\right)(1-\tau)\overline{X}Z.$$

Subtracting the interest charges on the borrowed funds leaves an income of

$$Y_U = (m/S_L)\left(\frac{V_L - \tau D_L}{V_U}\right)(1-\tau)\overline{X}Z - (m/S_L)(1-\tau)R_L$$

which will dominate Y_L if (and only if) $V_L - \tau D_L > V_U$. Thus, in equilibrium, both $V_L - \tau\, D_L > V_U$ and $V_L - \tau\, D_L < V_U$ are ruled out and (3) must hold.

III. *Some Implications of Formula* (3)

To see what is involved in replacing (4) with (3) as the rule of valuation, note first that both expressions make the value of the firm a function of leverage and the tax rate. The difference between them is a matter of the size and source of the tax advantages of debt financing. Under our original formulation, values within a class were strictly proportional to expected earnings after taxes. Hence the tax advantage of debt was due solely to the fact that the deductibility of interest payments implied a higher level of after-tax income for any given level of before-tax earnings (i.e., higher by the amount τR since $\bar{X}^\tau = (1-\tau)\bar{X} + \tau R$). Under the corrected rule (3), however, there is an additional gain due to the fact that the extra after-tax earnings, τR, represent a sure income in contrast to the uncertain outcome $(1-\tau)\bar{X}$. Hence τR is capitalized at the more favorable certainty rate, $1/r$, rather than at the rate for uncertain streams, $1/\rho^\tau$.[9]

Since the difference between (3) and (4) is solely a matter of the rate at which the tax savings on interest payments are capitalized, the required changes in all formulas and expressions derived from (4) are reasonably straightforward. Consider, first, the before-tax earnings yield, i.e., the ratio of expected earnings before interest and taxes to the value of the firm.[10] Dividing both sides of (3) by V and by $(1-\tau)$ and simplifying we obtain:

$$\frac{\bar{X}}{V} = \frac{\rho^\tau}{1-\tau}\left[1 - \tau\frac{D}{V}\right] \tag{31.c}$$

which replaces our original equation (31) (p. 294). The new relation differs from the old in that the coefficient of D/V in the original (31) was smaller by a factor of r/ρ^τ.

Consider next the after-tax earnings yield, i.e., the ratio of interest payments plus profits after taxes to total market value.[11] This concept was discussed extensively in our paper because it helps to bring out more clearly the differences between our position and the traditional view, and because it facilitates the construction of empirical tests of the two hypotheses about the valuation process. To see what the new equation (3) implies for this yield we need merely substitute $\bar{X}^\tau - \tau R$ for $(1-\tau)\bar{X}$ in (3) obtaining:

[9] Remember, however, that in one sense formula (3) gives only an upper bound on the value of the firm since $\tau R/r = \tau D$ is an exact measure of the value of the tax saving only where both the tax rate and the level of debt are assumed to be fixed forever (and where the firm is certain to be able to use its interest deduction to reduce taxable income either directly or via transfer of the loss to another firm). Alternative versions of (3) can readily be developed for cases in which the debt is not assumed to be permanent, but rather to be outstanding only for some specified finite length of time. For reasons of space, we shall not pursue this line of inquiry here beyond observing that the shorter the debt period considered, the closer does the valuation formula approach our original (4). Hence, the latter is perhaps still of some interest if only as a lower bound.

[10] Following usage common in the field of finance we referred to this yield as the "average cost of capital." We feel now, however, that the term "before-tax earnings yield" would be preferable both because it is more immediately descriptive and because it releases the term "cost of capital" for use in discussions of optimal investment policy (in accord with standard usage in the capital budgeting literature).

[11] We referred to this yield as the "after-tax cost of capital." Cf. the previous footnote.

$$V = \frac{\bar{X}^\tau - \tau R}{\rho^\tau} + \tau D = \frac{\bar{X}^\tau}{\rho^\tau} + \tau \frac{\rho^\tau - r}{\rho^\tau} D, \tag{5}$$

from which it follows that the after-tax earnings yield must be:

$$\frac{\bar{X}^\tau}{V} = \rho^\tau - \tau(\rho^\tau - r) D/V. \tag{11.c}$$

This replaces our original equation (11) (p. 272) in which we had simply $\bar{X}^\tau/V = \rho^\tau$. Thus, in contrast to our earlier result, the corrected version (11.c) implies that even the after-tax yield is affected by leverage. The predicted rate of decrease of $\bar{X}^\tau/V$ with D/V, however, is still considerably smaller than under the naive traditional view, which, as we showed, implied essentially $\bar{X}^\tau/V = \rho^\tau\text{-}(\rho^\tau - r)D/V$. See our equation (17) and the discussion immediately preceding it (p. 277).[12] And, of course, (11.c) implies that the effect of leverage on $\bar{X}^\tau/V$ is *solely* a matter of the deductibility of interest payments whereas, under the traditional view, going into debt would lower the cost of capital regardless of the method of taxing corporate earnings.

Finally, we have the matter of the after-tax yield on *equity* capital, i.e., the ratio of net profits after taxes to the value of the shares.[13] By subtracting D from both sides of (5) and breaking $\bar{X}^\tau$ into its two components—expected net profits after taxes, $\bar{\pi}^\tau$, and interest payments, $R = rD$—we obtain after simplifying:

$$S = V - D = \frac{\bar{\pi}^\tau}{\rho^\tau} - (1 - \tau)\left(\frac{\rho^\tau - r}{\rho^\tau}\right)D. \tag{6}$$

From (6) it follows that the after-tax yield on equity capital must be:

$$\frac{\bar{\pi}^\tau}{S} = \rho^\tau + (1 - \tau)[\rho^\tau - r]D/S \tag{12.c}$$

which replaces our original equation (12), $\bar{\pi}^\tau/S = \rho^\tau + (\rho^\tau - r)D/S$ (p. 272). The new (12.c) implies an increase in the after-tax yield on equity capital as leverage increases which is smaller than that of our original (12) by a factor of $(1 - \tau)$. But again, the linear increasing relation of the corrected (12.c) is still fundamentally different from the naive traditional view which asserts the cost of equity capital to be completely independent of leverage (at least as long as leverage remains within "conventional" industry limits).

IV. *Taxes and the Cost of Capital*

From these corrected valuation formulas we can readily derive corrected measures of the cost of capital in the capital budgeting sense of the minimum prospective yield an investment project must offer to be just worth

[12] The i_k^* of (17) is the same as ρ^τ in the present context, each measuring the ratio of net profits to the value of the shares (and hence of the whole firm) in an unlevered company of the class.

[13] We referred to this yield as the "after-tax cost of equity capital." Cf. footnote 9.

undertaking from the standpoint of the present stockholders. If we interpret earnings streams as perpetuities, as we did in the original paper, then we actually have two equally good ways of defining this minimum yield: either by the required increase in before-tax earnings, $d\bar{X}$, or by the required increase in earnings net of taxes, $d\bar{X}(1-\tau)$.[14] To conserve space, however, as well as to maintain continuity with the original paper, we shall concentrate here on the before-tax case with only brief footnote references to the net-of-tax concept.

Analytically, the derivation of the cost of capital in the above sense amounts to finding the minimum value of $d\bar{X}/dI$ for which $dV=dI$, where I denotes the level of new investment.[15] By differentiating (3) we see that:

$$\frac{dV}{dI} = \frac{1-\tau}{\rho^\tau}\frac{d\bar{X}}{dI} + \tau\frac{dD}{dI} \geq 1 \quad \text{if } \frac{d\bar{X}}{dI} \geq \frac{1-\tau\frac{dD}{dI}}{1-\tau}\rho^\tau. \tag{7}$$

Hence the before tax required rate of return cannot be defined without reference to financial policy. In particular, for an investment considered as being financed entirely by new equity capital $dD/dI=0$ and the required rate of return or marginal cost of equity financing (neglecting flotation costs) would be:

$$\rho^S = \frac{\rho^\tau}{1-\tau}.$$

This result is the same as that in the original paper (see equation [32], p. 294) and is applicable to any other sources of financing where the remuneration to the suppliers of capital is not deductible for tax purposes. It applies, therefore, to preferred stock (except for certain partially deductible issues of public utilities) and would apply also to retained earnings were it not for the favorable tax treatment of capital gains under the personal income tax.

For investments considered as being financed entirely by new debt capital $dI=dD$ and we find from (7) that:

$$\rho^D = \rho^\tau \tag{33.c}$$

which replaces our original equation (33) in which we had:

$$\rho^D = \rho^S - \frac{\tau}{1-\tau}r. \tag{33}$$

[14] Note that we use the term "earnings net of taxes" rather than "earnings after taxes." We feel that to avoid confusion the latter term should be reserved to describe what will actually appear in the firm's accounting statements, namely the net cash flow including the tax savings on the interest (our $\bar{X}^\tau$). Since financing sources cannot in general be allocated to particular investments (see below), the after-tax or accounting concept is not useful for capital budgeting purposes, although it can be extremely useful for valuation equations as we saw in the previous section.

[15] Remember that when we speak of the minimum required yield on an investment we are referring in principle only to investments which increase the *scale* of the firm. That is, the new

Thus for borrowed funds (or any other tax-deductible source of capital) the marginal cost or before-tax required rate of return is simply the market rate of capitalization for net of tax unlevered streams and is thus independent of both the tax rate and the interest rate. This required rate is lower than that implied by our original (33), but still considerably higher than that implied by the traditional view (see esp. pp. 276–77 of our paper) under which the before-tax cost of borrowed funds is simply the interest rate, r.

Having derived the above expressions for the marginal costs of debt and equity financing it may be well to warn readers at this point that these expressions represent at best only the hypothetical extremes insofar as costs are concerned and that neither is directly usable as a cut-off criterion for investment planning. In particular, care must be taken to avoid falling into the famous "Liquigas" fallacy of concluding that if a firm intends to float a bond issue in some given year then its cut-off rate should be set that year at ρ^D; while, if the next issue is to be an equity one, the cut-off is ρ^S. The point is, of course, that no investment can meaningfully be regarded as 100 per cent equity financed if the firm makes any use of debt capital—and most firms do, not only for the tax savings, but for many other reasons having nothing to do with "cost" in the present static sense (cf. our original paper pp. 292–93). And no investment can meaningfully be regarded as 100 per cent debt financed when lenders impose strict limitations on the maximum amount a firm can borrow relative to its equity (and when most firms actually plan on normally borrowing less than this external maximum so as to leave themselves with an emergency reserve of unused borrowing power). Since the firm's long-run capital structure will thus contain both debt and equity capital, investment planning must recognize that, over the long pull, *all* of the firm's assets are really financed by a mixture of debt and equity capital even though only one kind of capital may be raised in any particular year. More precisely, if L^* denotes the firm's long-run "target" debt ratio (around which its actual debt ratio will fluctuate as it "alternately" floats debt issues and retires them with internal or external equity) then the firm can assume, to a first approximation at least, that for any particular investment $dD/dI = L^*$. Hence, the relevant marginal cost of capital for investment planning, which we shall here denote by ρ^*, is:

$$\rho^* = \frac{1 - \tau L^*}{1 - \tau}\rho^\tau = \rho^S - \frac{\tau}{1 - \tau}\rho^D L^* = \rho^S(1 - L^*) + \rho^D L^*.$$

That is, the appropriate cost of capital for (repetitive) investment decisions over time is, to a first approximation, a weighted average of the costs of debt and equity financing, the weights being the proportions of each in the "target" capital structure.[16]

assets must be in the same "class" as the old. See in this connection, J. Hirshleifer, "Risk, the Discount Rate and Investment Decisions," *Am. Econ. Rev.*, May 1961, *51*, 112–20 (especially pp. 119–20). See also footnote 16.

[16] From the formulas in the text one can readily derive corresponding expressions for the required net-of-tax yield, or net-of-tax cost of capital for any given financing policy. Specifi-

V. *Some Concluding Observations*

Such, then, are the major corrections that must be made to the various formulas and valuation expressions in our earlier paper. In general, we can say that the force of these corrections has been to increase somewhat the estimate of the tax advantages of debt financing under our model and consequently to reduce somewhat the quantitative difference between the estimates of the effects of leverage under our model and under the naive traditional view. It may be useful to remind readers once again that the existence of a tax advantage for debt financing—even the larger advantage of the corrected version—does not necessarily mean that corporations should at all times seek to use the maximum possible amount of debt in their capital structures. For one thing, other forms of financing, notably retained earnings, may in some circumstances be cheaper still when the tax status of investors under the personal income tax is taken into account. More important, there are, as we pointed out, limitations imposed by lenders (see pp. 292–93), as well as many other dimensions (and kinds of costs) in real-world problems of financial strategy which are not fully comprehended within the framework of static equilibrium models, either our own or those of the traditional variety. These additional considerations, which are typically grouped under the rubric of "the need for preserving flexibility," will normally imply the maintenance by the corporation of a substantial reserve of untapped borrowing power. The tax advantage of debt may well tend to lower the optimal size of that reserve, but it is hard to believe that advantages of the size contemplated under our model could justify any substantial reduction, let alone their complete elimination. Nor do the data

---

cally, let $\tilde{\rho}(L)$ denote the required net-of-tax yield for investment financed with a proportion of debt $L=dD/dI$. (More generally L denotes the proportion financed with tax deductible sources of capital.) Then from (7) we find:

$$\tilde{\rho}(L)=(1-\tau)\frac{d\bar{X}}{dI}=(1-L\tau)\rho^{\tau} \tag{8}$$

and the various costs can be found by substituting the appropriate value for L. In particular, if we substitute in this formula the "target" leverage ratio, L^*, we obtain:

$$\tilde{\rho}^*\equiv\tilde{\rho}(L^*)=(1-\tau L^*)\rho^{\tau}$$

and $\tilde{\rho}^*$ measures the average net-of-tax cost of capital in the sense described above.

Although the before-tax and the net-of-tax approaches to the cost of capital provide equally good criteria for investment decisions when assets are assumed to generate perpetual (i.e., non-depreciating) streams, such is not the case when assets are assumed to have finite lives (even when it is also assumed that the firm's assets are in a steady state age distribution so that our X or EBIT is approximately the same as the net cash flow before taxes). See footnote 3 above. In the latter event, the correct method for determining the desirability of an investment would be, in principle, to discount the net-of-tax stream at the net-of-tax cost of capital. Only under this net-of-tax approach would it be possible to take into account the deductibility of depreciation (and also to choose the most advantageous depreciation policy for tax purposes). Note that we say that the net-of-tax approach is correct "in principle" because, strictly speaking, nothing in our analysis (or anyone else's, for that matter) has yet established that it is indeed legitimate to "discount" an uncertain stream. One can hope that subsequent research will show the analogy to discounting under the certainty case is a valid one; but, at the moment, this is still only a hope.

indicate that there has in fact been a substantial increase in the use of debt (except relative to preferred stock) by the corporate sector during the recent high tax years.[17]

As to the differences between our modified model and the traditional one, we feel that they are still large in quantitative terms and still very much worth trying to detect. It is not only a matter of the two views having different implications for corporate financial policy (or even for national tax policy). But since the two positions rest on fundamentally different views about investor behavior and the functioning of the capital markets, the results of tests between them may have an important bearing on issues ranging far beyond the immediate one of the effects of leverage on the cost of capital.

FRANCO MODIGLIANI AND MERTON H. MILLER*

[17] See, e.g., Merton H. Miller, "The Corporate Income Tax and Corporate Financial Policies," in *Staff Reports to the Commission on Money and Credit* (forthcoming).

* The authors are, respectively, professor of industrial management, School of Industrial Management, Massachusetts Institute of Technology, and professor of finance, Graduate School of Business, University of Chicago.

Errata

Page 436, equation 3: the first equality should read "$V_L = \frac{(1-\tau)\bar{X}}{\rho^\tau} + \frac{\tau R}{r}$."

Page 441: the first equality in the equation that is 5 lines from the bottom should read

$$``\rho^* = \frac{1 - \tau L^*}{1 - \tau}\rho^\tau."$$

A Theory and Test of Credit Rationing

By DWIGHT M. JAFFEE AND FRANCO MODIGLIANI*

Nonprice credit rationing by commerical banks and other intermediaries has attracted a good deal of attention in recent years, in part because of the role assigned to this phenomenon by the Availability Doctrine as developed by Robert Roosa [9] and others in the years immediately following World War II[1]. It is by now generally agreed that credit rationing, if it could be shown to be empirically widespread, would have important implications for an assessment of the effectiveness and timeliness of monetary policy as well as for our understanding of its *modus operandi*. But significant disagreement still exists whether credit rationing is consistent with rational bank behavior and whether it is an important empirical phenomenon. These two issues essentially define the goal of this study; namely, to provide affirmative answers to the following questions:

(1) Is it rational for commercial banks to ration credit by means other than price?

(2) Can credit rationing be measured? If so, are there significant variations in rationing over time and can these variations be accounted for?

With respect to the second question, empirical research has been hampered by the almost insolvable problem of directly measuring credit rationing. This has led to the use of proxy variables in the form of indicators of tight money such as interest rate levels or changes in interest rates. It is difficult to obtain conclusive results with such variables, however, since one cannot then really differentiate credit rationing from other symptoms of tight money. In this study, by contrast, we are able to derive and exhibit an operational proxy for credit rationing based explicitly on a theory of rational lender behavior.

The major contributions concerned with the first question have been provided in a series of complementary studies by Donald Hodgman [3], Merton Miller [8], and Marshall Freimer and Myron Gordon [1].[2] Although criticism of a technical nature has been raised with respect to the first two studies, the most recent of these works by Freimer and Gordon, provides a complete statement of the model. Consequently, it may seem surprising that even the rationality of credit rationing is still considered a debatable issue. The source of this paradox, we believe, is essentially that the authors have not addressed themselves to the relevant question. Before elaborating on this point, however, it is important to precisely define credit rationing.

In line with the generally accepted terminology, we propose to define credit ra-

* The authors are, respectively, assistant professor of economics at Princeton University and professor of economics and industrial management at Massachusetts Institute of Technology. The study was carried out in conjunction with the Federal Reserve-Massachusetts Institute of Technology econometric model sponsored by the Social Science Research Council with support from the Board of Governors of the Federal Reserve System. The authors also wish to express their thanks to other participants in the MIT-FRB project, and to Franklin M. Fisher, Stephen M. Goldfeld, Burton G. Malkiel, and Gerald A. Pogue for helpful criticism and suggestions. The views expressed in the paper are those of the authors alone.

[1] Credit rationing is discussed in this study only within the institutional framework of the commercial banking industry. Nonetheless, large sections of the paper, and particularly the theoretical model, could be applied equally well to other financial intermediaries.

[2] This list is not inclusive and references to other works can be found in the studies cited. A second aspect of the mechanism of credit rationing based on "customer relationships" is developed by Hodgman [3] and Kane and Malkiel [6] and is discussed further below.

tioning as a situation in which the demand for commercial loans exceeds the supply of these loans at the commercial loan rate quoted by the banks. Thus credit rationing is an excess demand for commercial loans at the ruling commercial loan rate. In addition, it is helpful to distinguish two forms of credit rationing depending on the status of the commercial loan interest rate. *Equilibrium rationing* is defined as credit rationing which occurs when the loan rate is set at its long-run equilibrium level. *Dynamic rationing* is defined as credit rationing which may occur in the short run when the loan rate has not been fully adjusted to the long-run optimal level.

This definition serves to bring into focus the basic challenge which must be met in order to establish the rationality of equilibrium rationing, namely: can it ever be rational for the bank to limit the loan to less than the amount demanded by the borrower when both the loan rate and the loan granted are chosen optimally, that is, to maximize profits. The problem of dynamic rationing differs only in that the commercial loan rate is set at levels consistent with short-run profit maximization.[3] In either case, three elements enter into the problem: the demand for loans, the supply of loans, and the determinants of the commercial loan rate. The shortcoming of the earlier studies already cited is that they concentrate on the determinants of the quantity supplied by lenders while neglecting the other two elements.[4]

[3] Previous discussions of credit rationing have studied the two forms of rationing independently: the theoretical justification of credit rationing was directed only at the equilibrium form; the empirical significance was considered only with respect to dynamic rationing. In our analysis we endeavor to integrate the two because our theory and the related empirical tests stress their common origin.

[4] The papers by Hodgman [3] and Miller [8] and the discussion of "weak credit rationing" in Freimer and Gordon [1] essentially just omit any reference to demand and the determinants of the rate. The discussion of "strong credit rationing" by Freimer and Gordon states the question properly but then assumes the answer, as shown in fn. 12.

It should be clear that information on the supply curve alone will generally not be sufficient to derive implications about credit rationing. For this reason, the development of our theoretical model of credit rationing integrates the demand for loans and the determinants of the loan rate with the supply of loans. The development of this model is given in Sections I and II of the paper. In Section I, analytic propositions concerning rationing are derived under alternative assumptions about market competition. In Section II, these results are then interpreted in the light of the institutional structure of competition in the commercial banking industry of the United States to provide the complete theory. Section III describes how our theory of credit rationing can be used to derive an operational credit rationing proxy. Section IV contains empirical tests of the theory as set out in Sections I and II using the credit rationing proxy derived in Section III.

I. *Some Analytic Propositions*

1. *The Bank's Optimal Loan Offer Curve*

The first set of propositions to be developed are concerned only with the bank's supply curve or offer curve for commercial loans. This offer curve is derived by generalizing the results obtained by Freimer and Gordon [1] for a rectangular density function of possible returns to the bank on commercial loan contracts. We shall then proceed to include a demand function and derive the implications of alternative forms of competition.

To start, consider a banker facing a large number of customers each wishing to finance its investment projects. As in the earlier literature, we define the outcome of the customer's projects as the firm's end of period value, denoted by x. We further assume that the bank views x as a random variable and summarize in the density function $f_i[x]$ the bank's subjective evaluation of the probability of different outcomes. In general, the density function $f_i[x]$ will be affected by the size of the customer's investment which, in turn, may be expected to depend on the size of the loan granted. For expository convenience, our formal analysis here will proceed under the restrictive assumption that the size of the project is fixed and therefore $f_i[x]$ can be taken as independent of the loan size granted. This assumption implies that the firm has alternative means of finance which can be used to complement the bank credit. It can be shown, however, that all the major conclusions reached here can be generalized to the case where the size of the project is not independent of the loan granted, provided the investment opportunity of the customer is subject to decreasing (expected) returns.[5]

The expected profit of the bank from the ith customer loan, P_i, is a function of the size of the loan made L_i, the loan rate r_i, and the density function f_i. It is helpful to assume the existence of a sure minimum outcome k_i and a maximum possible outcome K_i for the projects such that:

$$f_i[x] = 0 \qquad \text{for } x < k_i \quad \text{or} \quad x > K_i$$

Now let $R_i = 1 + r_i$ be the interest rate factor and thus $R_i L_i$ will be the total amount of the contract repayment (interest plus principal). Then the contribution of L_i to the bank's expected profits can be written as the difference between the total expected repayment by the firm and the total opportunity cost, i.e.:

$$(1) \qquad P_i = P_i[R_i L_i] = R_i L_i \int_{R_i L_i}^{K_i} f_i[x]dx + \int_{k_i}^{R_i L_i} x f_i[x]dx - I L_i$$

[5] Freimer and Gordon [1] conclude that there is a significant difference between the fixed size investment and variable size investment assumptions. However, this conclusion is based on an inconsistent definition of opportunity cost. In Jaffee [5] the essential equivalence of these two assumptions, using a proper definition of opportunity cost, is derived. See also fn. 11.

The first term in this expression represents the gross receipts of the bank if the outcome x is sufficiently favorable to enable the firm to repay the agreed amount $R_i L_i$ in full. The second term denotes the receipts if the outcome of the project falls short of the contracted amount. In this case, we assume the bank receives the entire outcome x, whatever it might be.[6] The last term represents the bank's opportunity cost, where $I = 1 + j$ and j is the opportunity rate. The rate is for the moment assumed constant and independent of the loan contract on the premise that the bank has unlimited access to a perfect capital market.[7]

The expected profit function (1) can be further simplified by adding and subtracting

$$R_i L_i \int_{k_i}^{R_i L_i} f_i[x]dx$$

and then integrating the second term of that expression by parts. This yields:

$$(2) \qquad P_i = P_i[R_i L_i] = (R_i - I)L_i - \int_{k_i}^{R_i L_i} F_i[x]dx$$

where

$$F_i[A] = \int_{k_i}^{A} f_i[x]dx$$

[6] In such cases of at least partial default, it is reasonable that the bank would incur some collections which should be deducted from the outcome x. While this refinement is neglected here, it can be shown that the character of our conclusions would not change if it were taken into account. See Jaffee [5] and Miller [8]. A similar remark applies to the cost of making and servicing a loan.

[7] The existence of well-developed markets in Federal Funds and Certificates of Deposits (*CDs*) make this assumption reasonable in normal periods. If these markets cease to operate in tight money periods, for example when the Regulation Q ceiling hinders the issue of new *CDs*, then the shadow price of funds would have to replace the market indicator as the opportunity cost. This may lead to dynamic effects, and these are considered below in the discussion of dynamic rationing (Section II.3) and in the empirical tests.

is the probability that x will be less than a.

An optimal loan to a customer is defined as the loan size which maximizes the bank's expected profits from that customer for a given loan interest rate.[8] The bank's offer curve for that customer is then the set of optimal loans corresponding to alternative possible loan rates. This offer curve can be derived from the first-order condition for the maximization of expected profit:

$$(3)\quad \frac{\partial P_i[R_iL_i]}{\partial L_i} = R_i(1 - F[R_iL_i]) - I = 0$$

This condition can be usefully rewritten in the form:

$$F_i[R_iL_i] = 1 - \frac{I}{R_i} = \frac{r_i - j}{1 + r_i}$$

Since the quantity $F_i[R_iL_i]$ is precisely the probability of default, (3) admits the following simple interpretation: the optimal loan is such that the probability of default is equal to the excess of the loan rate over the opportunity cost, normalized by the loan rate factor $R_i = 1 + r_i$.[9]

The offer curve can now be defined as the implicit solution to (3) for L_i in terms of R_i subject to the nonnegativity condition $L_i \geq 0$. We will denote this solution by $\hat{L}_i = \hat{L}_i[R_i]$. From (3) we can deduce several properties of this offer curve which will be used in developing our argument.

Proposition 1. The optimal loan offer curve defined by condition (3) (and drawn in Figure 1 has the following properties:

(1.1) $\hat{L}_i = 0$ for $R_i < I$

(1.2) $0 \leq \hat{L}_i \leq k_i/I$ for $R_i = I$

(1.3) $R_i\hat{L}_i \leq K_i$ for all R_i

(1.4) $\lim_{R_i \to \infty} \hat{L}_i = 0$

Proposition (1.1) follows from the nonnegativity condition and condition (3). Since the marginal expected profit of an additional loan $(\partial P_i/\partial L_i)$ is negative for all positive loan sizes whenever $R_i < I$, the best the bank can do under this condition is to extend no loan at all. Similarly, when $R_i = I$, condition (3) can hold only if $F_i[R_iL_i] = 0$; this implies $R_iL_i = IL_i \leq k_i$ which is equivalent to proposition (1.2). This means that the offer curve is a vertical line segment when $R_i = I$. In fact, in the case with no uncertainty in which F_i is identically zero, the offer curve is nothing more than this vertical line.

The logic of proposition (1.3) is that for any given interest rate factor R_i, the bank will not receive additional income from extending loans in amounts which exceed the solution of $R_iL_i = K_i$, because K_i is the maximum amount the firm could conceivably earn. Furthermore, loans cost the bank the opportunity rate I, and hence all solutions must satisfy the condition of proposition (1.3). *Thus the optimal loan is finite no matter how high the interest rate offered.*[10] From proposition (1.3) follows immediately proposition (1.4). It implies that as the loan rate grows larger and larger, the optimal loan does not follow course; to the contrary, at least after some point, the optimal loan will begin to decline as the rate grows and will eventually

[8] The formulation in terms of expected profits assumes, of course, a linear utility function for the bank. This makes it unnecessary to take into account higher order moments of the distribution of outcomes for the firm's projects and covariance of profits between customers. The rationale for this assumption is that banks service a large number of relatively diverse customers. In addition, a utility function with explicit risk aversion would leave unclear whether the existence of credit rationing in the model arises from the structure of the model or simply from the utility function.

[9] Since the empirically observed spread between the loan rate and the opportunity rate at which banks can secure or invest funds is typically small, this condition implies that banks should tend to assume quite modest default risk. This conclusion seems to be in agreement with bank loss experience on commercial loans.

[10] Although the maximum is finite, there may be multiple local maxima for the loan offer curve. In the discussion which follows, we abstract from this complication since it does not affect the results.

approach zero as the rate grows beyond bounds. The common sense of this surprising implication can be understood from the following considerations: (*i*) by making the size of the contracted repayment R_iL_i sufficiently large, default becomes virtually certain, and hence the bank can count on becoming the owner of all the net activities of the firm; (ii) as R_i rises, the amount L_i that the bank needs to invest to achieve this result grows smaller and smaller and approaches zero as R_i tends to infinity.[11]

Two other properties of the offer curve are also worth developing.

PROPOSITION 2. For a given interest factor R_i, expected profits decrease monotonically as the loan size varies from the optimal size in either direction.

The proof follows directly from (3), since

$$\frac{\partial^2 P_i[R_iL_i]}{\partial L_i^2} = -R_i^2 f_i[R_iL_i] < 0 \quad (4)$$

$$\text{for } k_i < R_iL_i < K_i$$

This also shows that the solution given by (3) is, indeed, a global maximum.

PROPOSITION 3. Expected profits increase along the offer curve for successively higher interest rate factors.

To derive this result, first substitute (3) into (1), which allows us to write the profit function along the offer curve as:

$$P_i[R_i\hat{L}_i] = \int_{k_i}^{R_i\hat{L}_i} xf[x]dx \quad (5)$$

But then,

$$\frac{dP_i[R_i\hat{L}_i]}{dR_i} = R_i\hat{L}_i f_i[R_i\hat{L}_i]\left(\hat{L}_i + R_i\frac{d\hat{L}_i}{dR_i}\right)$$

and by implicitly differentiating (3)

$$\hat{L}_i + R_i\frac{d\hat{L}_i}{dR_i} = \frac{1 - F_i[R_i\hat{L}_i]}{R_i f_i[R_i\hat{L}_i]}$$

and thus

$$\frac{dP_i[R_i\hat{L}_i]}{dR_i} = \hat{L}_i(1 - F_i[R_i\hat{L}_i]) > 0 \quad (6)$$

$$\text{for } k_i < R_i\hat{L}_i < K_i$$

which proves the proposition. An obvious and reasonable implication of this proposition is that the bank will obtain its maximum potential profits when allowed to charge an infinite interest rate. Of course, this only serves to emphasize that the offer curve is defined independently of the demand for loans and thus many points on the offer locus may not prove feasible for the lender.

2. *The Banker as a Discriminating Monopolist*

The optimal loan offer curve just derived can be interpreted as the bank's supply curve for the bank customer. It is interesting that this supply curve is "backward bending" as shown in Figure 1. In fact, Freimer and Gordon [1] base part of their argument for credit rationing on this characteristic of the supply curve alone.[12] Our

[11] A similar result holds for the variable size investment case. Although the optimal loan offer remains positive as the interest rate approaches infinity, the loan size approaches a finite asymptote. In contrast, Freimer and Gordon [1, p. 407] conclude that the optimal loan approaches infinity as the interest rate goes to infinity, because they only consider projects with an expected value exceeding the opportunity cost; but this contradicts the meaning of opportunity cost; see fn. 5.

[12] Reference is to the Freimer and Gordon [1] case of weak credit rationing. The terminology is misleading because one would normally not equate a backward bending supply curve with rationing. Freimer and Gordon also consider what they call "strong credit rationing," which conceptually is closely akin to our equilibrium rationing. For this case they argue that a bank sets a conventional interest rate (6 percent to be exact) and then grants loans to all customers up to the amount indicated by their respective bank offer curves. This analysis is inadequate for two reasons. First, the optimality of a 6 percent rate is essentially just assumed; banks do not charge rates below 6 percent because of convention; banks do not charge rates above 6 percent because their numerical examples suggest

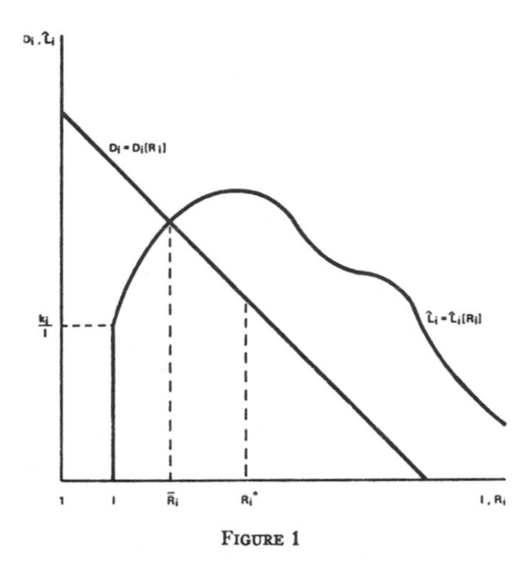

FIGURE 1

definition of credit rationing, however, obviously necessitates taking into account the demand for loans by the bank customer. Such a demand curve for the ith bank customer, denoted hereafter by $D_i = D_i[R_i]$, has been drawn in Figure 1. We assume a downward sloping demand curve, which vanishes for a sufficiently high interest rate factor and is finite even for a zero interest rate (or interest factor equal to unity). The boundary conditions for the demand curve are based on the characteristics of the underlying investment projects. At a zero interest rate the firm's demand for loans is bounded by the size of the investment projects, while the existence of some alternative means of financing suggests that at some sufficiently high interest rate the demand will become zero. The negative slope of the demand curve can be derived from the assumption that the firm has only limited access to these alternative means of finance. The implied limit on competition between banks for the customer's business is discussed further in Section II.

The conditions under which rational credit rationing will occur can now be seen with the aid of Figure 1. The ith firm's demand curve and the bank's offer curve to that customer are assumed to intersect at the interest rate factor $\bar{R}_i$.[13] If the bank chooses to charge an interest factor greater than $\bar{R}_i$, rationing will not occur since the loan demand is less than the loan offer at such an interest factor. In fact, if the firm were willing to accept a larger loan (which it is not by definition of the demand curve), the bank would increase its expected profits by providing such a loan (see proposition 2). On the other hand, if the bank chooses to charge an interest factor less than $\bar{R}_i$, then rationing will occur since in this region the bank's optimal loan offer is less than the amount demanded by the customer. The bank would only reduce its expected profits by increasing the loan offer to meet the demand. Thus the question of the rationality of credit rationing can be reduced to a consideration of the optimal rate factor to be charged by the bank, and its relation to $\bar{R}_i$.

Two critical variables enter into the bank's selection of the loan rate. First there is the question of the time horizon: in the long run, a rational banker would select the rate which maximizes his expected profits; but other constraints may preclude immediate full adjustment in the short run. This leads, of course, to our distinction between the cases of equilibrium rationing and dynamic rationing as already defined. We start by considering only the equilibrium case since it has been

that *customer* utility maximization occurs at lower rates. Secondly, even if the 6 percent rate is accepted as optimal, we have no way of knowing from their analysis whether rationing actually occurs, because the demand curve is never shown.

[13] The existence of at least one point of intersection is assured by the boundary conditions on the demand curve and proposition (1.4). Throughout the remainder of the paper we shall assume that, in fact, only one such point exists. Equivalent results can be obtained for the case of multiple intersections, but only at the cost of more complexity in the analysis.

the center of the theoretical discussion and since the short-run dynamic case is easily derived from the equilibrium case.

The second important variable influencing the bank's choice of rate is the nature of market competition. Because the degree of competition turns out to be a critical factor in determining the existence of rationing, it is worthwhile considering several different regimes from a purely analytic standpoint.

The first regime considered is the simple case of a discriminating monopolist. It is assumed that the bank maximizes its expected profits with respect to each customer separately and is free to charge each customer a different interest rate. Thus, we can take the bank's solution for the ith customer as typical:

PROPOSITION 4. Let R_i^* be the rate factor which maximizes the bank's expected profits when the bank is acting as a discriminating monopolist. Then:

(4.1) $R_i^* \geq \overline{R}_i$, which implies

(4.2) Credit rationing is not profitable for a banker acting as a discriminating monoplist.

The proof of this proposition is easily derived from Figure 1 and the properties of the offer curve. The bank will always charge an interest factor at least as high as $\overline{R}_i$ since; (i) expected profits increase along the offer curve for successively higher interest rates (proposition 3) and (ii) the loan $L_i(\overline{R}_i)$ is feasible by the definition of $\overline{R}_i$. We next observe that, in view of proposition 2, for any rate equal to, or larger than $\overline{R}_i$, the bank's profit will be higher the closer the loan is to the corresponding point on the offer curve. But since the demand curve places a ceiling on the feasible loan size, the bank will find the optimal rate R_i^* by maximizing profit along the demand curve constraint, which means that credit rationing will not be profitable. Indeed, as in the standard theory of monopoly under certainty, at the rate R_i^* the bank would be glad to lend more than the customer is prepared to take.

3. *The Banker Must Charge All Customers a Uniform Rate of Interest*

Now suppose that the banker is constrained to charge all customers the same rate though he can choose that rate freely and can also decide on the size of the loan to be granted each customer. We will show that under these conditions credit rationing may (and very frequently will) be profitable, i.e. at the common optimal interest rate, for some customers the most profitable loan for the bank to supply is less than the amount demanded.

To establish this proposition it is convenient to deal first with a subsidiary problem. Suppose that the bank faces only two customers and, for the moment, rule out credit rationing by requiring that the bank *must* satisfy the customers' demand at the chosen common rate.

The bank's expected profits under these conditions can be written as:

$$P = P_1[RD_1] + P_2[RD_2] \tag{7}$$

where R is the common rate factor charged both customers and the constraint of satisfying both demand functions is implicit in the notation. By differentiating this profit function with respect to the interest factor, we can obtain the first-order condition for the optimal interest factor, say R^*.

An important property of R^* can be obtained, however, without explicit reference to this first order condition. Let R_1^* and R_2^* be the optimal rate factors a discriminating monopolist banker would charge customers 1 and 2, respectively, and assume, without loss of generality, that $R_1^* < R_2^*$. It follows from this definition that the expected profit from each customer must be a concave function of R in the neighborhood of R_1^* and R_2^*, respectively. We shall go somewhat further and assume that the concavity of each expected profit function holds for all $R>1$.[14] We can then establish:

PROPOSITION 5. If R^* is the common rate factor that maximizes the bank's expected profit, we must have:

$$R_1^* \le R^* \le R_2^*$$

This result can be verified through use of a proof by contradiction. The assumption of concave expected profit functions implies that expected profits decrease monotonically as the absolute value of the spread between the actual rate to a customer and the discrimination monopolist rate increases. Thus, if the bank chose a common rate factor R^* that was less than both R_1^* and R_2^*, it would find that expected profits could be increased by increasing the rate factor at least to the level of R_1^*, thus contradicting the assumption that the original rate factor was optimal. Essentially the same argument shows that $R^*>R_2^*$ also leads to a contradiction.

We can now relax the restriction that the bank must satisfy both customers' demand function and show that, under these conditions, it will never pay to ration customer 1 but it may very well pay to ration customer 2. Specifically, we can establish:

PROPOSITION 6. For the common rate regime

(6.1) $R^* \ge R_1^* \ge \overline{R}_1$ implying it is not profitable to ration customer 1.

(6.2) $R_2^* \ge R^* \gtreqless \overline{R}_2$, implying that $R^* < \overline{R}_2$ is possible, in which case, credit rationing is profitable.

Proposition (6.1) follows directly from propositions 5 and 4. As for establishing (6.2), we need only exhibit a concrete example in which the condition holds. That it is, in fact, quite easy to construct such examples can be seen from the following considerations. First, going back to proposition 5, one can readily establish that the position of R^* within the range R_1^* to R_2^* depends on the relative size of the two customers (as measured, say, by the size of the loan demanded for any R in the critical range), and on the elasticity of the two demand curves. In particular, R^* can be made arbitrarily close to R_1^* by assuming that customer 1 is sufficiently larger than customer 2, and/or by assuming that the demand curve for customer 1 is sufficiently inelastic in the range of rates above R_1^*. By the same token, $\overline{R}_2$ can be made arbitrarily close to R_2^* by assuming a sufficiently elastic demand curve for customer 2. Thus, by appropriate choice of these functions, one can readily construct situations where R^* is lower than $\overline{R}_2$. The above construction also provides an interesting interpretation of proposition 6. The constraint of charging both customers the same rate R^* forces the bank to charge customer 1 a rate which is too high relative to R_1^* and hence, the customer is not rationed. On the other hand, the bank is forced to charge customer 2 a rate which is too low relative to R_2^*. If the rate is sufficiently low relative to $\overline{R}_2$, that is $R^* < \overline{R}_2$, then the second customer will be rationed.

The possibility of credit rationing also adds another dimension to the problem. In the case in which rationing does not occur, R^* is the optimal common rate charged by the bank and the customers receive loans

[14] The assumption of global concavity is not a necessary condition for proposition 6, to be proven below; the proof can be carried out with weaker assumptions. We have chosen to assume global concavity, however, because it leads, via proposition 5, to a particularly interesting demonstration of proposition 6.

of D_1 $[R^*]$ and D_2 $[R^*]$, respectively. But when customer 2 can be profitably rationed at R^*, the very existence of rationing changes the conditions of the problem and R^* need no longer be the optimal rate. Instead, there will exist a more general optimum optimorum rate, say $\hat{R}$, which yields the maximum expected profits after allowing for credit rationing of customer 2. $\hat{R}$ will just equal R^* in cases in which rationing is not profitable, but will generally differ from R^* when rationing is profitable. The fact that $\hat{R}$ may differ from R^* creates some difficulties in deriving the comparative static properties of the model, as will be apparent below. However, it does not affect our basic conclusion; proposition 6 remains valid even if R^* is replaced with the true optimum $\hat{R}$. For, as one can readily verify, $R^* \leq \overline{R}_2$ implies $\hat{R} \leq \overline{R}_2$, and conversely.[15]

Before proceeding to the generalizations of the propositions developed so far, it is worthwhile considering the special case of a risk free firm, that is a customer for whom the bank's subjective evaluation of default risk is zero.

> PROPOSITION 7. Neither a banker acting as a discriminating monopolist, nor a banker charging all customers the same rate, will ration a risk free customer.

The result of proposition 7 for the case of a discriminating monopolist is simply a special case of proposition 4 and follows directly from that proposition. To prove the proposition for a banker charging a common rate factor, it is important to recall from proposition 1 that the bank's offer curve for a risk free customer is a vertical line at $R=I$. Furthermore, it must be true that R^* (or $\hat{R}$) is greater than I if the bank's expected profits are to be positive. But this implies that $R^* \geq \overline{R}$ for the risk free customer, which on the basis of proposition 6 rules out the possibility of credit rationing.

We can now proceed to generalizations of the propositions developed in this part. First, consider a banker facing n customers and constrained to charge all n customers the same loan rate. Again, let R_i^* $(i=1,2,\ldots,n)$ denote the rate the bank would charge if acting as a discriminating monopolist and let $\hat{R}$ be the common "optimum optimorum" rate the bank charges when allowing credit rationing. Let us number customers in ascending order with respect to the monopolist rate; that is $R_i^* \geq R_{i-1}^*$ for $i=2,3,\ldots,n$. Proposition 5 can then be generalized to:

> PROPOSITION 5′. The optimal common rate $\hat{R}$ charged all customers must lie between the rate charged customer 1 and the rate charged customer n when the bank is acting as a discriminating monopolist. Formally, there exists an integer j, $2 \leq j \leq n$, such that $R_j^* \geq \hat{R} \geq R_{j-1}^*$.

Similarly, proposition 6 can be generalized to:

PROPOSITION 6′.

(6.1′) For any customers i such that $\hat{R} \geq R_i^*$, we have $\hat{R} \geq \overline{R}_i$ implying that rationing of these customers is not profitable.

(6.2′) In the case of customers for whom $\hat{R} < R_i^*$, we have $\hat{R} \gtreqless \overline{R}_i$ implying that rationing of some of these customers may be profitable.

The interpretation and proof of these

[15] We have previously established that $R^* \geq \overline{R}_2$ implies that R^* is already the optimum optimorum or $R^* = \hat{R}$; hence $R^* \geq \overline{R}_2 \rightarrow \hat{R} \geq \overline{R}_2$. Similarly $\hat{R} \geq \overline{R}_2$ implies that even when rationing is allowed, it is not profitable and therefore $\hat{R}$ must coincide with R^*, the maximum subject to the constraint that rationing is not permissible; that is $\hat{R} \geq \overline{R}_2 \rightarrow \hat{R} = R^*$ and therefore $\hat{R} \geq \overline{R}_2 \rightarrow R^* \geq \overline{R}_2$. But these two propositions together imply $R^* \geq \overline{R}_2 \Leftrightarrow \hat{R} \geq \overline{R}_2$, which in turn implies $R^* \leq \overline{R}_2 \Leftrightarrow \hat{R} \geq \overline{R}_2$.

propositions follows directly from the corresponding propositions for the case of two customers, and accordingly are not repeated here.

4. *Generalization to m Separate Customer Classes*

It is now easy to extend our conclusions about the rationality of credit rationing to the case in which the bank can assign customers to any one of, say, m classes, where within each class the bank must charge a single uniform rate. The principles which govern the assignment of customers to classes and the choice of the rate for each class can be readily inferred from the previous analysis:

(i) If the profit functions are all concave in the relevant range, then the optimal classification will be achieved by dividing the entire range of the set of R_i^* (the rate charged customer i when the bank acts as a discriminating monopolist) into m intervals and assigning to the same class all customers whose R_i^* falls in a given interval. If the profit functions are not concave, the principle for optimal classification becomes more complex; but in any event, it is clear there will exist a set of optimal group rates and a corresponding optimal classification for the customers, and that furthermore, each class will contain customers with different R_i^*s, as long as the number of customers exceeds the number of classes.

(ii) The optimum rate for any given class j, say $\hat{R}_j$, must fall somewhere between the smallest and the largest R_i^* of the customers in that class.

(iii) It will not be profitable to ration customers whose R^* is smaller than the group rate $\hat{R}_j$, but it may pay to ration those for whom R_i^* exceeds $\hat{R}_j$. In particular, rationing will occur whenever $\overline{R}_i > \hat{R}_j$.

(iv) The likelihood that it will be profitable to ration at least some customers in a class will be positively related to the heterogeneity of the R_i^* of the customers in that class and hence the likelihood of rationing will be inversely related to the size of m. Indeed, if m is allowed to be as large as the number of customers, that is, n, then the bank will be in the position of a discriminating monopolist and credit rationing will not occur.

There remains now to draw the implications of these results by combining the propositions developed so far with a number of considerations arising from the nature of competition in the banking industry.

II. *Competition in Banking and Credit Rationing*

1. *The Nature of Competition in Commercial Banking and its Implications for Credit Rationing.*

We have shown in Section I that a single bank, free to discriminate between borrowers by charging each customer its monopolist rate R_i^*, would not ration credit. A similar conclusion holds even if there are many banks, as long as they act collusively to maximize joint profits, relying if necessary on side payments. If all banks share the identical subjective evaluations of the profitability of borrowers' investment projects, then clearly the optimum rate R_i^* to be charged to the ith customer would be the same no matter which bank served him. Furthermore, even allowing for differences in the subjective evaluation of borrower risk and assuming an arbitrary initial distribution of customers between banks, the device of buying and selling customers would allow each bank and the industry as a whole to maximize profits. In this way a banker's Pareto optimum would be reached with each bank charging its customers the monopolist rate, and thus, again, no credit rationing would occur.

In this section we propose to argue that

this solution is in fact not feasible, at least in the present American economy. We suggest, instead, that banks can best exploit their market power, while remaining within the bounds set by prevailing institutions, by classifying customers into a rather small number of classes within each of which a uniform rate is charged, even though the membership of each class will exhibit considerable heterogeneity in terms of R_i^*.

First, even if there were but a single monopoly bank or a perfectly collusive banking system, the mere existence of usury laws would lead toward the indicated solution. Such laws would prevent the banker from charging any rate R_i^* which is greater than the legal limit. Thus all customers for whom R_i^* is larger than the ceiling would be classified together in the category with the ceiling rate. Since the monopolist rate R_i^* for each customer in this class would equal or exceed the uniform rate set for the class, namely the usury ceiling, it is apparent from the results of Section I that many, if not all, customers in this class would be profitably rationed.

Even aside from usury ceilings, the pressure of legal restrictions and considerations of good will and social mores would make it inadvisable if not impossible for the banker to charge widely different rates to different customers. A banker would tend, instead, to limit the spread between the rates and to justify the remaining differentials in terms of a few objective and verifiable criteria such as industry class, asset size, and other standard financial measures. An effort would no doubt be made to choose the criteria for classification so as to minimize the difference between the optimal classification of customers into rate classes and the categories dictated by the objective criteria, but a close approximation might be difficult to achieve.

The inducement to adopt a classification scheme of the type described is likely to be greatly strengthened when we take into account the fact that banks cannot openly collude, although they share a common desire to maintain rates as close as feasible to the collusive optimum. In order to prevent, or at least minimize, competitive underbidding of rates they would need tacit agreement as to the appropriate rate structure for customers, and thus a classification scheme based on readily verifiable objective criteria would appear as an efficient and effective device. Furthermore, to make the whole arrangement manageable, the number of different rate classes would have to be reasonably small. Finally, one can also readily understand how such tacit agreement on the structure of class rates could be facilitated by tying these rates through fairly rigid differentials, to a prime rate set through price leadership.

If we now superimpose the impact of usury ceilings along with the other legal and social constraints, it is clear that the entire structure of rates would tend to be compressed within narrower limits than would otherwise be optimal. This means, in particular, that the rate for each class would tend to the lower limit of the R_i^* spread appropriate for the customers in that class, with the possible exception of the lowest class rate reserved for the riskless or nearly riskless prime customers. The result is that widespread rationing would occur, particularly in the higher rate classes.

Finally, we may observe that the oligopolistic price setting pattern outlined above is likely to lead to a very sluggish and somewhat jerky adjustment of the entire rate structure as changes in underlying conditions generate changes in the optimal level and structure of rates. The considerations relevant here are well known from the literature on oligopolistic market structure and price leadership. It follows that when conditions are changing rapidly we might expect to find that the entire structure of rates would lag behind, and thus, for a while, would tend to be higher or lower than the optimal structure, depending on the direction of the change. These considerations provide the key to dynamic rationing to be elaborated below.

2. *Long-Run Equilibrium Credit Rationing*

We are now in a position to assemble the complete theory of credit rationing. We first take up equilibrium credit rationing which occurs when the loan rate is set at its optimal level. In Section I it was shown that credit rationing will be profitable, even in long-run equilibrium, as long as there is uncertainty of loan repayment *and* banks cannot discriminate perfectly between customers. In Section II.1 both of these conditions were verified as features of the commercial banking industry, and thus we conclude that equilibrium rationing is consistent with rational economic behavior.

This conclusion would remain basically unchanged if one recognizes that the bank's expected return and cost is affected by other contract terms such as loan maturity and compensating balance requirements. To be sure, if a bank could discriminate freely between customers with respect to such factors, there might be no occasion for equilibrium rationing. But while the empirical evidence is scanty, one would surmise that banks are limited in their power to discriminate with respect to these terms as well as the nominal interest charge. Similarly, our analysis can incorporate the benefits of maintaining long-run "customer relationships" (cf. Hodgman [4], Edward Kane and Burton Malkiel [6]) without invalidating our basic conclusions about the rationality of rationing.[16]

It is worthwhile to consider briefly the comparative static properties of equilibrium rationing in our model. The total amount of equilibrium rationing, E, can be written as the difference between loan demand and loan supply for those customers of the bank experiencing rationing:

$$E = \sum_{i=1}^{n} \max \left[D_i(\hat{R}) - \hat{L}_i(\hat{R}_i), 0\right] \tag{8}$$

The excess supply of loans to those customers to whom the bank would like to extend additional loans does not, of course, offset the rationing to other customers. The offer curve to a firm depends on the opportunity cost of the bank, I, and the firm's density function of possible outcomes, f_i, and hence E depends on these two factors and the firms' demand functions. Consequently, for purposes of comparative static analysis, one may consider the impact of changes in demand, risk, and opportunity cost on the amount of equilibrium rationing. Unfortunately, the evaluation of the impact of these changes turns out to be a very difficult process. In particular, the rationed or nonrationed status of customers may change because of the change in the underlying parameter. To at least illustrate the possible outcomes, however, we shall outline the case of a change in the opportunity cost I.

Two important results for the comparative static analysis are given in the following propositions:

PROPOSITION 8. A *ceteris paribus* increase in the opportunity cost causes the optimal loan offer curve to shift downward at every interest rate. Indeed, by implicit differentiation of equation

[16] Although the customer relationship and nonprice contract terms may serve to modify the importance of uncertainty in our theory of credit rationing, the bank's inability to discriminate perfectly in setting these terms is still critical. The need for such an element can be seen clearly in the attempts by Hodgman [4, p. 265] and Kane and Malkiel [6, p. 123] to rationalize credit rationing without appeal to such imperfect discrimination.

(3) we obtain:

$$\frac{\partial \hat{L}_i}{\partial I} = \frac{-1}{f_i R^2} < 0 \tag{9}$$

PROPOSITION 9. The common optimal rate factor R^* (applicable if the bank were constrained to satisfy all demand functions) is positively related to the opportunity cost I.

Proposition 8 is self-evident. Proposition 9 is in line with the standard theory of the firm in that an increase in marginal cost necessitates an increase in marginal revenue which takes the form of an increase in R^*. Because the very act of changing the parameter I may lead to a change in the rationed or nonrationed status of customers, as demonstrated below, special cases can arise in which $\hat{R}$ (the common optimal rate allowing for rationing when profitable) and I are not positively related, contrary to the relationship between R^* and I. Since such cases are distinctly abnormal, the obvious and reasonable situation being a positive relationship between I and $\hat{R}$, we shall proceed on the premise that proposition 9, is equally applicable to $\hat{R}$.[17]

With the aid of Figure 2, we can survey the impact of an increase in the opportunity cost from I_0 to I_1. From proposition 8, it is known that the offer curve will shift downward from the locus $\hat{L}_0$ to $\hat{L}_1$; and from proposition 9 it is known that the common optimal rate factor will increase, say from $\hat{R}_0$ to $\hat{R}_1$. Thus the net impact of a change in the opportunity cost on the maximum loan offered is the result of a shift in the offer curve and a movement along this curve, and the amount of equilibrium rationing may either rise or fall. These two alternative outcomes are illustrated in Figure 2. In the case of the demand curve D_1, the customer would move from a rationed to a nonrationed status, while for the case illustrated by the demand curve D_2, the opposite conclusion holds. Cases in which the rationing status remains unchanged are, of course, equally possible. Thus the effect of an increase in I on the size of rationing must remain uncertain. This result, however, should not be regarded as disturbing. What it implies is that in the long run, *no systematic relationship exists between the extent of equilibrium rationing and the absolute level of interest rates.*

[17] The abnormal conditions which lead to this abnormal result are discussed further in [5, p. 56 and p. 86].

3. *Dynamic Credit Rationing*

We define dynamic rationing as the difference between equilibrium rationing and the volume of rationing that arises when the actual rate charged customers, R, differs from the long-run equilibrium rate, $\hat{R}$. By this definition, dynamic rationing can be positive or negative, and we shall show that its magnitude will be positively associated with the spread, $\hat{R}$-R. Furthermore, we have already suggested, in view of the oligopolistic structure of the banking industry, that R is likely to adjust slowly to changes in $\hat{R}$, thus lending

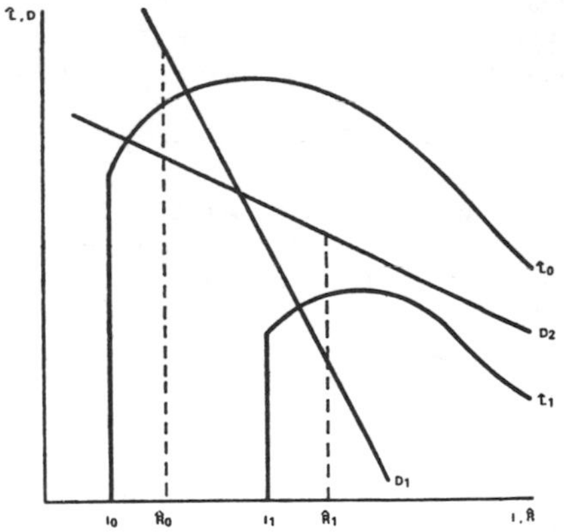

FIGURE 2

credence to the empirical importance of dynamic credit rationing. In fact, there is evidence that banks may tend to rely on some objective signal, such as changes in the Federal Reserve's discount rate, in determining the timing of loan rate changes, and hence, dynamic credit rationing would vary significantly depending upon Federal Reserve policy.[18]

It is helpful to begin by considering a system that starts in long-run equilibrium with a rate, $\hat{R}_0$, and then receives a shock that changes $\hat{R}_0$ to $\hat{R}_1$ while the quoted rate remains unchanged at $\hat{R}_0$. As we have seen, there are three main market forces that can change $\hat{R}$: a change in market interest rates leading to a change in the opportunity cost I; a shift in customer demand schedules; and a change in risk as may be indicated by a shift in $F[x]$. We shall first consider the effects of changing each of these factors, one at a time. Then by combining the results of these *ceteris paribus* experiments, we can examine more realistic situations in which several factors change simultaneously.

1. Consider first a change in market rates of return which, for convenience, may be summarized by some representative rate, r_M. a rise in r_M will directly increase the opportunity rate for funds invested in the loan portfolio. From propositions 8 and 9, we know that such an increase in I will lower all offer curves and also increase $\hat{R}$. Since the quoted rate remains at $\hat{R}_0$ and all the demand curves are unchanged, ***there must be an aggregate increase in rationing***. Our model also provides some information about the incidence of this increase. At one extreme, the risk free firms will still not experience any rationing because the offer curve for them is a vertical line.[19] At the other extreme, firms already rationed in the initial equilibrium will be rationed even more as the offer curve shifts down. Finally, among the risky firms initially not rationed, some will remain unrationed while others will experience new rationing, with the amount depending upon the extent of the shift.

Thus on the whole, the loan portfolio will shrink and the funds released by rationing will be shifted into other assets whose yield has increased (or be used to repay the now more costly borrowed funds). However, the opportunity cost I is now likely to fall relative to the market rate r_M because loans will be a smaller percentage of the total portfolio. This will tend to moderate, though not eliminate, the initial increase in rationing.

2. Consider next the effect of a downward revision of the anticipated distribution of outcomes; operationally, we may think of the initial distribution $F[x]$ being replaced by a new one $G[x]$ with $G[x] \leq F[x]$. As can be verified from (3), such a re-

[18] Empirical tests performed in an earlier work by one of the authors [5, Ch. 4] confirms the hypothesis that, in the period covered by our data, changes in the Federal Reserve discount rate were a major factor influencing the timing of changes in the commercial loan rate. It should be stressed, though, that such a relationship might not continue to hold in the future unless the Federal Reserve continues to operate the discount window in the customary fashion. Should the recent Federal Reserve proposal [11] to keep the discount rate closely in line with market rates be enacted, it is likely that the commercial loan rate would adjust more quickly toward its desired level. In this case, dynamic rationing in response to changes in market conditions would tend to die out faster than in the past. Thus discount rate policy is at least one way in which the Federal Reserve can influence the amount of credit rationing.

[19] This conclusion would not hold if the shift in I were so large as to exceed $\hat{R}_0$. In this case, the best course of action would be to cut off loans even to the prime firms, and a fortiori to all customers. But this case can be disregarded for the banks could be counted upon to respond promptly by raising their quoted rate, i.e., $\hat{R}_0$ would not remain unchanged in these circumstances. More generally in the usual theory of monopoly or oligopoly, if the equilibrium price rose because of a shift in either the demand or the cost function, and, for some reason, the market price was prevented from rising, rationing would occur only if the shift were such that the marginal cost would exceed the price. It appears, therefore, that dynamic rationing, just as equilibrium rationing, is intimately related to the uncertainty about the outcome of the loan.

vision results again in a downward shift in the offer curve, and in an increase in the R_i^* and hence in $\hat{R}$. Since the quoted rate has not changed, the maximum loan offered at that rate must tend to decline. With the demand unchanged, rationing must therefore increase for some of the customers, and the incidence of the increased rationing is entirely analogous to that of case 1. Once more, as loans shift out of the now less remunerative loan portfolio, the opportunity cost I may decline somewhat, mitigating the initial effects.

3. Much the same conclusion can be seen to hold for the case of a shift in all demand schedules, r_M and $F[x]$ constant, except that in this case, it is the demand curve which shifts while the offer curve remains unchanged. If I remains unchanged, then the initially rationed customers will experience more rationing because their increased demand is not satisfied at all; the risk free customers, in contrast, will receive larger loans and remain unrationed; and the initially unrationed risky customers will also obtain larger loans, but possibly not enough to match the increase in their demand. Furthermore, as funds flow into the loan portfolio (because some of the increased demand is satisfied), the opportunity cost of loans will tend to increase giving rise to additional rationing of the type under (1).

Normally, an increase in loan demand will tend to occur in periods of buoyant economic activity and hence will be associated with a rise in r_M (partly reflecting the higher demand in all markets and partly causing, in turn, a higher demand for bank funds), and also with an increase in the anticipated profitability of the investment projects, the latter producing a decrease in risk as measured by $F[x]$. The outcome is then a combination of the *ceteris paribus* results under (1), (2), and (3). The shift in $F[x]$ tends to raise the loan offered at the unchanged rate, $\hat{R}_0$; at the same time, the quantity demanded at that rate rises, and if I were unchanged, the effect on $\hat{R}$, as well as on rationing, would depend on the relative amount of the two shifts. Even on this basis, one would anticipate an increase in rationing because the demand curve is likely to shift further than the offer curve, reflecting an increase in the optimism of firms relative to that of the banks. But more fundamentally, I must rise, both because with I constant, more funds would flow into the loan portfolio causing I to rise relative to r_M, and because r_M itself will be rising. Hence the final outcome will tend to be the same as in the previous three cases. The extent of increased rationing will depend on the relative shift in $F[x]$, in the quantity demanded at the unchanged rate, and in r_M, and on whether, on balance, these shifts will cause funds to flow in or out of the loan portfolio. It is apparent, however, that the rise in I and in rationing will tend to be greater the smaller the elasticity of supply of funds to the banking system. The effect might be particularly severe if the ability of banks to attract funds were actually reduced, as happened in some recent episodes in which the Certificates of Deposit rates in secondary markets pierced the Regulation Q ceiling.

We may thus conclude quite generally that as $\hat{R}$ rises relative to $\hat{R}_0$, rationing will tend to increase; and the incidence of the increased rationing will tend to fall most heavily on customers who would be rationed in equilibrium, and will tend to affect the least, if at all, the riskless, or nearly riskless, prime customers.[20] One implication of this

[20] As we have argued in the text, the amount of dynamic rationing tends to be positively related to the spread between the equilibrium rate and the quoted rate. Actually, though this relationship must hold in the large, in some special circumstances it may fail to hold in the small. The special cases arise only when the slope of the demand curve exceeds the slope of the offer

result is worth stressing since it provides the key to our operational measurement of credit rationing set forth in the next section. Suppose that we were to classify all customers into two broad classes, the prime customers and all others. We should then expect that as the gap between $\hat{R}$ and R widens and dynamic rationing becomes more severe, loans to the riskless customers will tend to represent a growing share of the total loan portfolio.

This result can be given the following useful interpretation, which also serves to bring to light the common nature of equilibrium and dynamic rationing. In the presence of risk as to the outcome of the loan, reducing the size of the loan will increase the expected rate of return, by reducing the expected loss from insolvency of the firm. It is therefore quite understandable that a bank faced with a higher opportunity cost (whether from a rise in the market rate or in lending opportunities) and unable to raise the return by raising rates, will find it profitable to raise its return at least by upgrading the quality of its portfolio through a reduction in risk; the upgrading may take the form of shifting funds toward less risky customers, and/or of reducing loans made to risky customers, depending on the nature of the shift in underlying conditions.

III. *A Measure of Credit Rationing*

In this section we shall develop an operational measure of credit rationing which is based on the theory as developed in Sections I and II and which is used in the test of the theory presented in Section IV below. In principle, the volume of credit rationing should be measured by the difference between the loan demand and bank supply for rationed customers as defined by E in equation (8). The degree or relative incidence of credit rationing could then be measured by the ratio of the volume of rationing to the potential demand of rationed customers, or:

$$\hat{H} = \frac{E}{E + L_2} = \frac{D_2 - L_2}{D_2} \tag{10}$$

where D_2 denotes the demand of rationed customers and L_2 the volume of loans actually granted to them.

Unfortunately, the direct measurement of E and L_2, the components of $\hat{H}$, requires information on the *ex ante* customer demand and bank supply which is unlikely to be available, even in the future. The analysis of Section II.3, however, points to a possible, operational, proxy measure of the degree of dynamic credit rationing. As shown there, our model suggests that there should be a positive association between variations in dynamic credit rationing and variations in the proportion of the total loan portfolio accounted for by the risk free prime customers. Let us then denote by $L_1 \simeq D_1$, the volume of loans granted to these customers, and by L_2 and D_2, respectively, the loan granted and the loan demanded by all other customers. Our proposed operational proxy for the non-observable $\hat{H}$ is either of the following two:

$$H_1 = \frac{L_1}{L_1 + L_2} \tag{11.a}$$

or

$$H_2 = \frac{1}{H_1} = \frac{L_1 + L_2}{L_1} \tag{11.b}$$

The first measure, H_1, is simply the percentage of total loans which are granted to the risk free customers, and hence is positively related to the degree of rationing. The alternative proxy is its reciprocal and hence, is negatively related to the degree of rationing.

To see the relation between either proxy

curve. Since this can occur only at relatively high interest rates, indicating default risks well above levels bankers would consider acceptable, the case would seem to have little empirical relevance.

and the ideal measure $\hat{H}$, let

$$B = \frac{D_2}{D_1}$$

Then from (11) we obtain:

$$\text{(12.a)} \qquad H_1 = \frac{1}{[1 + B(1 - \hat{H})]}$$

$$\text{(12.b)} \qquad H_2 = 1 + B(1 - \hat{H})$$

since $L_1 = D_1$.

Differentiating (12) with respect to $\hat{H}$, yields:

$$\text{(13.a)} \qquad \frac{\partial H_1}{\partial \hat{H}} = \frac{B}{[1 + B(1 - \hat{H})]^2} > 0$$

$$\text{(13.b)} \qquad \frac{\partial H_2}{\partial \hat{H}} = -B < 0$$

The equations (12) show that for a given value of B, our proxies are monotonic functions of the ideal measure $\hat{H}$, and (13) confirms that the relation is in the direction expected. The functions relating either proxy to $\hat{H}$ involve as a parameter the relative demand factor, B, essentially because we have replaced the nonobservable D_2 with the observable D_1. This of course implies that any change in B will give rise to a variation in H_1 or H_2 which does not correspond to variations in $\hat{H}$. Hence, if there were sizable variation in B over time, our proxy measures of $\hat{H}$ could be subject to appreciable errors in measurement. Note, however, that even in this event, as long as H_1 or H_2 are used as dependent variables in a statistical test as we shall do below, these errors will not tend to generate bias in the estimated coefficients unless B happens to correlate with the behavioral determinants of $\hat{H}$.[21] Fortunately, the conclusions of Section II concerning the comparative static properties of the model and the classification of customers suggest that, at least in principle, these variables would not be correlated.

Some data problems are encountered even in attempting to measure the proxy developed in equations (11). Our source of data is the Federal Reserve's "Quarterly Interest Rate Survey" which records the volume of new loans granted by rate and size class during the first two weeks of the last month of the quarter. With this data, the percentage of loans granted to risk free firms (proxy H_1) can be at least approximated by the percentage of loans granted at the prime rate (and perhaps secondarily by the percentage of loans which were large in size). Unfortunately, in several instances the prime rate changed during the period of the survey, with the effect that one cannot distinguish between loans made at the new prime rate and loans made at this same rate while the old prime rate was still in effect. To circumvent this problem and secure a more reliable measure, we smoothed these quarters as well as possible. Following John Hand [2] who first used the data for this purpose, we combined the smoothed series with three other measures based on the distribution of loans by size through principal components analysis. More specifically, we calculated the first principal component of the following four series:

a) The proportion of total loans granted at the prime rate.
b) The proportion of total loans over $200,000 in size.
c) The proportion of loans over $200,000 in size granted at the prime rate.
d) The proportion of total loans $1,000–$10,000 in size.

The first three series should enter positively into the principal component and

[21] Because (12a) is nonlinear in $\hat{H}$, this statement will be true only for a linear approximation of H_1. If either proxy were being used as an independent variable, the problem of bias would be more serious. See, for example, Malinvaud [7, Ch. 10].

the fourth negatively, of course. The principal component has a mean of zero and standard deviation of unity and the four factor loadings were, respectively:

(a) .988

(b) .968

(c) .939

(d) −.959

This indicates that each series enters prominently and about equally into the principal component.

The principal component thus derived corresponds to the H_1 measure since the series (a) is analagous to H_1. Exploratory calculations indicated that the results would not be significantly affected by relying on the alternative H_2 measure derived from the reciprocal of series (a) to (d).[22] The solid line in Figure 3 is a plot of the seasonally adjusted principal component H to be used in the tests of the following section. The pattern of rationing indicated by the proxy seems quite credible throughout the period. Note in particular how the most recent pattern is consistent with what we might have expected, rising very high in the second and third quarters of 1966 and then falling off somewhat in the fourth quarter. Unfortunately this series cannot be computed beyond 1966 at the present time, since the information produced by the loan survey beginning in the first quarter of 1967 is not strictly comparable with the earlier information.[23]

IV. *A Test of the Model Using the Credit Rationing Proxy*

In this section we propose to use the credit rationing proxy to test the implications of our model as to the forces controlling variations in time in the extent of credit rationing. This test, relying on quarterly time series data for the years 1952 to 1965, will thus serve to shed light on three aspects of our problem: our theory of credit rationing, the effectiveness of the proxy variable based on the theory, and the existence of rationing as an empirically significant phenomenon.[24]

The principal implication of our theoretical model is that the main source of systematic variations in credit rationing is to be found in changes in dynamic rationing; and that these changes in turn are positively associated with the spread between the long-run optimal or equilibrium loan rate denoted hereafter by r_L^*, and the rate actually prevailing, r_L.[25] If we further assume that, to a first approximation, this association can be formulated as a linear relationship within the empirically relevant range, we are led to

$$H = a_0 + a_1(r_L^* - r_L) + \epsilon \tag{14}$$

Recall that, according to our model, when the commercial loan rate is at its long-run desired level, so that the second term of (14) is zero, we have only equilibrium

[22] We estimated a number of equations using the rationing model developed in Section IV for the specification of the independent variables, and the individual series (a) to (d), the principal component, and the reciprocal of each as separate dependent variables. The principal component yielded the best fit as expected, but comparable results were obtained with the other measures. We are grateful to John Hand for making his data on these series readily available.

[23] The difficulty arises from the fact that with the first quarter of 1967, the period of the survey was changed from the first two weeks of the last month of each quarter to the first two weeks of the second month of each quarter. Because of the strong seasonal component in the four series used to compute H, sufficient observations for the new survey period must be obtained before the new seasonal component can be reliably determined.

[24] It is important to note that success in this test will confirm the value of the proxy as a variable to be used in testing for the impact of credit rationing on the real sectors of the economy. Indeed, the first uses of the proxy for this purpose have been made in [2] and [5].

[25] r_L^* denotes an empirical approximation to the theoretical construct $\hat{R}$ developed above. In particular, r_L^* must stand proxy for the spectrum of optimal rates corresponding to the respective risk classes. Similarly, r_L stands for the spectrum of actual rates and is measured as the average rate on commercial loans compiled from the "Quarterly Interest Rate Survey."

$$r_L^* = c_0 + c_1\{r_T + b_1[(DEP/TB) - 1] - b_2D62 + b_2'C + b_3L/(A - L) + b_4\Delta[L/(A - L)]\} \tag{15}$$

rationing. On the microeconomic level, equilibrium rationing depends on the specific parameter values for the demand functions, density functions, and opportunity cost. But our investigation in Section II.2 indicated that no systematic relationship existed between the degree of rationing and changes in these parameters. Accordingly in (14), the constant term a_0 may be thought of as a measure of equilibrium rationing up to a stochastic error term which is included in the overall error term ϵ. When the quoted rate is above the equilibrium rate, the amount of dynamic rationing can be considered negative in the sense that rationing will be reduced below its equilibrium level, even though the actual amount of rationing can never be less than zero by definition. The dependent variable as measured by our principal component proxy will, in fact, take on negative values because the zero point for H is chosen arbitrarily. The arbitrary choice of origin is, of course, reflected in the constant a_0, and consequently one cannot distinguish between the level of equilibrium rationing and the scaling effect in the constant.[26]

We now turn to the important task of specifying the equilibrium commercial loan rate, r_L^*. Our theory indicated that the desired commercial loan rate would be at that level at which the marginal proceeds from a commercial loan, after adjustment for risk, would just equal the opportunity cost. We also know that this relationship will be valid for all other assets in the bank's portfolio. This means that the optimal commercial loan rate will tend to equal the market yield on any other asset held in the bank's portfolio after adjustment for risk, maturity, liquidity, and, possibly, any expectations concerning future levels of that rate. We are free, then, to choose as the standard of comparison, any security which is widely held by banks, the obvious criterion being practical expedience. Our choice, on this basis, is the bank's holdings of Treasury bills.

On the basis of the above considerations we are led to equation (15) as the specification for the desired commercial loan rate, where the notation will be defined as we proceed.

Consider first the bank's return on Treasury bills. It may be regarded as consisting essentially of two components. The first component, the Treasury bill rate, r_T, is straightforward. The second component is the liquidity value of Treasury bills, which is more involved and, in fact, accounts for the second, third, and fourth terms in the brackets. Our basic premise is that the liquidity yield of Treasury bills should decrease as the bank's holdings of these bills (TB) rises relative to its deposit liabilities (DEP). Our specification for this liquidity term takes the form b_1 $[(DEP/TB)\text{-}1]$ where b_1 (>0) is an estimated parameter.[27]

[26] Equation (14) can be rewritten such that the spread between the desired commercial loan rate and the rate actually quoted is a linear function of the degree of credit rationing. In addition, it has already been suggested that the timing of adjustments in the commercial loan rate depends on changes in the Federal Reserve discount rate. These two factors can be combined into a testable partial adjustment model of the determinants of the commercial loan rate in which the size of the desired adjustment depends on the degree of rationing while the speed of adjustment depends on changes in the discount rate. See fn. 18.

[27] The legal requirement that banks must maintain government securities in their portfolio as collateral for government deposits raises one conceptual problem. To the extent that this requirement necessitates holding

The liquidity value of Treasury bills has been reduced since about 1962, however, by the development of a broad and active market in Certificates of Deposits (*CD*'s), which affords the banks an important means for increasing their liquidity at short notice. The effect of the existence of this market may be measured by a simple shift parameter or dummy variable and this is included as the term $-b_2$ (*D*62) where *D*62 is a dummy variable which is unity starting in 1962-I and zero before then.[28] The value of the *CD* market is of course severely limited when the Regulation Q ceiling on *CD* interest rates is binding. This countervailing effect may be specified by an additional dummy variable which takes the value one in those quarters, if any, in which the secondary market rate for *CD*'s exceeds the ceiling rate. One would expect this dummy variable, denoted by *C*, to have a coefficient opposite in sign and of the same order of magnitude as the *CD* dummy variable *D*62.

The next to last term in equation (15) measures the share of the loan portfolio in total assets which, as suggested in Section II, should tend to affect the opportunity cost of funds for loans relative to market rates. In addition, this variable may be visualized as an adjustment of the required rate on loans for their relative illiquidity. We anticipate that this illiquidity should increase at an increasing rate as the ratio of loans to assets (or liabilities) grows and thus measure this effect as $b_3(L/(A\text{-}L))$ where b_3 (>0) is an estimated coefficient, A is total loans and investments, and L is the commercial loan portfolio of the banks. Finally, we should also consider changes in the liquidity ratio, since a dynamic short-run increase in loans which is beyond the control of the bank would have additional (although only transitional) liquidity cost, and this effect is accounted for by the last term in (15).

We have now almost completed the task of specifying the desired commercial loan rate. To obtain more generality we have formulated the desired loan rate as a linear function of the terms just summarized. The need for the linear function arises because we have not yet formally accounted for differences in risk and maturity between commercial loans and Treasury bills. The basic equation to be estimated can now be derived by substituting equation (15) into (14), which yields:

$$
\begin{aligned}
H = {} & (a_0 + a_1 c_0 - d_1 b_1) - a_1(r_L) \\
& + d_1(r_T) + d_1 b_1(DEP/TB) \\
& - d_1 b_2(D62) + d_1 b_2' C \\
& + d_1 b_3[L/(A - L)] \\
& + d_1 b_4 \Delta[L/(A - L)]
\end{aligned} \tag{16}
$$

where $d_1 = a_1 c_1$.

The coefficients of (16) were estimated using ordinary least squares from observations for the period 1952-II to 1965-IV.[29] (The year 1966 was omitted to enable us to carry out extrapolation tests reported below.) The results are as follows:

Treasury bills of some required amount, the correct variable for our analysis would be the free bills; that is, the bills held above the required amount. It has been suggested that, at least in 1966, such a restriction was a restraining influence on bill holdings. Legally, however, a wide variety of Federal and Local Government securities are acceptable as collateral and it is unlikely that more than a few banks, probably centered in New York City, held Treasury bills only to satisfy collateral requirements, even in 1966.

[28] We have also experimented with incorporating the *CD* term in the form of a multiplicative factor operating on the Treasury bill ratio itself. Since the two estimates are nearly identical, only the results for the linear form will be shown.

[29] The source of data for the independent variables is the *Federal Reserve Bulletin* with the exception of commercial loans. Commercial loans are the sum of industrial and commercial loans (from an unpublished Federal Reserve series) and nonresidential mortgage loans of the commercial banks (from the *Federal Reserve Bulletin*). The mortgage loans are included since they are made to the same customers as the shorter maturity commercial loans. All dollar magnitudes are seasonally adjusted and interest rates are measured as a percent.

$$(17)\quad H = -3.48 - \underset{(-5.3)}{1.16r_L} + \underset{(2.2)}{.296r_T} \quad (-7.0)$$

$$+ \underset{(1.2)}{.007DEP/TB} - \underset{(-7.8)}{1.27D62}$$

$$+ \underset{(1.6)}{.614C} + \underset{(8.0)}{26.7[L/(A - L)]}$$

$$+ \underset{(.92)}{9.0\Delta[L/(A - L)]}$$

$S_e = .350 \qquad R^2 = .84 \qquad D.W. = 2.02$
(T statistics shown in parentheses)

These estimates confirm the implications of our model in that all coefficients have the correct sign and the goodness of fit is respectable, taking into account the noise in the dependent variable which was discussed above. Note in particular the very significant negative coefficient of the commercial loan rate. This supports one of the most distinctive implications of our model, to wit, that a rise in the commercial loan rate given the optimal level of this rate as measured by the remaining variables in the equation, tends to reduce rationing as it reduces the demand and increases the supply. Similarly, the opportunity cost as measured by the Treasury bill rate, and the loan illiquidity variable, measured by the share of loans in the bank's portfolio, appear as the most significant factors tending to increase rationing, given the commercial loan rate. Although the Treasury bill liquidity term and the change in the commercial loan illiquidity term are not significant, this is probably due to multicollinearity since in the short run, with the level of total assets essentially fixed, banks may have to sell Treasury bills to meet unexpected loan demand.

The remaining variables are the dummies intended to measure the effect of *CD*'s. The coefficient of the *CD* dummy, *D*62, is both very significant and large (since the dependent variable has by construction unit variance). It suggests that the newly acquired ability of banks to attract and shed funds through *CD*'s contributed appreciably to a reduction of rationing. The contribution of the ceiling rate dummy *C*, on the other hand, is harder to assess because the ceiling was binding, and hence the dummy was one, only in the last quarter of the sample, 1965-IV.[30] Its coefficient has the expected positive sign but its magnitude, which we had expected to be roughly equal to that of the coefficient of *D*62, is instead only half as large. Yet this result makes good sense when we recall that the ceiling rate was effective only to December 6, which is just about in the middle of the two week period during which the loan survey is taken. Indeed, it suggests that if the ceiling had been effective throughout the period, then its effect would have come close to offsetting totally the contribution of the *D*62 dummy as expected.

The effectiveness of our model in explaining the behavior of the rationing proxy can also be judged from the plot of the values of H computed from equation (17) which is shown by the dotted line in Figure 3. The equation appears to track the broad movements of the actual series as well as the major turning points with leads or lags not exceeding one quarter. The largest errors correspond to a number

[30] The multiplicity of *CD* maturities and the thinness of the secondary market make it difficult to obtain a reliable indicator of those periods in which the ceiling is binding. In addition, an aggregation problem arises because the ceiling may be binding only for some banks or for some regions. The available information suggests, though, that until the last quarter of 1965 the ceiling rate was promptly raised whenever it threatened to become a significant hindrance to the issuing banks. In October and November of 1965, however, the secondary rate rose unequivocably above the ceiling and remained there until December 6th when the ceiling was again raised. See Willis [10] for further discussion of the secondary market for *CD*'s.

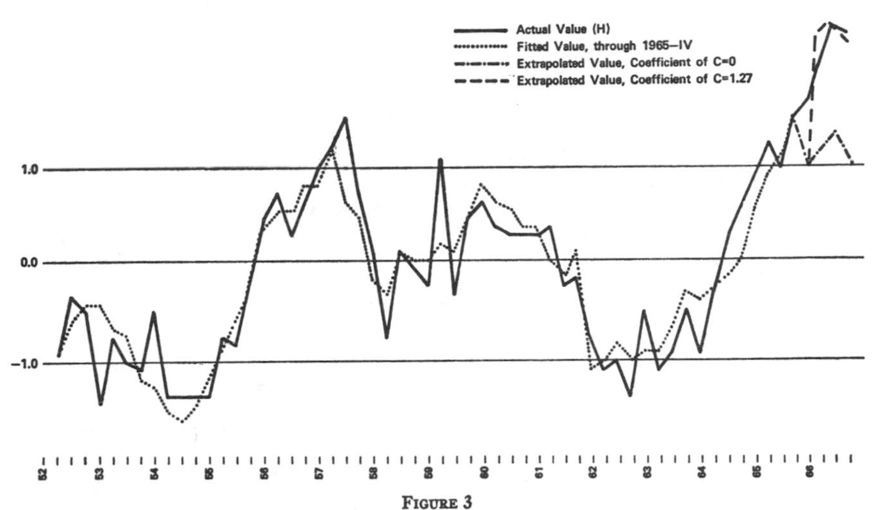

FIGURE 3

of one quarter spikes in H which may well reflect mostly noise in that series.

In Figure 3 we also present some extrapolations of our equation to the year 1966, which marks the end of the period for which usable data on the rationing proxy are presently available.[31] Unfortunately extrapolations of (17) to 1966 run into rather formidable difficulties because throughout the last three quarters the ceiling rate on CD's fell short of the secondary market rate. Nonetheless we feel it worthwhile to exhibit these extrapolations because of the tentative light they shed on the working of the ceiling rate. If one extrapolates (17) as though the ceiling rate dummy C were zero, one obtains the computed values represented by the dotted dashed line and as expected, this extrapolation very much underestimates the extent of rationing in the last three quarters. In order to allow for the ceiling effect, an alternative extrapolation of (17) was carried out for the last three quarters, represented in Figure 3 by the dashed line, in which the dummy variable C was assigned the value of one. In addition, since the ceiling rate was effective throughout these quarters, it was also assumed that the coefficient of C was equal numerically to that of $D62$. Stated differently, the alternative extrapolation assumes that a binding ceiling has the effect of undoing the loosening effect of CD's measured by the dummy $D62$. It is seen that this alternative fits the observations remarkably well.

These results, if taken at face value, have rather interesting implications for the *modus operandi* of ceiling rates as a tool of monetary policy. In particular they would support the view that, by allowing the ceiling rate to become a real hindrance to the ability of banks to attract new CD funds, the Federal Reserve could reduce significantly the availability of funds to the commercial bank customers of the banking system. This reduction would presumably occur to the benefit of customers of other intermediaries and/or of

[31] Cf. fn. 23.

those firms able to raise funds directly in the market. It should be recognized, however, that our evidence in support of this inference is at the moment rather limited and hence, quite tentative, until it can be confirmed by further experience under similar circumstances. Of course, by the time the system is again exposed to similar circumstances, it may have learned ways of evading or by-passing, at least partially, the constraint imposed by the ceiling.

REFERENCES

1. M. Freimer and M. J. Gordon, "Why Bankers Ration Credit," *Quart. J. Econ*, Aug. 1965, *79*, 397–416.
2. J. Hand, *The Availability of Credit and Corporate Investment*, unpublished doctoral dissertation, M.I.T. 1968.
3. D. R. Hodgman, "Credit Risk and Credit Rationing," *Quart. J. Econ*, May 1960, *74*, 258–78.
4. ———, "The Deposit Relationship and Commercial Bank Investment Behavior," *Rev. Econ. Statist*, Aug. 1961, *43*, 257–68.
5. D. M. Jaffee, *Credit Rationing and the Commercial Loan Market*, unpublished doctoral dissertation, M.I.T. 1968.
6. E. J. Kane and B. G. Malkiel, "Bank Portfolio Allocation, Deposit Variability, and the Availability Doctrine," *Quart. J. Econ.*, Feb. 1965, *79*, 113–34.
7. E. Malinvaud, *Statistical Methods of Econometrics*, Chicago 1966.
8. M. H. Miller, "Credit Risk and Credit Rationing: Further Comment," *Quart. J. Econ.*, Aug. 1962, *76*, 480–88.
9. R. Roosa, "Interest Rates and the Central Bank," *Money, Trade, and Economic Growth in Honor of John Henry Williams*, New York 1951.
10. P. B. Willis, "The Secondary Market for Negotiable Certificates of Deposits," paper prepared for the Committee for the Fundamental Reappraisal of the Discount Mechanism, appointed by the Board of Governors of the Federal Reserve System.
11. Board of Governors of the Federal Reserve System, *Reappraisal of the Federal Reserve Discount Mechanism*, Washington 1968.

Errata

Page 857, column 1, 7 lines below Proposition 5: "discrimination" should read "discriminating."

Page 857, column 2, first full paragraph, line 19: "inelastic" should read "elastic."

Page 863, column 1, paragraph 3, line 5: "a rise in r_M" should read "A rise in r_M."

Page 863, column 2, 2 lines from the bottom of the text: "$G[x] \leq F[x]$" should read "$G[x] \geq F[x]$."

Page 869, column 2, equation (16): there should be an additional term "+ e."

3 Some Economic Implications of the Indexing of Financial Assets with Special Reference to Mortgages

Franco Modigliani

I THE BASIC ROLE OF INDEXATION OF FINANCIAL ASSETS IN THE PRESENCE OF PRICE LEVEL UNCERTAINTY

As long as loan contracts are expressed in conventional nominal terms, a high and variable rate of inflation – or more precisely a significant degree of uncertainty about the future of the price level – can play havoc with financial markets and interfere seriously with the efficient allocation of the flow of saving and the stock of capital. Indeed it may be argued that this is one of the most damaging unfavourable implications of unpredictable inflation rates, potentially as serious as the capricious redistribution of income and wealth which, in the popular view, is the hallmark of a disorderly inflationary process. It has been suggested by many economists for quite some time now that these unfavourable effects on resource allocation as well as the redistributive effects can be eliminated or at least greatly alleviated by the device of 'indexing' financial contracts, especially long-term contracts. Indexation consists in denominating the principal and the interest in 'real terms', i.e. in terms of 'a suitable commodity basket'. In practice, this means that the nominal value of the principal is revalued periodically on the basis of an index of the changing nominal value of the stated basket, and that the agreed interest is to be applied to the revalued principal.

The reason for the unfavourable effect of inflation on financial markets and efficient allocation of resources and for the view that it can be remedied by indexation can be compactly stated as follows.

When the price level is stable (more generally, perfectly predictable) there exists in society one man-created intangible asset whose outcome is sure, namely that arising from loans to borrowers who are essentially default-proof. The existence of such an asset plays a fundamental role in the process of efficient allocation of capital because it permits separating the function of accumulating and holding wealth from that of managing physical assets and bearing the risk typically associated with such assets. Even though for society as a whole, capital or wealth must finally consist of physical assets (except for net claims on the government and the rest of the world) any individual can shed the risk associated with physical capital by holding at least some of his wealth in the form of claims fixed in terms of money as long as other members of society are prepared to assume more risk than they have wealth by issuing money fixed claims against themselves and using the proceeds to acquire physical assets or financial claims to such assets (equities). The sure contract can, in turn, form the basis for more complex 'intermediation' in which a financial intermediary is the initial borrower and, in turn, lends directly, or through further intermediaries, to the final borrower. This type of contract together with efficient and competitive financial markets permits physical capital to be allocated so as to produce the highest return adjusted for risk as assessed by all wealth holders through the market. The analysis of this process is the essential contribution of modern asset market theory.

When the future price level is uncertain, however, there is no asset which offers a sure outcome. If the uncertainty about future price levels becomes large enough the return from loan contract can become more risky than that from certain physical assets; hence holders of wealth may be induced to invest their wealth in such assets, even though from the point of view of society their real return may be small or even negative (e.g. gold), and this course of action will displace investment in potentially higher-yielding assets. This is the so-called flight into commodities (*corsa ai beni rifugio*) which may also contribute to kindling the inflationary process if the 'flight' is directed towards commodities with inelastic supply.[1]

This outcome may also be encouraged by the fact that monetary authorities quite frequently endeavour to stabilise interest rates, which prevents the nominal interest rate from changing enough to offset the expected changes in the rate of inflation. The result is that, when inflation is growing, even the *expected* real return from lending is reduced and may become negative, compounding the effect of greater uncertainty or dispersion around the expected outcome.

Even when this does not happen, and interest rates are allowed to rise to reflect increases in the expected rate of inflation, misallocation may be fostered by the fact that uncertainty about the price level may also

[1] If the supply is completely inelastic, as would be the case, e.g. with land, so that net investment can only be zero, the final result might well be an increase in consumption spurred by the rise in the (real) market value of private wealth, and a corresponding decline in investment.

tend to increase the risk of the outcome for the borrower, especially for long term contracts (when the nominal 20-year rate has reached, say 25 per cent because the expected rate of inflation over the next twenty years is 20 per cent, a 20-year loan may be quite risky for the borrower as well as the lender). Thus at least the volume of long-term loans may diminish because of the greater uncertainty about the average long-term rate of inflation, reducing the possibility of hedging against future movements of rates (even real rates).

Indexation prevents all this by reintroducing a contract with a 'reasonably' sure real outcome – regardless of the length of the contract and the actual future course of inflation – thus revitalising financial markets and re-establishing the possibility of intermediation and efficient allocation of capital. In addition, of course, indexation has desirable distributive effects in that it eliminates the capricious redistribution of income and wealth resulting from unforeseen inflation (or deflation).

It is sometimes argued that these redistributive effects may have some positive consequences in that inflation typically 'robs' the lender in favour of the borrowers, who on the average have a greater propensity to save and are more willing to bear risk. These effects would seem desirable in a society where both capital and willingness to assume risk are scarce. But the argument about the different propensity to save is, in my view, very doubtful – at least in the long run – on the basis of my own work and that of others on the life-cycle model of saving (cf. the results of a recent analysis of the Italian experience by Modigliani and Tarantelli).

Furthermore, the view that inflation systematically robs the borrower is valid only to the extent that nominal rates are prevented from reflecting the market's best estimate of the future rate of inflation. In this case, however, the inflation will also tend to produce, to a serious extent, the distortion in allocation referred to above. If, on the other hand, nominal rates do reflect an unbiased estimate of the future rate of inflation, lessening the misallocation problem, then the actual outcome is as likely to be a redistribution in favour of the lender as in favour of the borrower.

It has also been suggested that inflation may tend to reduce the overall level of saving and capital formation by reducing the expected real return on financial assets (when nominal rates are kept artificially low) and by causing the return on all assets to become uncertain. Unfortunately the validity of these propositions is hard to assess. As is well known, a fall in the rate of interest may either increase or decrease the rate of saving depending on whether the substitution or the income effect predominates, and at least some evidence suggests that income effect may be the dominant one (cf. Modigliani and Tarantelli and the references cited therein). Similarly recent work on the theory of saving under uncertainty (e.g. Dreze and Modigliani) leads to the conclusion that, under plausible assumptions about attitude toward risk (decreasing absolute risk aversion), an increase in uncertainty results in an *increase* rather than a *decrease* in saving, though in the case of uncertainty about rates of return either outcome is consistent with rational behaviour and plausible assumptions about tastes.

In summary, in the presence of substantial uncertainty about the future rate of inflation, indexation of financial assets would seem likely on balance to do considerably more good than bad, though one cannot rule out *a priori* some minor unfavourable effect. Many economists nowadays point to the Brazilian experiment with indexation as providing empirical evidence in support of the above conclusions, at least in extreme circumstances.

II THE SPECIAL CASE FOR THE INDEXATION OF MORTGAGES

More recently some economists have pointed out that a case may be made for the indexation of mortgage contracts that is even stronger than the general case made above. (See for example Poole, Baffi.) It can be argued that inflation may distort the allocation of resources between housing and other physical assets and variable rates of inflation may contribute to the instability of construction activity – even when inflation is largely predictable and adequately reflected in nominal rates; and that these problems could be relieved by the indexation of mortgages. As a result of these considerations research is presently getting under way at MIT to investigate in depth the theoretical as well as the practical issues involved in indexation of mortgages, and to compare indexation with alternative approaches to the stabilisation of construction by way of improved financial instruments. What follows is largely based on the preliminary and still tentative analysis developed in preparation for that project.

The propositions stated above about the unfavourable effect of high and variable rates of inflation on residential construction rest on two main considerations: (1) in most of the developed countries, the prevailing vehicle for financing residential housing, notably owner-occupied dwellings or small rental units, is the traditional level-payment mortgage; (2) the financing through this instrument is provided by specialised institutions such as savings banks or, in some countries, mortgage banks (frequently also connected with savings-type institutions). Under these conditions a high rate of inflation will tend to curtail the demand for housing, while variable rates of inflation are likely to produce instability in construction both through the demand for housing and through the availability of mortgage funds, for reasons detailed below.

II.1 DEMAND EFFECTS OF THE RATE OF INFLATION

The demand effect occurs because the high nominal rates of interest which result from the addition to the 'real' rate of interest of a premium roughly equal to the expected rate of inflation has the effect of increasing the level of the annual payment relative to the rate of earnings in the early year of the mortgage contract. This point is illustrated in column (1) of Exhibit I which shows the level annual payment required on a $30,000, 30-year mortgage. Assuming a 3 per cent real rate of interest, it is seen that with zero inflation (case No. 1) the first year (as well as all subsequent) payment amounts to $1,517; with a 2 per cent rate of inflation, and hence a 5 per cent nominal rate (case No. 2), it is nearly 25 per cent higher or $1,931; for a 6 per cent rate of inflation the payment is almost twice as high, $2,895. The reason for the positive association between rate of inflation and initial payment is that, in the presence of inflation, the constant nominal payment will imply an annual payment, which in 'real' or purchasing power terms, decreases in time at the rate of inflation. Thus with a 6 per cent rate of inflation, by the year 5, the real payment is $\$2{,}895/(1{\cdot}06)^4 = 2{,}294$; by the year 12 it is 1,525, or about the same as with no inflation and, thereafter, it becomes lower, being reduced in the terminal year to a mere 524. Of course the real present value of this declining stream of real repayments is always $30,000 no matter what the rate of inflation; it is precisely in this sense that the higher nominal rate corresponding to higher rates of inflation compensates for the gradual erosion of the purchasing power of the nominal stream. But precisely because the present value of the real stream must be the same and the stream is declining in time, it must start at a higher level. The higher the rate of inflation the greater the tilting in the rate of real repayment and hence the higher the initial payments. This point is illustrated graphically in Figure 1, which compares the behaviour of the real payment at successive dates over the life of the contract. (In this figure, the assumed real rate is 4 per cent and the mortgage is for $20,000.)

But why is the real rather than the nominal rate of repayment the important magnitude? The simple answer is that under generalised inflationary conditions the income of the typical home buyer may be expected to rise in the long run at a rate at least equal to that of the price index. In the limiting case where the growth of nominial income precisely equals the rate of inflation, the behaviour of the real rate of repayment in Figure 1 is proportional to the behaviour of the ratio of the nominal payment to nominal income. Columns (3) and (4) of Exhibit 1 provide a numerical illustration. One can see from column (4) that for that illustration, in the absence of inflation carrying the house will absorb some 15 per cent of the person's income throughout the life of the contract. But with a 2 per cent inflation the annual payment for the very same house will require 19·3 per cent of his income at the beginning of the contract, and will continue to absorb more than 15 per cent for some twelve years, though in the terminal year, it will take only 10·8 per cent. With a 6 per cent inflation it will absorb at the outset nearly 30 per cent of his income, declining to 5 per cent in the terminal year.[2]

It is obvious from this example that with conventional mortgage financing a rapid rate of inflation even if fully and correctly anticipated may be expected to reduce the demand for owner-occupied housing space by raising the ratio of annual payment to income in the early years of the contract. Exhibit 2, reproduced from Tucker (1973) shows that even the relatively modest increase in the mortgage rate that occurred in the US between 1963 and 1973, as a result of the relatively modest rise in the rate of inflation, has been sufficient to cause the initial payment, computed in column D (from an index of prices of new houses, the average mortgage rate and the prevailing length of contract), to rise appreciably faster than average wage income, shown in column E.

The nature of the unfavourable effect on the demand for housing of a higher nominal rate due to inflation is quite similar to that of shortening the length of the contract. This point is brought out graphically in Figure 2 which shows that a faster rate of inflation, much as a shorter maturity, forces the borrower to repay his real debt – or equivalently to accumulate equity in his house – at a faster rate. Of course the ratio of annual payment to income eventually declines as inflation erodes the purchasing power of the payment. But this only means that inflation causes the burden of owning a house to be very unevenly distributed over time. The extent of this unevenness is even greater than implied by column (4), when it is recognised that a major group of potential home buyers is represented by young households (cf. Baffi). This group can look forward to an increase in income even in the absence of inflation, both because of the general effect of productivity growth, which tends to raise all incomes, and because typically, even in the absence of productivity growth, income tends to rise with age, at least for a while (though the specific shape of the life cycle of income will be influenced

[2] On the assumption of a steady rate of inflation, $\dot{p}$, fully incorporated in the nominal rate $R = r + \dot{p}$, where r is the 'real' rate, the effect of inflation on the annual payment (which is also the initial real payment) relative to what it would be without inflation, is given by

$$(a) \qquad \frac{r + \dot{p}}{1 - (1 + r + \dot{p})^{-T}} \quad \frac{1 - (1 + r)^{-T}}{r}$$

T being the length of the contract. If the borrower's income is growing at the rate $\dot{p}$ then the ratio of nominal payment to nominal income in the nth year of the contract is proportional to

$$(b) \qquad \frac{(r + \dot{p})}{[1 - (1 + r + \dot{p})^{-T}]\,(1 + \dot{p})^{s}}$$

To find the number of years over which the ratio of annual payment to income is above the level prevailing with no inflation, one can equate (a) to $(1 + \dot{p})^{s}$ and solve for s.

by individual factors such as education, social institutions, etc.). Column (7) exhibits the share of income absorbed by the payment under the conservative assumption that income rises but 2 per cent per year. It is seen that even in the absence of inflation a conventional mortgage already implies a rather uneven burden over life. But if the rate of inflation reaches 6 per cent the unevenness becomes rather dramatic.

It should be apparent, in fact, that if the rate of inflation becomes very high the conventional mortgage contract becomes so onerous for the potential buyer as to become practically unusable, except possibly for those who already have the means to pay in cash a substantial portion of the price. To be sure, this problem could be remedied, in perfect markets, by recourse to second mortgages or similar devices. But such facilities are seldom readily available, and are unlikely to develop in an inflationary climate. On the contrary if, as frequently happens in such periods, the rate of interest on deposit is kept artificially low, and falls short of the rate of increase in the price of houses, there may be little hope for lower income groups, having a very limited menu of assets available beyond some type of savings deposit, ever to accumulate a sufficiently high equity to use as down-payment. One of the serious consequences of this situation is that, in many countries pressure has developed to provide relief for the home buyers through various types of government subsidies – e.g. direct contributions to the interest.

In addition to the above effect there may be unfavourable dynamic effects on construction from a *rise* in the rate of inflation if, as frequently happens, the seller of a house cannot transfer his mortgage to the buyer but instead must repay his loan. This tends to 'lock' the owner in the house he initially owns when a rise in the rate of inflation raises the mortgage rate on new contracts, and by selling his house he loses the benefit of the lower rate on the present mortgage.

II.2 SUPPLY EFFECTS

In addition to these demand effects, rapid changes in the rate of inflation have tended to have a destabilising effect on residential construction by destabilising the supply of mortgage funds – though the precise nature of this mechanism depends on the nature of the institutions providing funds to the mortgage market.

In the US and other countries, the bulk of these funds has come from specialised thrift institutions that secure funds through deposits – essentially a short-term liability – and then invest them in long-term mortgage assets. When a spurt of inflation raises money market rates these institutions find it hard to offer competitive deposit rates, because their earnings do not promptly adjust upward; in addition as the market value of their assets declines they may even approach technical insolvency. In order to limit the losses that these institutions would face if left free to raise competitively their deposit rates, as well as to hold down the overall level of long-term rates in order to minimise the negative effect of rising rates on these institutions and on potential home buyers, monetary authorities have imposed ceilings on the deposit rate that can be offered by the thrift institutions and by their close competitors, such as on time deposits at commercial banks. But ceilings have contributed to induce the public to switch their savings from traditional deposits to other types of assets (disintermediation). Thus even if the ceilings may have helped to protect the solvency of the intermediaries they have tended to dry up their inflow of funds and, hence, their ability to supply funds to the mortgage market, curtailing construction activity through supply of fund effects.

A similar mechanism has been at work even when, as in the case of Italy, mortgage funds come in part from the floating of mortgage bonds by specialised mortgage banks. This has come about because the mortgage banks have endeavoured to stabilise the price of their bonds in the face of rising long-term market rates on competing instruments, by limiting net new issues, even to the point of making negative new issues, using the repayment flows to buy back outstanding bonds. To pursue this course they have been led to ration funds at the artificially low rate they endeavoured to maintain (though the cost to the borrower has been allowed to reflect to some extent market rates through variations in the spread between the market price of mortgage bonds and the amount paid to the borrower).

II.3 THE ROLE OF INDEXATION IN ELIMINATING DEMAND AND SUPPLY EFFECTS

The institution of indexed mortgages (IM) could help considerably in eliminating both the demand and the supply effects. On the demand side, since the rate on an IM is a real rate, it should be largely independent of the rate of inflation, making the initial payment equally independent of inflation. It is true, of course, that if the anticipated inflation occurs the level of payment will rise precisely at the same rate as the price level as illustrated in column (2) of Exhibit 1. In fact in the presence of productivity – or real income-growth – the ratio of annual payment to income will still tend to decline in time as shown in column (8). However, this declining pattern is independent of the rate of inflation. Furthermore, it could be eliminated – or modified to any desirable extent – by combining indexation with another reform of the mortgage contract, namely non-level repayments. We need not be concerned here with this reform which is quite separate from indexation, but it should be pointed out that indexation can be readily combined with any appropriate contractual repayment schedule stated again in real terms, thus giving rise to a non-level repayment schedule in real terms. We may finally note that indexation should also greatly reduce, if not eliminate, the lock-in effect, since all available evidence suggests that the major source of variation in nominal rates is due to changing rates of inflation, and related changes in *expected* rates of inflation.

On the supply side, where mortgage funds come from mortgage bonds, indexed mortgages would be matched by the issue of indexed mortgage bonds. This instrument, one should expect, would be very attractive to investors, especially small investors, under conditions of high and uncertain rates of inflation as it would provide them with a hedge against inflation whether predicted or not. Hence it might, on the average, raise the flow of funds available for mortgages, especially if mortgages were the only, or main, type of indexed long-term instruments. More important, however, the indexed mortgage rate needed to equate the supply of mortgage funds with the stabilised demand for mortgage funds might be expected to be fairly stable, even in the face of wide movements in nominal rates on other instruments, in so far as these reflect changes in inflationary expectations unrelated to the real rate; there would, therefore, be little need for the mortgage banks to endeavour to stabilise the market price of indexed mortgage bonds by restricting issues and rationing funds.

Where the mortgage funds come from depository institutions, these again would now be in a position to offer indexed deposits, whose principal would be adjusted periodically to the price level, since any change in their liability due to such revaluation would be matched by similar changes in the value of their assets; and again the indexed deposit rate needed to maintain a stable inflow of deposits should remain reasonably stable despite inflation-induced variations in the nominal rates on competing financial assets. Alternatively the depository institutions could continue to offer nominal deposits but the rate they could offer on such deposits could be based on the contract (real rate on their indexed mortgages plus the rate of change of the price index: that is, the revaluation of principal could be treated as income currently available to remunerate depositors, on the ground that the mortgage could then be carried on their books at nominal value. Being able to pay such a nominal rate they might be expected to remain competive with market rates on competing short-term instruments.

When the rate of inflation is not only high but also subject to a high degree of uncertainty, the indexation of mortgages, as well as possibly of mortgage bonds and other instruments, such as deposits which are used to provide funds for indexed mortgages, would also achieve the desirable result of enabling borrowers and lenders to hedge against the risk of uncertain price fluctuations. This would be true even if indexation were limited to mortgages and mortgage market related instruments.

II.4 VARIABLE RATE MORTGAGES AS AN ALTERNATIVE TO INDEXATION

It is worthwhile noting briefly that the unfavourable effect of high (and variable) rates of inflation on the financial health of depository intermediaries and on the supply of funds might be also eliminated or reduced through another device which is also receiving considerable attention and has already been tried out to some extent (e.g. in the UK, in Canada, and to a very limited degree in the US), namely through so-called variable rate mortgages (VRM). In this version the interest rate charged to the borrower is not fixed in the contract but is allowed to float up and down being tied to some market rate, generally a short-term one. This approach clearly enables the intermediary to offer deposit rates competitive with other short-term market instruments and also disposes of the need for rate ceilings and other related disruptive devices. Furthermore, in so far as short-term rates reflect fairly accurately the actual rate of inflation over the life of the short-term instrument, VRM could also provide a reasonably good hedge against uncertainty of the price level.

However, in our view, this approach is distinctly inferior to indexed mortgages in three important respects: (1) the welfare of the borrower, (2) its effects on the level and stability of the *demand* as distinguished from the *supply* side of the market, and (3) the ability of the monetary authority to pursue an appropriate monetary policy.

The basis for propositions (1) and (2) can be most conveniently clarified by reference to Exhibit 3 which compares the annual payment required of the borrower under three alternative arrangements: conventional level mortgage (CLM) – block 1; variable rate mortgage – block 2; and indexed mortgage – block 3. The rate currently applied on the VRM is a nominal rate; hence it will be higher, the higher the rate of inflation, and so will the initial annual payment, just as in the case of CLM. Accordingly in the presence of high inflation VRM, in contrast to IM, has the same unfavourable effect on demand as CLM (see column 1 of Exhibit 3). In addition, if the rate of inflation, and hence the applicable interest rate *changes*, VRM will cause changes in the next annual payment which may be quite great and largely unrelated to the rate of inflation and hence to the changing income of the borrower. This can be seen by inspection of column (1) and (2) in the last row of the VRM block and by comparison with the corresponding figures for the IM block. If the rate of inflation rises from 3 to 5 per cent the scheduled payment under IM rises by 2 per cent above what it would have been if inflation had remained at 3 per cent, an increase commensurate with the likely effect of the higher inflation on the borrower's income. On the other hand, under VRM the scheduled payment rises from $1,453 to $1,798 or some 24 per cent; the reason for this much higher percentage change is that the higher inflation, by raising the nominal rate used in computing the constant payment for the rest of the contract, implies a further tilting of the real repayment schedule – a higher front-end load as it were. For similar reasons a decline in inflation produces a large percentage decline in the scheduled payment (cf. columns (3) and (4)).

Thus while the VRM approach protects the intermediary (and presumably insures a smoother supply of funds), it does so at the expense of imposing a good deal of additional real risk on the borrower, especially since short rates, as well as the short-run behaviour of $\dot{p}$, may be quite variable (see for example Kaufman). For the same reason it might do little to mitigate variability on the demand side. In contrast, IM tends to reduce the real risk to the borrower, as well as to reduce variability.

Some of these undesirable features of VRM can be eliminated by an alternative design, that has already been applied in some countries, under which the variable rate is used not to change the rate of annual payment, but rather the length of the contract, while the payment itself remains fixed. However, this alternative creates other difficulties, notably that the length of the contract can grow uncomfortably long, when the floating rate rises substantially above the one used in fixing the initial level of the annual payment; indeed the maturity will approach infinity if the rise in the rate is such that the fixed annual payment approaches the interest bill due on the remaining principal. This difficulty is intimately related to the fact that, in the presence of high rates of inflation, a level payment in nominal terms does not make much sense. Tucker (1973) and (1974), has suggested an interesting modification of the VMR which would combine it with the variable repayment scheme. His proposal relies on two basic ingredients: (1) the annual payment would be scheduled to rise in time at some constant rate which could be based initially on the rate of inflation expected at the time the contract was written: this would permit an initial rate of payment similar in size to that prevailing under IM; (2) the rate used in computing the annual payments would be revised periodically, as under VRM. But the change in rate would change neither the current payment nor the length of maturity but would instead change the rate of growth of the scheduled annual payment. Under some fairly reasonable assumptions this scheme would work in a way rather similar to indexed mortgages. But one can see little reason for preferring this roundabout 'imitation' to straightforward indexation.

Finally the IM retains one desirable feature of the traditional level mortgage under constant prices, that would be lost under any form of VRM, namely that it permits the borrower to hedge against future movements of the 'real rate', since this is fixed by contract. To have available such a hedging option would seem to be rather valuable when entering into a long-run commitment such as the acquisition of a house, considering the sizeable transaction costs associated with changing houses.

The third drawback of VRM listed above is suggested by the consideration that variations in the nominal rate affect very significantly the rate of payment of all mortgage borrowers. This feature is likely to generate a lot of pressure toward avoiding or delaying changes in nominal rates which might be desirable from a stabilisation point of view. Under IM, on the other hand, the payment rises only because of inflation and hence the pressures will be toward avoiding it, whereas changes in nominal rates as such would be of no consequence.

III THE EFFECT OF INDEXATION OF MORTGAGES ON OTHER FINANCIAL MARKETS

The considerations developed in section II suggest that considerable advantages might be anticipated from making available to borrowers an indexed mortgage instrument – possibly with non-level real repayment schedule – and to lenders indexed mortgage bonds, and/or deposits, or at least deposit rates reflecting more nearly the rate of inflation. However these conclusions were based, as it were, on a partial equilibrium analysis of the residential and mortgage markets, more or less in isolation. Before we can confidently advocate that legislation be adopted to make such an instrument available one has to give some consideration to at least two other major issues: (1) the effect of indexation on other financial markets and, (2) implications it may have on the effectiveness of traditional stabilisation policies and/or the stability of the economy as a whole. Both topics are being included in the pilot phase of the MIT project, and the best that I can do at this time is to report some preliminary thoughts on the issues and on the methodology by which the issues might be attacked.

The questions to be examined under heading (1) range all the way from whether there would, in fact, be a sufficient market for indexed mortgages and supporting instruments to warrant the costs of establishing such markets, to the issue of whether the introduction of such instruments would play havoc with the markets for conventional nominal instruments. The latter concern has been often put forward as an argument against allowing the introduction of any indexed instrument.

These issues can be partly attacked by examining the experiences of the few countries that have made use of such instruments in the post-war period. But it needs to be attacked also through the tools of economic analysis applied to financial markets, especially since the experience so far has been quite limited and for various reasons not too conclusive.

III.1 COUNTRY EXPERIENCES

A summary of experiences with indexation is provided in a recent OECD publication (1973).

The main countries which have had significant experience with these devices are Finland, Israel, and some Latin American countries, notably Brazil. In every case, indexation was applied more generally to instruments to finance housing. The most favourable experience seems that of Brazil, to which reference was made earlier. The one raising most questions is that of Finland. Exhibit 4, reproduced from the OECD publication, shows that the proportion of bond issues taking the indexed form rose rapidly to some 80 per cent from 1952 to 1956 and, thereafter, fluctuated between one-quarter and four-fifths, responding apparently positively, but with some lag to the rate of inflation in the recent past. However, the marginal rate was fairly uniformly above the average rate so that the share of the stock of bonds outstanding having indexed form rose fairly uniformly to 3/4 in 1967. In the case of deposits the trend is similar but at a lower level, reaching one-third by 1967. Unfortunately, in that year indexation was abolished, though apparently for reasons having little to do with market acceptance of the instrument as such. It appears that, following the devaluation of 1967, aimed at bringing under control the large trade deficit, it was felt necessary to abolish the indexation of wages. To secure labour consent to this step, indexation was abolished also on mortgages and other instruments. In Israel some forms of indexation (namely on foreign exchange) were abolished under circumstances somewhat reminiscent of those of Finland. This experience, which *prima facie* is not encouraging, will bear closer scrutiny. One lesson that it seems to suggest is that, at least in a small open economy subject to significant changes in terms of trade, the index used for indexation of financial instruments as well as of other contracts like wages should perhaps not be that of the basket of goods bought like a 'cost of living' index but that of the basket of goods produced, or domestic value added like the GNP deflator; in other words, it should aim to protect against redistribution of domestic income arising from wage or mark-up push, but not protect against changes in purchasing power due to changes in terms of trade. Had indexing been of this variety, it might have survived the devaluation.

III.2 SOME INFERENCES FROM ECONOMIC ANALYSIS

Several attempts have been made recently to examine the implications of the presence of indexed financial assets on the working of financial and other markets, as testified, for example, by the bibliographical references in recent studies – for example, one by the OECD cited earlier, and the essays by Scholtes. The most recent of these endeavours is represented by the just completed and still unpublished paper of Fischer which is especially valuable because of its rigour and promise for further development, and on which I will lean heavily in this section.

Fischer relies for his analysis primarily on the powerful approach developed by Merton for the study of individual saving and portfolio decisions under uncertainty and their implications for asset-market equilibrium. In this approach economic agents are assumed to make instantaneous and continuous decisions about their rate of consumption and the allocation of their wealth between the menu of assets available to them so as to maximise the expected utility of consumption over life. It is further assumed that investors' expectations about the return on assets as well as the behaviour of the price level, are identical and can be described by a continuous-time stochastic process, known as Ito process; the instantaneous stochastic distribution is essentially normal, though the resulting distribution of returns over any finite length of time is log normal. Fischer analyses a succession of models of increasing complexity, but for our present purpose it will be sufficient to concentrate on the results of his simplest model in which there is a single consumption good, and three assets: (1) a bond indexed on the consumption good with contractual non-stochastic real return r_1; (2) equity, with (instantaneous) expected return r_2, and (instantaneous) variance σ_2^2; (3) nominal bonds with contractual nominal return R_3. The price of the consumption good is also stochastic; the expected rate of inflation is π and its variance, which is also the variance of the rate of return on the nominal bond is σ_3^2. (Note that because the real rate of return on the nominal bond depends on the reciprocal of the price level, its expected real rate of return turns out to be $r_3 = R_3 - \pi + \sigma_1^2$.)

Assuming at first a deterministic labour income, Fischer derives the instantaneous demand equations for the three assets. Letting w_i denote the proportion of net wealth invested in asset i, and ρ the correlation coefficient between the real rate of return on equity and the rate of inflation, he finds

$$(1) \quad w_1 = 1 - \frac{A}{(1-\rho^2)\sigma_2\sigma_3}\left[\frac{(r_2-r_1)(\sigma_3+\rho\sigma_2)}{\sigma_2} + \frac{(r_3-r_1)(\sigma_2+\rho\sigma_3)}{\sigma_3}\right]$$

$$(2) \quad w_2 = \frac{A}{(1-\rho^2)\sigma_2}\left[\frac{r_2-r_1}{\sigma_2} + \frac{\rho(r_3-r_1)}{\sigma_3}\right]$$

$$(3) \quad w_3 = \frac{A}{(1-\rho^2)\sigma_3}\left[\frac{r_3-r_1}{\sigma_3} + \frac{\rho(r_2-r_1)}{\sigma_2}\right]$$

where A is a positive number measuring the so-called relative risk aversion. ($A = J_w/-WJ_{ww}$ where J_w is the 'derived' marginal utility of wealth, W.)

From these results he draws the conclusion that in order for the investor to choose to hold a positive quantity of indexed bonds, the contractual real rate of return on indexed bonds r_1 may have to exceed the expected real rate of return on nominal bonds (and hence *a fortiori* to exceed the nominal rate R_3 less the expected rate of change of prices). In other words, the indexed bond need not command a premium over the nominal bond; this result he finds striking and surprising since it runs contrary to the intuitive view that, with risk aversion, indexed bonds would be preferred to nominal bonds, other things being equal. A necessary condition for this counterintuitive outcome to occur is the not implausible one that the real rate of return on equity be positively correlated with the rate of inflation. Under these conditions some doubts might arise as to whether indexed bonds could, in fact, exist, or whether instead they might not be dominated by nominal bonds.

My own interpretation of his results, however, is rather different; specifically, they can be shown to imply that, at least, in a closed system without government, in which the *net* supply of both indexed and nominal bonds must be zero (i.e. the value of bonds privately held exactly offsets the liability of the private issuers) and, under the usual assumption of homogeneous expectations, indexed bonds dominate nominal bonds. That is, only indexed bonds would be issues and held, while the gross amount of nominal bonds issued and held would tend to be zero.

To establish this conclusion we merely need to note that the coefficient of the square bracket in (3) is necessarily positive under the assumption of risk aversion. Hence, if the quantity in square brackets were positive, then every transactor would have a positive net demand for nominal bonds; but since the net supply is zero, there would then be a positive excess demand for nominal bonds. By the same token, if the quantity in square brackets were negative, there would be an excess supply of these bonds. Hence the market can only clear if the relation between the rates is such that the quantity in brackets is precisely zero. But this means that at these market-clearing rates no one would either wish to lend or to borrow in the form of nominal bonds. In other words, the existence of the indexed bond would cause nominal bonds to disappear. This is clearly a rather remarkable result which, incidentally, readily generalises to the case where there is not one but many 'equities'.

One may throw some further light on this result by observing that, for the problem on hand, the demand equations derived by Fischer with Merton's approach are analogous to those obtained under the mean-variance approach of Tobin and Markowitz. It is well known that the basic result of their model is that, when there exists a sure asset, and a plurality of risky assets (in our case the equity and the nominal bond), for every wealth holder the optimum portfolio is a linear combination of the sure asset and a portfolio of risky assets; furthermore, the percentage composition of the portfolio of risky assets is the very same for all investors. In our case then, the optimum portfolio is a combination of the riskless indexed bond and of a portfolio containing the equity and the nominal bond in fixed proportions. But since the net supply of the nominal bond is zero, in market equilibrium, i.e. when the returns have been adjusted so as to clear all markets, the proportion of the nominal bond can only be zero.

With the help of Fischer's equations, we can establish just what the market clearing relation must be between r_1 and r_3. Specifically from (3) the necessary and sufficient condition for $w_3 = 0$ can be stated as

$$(4) \qquad r_3 - r_1 = -\rho\frac{\sigma_3}{\sigma_1}(r_2 - r_1)$$

This equation is readily recognised as the basic equation of the Capital Asset Price Model (CAPM) of Sharp-Lintner-Mossin, since

$$-\frac{\rho\sigma_3}{\sigma_1}$$

is the regression (or β) coefficient of the return of the nominal bond on the return on equity (which, when the net supply of bonds is zero, is also the return on the market portfolio). Since $r_2 - r_1$ must be positive under risk aversion, we can conclude that

$$r_1 \gtreqless r_3 \quad \text{as } \rho \gtreqless 0$$

This result, of course, conforms to Fischer's conclusion: however, it now appears that a positive correlation between the real returns on equity and the rate of inflation is both necessary and sufficient to make the market-clearing expected real rate on the nominal bonds smaller than the return on the indexed bond.

This result can be given intuitive meaning as follows. A positive value of ρ implies a negative correlation between the return on equity and the return on nominal bonds. But then lenders holding only indexed bonds could reduce portfolio risk by substituting nominal for indexed bonds. Hence, if r_3 equalled r_1, there would be a positive demand for nominal bonds. However, by the same token, people wishing to lever their portfolio would find nominal bonds unattractive, since the negative covariance of the return on equity with the real rate to be paid on nominal bonds implies that borrowing through nominal bonds rather than indexed bonds would increase portfolio risk. Accordingly they will be willing to pay a real rate on indexed bonds sufficiently higher to induce lenders to accept these instead of nominal bonds.

At the same time, Fischer's analysis suggests that if there existed in the market some positive net supply of nominal bonds – say because they were issued by the government or were the result of earlier contracts – the presence of indexed bonds would by no means have a disruptive effect on the market for nominal bonds. On the contrary, at least if ρ were positive, nominal bonds might well command a premium over indexed bonds.[3]

[3] Allowing for a net positive supply of positive nominal bonds, say issued by the government, would mean that w_3 would have to be positive for all private investors.

It should be added that Fischer shows that once we allow for a stochastic labour income, then it will no longer be the case that indexed bonds must drive nominal bonds out of existence, unless for all participants real labour income was uncorrelated with the real rate of inflation. But especially if for some participants interested in borrowing this correlation was negative, making for them the issue of nominal bonds relatively more attractive, then the two kinds of bonds could be expected to coexist. Dropping the assumption of homogeneous expectations would also work in this direction. It is also clear from the above reasoning that the presence of stochastic labour income would, on balance, act in the direction of a positive premium for indexed bonds if the correlation between real labour income and the rate of inflation was prevailingly negative, and of a negative premium in the opposite case.

In summary Fischer's results suggest that if inflation had no real effects on the economy (or to use an expression coined by Tobin, money were not only neutral but also 'superneutral') then the expected real rate of return would tend to be similar on both indexed and nominal bonds. On the other hand the well-known debate on the Phillips curve would lead one to expect a prevailingly positive correlation between (unexpected) inflation on the one hand and real labour income and return on physical assets on the other. Unfortunately, there is at present little empirical evidence to settle the issue, at least with respect to the effect of inflation on the return on equity, though casual observation suggests that, in recent years, the correlation has tended to be negative. The analysis, however, does suggest that in the case of indexed mortgages, considering also the advantages that such an instrument would offer the borrower, one should not be too surprised if the market-clearing real rate for such instruments were to exceed the expected real rate of nominal instruments.

IV EFFECTS OF INDEXATION OF MORTGAGES ON THE STABILITY OF THE ECONOMY

The analysis so far suggests that indexation of mortgages should help to stabilise residential construction without disrupting markets for nominal instruments. This conclusion, however, was based on a 'partial' equilibrium' analysis; to understand the full implications of such a reform one needs to consider also the interaction of construction with other components of aggregate demand and, in particular, effects on the stability of the economy as a whole and on the effectiveness of stabilisation tools, especially monetary ones. There seems little question that reliance on conventional mortgages and the specific institutional arrangements controlling this supply of mortgage funds, has helped to

It appears from (4) that if ρ were zero or negative, $w_3 > 0$ would require a negative premium on nominal bonds; but with ρ sufficiently positive and the net supply of nominal bonds sufficiently small, the premium could still be positive.

make residential construction very sensitive to monetary policy; and to bear the brunt of stabilisation policies through monetary tools. In particular, it would appear that it has made possible the containment of aggregate demand with smaller fluctuations in interest rates than might have been required otherwise. This is true both because the demand presumably responded in part to variations in *nominal* rates; and because the restraint has been obtained in part by quantity rather than by price rationing. One point is worth mentioning in this connection. While the measurement of real rates is extremely difficult in the absence of indexed instruments because of the difficulty of measuring price expectations, in so far as one can rely on past rates of inflation as at best a rough indication of expected rates, at least for the US there is little evidence of large changes in the real rates in the post-war period. This might well reflect the fact that, through residential construction, aggregate demand could be influenced by nominal rates alone.

IV.1 EFFECTS OF INDEXATION OF MORTGAGES IN THE PRESENCE OF EXOGENOUS CHANGES IN AGGREGATE DEMAND

With the indexation of mortgages residential construction, like other components of demand, should tend to respond mainly to real rates, and only through its effect on demand. Thus, if real rates were to remain stable, this reform should indeed tend to stabilise residential construction. But in the presence of exogenous changes in demand some components must adjust, and this means that, unless stabilisation rested on fiscal policy, real rates would have to fluctuate. Thus some instability in construction could not be avoided. Presumably, for given fiscal policy, the fluctuations would be smaller since other components would share more in the role of accommodating the exogenous changes. However, since it seems likely that the elasticity of construction with respect to real rates would be larger than for other components, variations in construction activity might still bear a major burden. The question here is fundamentally an empirical one. Some efforts are presently being made in the course of the MIT research to shed some light by simulation with econometric models – such as the MIT-Penn-SSRC model which has a well-developed housing and mortgage sector – though the model will require modifications to allow more explicitly for the likely effect of indexation on the demand for housing. These simulations should also help to throw light on the interaction between indexation, the conduct of monetary policy, the variability of real and nominal rates, and the overall stability of the economy and thereby help to assess the desirability of indexation.

IV.2 SHOULD CONSTRUCTION BE STABILISED?

For a full assessment, however, it is not sufficient to determine the effect of indexation on stabilising construction. Since this stabilisation must be at the expense of unstabilising other components, one also needs to be concerned with the issue of the social cost of instability of various components. A case might be made that residential construction is a particularly suitable sector to absorb fluctuations, for at least two reasons. First because of the durability of housing short-run variations in construction activity have but a small effect on the stock of houses and hence on the supply of housing services, although the force of this argument is considerably weakened by the geographical immobility of houses. But the very geographical dispersion of housing also means that construction activity is widely dispersed and hence variations in this activity produce equally dispersed variations in the demand for labour. Furthermore the skills of the construction labour force may be fairly readily transferable to other uses, such as non-residential construction. Also, in developing countries, employment in construction seems frequently to constitute the gateway through which labour enters the modern sector. Hence fluctuations in employment in this industry may tend to have smaller social costs than in other segments of the modern sector since the labour force can be more readily attracted and also more readily returned to earlier activities (though the evaluation of this social cost is a complex task). These arguments, as well as others pointing partly in the opposite direction (e.g. the effect on the supply price), need to be assessed carefully to reach a balanced judgement as to the relative costs of instability.

V SUMMARY AND CONCLUSION

The major themes developed in this paper, many of them in a preliminary and tentative form, can be summarised as follows:

(1) Indexation of financial activities can perform a very useful function in the face of substantial uncertainty about the future course of the price level. In addition to the traditional argument centring on the elimination of capricious redistribution of income and wealth, we have stressed its role in maintaining well-functioning capital markets with ample opportunities for financial intermediation, portfolio diversification and resulting efficient allocation of resources.

(2) A special case can be made for the indexation of mortgages, because inflation has major effects on the demand and supply of this instrument even when perfectly predictable. It reduces the demand for mortgages and housing by increasing the ratio of annual payment to income in the early years of the contract. Also because of the special nature of the institutions involved in the provision of mortgage funds, short-run variations in interest rates, even if due entirely to variations in expected inflation, produce sharp variations in the supply of funds. Both difficulties could be eliminated

or alleviated through indexation, possibly supplemented by variable real repayment schedules.

(3) It would seem perfectly possible to limit indexation to this instrument and perhaps to some related ones, in the sense that such a reform should not produce serious disturbances or dislocation in the markets for nominal assets. Indeed our analysis suggests that it would not be at all surprising if indexed mortgages were to command a higher expected real yield than corresponding nominal instruments.

(4) While indexation looms as a useful and powerful device for stabilising residential construction, one risks to exaggerate its effect if one considers the housing market in isolation. Taking into account the economic system as a whole suggests that the very forces which tend to stabilise construction must tend to unstabilise real interest rates and other components of demand, and the greater variation in real rates may be expected to feed back on to the housing market reducing the direct stabilisation effect.

(5) In assessing the desirability of mortgage indexation and the resulting likely stabilisation in construction, one must also assess the social costs of instability in residential construction versus instability in other sectors.

(6) Many of the conclusions summarised above, especially those under (2) to (5) must be regarded, at present, as tentative. Hopefully the research which is presently getting under way at MIT will help to confirm them, reject them or modify them and provide a firmer footing for those that survive.

EXHIBIT 1 Lifetime Comparison of Index-linked and Conventional Mortgages* ($30,000 30-year mortgage)

Year	*Annual payment*		*Payment/salary*					
	Conventional	*Index-linked*	*0% Real salary growth*			*2% Real salary growth*		
				Payment/Salary			*Payment/Salary*	
	Mortgage	*Mortgage*	*Salary*	*Conv.*	*Indexed*	*Salary*	*Conv.*	*Indexed*
Case 1	0% Inflation		3% Real interest				3% Interest on conv. mtge	
	(1)	(2)	(3)	(4)	(5)	(6)	(7)	(8)
1	1517	1517	10,000	15·2	15·2	10,000	15·2	15·2
5	1517	1517	10,000	15·2	15·2	10,833	14·0	14·0
10	1517	1517	10,000	15·2	15·2	11,972	12·7	12·7
15	1517	1517	10,000	15·2	15·2	13,323	11·4	11·4
20	1517	1517	10,000	15·2	15·2	14,623	10·4	10·4
25	1517	1517	10,000	15·2	15·2	16,160	9·4	9·4
30	1517	1517	10,000	15·2	15·2	17,786	8·5	8·5
Case 2	2% Inflation		3% Real interest				5% Interest on conv. mtge	
1	1931	1517	10,000	19·3	15·2	10,000	19·3	15·2
5	1931	1643	10,833	17·6	15·2	11,735	16·3	14·0
10	1931	1816	11,972	16·0	15·2	14,333	13·3	12·7
15	1931	2021	13,323	14·4	15·2	17,507	10·9	11·4
20	1931	2218	14,623	13·1	15·2	21,382	8·9	10·4
25	1931	2451	16,160	11·8	15·2	26,117	7·3	9·4
30	1931	2698	17,786	10·8	15·2	31,899	6·0	8·5

Case 3	4% Inflation		3% Real interest			7% Interest on conv. mtge		
1	2393	1517	10,000	23·9	15·2	10,000	23·9	15·2
5	2393	1780	11,735	20·4	15·2	12,712	18·8	14·0
10	2393	2174	14,333	16·7	15·2	17,160	13·9	12·7
15	2393	2656	17,507	13·7	15·2	23,164	10·3	11·4
20	2393	3244	21,382	11·2	15·2	31,268	7·7	10·4
25	2393	3962	26,117	9·2	15·2	42,207	5·7	9·4
30	2393	4839	31,899	7·5	15·2	56,973	4·2	8·5
Case 4	**6% Inflation**		**3% Real interest**			**9% Interest on conv. mtge**		
1	2895	1517	10,000	29·0	15·2	10,000	29·0	15·2
5	2895	1928	12,712	22·8	15·2	13,771	21·0	14·0
10	2895	2603	17,160	16·9	15·2	20,544	14·1	12·7
15	2895	3514	23,184	12·5	15·2	30,648	9·4	11·4
20	2895	4743	31,268	9·3	15·2	45,721	6·3	10·4
25	2895	6403	42,207	6·9	15·2	68,208	4·2	9·4
30	2895	8643	56,973	5·1	15·2	101,754	2·8	8·5

* All calculations assume continuous compounding of interest and inflation as well as payments on a continuous basis.

EXHIBIT 2*

Year	*A* Price index of new 1-family houses sold	*B* Contract rate for mortgages on new houses	*C* Average mortgage term on new houses	*D* Index of monthly payments required for level-payment mortgage of average term on standard house	*E* Index of average wage and salary income of employed civilians
		%	yr.		
1963	90·2	5·84	25·0	98·1	91·2
1964	91·1	5·78	24·7	99·0	95·0
1965	93·2	5·74	25·2	100·0	100·0
1966	96·6	6·14	24·7	108·6	106·5
1967	100·0	6·33	25·2	113·5	111·0
1968	105·1	6·83	25·5	124·4	118·5
1969	113·6	7·66	25·5	144·9	126·0
1970	117·4	8·27	25·1	158·7	131·9
1971	123·2	7·60	26·2	155·0	138·6
1972	131·0	7·45	27·2	160·7	146·7
1973 (est.)	143·0	7·72	26·3	181·6	156·0

Sources:

Column A: U.S. Department of Commerce, 'Price Index of New One-Family Houses Sold', *Current Construction Reports* No. C27–73–2 (Nov 1973).

Columns B and C: Table 'Terms on Conventional First Mortgages', *Federal Reserve Bulletin*, various issues.

Column D: Derived from columns A, B, and C, assuming same percentage down-payment in every year.

Column E: Index of series derived by taking the sum of ('total wages and salaries' plus 'proprietors' income' minus 'military wages and salaries') and dividing by 'total employed' (excluding armed forces), from US Department of Commerce, 1971 *Business Statistics* and various issues of *Survey of Current Business.*

* From Donald Tucker, 1973.

EXHIBIT 3 Computation of Annual Mortgage Payments Illustration

	(1)	(2)	(3)	(4)
Year	1	2	3	4
Real interest rate, *r*	3%	3%	3%	3%
Rate of inflation, *q*	3%	5%	5%	4%
Nominal interest rate, *i*	6%	8%	8%	7%
Years to maturity	30	29	28	27
Conventional mortgage				
Beginning principal	20,000·00	19,747·00	19,478·82	19,194·55
plus interest (6%)	1,200·00	1,184·82	1,168·73	1,151·67
less annual payment	1,453·00	1,453·00	1,453·00	1,453·00
Ending principal	19,747·00	19,478·82	19,194·55	18,893·22
Scheduled payment (next period)*	1,453·00	1,453·00	1,453·00	1,453·00
Variable rate mortgage				
Beginning principal	20,000·00	19,747·00	19,873·76	19,665·28
plus interest (nominal rate)	1,200·00	1,579·76	1,589·90	1,376·57
less annual payment	1,453·00	1,453·00	1,798·38	1,798·38
Ending principal	19,747·00	19,873·76	19,665·28	19,243·47
Scheduled payment (next period)*	1,453·00	1,798·38	1,798·38	1,627·23
Index-linked mortgage				
Beginning principal	20,000·00	20,166·99	20,707·15	21,236·13
plus interest (3%)	600·00	605·01	621·22	637·08
less payment	1,020·40	1,050·90	1,103·48	1,158·64
Ending principal	19,579·60	19,721·10	20,224·88	20,714·57
Ending principal (adjusted for inflation)	20,166·99	20,707·15	21,236·13	21,543·16
Scheduled payment (next period)*	1,050·90	1,103·48	1,158·64	1,205·12

* Annuity required to amortise principal over remaining life of mortgage at applicable rate of interest.

EXHIBIT 4 Index-tied Financial Assets in Finland

Year	Cost of living index change %	Bonds* so d during year			Bonds* outstanding at end of year			Deposits outstanding in all banking institutions		
		Total million marks	Index-tied		Total million marks	Index-tied		All term deposits million marks	Index-tied	
			Million marks	% of total		Million marks	% of total		Deposits million marks	% of total
1952	4·0	45	6	13·3	516	6	0·1			
1953	1·8	279	46	16·5	600	51	8·5			
1954	−0·5	142	96	67·6	675	145	21·5			
1955	−3·0	94	69	73·4	724	204	28·2	3,158	3	0·1
1956	11·4	121	102	84·3	901	284	31·5	3,230	225	7·0
1957	11·4	122	101	82·8	899	348	38·7	3,390	824	24·3
1958	6·5	210	111	52·9	924	412	41·6	3,852	833	21·6
1959	1·6	190	56	29·5	999	422	42·2	4,542	281	6·2
1960	3·3	216	173	80·1	1,077	544	50·5	5,405	151	2·8
1961	1·9	220	112	50·9	1,089	589	54·1	6,270	38	0·6
1962	4·4	486	299	73·6	1,295	807	62·3	6,707	68	1·0
1963	4·8	518	125	24·1	1,611	844	52·4	7,185	281	3·9
1964	10·4	478	224	46·9	1,803	919	51·0	8,158	1,287	15·8
1965	4·9	768	472	61·5	2,073	1,163	56·1	9,199	1,670	18·2
1966	3·9	704	427	60·7	2,221	1,468	66·1	10,437	2,217	21·2
1967	5·3	276	216	78·3	2,022	1,502	74·3	11,538	3,997	34·6

* Excluding Government indemnity bonds.

Source: OECD, 1973.

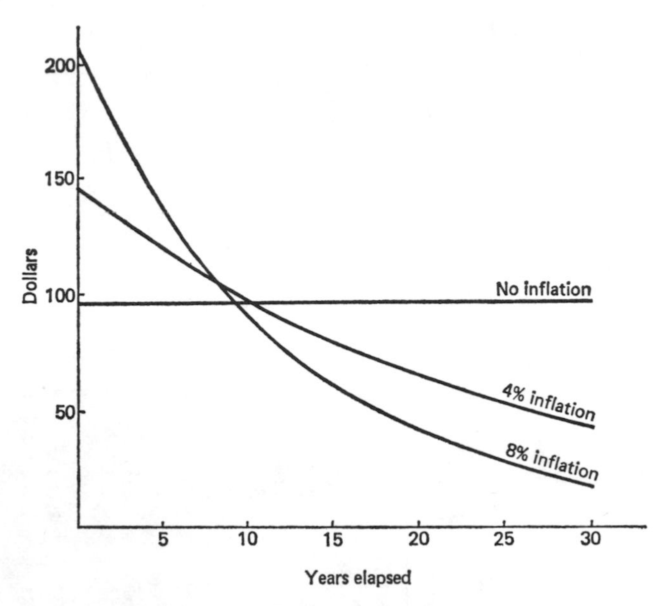

Figure 1. Real Value of Monthly Payments

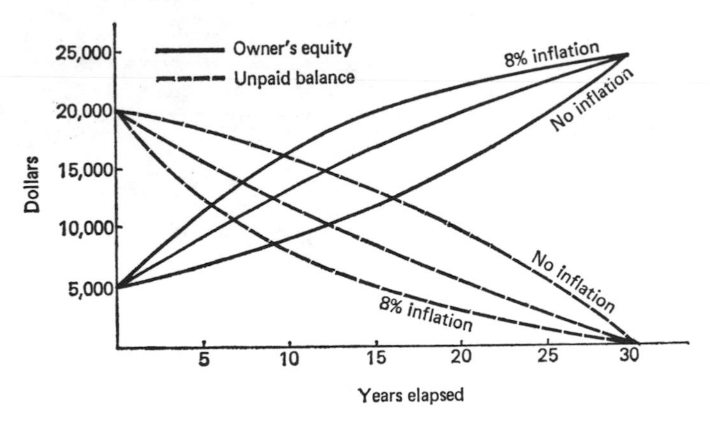

Figure 2. Real Value of Owner's Equity and Unpaid Balance

REFERENCES

Baffi, P., 'Savings in Italy, today', *Banca Nationale del Lavoro Quarterly Review* (1974).

Dreze, J., and Modigliani, F., 'Consumption Decisions under Uncertainty', *Journal of Economic Theory*, Vol. 5, No. 3 (Dec 1972).

Fischer, S., 'The Demand for Index Bonds', *Journal of Political Economy* (June 1975).

Kaufman, G. C., 'The Questionable Benefit of Variable-Rate Mortgages', *Quarterly Journal of Economics and Business*, University of Illinois (Autumn 1973).

Merton, R. C., 'Lifetime Portfolio Selection under Uncertainty: The Continuous-Time Case', *Review of Economics and Statistics* (Aug 1969), pp. 247–57.

Merton, R. C., 'Optimum Consumption and Portfolio Rules in a Continuous-Time Model', *Journal of Economic Theory* (Dec 1971), pp. 373–413.

Merton, R. C., 'An Intertemporal Capital Asset Pricing Model', *Econometrica*, (Sep 1973), pp. 867–87.

Modigliani, F. and Tarantelli, E., 'The Consumption Function in a Developing Economy and the Italian Experience', *The American Economic Review* (December 1975).

OECD, *Indexation of Fixed Interest Securities* (Paris, 1973).

Poole, W., 'Housing Finance under Inflationary Conditions' in *Ways to Moderate Fluctuations in Housing Construction*, Board of Governors, Federal Reserve System (Washington, 1972).

Poole, W., and Negri Opper, B., 'The Variable Rate Mortgage on Single Family Homes' in *Ways to Moderate Fluctuations in Housing Construction*, Board of Governors, Federal Reserve System (Washington, 1972).

Scholtes, C., The Indexation of Financial Assets: An Economic Analysis for Monetary Policy, Memoire presenté en vue de l'obtention du grade de Licencie et Maitre en Sciences Economiques et Sociales, Facultés Universitaires Notre-Dame de la Paix-Namur, 1972–1973.

Tucker, D. P., 'The Variable-Rate Graduated-Payment Mortgage', *Real Estate Review* (Spring 1975).

Tucker, D. P., 'Easing the Home Mortgage Burden', *Wall Street Journal* (12 June 1974).

Errata

Page 95, footnote 2, 2 lines below equation (*a*): "n^{th} year" should read "s^{th} year."

Page 100, paragraph 3, line 14: "VMR" should read "VRM."

Page 103, paragraph 1, last line: "σ_1^2" should read "σ_3^2."

Page 105, equation (4) and 3 lines below equation (4): "σ_1" should read "σ_2."

Page 105, footnote 3: at end of footnote add "(footnote contined on next page)."

Page 106: at beginning of footnote add "(footnote continued from previous page)."

PART II
Stabilization Policies

Inflation, Balance of Payments Deficit and their cure through Monetary Policy: the Italian example[*]

I

An examination of the evolution of the Italian economy during the years 1961-65 is very instructive for several reasons. It serves to illustrate the problems that beset a developing economy with large international trade when it first approaches full employment; it confirms the power of monetary tools in the control of aggregate demand; but, at the same time, it brings clearly to light the limitations of monetary (as well as fiscal) tools in dealing simultaneously with the task of maintaining full employment and balance of payments equilibrium in the face of a cost push; and, finally, it stresses the need for an effective incomes policy.

Between 1961 and 1963, Italy experienced a very fast growth of money wages and prices (1); during the same period the surplus of the balance of payments was converted into a deficit of sizable proportions (2). There is a rather clear evidence of monetary restric-

---

(*) The authors have received many helpful comments from Professors Forte, Graziani, Pasinetti and Sylos Labini and from Messrs. Fazio, Savona, Sideri and Trezza. Responsibility for errors rests solely with the authors.

(1) The yearly rate of growth of money wages for the period 1960-1966 was:

1960	+ 3.12%	1963	+10.71%
1961	+ 3.81%	1964	+14.54%
1962	+ 8.16%	1965	+ 8.48%

the cost of living index moved during the same period in the following way:

1960	+ 2.66%	1963	+ 8.79%
1961	+ 2.92%	1964	+ 6.49%
1962	+ 5.82%	1965	+ 4.34%

(*Source*: Alberto Campolongo: *La Politica dei Redditi*, Mediobanca, Milano, p. 67).

(2) The net outcome of the balance of payments was (in millions dollars):

1961	+ 577.4	1964	+ 773.9
1962	+ 50.4	1965	+1594.2
1963	−1251.8		

(*Source*: Relazioni della Banca d'Italia).

tions starting with the second half of 1963 (3). In any event, despite some claims to the contrary by the monetary authorities, at the beginning of 1964, whatever the cause, the economy entered a recession: employment, especially industrial employment, fell sharply, national income in real terms went up by less than 3% notwithstanding an increase of exports of some 13%, and investment dropped considerably. At the beginning of the summer 1964 the balance of payments exhibited again a surplus, which has been growing since then to reach the level of 1.6 billion dollars in the course of 1965.

During the second semester of 1965 and more so during the first half of 1966, the economy had shown signs of gathering momentum, but unemployment was still sizable and investment grew very slowly. Monetary indicators point (and did so starting with the second semester of 1964) to a non-restrictive monetary policy to which the economy failed to respond significantly (4).

---

(3) The net increase of the money supply between June 1963 and March 1964 was 533 billion lire, to be compared with 1,319 billions for the same period twelve months earlier and 907 billions for the following one. Especially when the figure for 1963-1964 is set against the figure for 1964-1965 — which was a year of depression and of rather abundant liquidity — one can see that in view of the wage and price increase we quoted in footnote one, from summer 1963 onwards the additional supply of money was very much restrained.

The best indicators of the tightness or easiness of monetary policy are two credit indexes. The first is the ratio of loans to total deposits of commercial banks. This index mounts regularly from 72.6% in December 1962 to 78.6 in December 1963 and to 78.5 in March 1964. After that it descends again to 74.4 by the end of 1964. The second index refers to the ratio of liquid assets (cash and money available on short call) to deposits. This ratio reaches its minimum (at 4.5%) in March 1964 and moves quickly up again before the end of the year to 6.0%, which is nearer to its customary level. Yields of bonds went up considerably during the first half of 1964, especially given the policy of trying to peg their courses which the central bank usually follows. They reach their maximum yield in June 1964 with 6.05% and then fall back to yields of roughly 5.50%.

(4) The ratio of loans to total deposits was at 68.7% in September 1965, at 67.7% in December, at 66.3% in March 1966, at 66.7 in June and 66.1 during August 1966. The ratio of liquid assets to deposits was 7.6% in September 1965, 5.4% in December; then it was 6.1% in March 1966, 4.5% in June and 6.0% in August.

National income in 1965 grew at 3.4% in real terms (a figure to be compared to rates of 5 and 6% in real terms for the period up to 1963). As in 1964, this result was largely due to the very fast rate of growth of exports (+19.9%), while investment was largely stagnant. The rate of growth is expected to be roughly 5% in real terms for 1966. But, once more, this result is to be attributed to the very good export performance (+13%). Investment is expected to increase by a mere 6%, which is less than an earlier forecast of some 8% increase.

Thus the picture of the economy is mixed, with some signs of greater momentum and some persisting signs of weakness of aggregate demand.

4

There appears to be a rather wide agreement among Italian economists, in and out of the Government, on the causes of the balance of payments crisis and of the ensuing recession. This explanation, originally put forward by the Bank of Italy (5), though rather unsatisfactory, has been uncritically accepted or at least has not been challenged in any systematic way.

It is unsatisfactory in our view for a number of reasons. For one thing, it blurs the role of monetary restraints in the determination of the downturn of the cycle and the subsequent improvement of the balance of payments. Furthermore, it stresses elements which are at best of secondary importance and on which the empirical evidence is not very impressive, while neglecting the role of other crucial mechanisms, and finally, it is not free of contradictions in its theoretical setting.

The purpose of this paper is to assess the validity of this explanation and to propose an alternative one. For convenience of exposition we have kept the case of an open economy quite separated from that of a closed one. Section 2 endeavours to formalize the model we are criticizing (we shall often call it, for brevity, the Bank of Italy's model) and to bring out its basic shortcomings. Section 3 presents the alternative model we propose. Section 4 discusses the nature of the Italian inflation and the determinants of wage movements. Section 5 deals with the case of an open economy, a case that should be of rather general interest for its analysis of the relationship between aggregate demand and the balance of payments. Conclusions and four appendices, providing a formal treatment of problems raised in the text, close the paper.

II

The annual reports of the Bank of Italy contain a very detailed analysis of past and present trends of the economy, together with an account of the monetary policy followed by the bank. The core of the report are the "Considerazioni Finali", "Concluding Remarks", by the Governor of the Bank, where a general appraisal of the economic situation is offered. The Considerazioni Finali for 1962, 1963 and 1964 basically deal with only one theme: the consequences on aggregate demand and on balance of payments of wage

(5) It was presented, in an organic way, in the annual report for 1964 (Rome, June 1965), but the same analysis is to be found in the reports for 1962 and 1963.

increases larger than the average increase in productivity per man. The Bank assigns a crucial role to the distribution of income between wages and profits in affecting both aggregate demand and the balance of payments. In particular, it holds that a redistribution of income from profits to wages will have an unfavourable effect both on investment, and thereby on aggregate demand, and on the balance of payments because of the increase in consumption expenditures which it induces (6).

The main lines of this explanation run as follows: the propensity to save out of wage-income is taken to be substantially lower than the propensity to save out of profit-income. Therefore, whenever money wages rise faster than productivity and prices do not match this rise so as to keep the rise in real wages within the rate of increase of productivity, the distribution of income is going to be modified in favour of wage incomes, the aggregate propensity to save for the economy as a whole will go down and the aggregate propensity to consume will go up.

The increase in the share of aggregate demand going into consumption will determine an increase in imports and hence a deterioration of the balance of trade. The reduction in profits and in the share of savings in national income is going to affect negatively investment for three basic reasons:

(a) a decreased supply of savings on financial markets (7);

(b) a disincentive effect due to the reduced self-financing opportunities available to firms;

(c) a disincentive effect due to the reduction of the rate of profit (8).

All these phenomena arise from the increase in money wages, the level of which the Bank considers largely exogenous. What are,

---

(6) Cf. the Bank of Italy's Report for 1964, where it claims: " These wage increases (those of 1962-63) tended to raise unit costs. Whenever this determined a rise in prices, the competitiveness of our economy was curtailed and foreign demand negatively affected. Whenever prices were unchanged, profit margins got squeezed. From this a lower propensity to invest followed, a smaller demand for capital goods and finally a smaller aggregate demand " (page 486).

(7) " If one compares the notable amount of new requests for bank credit with the limited amount of resources to be so employed, one has to conclude that the limiting factor has so far been and still is the insufficient amount of saving " (Annual Report for 1963 page 488).

(8) " To the extent that higher wages are matched by lower profits, the new distribution of income may well affect investment " (Annual Report for 1962 page 476-477).

then, the possibilities of monetary policy? The central bank, one infers from the Considerazioni Finali, has a choice between increasing the supply of money and, through this, determine an increase in prices which will keep the distribution unchanged, thus preventing the fall in investment which would otherwise take place and leaving the supply of money unchanged. In the latter case, the distribution of income is going to change with the consequences we have indicated above.

To help the understanding of this model, which is quite unusual for the stress it lays on distribution of income as the key variable controlling both aggregate demand and balance of payments, we shall make use of a diagram. For the rest of this and the following two sections we shall assume that the economy has no international trade. The assumption will be released in Section 5.

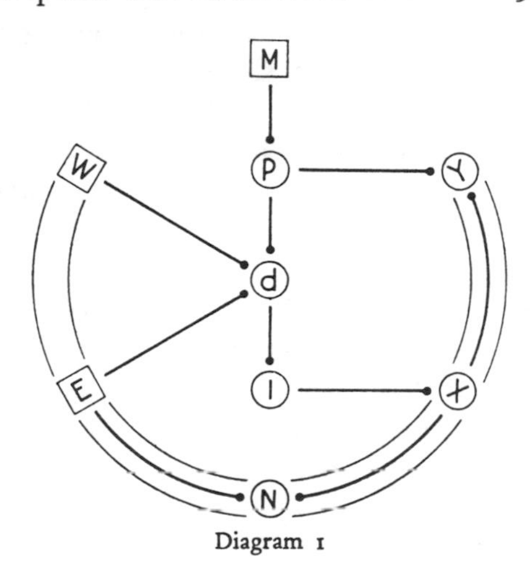

Diagram 1

There are three exogenous variables:

M : the supply of money
E : Productivity per man
W : the money wage rate

and six dependent variables

P : the price level
d : the distribution of income between wages and profits
I : the level of Investment
X : the level of Aggregate Demand in real terms
Y : National Income in money terms
N : the level of employment.

7

Circles around letters denote the endogenous variables. Boxes indicate the exogenous ones. Arrows denote the direction of causation among the variables. It is interesting to note that the model presented above has no feedbacks. Thus, for istance, the distribution of income is determined by two exogenous variables and by the price level, which is, in turn, determined by the exogenously given supply of money. The direct dependence of aggregate demand on distribution of income is also evident, and so is the role of the supply of money as the determinant of the price level.

It is necessary to emphasize the fact that this model has not been presented in this or any formal way in the Bank's reports. It is our interpretation based on a careful analysis of both the reports and the monetary policy followed in the course of the period 1961-1965. In particular, it seems to be the only way to put together the statement that balance of payments deficit and the fall in employment are to be explained by the same set of " real " circumstances, i.e. by a change in the distribution of income.

The model presented above rests on two crucial propositions. The first is that distribution of income is independent of the level of aggregate demand, being determined, instead, uniquely by wage bargain and the supply of money; the second is that investment and aggregate demand depend on the distribution of income. Let us examine both propositions starting with the second.

As we have seen, there are three mechanisms through which a change in the distribution of income is supposed to affect the level of investment and of aggregate demand (see page 6). We shall consider them in turn.

The first mechanism described by the Bank works through the supply of savings and has itself two components. First there is the empirical assessment that the propensity to save of wage earners is lower than that of profit earners; second, there is the analysis of the consequences of a fall in the aggregate propensity to save on investment and income.

As far as the empirical part is concerned, there are no Italian data which can be used to prove or disprove the point. The only indirect evidence (which goes against the Bank's thesis) is that up to 1963 the aggregate propensity to save had been going up in the Italian economy, notwithstanding a gradual change in the distribution of income in favour of wage income. Moreover, if one makes appeal to international comparisons of the average propensity to save, the available evidence suggests no significant association between the saving ratio and distributive shares (9).

However, we may take the first part of the proposition as an unsubstantiated assumption and inquire whether the change in the aggregate propensity to save which would follow, *ex hypothesi*, from a change in the distribution of income can *per se* affect the level of investment and of aggregate demand.

The answer to this question is that in general neither effect will follow. In one borderline case, i.e. when the economy is initially at full employment, investment may fall but aggregate demand will stay costant. The Bank's opinion, which appears to be shared by many Italian economists, seems to depend on a failure to distinguish clearly between investment demand, the supply of saving and the aggregate propensity to save. Denote respectively by I, S and X investment, savings and aggregate demand, all measured in real terms and let s stand for the average propensity to save and X^* for full employment income. We can then write, in their simplest form, the relationships among these variables as

$$X = I/s = S/s \qquad [1]$$

Now suppose that initially $X < X^*$, and consider the effect of a fall in s. Unless there is an independent change in investment demand, I will be unaffected by the change in s and hence S, the ex-post supply of saving, will also be unchanged. But this clearly implies that the fall in s must entail a *larger* and not a smaller level of aggregate income, X. What happens of course is that income must expand to make room for the additional consumption implied by the lower propensities to save. If, on the other hand, to the initial value of I and s corresponded a value of $X = X^*$, then, a fall in s must indeed force a contraction of investment to a lower level given by

$$I = S^* = sX^* \qquad [2]$$

where S^* denotes the new and lower level of aggregate saving at the unchanged full employment income. I, i.e. must now accommo-

---

(9) See Franco Modigliani, " The Life Cycle hypothesis of Saving, the Demand for Wealth and the Supply of Capital ", *Social Research*, vol. 33, No. 2, Summer 1966.

date itself to the lower supply of full employment saving (10), but obviously aggregate demand remains constant at the full employment level.

Thus, if a redistribution of income were in fact to lower s, unless the fall in s is accompanied by an independent downward shift in the Investment Demand schedule, its final effect would be to increase income, or, in the limit, to leave it unchanged. In short, there cannot be a deflationary effect due to the first of the three mechanisms listed above. The only change that might follow would be a change in the composition of aggregate demand, towards more consumption and less investment (11).

It appears, then, that if a redistribution of income has to have a deflationary effect on the economy, this must come about through significant disincentive effects on investment, that is, through the independent or combined effect of the mechanisms listed under (b) and (c) above.

Mechanism (b) emphasizes the role of the availability of self-financing on the level of investment. The argument applies mainly to business enterprises organized in the form of joint stock companies with shares traded in the stock exchange. These enterprises pay out part of their earnings as dividends, while retaining part to finance investment programs. Whenever their earnings fall, they have to make a choice between an unchanged dividend policy, an unchanged level of retained profits and an intermediate combination of those.

Yet, for mechanism (b) to be strictly correct, it would be necessary (i) that dividends should remain unchanged in the face of lower profits, and (ii) that the whole of retained profits be devoted to investment. Neither (i) nor (ii) can be taken for granted. The retention ratio is likely to depend jointly on the level of profits and on investment opportunities. A lower level of profits, coupled with unchanged investment prospects would lead firms to adopt a higher

---

(10) It is to be noted though that several economists (e.g. NICHOLAS KALDOR, "Alternative Theories of Distribution", in *Essays in Value and Distribution*, London, Duckworth, 1960) believe that the aggregate propensity to save cannot be taken as a parameter, insofar as it depends on the level of investment. Therefore, when $X = X^*$, instead of investment adjusting to the full employment supply of saving, it will happen that investment will bring forth a distribution of income compatible with full employment and that level of I.

(11) The composition of aggregate demand is very relevant to employment from a long period point of view. From the point of view of short run fluctuations, employment depends mainly on aggregate demand, not on its composition.

retention ratio. Nor are retained profits necessarily invested. They can be used to increase the firm's liquidity or to reduce past debts. Investment, on the other hand, can be financed out of decumulation of liquid assets.

We point out these possibilities to warn against assuming a strict dependence of investment on the level of profits through mechanism (b). It is probable, nonetheless, that a weaker form of dependence may be found to exist, with dividends rather inelastic to changes in total earnings, so that the impact of lower earnings is mainly felt on retained profits.

Let us assume therefore that when profits go down, self-financing opportunities are reduced. Even this assumption does in no way warrant the conclusion that, as a result, aggregate investment, and/or aggregate demand must fall. Indeed a reasoning analogous to that developed on pages 9 and 10 readily establishes that the reduction of internal funds can never imply a shrinkage in the overall availability of investible funds to the point where they become insufficient to finance the level of investment needed to maintain the initial level of aggregate demand.

To clarify this point we may usefully distinguish two possibilities. Suppose first that the fall in profits does not reduce the overall propensity to save. Then, since the level of investment required to support an unchanged level of income is itself unchanged, internal sources will indeed fall relatively to the required level of investment; *but* the fall in internal sources will be precisely compensated by an increase in the potential supply of saving from other sources. If, on the other hand, lower business saving is not compensated by higher saving of other transactors there will be a fall in the average propensity to save and therefore in the sum of internal and external sources at the initial level of income; but this overall reduction will just match the fall in the level of investment required to maintain the same level of employment with a smaller s.

It must be recognized, however, that the shrinkage of internal sources could create some difficulties, even though offset by greater availability of external sources, if firms are unwilling to substitute external for internal financing.

For instance, if new stock issues are needed to substitute for reduced sources of self-finance, the controlling group may fear that dilution of ownership might weaken its control over the firm. Similarly, other things being equal, a firm may be reluctant to increase its reliance on bank borrowing or on other forms of indebtedness (12).

In analysing the implications of such a phenomenon, it is well to distinguish between " absolute " and " relative " aversions. Absolute aversion means that firms will not substitute external for internal sources, regardless of the conditions under which the external funds might be made available. Such behaviour would indeed pose a serious problem, almost impossible to cope with through the tools available to the monetary authority. There is however very little evidence to indicate that absolute aversion was a problem of major proportions in Italy during the period under consideration, since the financial statistics reveal a notable upsurge of credit demand which the banks were unable to satisfy. We must therefore reject " absolute " aversion as a sufficient explanation for the fall in investment.

There remains the problem of relative aversion, i.e. an aversion which can be overcome by sufficient inducements. The importance of this phenomenon is hard to measure but we are perfectly willing to admit its existence and significance. Relative aversion merely implies that a fall in profits, and hence in internal sources, will tend to reduce investment, as long as the availability and cost of external sources is unchanged. In this sense its *modus operandi* is entirely analogous to the disincentive effect of lower rates of return on investment which constitutes mechanism (c) in our list of page 6.

We may therefore reword proposition (c) into the following very plausible assertion which covers also the viable portion of mechanism (b): a fall in current profits, by reducing both the expected rate of return on investment and the availability of " preferred " internal sources, will tend to reduce the incentive to invest, as long as the cost and availability of external sources remains unchanged. Stated more formally, this proposition says that the rate of Investment I, depends, among other things, on the current rate of profit, with the property

$$\frac{\partial I}{\partial \pi} > 0 \qquad [3]$$

Just what does [3] imply for the effect of a fall in profit on aggregate demand, X? Clearly from [3] and [1] it does follow that a fall in π will reduce X, as long as other things are equal;

(12) For a fuller treatment of this question, see Franco Modigliani and Merton H. Miller, " The Cost of Capital, Corporation Finance and the Theory of Investment ", *American Economic Review*, 1958, pp. 261-296.

12

and these other things include in particular the average propensity to save, s and the cost and availability of outside financing, which for brevity we associate with r. But of course other things cannot be assumed equal. In particular, according to the Bank's model, s itself is an increasing function of π, or

$$[4] \qquad \frac{\partial s}{\partial \pi} > 0,$$

so that a fall in profits will determine a fall in the average propensity to save. Thus, the negative effect on investment will be partially, totally, or even more than totally offset by the higher income multiplier. The net effect on X will depend on the relative weight of the change in I and the change in s. In formal terms, as is shown in Appendix 2, the outcome depends on the elasticity of investment with respect to profits and on the elasticity of the average propensity to save with respect to the same variable. If the first is larger than the second, national income will fall, if the two are equal, national income will be unchanged, and if the latter outweighs the former, national income will tend to increase (provided it is not bounded from above by the full employment ceiling).

Finally, even if the values of these elasticities are such that, for given r, X would fall, there is no reason why r should not be reduced as well (as a result of monetary policy) to affect positively I through credit conditions or greater credit availability. A change in r may therefore act as an incentive and balance the disincentive effect of a relative aversion to external forms of finance or low realized profit levels. The conclusion of our analysis of mechanisms (b) and (c), then, is that there is no *a priori* reason to expect a fall of realized profits, to cause automatically a fall in aggregate demand especially if monetary authorities are willing to take the steps that might be needed to counterbalance disincentive effects coming from low profit margins.

Let us summarize the conclusions we reached concerning the influence of a redistribution of income on aggregate demand.

1. The reduction of self-financing opportunities consequent upon a fall of profits may determine a fall in investment only in the hypothesis that firms have a total aversion against the use of external sources of finance. The evidence in support of this phenomenon is very scanty.

2. If, for the preceding or for other reasons, the inducement to invest tends to fall as profits fall, an increase in the average propensity to consume is to be welcomed rather than regretted and resisted. In fact, such an increase helps to maintain a high level of aggregate demand and employment.

3. An appropriately expansionary credit policy may be able to counterbalance the disincentive effects of a reduction in profits, should this prove powerful enough.

On the basis of the above considerations we are led to the view that the inversion of the cycle around the turn of 1963 cannot be accounted for by the fall of profits and the incentive to invest, unless there had not also been an active policy of monetary restraint to put a brake on the system. With this assertion we certainly do not wish to deny (1) that in the course of the inflation forces were developping which were making the continuation of the boom increasingly precarious, and therefore also making the system more vulnerable to a policy of monetary restraint, and (2) that the contraction was accelerated and magnified by rather ill-timed contractive fiscal measures hitting the system at a time when the monetary measures were already working their deflationary effects (namely in the spring of 1964). Nor do we want to leave the impression that in our view the Central Bank should be blamed for the restraint and the contraction that followed. At the moment we are concerned only with trying to understand the phenomena that occurred and their causes, leaving for the concluding section the task of drawing some inferences as to what might have been the most desirable course for monetary (and fiscal) policy.

As a final point before leaving this matter, it is important to note that if the Central Bank is concerned with encouraging investment in the face of a fall in the expected return from investment — whether originating in a fall in profit margins or in a fall in demand and the emerging excess capacity — it cannot confine itself to making credit more readily available; it must also take active measures to reduce its cost.

In Italy, interest rates are pegged to a level which has been largely constant (and at any rate inflexible downwards) during the post-war period. In particular, there exists a banks' agreement on credit terms, whose provisions have hardly changed in this period. Moreover, the Central Bank actively operates on financial markets to keep the yield of public debt roughly constant. This behaviour exerts a stabilising effect on prices of long-term bonds available on the financial market, so that their yield doesn't vary very much through time. By and large, the Italian Central Bank prefers to operate through the availability of credit rather than through its cost. This policy may certainly exert a restraint, when demand exceeds the supply of credit, because " de facto " interest rates tend to go up and availability effects are quickly felt by firms. But it is very doubtful whether this policy can provide a stimulus to expansion. In technical terms, if the marginal efficiency of capital schedule has moved inwards, lower interest rates are a necessary condition (even if not sufficient) for keeping the level of investment unchanged (13). These considerations may help to explain the very disappointing performance of domestic investment in the last two years, when long-term interest rates remained quite high despite the supposed ready availability of credit, and seem to suggest the opportunity for Italian monetary authorities to reconsider their policy of pegged interest rates.

III

In the last section we have shown that distribution of income, alone, cannot determine aggregate demand. In this section we propose to argue that the opposite is true, i.e. that the distribution of income is determined by the level of aggregate demand which in turn is shaped by quite different forces, including monetary and fiscal policy.

For the moment, we find it convenient to retain the assumption that the economy has no international trade relationships and that money wages are fixed through an exogenous bargaining process between unions and business organizations. These two restrictive assumptions will be discarded in the two sections following the present.

To make the discussion simpler and to compare our model with the one discussed above, we have formalised it in a diagram (see also Appendix 1).

For the definition of the symbols, see diagram 1, page 7. The only difference between the variables appearing in the two dia-

---

(13) It may be, though, that the responsiveness of investment to lower interest rates is small and that investment is basically inelastic with respect to the rate of interest. But until a policy of flexible interest rates is attempted, no information on this elasticity will be available.

grams is that, in ours, there is no variable denoting the distribution of income and there is a variable, r, denoting the conditions and availability of credit. Boxed letters indicate exogenous variables. But since wages will be shown (in section IV) to be only partially exogenous, their box is not solid. Circled letters denote endogenous variables.

Given the level of money wages, the question of what determines the distribution of income boils down to that of what determines (a) the level of aggregate demand, (b) the level of prices.

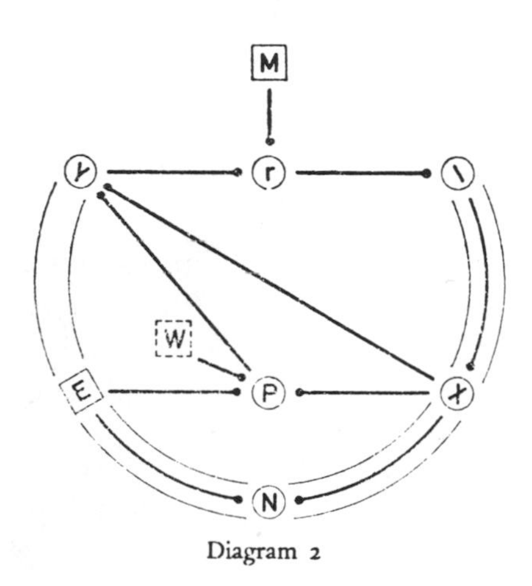

Diagram 2

In the Bank's model, there are partially conflicting statements on the determinants of the level of prices, but, by and large, one can say that, in that model, prices directly depend on the supply of money. Our view is different. We hold that an increase in money wages, larger than productivity, will affect prices even if the quantity of money is unchanged. Given the money wage, the price level depends on productivity per man, E, and the level of aggregate demand. Precisely, for given X and E, the price level, P, will be approximately proportional to the level of money wages. Conversely, for given W, an increase of X will tend to be accompanied by a higher price level.

This conclusion is borne out by various considerations: one was originally advanced by Lord Keynes in the *General Theory*, where the relationship of aggregate demand to the price level is clearly spelled out for the case of a perfectly competitive system. According to this view, real wages tend to the level of the marginal productivity of labour. The latter, in the short run, is a decreasing function of

16

the level of employment and of aggregate demand. Therefore, given X, real wages are determined. And the price level will be set in such a way as to make money wages correspond to that level of real wages (14).

A more satisfactory approximation to the working of modern economies is to be found in models of oligopolistic behaviour, where the emphasis is on " mark-up " procedures for price determination. According to this view, firms set prices in such a way as to cover direct costs and to secure a given profit margin. The price fixed must be consistent with a " normal " rate of utilization of plant and machinery. In this case a change in money wages (in excess of productivity increases) will tend to be transferred on prices as long as the rate of utilization of capacity is maintained. However the " mark-up " is influenced also by the rate of utilization of capacity, and tends, therefore, to rise with output in the short run. We may also note, for later reference, that when the economy is open, international competition will influence the " mark-up " in much the same way as capacity. In that case, profit margins may be squeezed without a change in the level of aggregate demand or in the degree of utilization of plants, if domestic costs rise relative to foreign costs and prices.

Thus, both in the keynesian and in the oligopolistic model, real wages depend on aggregate demand and employment. This means that, for given X, money wages and prices move together. Changes in aggregate demand, however, will affect the proportionality factor between W and P and in general we will expect that, given productivity per head, real wages will move in the opposite direction of aggregate demand.

We are now in a position to analyse the relationship between the supply of money and the price level. As diagram 2 shows, the supply of money affects the price level through its influence on aggregate demand. It is in fact the latter that, together with E and W, sets the price level. The relationship between M and X can

(14) We are aware that a number of empirical studies on the relationship between the level of output and productivity per man seem to indicate that the two move in the same direction in the short run. This may be taken as a disproof of the perfectly competitive model of the General Theory, in the sense that real wages would not go down when employment goes up and that therefore the price-wage ratio need not increase together with output. On the other hand, these results are open to further discussion, and, moreover, the relationship that we have put as a basis for our analysis, i.e. that, *for given X*, the price-wage ratio tends to be constant, is valid even if the other relationship may be doubted.

be spelled out in greater detail: M influences r; r in turn influences investment expenditures, encouraging or discouraging them, as the case may be. Investment expenditures determine income through the investment multiplier. There is a feedback in the model insofar as the level of money income determines the demand for money and therefore the level of r (15).

A useful way to make the working of our model clear is to suppose that, starting from an initial equilibrium position, money wages rise by a given amount (supposing, for simplicity, that productivity is unchanged). Let us assume that monetary authorities leave the supply of money unchanged. From the considerations developed above, if aggregate demand were unchanged, prices would increase in the same proportion. The demand for money (coming from an expanded volume of monetary transactions) will be pushed up and will exert a pressure on the available stock of money. Thus strains will develop on financial markets, with money being less readily available and with its cost increasing. There will be a larger demand for bank loans leading to higher rates and an increased rationing of credit. And there will be larger issues of bonds and liquidation of bank holdings which can only be absorbed by the public at higher interest rates.

Given its greater cost and lower availability, money will circulate faster, with operators trying to economize on cash holdings relative to transactions. But real aggregate demand too will bear the burden of this scarcity. Firms will consider the opportuneness of cutting some of their planned expenditures which are now more costly and more difficult to finance. It will be mainly new orders of plant and equipment which will be considered the first candidates for these reductions, because of their greater volatility, though current operations may also be somewhat affected.

With aggregate demand being reduced, prices will not be pushed up to the full extent of the wage increase. Eventually the system will settle down to a new position characterized by a higher level of aggregate money demand, a lower level of real aggregate demand and employment, a higher rate of interest and an increased velocity of circulation of money. Since prices rise by a lesser amount than money wages, real wages (of the employed) will be higher than before, and profits per unit of output will be lower. Total

(15) See Appendix 1.

profits, on their part, will be reduced for two reasons: because profits per unit of output are lower and because the total volume of output has shrunk. Nevertheless, distribution of income, i.e. the shares of wages and profits in national income, may move either way (16).

Can monetary policy prevent all this from happening? and at what cost? The answer depends basically on the behaviour of money wages. If they are constant at the new level they have reached, as we suppose throughout this section, then the answer to the first question is positive. If, on the contrary, their rate of change depends on aggregate demand or if unions are determined to reach a given *real wage rate*, then the aims of monetary policy will be frustrated.

Let us assume for the moment that wages are constant at their new level and suppose that monetary authorities set the money supply so as to keep real aggregate demand at the level it was before the wage increase (17). In this case, it is to be expected that real wages will not change, i.e. that prices will grow by the same amount as money wages. Thus, the distribution of income between wages and profits will be unchanged (as a by-product of a constant level of real aggregate demand).

The causal link in our model is exactly the reverse of the one stressed in the Bank's model. Whereas, in ours, the distribution of income is determined by aggregate demand, in the Bank's model distribution of income determines aggregate demand. The fact that both models consider an expansion of the money supply as a necessary condition for preserving a given level of employment does not change the basic fact that the working of the two models is fundamentally different (18).

---

(16) Distribution of income depends on the elasticity of employment and the elasticity of prices with respect to aggregate demand. When output falls, real wages are higher and unit profits lower. But the share of wages in the (lower) output depends on the number of employed workers as well as on their (higher) wage. If employment is reduced by a large enough amount, the share of wages in output may be lower than before. If one is willing to use the notion of a marginal rate of substitution of capital and labour, the final result depends on the elasticity of substitution between these two factors of production.

In practice, even when the share of wages is reduced, it is probable that profits, in a strict sense, are reduced too as a share of national income, the share of interest and rents (which are rather more inflexible than profits) having increased to account for the difference.

(17) Question: how can monetary authorities know the "appropriate" level of the money supply? The answer is that (at least in theory) they can implicitly find it simply by enforcing a constant interest rate (or set of interest rates), i.e. by releasing money whenever credit and financial conditions become tight, and recalling it when they are too loose.

(18) To mention another difference: we expect velocity of circulation of money to change when credit conditions change, whereas the Bank's model would seem to implicitly

To assert that monetary expansion is a *necessary* condition for preserving employment in the face of a wage push does not imply that such a response is *desirable* or even that it is *sufficient* to achieve that goal. Even if it were sufficient, the monetary authority would still face a difficult dilemma between maintaining employment at the cost of higher prices or maintaining the initial price level at the cost of lower employment. Under certain conditions this dilemma might not be too hard to resolve. *If* one could be sure that wages would not respond to higher prices by further escalation, and *if* balance of payments effects could be disregarded, then a monetary expansion would also prove sufficient to preserve employment. In this case, we, at least, would have no qualms in opting for monetary expansion on the ground that a once and for all rise in prices is a lesser evil when compared with a permanent, or at least protracted, fall in employment. Unfortunately, in general, neither of the above " ifs " could be expected to hold in Italy, as we shall indicate in the following two sections.

IV

In this paragraph we want to address ourselves to the question of the determinants of wage behaviour. In particular, we want to inquire whether it is justifiable to treat money wages as a purely exogenous variable.

Keynes's view was that, by and large, so long as there exists some unemployment, money wages are rigid (both downwards and upwards). At full employment, they tend to move in response to demand changes. Contrary to this view, post-keynesian analysis has emphasized a number of mechanisms which tend to impart an upward thrust to money wages even when the labour force is partially unemployed. Some of these mechanisms link the level of money wages to the price level; some others link the level (or, more exactly, the rate of change) of money wages to the level of employment.

A typical mechanism, linking money wages and prices, is the so-called " sliding scale " clause in wage contracts which provides for an automatic wage adjustment to the price level. When these clauses are effective, an upward movement of wages, inducing — as

deny this. In particular we would expect velocity of circulation to increase when money becomes tight so that an unchanged quantity of money would be accompanied by a higher Y, with P going up somewhat and X being somewhat reduced.

we have seen in the last section -- an upward revision in prices, will lead to further wage and price increases. Therefore monetary policy can be successful in preventing a squeeze in aggregate demand and employment only if the central bank is willing to let the supply of money expand in step with wages and prices.

There are two distinct possibilities. The sliding scale mechanism may provide only for a partial adjustment of wages to prices (19). In this case an expansionary monetary policy aiming at a constant level of employment will determine a damped wage-price spiral. But there is no way of knowing what will be the level of wages and prices that will prevail when a stable situation is reached again.

If, on the other hand, the sliding scale mechanism provides for a full adjustment of wages to prices or if trade unions bargain the money wage on the basis *of a level of the real wage they aim at*, an expansionary monetary policy will give rise to an undamped wage-price spiral with prices and wages growing at the same rate.

It is interesting to note, however, that, even in this case, monetary policy may still be able to keep the level of employment unchanged at its initial level, provided there is a certain lag between price changes and wage adjustments. In fact, if monetary expansion immediately follows a wage increase, but wages are adjusted to the new (higher) prices only after a time, although wages and prices grow at the same rate, real wages never exceed that level compatible with the pre-existing level of employment (20).

The previous result depends on the lag structure we have assumed, namely, an immediate adjustment of prices to wages and a delayed adjustment of wages to prices. But if the lag between price adjustment and wage adjustment is in itself a function of the rate of inflation, it will decrease through time with trade unions insisting on shorter and shorter periods between successive wage adjustments. In this case the rate of inflation itself will increase through time (21).

---

(19) This is the case for Italy, where the " scala mobile " provides for a wage increase of 0.6% for every 1% increase in the cost of living index.

(20) One can easily construct a symmetrical, although less plausible, case, i.e. a situation in which monetary policy reacts to wage changes after a lag of time, whereas wages are instantaneously adjusted to the level of prices (say through a perfect " sliding scale " mechanism). In this case the level of employment will be the one implied by the maximum level of real wages, because monetary policy will manage to inflate aggregate demand just for a fraction of time, but this will not be sufficient to push employment to a higher level, the following wage change undoing what monetary policy is trying to achieve.

(21) See Appendix 3 for a formal discussion of this point.

The mechanisms we have discussed so far are independent of the behaviour of employment. In recent years, following a pioneering study by A.W. Phillips (22), there has been a remarkable interest in testing the hypothesis that the rate of change of money wages is a function of the unemployment rate. In its most common formulation, the hypothesis is that the rate of change of wages is a decreasing function of the unemployment rate.

If this relationship was found to exist, given the rate of growth of productivity per man, the constancy of the price level would require that wages increase at a specified rate, and this would in turn determine the rate of unemployment which should prevail in the economy. A monetary or fiscal policy aiming at a higher level of employment would result in a continuous increase of wages and prices.

The Phillips relationship is not easy to establish, mainly because of the simultaneous appearance, when employment is high, of various phenomena that can explain rapid wage changes. This poses rather complicated econometric problems (23).

Even apart from these difficulties, we do not think that this analysis can be used to interpret the Italian situation between 1961 and 1965, for one basic reason. The countries for which this relationship has been shown to be statistically significant are countries where unemployment is a cyclical phenomenon due to fluctuations of effective demand around its full employment or quasi-full employment level. In Italy, on the other hand, except for the years 1964 and 1965, the change in employment has been largely unidirectional. During the last years of the '50s and the first years of the '60s Italy has moved from a situation of "structural" unemployment to a situation of near full employment. Wage changes taking place in these conditions should not be interpreted against the background of a cyclical model like a Phillips curve (24).

On the whole, we are inclined to think that the high rate of inflation of 1962-1963 is to be explained as a cost-push phenomenon

---

(22) A. W. Phillips, "The Relation between Unemployment and the Rate of Change of Money Wages in the United Kingdom, 1861-1957", *Economica*, 1958, pp. 283-299.

(23) For a critical view of Phillips Curves see, for instance, E. Kuh, "Wage Changes and their Determinants", M.I.T. unpublished, 1966.

(24) Recently, this topic has attracted some attention among Italian economists and lately an attempt to fit a "Phillips curve" to Italian data has been made by A. Campolongo in the work we quoted in footnote 1.

coupled by an expansionary monetary policy aimed at preserving the level of employment (25). It may well be, though, that some demand pull elements have been contributed initially by the central bank's attempt at maintaining the level of investment in the face of a reduced propensity to save. But, since we do not have clear evidence to substantiate this hunch we mention it only as a possibility (26).

The inflationary process was halted by the policy of monetary restrictions enforced in the fall of 1963. The slack in domestic demand and the pressure of the foreign competition at home and abroad restrained prices from rising too much, and the resulting fall in employment reduced the strength of trade union demands. Although wages and prices were never completely halted in this period, they were kept sufficiently in check and this contributed to the rapid improvement of the balance of payments.

Consideration of the mechanisms we mentioned and in particular of the " sliding scale " adjustment clause should have led monetary authorities in 1961 to doubt the opportuneness of an expansionary monetary policy and should have suggested instead a less buoyant policy. These considerations apply even more forcefully when the balance of payments aspects are taken fully into account, as we will show in section V.

---

(25) Italian unemployment never fell below some 2% of the total labour force (at least according to one of the available sets of statistics). But this situation was close enough to full employment to make the labour market very tight. In fact, one has to consider where unemployment was mostly located. The industrial areas of the North had reached full employment of the local population some time before 1961. At that time workers were imported from Central and Southern regions of Italy. At least three causes contributed to higher wages:

(a) the proper cost of transferring workers from agricultural areas into industrial regions;

(b) the necessity for Northern Italian firms to compete for immigrant labour with other industrial areas of the Common Market where wages were, at the beginning of the period we are studying, higher than in Italy;

(c) the very high wages (relatively to other firms) paid within the Northern regions of Italy by the largest and most advanced firms, like FIAT, to attract workers from other firms of the area, thus compelling the other firms to raise in turn their wages to keep skilled workers with them.

(26) It is actually possible that during this period there was an upward movement of the propensity to consume of the economy as a whole (it is of no consequence, at this point, to discuss whether it was due to a redistribution of income from profits to wages or to the other causes) that would have called for a lower amount of investment to keep the level of employment unchanged. To press for an unchanged level of investment, when employment was nearly full, may have powerfully contributed to wage increases through the pressure of demand.

V

Models of income and price determination that take into account the complications arising from international trade are rather difficult to describe and analyse in plain English. We have tried to formulate diagrammatically (leaving to Appendix 4 its further formal exploration) the one we think to be appropriate to the Italian situation.

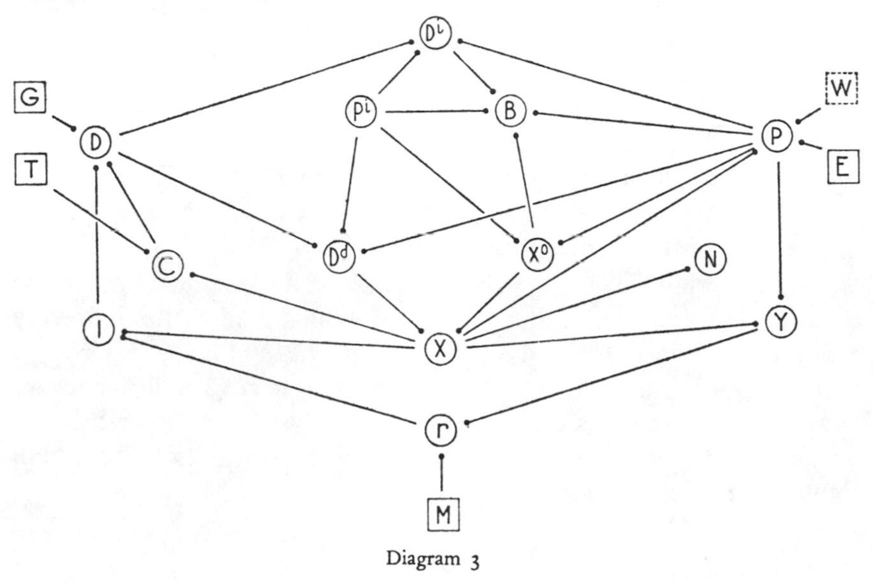

Diagram 3

The symbols appearing for the first time are:

- G : Public expenditure in real terms
- T : Taxes in real terms
- D : Aggregate demand in real terms
- D^d : Aggregate demand in real terms for home produced goods
- D^i : Demand for imports in real terms
- X^e : Demand for exports in real terms
- X : Real national income
- P^i : International price level
- B : Balance of Payments deficit or surplus (— B: deficit; + B: surplus) on current account

E, W, M, r, P, Y, N, C, I, are defined as in the preceding sections. Boxes denote exogenous variables (with the proviso that wages are only partially exogenous and thus their box is not solid) and circles the endogenous ones.

The basic difference between the case of a closed economy and that of an open economy is that, in the former, aggregate demand and national income necessarily coincide, while in the open case, they will in general be different. The difference is accounted for by the balance of payments deficit or surplus. In fact, aggregate demand (i.e. the sum of consumption, investment and public expenditure) does not become entirely national income, because part of it is spent on imported goods. On the other hand, national income includes that part of aggregate demand which is not spent on imported goods, as well as the demand coming from abroad.

The fundamental relationships are therefore

[5] $$Y \equiv PX \equiv PD + B$$

in money terms, or

[6] $$X \equiv D + B/P$$

in real terms.

The case of an open economy requires therefore both an analysis of the forces controlling aggregate demand and of those controlling national income. Since there are several feedbacks in the model, a literary exposition of these relationships is very complicated indeed. It is possible, though, by using an appropriate set of simplifying assumptions, to represent diagramatically the relationships we are most interested in, that is, the relationships among money wages, the price level, national income and the balance of payments.

The first relationship we want to derive is that between real aggregate demand and net balance of trade in real terms. For the balance of payments, we have the definitional identity

[7] $$B = PX^{e} - P^{i}D^{i}$$

which can be expressed in real terms as

[8] $$B/P = X^{e} - P^{i}D^{i}/P$$

Aggregate demand in monetary terms is, on the other hand,

[9] $$PD = PD^{d} + P^{i}D^{i}$$

25

Let us assume, as a first approximation, that import expenditure is proportional to aggregate demand in money terms, but that the factor of proportionality, which we denote by k, is a function of the ratio of internal to international prices (27), or

$$[10] \qquad k = k\,(P/P^i)$$

k represents the average and marginal propensity to import; its value lies between 0 and 1 (28). For a given P/P^i, we will have

$$[11] \qquad P^iD^i = kPD$$

Substituting [11] into [4] we derive

$$[12] \qquad \frac{B}{P} = X^e - kD$$

It is convenient at this point to introduce a second simplifying assumption, namely, that the internal price level can be taken as proportional to the money wage, with the proportionality factor changing over time as productivity rises, but independent, in the short run, of the level of economic activity (29).

It can be shown that the result of our analysis would not change in any significant respect if we acknowledged that in the short run the mark-up of prices on wages is likely to rise with the rate of utilization of capacity, as indicated in section 3. But since this refinement would considerably complicate the presentation we shall treat it only sketchily in footnotes and in the appendix.

With P uniquely determined by W and with P^i taken as a *datum*, it follows that W uniquely determines k, and, by virtue

---

(27) While we were reading the galley proofs of this paper, it was suggested to us by Professor Sylos Labini and by Dr. Bruni that recent econometric testing has led them, independently, to conclude that the ratio of internal to international prices is not significant in explaining the level of the demand for imports in Italy. The main explanatory variable seems to be aggregate demand.

(28) Average and marginal propensities need not coincide. A more general formulation of equation [8] is:

$$[8'] \qquad P^iU^i = k\,(PU)^\theta$$

In this case the average propensity to import is greater, smaller or equal to the marginal one according to whether θ is smaller, greater or equal to 1.

(29) This approximation is not altogether unsatisfactory, if we limit ourselves to considering small variations of X and provided $X < X^*$ (where the asterisk denotes the full employment value of X).

26

of [12], also the relation between the value of imports and the level of real aggregate demand D. As for exports, to a good first approximation, they may be expected to depend on world demand and on the ratio of domestic to international prices. But with world demand and prices taken as a *datum* we can conclude that also the level of exports, X^e, is uniquely related to W (30).

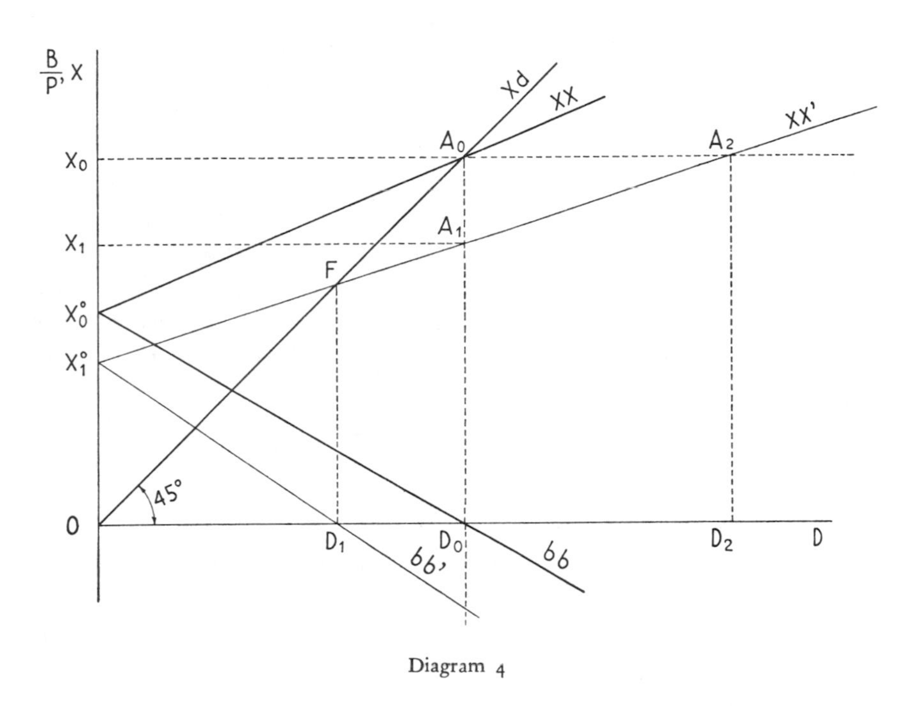

Diagram 4

Equation [12] is now seen to imply that, for a given level of money wages, say W_0, B/P is a linear function of D with intercept X^e_0 and slope $-$k. In diagram 4, this linear relationship is represented by the line *bb*. The relationship indicates that the balance of payments tends to worsen when D rises, because imports increase whereas exports are constant. There is a level of aggregate demand, D, let us call it D_0, for which *bb* cuts the x-axis and thus $B=0$. For

(30) Both *a priori* considerations and the empirical evidence suggest that, for given W and P_i, X^e may be also affected by the rate of utilization of domestic capacity. Taking this effect into consideration would affect the analysis as much as recognizing the dependence of the mark-up on the level of domestic activity. Cf. footnote 31 below.

27

values of D smaller than D_0, B is positive and for D greater than D_0, B is negative.

On the same diagram we can represent the relationship between real national income, X, and real aggregate demand D. Equations [6] and [12] together imply that X, under the assumptions made above, is a linear function of D, being the sum of a linear function of D and of D itself. From the *bb* line we can derive the relationship between X and D. We know that the equation of the straight line going through the origin with an angle of 45° is $X = D$. We will call it the *xd* line. If, for any D, we sum the ordinate of *xd* to the corresponding ordinate of *bb* we get a new line, which we may call *xx*, which represents equation [6]. The ordinate of the point where *xd* and *xx* cross indicates the level of real national income leaving the balance of payments with neither deficit nor surplus (31).

Diagram 4 indicates therefore that there is a unique relationship between aggregate demand, national income and the net balance of payments position. When D goes up, so does national income. B, on the other hand, tends to worsen.

Figure 4 focusses on the dependence of income on aggregate demand. As is apparent from diagram 3, it is also true that D depends on X. This second relation, however, not exhibited in figure 4, is mediated by the policy variables G, T and M controlled by fiscal and monetary authorities. Thus, to a given level of D, there corresponds a given level of X, whereas to a given level of X

(31) If we now abandon the assumption that P is independent of the level of X, and assume that, for given W, P is higher, the higher is national income, the relationships between B/P and D and X and D are no longer linear. *bb* and *xx* (which is still the sum of *bb* and *xd*) become concave towards the origin. The uniqueness of these relationships, which is what we meant to stress, is preserved. Diagram 5 indicates the modifications to introduce in diagram 4 in this non-linear case. If exports are negatively influenced by the level of demand (cf. footnote 30), the curvature of *bb* will be greater and the level of d consistent with $B = 0$, correspondently lower.

Diagram 5

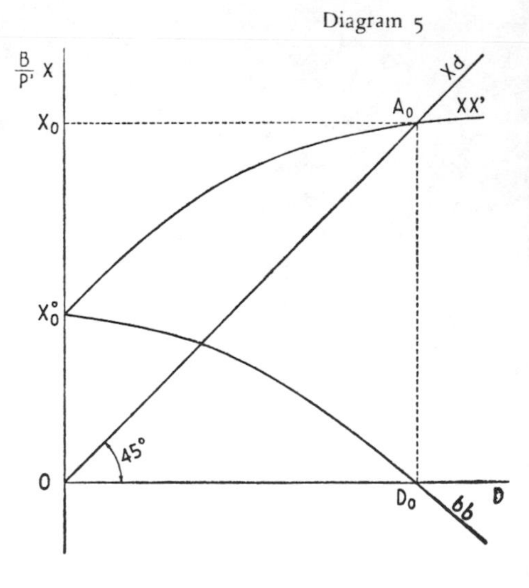

28

may correspond many different values of D depending on the values taken by G, T and M.

The graphs in figure 4 discussed so far correspond to a given money wage, W. A higher level of money wages under our assumptions implies a higher level of prices. This will affect both the intercept and the gradient of the *bb* and the *xx* line. In particular, a rise in prices will increase the propensity to import and therefore make *bb* steeper. At the same time, it will decrease exports and therefore lower the intercept of *bb* on the y-axis. As far as *xx* is concerned, both its slope and intercept are reduced. It follows that the level of aggregate demand which leaves $B=0$ is lower than before. We indicate this new level with D_1. A lower level of X, will correspond to it, as the ordinate of the point F in diagram 4 shows (32).

Some applications of the model

With the help of this framework, we can now examine the consequences of an increase of money wages in excess of the increase in productivity. Let us first suppose that the supply of money is unchanged.

As in the closed economy, firms will react to the increase in costs with an increase in prices. Since international prices are independently set, the higher internal prices will adversely affect aggregate demand on four different counts:

(a) exports (and therefore production and employment) will be reduced. The size of this reduction depends on the elasticity of exports with respect to internal prices (33);

(b) for a given level of aggregate demand in real terms, higher domestic prices push up the demand for imports and decrease the demand for home produced goods. The fall in D^d will reduce X. Again the effects will be more or less strong according to the elasticity of D^i with respect to P (see footnote 27);

---

(32) This conclusion may be easily generalized to the non-linear case discussed in footnote 31.

(33) Demand for exports should be rather elastic because an increase in prices of the exporting country sets two effects in motion: a reduction of consumption in foreign countries of the now more expensive commodity and a shift of purchases from the market where prices have risen to foreign markets.

(c) since D depends on X as X on D, a smaller X will generate a smaller D, which in turn will again reduce X. Part of the reduction in D will be absorbed by the reduction of D^i. There are, in other words, " multiplier " mechanisms leading to a reduction in X larger that the one determined by the initial reduction of D^d and X^e;

(d) finally, the price increase will tend to raise the level of money national income. The expansion of Y will tend to push r up (for an unchanged supply of money) and to reduce D and X in this way. This mechanism is common both to the closed and to the open economy (34).

Thus, employment and national income go down when money wages go up and the supply of money is unchanged. The balance of payments, however, can go either way. In the first place, although the price increase tends to reduce the volume of exports, the increase in their unit value prevents their value (PX^e) from falling as much and may even increase it, if the price elasticity of the demand for exports is less than 1. In the second place, although the price increase tends to direct demand towards imported goods, the fall in income which follows from it, works in the opposite direction i.e. towards a containment of imports. Thus an increase in money wages, even if coupled with a constant money supply, will normally lead to a deterioration of the balance of payments though the opposite result is not impossible if the demand for exports is inelastic and the fall in national income appreciable.

Diagram 4 may be used to illustrate this conclusion. Suppose that *xx* and *bb* and *xx'* and *bb'* represent respectively the relationship between income, aggregate demand and balance of payments before and after the wage and price increase, and suppose that in the former situation, aggregate demand be D_0, so that $B=0$. In the new situation B depends on the new level of D. If aggregate demand is reduced but not beyond D_1, B becomes negative; if, on the other hand, D falls below D_1, B will become positive.

---

(34) It is interesting to note, however, that this mechanism may not work or may work in the opposite direction. In fact if X falls by a sufficiently large amount (because of the three other mechanisms discussed in the text), Y may be reduced too. In this case the demand for money will be reduced and so the rate of interest may fall and in turn reduce the negative effects on demand and income deriving from the first three mechanisms.

The question we want to discuss now is whether, through monetary or fiscal tools, employment could be kept constant in the face of a money wages push and how such policy would affect other relevant variables.

Let us first suppose that wages move *una tantum*, whatever the behaviour of prices and employment. In this case, our model brings forth three conclusions:

(a) it is possible in general to keep employment and national income constant, provided fiscal and monetary policy are used, jointly or separately, to bring about a sufficient expansion of aggregate demand in money terms;

(b) to preserve the level of employment, it is not sufficient to keep real aggregate demand unchanged, as was the case for the closed economy; it is now necessary *to increase real aggregate demand* and therefore to increase aggregate demand in *money terms* proportionally more than wages and prices;

(c) an unchanged level of employment will necessarily be accompanied by a worsening of the balance of payments. The extent of this worsening depends on import and export elasticities (with respect to internal prices) and on the extent of money wage increases.

To establish the foregoing assertions, we can make use once more of diagram 4. Let us suppose that, after the price increase, the two relevant curves are *bb′* and *xx′*. Assertion (a) is the direct consequence of the dependence of X on D. Any level of X (up to full employment) can be reached, provided D is high enough. In particular, the level X_0 can be preserved, where X_0 is the level of national income preceding the wage and price increase.

As for assertion (b), we can start by noting that if D is unchanged at the level D_0, in the new situation represented by the *bb′* and *xx′* lines, national income would go down from X_0 to X_1. To keep X at the X_0, D has to increase from D_0 to D_2. D_2 is the abscissa of A_2, that is, of the point where *xx′* cuts the line X_0A_0, and is necessarily larger than D_0. Since for an unchanged level of employment, the wage-price ratio is unchanged, aggregate demand in money terms must increase by a larger amount than the increase in wages (35).

(35) Denoting with $\omega = W_1/W_0$ the ratio of wages in two successive moments, if employment is constant at X_0, $P_1/P_2 = W_1/W_0 = \omega$. Since X_0 corresponds, in the new situation, to D_2, with $D_2 > D_1$ we shall have $P_1D_2/P_0D_0 > \omega$.

The third conclusion can also be readily verified from the diagram. Given the new position of *bb*, B would be negative even if D were to remain at D_0. This conclusion is reinforced if D has to increase to D_2 in order to keep employment unchanged.

Similar, but even more pessimistic, conclusions follow if wages rise further in response to the initial increase in prices because of mechanisms like the " sliding scale " or because of trade union insistence on a specified level of *real* wages.

In this case too, it is possible to preserve a given level of employment, but the consequences on the balance of payments will be all the worse because of successive wage and price increases. The explicit consideration of the balance of payments therefore makes even more doubtful a policy of monetary expansion when prices and wages tend to move in step.

On the other hand, international trade opens two avenues for moderating the wage-price spiral, which do not exist in the closed economy. In the first place, prices tend to increase less in an open than in a closed economy. This is due to the strength of international competition both inside the country and in foreign markets. Therefore the wage-price spiral is weaker.

In the second place, since part of the wages is spent on imported commodities, their real purchasing power is increased (insofar as international prices are unchanged). Therefore, if wage movements are determined by unions aiming at a given level of real wages, the wage-price spiral will grow weaker through time (36). It is to be stressed, though, that the burden of this milder inflation is borne by the balance of payments, that will turn negative, even under the favourable hypothesis of a final disappearance of the wage-price spiral.

On the basis of the conclusions we reached in this section, we can examine the opinion, which is largely current in Italy, that the deterioration of the balance of payments in 1963 can be traced to the change in the composition of aggregate demand and in particular to the increase in consumption following the redistribution of income from profits to wages. We may note, in the first place, that in our analysis, thus far, we have had no occasion to refer to the composition of demand. This feature is due to the

(36) Moreover, if productivity per man is rising, and unions aim at a given real wage, the rate of inflation will tend to decrease through time for this reason too.

simplifying assumption, introduced in equation [11], that expenditure on imported commodities depends on the *level* of aggregate demand and *not on its composition.* When this assumption is abandoned, the relationship between national income, aggregrate demand and the balance of payments is no longer independent of the composition of aggregate demand. But it is not possible to establish, on a *a priori* basis, whether a change in the composition of demand, towards greater consumption and smaller investment is going to affect favourably or unfavourably the balance of payments. The answer depends on the marginal propensity to import of the two large classes of commodities. A change in the composition of demand towards greater consumption will affect adversely the balance of payments *only if the marginal propensity to import is larger for consumption than for investment goods.* If the reverse case is true, the balance of payments will improve and if the two propensities are equal, composition does not make any difference (see Appendix 4 for further discussion of this point).

To the best of our knowledge, no reliable estimates are available at present as to the relevant marginal propensities, i.e. the response of imports to a marginal increase respectively in consumption and investment expenditure. A superficial examination of the data casts serious doubts on the hypothesis that the marginal propensity is higher for consumption goods than for investment goods; indeed, at least in terms of average propensities, the reverse is definitely true. In any event a numerical example provided in Appendix 4 shows that the difference between the marginal propensities would have to be quite large for the composition of demand to have any appreciable effect on total imports (37).

Our analysis implies instead that the worsening of the balance of trade is to be attributed to the cost and price inflation resulting initially from the wage push fed by an expansionary monetary policy, aimed at maintaining full employment in the face of rising prices, which brought into play the wage-price spiral mechanisms outlined in section IV.

---

(37) A recent econometric analysis, again reported to us by Professor Sylos Labini, while we were reading proofs of this paper, estimates the propensity to import investment goods to be consistently higher than the propensity to import consumption goods. Furthermore, it appears that in the years after 1960 both propensities moved up, still preserving, though, their relative position. This may be due to internal price increases or to lower barriers on imports (especially from Common Market countries) or to both effects together.

It is true that in 1963 there were unusually large increases in certain imports of consumption goods, notably meat and cars. This phenomenon caught the attention of contemporary observers and led them to associate the deterioration of the balance of payments with the increased consumption and the latter with the shift in the distribution of income. But even apart from the distinct possibility that these sharp increases may have reflected in part transitory phenomena, what is usually forgotten is the equally remarkable increase in investment goods imports in 1963 and the subsequent sharp decrease accompanying the abatement of investment in the following period, which contributed very significantly to the improvement of the balance of payments. Of course, we are not denying that a fall in consumption would have reduced imports of consumption goods; the point is that such a fall, if not offset by a corresponding expansion of investment demand, would have led to a fall in income and employment, while, if offset by the expansion of investment, would have merely led to a replacement of imports of consumption goods with (possibly larger) imports of investment goods.

VI

From the discussion of the preceding sections, the differences between our model and that of the Bank should be apparent.

Both analyses agree that the origins of balance of payments and inflationary problems in Italy are to be found in the large increase in money wages, far beyond the increases in productivity, which unions managed to obtain during 1961 and 1962. But from this common starting point, the two models move in different directions.

According to the Bank's model, the unfavourable consequences of the wage surge spring from the threat of an income redistribution which would increase the average propensity to consume. This would, on the one hand, reduce employment and aggregate demand and, on the other, generate a deficit of the balance of payments.

According to this analysis the Bank, through the great monetary expansion of the period 1961-63, aimed at protecting the level of investment and employment by making it possible for the higher wages to be reflected into higher prices, thus preserving the initial distribution of income.

The Bank however could not entirely prevent some redistribution of income, in part because it was cramped by balance of payments considerations. The redistribution of income together with the rising prices caused a deterioration in the balance of payments in 1962 and, more dramatically, in 1963, and also gradually worked its unfavourable effects on investments, determining the fall in employment and output of the years 1964-65 (38).

Our own analysis concurs with that of the Bank in some respects but differs crucially in several others. It agrees with the conclusion that the unrestrained monetary expansion of the early years permitted the maintenance of the level of employment in the face of the wage push, through the expansion of aggregate demand; but it suggests that it was the expansion of demand that kept within bounds the redistribution of income, and not the other way around. It further implies that in the absence of direct and effective controls over wages, the chosen course of action was bound to bring into play a wage-price spiral, causing in turn growing deterioration of the balance of payments. It could not therefore provide a permanent solution but only postpone the day of reckoning. Clearly, with limited international reserves, a country cannot indefinitely cope with a large and growing deficit. Conceivably devaluation might provide some transitional relief by improving the competitive position of the domestic product. But unless a country is prepared to embark on the road of repeated devaluation (probably at shorter and shorter intervals) sooner or later it will have to put an end to rising prices by checking the expansion of aggregate demand, through monetary and/or fiscal measures, and accepting the consequent unavoidable contraction in real income and employment.

The alternative course of action would have consisted in containing aggregate demand from the very beginning, thus preventing prices from increasing beyond a limited and unavoidable response to increased unit costs, but at the same time accepting immediately the resulting increase in unemployment. Because of this costly consequence, this alternative seems very unattractive and this may help to explain why it was not adopted as soon as the danger of inflation became apparent. It must be remembered however that, if our analysis is valid, sooner or later the fall in income and employment is unavoidable. Furthermore, this harsh medicine also tends to pave the way for a gradual return to full employment with a satisfactory ex-

---

(38) The reader may find it useful to take a fresh look at the passage on pag. 486 of the Relazione annuale 1964 cited in footnote 6.

ternal balance. It is in fact reasonable to suppose that the combined effect of unemployment and depressed profits will tend to reduce wage demands and awards, containing the wage increases within the increases in productivity, thus leading to stable or possibly falling prices. Under these conditions, and especially if foreign prices exhibit some rising trend, the competitive position of the economy will gradually improve. In terms of our figure 4, this means that the line *bb* which had been pushed towards the origin by the initial push of wages and prices will tend to shift gradually back, raising the level of aggregate demand and employment consistent with external balance.

The developments of the Italian economy seem to conform rather well with our analysis, with one possible exception, to wit the painfully slow recovery of employment since 1964. However, the fact that the balance of payments has exhibited a substantial and growing surplus in the last two years indicates that this result must be attributed to a failure of monetary and fiscal authorities to reflate aggregate demand at a sustained pace still consistent with the requirement of external balance.

The upshot of the above discussion is that the only real dilemma posed by the initial wage push is, fundamentally, one of timing. Is it preferable to adopt a restrictive stand from the beginning or can something be gained by postponing the harsh treatment?

Our analysis suggests a rather unequivocal answer to this question: the sooner the better. The reason for this conclusion should be clear. The longer the span of time over which the inflationary spiral is allowed to proceed, the higher will be the price level reached by the time the inflationary process is checked. Now, from figure 4, we know that a high price level implies a lower and steeper *bb* curve; and this in turn implies that the higher the price level, the lower will be the level of aggregate demand and employment consistent with external balance. Thus, when a policy of containment is finally adopted in order to reestablish external balance, it will be necessary to create *more* unemployment and the process of reabsorption of it will be more drawn out.

Our model enables us also to throw some light on an issue that has received considerable attention in recent years, namely, whether it is preferable to control aggregate demand though monetary or through fiscal tools. Central banks frequently seem to favour the latter; but apart from the very understandable desire of the monetary authority to shift the burden of unpopular measures to the Government, is there any valid ground for choosing? The prevailing view among economists nowadays is that the two tools differ primarily in terms of their effects on the *composition of demand*. Monetary tools tend to affect investment and fiscal tools to influence consumption. This proposition provides a useful first approximation though it admits of significant exceptions: fiscal policy can be used to provide incentives or disincentives to invest and monetary policy may have some effect on consumers' investments in durable goods, which are conventionally treated as a component of consumption.

According to our model, the behaviour of employment and of the net external balance on current account depends, to a first approximation, only on the behaviour of aggregate demand and not on its *composition*. It follows that, given some target level of aggregate demand, it is immaterial, at least to a first approximation, whether the target is aimed at through monetary or fiscal tools. This does not necessarily mean that there are no grounds at all for choosing; it does mean, however, that the choice should rest on considerations other than their differential effects on the balance of payments. Among these other considerations one might mention in particular: (a) speed of enforcement and flexibility; (b) effects on capital movements; and (c) long run effects on the stock of physical capital. It would take us too far afield to pursue items (b) and (c). However, with respect to item (a), we suspect that in Italy, and in most other countries, the monetary tool offers distinct advantages, especially when the goal is to reduce aggregate demand.

For the sake of completeness it must also be acknowledged that fiscal tools can be used not only to control aggregate demand but also to influence the demand for specific commodities. It follows that, in principle, fiscal measures could be relied upon to modify the relation between aggregate demand and employment on the one hand and the current balance on the other, by steering demand towards domestic products or products with lower import content. In terms of our figure 4, such measures would have the effect of shifting the *bb* curve away from the origin. It is doubtful however that such selective tools offer much room for manoeuvring in view of existing international agreements designed to prevent or severely limit their use.

Franco Modigliani
Giorgio La Malfa

Cambridge, Mass.

37

APPENDIX

APPENDIX I: *A model of the interaction of real and monetary phenomena in a closed economy.*

Notation:
X = Real national income
Y = Money national income
P = The price level
W = The money wage
r = The rate of interest and credit conditions
C = Consumption
I = Investment
M = The quantity of money
N = Employment
G = Public expenditure
T = Taxes

The model:
[1] $X = C + I + G$
[2] $I = I(r, X)$
[3] $C = C(X, T)$
[4] $N = N(X)$
[5] $P = P(W, X)$
[6] $Y = PX$
[7] $r = L(M, Y)$

There are seven unknowns: X, I, C, N, P, Y, r. The solution of the system depends on the parameters: M, W, T and G. The model is very much simplified, but it preserves the central feature of our analysis, that is, the interrelationship of monetary and real phenomena expressed in equations [1], [2], [5], [6] and [7] (39).

(39) For a fuller analysis of a model of this sort, see FRANCO MODIGLIANI, " The Monetary Mechanism and its Interaction with Real Phenomena ", *Review of Economics and Statistics*, No. 1, part 2, 1963, pp. 79-107.

38

APPENDIX II: *Effects of income redistribution on national income.*

We assume that investment is a function of actual profits. Denoting investment by I and profits by π, we write (40):

$$I = I(\pi) \qquad [1]$$

If investment positively depends on profits, we shall have:

$$\frac{dI}{d\pi} > 0 \qquad [2]$$

The average propensity to save, s, depends on the distribution of income, so that we may write in general:

$$s = s(\pi) \qquad [3]$$

If there are only two classes of income, wages and profits, s will change with a change in the distribution of income if the propensities to save of the two classes differ. If they are different, it is, *a priori*, reasonable to expect s to be an increasing function of π. Thus we have

$$\frac{ds}{d\pi} \geq 0 \qquad [4]$$

National income depends on I and s. The relationship is

$$X = \frac{I}{s} \qquad [5]$$

where X stands for national income.

The effect of a change in profits on national income is:

$$\frac{dX}{d\pi} = \frac{\partial X}{\partial I}\frac{dI}{d\pi} + \frac{\partial X}{\partial s}\frac{ds}{d\pi} \qquad [6]$$

and since $\frac{\partial X}{\partial I} = \frac{1}{s}$ and $\frac{\partial X}{\partial s} = -\frac{I}{s^2}$, by substituting in [6], we get

$$\frac{dX}{d\pi} = \frac{1}{s}\frac{dI}{d\pi} - \frac{I}{s^2}\frac{ds}{d\pi} \qquad [7]$$

It follows that the sign of $\frac{dX}{d\pi}$ depends on the sign of

$$\left[\left(\frac{1}{s}\frac{dI}{d\pi}\right) - \left(\frac{I}{s^2}\frac{ds}{d\pi}\right)\right]$$

(40) In fact we should write $I = I(\pi, r)$, but since we will assume that r is constant, we can specialize the function into the form [1].

39

Let us put this expression in a more readily interpretable form by multiplying both terms by $s\pi/I$. We can conclude that

$$[8] \quad \begin{cases} \frac{dX}{d\pi} > 0 \text{ if } \frac{\pi}{I}\frac{dI}{d\pi} > \frac{\pi}{s}\frac{ds}{d\pi} \\ \frac{dX}{d\pi} = 0 \text{ if } \frac{\pi}{I}\frac{dI}{d\pi} = \frac{\pi}{s}\frac{ds}{d\pi} \\ \frac{dX}{d\pi} < 0 \text{ if } \frac{\pi}{I}\frac{dI}{d\pi} < \frac{\pi}{s}\frac{ds}{d\pi} \end{cases}$$

$\frac{\pi}{I}\frac{dI}{d\pi}$ and $\frac{\pi}{s}\frac{ds}{d\pi}$ are two elasticity coefficients, namely, the elasticity of investment with respect to profits and the elasticity of the propensity to save with respect to profits. If the former is larger than the latter (as is indeed the case if $\frac{d\pi}{ds} = 0$) a redistribution of income will reduce national income, if the reverse is true, national income will increase, and if the two elasticities are equal, national income will be independent of the distribution of income.

Let us now consider the case of extreme propensities to save, namely, that profits are completely saved and wages completely consumed. In this case [2] becomes $\frac{dI}{d\pi} = 1$ and [4] becomes $\frac{ds}{d\pi} = \frac{1}{X} = \frac{s}{I}$

Inserting these values in [7], we can rewrite it as

$$[7'] \quad \frac{dX}{d\pi} = \frac{1}{s} - \frac{Is}{s^2 I} = 0.$$

In this case, national income is independent of income distribution, although investment and the propensity to save both depend on it.

Appendix III: *The dynamics of cost inflation.*

In this appendix we shall give two examples of the way in which the wage-price relationships we discussed in section 4 may give rise to an inflationary process.

Let us assume that prices depend on wages according to the linear relationship

$$[1] \quad P_t = \alpha W_t$$

where P_t is the price level at time t, W_t the money wage rate at time t, and α a constant greater than 1.

Let us suppose, moreover, that wage bargaining by the unions is aimed at a given real wage rate, say

$$[2] \qquad \frac{W_t}{P^e_t} = \beta$$

where β is a constant greater than 0 and P^e_t is the price level expected for time t, and let us finally assume that union expectations are static, as far as prices are concerned, i.e., that they expect prices at t to be the same as prices at time t-1. This may be written as

$$[3] \qquad P^t_e = P_{t-1}$$

Supposing wage negotiations to be successful, money wages at time t will be $W_t = \beta\, P^e_t = \beta\, P_{t-1}$. Making use of [1] we get

$$[4] \qquad W_t = \alpha\, \beta\, W_{t-1}$$

This is a difference equation of first order with solution

$$[5] \qquad W(t) = W(0)\, (\alpha\, \beta)^t$$

where W(t) are wages at time t and W(0) is a constant to be determined by the initial conditions of the system.

For inflation to arise we must have

$$[6] \qquad \alpha\, \beta > 1$$

in this case wages rise through time. If $\alpha\beta = 1$ wages are constant and if $\alpha\beta < 1$ money wages tend to fall through time.

Price movements may be described in an analogous way, i.e. (by substitution of [1] in [4])

$$[7] \qquad P(t) = P(0)\, (\alpha\, \beta)^t$$

with prices rising, staying constant or falling according to the value of $\alpha\beta$.

The meaning of condition [6] is that the price-wage ratio imposed by firms (α) is larger than the price-wage ratio desired by the unions ($1/\beta$). Since unions manage to get wages to rise to the extent they desire but firms adjust prices to the new wage levels, inflation follows.

Our second example illustrates the possibility, which we referred to in section IV, of a growing rate of inflation through time.

Let us keep equation [1] and insert in lieu of [4]

$$[4'] \qquad W_t = \beta_1\, P_t + \beta_2\, P_{t-1}$$

where

$$[8] \qquad \beta_1 + \beta_2 = \beta \text{ and } \beta_i \geqslant 0 \; (i = 1,2).$$

with β_1 depending on the recent rate of increase of prices and tending to β. This formulation reflects the hypothesis that union tend to shorten the period between successive bargaining periods when prices react, by rising, to wage increases. [4′] may be rewritten in the form $W_t = . \frac{\alpha\,\beta_2\,W_{t-1}}{(1 - \alpha\,\beta_1)}$ a difference equation whose solution is

$$[5'] \qquad W(t) = W(0)\left[\frac{(\alpha\beta_2)}{(1 - \alpha\beta_1)}\right]^t$$

[5′] will determine a positive rate of increase of wages and prices if

$$[6'] \qquad \alpha\,\beta_2 > 1 - \alpha\,\beta_1$$

By using condition [8] we can show [6′] to be equivalent to [6]. In fact, $\alpha\beta_2 = \alpha(\beta - \beta_1) = \alpha\beta - \alpha\beta_1$ and substituting this expression in [6′] we get $\alpha\beta > 1$.

We shall now denote with λ the expression $\frac{\alpha\,\beta_2}{1 - \alpha\beta_1}$ and find out how it varies when β_1 changes.

In the first place, for $\beta_1 = 0$, $\beta_2 = \beta$ and [5′] and [5] become equal. Let us now take the derivative of λ with respect to β_1:

$$[9] \qquad \frac{d\lambda}{d\beta_1} = \frac{-\alpha(1 - \alpha\beta_1) + \alpha\,(\beta - \beta_1)\alpha}{(1 - \alpha\,\beta_1)^2} = \frac{-\alpha + \alpha^2\,\beta}{(1 - \alpha\,\beta_1)^2} = \frac{\alpha\,(\alpha\,\beta - 1)}{(1 - \alpha\,\beta_1)^2}$$

If $\alpha\,\beta > 1$, [9] will be positive. This indicates that the rate of inflation is a positive function of β_1. Moreover for $\beta_1 = 1/\alpha$ the denominator of [9] is null. On the other hand, condition [6], if satisfied, guarantees that the numerator of λ is bound away from 0 when $\beta_1 = 1/\alpha$. Thus the rate of inflation tends to increase without limit.

Appendix IV: *A model of the interaction of real and monetary phenomena in an open economy.*

Notation:

X = Real national income

Y = Money national income

P = The price level

P^i = The international price level

D = Aggregate demand in real terms

D^d = Aggregate demand in real terms for home produced goods

D^i = Aggregate demand in real terms for imported goods

X^e = Exports in real terms

42

Q = World demand
B = Net balance of payments in money terms
W = The money wage rate
r = The rate of interest and credit conditions
C = Consumption
I = Investment
M = The quantity of money
N = Employment
G = Public expenditure
T = Taxes

The model - Identities and definitions:

[1] $$X = D^d + X^e$$

Definition of real national income: domestic output for home use + exports.

[2] $$PD = PD^d + P^iD^i$$

Definition of aggregate demand in money terms: expenditure on domestically produced commodities and services + import expenditure.

[3] $$D = C + I + G$$

Real aggregate demand: Consumption + investment + public expenditure.

[4] $$B = PX^e - P^iD^i$$

Value of exports - Value of imports.

[5] $$Y = PX$$

Money national income.

Other equations:

[6] $$N = N(X)$$

Employment as a function of national income.

[7] $$X^e = X^e(Q, P, P^i)$$

Exports depend on world demand, national and international prices.

[8] $$P^iD^i = D^i(PD, P, P^i) = Pf(D, P^i/P)$$

Imports expenditure is a function of aggregate demand in money terms, internal and international prices. It is homogeneous of the first degree in the

43

three variables and can therefore be written in either of the two forms. From [8] we derive as an implication: $D^d = D - \frac{P^iD^i}{P} = D - f(D, P^i/P)$.

$$[9] \qquad P = h(X/X^*)W$$

Prices are proportional to the ratio of wages to productivity per man. Since productivity may be taken as constant in the short period, prices are proportional to money wages, the proportionality factor being given by the ratio of actual to full employment national income.

$$[10] \qquad I = I(r, X, P^i/P)$$

Investments depend on the rate of interest, on real national income and on the ratio of international to internal prices.

$$[11] \qquad C = C(X, P^i/P, T)$$

Consumption depends on national income, the ratio of international to internal prices and tax policy.

$$[12] \qquad r = L(M, Y)$$

The rate of interest depends on the money supply and money national income.

Properties of the model. The role of aggregate demand.

There are 12 endogenous variables in this model. They are: X, D^d, X^e, D, D^i, C, I, B, P, Y, N, r.

There are three exogenous ones: P^i, Q, W, and three instrumental (or policy) variables: M, T, G.

The model we have presented has an interesting property, which is at the base of the analysis carried in the text. The property is that, if one takes equations [1], [2], [4]-[9], these 8 equations contain 9 of the 12 endogenous variables. Therefore it is possible to solve this sub-system for 8 of its unknowns as a function of the remaining one. For instance, every variable of it can be expressed as a function of real aggregate demand, D. Figure 4 of the text and figure 5 in footnote 31 represent the relationship between balance of payments and aggregate demand and between real national income and aggregate demand.

The four remaining equations can be used to analyse the relationship of D to X, a relationship influenced by the policy variables, M, T and G. It is interesting to note that these three variables do not appear in the sub-system [1], [2], [4]-[9].

44

If monetary or fiscal policy aims at attaining a given level of X, say X, this adds one equation to the system and sets a constraint between the three policy variables in the sense that, given two of them, the third one has to assume a certain specified value. The same is true if one intends to have any other endogenous variable assume a given value, say $B = \overline{B}$. It is not possible, though, in our model, for two endogenous variables to assume exogenously prescribed values, unless they are, by fluke, mutually consistent. Thus, in general, an economy cannot aim, at the same time, at a certain level of X — say to full employment national income — and at a certain level of B — say $B = 0$. In this case, for the two conditions to be satisfied an exogenous variable has to become endogenous. The most likely candidate should be W. There exists in general a value of W — say W* — such that $X = X^*$ and $B = 0$. What is this value of W? It is the value implied by X* in equation [9] once the internal price level consistent with $B = 0$ has been determined from equation [4] and the rest of the system. We may reach exactly that value by chance or it may be brought to that level if it is lower. It is difficult, though, that it could be brought to that value if it is too high, as is usually the case. In these circumstances, the same results might be achieved through a currency devaluation, that is, through a change in the ratio of internal to international prices. If W is fixed in money terms and does not move, then this measure might prove effective. Changes of W will, on the other hand, largely frustrate the purpose of the devaluation.

A generalization of the model. The effect of the composition of aggregate demand on the balance of trade.

Some of the properties of the model we have been discussing depend on the form of equation of aggregate demand. To be more general, we may rewrite [8] as

$$[8'] \qquad \frac{P^i D^i}{P} = f\,(C, I, G, P^i/P).$$

Denoting with f_C, f_I and f_G the partial derivatives of [8′] with respect to C, I and G, we can still get [8] in the special case of $f_C = f_I = f_G$. In general, however, B is not independent of the composition of demand. It can be shown, though, that changes in the composition of demand can have but limited effects on B/P.

To establish this result we have to measure the effect on B/P of a change in consumption accompanied by a compensating change in investment. Let us start from the fundamental identity $X = U + B/P$ which can be rewritten, by using [3], [4] and [8'], as

$$X = C + I + G + X^{\bullet} - f(C, I, G, P^{i}/P) \qquad [13]$$

Differentiating equation [13] totally with respect to C and imposing the condition that X is unchanged, we get

$$0 = 1 + \frac{dI}{dC} - f_C - f_I \frac{dI}{dC} \qquad [14]$$

which can be written as

$$\frac{dI}{dC}\bigg|_{X=\bar{X}} = - \frac{1 - f_C}{1 - f_I} \qquad [14']$$

We now differentiate [4] with respect to C and get

$$\frac{dB}{dC} = - P\left[f_C + f_I \frac{dI}{dC}\right] \qquad [15]$$

Substituting [14'] in [15] we get

$$\frac{dB}{dC}\bigg|_{X=\bar{X}} = - P\left[f_C - f_I \frac{(1 - f_C)}{(1 - f_I)}\right] = - P \frac{f_C - f_I}{1 - f_I} \qquad [16]$$

which can be rewritten (P being constant for this analysis) as

$$\frac{dB}{d(PC)}\bigg|_{X=\bar{X}} = - \frac{f_C - f_I}{1 - f_I} \qquad [17]$$

If $f_C = f_I$ the balance of payments is unaffected by a change in the composition of demand. If the former is smaller than the latter, to increase consumption will improve B, and if the propensity to import consumption goods is greater than the propensity to import investment goods, an increase in consumption will worsen the balance of payments. But, even in this case, the effects on the balance of payments are likely to be small unless the two propensities differ by a sufficiently large amount.

A numerical example may be useful to make the order of magnitude of the phenomenon quite clear. In 1963, Italian imports represented roughly 18% of aggregate demand. We may take this figure as an approximation to the marginal propensity to import and consider it a weighted average of the marginal propensity to import consumption and investment goods. Let us suppose that f_C is 30% higher than f_I. Since consumption represented roughly 85%

46

of national income, we can calculate that f_I is approximately 0.15 and f_C is 0.20 Inserting this data into [14'] and [17] we get respectively

$$[18] \qquad \frac{dI}{dC} = -\frac{0{,}80}{0{,}85} = -0.94.$$

and

$$[19] \qquad \frac{dB}{d(PC)} = -\frac{0{,}20 - 0{,}15}{1 - 0{,}15} = -0{,}06.$$

Thus, a reduction in consumption of the order of a thousand billion lire, compensated by investments for roughly 940 billion lire (which is as high as 13% of total investment in 1963), would improve the balance of payments by some 60 billions, barely a 1% of total imports of 1963.

Moreover, as noted in the text, there are no indications that f_C is larger than f_I. On the contrary, some evidence, which we have already referred to, points in the opposite direction.

F. M. - G. L. M.

Errata

Page 18, last paragraph, line 1: "aggregate demand" should read "aggregate real demand."

Page 18, last paragraph, line 4: "aggregate money demand" should read "aggregate nominal demand."

Page 26, line 9: "Substituting [11] into [4]" should read "Substituting [11] into [8]."

Page 26, footnote 28: equation [8'] should read "$P^iD^i = k(PD)^\theta$."

Page 27, first line: "[12]" should read "[11]."

Page 28, footnote 31, 2 lines from the bottom: "d" should read "D."

Page 29, line 12: delete comma after "A lower level of X."

Page 40, 4 lines after equation [8]: "$\frac{d\pi}{ds} = 0$" should read "$\frac{ds}{d\pi} - 0$."

Page 46, line 1: "$X = U + B/P$" should read "$X = D + B/P$."

The 1974 Report of the President's Council of Economic Advisors: A Critique of Past and Prospective Economic Policies

By Franco Modigliani*

I. How Good a Year Was 1973?

Judged by traditional standards, the year 1973 might appear as a success story for economic policy makers. Real *GNP* rose by just about 6 percent relative to 1972, a rate of growth right at the midpoint of the rosy forecasts made at the beginning of the year which clustered unusually narrowly around 6 percent; employment rose by well over 3 percent; productivity (in the private sector) by nearly 3 percent; and hourly wages (adjusted for overtime and industry shifts) rose a relatively modest 6.2 percent, the lowest figure since 1968 and almost puny when compared with the experience of many other industrial countries. Even the *GNP* deflator increased but 5.5 percent, clearly outside the fashionable forecasted range of 2.5 to 4 percent, but still not outlandish in this era of worldwide inflation, quite commonly at the two-digit rate.

Needless to say, these figures, the kind one would probably hear widely quoted if this were election time, are extremely misleading; they largely reflect the total inadequacy of the customary year-over-year comparisons. The truth is that, by most standards, 1973 was more nearly a debacle than a success story for economic policy, with the country gripped by the worst rate of inflation of any postwar peace year, with many commodities hard to get at times, both for consumers and for producers, with temper-raising gas queues a frequent sight at the turn of the year, and the dollar—no longer as sound as a dollar!

Measured from fourth quarter to fourth quarter (the standard that I shall use hereafter unless otherwise stated),[1] the rise in the *GNP* deflator was 7.1 (7.7 if measured by a fixed weight price index, Table C-4); but wholesale prices rose 17 percent—more than 30 percent for farm products and processed food and 12 percent for industrial commodities—and the cost of living by 8.4 percent. Furthermore since the increase in hourly wages during 1973 itself was only 6.7 percent, real hourly wages adjusted for overtime and industry shifts *declined* rather steadily throughout the year by a total of nearly 2 percent, and

* Massachusetts Institute of Technology. I am indebted to my colleagues, Stanley Fischer, Robert Merton, Paul Samuelson, and Lester Thurow, for reading a preliminary draft and making valuable suggestions, as well as for the opportunity I have had to discuss with them, on numerous occasions, many of the issues analyzed in this review. I also wish to express my thanks to Albert Ando for help in designing the simulations reported in Section IV and in interpreting them.

[1] This measure, it should be acknowledged, is not without shortcomings of its own, mainly that it is independent of the path followed by the variable within the year. One might remedy this shortcoming by taking as a measure the average quarterly growth above the last quarter of the previous year (which is equivalent to a weighted average of the quarterly growth, weighted 4, 3, 2, 1). For my present purpose, however, I feel that the last quarter to last quarter measure is the most suitable, though recognizing that, because the growth of *GNP* was by far largest in the first quarter, this measure may somewhat underrate the performance of the year.

real weekly earnings declined even more, by 3.1 percent. This is a performance without precedent on similar scale in the postwar *U.S.* economy, except possibly for 1951. Nor, surprisingly enough, were these soaring prices and reduced real wages the hallmark of a "capitalist paradise." There was no great leap in corporate profits, which in real terms increased only 5 percent, while total property income (profits plus interest plus rents) increased a much more modest $3\frac{1}{2}$ percent—an apparent puzzle which will be resolved shortly. And, to boot, despite the rise in profits, the stock market, reflecting among other things the deep anxieties of the country, lost 20 percent in the course of the year. Since there was but one important exogenous shock in 1973 that could not reasonably have been anticipated, namely the so-called Arab oil embargo, and that came only at the tail end, one would be led to conclude that the disastrous performance outlined above was largely the result of an ill-conceived and ill-implemented economic policy.

In advance of reading the Economic Report of the President I had been inclined to this conclusion, attributing the poor record to four major policy mistakes: i) an overexpansionary aggregate demand policy, both fiscal and monetary in 1972, especially in the last half of the year, and in early 1973; ii) inadequate provisions for expanding agricultural output after the sales to Russia and China; iii) encouraging or at least tolerating the depreciation of the dollar, especially after the February devaluation and through the third quarter; iv) the retention, and even more, the poor management of an extensive system of controls on prices, wages, etc.

Holding these views, which I had partly expressed in print,[2] I looked forward eagerly to study the Council's Report to see whether it would provide grounds for modifying these negative judgements, or explanations of what had caused the errors.

[2] Notably in a series of articles in the Milan, Italy, newspaper *Corriere Della Sera*.

II. The Council Account of Developments and Policy in 1973

A study of the Council's account of developments and aggregate demand management in 1972–73 seems to me to provide little ground for modifying my prior view that the Administration and the Council managed to repeat the terribly costly error committed by the Democratic Administration in the mid-1960's, namely that of permitting the rate of expansion of the economy to accelerate as we were getting closer to full utilization of resources. In 1963, when unemployment stood at an average of 5.7, the rate of growth of *GNP* was but 4.4; in 1964 with unemployment down to 5.2, it was 4.5, but in 1965, which opened with unemployment down to 5 percent, growth accelerated to 8.2 percent bringing unemployment to the critical area of 4 percent; and, as that line was being crossed at the turn of the year, the growth was allowed to leap to over 9.4 percent in the fourth quarter and 8 percent in the first quarter of 1966. Lack of resources finally slowed down the growth in the rest of the year to below 4 percent, but at the cost of putting pressure on prices which in some months grew at a rate approaching 10 percent at wholesale and 6 percent for the cost of living. This opened up the inflationary era from which we are still unable to extricate ourselves.

Ever since that disastrous experience I had been in dread of a "second," and as the Nixon Administration game plan developed, my worries kept increasing. By July of 1971, the Administration had brought unemployment back to the 6 percent area, income was growing at a sluggish 3 percent or so, yet no fiscal actions were being taken to speed the recovery and the monetarists were giving hell to the Federal Reserve because the money supply in the previous six months had grown at over 12 percent. At that time, testifying before the Joint Committee on the Economic Report, I pleaded for more stimulating policies, explaining that, given the fiscal inaction, there was nothing wrong with a 12 percent growth of M_1 at that time, and that, anyway, the M_1 series, and especially the seasonal adjustments, were too unreliable to warrant paying attention to every wiggle of the annualized rate of growth of M_1,[3] and finally expressed my alarm in the following rather frank terms: "What I am concerned with is the following thing, that if we have a slow recovery in 1971, as we seem to have and we are approaching election time, there will be all kinds of measures taken to stimulate the economy quickly at that time, to be sure we get through the election time with a reasonable level of employment, and then we will be picking exactly the wrong tactic; namely, going slowly when we are far away from the full employment goal, and running quickly when we get close to the goal, with a large chance to overshooting it" (1971, p. 123).

I submit that this statement came pretty close to anticipating correctly one of the major causes of trouble in 1973 (though I shall leave it to the reader to decide whether my suggested motivation was the relevant one!). In 1972, as unemployment was moving rapidly down, the rate of growth accelerated to 7 percent; in the last (and election) quarter, with unemployment down to just over 5 percent, the rate of growth exceeded 8 percent.

All this was achieved through a monetary-fiscal policy mix which was extraordinarily expansive throughout the year and became even more so at the year's end. The actual federal government budget deficit on *NIA* account was $16 billion, a figure which further rises possibly by as much as $9 billion, if one accepts the suggestion of the Economic Report (pp. 29–30) that, in terms of effect on consumers' expenditure, overwithholding in 1972, estimated at some $9 billion, should be primarily treated as an addition to the stock of claims of the private sector against the government, rather than as ordinary tax. With this correction, the Council estimates the full employment deficit in 1972 at $7 billion, using the conventional measure of "full employment" (4 percent unemployment) and at over $10 billion using a variable measure of "full-employment unemployment" corrected for labor force composition, as now recommended fairly persuasively by the Council (p. 30 and Table 1). If one does not accept fully the overwithholding correction, then the full-employment deficit would be lower, possibly, in the limit, down to $1.5 billion; however, since the Council seems to regard close to full correction as appropriate, it could hardly fail to regard 1972 fiscal policy as highly stimulative. Furthermore, in the year's last quarter, a sudden spurt of expenditure brought the actual deficit to an annual rate of $23 billion, implying a full-employment deficit of $19 billion (presumably corrected for overwithholding, Table 17, p. 80). To be sure, some $10 billion of this increase represented the first installment of the new revenue sharing system, and was therefore partly offset by an increase in the surplus of state and local governments; still the combined full-employment surplus for all governments, as estimated by the Council, fell by some $11.5 billion (Table 17, last column).

As for monetary policy, throughout 1972 money (by which I always mean M_1), grew at a rate in excess of 9 percent. But, what is to me more significant is that long-term interest rates, which had been al-

[3] Since that time the estimate of M_1 for that period has been increased by some $6 billion, or 3 percent, and the implied rate of growth for the first six months has been revised down from 12.3 to 10.9 percent.

lowed to rise in the first half of 1971 when unemployment was holding steady at 6 percent, were still falling, or at their lowest point, at the turn of 1972. Thus the mortgage rate, as measured by the FHA new home mortgage yield, stood at 7.57 as compared with nearly 8 in mid-1971 and the AAA new issue rate, computed by the Federal Reserve, stood at around 7.1 as compared with about 8 percent. It seems hardly surprising then that, in the first quarter of 1973, which opened with unemployment down to 5 percent, the growth rate of real *GNP* accelerated further to a mammoth 8.6.

My hunch that such an outlandish rate of expansion—roughly twice the long-term rate of growth—was highly inappropriate under the circumstances, much as the corresponding rate in the first quarter of 1966, receives strong support from some simple calculations exhibited in Table 7 of the Report. These calculations are based on the consideration, by now widely accepted by students of the unemployment syndrome, that for a given state of demand pressure—as measured, say, by overall vacancies—demographic groups of different age, sex, race, etc., may have different specific rates of unemployment (because of differential frequency of quits or layoffs, or entering and leaving the labor market, for example). If, then, the composition of the population changes significantly over time, the same state of demand will imply a different overall rate of unemployment; in particular, if the composition shifts toward groups with higher specific unemployment rates, as has happened in the United States since the mid-1950's, then the overall rate will rise, and the target full-employment level of unemployment must be raised accordingly.

One simple way to make a rough allowance for changes in composition is to compute a "standardized" unemployment rate for every year, by weighting the unemployment rate of each group in that year by a standard labor force composition, say that of a specific year, which thus serves as a sort of base year. Table 7 shows that if one uses as the base year 1956, in which unemployment was 4.1 percent, or very close to what was considered then the full-employment rate, then in 1972, the actual unemployment rate of 5.6 percent is equivalent to a standardized rate of only 4.9, and the actual 1973 rate of 4.9 percent is equivalent to a standardized rate of but 4.1 percent—the same as in 1956. This is clearly a striking result. It confirms my view that the end of 1972, when the actual unemployment rate was down to 5.3 percent and the corresponding standardized rate down to but 4.6 percent, was a time calling for a very moderate rate of expansion of aggregate demand, not significantly higher than the long-run growth of 4 to 5 percent.

It should be recognized at this point that the Council's calculations might tend to overstate the tightness of the labor market in 1972–73 relative to 1956; the reason for this conclusion is that, in the two years the group-specific rates of unemployment were by no means identical. Specifically, in both years the rate of unemployment (hereafter *U*) for the prime groups, male 20 years and over, was the same or lower than in 1956; but the *U* for all other age groups (except females over 55) was higher, sometimes appreciably. Under these conditions, the results are not invariant under the choice of the base year. In particular, since in 1956 the prime group was relatively more abundant than in the later years, if we use 1973 as the base year, the standardized *U* for the more recent year will rise relatively to that of 1956. Thus, using 1973 weights the standardized *U* for 1956 is found to be 4.6, instead of the actual 4.1 (see fn. 3 to Table 1), which is somewhat lower than the actual rate in 1973, namely 4.9. In other words, in terms of 1973 weights the labor market in 1973 was a little less tight than in 1956. But the difference was not large enough to change my conclusion about the need for extreme caution, expecially since, as already noted, the critical, male-prime-age, labor market was tighter in 1972–73.

The interesting question at this point is whether the Council realized in late 1972 just how tight the situation was getting; the Report does indicate that the extraordinary rate of growth of the first quarter of 1973 was unexpected, and, since most other forecasters failed equally, I would not be prepared to blame the Council seriously for this failure. However, there is no indication that the tightness of the labor market was appropriately appreciated; quite the contrary, the January 1973 Report stated as its goal for 1973 to "... reduce the rate of unemployment to the neighborhood of $4\frac{1}{2}$ percent by the end of 1973 ..." and that "This does not imply that in present circumstances $4\frac{1}{2}$ percent is necessarily the floor to the unemployment rate" (p. 73). These are amazing statements from the vantage point of the 1974 Report and one wonders why what was so obvious at the end of 1973 was apparently not even conceived of a year earlier, especially on the part of a Council that on the whole had been rather conservative in its unemployment targets.

To be sure, the 1974 Report stresses the fact that, from the beginning of 1973, fiscal policy stopped being highly stimulative. But neither did it become very restrictive. The budget shifted to a full-employment surplus of about $3 billion by the conventional measure (Table 17) implying probably a budget balance on the Council preferred measure (inferred from a comparison of the two alternative measures of full-employment surplus for 1973, provided in Table 1, cols. 2 and 4). This measure, it should be acknowledged, however, tends to understate the restraining impact of fiscal policy, for the change from deficit to surplus was achieved primarily by holding outlays fairly constant while receipts were rising, and one must therefore allow for the "balanced budget multiplier" effect.

Looking next at monetary policy, in the first half of 1973 the money supply continued to rise at the hefty rate of nearly 8 percent. According to the data, the growth was rather erratic but I would not make much of this, especially since I mistrust the seasonal adjustment. Short-term interest rates rose fairly sharply by somewhat over 200 basis points; but long-term rates rose slowly and moderately, the new issue rate by 50 basis points and the mortgage rate by only 20, and both rates remained well below the peaks of the high unemployment period of mid-1971.

Unfortunately the 1974 Report's discussion of Monetary Policy in 1973, occupying but a page or so (pp. 83–84), is rather uninformative, and one cannot gauge whether, on the whole, the Council approved or disapproved the relatively expansionary policy being pursued, especially in the first half of the year. This is perhaps understandable in terms of the rather delicate relation and unclear division of power and responsibility between the Council and the Federal Reserve, a point on which I shall touch again later.

Finally in 1973 a further strong stimulus was provided to the economy by allowing, and even encouraging, the dollar to depreciate through the first half of the year. The associated swing in net exports added directly some $3.5 billion to aggregate demand (presumably adding as much, to "offset to saving") in the first quarter, about one-tenth of the total increase in first quarter demand, and $8.5 billion over the year, again close to 10 percent of the total increase in demand; and this quite aside from multiplier effects and direct effect on *U.S.* domestic prices, both through imports and exports channels. The Report explicitly acknowledges these pervasive and, under the circumstances, undesirable effects of the depreciation on prices and aggregate demand. The effect on aggregate demand via net exports is attributed in part (pp. 55–56) to causes other than the depreciation, namely the boom and low food supplies in the rest of the world. At the same time, the list fails conspicuously to mention the effect of controls in Phase III and thereafter, such as the effect of price controls on exports and imports (although these too are acknowledged later in ch. 3's discussion of inflation control and in ch. 5, p. 190). Similarly the effect of devaluation on prices is explicitly recognized in chapter 3 (see p. 93). What is, however, conspicuously missing is an explanation and defense of the policy of letting the dollar continue to depreciate. There was a widespread feeling that the 10 percent official depreciation of February 12 was already somewhat on the high side. I shared this view with many other international trade specialists, such as Richard Cooper. But, as the Report recognizes (p. 186), there was an even more widespread feeling that the further depreciation in the second quarter by " . . . about 11 percent in terms of most of the EC currencies floating jointly and 5 percent in terms of the trade-weighted average of 14 currencies" (p. 185), (6 percent from March 19 to July, see pp. 92–93), was totally unwarranted and hence undesirable. I, for one, expressed this view both in print[4] and in private communications to the appropriate *U.S.* authorities. Nor have the events since provided any ground for changing that view.

The Report appears to foster the impression that this devaluation reflected the behavior of other central banks and not a *U.S.* game plan: " . . . when large-scale market intervention [by foreign central banks] failed to restore stability to foreign exchange markets, fixed exchange rates were abandoned; consequently the dollar fell . . . " (p. 183). But the simple truth is that the United States could have intervened on its own—and quite effectively as was shown by later experience in July—and that foreign Central Banks had stopped intervening when it became clear that the United States was not prepared to cooperate in an effort to support the dollar and, indeed, was not at all interested in the dollar being supported. On this point the Report states that in the third quarter " . . . there was limited intervention, by a number of central banks *including the United States, to prevent the dollar from rising*" (p. 183, italics added).

The peak of absurdity in our foreign exchange policy was reached in the third quarter of 1973 when we began to impose a variety of export restrictions, detailed in Table 24 of the Report, thus removing the only conceivable ground for the deep devaluation, namely to improve the current account balance. It would obviously have been far better from every point of view to push up the foreign value of the dollar and to impose export duties—as other countries have done—(whatever one finally concludes about the wisdom, from a longer run point of view, of limiting specific exports).

Chapter 2 also helps to make some sense of the apparent paradox mentioned in my opening paragraph, of a simultaneous sizable decline in real wages, reasonable growth in productivity, and yet, no substantial rise in profits and property income. The resolution of this puzzle actually involves a rather long chain, of which the Report covers only the last few links (pp. 74–75). In the first place, one finds that the share of labor in national income was essentially stable. The moderate rise in property income and the substantial rise

[4] In the *Corriere Della Sera* articles referred to earlier.

in farm income by nearly 45 percent in current dollars and 33 in terms of purchasing power—which, incidentally, was a good development from the point of view of reducing income inequalities—was offset by a substantial decline in the profits of nonfarm, noncorporate business, and professional incomes. The share was equally stable in terms of *GNP*, or Private *GNP*, and actually rose by about $1\frac{1}{2}$ percent in terms of Private Nonfarm *GNP*, after noncorporate business profits are corrected for imputed labor income. Hence real property income—outside farms—rose roughly as much as real output. But this rise *within* the year was only 4 percent (4.2 for private nonfarm) rather than 6 percent when measured year over year. As mentioned earlier, profits rose a little more and total property income a little less. But under these circumstances one would expect real wages to rise as much as productivity. Why, instead, did they decline significantly?

One part of the explanation is that productivity rose very little in the course of 1973. The increase in real output was achieved in fact by a quite sizable increase in employment—some 3.5 percent—and an almost equal increase in man-hours—3.4 percent for the private nonfarm economy—because hours worked apparently fell slightly. (However, the Report raises some reasonable doubts about the reliability of the hours worked series, p. 58.) Thus, measured productivity rose by less than 1 percent, the increase being concentrated in the first quarter, after which it tended to decline slightly. The second major explanation lies in the fact that even though hourly wages rose 6.7 percent, compensation per man-hour rose 8.2 percent (8 percent for private nonfarm). The difference between these two figures is accounted for, primarily, by the increase in "other benefits" (nearly 1 percent) " . . . the major part of which in 1973 came from the increase in employers' social security taxes in the first quarter" (p. 70), the rest being due to overtime and interindustry shifts. Since the private *GNP* deflator rose by just over 7 percent, real compensation per man-hour *measured in terms of the output produced* did rise by nearly 1 percent. For the nonfarm sector the increase was even larger, 2.5 percent, as the deflator rose by only 5.5, because of the 1.6 percent increase in the labor share. However, real wages are expressed in terms of consumables and not in terms of output produced. Now the price of consumption goods tended to rise relative to that of domestic output basically because of the sharp rise in import prices (26 percent), and even more relative to that of domestic nonfarm output (value-added) because of the surge in farm prices. Indeed, the consumption deflator rose by 7.4. However, the decline of real hourly wages was in terms of the cost of living index (*CPI*) which, as indicated, rose by 8.4. The difference between the two measures of the cost of consumables comes in part (about .5, p. 75) from the fact that the *CPI*, in contrast to the implicit deflator, uses fixed weights. The rest of the difference is due to the fact that the basket of goods used in the *CPI* is different from that in the implicit deflator; for example, it tends to give more weight to food which rose sharply.

The result of this long chain can be conveniently summarized by using the same links to explain another puzzle which is really the other side of the same coin: why did the *CPI* rise by as much as 8.4 percent when hourly wages rose only 6.7 and the profit share (the markup) actually declined? It should by now be apparent that the answer lies partly in the growing gap between hourly wages and the cost of labor to employers, through social security and other fringe benefits; this gap rose especially rapidly in 1973, the very year in which productivity grew very little. The balance of the explanation is that the *CPI* rose much more than the implicit nonfarm deflator. This, in turn, can be accounted for in part by the sharply rising farm and import prices which caused a deterioration in the "terms of trade" for the domestic nonfarm sector; the remaining discrepancy between the *CPI* and the consumption deflator is due to the more questionable difference in composition between the basket of consumption goods actually consumed and the basket used in computing the *CPI*.

The moral of the story is, of course, that unless and until farm output expands and farm prices and import prices fall back, real labor income—including fringe benefits—must *pro-tantum* decline; and that a year in which productivity rises little is not the best suited for sizable increases in social security and other payroll taxes, at least if one cares for price stability.

The fact that all these unfavorable factors happened to hit the *U.S.* economy at the same time might well be considered a piece of bad luck for which the Administration could not be seriously blamed. It should also encourage some optimism about the future of inflation without the need to create a high rate of unemployment, just by avoiding a rapid expansion of demand when unemployment is already down to 5 percent. However, I am not quite prepared to go along with the first proposition about bad luck for the reason that at least two of the unfavorable factors—the high price of farm products and the high price of imports—can be attributed in some part to Administration action or inaction. A third factor, the poor performance of productivity, can also be at least partly attributed to an excessive expansionary policy in the presence of what should have been perceived as a relatively tight labor market and relatively tight productive capacity situation. I also suggest that it might well be attributed in part to the presence, and poor management, of price and related controls, a topic to which I now turn.

III. Did the Controls Help or Hinder—and How Much?

This issue is examined in chapter 3, which also gives a summary account of the major control measures and their administration. It was widely understood in the profession that the Council as well as Secretary Schultz had not been enthusiastic supporters of price controls—to say the least—a position which incidentally I also shared.[5] It was rumored, if only in jest, that its members were of two minds about its numerous failings since they vindicated their opposition and might also serve to immunize the public and Congress against the repetition of such arbitrary interferences with the system. This teach-you-a-lesson view certainly received support from the following characterization of price controls offered by Secretary Schultz in an interview to the Boston Globe: "It was a disaster from an economic view, but a great thing from an educational point of view." (!)

I was therefore very much intrigued by whether the Report would paint the episode as a success or as a failure. By and large it steers an intermediate or neutral course, at least in the summary conclusions: " . . . no one can disprove the thesis that the controls had a significant effect, although 1973 makes it a hard thesis to believe" (p. 108). These conclusions rely partly on an earlier section on "The Effectiveness of Controls"; this contains a theoretical disquisition, pp. 99–103, which I find rather muddy, the essence of which is that " . . . whether controls restrained the rate of inflation boils down to whether it can be demonstrated that they either restrained the rate of spending or increased the rate of production" (pp. 100–

[5] See my testimony before the Joint Committee cited earlier.

01). The effect on the rate of spending "... might show up in a lower ratio of spending and income to the money supply, or even in a lower money supply, if ... the Federal Reserve felt less need to permit monetary expansion" (p. 101). The main effect conceived on the supply side is of the classic type analyzed by Joan Robinson or in Abba Lerner's counter-speculation proposal: a ceiling on price by making marginal revenue coincide with price might raise marginal revenue and increase output. This framework might be a useful tool of analysis at the micro level but its macro relevance is rather questionable. Yet it is apparently on the basis of this type of analysis that the Report suggests that one cannot "... rule out the possibility that inflation might have been even greater in 1973 without controls. We think it could not have been much greater, however, since with the controls the rate of spending was high relative to the money supply, and output was low relative to the labor supply" (p. 108).

My own analysis of the effectiveness of controls, and I suspect that of many other colleagues, would have gone along very different lines. For some time now, I, as well as many others, have found that the behavior of aggregate wages and prices can be rather effectively analyzed in terms of a model both consistent in the theoretic sense and empirically useful. It consists of a generalized Phillips curve explaining hourly compensations in terms of unemployment, price expectations, and institutional variables (social security taxes, minimum wage legislation) and of a price equation in which the price level (and the real wage) is determined by an oligopolistic markup à la Sylos-Baine[6] on (long-run minimum) unit labor and raw material costs, with the markup stable in the relevant medium run, except for some upward and downward shading in response to the rate of utilization of capacity.[7]

Because of the lagged adjustment of wages to prices and prices to wages, this model implies that, once an inflationary process gets underway (say because of temporary excessive demand pressure on the labor market), it will take a rather long time for it to abate even if the rate of unemployment is kept substantially above the level consistent with reasonable long-run price stability. In terms of this structure, wage controls might be effective by holding down money wage increases, especially in the more highly unionized sector, partly by sheer decree and partly by reducing expectations of future price increases; and price controls might be effective partly by making wage controls acceptable to organized labor and partly by reducing the markup.

When the equations of such a model are estimated through a period ending in the third quarter of 1971, it is generally found that there is very little evidence of wage controls per se being effective in the sense that, given price behavior, there is no evidence of wages behaving significantly differently from the past. There is instead evidence of price controls being moderately effective in the sense that the markup on costs declines through the fourth quarter of 1973 (the end of Phase II) and then tends to move back toward the historical level, but by no means catching up with it at the end of 1973. The lower level of prices in turn has a feedback effect on wages, which feeds back on prices and so on, so that altogether one finds a non-negligible effect of Phase II on wages and a stronger one on prices, and similar effect

[6] See the author (1958).

[7] This structure, which is used in the MIT-PENN-Social Science Research Council (*MPS*) econometric model of the United States, is described in George de Menil and Jared Enzler.

on wages for Phase III, together with a more moderate one on prices.[8] On the basis of this evidence, obviously subject to many qualifications and uncertainties, I would be inclined to conclude, very tentatively, that Phase II was moderately successful and even Phase III helped, at least in the sense of slowing down the rebuilding of the markup.

However, these judgments, which at least for Phase II broadly agree with the Council's evaluation in the 1973 Report, relate only to the *aggregate* level of wages and prices, under *given* aggregate demand and productivity. To assess the overall effect we need to be concerned also with the effects of controls on these two other variables. Here it seems to me that the record must be assessed as rather negative in 1973. As the Report admits, price controls are likely to have stimulated exports, and hence aggregate demand pressure. The widely reported difficulty of procurement for many products cannot but have contributed to the very poor performance of productivity, something which the Report again acknowledges as likely on page 101. In addition, the unavailability of commodities to the consumers contributed of course to reduced welfare, even if this is not caught in our measure of real income and *GNP*.

The worst episode in the history of controls was clearly Phase III$\frac{1}{2}$ and particularly the notion that by freezing the prices of meats and poultry one could indirectly control the prices of feedstuffs—even though these were not directly controlled—because of the derived demand nature of the demand for these products. This maneuver could not possibly have worked given the fact that the inputs were storable, and prices were expected to be higher later, especially since the freeze was announced to last but two months. This policy led to the thinning out of supplies and contributed to the increase in food prices during August at the mammoth rate of some 80 percent at annual rates, an inference supported in part by the decline in food prices in the next two months following the end of the freeze.

On balance then one might agree, though on rather different grounds, with the Report's conclusion that the overall net effect of controls is hard to assess (except for Phase III$\frac{1}{2}$, which was definitely disastrous), but that on the whole, in 1973, given the erroneous aggregate demand management, the controls did appreciably more harm than good. One of the sad aspects of this conclusion is that it may have deprived us permanently of a device which, used extremely sparingly under conditions similar to those of 1972, might have been a useful addition to our almost empty box of tools to bring inflation to a rapid halt—without repeating the Great Depression!

IV. Targets and Policies for 1974—and their Consistency

Chapter 1 of the Report lays out a target path for real *GNP* for the year 1974, together with its implications for unemployment and prices, and with an outline of the fiscal and monetary policy designed to achieve that target. It is made clear that the figures for the first couple of quarters are more in the nature of a forecast than of desired rates because, given the lags in the response to policy, that initial period is largely beyond the reach of policy options, as of the time the Report was written. However, the path for the balance of the year is truly a "goal" as well as " . . . a prediction of what will be achieved if the planned policy is carried through" (p. 28). In this section I propose

[8] See, for instance, Robert Gordon, pp. 775–78, especially Table 1. The wage-price equations of the *MPS* model leads to very similar inferences.

to analyze the content of the chapter from three points of view: i) the appropriateness of the real output and employment targets; ii) their consistency with the associated price behavior; and iii) the consistency between the targets and the policies prescribed to achieve them.

The Report foresees for the first half "A slow rate of economic expansion . . . and possibly a decline, with rising unemployment" (p. 27). For the second half the target is essentially that of holding unemployment steady at the midyear level, by endeavoring to keep the growth of real *GNP* at roughly the long-run full-employment rate of 4 percent. This path implies a growth of real *GNP* of about 1 percent over 1973 and 1½ percent within the year. No specific estimate is offered as to how high unemployment will have risen by midyear, but one can infer that it must be somewhere above 5.5 but short of 6, from the statement that "Unemployment for the year will be a little above 5½ percent" (p. 28).

Relying on the forecasts of reliable analysts as well as on projection based on the *MPS* model I found myself in basic agreement with the assertion that policy could do little about the first half of the year, though I would like to know to what extent the rise in unemployment reflects the goals of policy pursued by the Administration in the second half of 1973, when economic conditions in the first half of 1974 were still within its control. The provisional first quarter figures, which in the meantime have become available, confirm that real *GNP* declined, and at a substantial rate, presumably larger than the Council expected and even larger than that of the most pessimistic forecasters.

As for the target in the second half, I share the view that it would be a mistake to try to reduce unemployment rapidly, but see little justification for going as far as holding it constant in the 5¾ range. I would much have preferred a goal of a modest reduction from the peak figure say down to 5½ or just below, which, in my view, would have negligible cost in terms of inflation. This would require a rate of expansion closer to 5–6 percent on the average for the second half, bringing the year growth to 3–4 percent, but without raising very much the year-to-year growth. But these are relatively minor differences, especially if one has adequate humility about our ability to perform "fine tuning."

What is somewhat more serious is that, in my view, the Report is too optimistic about the behavior of prices consistent with the target real path; though opinions are divided on this point, my own model, as well as many others, suggests that the increase in the deflator year over year is likely to be closer to 8 percent than to the 7 percent projected by the Council. The first quarter figures suggest that even 8 may be optimistic, though I am not willing to be significantly swayed by the nearly 11 percent increase in the deflator reported for the first quarter. With this more realistic price forecast, the target path of money *GNP* should presumably involve a year-to-year growth just short of 9 percent rather than 8 percent (and a within-year growth of just about 9).

We now come to the most serious issue, that of appropriate policies. For fiscal policy the Report proposes a shift from a $13.5 billion full-employment surplus to a $1 billion deficit (based on the variable unemployment rate recommended by the Council). Together with this fiscal policy it recommends a monetary policy formulated—not surprisingly—in terms of "monetary aggregates" and more specifically in terms of M_2 (money plus time deposits except large CD's). M_2 is to increase at the rate of 8 percent on the ground that "For more than a decade the proportionate increase of money *GNP* tended to be the same as that of M_2, though in some years the deviations from this proportionality were substantial . . . " (p. 32). The Report further suggests that this growth of M_2 would require a growth of M_1 of the order of 5 percent.

In cooperation with Wharton EFA, Inc. at the University of Pennsylvania, we have tried to simulate on the *MPS* model the effect of pursuing the Report's fiscal policy (as interpreted in the Wharton model), together with an 8 percent growth of M_2.[9] The basic result of the 8 percent growth of M_2 is that, beginning with the third quarter, the rate of growth of real *GNP* is *distinctly below* the Council projection: 2.5 percent in the third quarter and 3.4 in the last, with a within-year growth rate of only 1 percent, a year-to-year growth rate of about .7, fourth quarter *GNP* lower by $\frac{1}{2}$ percent and unemployment rising to 5.9. Furthermore the initial conditions for 1975 are seriously unfavorable; if the 6 percent growth of M_1 is continued into the first quarter, unemployment rises to 6.2, a figure which would not be significantly affected by an alternative growth of M_1 in that quarter, within reasonable limits.[10]

The reasons for these striking results are best understood by comparing them with the result of an alternative simulation in which monetary policy has been set so as to produce closely the real path targeted by the Council. It turns out that the required policy can be characterized as one of keeping the short-term interest rate—measured operationally by the 4–6-month prime commercial paper rate series—at around 8 percent, just a shade below the actual average level in the first quarter (8.3). The growth of M_1 required to achieve this result is about 8 percent within the year (which implies only 6.5 percent year over year, because of the flatness of M_1 in the second half of 1973). This implication for M_1 is hardly surprising considering that target money *GNP* rises by 9 percent and that, for a change, short rates are required to move slightly down within the year to achieve the stipulated real growth of *GNP*. The corresponding growth of M_2 is 10 percent within the year (as well as year over year), again reasonable under the circumstances.[11] The trouble with the Council recommended monetary policy is that the inadequate expansion of M_1 it implies perforce leads to sharply rising short-term rates: the implied commercial paper rate rises from 8.3 in the first quarter of 1974 to 9.5 in the last and 10.5 in the first quarter of 1975, the highest level in recent history. Similarly, the long-term corporate bond rate which, even under the "control" simulation, rises from the first quarter 7.9 to 8.1 would, with the Council's policy, rise to 8.6 by the first quarter 1975. These high rates would reduce real *GNP* by 1 percent ($9 billion) by early 1975 (residential structures by 10 percent, fixed investment by 1.3, consumption by .5).

The strong effect on residential construction comes partly from the fact that under present ceiling rates, the flow of savings into thrift institutions is adversely affected. This effect extends to time deposits and causes an 8 percent growth of M_2 to require a relatively larger (6 percent) growth of M_1 in the *MPS* simulation of the Council's policy. An alternative simulation of the Council's policy was therefore carried out, appropriately raising ceiling rates so as to maintain the recent historical relation between the growth of M_1 and M_2. We then find that an 8 percent growth of M_2 can be achieved with a growth of M_1 of only 5.5 percent. However, the results in

[9] The simulations were carried out by William Fitzgerald in consultation with Albert Ando. It might be noted that the 8 percent growth of M_2 turns out to require a growth of M_1 of around 6 rather than 5 percent partly for reasons mentioned below.

[10] For further details see the release by Wharton EFA, Inc., "MPS Model Forecasts, March, 1974—Experiment III."

[11] See the release cited in fn. 10.

terms of real *GNP* are essentially unaffected. The reason is that both short and long rates are roughly the same under either simulation of the Council's monetary policy for the reason that the rise in time deposit rates reduces the demand for money approximately as much as the reduction in supply.

It is of course entirely conceivable that the simulations from the *MPS* model are way off, and that the explanation suggesting their plausibility is equally wrong. Nonetheless I would urge the Council and the Federal Reserve to consider seriously the possibility that the achievements of the Council's own modest targets will require more growth of the monetary aggregates than recommended in the Report: in particular, the growth of M_2 should be closer to 10 than to 8 percent and that of M_1 closer to 8 than to 5. An 8 percent growth of M_1 was entirely too steep in the first half of 1973, given the moderate inherited rate of price rise, and in the face of unemployment that was low and falling, all of which created the need to raise promptly long-term rates to restrain an economy already overheated by past policies. But, in view of the present inherited high rate of inflation, the many nonrepetitive forces which have generated it, and the fact that unemployment is well on its way to pass the $5\frac{1}{2}$ percent mark by midyear, an 8 percent rate of growth of M_1 appears to me and to many others entirely appropriate to nudge down, not up, interest rates in order to support housing and other components of demand.[12]

What needs to be stressed is that the higher proposed rate of growth of M_1 and M_2 is no more than what is needed to achieve the Council's own modest target of a rate of unemployment above $5\frac{1}{2}$ percent throughout the second half of the year, and hence does not imply a higher rate of inflation than what is realistically consistent with that target.

My plea acquires a special urgency at this writing as the Federal Reserve appears to be terribly concerned over the fact that, since the beginning of the year, M_1 has grown at something like 8 percent and M_2 at something like 10, and is reacting by driving the Federal Funds rate above the 11 percent range, which in turn has already raised the commercial paper rate above 10 percent (instead of down to 8) and the corporate bond rate to the $8\frac{1}{4}$–$8\frac{1}{2}$ range. Does the Council and the Federal Reserve believe that these rates are consistent with Council's targets? Or has the Council abandoned even its modest targets? Or have they been abandoned, or even never accepted, by the Federal Reserve? The latter is perhaps the most disquieting possibility, since I hold strongly the view that it is for the Administration to set *GNP* targets (in cooperation of course with the Fed), and for the Fed to use its skills to achieve these targets—or persuade the Administration to change them—but not to aim at targets of its own.

V. Concluding Remarks

Because the previous sections are so critical of the Council's record, when I started on this manuscript I had hoped to devote some space to praise other sections of the Report and especially chapter 5 dealing with the distribution of income, which I have found a very useful and informative summary of past work, enriched by some results still unknown to me, and have enjoyed reading also in the light of my interest in the life cycle. Unfortunately the pressure to concentrate on urgent policy issues prevents me from saying any more. I do hope, however, that

[12] Almost identical conclusions have been set forth in a paper presented by Gordon in 1974, which the reader might find helpful since it provides a careful literary justification for the price forecast yielded by the *MPS* simulation, and a "monetarist-type" explanation of why a more expansionary policy is needed.

my criticism will be taken in the spirit in which it is offered—as an earnest endeavor to learn from past mistakes. And having been so candid in my criticism, I must be equally candid in acknowledging that I am glad indeed that it was not *my* responsibility to make decisions in the tough circumstances of last year and to write the Report, with Herbert Stein writing this review!

REFERENCES

G. de Menil and J. Enzler, "Prices and Wages in the FR-MIT-Penn Econometric Model," in *The Econometrics of Price Determination Conference*, Washington 1972.

R. Gordon, "The Response of Wages and Prices to the First Two Years of Controls," *Brookings Papers*, Washington 1973, *3*, 765–78.

———, "The Consequences of Inflation for Monetary Policy," presented at the Conference Board's Fifth Annual Midyear Outlook Conference, Chicago, Apr. 10, 1974.

A. P. Lerner, *The Economics of Control*, New York 1944.

F. Modigliani, "New Developments on the Oligopoly Front," *J. Polit. Econ.*, June 1958, *66*, 215–32.

———, *Testimony, Hearings before the Joint Economic Committee on the Economic Report*, 92d Congr. 1st sess., July 7, 8, 20, 21, 22, 23, 1971.

J. Robinson, *The Economics of Imperfect Competition*, London 1933.

U.S. Council of Economic Advisers, *Economic Report of the President*, Washington, Jan. 1973.

———, *Economic Report of the President*, Washington, Jan. 1974.

Errata

Page 548, column 1, last line: ''understate'' should read ''overstate.''

Monetary Policy for the Coming Quarters: The Conflicting Views

FRANCO MODIGLIANI AND LUCAS PAPADEMOS*

I. The Problem

IN the course of the third quarter of last vear, the economy finally began an energetic recovery from the postwar period's longest and deepest contraction which lasted nearly six quarters, and was accompanied by a reduction of real output of over 7 percent, and unemployment rates in excess of 9 percent. This recovery can be expected to continue at a moderate pace into the next two to three quarters, and more or less independently of what monetary policy might be pursued in the near future (within reasonable limits) in view of the substantial lag in the response of the economy to policy actions. Thus the policies pursued over the coming quarter or two cannot have a significant impact until the second half of 1976 and thereafter.

On the other hand, what happens after the middle of this year is very much dependent on policies in the coming quarters, and in particular on monetary policy, which is the subject of this article. Furthermore, the stakes involved in choosing an appropriate policy are quite high, as most observers agree that by the middle of 1976 we will still be facing a serious case of stagflation, with an uncomfortably high rate of inflation, upward of 5 percent, and a rate of unemployment not far from 8 percent. These considerations help to explain, in part, the wide interest in the issue of the appropriate policy for the coming quarters.

But that interest has also been kindled by the fact that the policy recommendations put forth by the economic profession have tended to be sharply polarized.

At one pole one finds the so-called monetarists and monetarist sympathizers, whose prescription is a very simple one: over the

---

* Franco Modigliani is Institute Professor and Professor of Economics and Finance at the Massachusetts Institute of Technology and President of the American Economic Association. Lucas Papademos is an Assistant Professor of Economics at Columbia University.

The authors would like to express their thanks to Phillip Cagan, Rudiger Dornbursh, Stanley Fisher, Benjamin Friedman, Robert J. Gordon, Arthur Okun, Edmund Phelps, and William Poole for valuable comments on earlier versions of this paper. We would also like to thank David Modest for his excellent research assistance.

The New England Economic Review is produced in the Research Department. Mrs. Ruth Norr is the Editor. The authors will be glad to receive comments on their articles.
Requests for additional copies should be addressed to the Research Department, Federal Reserve Bank of Boston, Boston, Massachusetts 02106.

coming year the money supply should rise at a stable rate which, by and large, coincides with the announced current target of the Fed—4½ to 7½ percent. No doubt some would prefer the upper and some the lower limit of the range. But what clearly characterizes this group is: (1) the emphasis on strict adherence to some preselected rate of growth of some monetary aggregate, independently of what might be happening to interest rates or, for that matter, to any other variable; (2) the fact that the prescribed rate of growth, typically not more than 7½ percent, is small when compared with the rate of growth of money income which is foreseeable for the coming quarters, and even more when compared with the increase that would be needed to make substantial progress in reabsorbing the current massive unemployment; (3) the widely professed concern that "higher target rates for the money supply . . . would soon lead to accelerated inflation," and even "that a fresh burst of double-digit inflation [would] develop, and before long, bring on another recession." [1]

At the other pole, one finds a set considerably more varied in terms of their analysis of the situation, value judgments and recommendations, at least over a longer horizon. What they share in common is: (1) the view that economic policy should aim at a substantial and prompt reduction of unemployment, because of its high social and economic costs and because such a reduction is fully consistent with an orderly liquidation of current inflation; (2) the solid conviction that achievement of this target depends crucially on the pursuit of an appropriate monetary policy and that such a policy calls for the Fed to increase the money supply for a while at a rate well above 7 percent, at least to the extent that failure to follow this course would result in a significant increase in short-term interest rates, as seems likely. Not abiding by this prescription would in their view almost certainly cause the recovery to falter by the end of this year, at a time when unemployment will still be unbearably high; (3) substantial agreement that holding the line on interest rates and letting the money supply rise at a fast rate, while appropriate during the early phase of the recovery would no longer be appropriate once the recovery was well under way, and that accordingly monetary policy should not be framed in terms of maintaining for any significant length of time any particular rate of growth of M_1, or for that matter, any particular level of interest rates.

Our own view falls squarely within this latter pole, as will be apparent from the next section in which we present in more detail our policy recommendations, and also set forth the analytical framework and empirical evidence that supports them. We do not, of course, wish to suggest that our analysis and formulation would be shared *in toto* by all those who broadly share our real targets and policy prescription. We believe nonetheless that the agreement on prescriptions does in fact result from a broad similarity in the approach to the problem as well as in the assessment of social priorities.

Finally, in the concluding section we endeavor to clarify the sources of the great current cleavage in the economic profession as to the appropriate near-term monetary policy. It is argued that the chasm is much less related than is commonly believed to difference in analysis as to the basic nature of the monetary mechanism and much more to (i) differences in views as to the proper role of discretion in

[1] Statement by Federal Reserve Chairman Arthur F. Burns, before the Committee on the Budget, U.S. Senate, September 25, 1975. This citation should not be construed as implying that we classify Dr. Burns as a monetarist.

economic stabilization, reflecting in part empirical judgments about the length and stability of response lags and in part ideological preferences, and (ii) different assessments about the relative costs and the available trade-offs between unemployment and inflation.

II. Real and Monetary Targets for the Coming Quarters

A. Overview

Our point of departure is the proposition that stabilization policy should be designed to achieve explicitly stated employment, real income and money income targets, which should of course be deemed attainable and mutually consistent. This seemingly obvious proposition is at odds with the past practice of the monetary authority of indicating no target at all, or, more recently, of stating targets entirely in terms of monetary aggregates without explicit indications of what these intermediate targets are designed to achieve in terms of final goals.

With the country suffering from an acute case of stagflation—mass unemployment of a size not seen since the Great Depression and a rate of inflation considerably reduced from the peak of last year but still painfully high—the challenge we face is clearly that of speedily reducing both unemployment and inflation. But are these two goals consistent with each other? More specifically, how far, if at all, can unemployment be reduced without compromising the target of a continued orderly reduction in inflation?

In this section we endeavor to provide an answer to this question and to draw its policy implications. It is shown that the historical experience clearly supports the proposition that there exists some *critical* rate of unemployment such that, as long as unemployment does not fall below it, inflation can be expected to decline—at least as long as there is some nonnegligible inflation to begin with. We label this critical level the Non-Inflationary Rate of Unemployment, or NIRU for short. We find that, at the present time, NIRU can be estimated at somewhat below 6 percent. We conclude that we can afford to, and should therefore aim at, reducing unemployment with deliberate speed down to the NIRU level. We next examine the path of real output which is consistent with this unemployment target and finally outline the economic policy and in particular the monetary policies which are called for in the coming quarters to achieve these real targets.

B. The Non-Inflationary Rate of Unemployment

There is prevailing agreement among economists that at least in the short run there is an inverse relation between the course of inflation and the rate of unemployment, a relation that has come to be labeled as the Phillips curve, after the man who pioneered the study of this relation.[2] Important differences do exist concerning the long-run nature of this relation. Nonetheless, all major views can be shown to imply the existence, at any point of time, of a critical level of unemployment that corresponds to our NIRU concept.

One view, subscribed to by most monetarists and also by some nonmonetarists, holds that the long-run Phillips curve is "vertical," that is, that there exists at any point in time a critical rate of unemployment—the so-called "natural

[2] The term Phillips curve usually refers to the relation between the unemployment rate and the rate of change of wages rather than of prices. However, from the wage-Phillips curve, one can derive a price-Phillips curve by taking into consideration the relation of prices to labor cost. See Section D below.

4

rate"—which is consistent with a constant rate of inflation. The line VV′ shown in Figure 1 illustrates a vertical Phillips curve. Unemployment rates consistently below the natural rate will tend to be accompanied by accelerating inflation, while unemployment in excess of that rate will be associated with decelerating inflation.[3] Obviously this view implies the existence of a NIRU which coincides with the natural rate (as indicated by the direction of the arrows from points A and B respectively).

The other major, more traditional, school of thought holds that even in the long run there exists a stable inverse relation between the rate of inflation and the rate of unemployment. This long-run Phillips curve is supposed to be of the form shown in Figure 1 as PP′, with the exact nature and position of this curve controlled by a number of other variables which will be discussed later. This nonvertical view of the long-run Phillips curve also implies the existence of a NIRU since it implies that for any given unemployment, inflation will keep decreasing as long as it is above the value implied by the long-run Phillips curve. The NIRU can, therefore, be determined by defining a "negligible" rate of inflation. It is given by the unemployment rate that corresponds to that negligible rate according to the Phillips curve.

This proposition can be illustrated with the help of Figure 1. The height of the horizontal line, abc, represents the assumed negligible rate of inflation. NIRU is then the value of unemployment corresponding to the point, b, at which the horizontal line cuts the Phillips curve. It is the NIRU because, for any unemployment rate to the right of this point, as long as inflation were above the negligible rate —above the horizontal line—it could be expected to move down toward the Phillips curve as shown again by point B. For our purposes, the only difference between the vertical and nonvertical school is that, for the former, the rate of change of prices must necessarily decline for unemployment above NIRU, even if it was zero or negative to begin with; whereas for the latter it may increase if inflation was initially below the Phillips curve, at a point such as C.

Because the existence of a NIRU is conceptually consistent with both major views about the nature of the trade-off, we can try to identify its value empirically without confronting the problem of the shape of the long-run Phillips curve.

C. Estimating NIRU—A Graphical Approach

Postwar data strongly suggest that there exists a stable NIRU that can be located within fairly narrow bounds. The evidence presented in Figure 2 clearly supports this conclusion. The horizontal axis measures the rate of unemployment, and the vertical axis measures the acceleration, or *change*, in the rate of inflation in a given year. Inflation is measured by the rate of change of the annual average of the consumer price index excluding food—referred to hereafter as pcx. We use this price index because year-to-year changes in food prices reflect, to a considerable extent, circumstances specific to agriculture, such as weather, rather than demand pressures.

Unemployment is measured by a rate which has been adjusted for changes in the composition of the labor force. This was done for the following reason: the official rate measures unemployment by weighing the unemployment rates of various groups by their share in the

[3] Recent analysis based on the hypothesis about the "rational" formation of expectations by economic agents implies that any attempt to permanently peg the unemployment rate below the "natural" rate is bound to be frustrated.

5

Figure 1

ILLUSTRATION OF THE NIRU UNDER ALTERNATIVE VIEWS ABOUT THE LONG-RUN TRADE-OFF BETWEEN INFLATION AND UNEMPLOYMENT

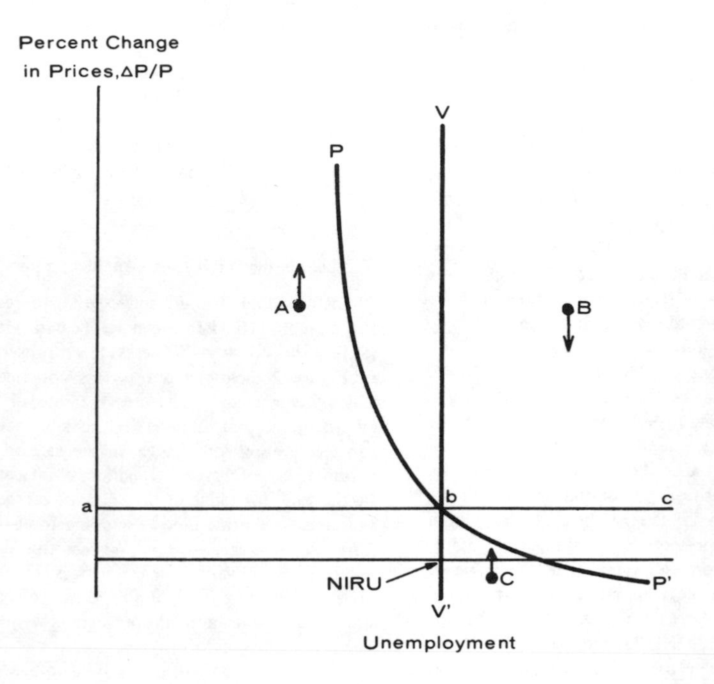

Figure 2

RELATION BETWEEN THE UNEMPLOYMENT RATE AND THE CHANGE IN INFLATION, 1953-1974

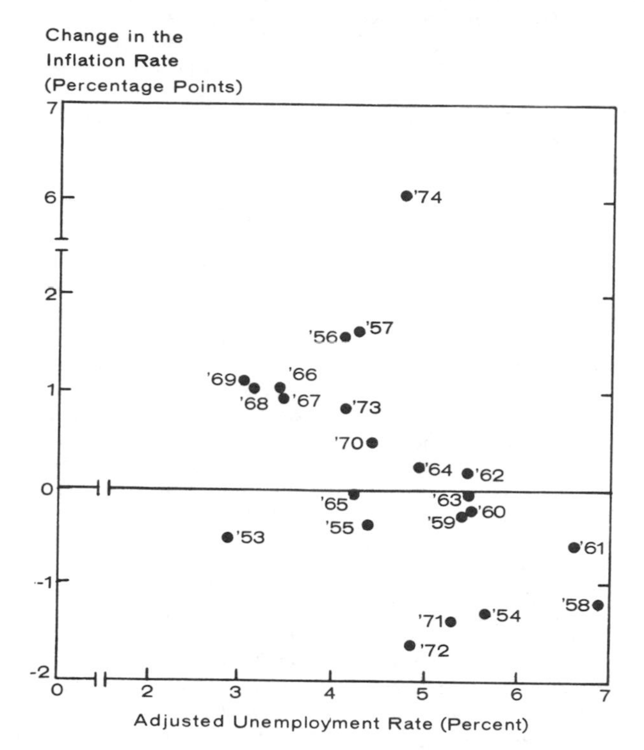

Sources: The data for the adjusted unemployment rate were provided by the Council of Economic Advisers. The rate was adjusted using the 1956 composition of the labor force to compensate for the changing composition of the labor force over time. The change in the inflation rate is measured by the rate of change of the annual average of the consumer price index excluding food, from the National Bureau of Economic Research Data Bank.

labor force. It is by now well established that, under given conditions of demand pressure (as measured, for example, by vacancies), different demographic components of the labor force are characterized by different unemployment rates. If the composition of the labor force changes in a significant way, and high unemployment groups, such as teen-agers, increase their share in the labor market, as has been the case in recent years, then the official unemployment rate will progressively overestimate the overall labor market slack. We, therefore, use as a measure of demand pressure, an "adjusted" unemployment rate, UA, provided by the Council of Economic Advisers, which is based on a constant composition of the labor force—in our case the composition of 1956.

The points plotted in Figure 2 show the relation between UA and the corresponding change in the inflation rate for each year from 1953 to 1974. Points above the solid horizontal line are years in which inflation increased, and points below it are years in which inflation decreased. A close examination of the graph leads to the conclusion that over the period covered, the NIRU was at most 5 percent. This inference rests on the consideration that in the years corresponding to points falling to the right of the vertical line, drawn at 5 percent, inflation consistently decreased—with but one minor exception. The exception is 1962, and it is minor in that inflation increased but negligibly (.2 percentage point). Even if this exception does not reflect mere errors of measurement, it is not inconsistent with a 5 percent NIRU because 1962 followed a year in which inflation was at a very low rate. Under such circumstances, if the Phillips curve is not vertical, inflation may speed up merely to reach the low rate of inflation implied by the long-run Phillips curve (as indicated by point C in Figure 1).

The NIRU could be somewhat lower than 5 percent, but the figure is ambiguous on the issue, because the next three lower observations, lying between 4.8 and 5.0 percent, are subject to certain special factors. The year 1964 is similar to 1962 in that it followed a year characterized by a very low inflation rate. Price and wage controls marked 1972, and the sharp deceleration must be partly attributed to the controls rather than the prevailing demand pressure. Finally, 1974 was characterized by unusually large increases of raw material prices in that year, and food prices in the preceding year. As will be shown below, the outlying behavior of that year (and of 1953) can be accounted for by the movements of these "exogenous" prices.

Turning next to the leftward portion of the diagram, it is seen that in nine years UA equals or falls short of the vertical line drawn at 4.3 percent. In all but two of these years, the rate of inflation increased noticeably. The exceptions are the years 1953 and 1965. The year 1953 (like 1974) was characterized by exceptionally high movements of exogenous prices, though this time in a downward direction. The year 1965 was again somewhat special because of the elimination or reduction of excise taxes at midyear. Thus the evidence strongly suggests that a UA of about 4.3 percent represents what could be labeled the inflationary rate of unemployment, which policy-makers should vigorously avoid because it leads to increasing inflation. In this region, the Phillips curve might be quite steep, if not vertical. On the other hand, for the two remaining years in which UA fell between 4.3 and 4.8 percent (1955 to 1970), the response of inflation is not so consistent.

To summarize then, Figure 2 provides strong support for the hypothesis that in terms of our adjusted measure of unemployment, UA, the value of NIRU can be placed somewhere in the region between 4.3 and 5.0, which is shaded in the graph—probably toward the upper end.

D. Estimating NIRU by Alternative Methods

The conclusion suggested by Figure 2 is confirmed by additional tests designed to obtain an estimate of NIRU by an alternative and more objective method of analysis, and to test robustness by relying on different measures of the unemployment and inflation rates. The analysis recognizes that unemployment is not the only force that may affect the dynamics of inflation. Cyclical changes in productivity, inflationary expectations, the past history of the inflationary process, as well as "external" shocks such as large changes in the prices of imports and farm goods will influence the movements of prices of the domestic nonfarm economy.

To assess the contribution of these additional factors to the rate of inflation, and thus obtain a more reliable measure of the role of unemployment and of the value of NIRU, we have estimated equations expressing the rate of inflation in a given year in terms of the rate of unemployment and the rate of change of productivity in the same year, the rate of inflation in the previous year, the current rate of change of a price index of imports excluding food, and the lagged rate of change of an index of farm prices. This equation can be thought of as a "reduced form" relation resulting from the interaction of two basic equations: (1) a price equation according to which prices adjust gradually to a target level determined by unit labor costs and exogenous input prices; unit labor costs in turn depend on wages and productivity; and (2) a Phillips wage equation relating changes in wages to unemployment and previous changes in prices of the basket of goods bought by workers, including food as well as nonfood prices. The effect of past inflation on wages may partly reflect expectations about future inflation.[4]

Equations were estimated for the period 1953-1971, so as to avoid distortions resulting from the Korean War at one end and from price and wage controls at the other. The results, which are reported and discussed in more detail in an earlier paper,[5] can be summarized here as follows:

(1) All the variables are found to contribute significantly to the explanation of inflation in the hypothesized direction, and together account rather well for the behavior of inflation in the years since the Korean War. This can be gauged from Figure 3a which compares the actual course of inflation with that predicted by the equation. For the last four years, 1972-1975, the computed values represent extrapolation of the equation beyond the period of fit. The equation is seen to overestimate inflation

[4] In principle, the relation between prices and wages expressed by the price equation should allow for a possible effect of the rate of utilization of capacity on the markup. Accordingly, the "reduced form" should include two separate indicators of demand pressure: the rate of utilization of capacity and the rate of utilization of labor force as measured by the unemployment rate. Because these two measures are highly correlated, we were unable to estimate a significant independent effect for the capacity utilization, and accordingly this variable is not included in the equation reported in footnote 5 below.

[5] See F. Modigliani and L. Papademos, "Targets for Monetary Policy in the Coming Year," *Brookings Papers on Economic Activity*, 1:1975, pp. 141-163. The basic equation referred to in the text is:

$$\underset{}{p\dot{c}x} = \underset{(0.73)}{-0.42} + \underset{(2.4)}{8.2(1/ua)} + \underset{(0.10)}{0.68p\dot{c}x(-1)} - \underset{(0.10)}{0.24\,\dot{\pi}} + \underset{(0.044)}{0.081p\dot{m}x} + \underset{(0.033)}{0.059\dot{p}f(-1)}$$

Standard error $= 0.58$; $\bar{R}^2 = 0.88$; DW $= 1.80$ *(Cont.)*

9

somewhat in the years 1972 and 1973, which is what one would expect if price controls had some effect in temporarily repressing inflation.[6] It is worth stressing, for later reference, that according to our equation, nearly 60 percent of the 10 percent inflation rate in 1974 is accounted for by the effect of the sharp increase in farm and import prices, reflecting in part the effect of oil and the devaluation; another 10 percent is accounted for by the poor performance of productivity relative to trend. Thus, only one-third of the overall inflation, or less than 3 to 4 percentage points, are attributable to demand pressures—a little less than one-fourth to the received rate of inflation, and only about one-tenth to current demand pressure as measured by the unemployment rate (after allowing for normal productivity growth).[7]

(2) The equation implies that a change in inflation is negatively associated with the past rate of inflation, a result consistent with the traditional rather than with the vertical Phillips curve hypothesis—(though the dependence is rather weak, suggesting that the vertical hypothesis may be a good approximation, at least for low rates of unemployment). Accordingly, in order to estimate NIRU we must specify what can be considered a "negligible" rate of inflation. Choosing for this purpose a rate of 2 percent and assigning to all the other variables in the equation their average value over the period of estimation, we obtain an estimate of NIRU in terms of our adjusted index of unemployment of 4.8 percent, which agrees closely with the conclusions suggested by Figure 2.

Footnote 5 (Cont.)

SOURCES: Adjusted unemployment rate—Council of Economic Advisers; price index of imports—U.S. Department of Commerce, *Indexes of U.S. Exports and Imports by Economic Class: 1919 to 1971* (1972), and Department of Commerce, *Overseas Business Reports,* various issues; consumer price index excluding food—NBER Data Bank; productivity and price index of farm products—MPS Data Bank.

a. The equations are estimated from annual data for 1953-71. The numbers in parentheses are standard errors.

b. UA = unemployment rate, standardized for composition of the labor force

$\dot{p}$ = rate of inflation measured by the rate of change of the consumer price index excluding food

$\dot{\pi}$ = rate of change of productivity in the private nonfarm business sector

$p\dot{m}x$ = rate of change of price index of imports excluding crude and manufactured foods, constructed from the index of crude materials, semimanufactures, and finished manufactures, published by the U.S. Department of Commerce (see sources above). It is a Paasche index calculated by dividing the sum of the values of the three components by the sum of their quantity indexes weighted by the values of the base year (1967).

$\dot{p}f(-1)$ = rate of change of price index of farm products, lagged

For other specifications, see F. Modigliani and L. Papademos, *op. cit.*

[6] It has been suggested that the inflationary pressures in 1973 reflected in part production bottlenecks arising more from a shortage of capacity than from the unavailability of labor. The fact that our equation overestimates inflation in this year would suggest that capacity bottlenecks did not play a major independent role.

[7] The estimated effect of import prices on inflation is larger than can be accounted for by the share of imports in the basket of goods measured by the nonfood CPI. It may reflect an indirect effect of the price of imports competing with domestic goods on the domestic markup. Yet the overestimation of the 1974 inflation rate by 1 percentage point (see Figure 3a) suggests the possibility of some upward bias in the coefficients of the "exogenous" prices. Because of the dominating position of the United States in world trade, over the period covered, the behavior of import prices may be influenced by U.S. domestic prices.

The presence of import and food prices in the equation also has the significant implication that a cessation of the favorable trend in the terms of trade between domestic nonfood output on the one hand and imports and food on the other, which prevailed over the postwar period, would tend to raise the NIRU. However, it seems likely, although not certain, that such an effect would be but transitory.

Figure 3

ACTUAL AND PREDICTED INFLATION RATE, 1953-1975

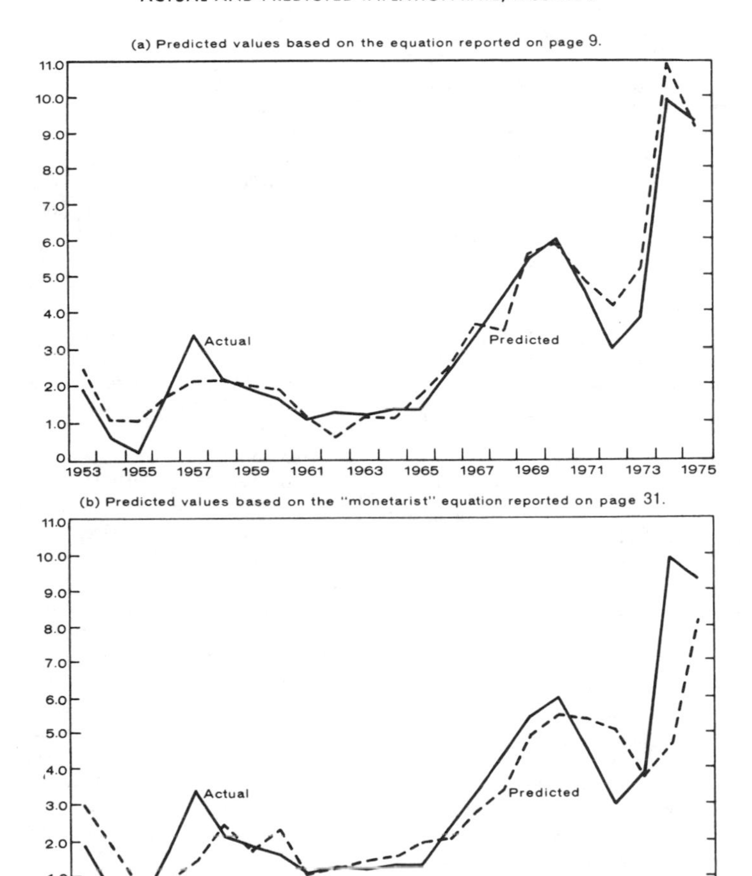

Note: The inflation rate is measured by the Consumer Price Index excluding food. The equations are estimated over the period 1953-1971; the predicted values beyond 1971 are extrapolations.

(3) According to our equation, the short-run effect of unemployment on inflation is rather modest. For example, in a given year a reduction of unemployment from 6 percent to 5 percent would increase the inflation rate by only one-third of a percentage point. Furthermore, the equations imply that the trade-off would be even smaller for higher unemployment rates.

(4) Deviations of the rate of change of productivity from its trend is found to exert a strong inverse effect on price changes, an effect which, as noted, appears to play an important role in 1974. This effect, combined with the well-known tendency for productivity to decline when unemployment rises, and conversely, may also help to explain why inflation generally appears to respond sluggishly to changes in output and employment.

(5) We have also tested, but found no evidence for, the view that the rate of inflation depends not only on the current level of unemployment, but also on how rapidly unemployment is declining. There is some evidence to support this view in the case of wage changes. However, there is also evidence that prices depend partly on lagged wages, and hence lagged unemployment. Under these conditions, given the unemployment rate in a particular year, a higher rate in the previous year will have two counteracting effects on inflation; it would tend to raise the rate of inflation because of the rate-of-change effect on wages, but would tend to lower the rate because of the lagged response of prices to unemployment. Our results suggest that, for the average change of prices from a year to the next, these two opposing effects tend largely to offset each other.[8]

To summarize then, correlation methods support the earlier graphical analysis about the magnitude and stability of NIRU: past experience clearly indicates that as long as adjusted unemployment exceeds some critical level, which can be estimated at around 4¾ percent, and so long as other variables—productivity, food and import prices—behave normally, inflation can be expected to decline, at least as long as it exceeds some 2 percent.

For the purpose of setting policy targets, the above estimate of NIRU for *adjusted* unemployment must be translated into a corresponding estimate for *unadjusted* (i.e., actual) unemployment. The noninflationary rate of unadjusted unemployment, or NIRUU for short, coincides with NIRU, by definition, in the year 1956. However, since then, and especially since the mid-sixties, the unfavorable shifts in the composition of the labor force, referred to earlier, have caused NIRUU to drift up, even though NIRU appears to have been stable. Given the current composition of the labor force, NIRUU can be estimated at about 0.8 above NIRU, or at some 5.6 percent.

To examine the possible sensitivity of this estimate to alternative measures of the rates of inflation and unemployment, the above equation was reestimated: (1) by replacing our adjusted unemployment by another frequently used measure of labor market tightness, the unemployment rate for married men, a measure that is also relatively insensitive to shifts in the composition of the labor force, and/or (2) by replacing the CPI excluding food by the private nonfarm business deflator. All the estimated equations implied a current value

[8] Additional tests performed with quarterly data confirm this inference. They show that the annual rate of change in prices depends on a distributed lag of quarterly unemployment rates in such a fashion that when aggregated to annual responses the rate of change effects and the lagged level effects cancel each other.

for NIRUU around 5.7 percent which agrees closely with the previous estimate.

What happens to NIRUU in the coming years will depend of course on forthcoming changes in the structure of the labor force. Fortunately the available information suggests that the unfavorable trends of the last decade are coming to an end so that, as long as NIRU remains stable as in the past, NIRUU can also be expected to remain around the current levels in the near future, while by the end of the decade it may even begin to drift down again.[9]

Considering the robustness of the empirical estimate of NIRUU under alternative specifications and the reasonable expectation that the factors that affect this value will not change significantly in the near future, we conservatively propose a rate of unemployment of around 6 percent as the operational interim unemployment target.[10]

E. The Appropriate Path of Real and Money Income to Achieve the Target

Our aim of reducing unemployment toward 6 percent with deliberate speed, from the fourth-quarter rate of some 8½ percent, is based on value judgments about the social and economic costs of unemployment and loss of output. From this point of view, the sooner this task is accomplished, the better. But a number of considerations suggest aiming to achieve the target in about two years to avoid the risk that an extraordinary large rate of expansion might strain the economy.

This conclusion is supported by an examination of the path of real output, as measured, say, by real GNP, which would be required to meet this timetable. To this end we may first ask how much of an increase in output would be required to reduce unemployment from the current 8½ to the 6 percent target. To estimate this gap, one can make use of a well-known empirical regularity known as "Okun's Law" according to which it takes roughly a 3 percent expansion of output to reduce unemployment by 1 percent. On this basis, output could be estimated presently at some 7 to 8 percent below the level consistent

---

[9] This is the conclusion reached by M. Wachter in "The Changing Responsiveness of Wage Inflation Over the Postwar Period," *Brookings Papers on Economic Activity*, forthcoming—though using a somewhat different approach to the estimation of NIRU.

[10] Mention should also be made here of some results based on a different indicator of labor market demand pressure which has received some attention of late, namely, a measure of employment relative to working age population (see e.g., Geoffrey Moore, "Employment vs. Unemployment as a Guide to Full Employment," unpublished NBER paper). Such an indicator may well have advantages in gauging short-run variations of demand pressure since it bypasses the difficult problem of reliably measuring who is in the labor force. However, over longer periods of time, it might have an increasing upward bias if the labor force participation has tended to increase, as has been true in the United States, especially since the early 1960s.

If in the equation of footnote 5 one replaces the variable UA with the employment ratio referred to above (civilian employment plus Armed Forces divided by noninstitutional population 16 years and over), one finds that the fit is only marginally poorer (standard error = 0.59), and the estimated role of the other variables is roughly similar. Also, on extrapolation, the equation accounts quite well for 1974. If one uses the equation to estimate a "Non-Inflationary Rate of Employment," analogous to our NIRU, one obtains a value of just over 57.2 percent. This compares with an actual employment ratio of 56.6 in the last quarter of 1975. Thus, the employment ratio would currently be less than 1 percent below the acceptable target, suggesting substantially less slack than would be implied by the 2½ percentage point difference between current unemployment and the 6 percent NIRU target. Some—but only a small part —of the difference can be accounted for by the fact that the unemployment rate fluctuates cyclically more than the employment ratio. The rest of the rather large gap cannot be readily accounted for, and is therefore rather a puzzle. In our view, it reflects primarily the long-run bias of the employment measure referred to above, and accordingly we see no ground for modifying our estimate of the current slack. However, it may also be taken as an indication of the possible margin of uncertainty in our estimate of NIRU.

with our target. This estimate must be recognized as subject to a more than usual margin of error because of the extraordinary decline in productivity and the large growth in the labor force since the beginning of the contraction, but is supported by alternative methods of estimation. Over the two-year span allowed to reach the unemployment target, labor force and productivity growth can be expected to raise the target level of GNP by another 7 percent. Thus, over the two years, income should grow by around 15 percent, or at an average annual rate of 7 percent. However, to minimize the danger of overshooting the NIRU target, and to insure consistency of the course of recovery with the desirable long-run growth path, it would be optimal for output growth to decelerate as we get close to the target. Therefore, we suggest that the optimal path should not lead to recovery at a uniform pace; rather the rate of growth should be faster in the first year, when there is still plenty of slack, and less rapid as the target is approached. Indeed, in the final quarter the growth rate should not be much above the long-run figure of a 3½ to 4 percent. Hence, for the first year, we should aim at a real GNP growth rate of 8 percent, or even somewhat higher.

An expansion of this magnitude is large by historical standards, but in our view there is little ground for concern that it would create new inflationary pressures considering the conspicuous slack in the economy. The conclusion is supported by the lack of evidence, reported earlier, that inflation is significantly increased by a fast reduction of unemployment accompanying a rapid growth, at least within the limits of historically experienced growth rates. A growth of 8 to 9 percent for a few quarters is certainly within the confines of this experience. Indeed, the recoveries from the Great Depression, as well as from the 1958 contraction, have been marked by growth rates of this magnitude and even higher without significant inflationary pressures. The vigorous 12 percent rise in real GNP during the third quarter of last year accompanied by a reduction in inflation points in the same direction. On the other hand, aiming at a 6 percent unemployment rate in a period appreciably less than two years would require initial growth rates in the two-digit range for several quarters, which might involve unwarranted risks of excessive demand pressure.

F. Implications for Monetary Policy

1) Interest Rate Targets

Our analysis of the modus operandi of monetary policy, of the lags it involves, and of the trends at work in the immediate future lead us to the conclusion that to achieve this output target would require, in the coming quarters, a combination of an aggressive monetary policy and some temporary fiscal stimulus.

These conclusions rest in the first place on our view of the mechanism through which the money supply affects demand and output. Put very schematically, the essence of this mechanism is that, through the control of reserves, the Federal Reserve affects quite promptly the money supply and interest rates, and interest rates in turn through a variety of channels including cost of capital, relative prices, wealth and availability effects, affect all major components of demand (see below). But the evidence suggests that the response of output to interest rates is gradual; it appears to reach significant proportions only after two to three quarters and to approach its full effect only after four to six quarters. For this reason, the behavior of output over the next two quarters must be regarded as largely beyond the reach of monetary policy. It is by now a variable to be forecasted rather than a controllable target.

The likely growth over the first half of 1976 is generally forecasted at 5 to 6 percent. This sluggish growth is roughly in line with the Administration's announced targets for 1976, but is glaringly inconsistent with our optimal path. In particular, this forecasted growth implies that by mid-1976 unemployment is unlikely to be much different from 8 percent. To pursue our path would require over the coming quarters, policies designed to increase the momentum of the current sluggish recovery, and aimed at achieving the advocated 8 to 9 percent growth rate at least in the second half of the year.

It is our considered conclusion based both on judgment and on more formal simulation of the response of the economy to alternative policies using the MIT-Penn-SSRC econometric model of the United States that because of the long lags of monetary policy, it would be very hard and even undesirable to aim for this target without the help of *some* temporary fiscal stimuli. To be sure, many temporary fiscal stimuli, including the popular temporary reduction of personal income taxes, run into the same difficulty as monetary policy, namely that they take time to produce an effect but then continue to do so long after the stimuli have been withdrawn. However, there are other instruments, such as a temporary reduction in excise taxes, or a temporary reduction in social security contributions of both employers and employees, whose effect can be expected to be quite prompt and very much concentrated in the desired span of time. Unfortunately we can see no hope that those responsible for stabilization policies would be amenable to pursuing such a program. Under these conditions, a good case can be made for an aggressively expansionary monetary policy aimed at a further reduction in interest rates for some time to come; but at the very least, interest rates should not be allowed to rise over the next two to three quarters. This second best policy of merely holding the line on interest rates is unlikely to achieve our target, but allowing interest rates to rise significantly above current levels would surely produce downward pressure on many components of demand leading to a path of output below the target, and by non-negligible margins.

First, as is well known, a substantial rise in interest rates would have a generally unfavorable effect on private investment which has been declining since the last quarter of 1973. This is particularly serious at a time when there is much longer-run need for added capacity and so much concern with a forthcoming shortage of capital. But the negative effect will be particularly severe and rapid on housing, which has suffered a general decline since early 1973 that dramatically accelerated during the monetary squeeze of mid-74, and which only recently is recouping along a hopeful but uncertain path. As is well known, the severity of the impact on housing would be accentuated not only because of the increase in the cost of financing, but mainly by the relative shortage of financing that will result from the loss of deposits by the thrift institutions as market rates rise above their interest ceilings. It is this disintermediation process which can be expected to materialize as interest rates rise substantially above current levels that motivate our stress on holding the line around these levels.

Higher interest rates will also tend to affect consumer demand adversely by inducing unfavorable developments in the stock market and, to a lesser extent, by raising the cost of financing purchases of durables, such as automobiles.

Finally, they will have an unfavorable influence on the expenditure of state and local governments whose finances are already shaken by the New York crisis. Although the magnitude of this effect may be moderate and gradual, it will add to the observed and projected slowdown in state and local spending.[11]

2) Money Supply Targets

We may consider next what are the implications for the behavior of the money supply of our minimal "compromise" target of maintaining interest rates for the next two to three quarters on the low side of current levels. The answer to this question will depend upon the growth of output that will actually be achieved, the expected rate of inflation and the short-run behavior of the demand for money. In the immediately coming quarters, prices are expected to increase at a rate of 5 to 6 percent. If over this period output were to grow at a rate consistent with our optimal path, or roughly 8 percent, then money income growth would be close to 14 percent. If the demand for money were stable, i.e., consistent with past experience, then to accommodate this rise in income, while maintaining interest rates constant, would require an average growth of money around 10 to 11 percent.[12] Actually, as indicated earlier, the growth of output is more likely to fall initially on the low side of 6 percent, and in this case the required growth of money would be somewhat around 9 to 10 percent.

These estimates assume that the demand for money for given income and interest rates is both stable and in line with historical experience. The evidence suggests, however, that since the middle of 1974, the demand for money has tended to be both lower and less stable than past relations indicate.[13] This behavior probably does reflect in part some recent financial innovations. These include the appearance and initial rapid growth of the so-called money management funds, the spread of what amounts to "checkable" forms of saving deposits, which are not now included in the money supply, and more recently the fact that firms and local governments are allowed to hold savings deposits. But these innovations are unlikely to account fully for the experience of the last year, which therefore remains somewhat of a puzzle. Should the downward drift in the demand for money continue in the coming quarters, then a maintenance of current short rates might require a growth of money which could be appreciably below the above estimates. On the other hand, at least part of the recent decline might be of a transient character, in which case the decline would not continue and there might even be a partial return toward the historical relation. In this case, the required money growth might well be higher than indicated.

---

[11] We have obtained a rough estimate of the gross impact on output of an increase in the interest rates from simulations of the MPS model over the coming quarters for two different constant interest rate policies (allowing the money supply to expand appropriately to enforce these paths.) The cumulative effect of a policy that would maintain interest rates at a level higher by 200 basis points (say from 5 percent to 7 percent) for three quarters would be to reduce real GNP by some $8 billion, or 1 percent, by the third quarter, and some $12 billion by the fourth quarter.

[12] On the basis of historical experience, the growth in money needed to accommodate a given growth in income while holding (short-term) interest rates constant can be estimated to equal the rate of inflation plus some two-thirds of the growth in real income. See, e.g., S.M. Goldfeld, "The Demand for Money Revisited," *Brookings Papers on Economic Activity*, 3:1973, especially Tables 9 and 13.

[13] As will be discussed in the next section, the downward shift in the demand for money can be equivalently described in monetarist terminology as a rise in the velocity of money independent of a rise in interest rates.

To sum up, the best judgment that one can make from historical experience as to the rate of growth of money needed to hold interest rates around current levels over the next two to three quarters is around 9-10 percent, but we would not be too surprised if that number turned out to be as high as 12 or instead to fall short of the current target range. This is a large margin of uncertainty, but fortunately there is no need to be concerned about it, since our policy target is stated in terms of interest rates, not in terms of money supply. The interest rate target can be enforced by the Federal Reserve directly without any need to decide in advance what growth rate in the money supply or in reserves will be required to achieve it. Indeed, the great uncertainty about the demand for money is one major reason why, at the present time, the target of monetary policy is best stated primarily in terms of interest rates rather than in terms of growth of money.

If we were to state our target as, say, a 9 percent growth of money, we would be faced with a large uncertainty as to the behavior of short-term rates that this policy would generate. If the demand for money moved back to the historical pattern, or exhibited an erratic increase, a 9 percent growth of the supply would prove insufficient and market rates would rise possibly quite quickly, as happened in the second quarter of last year. If, on the other hand, the demand continues its recent decline, then enforcing rigidly a 9 percent growth could well result in lower interest rates, possibly to the point of being excessively low and overstimulating the economy.

The large margin of uncertainty and the wide range of possible outcomes for the growth rate of money further imply that neither the Federal Reserve nor the public need panic if the maintenance of the current level of interest rates for the next two to three quarters were to require in some quarters a rise in the money supply, well above 10 percent. There is no danger that such a growth rate for the next two or three quarters would lead to increasing inflation contemporaneously or even at some later date, as long as it resulted from maintaining current interest rates, rather than from a policy of forcing them down. Indeed as we have indicated, a policy of holding the line on interest in the near future is, if anything, overly conservative. It implies a path of unemployment above our optimal path, which in turn was selected precisely with a view to insure a continued decreasing trend in inflation toward a negligible rate.[14]

The only valid consideration that should lead the Federal Reserve to resist a rapid growth of money and let interest rates rise would be substantial evidence that this rapid growth was not due to a recovery of the demand for money, but instead to a growth of real income in excess of 9 percent. Furthermore, in the face of such evidence—or of evidence that the growth of income was threatening to exceed 8-9 percent in the second half of the year and beyond—the Federal Reserve should enforce higher interest rates regardless of how fast the money supply was rising.[15] Conversely, evidence that the prospective rate of growth of output was falling well below target should lead the Fed to enforce appreciably lower interest rates, and again regard-

---

[14] The effect on inflation of a transiently rapid growth of money in recovery is discussed more fully in Section IIIC3.

[15] Such a course of action might also be justified by evidence of a current or prospective rate of inflation persistently in excess of 6 percent, though in this case some consideration would have to be given to whether the behavior of prices reflected unexpected growth of wages or the behavior of "exogenous" prices.

less of whether the money supply was rising fast or slowly.

III. What Lies Behind the Cleavage

Having made the case, and hopefully a convincing one, for the type of policy recommended by those at the nonmonetarist pole, we must face the question: how could the monetarists possibly come up with a sharply different one? In particular, why are their monetary policy targets stated exclusively in terms of growth rates for monetary aggregates with no reference to the appropriate course of interest rates? And why is the upper limit of their growth target for money so much lower than that advocated by or acceptable to nonmonetarists? In the concluding section we attempt to answer these questions, sorting out the role of differences in basic analysis, in empirical assessments, in value judgments and in ideological preferences.

A. The Role of Differences in Basic Theoretical Approach

It is frequently supposed that the difference in the policies advocated arises from a basic theoretical disagreement about the role of money in the economy with the monetarists holding that only money matters, and the nonmonetarists arguing that money matters not at all. The previous section should be sufficient to show that the position attributed to the nonmonetarists is utterly false. Indeed, if we held the view that money was unimportant we would not be making our passionate plea against a no-more-than 7 percent money growth policy. But the position vulgarly attributed to the monetarists is also grossly oversimplified. The truth of the matter is that after years of heated but also constructive debate, it has become apparent that there are no really basic differences of analysis. Both the monetarists and at least that set of nonmonetarists that believe money to be important (which by now probably includes most macroeconomists), do agree: (i) that a change in the quantity of money changes aggregate spending primarily by affecting the relative returns of different assets, relative prices and wealth, (ii) that initially the effect on spending takes partly the form of a change in output and partly that of change in prices, and (iii) that given time enough—in the long run—the effect on output dwindles and only the effect on prices remains. Similar basic agreement appears to exist with respect to the short-run and long-run effects of fiscal policies or changes in government spending and taxation.

Some difference might exist with respect to the long-run Phillips curve to which reference was made in Section II. But as was pointed out there, these differences might be significant at best with respect to whether *high* unemployment would *eventually* lead to an explosive *deflation*—an issue of purely academic interest at this juncture. The essential point is that both sides would largely agree that an endeavor to keep the unemployment rate too low—below what we have labeled the NIRU—for a sustained period of time would have unacceptable implications for inflation.

The broad consensus about the nature of the monetary mechanism and about the long-run response to monetary and fiscal policies, however, leaves room for disagreements in empirical assessments of the value of parameters controlling the short-run response of the system and its time path, and about the stability of these parameters and hence of the responses. These disagreements in turn have important implications for the role of stabilization policies, and finally for differences in views

18

as to the appropriate targets for monetary policy.

B. Rules Versus Discretion and the Choice of Monetary Targets

1) The Proper Role of Discretion in Economic Stabilization

Despite references to "long and variable lags," monetarists frequently appear to reason as though the "long run" in which the effect of money is reflected entirely in higher prices was reached rather promptly and independently of the degree of slack in the economy. More generally, in their view, whenever a shock occurs, including those produced by monetary or fiscal policy, the economy tends to revert fairly promptly to its long-run equilibrium position, and in particular toward its natural rate of unemployment—though the precise shape or length of the path to equilibrium cannot be foreseen with any precision.

This view of the working of the economy provides one basis for the monetarists' opposition to discretionary stabilization policies on the twin grounds that (i) there is no "clear and present" need for such policies to counteract exogenous shocks, and that (ii) such policies are on balance likely to do more harm than good. The second conclusion is supported by the consideration that the response to policy actions takes some time, and that we cannot reliably foresee either the precise path of response, nor what the economy would do in the absence of policy. One wing of monetarists, of recent formation but rapidly expanding, infers this instability of the response from the so-called Rational Expectations Hypothesis. The response of the public, and hence of the system, to policy actions must depend on expectations about the future path of the economy; but rational expectations must take into account the effect of the policy itself. Thus, the actual response to policy will tend to differ from what one would estimate to be in designing the policy. These considerations lead monetarists to the conclusion that these shocks from stabilization policy are more likely to cumulate than to offset the exogenous shocks —and this even if the discretionary policy was run by the most competent economist in the best conceived general interest.

For many monetarists, however, the opposition to discretionary policy also stems in large measure from the conservative outlook they tend to share and which leads them to oppose any active role for the government, especially in economic matters. For them, the government has no business in business, since any discretionary responsibility assigned to the government would be bungled and/or misused. In the specific case of stabilization policies, they argue that the government will tend to choose policies far inferior to the "best," both because of sheer incompetence and because those in power will try to manipulate these tools for their own short-run political advantage.

On the basis of these considerations, the monetarists advocate the elimination of all discretion in monetary policy by reducing the Federal Reserve's responsibility and obligation to that of increasing the money supply at a constant rate, forever. Just what that rate might be is of secondary importance, as long as it is known and constant in time. The monetarists generally agree that, with this policy, the economy may still be buffeted around by exogenous shocks, and that, in principle, there exists a nonconstant rate of growth path of money that could offset these shocks. But, because of ignorance as well as political pressures, granting the authorities the responsibility and discretionary powers to find and follow this path would result in an actual path worse than that produced by the constant growth rule.

The nonmonetarists for their part have assembled a lot of evidence that, in their view, clearly establishes that the path to the final long-run position for the economy as a whole is quite a long one, lasting many years, and that it will frequently involve oscillations around the "long-run" position[16]: some of this evidence even suggests that under certain conditions the economy may not be stable, i.e., it may not tend, by itself, to converge to the long-run position, unless helped along by appropriate stabilization policies. Accordingly, the long-run equilibrium is of little interest and the agreement with the monetarists about its nature is consistent with wide disagreement in matters of policy. What counts is the response in the first few quarters, since the response farther in the future will be drowned out by intervening shocks, and in any event can be readily undone by intervening actions. The nonmonetarists' evidence suggests that the initial response is reasonably predictable. Hence, they conclude that as long as the economy continues to be subject to serious shocks —such as the Vietnam War, the Great Society, the Oil Crisis and the crop failures, to mention just a few of the more recent ones—there is a need for stabilization policies. They further maintain that we have enough knowledge to devise changing policies which will make a substantial contribution to the stability of the system.

As to whether the government can be trusted to administer an effective stabilization program, nonmonetarists generally take a pragmatic view. They do not believe in any law of nature according to which the government is either totally good or totally evil, either superman or submoron. Decisions as to whether and how much discretion is beneficial should depend on how badly things work out if the government is kept out, versus how well the government can perform its task, and this in turn depends on changeable institutions. Of course, discretionary power can be misused for political considerations and some will in fact point to the period from 1966 to 1973 as providing glaring illustrations of malpractice. But this possibility merely calls for greater public vigilance within the frame of existing institutions and continuous search for improving the institutions. To illustrate, many analysts from all segments of the spectrum have been pressing for some time to greatly reduce, if not eliminate, the cloak of secrecy which surrounds the Federal Reserve choice of monetary targets, and its discretion and secrecy in the choice of real targets, and can point with satisfaction at progress that has been made, notably within the last year, toward changing this situation. Similar progress has been made for fiscal policy through the improved budget-making congressional procedures. One can look forward to further improvements even without aspiring to utopian perfection.

2) Some Empirical Evidence

A more important consideration is that the evidence in no way supports the proposition that discretionary stabilization policies, as they have actually been operated since the end of the Second World War, have produced results which are worse than could be expected in the absence of such policies. There is, for instance, ample evidence that in this period, at least until around 1970, the economy has been

[16] See, e.g., G. Fromm and L.R. Klein, "A Comparison of Eleven Econometric Models of the United States," *The American Economic Review*, Papers and Proceedings, May 1973; and C.F. Christ, "Judging the Performance of Econometric Models of the U.S. Economy," *International Economic Review*, February 1975.

distinctly more stable than in earlier decades, and this even if one disregards the Great Depression. Furthermore, this is broadly true not only for the United States but also for other industrial countries. Indeed, it has been suggested that the inflationary climate that has developed since the late sixties can be traced to the fact that stabilization policies were, if anything, too successful. As a result, governments became too ambitious in their targets and tried to steer a course too close to the danger area (such as our NIRU). Insofar as there is a grain of truth in this evaluation, it calls for scaling down targets not for *abolishing* discretionary stabilization policies.

Finally, the years since 1970, which have been characterized by a rising influence of monetarism, have provided us with a quasi-experiment throwing some light on the effectiveness of the monetarists' prescription of a stable growth of the money supply in keeping the economy stable. Since the turn of the decade, the Federal Reserve has shifted toward primary reliance on enforcing targets stated in terms of money supply and other monetary aggregates, and from the beginning of 1970 until the middle of 1974, the money supply and most other aggregates have actually increased at reasonably stable rates—certainly far more stable than in previous years. The results seem to have been distinctly unfavorable, much as the nonmonetarists feared: at no time since the Koren War has the economy been so unstable as well as so sluggish in its growth, as during the last few years.

These propositions are illustrated in Figure 4A. The top panel on the left side shows the growth rate of the money supply (M_1) from 1970 to the second quarter of 1974. Each bar represents the growth of M_1 for the year terminating in the quarter indicated, and beginning in the corresponding quarter of the previous year. (Thus the first column relates to the year terminating in 1971.1.) This so-called 4-quarter change is used here to summarize the data both to bypass the problem of possible faulty seasonal adjustment, and because short-run vagaries are, by general agreement, of little concern especially when they may reflect in part difficult-to-estimate seasonal adjustments. The solid horizontal line cutting across the bars denotes the mean rate of growth for the period, which amounts to 6.8 percent. The modest magnitude and alternating sign of the deviations of the individual bars from the mean indicate that the period may be characterized as one of reasonably stable growth of money around a 6.8 percent trend. To measure just how stable the growth was from quarter to quarter, we have computed the average absolute deviation of each quarter's growth from the mean. This statistic is represented in the figure by the distance between the dotted line above (or below) and the solid line denoting the mean. For the period in question, the average deviation is rather moderate, ¾ of 1 percent.

The second panel on the left-hand side provides the same information for the monetary base, a quality which monetarists have frequently mentioned as a good candidate for *the* aggregate that should rise at a constant rate. Here the stability is even more striking, as the average deviation is below ½ of 1 percent.

To support our statement that this variability of the growth rate is distinctly smaller than was typical of earlier years, we show in the second column of panels of Figure 4A the same information for the preceding four years, terminating at the end of 1970. The smaller variability in the growth of either M_1 or the base in the most recent period is visible by inspection, and is confirmed by the fact that the average deviation in the earlier period is twice as large for M_1 and 2½ times as large for the base.

As a further confirmation of this result, the smaller panels in the last column summarize the information for a longer span of years, namely the entire decade terminating in 1970. Here, to save space, we exhibit only the mean value—the solid horizontal—and the mean absolute deviation. It is seen that for both M_1 and the Monetary Base, variability is very nearly the same for the entire decade of the sixties as for the terminal years of the decade.

As indicated earlier and discussed further in the next section, adherence to a constant money growth rate target can be expected to result in greater instability of short-term interest rates. This expectation is fully borne out by the data graphed in the third panel of the figure. They show the quarter-to-quarter change in the commercial paper rate. In the era of stable money growth (left panel), the average change was 110 basis points, and even if we take out the mean growth reflecting the rising trend of this period, the average deviation from the mean is 106 basis points. This variability is 2.3 times as large as in the previous four years, and three and a half times larger than in the previous decade!

The crucial question now is whether the greater stability in the growth of monetary aggregates and resulting greater instability of interest rates have produced the favorable effect in stabilizing the economy heralded by the monetarists. Figure 4B endeavors to provide some evidence on this question with reference to three selected broad indicators. The first is the growth rate of real GNP, measured again by the four-quarter change to eliminate transient short-run fluctuations including those due to faulty seasonals, strikes, and the like. The result is rather striking: in the last four years the average growth rate is appreciably lower—2 percent as against 2.6 in the previous four years, and 4.5 in the previous decade, and in addition, we note a major deterioration in the stability of the economy as measured by the average deviation: the fluctuations of the growth rate around its trend in the most recent period are nearly three times as large as in the previous four years, or in the last decade.

The next panel measures instability by the four-quarter variations in unemployment; the verdict is seen to be similar even if not quite as dramatic.

The last panel, relating to the rate of inflation, should be of special interest for anyone who accepts the "crude" monetarist proposition that the rate of inflation is closely associated with the rate of growth of the money supply. If this proposition were valid, then one would expect that in the recent period of fairly steady monetary growth, the rate of inflation should be steady. Because the growth of money was hefty (see panel 1), the rate of inflation would be undesirably high, but it should at least be relatively constant. The last panel shows that the average rate is indeed higher, but is also far more unstable than in the earlier period. The average deviation is five times larger than in the previous four years and 2¼ times as large as in the previous decade. In other words, the stabilization of the monetary aggregates—which is of no relevance per se—has been at the expense of more instability not merely in interest rates, but also in all the truly relevant variables: output, employment and even prices.

While the evidence we have adduced is striking, the reader should not interpret it as establishing that discretionary policies are clearly superior to a stable growth rule in terms of stabilizing the economy. For instance, the greater economic stability of the two decades up to 1970 as compared with earlier periods, might reflect in part the presence of stronger "built-in stabilizers"—i.e., devices which cause the government deficit to move countercyclically, such as high marginal tax rates, unemployment compensation and the like. Again, the period of experiment was clearly one marked by significant exogenous shocks, notably the oil crisis. What we can say,, however, is that the evidence in no way supports the monetarist contention that past instability was the result of an unstable growth of money prompted by a vain attempt at stabilizing the economy, or that a stable growth of money would be conducive to a reasonably stable economy. On the other hand, it is consistent with nonmonetarists' conclusion that rigid adherence to a constant growth rate would produce a rather unstable economy, especially in the presence of serious disturbances as in the current troubled period. And in the absence of such disturbances, the nonmonetarist prescription would, of course, also lead to a stable growth of money.

3) The Issue of Interest Rate Targets

Objection in principle to discretionary policy also largely explains why the monetarists typically ignore interest rates, and vigorously oppose interest rate targets, while at least some of those at the nonmonetarist pole tend, especially at this time to stress an interest rate rather than a money supply target.

The monetarist opposition to interest rate targets is based on several arguments. The main and best known is that the level of (nominal) interest rates needed to achieve a target rate of output and price behavior—call it the warranted level—will tend to change over time as a result of gradual changes in the economy (capital accumulation, technology), of shocks, and of expectations about the rate of inflation. Under these circumstances, if the Monetary Authority should adopt a given interest rate target and stick to it forever, the consequences, given time enough, could, and probably would, be disastrous, leading to explosive inflation or prolonged unemployment and deflation. The nonmonetarists basically agree with this assessment; the difference lies in drawing the implications.

In view of their basic objection to allowing any discretion to the policy-maker, the monetarists naturally draw the conclusion that interest rates cannot provide a suitable target, and opt instead for a constant money growth rule, whatever interest rates it might bring about. They bolster this position with the expectation that a stable monetary growth would tend to stabilize the economy, and therefore also interest rates. Possible fluctuations in interest rates resulting from a rigid money supply rule would be short lived and have no significant effect on economic activity. However, these propositions receive little support from the evidence just reviewed.

The nonmonetarists are far less monolithic in their views as to whether and when interest targets are desirable, but they would concur that, insofar as they are used, interest targets, just as money growth targets, have to be adjusted flexibly to varying circumstances. Many would further hold that if this is done, there is, in the relevant short run, no intrinsically greater danger in an interest rate target than in a money supply target. The advantage of in terest rates as a target, is that, as noted earlier, monetary policy basically affects spending through the channel of interest rates; it is the change in interest rates that generates the relative return, the price and wealth effect that finally influence spending. Thus, even if one chooses the money supply as a target, one must do so in the light of the interest rates that

Figure 4

STABILITY OF SOME ECONOMIC INDICATORS OVER SELECTED PERIODS *

A. FINANCIAL INDICATORS

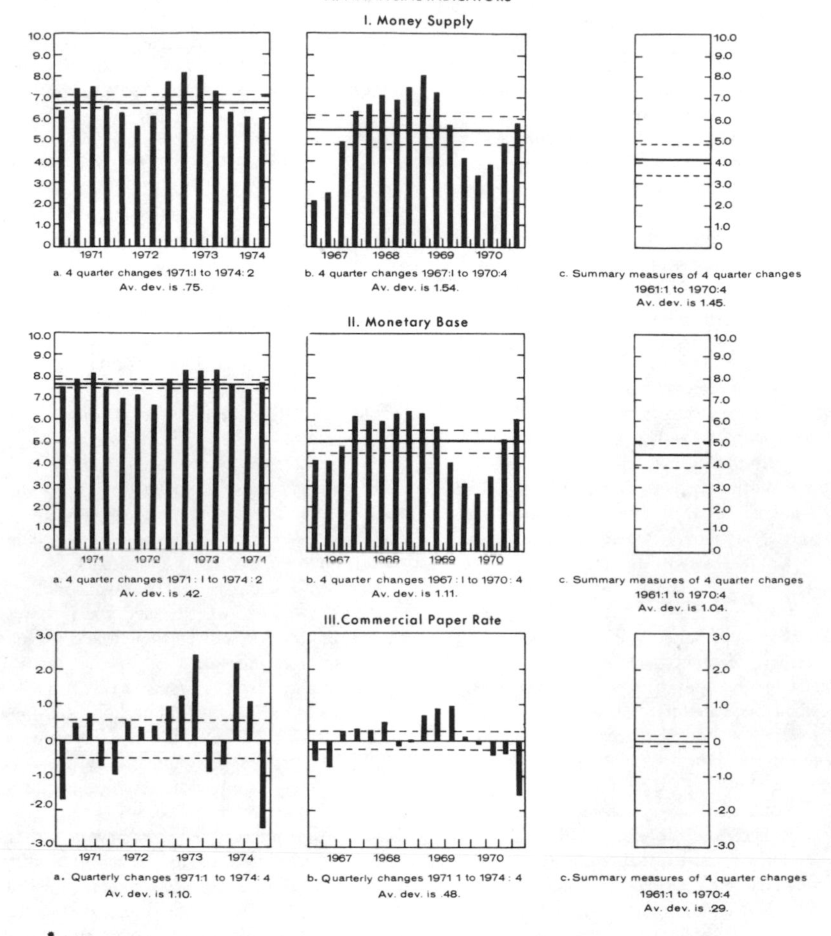

* The solid horizontal line in each panel denotes the mean value of the variable while the distance between the solid and dashed horizontal lines in each panel denotes the absolute average deviation from the mean (except in III and V where the average deviation is measured around zero).

Figure 4 (continued)

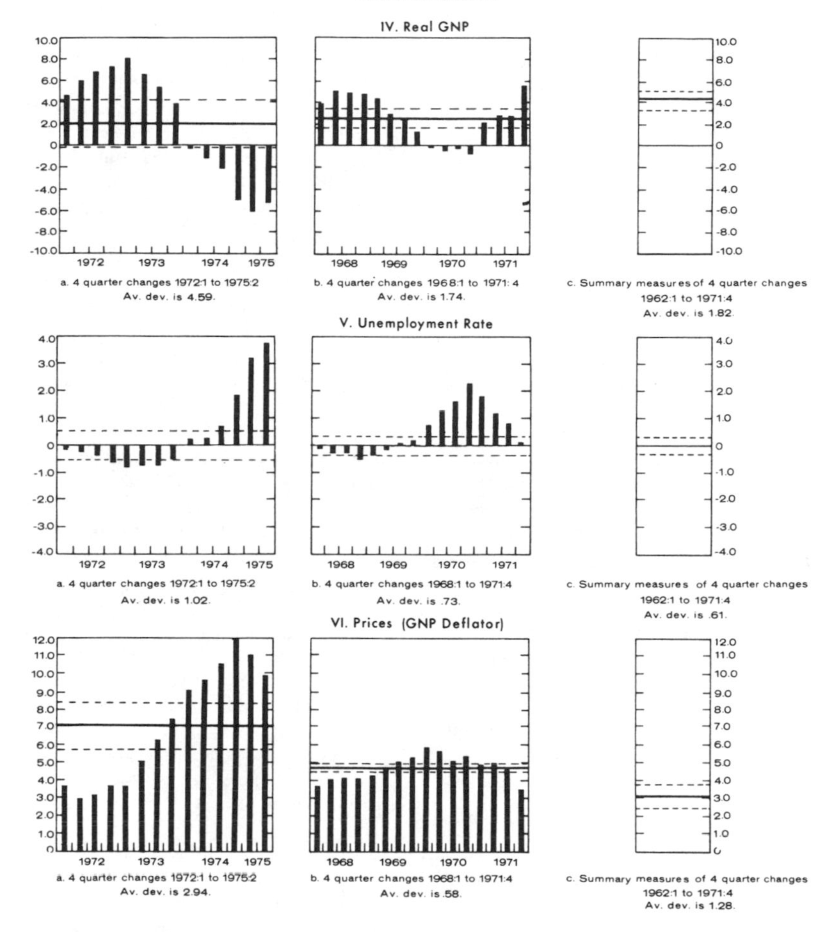

** The behavior of the real indicators is exhibited for a time interval beginning one year later than for the financial indicators in order to make some allowance for the lag with which monetary variables are presumed to affect output and prices.

Source: National Bureau of Economic Research Data Bank

will result; hence one might as well state the target directly in terms of interest rates. Of course, if one had accurate knowledge of the warranted interest rate path, and of the money supply needed to achieve that path (i.e., of the money demand function) one could as well opt for a target money supply path—but this path would generally not involve a constant rate of growth.

In reality our knowledge both of the warranted path of interest rates and of the money supply needed to bring it about is subject to errors and uncertainties. Recent work on the problem of optimal stabilization policy has established that under these circumstances, the optimal procedure can be described as one of straddling between the two targets. That is, one should start out with a money supply and an interest rate target which are consistent with each other in terms of our a priori fallible knowledge of the economy's structure. As long as these two targets prove to be in fact consistent, both targets can be enforced simultaneously. On the other hand, if and when they turn out to be inconsistent with each other, then neither of them should be enforced rigidly at the expense of the other. Instead, one or both should be modified and updated so as to make them again consistent ex-ante, by appropriate procedures which also take into account any available information on the extent to which the final targets—output and prices—deviate from the intended path.[17] The essential point is that, except possibly in unrealistic limiting cases, it is generally not optimal to stick to an exclusive money supply target, let alone a constant growth one.

[17] See e.g., W. Poole, "Optimal Choice of Monetary Policy Instruments in a Simple Stochastic Macro Model," *Quarterly Journal of Economics*, LXXXIV, May 1970; and B. Friedman, "Targets, Instruments and Indicators of Monetary Policy," *JME*, Vol. 1, October 1975.

By the same token, of course, it is also generally not optimal to adhere to an exclusive interest rate target. The reason we have placed primary stress on this target here reflects the nature of our recommendation and some special circumstances of the moment.

First, we must recall that our interest rate target is higher than what we regard as the optimal one, and is a compromise dictated by institutional feasibility considerations. The probability that new information accruing over the next two to three quarters will indicate that this target is too low is, in our view, negligible—though we have allowed for this possibility.

Second, our choice of targets is intimately related to the prevailing level of interest rate ceilings, and the judgment that an appreciable rise above this threshold would be likely to produce serious repercussions on the already problematic recovery of housing.

Finally, there is the problem of the recent instability of the demand for money to which reference was made above, and which militates against a rigid money supply target since its interest rate implications are subject to a large margin of uncertainty. As noted earlier, if this instability continues in the near future, pursuit of an interest rate target may well be accompanied by sizable short-run swings in the growth of money, even if money income stays within the anticipated and prescribed path. Such swings have in fact occurred recently, notably in the second quarter of last year. To nonmonetarists, these short-run swings in money growth rates to accommodate short-run fluctuations in money demand have no significant undesirable consequence; on the contrary they are quite appropriate in that, in the words of Chairman Burns, "to maintain a constant growth rate of the money supply, could lead to sharp swings in interest rates and risk damage to financial markets and the economy."[18] The monetarists on the other hand seem to hold that swings in the growth rate of money have serious destabilizing effects on the economy independently of the circumstances and the course of interest rates, while swings in interest rates have none. This difference in assessment provides one further reason why monetarists want a constant money growth target, while nonmonetarists want short-run stability of interest rates.

To our regret, we are unable to provide a rationale for the monetarists' assessment of the comparative unstabilizing effects of *short-term* variability in the growth of monetary aggregates versus variability in short-term interest rates. First, there is the question that the short-run stability of some monetary aggregates may only be achieved by unstabilizing others. A second, and more serious, consideration is that interest rates clearly affect directly income, wealth, costs and profits of millions of people, whereas it is pretty hard to see how a change in any particular monetary aggregate could directly affect anybody except through interest rates. (Rationing effects could conceivably be important but could hardly be invoked by the monetarists who generally regard them as nonexistent or utterly unessential.) The only explanation we can find for the monetarists' puzzling ranking is concern that agreeing to a different ranking might raise questions about the virtues of the constant money growth rule.

C. Why the Difference in the Maximum Acceptable Rate of Growth of Money?

The considerations developed so far throw light on why the monetarists' advice is cast entirely in terms of a money supply target, while at this time the nonmonetarists stress also, if not primarily, the interest rate target. There still remains the question as to why the monetarist target is so distinctly lower than that advocated by the nonmonetarists, be it directly or indirectly as the most probable implication of their interest target. As we see it, in respect to this issue, the similarity of advice within the monetarist pole conceals important differences of reasoning and judgment.

1) Rules Versus Discretion Once More

There is first of all a group of "purists" whose support of the moderate growth rate target can be traced to an issue of principle, rather than to the specific circumstances.

The issue of principle is that the rate of growth of the money supply must be held at the same constant rate indefinitely, or at least for very long periods. They would not tolerate a maximum growth rate of the magnitude envisaged at the nonmonetarist pole for the near future, for, by general agreement, such a growth rate would most certainly be too high beyond two or three quarters. Their 5 to 7 percent target already represents somewhat of a departure from their standard range which is much closer to zero, a departure presumably prompted by the recognition that the current circumstances do justify some exception; as the inflation abates, they will (justifiably) feel bound to lower the present target. A target above 7 percent with its implication of more frequent revisions would just be too much of a departure. These issues of principle probably play some role also for the others at the monetarist pole, but are reinforced, and even overshadowed by various other arguments examined below.

[18] Statement by Chairman Burns, *op. cit.* Again, this citation should not be construed to imply that we classify Dr. Burns as a nonmonetarist.

2) How Fast Should Unemployment Be Reabsorbed: Available Trade-Offs and the Relative Cost of Unemployment and Inflation

A second and equally important reason for the discrepancy in money growth targets can be traced to basic differences in views as to how fast we should endeavor to reduce unemployment and hence how large is the desirable growth of output over the coming quarters. Monetarists are in no rush to reduce unemployment as long as the rate of inflation remains high, and hence favor a slow recovery, at least for the moment. Nonmonetarists, on the other hand, though agreeing on the need to maintain some slack in order to insure a continued decline of inflation, see no justification for the current extremely high rate and are anxious to see a rapid reduction to more reasonable levels. These different views reflect both differences in value judgments as to the relative costs of unemployment and inflation, and significant disagreement in the assessment of the trade-off between inflation and unemployment.

With respect to costs, the monetarists are inclined to view inflation as a most serious (if not mortal) disease which erodes the very fabric of society by capriciously redistributing wealth and income, and siphoning off resources from the private sector to the government (through the effect of progressive taxes and tax brackets defined in nominal terms). The nonmonetarists generally agree that inflation is a serious social and economic problem, though many would argue that the costs of inflation can be considerably reduced by appropriate reforms including the indexation of the tax system, the elimination of government-imposed ceilings on thrift institutions, and so on. These reforms, by reducing the cost of inflation, would justify less reliance on the high rate of unemployment in order to reduce inflation.

There are more important differences in the assessment of the cost of unemployment. Monetarists, though acknowledging in principle that unemployment has social costs, are frequently inclined to treat it in what appears a rather cavalier fashion. They argue that much of the direct economic loss visited on the unemployed is made up through unemployment compensation, that by all available evidence unemployment is but a transient state even when the overall unemployment rate is high, and that many remain unemployed simply because—partly as a result of unemployment compensation—they are unwilling to accept jobs available, at least in other locations or in other occupations.

The nonmonetarists, on the other hand, view an unnecessarily high rate of unemployment as a most serious blight as well as an inexcusable waste of productive resources. They point out that even under present liberalized arrangements, unemployment compensation covers on the average not much more than 60 percent of the unemployed (ranging in 1975 from a minimum of 56 percent in October to a maximum of 72 in April), leaving 2 to 3 millions unprotected; and that the incidence of unemployment is very uneven, falling most heavily on the lower economic strata and on minorities and teen-agers. They accordingly see unemployment as contributing to social disintegration and crime, and also to fomenting social strife, as those who remain employed see themselves bearing the cost of welfare and other programs to support idle members of society. As for the proposition that many unemployed are voluntarily so, they point out that the experience clearly demonstrates that when jobs are readily available, as indicated, e.g., by a rise in job openings, those presumed voluntarily unemployed move en masse out of the ranks of the unemployed.

Finally, unemployment implies a loss of output which empoverishes the whole society. Even if we accept our very conservative interim unemployment target of 6 percent, the present unemployment rate of close to 8½ percent implies a loss of output of over $100 billion a year. This massive additional output would not only improve the lot of those leaving the ranks of the unemployed, but would also contribute to the solution of many other problems. It would for instance provide additional investment to relieve the shortages of capacity that plagued us in 1973 and reduce the shortage of capital widely anticipated for the coming years. Similarly, by raising tax revenues, it would help to reduce the large government deficit that is of so much concern to the financial community, and it would equally contribute to improve the tottering finances of local governments and to relieve the pressure on taxpayers by shifting the now unemployed from the role of recipients to that of contributors.[19]

These differences in value judgments interact with differences in empirical judgments as to the nature of the short-run trade-offs between unemployment and inflation. There is in the monetarists' camp a tendency to argue as though the trade-off problem did not really exist in the sense that squeezing the inflation out of the system would require a fixed total amount of unemployment in excess of the NIRU. In this view, the only choice would be how best to spread that fixed total amount of unemployment-years over time: if we take more unemployment earlier we will have to take that much less later. If this view was empirically valid, the monetarists would have a good case for proposing a gradual reduction in unemployment toward NIRU; for tolerating higher unemployment at the initial stage of the recovery would produce a faster decline in inflation without requiring a cost in terms of an increase of unemployment-years. This view of the trade-off would be valid if both (1) the change in inflation was independent of the previous path of inflation, and (2) if the marginal effect of unemployment on inflation was the same at any level of unemployment. But all the empirical evidence about the nature of the trade-off, including our own equation in Section II, suggests that these two conditions do not hold. Under the circumstances, one can not avoid the dilemma of choosing between a gradual reduction of unemployment (a higher total of unemployment-years) in order to secure a faster reduction of inflation, or a rapid reabsorption of unemployment (implying lower unemployment-years) which would also be accompanied by declining inflation, but along a higher price path.

The precise trade-off between unemployment-years and average inflation along alternative paths depends on parameters of the Phillips curve. Nonmonetarists point out that all we know about the values of the relevant parameters suggests that a higher average path of unemployment will contribute relatively little to the reduction of inflation. This conclusion can be illustrated by using the equation reported in Section II to compare the path of inflation accompanying two alternative paths of approach to the NIRU target. In the first path, the return to NIRU is spread over four years with unemployment declining linearly until 1980. The second is our recommended path of reaching NIRU in two years (and remaining there until 1980). By the end of the

[19] For a fuller systematic analysis of the nature and magnitude of costs associated with unemployment and inflation, see E.S. Phelps, *Inflation Policy and Unemployment Theory*, New York: Norton Co., 1972.

four-year period, the difference in the inflation rate is only about one-third of a percentage point, and the difference in the price level is about 1.2 percent.[20] This discrepancy would be even smaller if, as seems likely, the faster increase in output that would accompany the recommended path would be counted on to have favorable effects on productivity counteracting the modest unfavorable effects on wages. But if the gains in terms of lower inflation are small, the output loss is significant; the high unemployment path implies a loss in output of about $110 billion. Such calculations in combination with the high cost associated with the loss of employment and output relative to inflation explain the nonmonetarist policy prescription of aiming at a rapid initial decline of employment.

3) Inflationary Potential of a Fast Growth of Money

It must be acknowledged that opposition to a rapid growth of money does not reflect exclusively the assignment of a relative low cost to unemployment. There appears to be also a widespread concern, fanned by crude monetarism, that the temporary rise in the rate of growth of money, which the nonmonetarists' prescription might entail, would unavoidably produce a fresh increase of inflation, despite the large slack in the economy. This view results from a basic confusion between the long-run effect on inflation of a maintained growth rate of money and the short-run (or even long-run) effects on inflation of a transient acceleration when there is plenty of slack in the economy.

There is no disagreement that a sustained increase in prices cannot be maintained over a long period of time without a commensurate rate of money growth. But it is wrong and misleading to conclude from this long-run proposition that the only cause of inflation is excessive money growth, and/or that a monetary expansion has a direct effect on prices other than through its effect on aggregate demand, and thus finally on capacity utilization. This distinction is important because our recommendation does not involve maintenance of a high rate of money growth over a long period of time during which the economy operates under normal (close to full employment) conditions. Rather it advocates a course which may lead to a temporary acceleration of the money supply during a period plagued by a substantial underutilization of available resources, to the extent needed to bring the money stock back to a level where it should have been if the economy was operating along its long-run full employment path and with a stable demand for money. Is there any reason to fear that such a policy would produce a new burst of inflation? More generally, is there any evidence that an acceleration in the money supply necessarily leads to a corresponding acceleration of inflation?

To test this hypothesis, we can examine the relation between the acceleration of money and the acceleration of inflation, during the 22 years of the post-Korean period. One finds that these two quantities have moved more often in *opposite* directions than together, and that their correlation is about *zero*. Allowing for a lagged response of prices to money scarcely changes this result; similarly, simple relations between inflation and money growth rates fail to exhibit any systematic effects.

[20] These results do not depend to a significant extent on the nonlinearity of the Phillips curve. If one repeats the same calculations for an equation in which 1/UA was replaced by UA, one finds that the difference between the terminal inflation rate generated along the two alternative paths is two-thirds of a percentage point, and the difference in the terminal price level is 2.4 percent.

The only way to obtain a meaningful and significant relation between inflation and the rate of money growth is by allowing for the compound effect on prices of monetary growth over a long stretch of previous years.[21] This outcome is, of course, consistent with the previous statement, which both monetarists and nonmonetarists accept that, in the long run, the rate of inflation is roughly equal to the rate of growth of money, up to a constant reflecting the growth trend of income and possibly of velocity. But the outcome is also perfectly consistent with our analysis presented in Section II, which established that the behavior of inflation can be accounted for quite closely, exclusively in terms of real causes—aggregate demand as reflected in the utilization of the labor force, productivity and exogenous prices—without any explicit reference to money. The reason is, of course, that money is *one* of the important forces (though not the only) shaping aggregate demand in the short run, and probably the most important in the long run. In this light it is interesting to compare the graph in the bottom panel of Figure 3, which exhibits the actual course of inflation with that "predicted" by the monetarist equation, with the top panel providing the same information for our "real" equation of Section II. It is seen that the monetarist equation reproduces the broad sweep of history but it catches much less closely the short-run movements. In particular it fails completely to account for the 10 percent inflation of 1974, predicting a rate of but 4.7 percent. This failure is fully consistent with our evidence that the 1974 burst was only fractionally the result of aggregate demand pressures.

For our present purpose, however, the critical question is whether money has any *direct* effect on prices over and above its *indirect* effect as a determinant of the real variables incorporated into our real equation. It has been suggested for instance, that a rapid growth of money would generate expectations of higher prices and thus lead price setters—be they firms or unions—to enforce higher prices and wages, independently of real conditions. One may well be skeptical of the validity of this hypothesis which assumes an obviously irrational behavior on the part of economic agents—rational agents would look at the real variables current and prospective, such as sales and unemployment not at the current rate of growth of money as such. But admittedly this hypothesis cannot be ruled out a priori. Fortunately it can be readily tested by adding variables measuring the monetary growth rate to our real equation of Section II. If money has an *independent* effect on inflation, than the coefficient of such variables should be positive and significant.

The result of the test is striking and unequivocal; when the rate of change of M_1, current and lagged one or two years, are added to the equation, singly or in combination, the estimated coefficients turn out to be *negative,* although not very significant. The safe conclusion then is that absolutely no evidence supports the view of a systematic *direct* effect of the rate of growth of the money supply on inflation, as distinguished from its indirect effect in contributing to determine aggregate demand in relation to the available labor force and possibly other determinants of productive capacity.

[21] Among several specifications estimated with annual data for the 1953-1971 period, the best "monetarist" equation was

$$\dot{p} = 0.09 + \underset{(.12)}{0.27}\dot{M}(-1) + \underset{(.15)}{0.71}\dot{p}(-1);\ \bar{R}^2 = .75,$$

standard error = 0.83; $\dot{p}$ is defined as in footnote 6 and $\dot{M}$ is the growth rate of the money supply (M_1); the numbers in parentheses are standard errors.

The essential implication of these tests for the formulation of current policy is that even if the rate of money growth required initially to enforce our interest rate target turned out to be well above 7 percent, there should be no cause for concern. A high growth is perfectly consistent with decreasing inflation, as long as the underlying interest target did not cause unemployment to fall below NIRU. But, as we have seen, that interest rate target is actually on the conservative side, and such that unemployment could be expected to remain above NIRU for quite a few quarters; nor could it set in motion overexpansionary forces such that they could not be readily offset before NIRU was reached.

The conclusion that a rapid growth of money in the course of recovery from a deep contraction is fully consistent with little inflation is also supported by earlier experiences for which one must go back to the period before the Second World War. Throughout the four years of recovery from the Great Depression from 1933 to 1937 the money supply grew at an annual rate of about 10 percent, real net output at a rate of 12 percent, but the rate of growth of the cost of living was below 3 percent and the consumer price index excluding food rose even less. Moreover, it is generally agreed that the modest inflation rate can be attributed to a considerable extent to "autonomous forces raising wages and prices" during those years.[22] Nor did that period's money growth induce inflation with some lag. Prices remained flat until mid-1940. Similar instances of "explosive" monetary expansion accompanied by a moderate or negligible rise in prices have been observed during two earlier rebounds from deep depression: during the 1879-1882 and 1896-1899 expansions, the stock of money rose at an annual rate of some 11 and 9 percent respectively, while the corresponding rise in prices was only 2.4 and 1.5 percent.[23]

More recently, monetarist-bent analysts, especially from the financial community, have produced a more sophisticated and novel argument against a high growth rate of money. It is claimed that an attempt at holding the line on interest rates by allowing money to grow rapidly is bound to be self-defeating. The reason is that lenders would interpret this growth as heralding an acceleration of inflation, and hence higher future short-term rates, and therefore, would hold out for higher long-term (nominal) rates. The higher long-term rates in turn would reduce aggregate demand. This argument is specious if not outright fallacious for it not only assumes that lenders' expectations are based on irrelevant information, but it further assumes that the borrowers' are not. For if the borrowers agree with the anticipation of higher inflation, then the increase in long-term nominal rates will leave real rates unchanged and hence have no unfavorable effect on investment. In view of the publicity that the above argument has received, we cannot rule out the possibility that, for brief periods, the financial markets might react perversely with some danger of adverse consequence. But we believe that the effect would at worst be transient. Furthermore, it could be avoided altogether if, in the process of following the general policies advocated here, the Federal Reserve spelled out clearly the nature of implications of this policy.

---

[22] M. Friedman and A. J. Schwartz, *A Monetary History of the United States, 1867-1960*, Princeton: Princeton University Press, 1963.

[23] *Ibid.*, p. 497.

4) Some Further Arguments Against a Temporary High Money Growth

Two more arguments against fostering or even tolerating a rapid growth of money in the coming quarters need to be reviewed briefly.

There are first some who are concerned that a rapid reabsorption of unemployment and implied rapid expansion of output would generate serious upward pressure on prices, despite the huge current slack. We have already examined this concern and found that it has no empirical support, particularly when dealing with the initial phase of recovery from a substantial contraction.

There is finally a view that appears to support a modest growth rate of money in the expectation that velocity will rise sharply in the current recovery, and as a result, this growth target will be consistent with a growth rate of GNP not very different from that sought by the nonmonetarists.[24] This argument is quite plausible and deserves close scrutiny.

It is true that velocity has typically risen appreciably in the early quarters of a recovey. This can be seen, for instance, from the data reported in Table 1 which summarizes the experience for each of the postwar recoveries since the 1952 Accord (releasing the Fed from the commitment to peg interest rates on government securities). Column (1) reports the average annual growth of velocity (measured by the difference between the rate of growth of income and money) for the first six quarters of the recovery. It is seen that on the average, velocity rose in these quarters at a 5 percent rate, well above the average for the entire period, or 2.7 percent. This held true for each recovery except the last, when the increase was only slightly above average.

There is also little doubt that velocity will rise again in coming quarters of the current recovery if the growth of money supply is kept within 7 percent. Indeed, as was pointed out earlier, the course of income over the next two to three quarters is largely independent of the path of money supply over these quarters. It was further indicated that the growth of money income is likely to be in the order of at least 10 percent on the average, and possibly substantially larger, at least in some quarters. If, then, the growth of M_1 is within 7 percent, velocity must of necessity rise at an annual rate of at least 3 percent, and probably appreciably more.

But whether these propositions justify the conclusion that a 7 percent growth is consistent with nonmonetarist-like real targets, depends entirely on whether or not the rise in velocity is accompanied by a significant rise in interest rates.

Now, barring a further downward shift in the demand for money schedule (a reduction of cash holding for a given level of transactions and interest rates, relative to historical behavior), an appreciable rise in velocity can occur *only* in concomitance with a rise in interest rates. And, in fact, in every one of the post-Korean recoveries, interest rates rose substantially, except in the latest for which the rise in velocity was barely above trend. Since it has already been argued that a significant rise in interest rates over the coming two quarters is inconsistent with maintaining the momentum of the recovery beyond the middle of 1976, one must conclude that a 7 percent money growth is inadequate—as long as the demand for money behaves in accordance with historical experience. Indeed, the reason why it was rejected earlier is precisely the

[24] See, for instance, the views attributed to Chairman Burns by Edwin Dale, Jr. in his column "Economic Paradox" in the *New York Times*, November 26, 1975.

Table 1

HISTORICAL MOVEMENTS OF MONETARY VELOCITY AND SHORT-TERM INTEREST RATES

	Average $\%\Delta GNP\text{-}\%\Delta M_1$	*First Quarter RCP*	*Final Quarter RCP*
All post-Accord quarters, 1953:Q1-1975:Q2	2.7	2.33	5.92
Six-quarter post-trough intervals			
1954:Q4-1956:Q1	5.8	1.31	3.00
1958:Q3-1959:Q4	5.0	2.13	4.76
1961:Q2-1962:Q3	5.7	2.86	3.33
1971:Q1-1972:Q2	3.3	4.59	4.58
Average for four post-Accord post-trough intervals	5.0	—	—

$\%\Delta GNP$ = quarterly percentage change, at annual rate, of seasonally adjusted current-dollar gross national product

$\%\Delta M_1$ = quarterly percentage change, at annual rate, of seasonally adjusted narrow money stock

RCP = 4-6 month prime commercial paper yield

SOURCE: Adapted from Benjamin Friedman, "Monetary Policy for the 1976 Recovery," *New England Economic Review*, January/February 1976, p. 7.

likely inconsistency of this growth with the appropriate course of interest rates.

There remains the possibility that the rise in velocity would not be accompanied by higher interest rates because of a significant and continued fall in the demand for money. This outcome cannot be ruled out, in view of the apparent downward drift in the money demand discussed in Section II. If this eventuality materializes, then indeed a modest growth of M_1 could be entirely consistent with the nonmonetarist recommendations and targets. However, it is hard to see how one could confidently base one's prescription entirely on the realization of this chancy event. It would seem that anyone supporting a 7 percent money growth limit on this ground would be on far safer ground by formulating his target in terms of interest rates (possibly conditioned on the course of income); for if the downward shift in money demand does not occur, then the 7 percent prescription would no longer be justified; whereas if it does occur, then the interest rate prescription would automatically lead to a modest growth of money supply.

IV. Conclusion

We have made an effort to provide a comprehensive and fair review of the differences in analysis, in empirical judgments and in value judgments that underlie the two positions. We suggest, however, that in order to choose between the alternative prescriptions, one does not have to accept or reject the entire position of either school.

From an operational point of view, agreement with our policy prescription requires only acceptance of a few propositions that can be largely reduced to the following—*value judgments:* that a prompt reduction of unemployment is highly desirable, at least as long as it is consistent with a declining trend of inflation, even if it requires at least temporarily abandoning rules for discretion; *empirical judgments:* i) that as long as unemployment remains above our interim 6 percent target, inflation can be expected to trend downward (at least until it has reached modest proportions), and ii) that a significant increase in interest rates beyond the critical disintermediation range in the near future has a high probability of slowing down the recovery to a pace inconsistent with a rapid reduction of unemployment toward the interim target.

Anyone who subscribes to the above propositions should reject the monetarists' prescriptions and favor our alternative recommendations for the near future. And, for the longer run, he should also see the merit of the non-monetarist position that money is too important to be left to the monetarists.

Errata

Page 31, column 2, paragraph 2, line 23: "than the coefficient" should read "then the coefficient."

ESSAYS IN INTERNATIONAL FINANCE

No. 130, December 1978

THE MANAGEMENT OF AN OPEN ECONOMY WITH "100% PLUS" WAGE INDEXATION

FRANCO MODIGLIANI

AND

TOMMASO PADOA-SCHIOPPA

INTERNATIONAL FINANCE SECTION

DEPARTMENT OF ECONOMICS

PRINCETON UNIVERSITY

Princeton, New Jersey

1 Introduction

The purpose of this essay is to analyze the relationships among inflation, aggregate demand, external deficit, and government deficit in an open economy where wages are set from time to time in nationwide bargaining and protected by indexation at a rate of 100 per cent or more against changes in prices. We shall label this economy "100% plus." Our analysis will help us to identify economic policies that can be pursued in such an economy to reduce inflation and unemployment simultaneously.

A concrete example of a "100% plus" economy is provided by Italy, where an agreement was reached in early 1975 on a novel form of cost-of-living adjustment. All covered workers (the bulk of the labor force) were granted the *same* number of lire per point change in a designated cost-of-living index, *independently* of each worker's wage level.

The long discussion that has followed this agreement seems to have established the following points: (a) a large range of wages, and probably the majority of the wages of industrial workers, are now indexed at more than 100 per cent; (b) total wages in industry are indexed at about 96 per cent; (c) with continuing inflation, the system of wages would converge in time toward a unique real wage protected by 100 per cent indexation. An agreement of this type also has important redistributional effects, of course, because a persistent inflation will gradually reduce the initial wage spread (except to the extent that the spread might be regenerated through wage drift or new wage contracts). It will also tend to generate redistributive and distortive effects between industries by causing a relative increase in the labor costs of sectors relying more heavily on less skilled, lower-paid labor.

In the simple aggregative model on which we shall rely for our analysis, we neglect these redistributive aspects, which are specific to Italian institutions, and focus our attention instead on the implications of a high degree of overall wage indexation, possibly exceeding 100 per cent. This, incidentally, is the aspect that has received less consideration by economists who have analyzed Italian wage indexation, their thinking being conditioned by an intellectual climate where distributional problems have

This paper is an extensive revision of an earlier Italian version that appeared in *Moneta e Credito,* 30 (1° trimestre, 1977), under the title: "La Politica Economica in una Economia con Salari Indicizzati al 100 o Piú." The authors wish to express their deep appreciation to the many colleagues who read and criticized various drafts of the paper, in particular to Nino Andreatta, Lucio Izzo, Bruno Sitzia, Rudiger Dornbusch, Andrew Abel, and Jeffrey Sachs.

1

more importance than problems of growth. By considering only aggregate effects, however, more light can be shed on what looms these days as the most fundamental of all distributional problems, that between employed and unemployed.

We shall assume that the major objective of the political authority is to keep economic activity and employment at a high level while assuring a condition of price stability that will keep the external deficit within limits that can be financed. For more than forty years, this problem has been at the core of both macroeconomic thinking and economic policy. In a "100% plus" economy, however, it presents features that are significantly different from the usual ones. Our essay tries to shed light on these issues.

Some Propositions

In what follows, we endeavor to establish a number of propositions about the relationships among the real contractual wage, national income, inflation, and external balance, and about the effectiveness of various policy measures in a "100% plus" economy. For the convenience of the reader, we summarize here the major propositions that emerge from our analysis.

Proposition 1. For given levels of productivity and indirect and social security tax rates, there exists, for each level of the contractual real wage, at most one level of output and employment that is consistent with price stability. This critical level is referred to hereafter as the "noninflationary rate of output," or the NIRO.

Proposition 2. If output is maintained above the NIRO by appropriate demand policies, then, even if output is maintained below full employment, a process of continuous inflation will be set into motion. The rate of inflation will tend toward a steady value that is higher the greater the excess of output over the NIRO. There is thus a tradeoff between the rate of inflation and output, and it is monotonically increasing.

Proposition 3. The critical level of output and the tradeoff mentioned in proposition 2 are adversely affected by an increase in unit labor cost from any source, particularly by a rise in the contractual real wage or by a fall in productivity.

Proposition 4. Given the value of all the parameters listed in propositions 1 and 3, the rate of inflation will tend to be an increasing function of the frequency with which wages are adjusted for intervening changes in the escalator price index (unless, of course, output is at the critical NIRO level).

Proposition 5. It follows from proposition 2 that output can be maintained at any constant level above the NIRO if, and only if, the money

2

supply is allowed to grow at a constant rate appropriate to accommodate the rate of inflation associated with that output level. This result further implies that neither a one-time change in the money supply nor changes in fiscal-policy variables can permanently keep output above the NIRO for a given money supply.

Proposition 6. Neither the NIRO nor the tradeoff between inflation and the excess of output over the NIRO can be affected by the standard fiscal instruments (government expenditure and income taxes) or by monetary policy. These generalizations must be qualified only in the sense that the noninflationary rate of employment may be affected by direct government employment policies.

Proposition 7. It follows from propositions 5 and 6 that fiscal policy can affect the *rate* of output only temporarily. Fiscal policy does, however, control the *composition* of output between the private and public sectors and between consumption and investment (contributing thereby to the determination of the real money supply). In the longer run, of course, the share of output devoted to investment will have effects on the tradeoff via productivity, and hence on unit labor costs.

Proposition 8. Proposition 6 does not hold if the fiscal action takes the form of an increase in indirect taxes. In the "100% plus" economy, such an increase cannot be used alone to shift the rate of inflation. But, because it is equivalent to a rise in direct unit costs, it produces an unfavorable shift in the entire inflation-output tradeoff, lowering the NIRO in the process. The increase in tax rates will generally reduce the deficit, but only at the cost of a permanent increase in inflation. It is not only a wasteful device for the purpose of making room for additional investment but it is inequitable. The only way that higher inflation can be avoided is by accepting a lower level of output, which may even imply a lower rate of investment, since in the "100% plus" economy the higher indirect taxes will fall largely, if not entirely, on profits.

Proposition 9. Proposition 8 applies equally well to a change in social security taxes, and for this reason a reduction in those taxes may appear to be a promising device to reduce inflation. However, if the reduction in social security taxes is financed by a corresponding increase in indirect taxes, the two tax changes will tend to offset one another, with little net beneficial effect on the NIRO.

Proposition 10. Given the rate of output and the associated rate of monetary growth, the rate of inflation is entirely independent of the magnitude of the real deficit or surplus in the government budget (except for limiting cases, and with due regard to the long-run effects of the deficit on the tradeoff via investment, mentioned under proposition 7).

3

Proposition 11. All the above propositions hold for the open economy with relatively minor modifications. The main qualification relates to propositions 1 and 6, to the extent that fiscal policy can be used to affect the volume of imports directly for a given level of aggregate income and given terms of trade. However, the mechanism driving inflation when output exceeds the NIRO differs in some important respects in the open economy. In the closed economy, inflation is driven basically by the inconsistency between the contractual real wage and the real wage that firms are prepared to pay to produce that output. In the open economy, this mechanism is overshadowed by the external deficit that develops when output exceeds the NIRO and causes a depreciation of the exchange rate, which fosters inflation and, in turn, leads to a further depreciation.

With the help of a simple aggregate model, we establish these propositions first for a closed economy in section 2, and then extend them to an open economy in section 3.

2 The Closed Economy

The Price-Wage Sector

The model. For the purpose of our aggregate analysis, the determinant of the price level can be modeled by means of the following equations:

$$P = (mWs/\pi)t \tag{2.1.1}$$

$$m = m(Q); \qquad m' \geqq 0;\ Q \leqq Q^0\ , \tag{2.1.2}$$

where P = overall price level, W = nominal hourly wages, π = output per man-hour, $s = 1$ + social security tax rate, $t = 1$ + rate of indirect taxation, Q = aggregate real output, and Q^0 = capacity output.

In equation (2.1.1), Ws denotes the cost of labor, including social security taxes, and therefore Ws/π measures unit labor costs. According to equation (2.1.1), price per unit of output, measured at factor cost, can be approximated in the short run by the expression mWs/π. Here the coefficient m denotes the relation between price at factor cost and unit labor cost, so that $m - 1$ represents the so-called "markup" on direct unit labor costs. Equation (2.1.1) can accordingly be regarded as an identity or as a definition of m.

The basic behavioral hypothesis is provided by equation (2.1.2), which states that, at least in the short run, the markup can be treated as a constant (if $m' = 0$) or as a stable increasing function of the rate of output. This formulation follows directly from the well-known Sylos Labini-Bain model of oligopolistic competition, which has already found ample con-

4

firmation in empirical studies (except that in that model π should be interpreted as "normal" or long-run productivity). In that model, too, the markup may have some tendency to decrease when there is a reduction in the rate of plant utilization, because oligopolistic discipline may weaken under such circumstances. However, the specification of $m' > 0$ is equally consistent with the classical model of short-run decreasing returns and market price determined by the short-run marginal cost (except that, in this case, π must be understood as a coefficient that can be deduced from the production function).

The market price P is obtained by multiplying the price at factor cost by the rate of indirect taxation t, which by hypothesis has no effect on the markup.

Equation (2.1.1) assumes that price adjusts promptly to variations in unit costs. In reality, for various reasons, the adjustment can be expected to occur only gradually. This phenomenon might be modeled by rewriting equation (2.1.1) in the following form:

$$P = g[(mWs/\pi)t] + (1 - g)\, P_{-1}; \qquad 0 < g \leq 1\,. \tag{2.1}$$

Assuming for the moment that the rate of indexation is precisely 100 per cent, the determinants of wages for the type of economy with which we are concerned can then be formalized by the equation

$$W = \mu P_{-1}\,. \tag{2.2}$$

Here, μ denotes the real wage established at the time of the latest national wage contract and preserved thereafter through indexation for the entire period during which the contract holds. The quantity μ is, accordingly, a parameter of the model. At the moment of the next national bargaining period, it becomes a variable determined by such forces as demand conditions, availability of labor, and the bargaining strength of the two sides.

The wage rate is assumed to depend on the *lagged* price level, in recognition of the fact that the labor contract does not (and cannot) prescribe a continuous contemporaneous adjustment of wages to prices. Rather, it establishes that the "correction" is to occur at stated intervals. In the case of Italy, for example, the adjustment is at present once a quarter. Note that the one-period lag formulation of equation (2.2) is consistent with any adjustment interval, provided this interval is conveniently chosen as the unit of measurement of time.

It is also worth noting that, in view of the lag of wages behind prices, the real wage at any point can differ from that established at the time of the contract; in this sense, the escalator clause does not totally insulate real wages from the effect of inflation.

5

If we now substitute equations (2.1.2) and (2.2) into equation (2.1), divide through by P_{-1}, and rearrange terms, we obtain $(P - P_{-1})/(P_{-1}) \equiv \dot{p} = g[m(Q)A\mu - 1]$, where $A \equiv (st)/\pi$. Here, $\dot{p}$ denotes rate of inflation per unit of time—for instance, the quarterly rate of inflation if the interval between successive adjustments of wages is one quarter. The annual rate of inflation, which we will denote by p, can then be approximated by

$$p \simeq ng\ [m(Q)A\mu - 1]\ , \tag{2.S.1}$$

where n denotes the number of wage adjustments per year[1] (e.g., 4 in the case of Italy).

The relationships among employment, inflation, and contractual real wages. Equation (2.S.1) enables us to establish several useful results, which can be conveniently illustrated by means of Figure 1. The rising curve denoted by B is a graphic representation of the markup function $m(Q)$ multiplied by the parametric constant A. From equation (2.1.1) we can infer that this curve represents the value of the ratio of price to wages that business firms will require in order to produce a given output. The slope of this curve at any point measures the sensitivity of the markup to variations in aggregate output.[2] The straight line parallel to the Q axis is the graphic representation of $1/\mu$. Since μ is the real wage imposed by union contracts, $1/\mu$ can be thought of as the value of P/W that is imposed by labor and is therefore denoted as L.

Equation (2.S.1) tells us that, for any given level of output, the rate of inflation P is proportional to the distance between curves B and L in Figure 1. Accordingly, there will exist (at most) one rate of output at which the price level will tend to be stable, namely the abscissa of the point of intersection of the two curves, denoted by $\hat{Q}$ in the figure. This output is the noninflationary rate of output, or NIRO, referred to in proposition 1. In terms of equation (2.S.1), the NIRO is that value of output, $\hat{Q}$, which satisfies $m(Q)A\mu - 1 = 0$. Note that there may not be a NIRO within the relevant range if curve B is horizontal or sufficiently flat.

It is also apparent that at any given point in time there is a single value of the real wage that is consistent with price stability *and* full-employ-

[1] In (2.S.1) we approximate $(1 + \dot{p})^n - 1$ with $n\dot{p}$.

[2] The hypothesis underlying the figure that $m' > 0$, which is supported by empirical evidence for a number of countries, is convenient when dealing with a closed economy in that it helps ensure price stability for some positive rate of output. If $m' = 0$, price stability would be impossible at any output whenever real contractual wages exceeded the level consistent with full employment. However, in the open economy, whether m' is positive or zero turns out to be of little consequence.

6

Figure 1

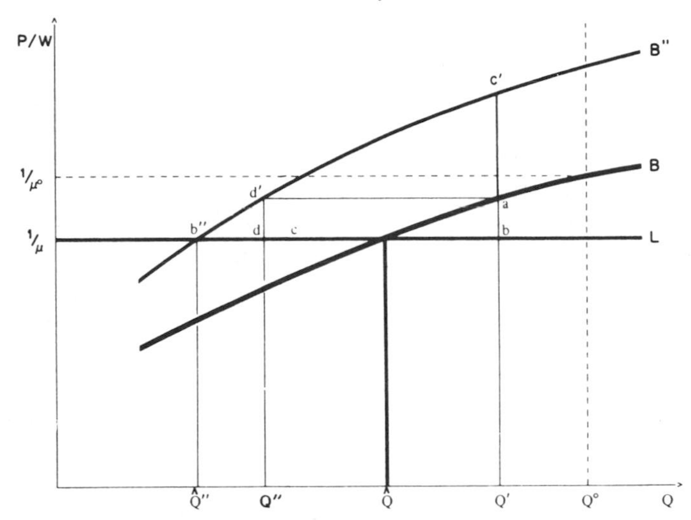

ment output, say Q^0. It is the value given by $1/\mu^0 = m(Q^0)A$ and is represented in our figure by the dashed horizontal line that intersects B at Q^0. Whenever the value μ exceeds μ^0, full employment becomes inconsistent with price stability.

If, through appropriate aggregate demand policies, the authorities succeed in maintaining output at some level higher than the NIRO, such as Q' in Figure 1, then, even if Q' is below the full-employment level, the outcome must be steady inflation, at a rate increasing with the excess of Q' over the NIRO (proposition 2). In Figure 1, this rate is proportional to the vertical distance between points a and b.

Recall that the height of curve B is proportional to A. Hence, it is directly proportional to the rate of direct and social security taxes and inversely proportional to productivity. Similarly, the height of curve L is inversely proportional to the contractual real wage. We can conclude, therefore, that an increase in real unit labor cost, from whatever source, will uniformly impair the tradeoff between inflation and output. In particular, it will lower the value of the NIRO (proposition 3).

If the curves B and L in Figure 1 do not intersect in the relevant range of outputs, or, equivalently, there is no value of output that makes the right-hand side of (2.S.1.) equal to zero, inflation will occur at all relevant levels of output, although the rate will still be an increasing function of output as long as curve B has any positive slope at all.

Equation (2.S.1) also shows that for given values of A and μ, the rate

7

of inflation corresponding to any output larger than the NIRO is proportional to ng, and hence presumably will tend to be higher the greater the frequency, n, with which wages are adjusted for the changes in the cost of living (proposition 4). Indeed, if the value of g were independent of n, the rate of inflation would grow in proportion to n. For example, let us suppose that the distance between the two curves in Figure 1 is 6 per cent and the adjustment of prices to wages in the course of the quarter is very rapid, say, $g = 1$. In this case, the rate of inflation would be 6 per cent per year if the adjustment occurred once a year. But if the adjustment occurred once a quarter, so that $n = 4$, the rate of inflation would be approximately 24 per cent per year [more precisely $(1.06)^4 - 1 = 26$ per cent per year].

In general, however, unless the speed of adjustment is very high, the adjustment per period, g, may be expected to decrease as the adjustment period becomes shorter (as n rises). Accordingly, ng will tend to change less than proportionally to n. To illustrate, suppose the adjustment is 30 per cent within one quarter. The adjustment within a one-year interval will then be 76 per cent.[3] In this case, if wages adjust once a quarter ($n = 4$), the annual rate of inflation will tend to be 7.2 per cent per year. Cutting down the frequency to one adjustment per year will reduce the annual rate of inflation to 4.6 per cent per year, or by a factor of less than 2, even though n has been reduced four times.

Equation (2.S.1) and the three propositions based on it apply directly to the case in which indexation is at the 100 per cent rate. But the analysis can be extended without difficulty to the case in which indexation is not at that rate, particularly when it is higher. In this case, in fact, the real wage rate implied by the original contract becomes a function of the price level, taking as a base the level prevailing at the time of the last contract: the parameter μ must be replaced by the variable $\mu(P)$, with $\mu' \gtreqless 1$ according to whether indexation is higher than, equal to, or lower than 100 per cent. We do not propose to give a formal treatment of this case here, and it will be neglected in what follows. But the qualitative effect can easily be seen, since the price level is simply the integral of inflation. For instance, if indexation is above 100 per cent and output is maintained at a level higher than the initial NIRO, the horizontal line L in Figure 1 will decline in time as the price level rises, causing a progressive decline in the NIRO and a steadily increasing rate of inflation, which in turn will displace L downward at an increasing rate. Clearly, the system is unstable except in the neighborhood of the NIRO implied

[3] If we denote by g_o the annual rate of adjustment and by g_n the rate of adjustment for a period of $1/n$ years, then $(1 - g_o) = (1 - g_n)^n$.

8

by the initial real wage. For the same reason, indexation at a rate lower than 100 per cent is stabilizing insofar as it tends to cause the line L to rise, thus tending to cause inflation to die down, although in this case, line L is likely to make a large downward jump when the labor contract is renewed.

Some implications. What makes it possible to maintain output at a level higher than the NIRO, even at the cost of a high rate of inflation? The answer to this question is simple in the limiting case in which the speed of adjustment of prices to costs is unitary. In this case, it is obvious from equation (2.1) that the markup will remain continuously at the level appropriate to Q'. This means that the real wage or its reciprocal, P/W, will remain precisely at the level "required" by firms in order to produce that output, and this independently of the contractual real wage. In Figure 1, the realized value of P/W will always fall on curve B, whatever the position of curve L. For instance, if output is at Q', it will be given by the ordinate of point a. This result comes about through the lag in the adjustment of money wages. It does not follow that the contractual real wage has no role to play, but its role is reduced to determining the rate of inflation: the larger the real wage established in the contract (that is, the lower line L relative to the level that is appropriate to output Q'), the higher will be the rate of inflation.

When the speed of adjustment of prices to costs is distinctly below 1, the situation becomes somewhat more complex. In this case, the effective real wage or its reciprocal, P/W, will fall between the contractual level $1/\mu$ corresponding to line L and the equilibrium level required by firms on curve B. In Figure 1, if output is maintained at Q', the realized P/W will be represented by a point on the line $Q'a$ in the interval ab. The closer g is to zero, the closer to b the point will lie, and conversely. In this case, obviously, the contractual salary influences the effective real wage. As μ increases and line L falls, the value of P/W will fall also, although at the same time inflation will increase.

This last result must be interpreted with caution because it assumes that the speed of adjustment of prices is constant, whereas there are good reasons to suspect that it is variable. The speed of adjustment may be low when the cost increase is at least partly unexpected, is of modest size, and does not hit all firms in the system simultaneously and uniformly. But when a high rate of inflation becomes chronic and generalized, there is reason to think that the speed of adjustment will tend to grow and approach unity.

This consideration suggests that the conclusion based on equation (2.S.1) (that to any value of output higher than the NIRO there cor-

9

responds a stable rate of inflation) is likely to hold only in the short run. If the inflation rate given by this equation is high, the speed of adjustment and therefore the inflation rate itself are more likely to increase in time, so that, for that same level of output, there will be a growing and not a constant rate of inflation. This process will reach a limit when the speed of adjustment becomes unity. However, one must also recognize that as this begins to happen and the rate of inflation rises, real wages will shrink because of the lag in adjustment. The unions will then try to increase the frequency of cost-of-living adjustments, in order to defend the real wage. The result, of course, will be a further increase in the rate of inflation, while the benefit to real wages will tend to be smaller the closer the speed of adjustment has come to unity.

In summary, even though it is possible in the short run to maintain levels of output distinctly higher than the NIRO, possibly at the cost of a high but stable rate of inflation, this equilibrium tends to become unstable in the longer run. The only stable level is in the neighborhood of the NIRO. In this sense, the contractual real wage or, more generally, the unit labor cost corresponding to this real wage has a fundamental role to play in determining the level of output and employment that the system can hope to achieve and maintain.

Determinants and Control of Aggregate Demand and the Inflation Rate

The model and its steady-state properties. So far, we have treated the level of output as an exogenous variable, concentrating on its effect on the inflation rate. It is useful at this point to endogenize output in order to examine how far output and inflation can be controlled through monetary and fiscal policies, and whether such policies can affect the tradeoff between inflation and output.

For this purpose it is sufficient to limit ourselves to a highly aggregated type of macro model of the Hicksian IS-LM type. Starting from the well-known identities of the national accounts and taking into account the consumption function and the fact that it depends on income net of direct taxes and social security taxes, we can approximate aggregate demand for a closed economy with the following equations:

$$X = Q + (W/P)G \,, \tag{2.3.1}$$

$$Q = Q(st,\ \theta,\ (W/P)G,\ Q_g,\ Q_i) \simeq \{(st)\ /\ [st - c(1 - \theta)]\}\ [(Q_g + Q_i) + c(1 - \theta)(W/P)G] \,, \tag{2.3.2}$$

where X = real national product, Q = real value added by the private

10

sector, G = employment in the public sector, Q_g = purchase of goods by the public sector, Q_i = private investment, and θ = rate of direct taxation.

The approximation in equation (2.3.2) holds insofar as the consumption function can be approximated linearly in the relevant interval.[4] We next assume, for the sake of simplicity, that net investment can be expressed as a function of the rate of interest r, that is,

$$Q_i = f(r) . \tag{2.3.3}$$

But note that our analysis could be repeated without significant changes if we assumed that investment depended instead on the rate of growth of credit, expressed in real terms.[5]

Finally, we add an equation that expresses the demand for money:

$$M/P = k(r)X ; \qquad k' < 0 . \tag{2.4}$$

If we take as given the value of M/P and approximate the value of W/P in equations (2.3.1) and (2.3.2) by the real contractual wage μ, the three equations (2.3) with equation (2.4) form a closed system in the four unknowns, X, Q, Q_i, and r. It is therefore logically possible to solve the system for each of these four variables as a function of M/P and of fiscal parameters. In particular, the solution for Q can be expressed in the "reduced form"

$$Q = F(M/P , st , \theta , G , Q_g) , \tag{2.S.2}$$

where, denoting by F_x the partial derivative of F with respect to the argument x, we know that $F_{M/P}$, F_G , $F_{Q_g} > 0$ and F_{st} and $F_\theta < 0$. If investments were related to the real credit flow, this variable would replace M/P in (2.S.2), assuming the nominal credit flow to be directly controlled by the central bank.

In Figure 2, the curve labeled F shows the relation between Q and M/P for a given value of the fiscal parameters. An increase in G or Q_g will shift the entire curve upward, whereas an increase in the coefficients of taxation θ, s, and t will shift it downward.[6]

[4] The hypothesis that s and t appear as a product in (2.3.1) is also a convenient approximation (see footnote 8 below).

[5] In principle, the right-hand side of equation (2.3.3) should contain the expected rate of change of prices along with the nominal rate of interest r. This refinement would seem particularly desirable in our analysis, which deals with the path characterized by differing maintained values of inflation. Nonetheless, we have chosen to neglect this effect in what follows. Omitting it does not appear to bias the analysis, in the sense of significantly affecting any of our conclusions, whereas taking it into account would greatly complicate the graphical presentation (see footnote 6 below).

[6] It is easy to verify, for example, that if one measures the expected rate of inflation by the actual rate p, the locus F in Figure 2 would no longer be independent of the

Figure 2

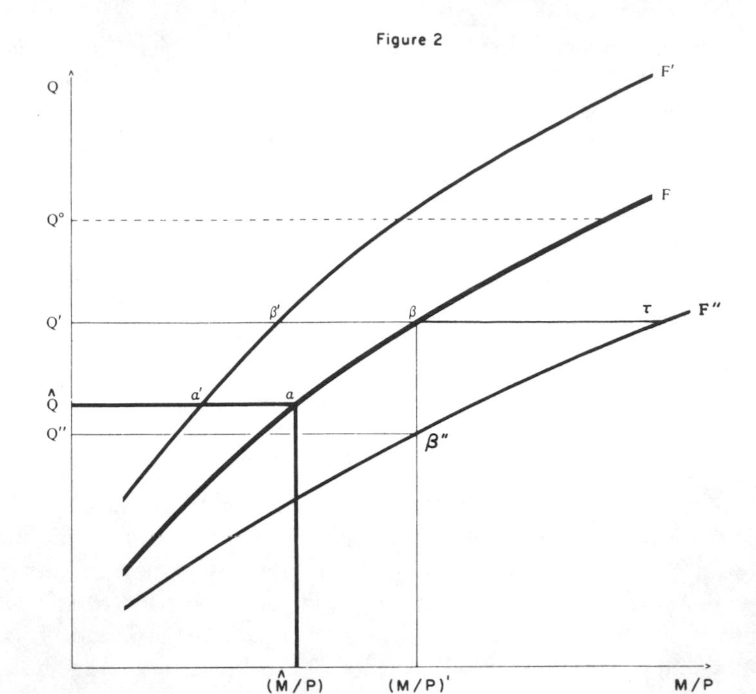

Let us suppose that the quantity of money, M, is fixed by the monetary authority, but let us regard P as an endogenous variable. In this case, equation (2.S.2) in the two variables Q and P, together with equations (2.1) and (2.2) in the variables P, W, and Q, form a closed system of three equations in the three variables P, W, and Q. If we combine the curves in Figures 1 and 2, it is easy to show that this system tends toward a unique solution (provided there is a unique NIRO, $\hat{Q}$): $Q = \hat{Q}$; $\hat{P} = M/F^{-1}(\hat{Q})$; $\hat{W} = \mu\hat{P}$, where F^{-1} is the inverse of the function F. This solution is indicated in Figure 2 by point α at the intersection of curve F with the horizontal straight line $\hat{Q}$.

That this must be the only stable solution follows from the fact that if the system were initially at some point such as β in Figure 2, where output exceeds the NIRO, Figure 1 asserts that there would be a positive

parameters of equations (1.1) and (1.2), and hence of the position of the two curves in Figure 1. Note also that if Q_t depends on the real rate, the curve F could conceivably have a negative slope—if the elasticity of demand for money with respect to the nominal rate, the elasticity of investment with respect to the real rate, and the responsiveness of inflation to output were all sufficiently high.

12

rate of inflation. But that means that P would be rising. Hence, for given M, M/P, and aggregate demand, Q would be shrinking along the curve F. A reduction in the real money supply (or in the real supply of bank credit) through higher interest rates (or tighter credit availability) would reduce the demand for investment and other durable goods, and hence aggregate demand. The system can find a resting point only when it reaches point α, where prices, and hence the real money stock, are stable.

The limits of conventional monetary and fiscal policy. From Figure 2, it follows immediately that in the "100% plus" economy the level of output and employment in the private sector can be increased only temporarily by the standard tools of fiscal policy—changes in government expenditure or direct taxes—as long as the money supply remains fixed. The same holds for a once and for all change in the money supply. Neither of those policies can keep output above the NIRO indefinitely (proposition 5). Furthermore, if equations (2.1) and (2.2) and the corresponding curves in Figure 1 are not affected by standard fiscal and monetary parameters, such policies are also powerless to affect the NIRO and the entire tradeoff between output and inflation, as stated in proposition 6.

The fact that conventional fiscal policy does not have permanent effects on aggregate output does not mean that it has no real effects. On the contrary, it will generally have important effects on the *composition* of output (proposition 7). Thus, an increase in government expenditure Q_g or G, a reduction in direct taxes, or an increase in transfer payments will have the effect of shifting upward curve F in Figure 2, as indicated by curve F'. This will initially move the system to a point corresponding to β' and a level of output Q' higher than $\hat{Q}$. But the process of inflation that gets underway when output exceeds the NIRO will tend to bring the system back toward the NIRO, at α' on F', by causing a gradual decrease in the real money supply that ends with a return to the NIRO. If the expansionary fiscal policy takes the form of additional government purchases, they will occur entirely at the expense of private demand, particularly of private investment. These will tend to decline because of the reduced availability of investment funds resulting from the increase in demand by the public sector to finance its increased deficit, which will also tend to be reflected in an increased cost of funds. If fiscal policy is carried out through a reduction in direct taxes or an increase in transfers, private consumption will increase, but again entirely at the expense of private investment. In other words, the "100% plus" economy behaves in accordance with well-known monetarist propositions. The fiscal maneuver

13

has no effect on the level of output and employment, since any expenditure it may increase will crowd out an equal amount of other expenditures (proposition 7).

The above considerations suggest that in a highly indexed economy expansionary fiscal policy of the conventional type may not merely be useless but actually undesirable, because its final outcome is a reduction in private investment. If the goal is to encourage investment, a case can thus be made for a *restrictive* fiscal policy despite the presence of excessive unemployment. The initial effect of such a restrictive policy may be a further reduction in the level of output, but this effect is transitory: if the money supply remains stable, the deflation resulting from the initial fall in output will have the effect of increasing the real money supply and investment, finally bringing output back to the NIRO. Furthermore, a carefully designed policy could attempt to avoid the initial contraction. The fall in consumption demand could be made to coincide with an increase in investment demand by an initial expansion of the money supply designed to bring about the required higher level of the real money supply.

Contrary to the monetarist tenet, there is one conventional fiscal measure, the expansion of public employment, that can increase total employment even though it cannot increase private output. In Figure 2, this action also has the effect of shifting curve F upward. As we have seen, this has no effect on the NIRO or employment in the private sector. Nonetheless, it will increase employment in the public sector, and hence total employment. But this operation, too, has a cost in terms of reduced investment, in that the newly employed in the public sector will increase their consumption. This result could be avoided by an appropriate increase in direct taxation. In this case, what would happen is that in effect those employed in the private sector would yield a portion of their consumption to those newly employed in the public sector.

In this sense, the swelling of public employment can offer a solution to the unemployment-inflation dilemma. It has even been suggested that such a development may explain certain aspects of the situation in countries like England and Italy. It should be clear, however, that this is a sick type of solution which replaces productive private jobs with presumably less productive public employment and which, in the long run, will tend to worsen the situation by reducing investment and incentives in the private sector.

We believe, nonetheless, that the above considerations are of some relevance to those who suggest that the root causes of stagflation are to be found in excessive public employment and the resulting waste of man-

14

power in that sector. Our model suggests that the first effect of a reduction of waste through a reduction of wasteful public employment will be the reduction of total employment unless a simultaneous expansion occurs in the private sector. But private-sector demand cannot expand as long as there is no reduction in the real unit labor cost. Accordingly, the argument that has been frequently advanced by labor spokesmen, for instance in Italy, that there is no point in focusing on real wages and productivity until the waste in the public sector has been eliminated is totally in error. We would suggest that the very opposite is true. There is no point in focusing on waste and overemployment in the public sector until a solution has been found to the problem of expanding private output without inflation—that is, to the crucial problem of reducing unit labor costs.

Output can be maintained at some level Q' above the NIRO only if the nominal money supply expands at a rate sufficient to support the rate of inflation that must accompany Q'. Conversely, if the money supply grows at some constant rate $\dot{M}$, output must tend toward a constant rate, say Q', such that the accompanying rate of inflation matches $\dot{M}$. For, as long as output is less than Q', the inflation rate will be lower than $\dot{M}$, causing the real money supply, and hence output, to rise toward Q', and similarly for output above Q'. This establishes the first part of proposition 5. With the equilibrium level of output determined by the growth of money, fiscal policy again plays the role of determining the composition of output (and the real money supply, M/P) as stated by proposition 7. In Figure 2, for example, the same Q' is consistent with the fiscal parameters underlying curve F and leading to equilibrium at β with money supply $(M/P)'$, or with a "looser" policy resulting in the curve F' and equilibrium at β'. Here the real money supply is lower because the looser policy means that more public or private purchases have crowded out investment through tighter credit and higher interest rates.

One significant implication of the proposition just established is that the rate of inflation is independent of the level of government deficit or surplus (proposition 10). This proposition is clearly at odds with a point of view which is widely held, especially in the financial community, and which is encouraged by the fact that inflation in both England and Italy has been accompanied by very large government deficits. To be sure, the government deficit has a negative effect on investment, and from this point of view there may be good and sound reasons to oppose it, especially since a low rate of investment reduces the chances of offsetting the increase in real wages with increases in productivity. Nonetheless, our results indicate that, in the short run, it is erroneous to attribute either inflation or unemployment to the deficit as such.

15

The notion that there is a direct connection between deficit and inflation arises from the unwarranted view that the deficit is the cause of monetary expansion because the central bank is somehow required to acquire and thus monetize the issues of public debt that must be floated to cover the deficit. In reality, in a country sufficiently developed to be able to rely on a wide market for securities, there is no logical reason why government securities should be placed with the central bank rather than in the market. Of course, if the central bank wants to maintain output at the level Q', it must necessarily expand the money supply at a rate consistent with this target. If it does not buy public issues, it will have to monetize an appropriate quantity of private issues. But refusal to monetize a certain volume of public debt will have no effect on interest rates as long as purchases of public securities are replaced by purchases of private debt. If they are not, interest rates will be driven up, but for the reason that the money supply is not growing at the rate required to support the rate of output Q'. In other words, to maintain output at Q' the central bank must monetize enough debt, either public or private, to cause an increase in the money supply at a rate consistent with Q'. But, at least as a first approximation, the division between public and private debt of the securities issued or bought is unimportant.[7]

Finally, let us touch briefly on a semantic issue. Even though the inflation we have described could not be sustained without a commensurate growth of the money supply (or credit), we see little value in asserting that it is "caused" by excessive money creation, thus equating it with the customary type of inflation in which "too much money chases too few goods." At Q' effective aggregate demand is not excessive because there are unutilized resources, possibly of considerable magnitude. It seems far more enlightening to say that, given the excessive unit cost of labor, if output is to be kept from contracting below Q' the central bank has no choice but to expand the money supply at a rate consistent with Q', even if this means a large expansion. There is usually a hope that the rapid growth of money can soon come to an end as the result of some break that will again make full employment consistent with price stability.

The effects of a change in indirect taxation. The possible role of other tools of fiscal policy remain to be considered, particularly the role of indirect and social security taxes, either singly or in combination with direct taxation. In Italy, for instance, increases in indirect taxes have been frequently suggested, and occasionally used, to reduce inflation. The

[7] The deficit can become an independent cause of inflation only when it exceeds saving at current output—or in fact that portion of such saving that the public would like to invest in fixed money claims.

16

higher taxation is held to reduce inflation by reducing aggregate demand, both directly and through a decline in the government deficit, resulting in a reduced growth of the money supply. In addition, the lower deficit is supposed to make room for more investment. However, our analysis suggests that in the "100% plus" economy this policy is ineffective and indeed harmful, as indicated in proposition 8.

Clearly, raising indirect taxes will reduce the government deficit, even though the increase in revenue due to the higher tax rates will be partly offset by a reduction due to the drop in income. But, as we have seen, a reduction in the government deficit has no direct effect on the rate of growth of money or on inflation in any other way. The only possible beneficial effect that could be claimed for higher indirect tax rates is that, by reducing consumption and the deficit, they might free resources for more investment. We contend that higher indirect taxes are a very poor tool to achieve this end, and, in fact, might be able to achieve it only at the cost of aggravating the inflation.

These conclusions may be illustrated by means of Figures 1 and 2. Suppose, in Figure 2, that we start at β on F with ouptut Q', and that the rate of indirect taxation t is increased, lowering curve F to, say, F''. If output remains at Q', the new equilibrium point will be at γ, implying a higher M/P, a lower interest rate, and higher investment. The trouble is that maintaining output at Q' would require accepting a substantially higher rate of inflation and a correspondingly higher growth rate of money. The reason is that an increase in t is equivalent to an increase in direct unit costs, and hence, as is apparent from equation (2.S.1), must shift the entire curve B upward in Figure 1, to curve B''. Thus, at the original output Q', the rate of inflation will be proportional to bc' instead of ba in Figure 1. More generally, the rise in t produces an overall deterioration of the tradeoff between employment and inflation.

The final effect of the higher tax rate on inflation and output will of course depend on what point is chosen on the new B'' curve as an appropriate choice of output and supporting growth rate of money. Note that if the output chosen is any larger than Q'' in Figure 1—for which the ordinate of the new B'' curve is the same as the ordinate of the initial curve B at the initial output Q'—the result will be not only *less* employment but also *more* inflation (which would, of course, require a faster growth of M). On the other hand, if the authorities are prepared to accept an output as low as Q'' or lower to prevent a rise in inflation, they cannot even be sure that there will actually be a rise in investment, which is presumably the only ground on which the rise in taxes could be justified. The reason is that the decline in deficit due to the higher taxes will be offset at least in part, and possibly more than fully, by the fall in saving and the reduced receipts from pre-existing taxes resulting from the reduction in output. Put differently, if the reduction in output needed to prevent a rise in inflation is large enough, it could exceed the decline in consumption brought about by the higher taxes and the fall in income, in which case there would be a *decline* in investment.

This surprising result (proposition 8) reflects the fact that in the "100% plus" economy indirect taxation cannot touch real wages (except possibly to the extent that it leads to a rise in inflation). To be sure, firms will endeavor to shift the tax forward, which results in the indicated upward shift of B, increasing the rate of inflation at any Q'. But, because of indexation, they can only partially succeed, and then only to the extent that inflation increases. In the final analysis, firms will bear the brunt of the tax through the lower markup they will be led to accept as a result of the fall in output that must come about to the extent that the monetary authority refuses to accommodate a higher rate of inflation. We can conclude, therefore, that in the "100% plus" economy, indirect taxes, if they are included in the escalator basket, represent a very ineffective, wasteful, and inequitable tool to reduce inflation or increase investment.

The possibility that an increase in indirect taxes is more likely to increase than to decrease inflation has led some to suggest that inflation could be reduced by *lowering* social security taxes. This suggestion has some merit. Indeed, since both taxes affect the outcome only through equation (2.1.1) and they enter symmetrically—as the product st—the reduction of social security levies must uniformly improve the tradeoff between inflation and output by lowering the B curve. By the same reasoning used to analyze the effect of indirect taxes, it can be established that, because of this improvement a cut in social security levies *could* simultaneously achieve higher output, lower inflation, and higher investment, despite the likely higher deficit.

Of course, it would be possible to reap the full benefit of the improved tradeoff from lower social security levies while avoiding any unfavorable effect on investment via a higher deficit by using other indirect taxes to replace the lost revenue. In a country like Italy, where indirect taxes have traditionally been easier to manipulate, it has been natural to propose the use of such taxes. However, in view of the symmetry noted above, it is obvious that raising the revenue by indirect taxes must largely undo whatever is gained by lowering social security taxes, with no net effect—at least as a first approximation (proposition 9).[8] For a closed

[8] The effect is not complete because the two taxes are likely to have different tax bases. The tax base for social security is only the wage bill, whereas the base for

18

economy, this result may seem fairly obvious. But, as will be shown presently, it continues to hold in an open economy, even if indirect taxes are rebated to exporters while social security levies are not.

Note, finally, that lowering social security taxes can be quite effective if the loss of revenue is made up by direct taxes. The reason is that the replacement of revenue will leave unchanged the fiscal-policy curve F and the equilibrium point β in Figure 2, but curve B shifts down in Figure 1, improving the tradeoff between output and inflation. The improvement in the tradeoff can be used to secure some mix of inflation abatement and output expansion, including higher investment.

3 The Open Economy

The Model

The price/wage sector. International trade affects the price equation in two important ways. First, unit costs will include not only labor costs but also the cost of imported raw materials. Second, prices may be directly influenced by foreign prices through foreign competition in both international and domestic markets. Hence, for an open economy, we are led to modify equation (2.1.1) as follows:

$$P = m[d_1(Ws/\pi)t + d_2 i] + d_3 i \,. \qquad (3.1.1)$$

Here, i is the domestic price in domestic currency of imported goods, which in turn can be expressed as:

$$i = eP_e t \,, \qquad (3.1.3)$$

where e = exchange rate (domestic price of foreign currency, which we refer to as "the dollar") and P_e = level of foreign prices expressed in "dollars." The markup equation (2.1.2) maintains its original form.

Allowing again for a gradual adjustment, equation (3.1.1) can be rewritten as:

---

indirect taxes also includes return of capital, profits, etc. As a result, a decrease in social security rates coupled with a rise in indirect tax rates that leaves unchanged the total revenue from indirect taxes may lead to a price decline. This effect, brought to our attention by R. Paladini and C. Casarosa, is modest, however. To illustrate, a constant revenue $\bar{T} = (t-1)ms(W/\pi) + (s-1)(W/\pi)$ requires that $t = [1 + \bar{T}\pi/W) + s(m-1)] \,/\, sm$. Substituting that expression for t into (2.1.1), we obtain $\eta_{Ps} = (m-1)\,/\,mt$, which is close to zero for plausible values of m and t. It is interesting to note that whatever effect is obtained through such a policy comes about because it affects profits asymmetrically, leaving unchanged their purchasing power in terms of labor while reducing it in terms of final goods (including investments). One might think that a systematic exploitation of this effect would eventually lead firms to increase m.

$$P = g\{m[d_1(Ws/\pi)t + d_2i] + d_3i\} + (1 - g)P_{-1} . \quad (3.1)$$

The wage equation must also be modified to take into account the fact that the basket of goods used to compute the escalator index will include not only domestically produced goods but also imported goods. Accordingly, equation (2.2) becomes:

$$W = \mu(a_1P_{-1} + a_2i_{-1}) , \quad (3.2)$$

where μ is defined so that $a_1 + a_2 = 1$, and therefore a_2 represents the weight of imported goods in the escalator basket. If the index were based on domestic value added, as has sometimes been suggested, then a_2 would be *negative* and correspond to the import content of domestic output.

The balance-of-payments constraint. Another essential feature of the open economy is the necessity to balance the foreign accounts, that is, to offset imports by exports, or at least to maintain the difference within limits determined by the availability of foreign reserves. This constraint can be formalized by means of an equation that expresses the current-account balance, or excess of exports over imports.

The volume of exports Q_e can be approximated in the short run as a function of the ratio of foreign prices P_e to domestic prices expressed in "dollars," net of indirect taxes, which are typically rebated on exported goods, P/et. It will also depend on world demand, but this can be taken as exogenous for present purposes and hence disregarded. Therefore,

$$Q_e = \phi[(eP_et)/P] = \phi(i/P) ; \qquad \phi' > 0 . \quad (3.5.1)$$

We will initially assume that the volume of imports can be approximated as a function of real income produced Q and the ratio of external prices expressed in domestic currency and inclusive of indirect taxes, $eP_et = i$, to domestic prices P, or:

$$I = \psi(i/P, Q) ; \qquad \psi_{i/P} < 0 ; \qquad \psi_Q > 0 . \quad (3.5.2)$$

The choice of Q as the "income" variable in the above equation has been adopted for convenience. It is, however, open to several objections, which will be reviewed in a section below where we also indicate how much we must modify our conclusions if we discard this assumption.

Using (3.5.1) and (3.5.2), the balance on current account expressed in dollars is given by

$$B_e = (P/et)Q_e - P_eI = P_e[(P/i)\phi(i/P) - \psi(i/P,Q)] . \quad (3.5)$$

Thus, for given external prices, the balance is a function of relative prices i/P and real income Q. From (3.5) and (3.5.2), it is obvious that

20

an increase in real income, with constant relative prices, increases imports and will reduce the current-account surplus or increase the deficit. We will also assume that the price elasticity of the demand for imports and exports is sufficiently high in the relevant time period to ensure that a rise in domestic prices expressed in dollars will result in a reduction in the current-account balance expressed in dollars.

From equation (3.5) it can then be deduced that, for any value of real income, there is only one value of relative prices that is consistent with current-account balance (or, more generally, with any pre-assigned value of the real balance). Furthermore, this value of relative prices is clearly an increasing function of real income. For if income, and hence imports, increase to maintain an unchanged current-account balance, the relative price of domestic goods must decline, making domestic products more competitive and thus stimulating exports and discouraging imports.

Determinants of aggregate demand. Equations (2.3.1) to (2.3.3) and (2.4) of the closed economy hold in the open economy as well, except that when we allow for the role of exports and imports, the function Q of (2.3.2) must include among its arguments the ratio of domestic to tax-adjusted foreign prices, P/i. From these equations we can therefore derive a reduced form that is a straightforward generalization of (2.S.2):

$$Q = F(M/P\,, st\,, \theta\,, G\,, Q_g\,, P/i)\,, \tag{3.S.2}$$

where $F_{M/P}\,, F_G\,, F_{Q_g} > 0$ and $F_{st}\,, F_\theta\,, F_{P/i} < 0$.

We can now proceed to examine how these various modifications affect the conclusions reached for the closed economy.

Real Contractual Wages, Employment, External Equilibrium, and Inflation under a Fixed Exchange Rate

Implications for the price-wage sector. Substituting (3.2) into (3.1), taking into account (2.1.2), and dividing by P_{-1}, we obtain a formula for the rate of inflation that is equivalent to (2.S.1):

$$\begin{aligned} p = ng\{m(Q)A\mu a_1 + [m(Q)\,(A\mu a_2(i_{-1}/i) \\ + d_2) + d_3]\,(i/P_{-1}) - 1\}\,, \end{aligned} \tag{3.S.1}$$

where now $A \equiv d_1 st/\pi$.

The first term in the curly brackets is basically the same as the first term in (2.S.1). But now there is a second term, which has the effect of radically changing the implication of this equation, because it includes the quantity i/P_{-1}. The behavior of this magnitude will depend in general on the behavior of the exchange rate, as it appears in the definition of i in (3.1.3). Let us suppose for the moment that we are in a regime of fixed

21

exchange rates and that foreign prices expressed in dollars are stable. In this case, it is clear that i is a constant (and therefore also $i_{-1} = i$), but i/P_{-1} is a variable because P changes unless the rate of inflation p is zero. Equation (3.S.1) tells us that for any initial value of P,

$$p \gtreqless 0$$

according to whether

$$P_{-1} \lesseqgtr \{[m(Q)(A\mu a_2 + d_2) + d_3]/[1 - m(Q)A\mu a_1]\}\, i\,.$$

It follows that, regardless of its initial value, P will tend through time toward an equilibrium value that is given by the right-hand side of this inequality. For if P is initially smaller, prices will be rising, and vice versa, bringing P toward its critical value. At the critical value, inflation is zero and therefore P will remain stable. From an economic point of view, this result means that, in contrast to a closed economy, where an excessive real wage implies a constant inflationary process for sufficiently high income levels, in an open economy under a fixed exchange rate, as long as output does not exceed the full-employment level, the inflationary process will tend to die down independently of the real wage obtained by the trade unions.

To clarify the mechanism leading to these results, let us start from some output and a corresponding equilibrium of P/i and suppose that the real contractual wage makes an upward jump. Equation (3.1) tells us that, keeping output constant, in the first period following the wage rise the price level will rise by a finite amount. The first round in wages thus causes a first round in prices. But the latter will be smaller than the former, both because a part of the cost (the cost of imported raw materials) remains unchanged and because prices of international competitors are fixed. The increase in prices generates, through indexation, a second round in wages. But this wage rise will be smaller than the first round in prices—and *a fortiori* smaller than the first round in wages—because prices of imported goods in the basket remain unchanged. The second round in prices will again be smaller than the second round in wages—and *a fortiori* smaller than the first round in prices—and so on. In this way, the initial shock tends to produce increments in the price level that gradually die out while the price level approaches its new equilibrium level.

Some features of this process are worth noting. First, at its end, the real wage will have increased by the amount established in the wage contract. However, the ratio of wages to domestic prices will increase less than the real wage because prices of imported goods stay constant

22

and the gain in purchasing power over these goods offsets the loss in purchasing power in terms of domestically produced goods. Second, although output is assumed constant, while the system is approaching a new equilibrium through a price-wage spiral the rate of profit will be falling. The reason is that international competition on foreign and domestic markets prevents firms from passing through to prices the entire increase in labor costs.[9] Finally, we observe that the inequality above implies that, for a given value of i, the equilibrium price is an increasing function both of the real contractual wage μ and of the level of output. This follows directly from the fact that an increase in either variable increases the numerator and reduces the denominator of the expression that multiplies i in the above inequality. Therefore, for a given value of i the relationship of P/i to Q may be represented by an increasing curve such as FL^0 in Figure 3. This curve corresponds to a given real wage rate, μ^0. A larger value of μ will be represented by a higher curve, such as FL''. The notation FL is a reminder that these curves represent the value of P/i that, for any given Q and μ, is consistent with price stability, in the sense that it is compatible both with the markup required by *firms* and with the real contractual wage secured by *labor*.

The balance of payments constraint. The fact that the open economy, unlike the closed economy, can reach an equilibrium with stable prices for any level of the real wage and any level of output less than Q^0 may make it seem that international trade opens the gate to an earthly paradise where one can have everything—full employment, price stability, and unlimited real wages—although at the expense of profits. But, in reality, this is not true—unless the rest of the world is ready to finance indefinitely any deficit in the balance of payments. What actually happens is that as the real wage increases for any given output, the domestic price also rises, causing an increase in the ratio of domestic to foreign prices, P/i. But, as we know from equation (3.5), this increase tends to produce an increasing deficit on current account. Thus, the need to balance the foreign accounts implies the existence of a tradeoff between real wages and output just as in the closed economy, although apparently through a different mechanism. The nature of this mechanism can be made clear by drawing another curve in Figure 3 labeled $B_c(0)$ derived from equation (3.5). Curve $B_c(0)$ shows the value of P/i that is needed for any given value of Q in order to ensure current-account balance (or, at least, to

[9] Let us denote with R gross unit profit, or the excess of income over direct costs. From (3.1.1), we have $R = m - 1 + [d_3 i/(AW + d_2 i)]$, where $A \equiv (d_1 st)/\pi$. Substituting for W from equation (3.2), $R = m - 1 + \{d_3 i / [A\mu a_1 P + (A\mu a_2 + d_2)i]\}$, which clearly shows that $(dR/dP) < 0$, provided d_3 is positive.

contain the deficit to a size consistent with the availability of foreign reserves). Curve $B_e(0)$ is decreasing, as was shown earlier.

With the help of Figure 3 we can establish first that for given values of productivity and tax parameters there is only one contractual real wage compatible with full employment, external equilibrium, and price stability. It is the real wage μ^0, corresponding to curve FL^0 intersecting the schedule $B_e(0)$ at point *d*. We can verify that point *d* satisfies all three conditions simultaneously. First, it corresponds to a full-employment income because it lies on the vertical line passing through Q^0. Second, it lies on the schedule $B_e(0)$ and therefore implies external equilibrium. Third, it lies on curve FL^0, corresponding to μ^0, and therefore at point *d* there is stability of P/i, and hence of P, for a given i.

From Figure 3 we can verify next that if the real wage rate is higher than μ^0, then at most two of these conditions can be satisfied, but never all three simultaneously. Assume, for instance, that the real wage rate, initially set at μ^0, is raised to μ'', corresponding to FL'', and that an appropriate management of aggregate demand achieves the aim of maintaining full employment, or Q^0. From our earlier analysis, we know that, as a consequence of the increase in the real wage rate, an inflationary process will be set into motion that will gradually bring the economy from point *d* to point *f*.

Figure 3

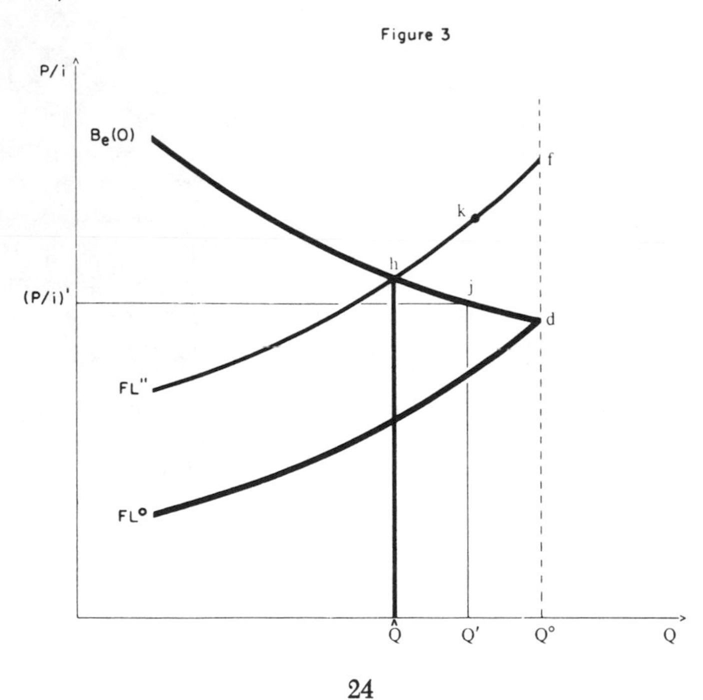

24

As this process unfolds, there will first be an increasing squeeze on profits, as domestic producers are unable to pass through the entire rising labor cost to higher prices because the prices of foreign competitors are unchanged, and then a growing current-account deficit.

By the time point f is reached, the inflation will have died down, so that this point satisfies two of the three conditions—full employment and price stability. But still f is not a stable point, because it fails to satisfy the third condition—external balance. In view of the deficit incurred at f, and indeed all along the path from d to f, and of limited reserves, the government will sooner or later be forced to abandon the effort to defend the initial exchange rate and to accept a devaluation to re-establish external balance. If it endeavors to accomplish this task while keeping output at Q^0, it will have to increase the price of the "dollar" by a percentage equal to fd/dQ^0 in Figure 3. The impact of this operation is to increase i and thus reduce the value of P/i in such a way as to lower point f until it coincides with the original point d. It thus re-establishes external equilibrium and the initial level of profits. However, devaluation, like a drug, can provide only temporary relief. Since the devaluation does not move curve FL'', point d, which lies below it, is no longer a point of price stability. Hence, the devaluation sets in motion a new wave of inflation carrying P/i back from d to f. Furthermore, the new price and wage spiral will be accompanied by a new gradual profit squeeze and by a loss in competitiveness that recreates the initial deficit at the new, depreciated level of the exchange rate. After a period of time, which is shorter the greater the speed of adjustment and the frequency of wage adjustments through the escalator, the effect of the drug will wear off and the system will be back at point f, with the same foreign imbalance and the same pressure to devalue. The only difference will be that the national currency has depreciated in terms of purchasing power both domestically and externally. Moreover, if the alternation between d and f is repeated, it is likely that the time required for the trip will shorten and that devaluation will tend to occur even before the system reaches point f and price stability. The expectation of a devaluation will create speculative pressures that will make it even more difficult to support the existing exchange rate, especially in the face of dwindling reserves.

We can conclude, therefore, that the attempt to hold output at Q^0 when curve FL lies above point d at that output must unavoidably result in a process of more or less continuous inflation. It is further apparent from Figure 3 that a similar conclusion must hold for any other output above the output $\hat{Q}$ defined by the intersection of $B_e(0)$ and FL''. For instance, at Q' there will be cycling between the poles j and k, which will again be

25

accompanied by continuing inflation, although presumably at a lower average rate because of the shorter distance between the poles. The only output consistent with price stability, or the NIRO, given the exchange rate is $\hat{Q}$, because point *h* falls on FL''; $\hat{Q}$ also assures the stability of the exchange rate because *h* falls on $B_e(0)$ and hence satisfies the external-balance constraint. We have thus established that proposition 1 and the first part of 2 remain valid in the open economy. Furthermore, since a rise in the contractual real wage, or in unit labor costs from any source, raises curve *FL* and thus shifts the NIRO to the left, proposition 3 also holds. Finally, under the assumption that, as a first approximation, imports depend on *Q* and not on its composition, proposition 6 also remains valid, since fiscal parameters cannot affect either the *FL* locus or the $B_e(0)$.

In a closed economy, the simultaneous achievement of full employment and price stability when μ exceeds μ^0 was prevented by the inconsistency of the contractual real wage rate with the markup required by firms. In an open economy, however, the problem goes deeper and extends beyond what might seem to be arbitrary and greedy demands by labor or the collusive behavior of business. The point is that μ^0 is the only real wage rate consistent with a ratio of domestic to foreign prices such that foreign demand for domestically produced goods is sufficient to pay for what the country wants to purchase abroad under conditions of full employment. Or, equivalently, it is the only real wage rate at which domestic and foreign demand for domestically produced goods is such as to absorb full-employment output with equilibrium in the balance of payments. On the other hand, the real wage rate μ'' implies a relative price such that foreign demand makes it possible to cover what the country desires to import only at a level of output $\hat{Q}$, which is below full employment.

While our analysis so far has enabled us to conclude that maintenance of output at a level above that consistent with the contractual real wage must give rise to an inflationary process, it does not enable us to trace out the laws of motion of the system as we could in the case of the closed economy. The reason is that the inflationary process goes through the exchange rate, and under fixed or managed exchange rates the authorities typically have some choice, especially in the early stages of the process. There is, however, one limiting case in which choice vanishes—when, either owing to a lack of foreign-exchange reserves or by voluntary decision, the authorities refrain from intervening in the foreign-exchange market and therefore the exchange rate is freely floating.

In this case, analyzed briefly in the next section, the path of the system, and in particular of inflation, can be specified more closely and can be shown to be analogous to the path characterizing the closed economy and summarized in proposition 2.

The Floating Rate

The consequences of maintaining income above its NIRO level. The essential implication of a floating exchange rate is that the rate will tend to adjust continuously so as to keep the ratio of foreign to domestic prices at a level consistent with current-account balance (or with a manageable deficit). Thus, if the management of aggregate demand succeeds in keeping output at some given level, say Q' in Figure 3, the exchange rate must be such as to generate the value of i/P corresponding to the ordinate of point j on $B_e(0)$. More generally, to any maintained value of Q there will correspond a value of i/P enforced by exchange-rate adjustments, given by the reciprocal of the ordinate of curve $B_e(0)$. Denote this value of i/P by $i/P(Q)$. Using this relation, we can express the variable i in equation (3.1) in terms of P and Q: $i = i/P(Q) \times P$. In other words, the movement of the market exchange rate ensures that foreign prices, expressed in domestic currency, move *pari passu* with (or proportionally to) domestic prices P, with the proportionality factor an increasing function of Q. Substituting for i in (3.1) and solving for P, we obtain

$$P = \frac{gm(Q)AW + (1-g)P_{-1}}{1 - g[m(Q)d_2 + d_3]\,(i/P)(Q)}\,. \tag{3.6}$$

By setting $g = 1$, it is possible to derive from this equation the value of the ratio P/W necessary for the equilibrium of firms:

$$(P/W)^F = [m(Q)A] \,/\, \{1 - [m(Q)d_2 + d_3](i/P)(Q)\}\,. \tag{3.6a}$$

Similarly, substituting for i in the wage equation (3.2), we obtain

$$W = \mu[a_1 + a_2(i/P)(Q)]P_{-1}\,, \tag{3.7}$$

remembering that $i_{-1}/P_{-1} = i/P = i/P(Q)$. Therefore, the value of P/W implicit in the real contractual wage is given by

$$(P/W)^L = 1 \,/\, \mu[a_1 + a_2(i/P)(Q)]\,. \tag{3.7a}$$

Dividing both sides of (3.6) by P_{-1} and using (3.6a) and (3.7a), we arrive at the following fundamental dynamic equation, which describes the behavior of inflation under a regime of floating exchange rates:

$$\dot{p} = g\,\frac{1 - [m(Q)d_2 + d_3](i/P)(Q)}{1 - g[m(Q)d_2 + d_3](i/P)(Q)}\left[\frac{(P/W)^F - (P/W)^L}{(P/W)^L}\right]. \tag{3.S.1'}$$

27

This equation gives the rate of inflation per unit of time equal to the period of adjustment. The annual rate p is obtained again by multiplying the right-hand side by n (bearing in mind that the value of g has to be simultaneously adjusted).

It is obvious that the equation above is very similar to the corresponding equation (2.S.1) of the closed economy. When the contractual real wage rate obtained by the unions exceeds the rate that is required by firms to produce an output Q', an inflationary process gets under way at a constant rate proportional to the difference between these two quantities. Moreover, the constant of proportionality depends again on the velocity of adjustment of prices to costs, g, and on the annual frequency of escalator adjustments. We have thus established that proposition 2, as well as 3 and 4, applies equally to the open economy.

There are differences, however, between the equations of the open and closed economies that have some bearing on other propositions. In the closed economy, $(P/W)^L$ was a constant $1/\mu^0$, while in the open economy it is a function of output through the term $i/P(Q)$ appearing in the denominator of (3.7a). Since i/P is an increasing function of output for a given μ, $(P/W)^L$ is itself a decreasing function of output. It decreases because, as income increases, the terms of trade deteriorate. To keep the real wage rate constant, the increase in the real cost of the imported goods has to be compensated by a higher purchasing power of wages in terms of domestic goods. This conclusion is illustrated in Figure 4, which is analogous to Figure 1. The relationship between $(P/W)^L$ and Q for a given real wage μ^0 is represented by the *decreasing* curve labeled L^0, while the corresponding curve in Figure 1 was horizontal. Clearly, a higher contractual wage rate would shift the curve proportionally downward.

The rising curve labeled B^0 represents the behavior of $(P/W)^F$ given by (3.6a) for a given value of A. As in the closed economy of Figure 1, it is an increasing function of Q. In Figure 1, however, the B slope reflects only the effect of the level of aggregate demand on the markup, while in the open economy the slope would be positive even if the markup were constant (and, within limits, even decreasing). As is apparent from (3.6a), in fact, an increase in Q, through the deterioration of the terms of trade, determines an increase in the cost of raw materials with respect to P that has to be compensated by a reduction in the relative cost of labor. Moreover, m appears also in the denominator of (3.6a); for this reason also, curve B^0 of the open economy has a greater slope than curve B of the closed economy for given values of A and m'. It could be concave

28

Figure 4

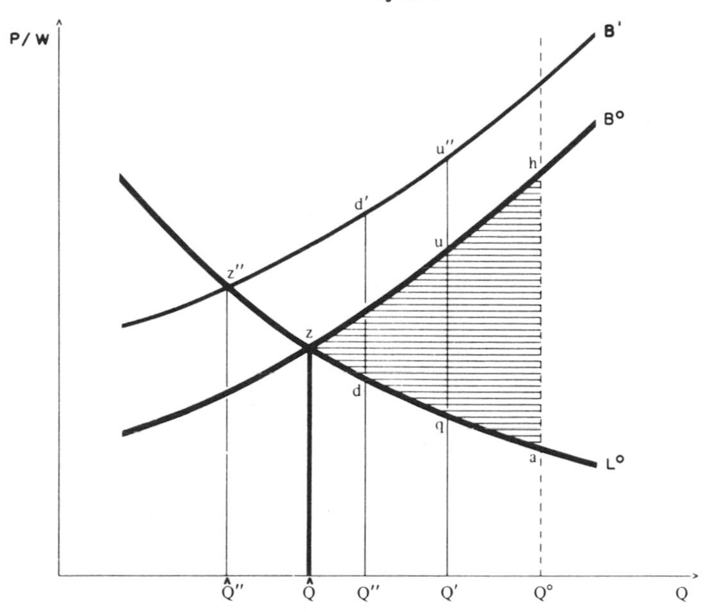

with respect to the horizontal axis, even if, as is likely, it would be convex in a closed economy.

Figure 4 can be interpreted exactly like Figure 1. Suppose the value of A is such as to produce curve B^0 and the value of μ, say μ', results in curve L^0. Suppose that aggregate output is maintained at Q'. Let us draw the perpendicular through Q', intersecting curve L^0 at q and curve B^0 at u. The fundamental equation (3.S.1′) tells us that, at that level of income, the economy will be characterized by an inflationary process at a constant rate that is proportional to uq/qQ', with a coefficient of proportionality that increases with n. The figure also confirms that for the given real wage there is a unique NIRO, namely the level $\hat{Q}$ corresponding to point z, at the intersection of the two curves.

The schedule B^0 holds for a given $A \equiv d_1 st/\pi$. An increase in indirect taxation or in social security levies changes A proportionally; therefore, as can be verified from (3.6a), it shifts the curve proportionally. This is shown by curve B', which indicates the effect of higher taxation. It reduces the NIRO from $\hat{Q}$ to $\hat{Q}''$. If Q remains at Q', the rate of inflation increases in proportion to $u''q/uq$. That means that proposition 8 is valid also in the open economy.

We can now consider proposition 9 about the effect of a reduction in the social security tax rate that is financed by an equivalent increase in the indirect tax rate. It has been suggested that this reduction, designed to lower curve B without increasing the government deficit, could be effective in an open economy even if it could not succeed in a closed economy. Although the operation would leave unchanged the total tax burden on firms, the reasoning is that it would shift the burden toward indirect taxation and, under prevailing international agreements, indirect taxes can be rebated to exporters, while social security taxes are not.

Our analysis enables us to show, with the help of Figure 4, that these reasons are invalid and that proposition 9 holds in an open economy. First, we can verify that the coefficients s and t do not appear at all in equation (3.7a) and hence cannot affect curve L. Next, we see that s and t affect equation (3.6a) through the coefficient A, in which they enter only as a product. Therefore, a simultaneous change in s and t that leaves their product unchanged does not in any way modify either of the two curves in Figure 4. Accordingly, it cannot change their point of intersection z or the rate of inflation that exists at any level of output larger than the NIRO.[10]

To understand this rather surprising result, observe from Figure 3 that, if Q is maintained at Q', P/i maintains the value of $P/i(Q')$. Thus the operation leaves unchanged the ratio P/etP_e. But since the foreign price in dollars, P_e, can be taken as given, it follows that the operation also leaves unchanged $(P/t)/e$, the price of exported goods in dollar terms. It must therefore increase P/e (the domestic price in dollar terms) in proportion to the increase in indirect taxes. The increase in the domestic price derives from the fact that, as indirect taxes increase, the cost of imported raw materials increases immediately in proportion, and wages also rise soon enough through the effect of imported goods in the escalator basket. The increase in these costs determines an increase in prices that raises the wage rate again, until prices of imported goods, wages, and domestic prices are all increased in the same proportion as indirect taxes. At this point, the competitiveness of foreign goods on the domestic markets is back at its initial level, leaving imports unchanged. On the other hand, the refund of the tax on exported goods exactly compensates for the increase in the cost of production. This explains why the price of exported goods in dollar terms is unchanged, leaving unchanged also the competitiveness of domestic products on foreign markets.

When we apply our negative conclusion to a concrete situation, we must of course allow for possible discrepancies between the real world

[10] But see our qualifications on the equivalent proposition for the closed economy.

30

and our streamlined description. For example, if there are costs of collecting and refunding taxes, or a different degree of evasion for the two forms of taxation, which is very possible, there may be net losses for society or a difference in the net revenue from the operation. The conclusion should also be modified if indirect taxes fall selectively on goods that are not part of the basket. In that case, the operation would be effective in reducing real wages, and the unit cost of production would increase by less than indirect taxes. These modifications can easily be worked out by the reader once the basic mechanism is clear.[11]

The limits of monetary and fiscal policy. We have seen that in an economy with floating rates we can assume that the balance on current account is always zero (or some exogenously given value), so that in equation (3.5) we can replace B_e with a constant. If we then solve (3.5) simultaneously with the reduced form (3.S.2) for Q and (P/i), we obtain an expression for Q in which the ratio (P/i) has been eliminated. The form of this equation is identical to equation (2.S.2) of the closed economy. This enables us to extend to the open economy the validity of propositions 5 and 10, to the effect that a necessary (and sufficient) condition for maintaining income at any level Q' above the NIRO is the growth of money at a rate equal to the rate of inflation appropriate to Q' while the deficit or the surplus in the government budget has no effect on the rate of inflation.

We must still consider the effect of changing indirect taxation and show that the criticism of its effectiveness expressed in proposition 8 remains basically valid in the open economy. To this end, note first that an increase in such taxes must again have an unfavorable effect on the inflation-output tradeoff and lower the NIRO. Indeed, it can be seen from equations (3.6) and (3.7) that a rise in t (a factor of A) must shift up the entire B curve, e.g., from B^0 to B' in Figure 4, while leaving the L curve unchanged. Thus, in order to prevent a rise in inflation, the higher taxes must be accompanied by a reduction of output from Q' to at least Q'', where the distance dd' to the new B curve from the unchanged L curve is the same as the distance qu of the old curve. Because of this required fall in output, a portion of the intended effect on investment of the larger tax receipts will again be wasted. The only difference is that in the open economy the dead-weight loss of output from Q' to Q'' will tend to be smaller than in a closed economy (compare Figures 4 and 1). This is because the B curve is bound to be steeper in the open economy than in the closed economy, and in addition the L curve slopes down in

[11] See, in particular, footnote 8.

Figure 4 instead of being horizontal, as in Figure 1. As a result, in the open economy there is a greater possibility of obtaining more investment without having to accept higher inflation, although this will always require a reduction of output at least as large as the distance from Q' to Q''.

Even with this qualification, there seems to be no ground for changing our conclusion that if an attack on the problem of inflation and a trade deficit is to be made by tightening fiscal policy, it is definitely preferable, for reasons of both equity and effectiveness, to use direct taxation. In a fully indexed economy, whether closed or open, indirect taxes, unlike direct taxes, fall entirely on profits; in addition, they produce unfavorable inflationary side-effects that may even nullify the desired reduction in inflation.

The Managed Rate: The Three Poles of Economic Policy

We can conclude our analysis of the open economy by considering the regime in which the exchange rate is left free to float only occasionally, while most of the time the authorities intervene on the market to fix the rate or to limit its depreciation. In the long run, the cumulative increase in prices and the external depreciation of the currency in such an economy cannot vary significantly at the same level of income from those in the economy with a floating exchange rate (if the cumulative deficit is kept at roughly the same level).

The major difference in the real world, as illustrated by the Italian case, is that depreciation tends to occur in steps, followed by periods of more rapid inflation. Such a process was described earlier with reference to Figure 3, in terms of the oscillation of the economy between the two poles d and f. Reality is more complex. During the inflationary process that starts at d, the deterioration of the current-account balance will tend to reduce income and employment, so that the economy moves not from d to f but rather tends to take a northwest direction toward a point such as k on the FL'' curve. Accordingly, in the vicinity of k pressure to depreciate comes not only from the deficit but also from a "devaluation coalition" including businesses suffering from the profit squeeze and possibly also portions of the labor force. The high average level of inflation that characterizes the economy's movements between d and k generates from time to time strong pressures for policies to stop, or at least reduce, inflation. Thus, a period of restrictive policies, both fiscal and monetary, will begin. After a devaluation has brought the economy to point d, the central bank may decide not to create enough money to finance the increase in prices on the path from d to k. At this point, income will start to fall (relative to the increase in productivity, which for convenience we have

32

omitted from our analysis) toward the NIRO, where the balance of payments is in equilibrium and inflation tends to disappear. But such a policy is short-lived: sooner or later, it will yield to the pressure of public opinion rebelling against the depressed state of the economy, the high level of unemployment, and the losses of firms. A period of reflation will thus follow, raising income toward Q^0, but only at the cost of renewed inflation pushing the system toward f, with a large deficit in the balance of payments and eventually a new depreciation. Therefore, the economy does not move between the two poles d and f, but rather between the three poles d, h, and f or k, each of which satisfies only two of the conditions of full employment, price stability, and external equilibrium. The wandering between these three poles may be appropriately described as the "infernal cycle."

Allowing for Fiscal- and Monetary-Policy Effects on the External Balance

So far in our analysis, we have relied on the convenient simplifying assumption that the main determinant of imports, aside from the terms of trade, is a broad measure of income, which we have identified with aggregate private output Q. In reality, both *a priori* considerations and empirical evidence suggest that aggregate imports may also be affected by the composition of domestic demand, because components such as consumption, investment, and government expenditure may differ appreciably in terms of their import content. This qualification could be of some consequence for our conclusions, since the composition of demand for given income (or real national product) can, within limits, be affected by monetary and fiscal policy.

From a formal point of view, the import equation (3.5.2), and hence the external-balance equation (3.5), should be "generalized" to include among its arguments, in addition to i/P and Q, fiscal parameters such as those appearing in equation (3.5.2). [On the other hand, it is not necessary to display M/P, since from (3.5.2) this variable can be expressed as a function of Q and the fiscal parameters.] In this generalized-balance equation, the effect of a change in a given fiscal parameter depends on the response to this change by various components of demand (subject to the constraint that Q be constant) multiplied by the import content of each component. A rise in the rate of direct taxation will reduce consumption and hence imports of consumption goods. If the other fiscal parameters are unchanged, it must increase investment (through an appropriate rise in the real money supply) and investment imports. The net effect will be to increase or decrease imports depending, roughly, on

33

whether investments have a higher or smaller import content than consumption, per unit of expenditure.

To see the implications of this "generalization" for our analysis, consider first Figure 3. The B_e curve in this figure was derived from (3.5). If some fiscal parameters are among the relevant arguments of this equation, the ordinate of this curve for any given Q will not be unique but will instead depend on the value of these parameters. In other words, P/i can be made to rise or fall by changing these parameters, depending on whether the change makes for a composition of demand leading to more or less imports for the given Q. Similarly, curve B^0 in Figure 4 was obtained from (3.6a) after expressing i/P in terms of Q through (3.5). Hence, in principle, the ordinate of this curve can also be affected by the choice of fiscal parameters; the same holds for curve L.

We must then conclude that proposition 6 no longer strictly holds in the open economy: fiscal policy can affect the NIRO and the whole tradeoff between inflation and output. It can do so within the limits—presumably fairly narrow in practice—in which it can affect imports for a given income by affecting the composition of demand.

We suggest, however, that this generalization need not significantly influence our analysis or the relevance of our conclusions. Although the locus in Figure 3 might be regarded as a band rather than a curve, in practice the width of this band can generally be taken to be fairly narrow. Second, the band can be reduced to a curve by considering only its upper boundary. In other words, with any Q we can choose the value of P/i corresponding to the lowest level of imports obtainable through fiscal-policy choices. This formulation has serious limitations, however, for it implies that the composition of output is of no concern to the policy-makers except as it affects imports. It also ignores the consideration that structuring fiscal policy with the sole aim of curbing imports to the utmost may violate the international rules of the game and invite retaliation.

A more useful interpretation of the B_e curve is that it represents the result of a stepwise maximization: for every Q it gives the value of P/i corresponding to the composition deemed most desirable with respect to its effects on imports and to any other relevant effect. The resulting single relationships between P/i and Q can be relied upon to produce unique B and L curves in Figure 4. With this interpretation, Figures 3 and 4 and the analysis based on them remain relevant.

Finally, we should recognize some possible effects of fiscal policy by means of capital movements. Moving policy toward an easier fiscal and tighter monetary stance should tend to attract capital (at least short-term), making it easier to finance a deficit while avoiding depreciation. Clearly, this approach cannot offer a lasting solution to the problem either, although it can be useful in providing temporary relief.

To conclude, in the open economy fiscal policy may play some role in determining the NIRO and the rate of inflation for given output, working through the composition of demand and short-term capital movements. But this role is likely to be narrow once other long-run implications of the composition of demand and of foreign indebtedness are taken into account. In general, therefore, fiscal policy cannot be counted upon to contribute much by itself toward a solution of the three-way problem of achieving full employment, price stability, and external equilibrium, but it can help to make it more manageable for a limited time.

4 Conclusions

We can now briefly review to what extent and in what forms economic policies can help to get the "100% plus" economy out of the infernal cycle and achieving simultaneously the basic objectives of full employment and price stability and the subsidiary objective of external balance on which the first two depend.

Our results can be summarized most conveniently in terms of Figure 3. The infernal cycle can come to an end only if there is conjunction of poles h, f, and d, defined respectively by the intersection of the B_e curve (representing external equilibrium) and the FL curve (representing the tradeoff between output and terms of trade) with each other and with the line representing full-employment output. Our first conclusion is that the conventional tools of macroeconomic policy—monetary and fiscal management—cannot be relied upon to produce significant shifts in the position of these curves. Hence, these tools cannot be helpful unless the three poles overlap to begin with, i.e., unless the NIRO corresponding to point h coincides with full employment. In that case, the task of stabilization policies is reduced to the traditional one of ensuring that aggregate demand equals full-employment output. What, if anything, can be accomplished then through less conventional policies?

Lowering the Sights

The most straightforward solution—even though it is not really economic, and hence may appear trivial to the economist—is to redefine the targets. The community could choose to shave the full employment (or at least the full-employment hours) target so as to make it coincide with the NIRO. In Figure 1, moving Q^0 to the left until it meets $\hat{Q}$ is

35

indeed one way to make the three poles coincide. This solution may be particularly attractive if the "establishment" consists of the employed, if the employed are able to protect themselves from encroachment by the unemployed, and if unemployment relief is minimal—a set of circumstances reminiscent of Italy in recent years. If, however, unemployment is a threat to everyone, or if the employed have to contribute generously to the unemployed, a better solution may be forcible work sharing through reduced hours but at the original hourly rates. All of these are distasteful solutions, the contemplation of which may help to make other solutions more acceptable.

Giving up the second target—price stability—and accepting the high permanent rate of inflation associated with a satisfactory rate of employment might appear to be another way out of the infernal cycle. It would seem to permit an end to stop-and-go policies and to the vagaries of inflation associated with the vain effort to defend the exchange rate, only to abandon it periodically under pressure. But this solution, even aside from its considerable costs, if only because of pre-existing contracts, runs into the difficulty that it is unlikely to be lasting. Indeed, the inconsistency between the contractual real wage and the wage required by firms at output above the NIRO is reconciled by inflation only through a process of "fooling" at least one party—a process that creates social tension and tends to be unstable. To reduce this fooling, adjustment of wages to prices and prices to wages must become faster and faster, leading to accelerating inflation.

Obviously, the third target—external balance—is not one that the community can renounce unilaterally.

Reducing Unit Labor Costs

A second set of solutions revolves around measures to lower the tradeoff between output and terms of trade by achieving a reduction in unit labor cost. The most obvious and direct way to do this, of course, is to reduce real wages, but such a measure is likely to meet the stiffest resistance. Increased productivity is an alternative which, if available, may be less painful. This approach is particularly promising where unions have previously encouraged or tolerated a fall in productivity through absenteeism, featherbedding, and other restrictive practices inside the firm, or through limitations on the use of the plant (on holidays, for multiple shifts, etc.).

One problem with this approach is that, although increased productivity will shift the *FL* curve in Figure 3 down and move the NIRO to the right, it will also reduce the employment level associated with any given

36

output. Hence, it may be hard to "sell" such a program to labor without a commitment to expand output proportionately more than the increase in productivity. Whether such a commitment is consistent with a reduction in inflation depends on the slope of both the FL and the B_e curves in Figure 3. In fact, if we were to measure employment E instead of Q on the abscissa, we would find that an increase in productivity has the effect of shifting both curves down. Accordingly, their intersection, which defines the noninflationary rate of employment, will not necessarily shift to the right. For this to happen, the B_e curve would have to be flat—changes in the terms of trade would have to produce large changes in the level of income consistent with external balance.

Indirect Approaches

Aside from these direct approaches, a number of tax "finesses" and related contrivances are possible. We so label them because they generally turn out to be disguised ways of enforcing one of the above direct methods, relying on some form of tax illusion.

One measure that has found considerable support revolves around the reduction of social security levies. Abstracting from institutional details, such a reduction is tantamount to a subsidy to firms proportional to labor costs. Since this measure again lowers unit labor costs and thus the FL curve in Figure 3, it will bring points h, f, and d closer together. However, unless it is offset by other measures, the reduction will increase the public deficit, possibly reducing the resources available for investment. This outcome is by no means certain, however. The expansion of output that becomes possible without increasing inflation above the original level reduces the deficit and also provides increased saving, which may exceed the residual increase in the deficit. Yet this approach is sure to run into strong "conservative" opposition as destructive of wealth, since, in the final analysis, it involves using saving to subsidize current income in order to reconcile demands for shares of income that exceed 100 per cent. What is forgotten is that the alternative way of reconciling these demands, through lower output and saving, may be even more wasteful.

To prevent or reduce a rise in the deficit, outlays might be reduced first. Ideally, this should be done not by curtailing real benefits but just by eliminating waste. But this approach, if feasible, should be classified under the heading of increased productivity. If it is not feasible and outlays can be reduced only by a curtailment of benefits, the effect is akin to a cut in real wages. The alternative is to offset the lower receipts by means of other taxes. A rise in income taxes to subsidize labor costs is really an indirect way of enforcing a wage cut, to the extent that the self-

37

employed manage to escape taxes. Indirect taxes provide an alternative only if they are *not* included in the escalator index, so that they imply at least a partial reduction in real wages. Otherwise, the result is a total or near-total washout. On the other hand, when indirect taxes *are* included in the escalator index, a reduction in such taxes becomes one possible device to reduce the *FL* curve, acting much like a reduction in social security taxes.

Improving the Tradeoff between Employment and a Sustainable Current-Account Deficit

Let us begin again by considering the use of standard macro tools. Since these tools can be used to affect the way demand is divided into its major components—consumption, investment, and government acquisitions—they might also be used to raise the B_e curve to the extent that the components of demand are characterized by appreciably different marginal propensities to import. But the room for maneuver is circumscribed by insufficient differences in the propensities and by the practical limits to modifying the composition of output. The composition of demand can also affect the B_e curve by influencing the domestic rate of return—at least on financial assets—and thereby short-term capital movements, but these effects are transitory.

Micro tax policy might also help to raise the B_e curve by imposing differentially high rates on commodities that are primarily imported, as against those produced at home. But heavy reliance on this approach invites retaliation, which shifts the curve back down.

A third approach to raising the B_e curve is by a policy of outright protectionism and self-sufficiency. The wide support for this approach rests on the perception that what stands in the way of full employment and price stability is the deficit that develops short of full employment as output crosses the NIRO. It is therefore tempting to conclude that the problem could be solved by impeding imports—whatever the cost to foreigners—and replacing them with domestic goods.

In reality, as we have argued, the problem lies in an excessive real unit labor cost, and protectionism cannot solve this problem: On the contrary, it can only exacerbate it. True, protectionist measures will tend to raise the B_e curve, but only so long as they do not incite retaliation. Domestic production is more expensive than the foreign goods it replaces, however, so that self-sufficiency tends to have the same effect as a fall in productivity: it shifts the *FL* curve up even more than the B_e curve. Thus, in the end, the three poles are moved farther apart instead of coming closer together. These conclusions should be qualified to the extent

38

that the reduction in imports might result in an appreciable improvement in the terms of trade, but it is precisely under such circumstances that retaliations are most likely, leading finally to reduced trade and universal loss.

These considerations do not deny the usefulness of incentives to domestic production of import substitutes, when that is possible at competitive prices, or to increased international competitiveness of domestic goods. But import substitution and increased competitiveness are most likely to come about through higher productivity.

In summary, the economist can suggest a variety of policies to attack the stagflation and associated exchange-rate instability that haunt the "100% plus" economy. But short of consenting to live with the disease, there is finally only one sound remedy: increased productivity relative to real wages. The handful of other devices tend, at best, to provide transitory relief—a breathing spell that can be useful only if the more fundamental cure is on the way.

39

PART III
Essays in International Finance

A Suggestion for Solving the International Liquidity Problem

Since it has not yet been possible to explain satisfactorily the facts about the demand for international reserves, the authors propose to modify the facts so they will generate a predictable and operationally stable demand for reserves.

Preamble

Exactly seven years ago, in March 1959, the *Quarterly Review* of the Banca Nazionale del Lavoro published the first of two articles by Professor Robert Triffin and touched off the debate on international liquidity. Since then, a multitude of plans has appeared, a host of conferences has been convened, and high-level negotiations have been begun. A significant consensus has emerged on several of the major issues, but no single plan has been adopted. It is not our purpose to survey the debate or even to review the principal issues. We hope, instead, to furnish a way out of the impasse by offering a fresh approach to the whole problem. It will, at first glance, seem to be a radical plan, but does not really involve any major departure from the principles of economic policy and conduct to which most major governments seemingly subscribe.

It is by now generally agreed that an adequate functioning of the system of international settlements under fixed parities requires that gold be supplemented, or even replaced, by some kind of intangible credit instrument. The main problem blocking adoption of a particular plan is how to determine, and who will control, decisions as to the rate at which total reserves should change over time. The problem is deep rooted, reflecting the difficulties encountered in developing adequate criteria to determine whether a given aggregate amount of reserves is " excessive ", exerting inflationary pressures on the world economy, or instead " inadequate ", exerting pressures toward deflation and unemployment. The widespread concern that an international authority responsible for creating new

3

reserve instruments would err in the direction of overissue has also created a reluctance to accept a new instrument in competition with gold. These problems have been nicely focused by the concluding remarks in the section on " International Liquidity Arrangements " in the *1966 Annual Report of the Council of Economic Advisers*:

> In any event, it is essential that the negotiations (for the establishment of new international liquidity arrangements) provide for (1) efficient as well as equitable rules for the creation, distribution, and use of new assets; (2) smooth integration of new assets within the existing framework; (3) the appropriate degree of expansion in the over-all volume of international liquidity which will foster sound world economic growth.

The plan outlined below is designed to provide a workable answer to each of these problems. It does so, basically, by requiring that each member country state explicitly its reserve target and undertake, through domestic and international economic policies, to maintain its reserves close to its target. The aggregate of all targets, in turn, provides a basis for determining the aggregate need for reserves. In addition, the plan includes an automatic mechanism which will tend to stabilize the purchasing power of a new international monetary unit. This mechanism would make the new unit quite desirable to hold (i.e., a satisfactory store of value), and suitable as a unit of account for international transactions.

In what follows, it will be convenient to have a compact name for the proposed new international monetary unit. We shall label it the Medium for International Transactions or, in brief, the MIT.

In order to bring out most clearly the basic properties and goals of the proposed system, we find it convenient to describe how the system could be set up and would function, disregarding received institutions and the legacy of the past as embodied in the present distribution and composition of international reserves. This will be done in section I, below, where we assume that the MIT is the sole legal tender for international transactions between central banks. Next, in section II, we show how the system could be modified to permit the continued use of gold, along with the MIT. Finally, in section III, we attempt to deal with some of the issues that will have to be resolved if the participating countries are not prepared to disregard the past. Needless to say, the problems involved in liquidating received positions or integrating them into the new system are largely political, and would have to be settled at the bargaining table. Hence our contribution *qua economists* must perforce be confined to identifying the major problems involved and outlining the main alternatives.

I. Outline of the Plan and Its Operation. The "Ideal" Version

1. Every member country shall accept a target reserve, expressed in units of MIT's, to guide its relations with the international monetary system. This target, denoted hereafter by T (for target) will be given by an agreed "formula" for each country, which will take into account its foreign trade and some measure of the variability in its balance of payments, based on historical experience.

We shall say more about the formula at the end of this section, once the role of the target reserve has become clear. Suffice it to note here that, given the formula, a country's target reserve will vary over time as its foreign trade and the variability in its balance of payments change over time. We therefore use T_t to denote the target reserve given by the formula, at a particular date t. If trade continues to expand in the future, as it has done in the past, targets will tend to grow over time.

2. At the start of the plan, the MIT bank (successor to the present IMF) shall credit each country with a demand deposit equal to the value of the target given by the formula at the opening date. This deposit might be secured by depositing with the MIT bank an equivalent amount of the country's own currency. At regular intervals, say once a year, the target shall be recomputed and each country shall receive from the MIT bank an additional credit to its deposit, equal to the increment in its target during the intervening year. (If the latest target happens to be smaller than the previous year's target, then the country's deposit shall be debited accordingly.)

Thus, at any date, the cumulated total of MIT's credited by the MIT bank to a country will precisely equal its target (subject, however, to the modification proposed in 5 below).

3. (a) Participating countries shall agree to use that MIT as the sole instrument to settle balances arising from international transactions (except as noted under 3 (b) below). Specifically, each country's

central bank shall agree to buy from, and sell to, other central banks, on demand, its national currency against MIT's and *only* against MIT's, at a rate of exchange established by that central bank. As under the present system, however, central banks may be allowed to fix a small percentage spread between their buying and selling prices.

(b) Member central banks shall agree not to hold, directly or indirectly, foreign currencies, except the small amounts required for day-by-day transactions in the foreign exchange markets. Allowable foreign-currency balances could be specified as a percentage of the target reserve, or as an absolute amount (measured in MIT), whichever is larger.

As a result of the transactions described under 3, each country's reserves, as measured by its balance with the MIT bank, will fluctuate over time, even though the worldwide aggregate of MIT deposits, or aggregate reserves, will be precisely equal to the sum of all targets (except as noted under 5 below). Denote by R_t the actual reserve of an individual country at date t. We now introduce the following clause which constitutes the very heart of our plan:

4. Participating countries shall strive to keep their reserves close to their targets at all times, by appropriate domestic and international economic policies.

The relation between the reserve and the target for each country can be conveniently summarized by a single number expressing the excess or deficiency of actual reserves as a percentage of the target itself. This summary measure will be labeled the *measure of imbalance* and denoted by I_t. It is given by the formula:

$$I_t = \left(\frac{R_t - T_t}{T_t}\right) 100$$

The imbalance measure may be positive, reflecting past or current balance of payment surpluses, or negative, reflecting past or current balance of payments deficits.

The obligation laid out in 4 can thus be restated as that of maintaining I_t close to zero at all times. This implies that all countries having an imbalance, whether positive or negative, accept the obligation to help in the adjustment process. The next clause spells out procedures insuring compliance with this basic obligation:

5. (a) Whenever a country's measure of imbalance departs significantly from zero it shall take appropriate policy measures to reduce the imbalance. If, however, the measure of imbalance remains within preassigned limits, henceforth called the *normal range*, the country shall be under no immediate obligation to take any measures.

For the sake of concreteness, we shall take the normal range to be between plus and minus 50 per cent, implying a cumulative surplus or deficit in a country's balance of payments not exceeding 50 per cent of the target reserve. For values of I_t in the normal range, limitations on a country's freedom of action should only be of a negative character: a country should not increase impediments to its foreign trade or to the convertibility of its currency and should not change the MIT par value of its currency. (Circumstances might occasionally warrant exceptions to this rule; a country in the normal range, but with severe unemployment, may desire to devalue in order to prevent a loss of reserves as it expands domestic demand. In such cases, however, the action would require approval by an appropriate supervisory organ of the MIT bank.)

(b) If a country's imbalance falls outside the normal range, through failure to take appropriate measures early, or because such measures have proved ineffective, or for other reasons, the country shall submit to the MIT bank, for its approval, a program of action designed to eliminate the imbalance within a reasonable span of time, account being taken of all the relevant circumstances. The MIT bank shall also be responsible for monitoring the execution of the program and recommending modifications in the light of subsequent developments, as long as the imbalance remains outside the normal range.

The process of adjustment described in clause 5 could be made more effective if, besides avoiding excessive departures from target in any one year, countries agreed to avoid *sustained* imbalances of either sign, even within the normal range. Imbalances maintained over a long period would in fact tend to complicate the process of adjustment for other countries, and might also interfere with the price stabilization feature of the plan described under 6 below. Ways of making this commitment operational need not be dwelt upon here in detail. In essence, a country would be deemed to have moved outside the *normal range* not only if its current imbalance, I_t, had fallen outside the 50 points band, but also if a moving average of I, including 2, 3, ...n terms, had fallen outside some agreed upon bands, which would be narrower the larger the value of n.

We recommend that the menu of measures open to countries with imbalances be rather broad — as long as they are not discriminatory in nature — broader than the IMF and other international organizations have typically been willing to accept. For a country with a positive imbalance, the acceptable measures might include reflationary measures (if the country also suffers from inadequate aggregate demand or its price level has been declining), fiscal and interest rate encouragements of capital exports and discouragements of capital imports, and revaluation of its currency relative to the MIT. A country with a negative imbalance should be encouraged to rely on deflationary fiscal and monetary measures if confronted with excessive domestic demand and/or rapidly rising prices, but should otherwise be encouraged to provide incentives to capital imports and disincentives to capital exports, to devalue its currency or to apply broad based supplemental import duties and export subsidies, especially if the difficulty appears to be transient. In short, when reviewing a country's policies, the supervisory organ of the MIT bank should be instructed that policies likely to operate at a significant domestic cost — be it rising prices or unemployment — should not be imposed or even encouraged except as measures of last resort. We stress this point in the belief that it is both necessary and appropriate to provide participating countries with considerable freedom of action if they are to accept the curtailment of sovereignty implicit in our plan.

Should a country fail to comply with the provisions of clause 5 (b), penalties might be invoked. In the case of a country with an excess imbalance which declines to submit an acceptable program of corrective measures, the sanction might take the form of an annual fine that recaptured some stated percentage of its balance in excess of the normal range, the percentage itself increasing with the imbalance. (If, for example, the rate of fine is set equal to the excess of I_t over 50 per cent, and that rate is itself applied to I_t in excess of 50 per cent, a country with reserves equal to twice its target,

8

hence an I_t of 100, would lose one-quarter of its surplus reserves in a single year.) The proceeds of the levy could be distributed among the remaining countries in proportion to their targets. In the case of a country with a large negative imbalance, levying of a fine might not prove too satisfactory, since that would reduce further the country's reserves. Appropriate penalties might involve the loss of other prerogatives, such as voting rights and distribution privileges, and in the limit, the blocking of any balances remaining in its MIT account. On the other hand, compliance could be rewarded by providing limited overdraft privileges to pace out difficult adjustment processes.

Since we strongly advocate a freer use of changes in individual parities as a means of adjustment, we should also like to urge that serious consideration be given to the possibility of making them by a series of small steps at frequent intervals — rather than in one discontinuous jump — with each step limited to, say, ½ per cent once a month. If these monthly changes in par values were kept within the customary parity points, there would be little incentive to disequilibrating speculation, and forward markets could ensure a smooth adjustment.

The scheme described so far would already be quite helpful in creating the appropriate quantity of international reserves, determining the distribution among countries of the initial supply and successive increments, and distributing the burden of adjustment between surplus and deficit countries. However, it would not be proof against inflation or deflation. If some countries promoted inflation or deflation, they would place a part of the burden of adjustment on other, "well behaved" countries. Furthermore, there would be no assurance that the purchasing power of the MIT would remain stable over the long run. We propose to handle this problem by the following modification of clause 2:

6. At regular intervals, the statistical office of the MIT bank shall compute an index of prices, in terms of MIT's, of internationally traded commodities and services, with weights reflecting their importance in world trade. (Alternatively, weights reflecting the importance of the commodities and services in world production rather than trade might deserve consideration.) Let P_t denote the standing of this index relative to the base year (the year in which the plan goes into effect). The aggregate amount of reserve credit granted to each country at date t shall then be made equal, not to

T_t as in clause 2, but to T_t/P_t, i.e., to the target expressed in MIT's deflated by the price index.

Under this clause, an increase in prices above the base year level, $P_t - P_o$, will cause the total of actual MIT reserves to fall short of the total of targets by a factor $(P_t - P_o)/P_t$. (If, for example, prices have risen 10 per cent, P_t would equal 1.1, and the aggregate of reserves outstanding would be below the aggregate of all targets by $\frac{.1}{1.1} \simeq$ 10 per cent.) Thus, even though some individual countries could still be above their targets, the typical member would be under more pressure to deflate than to inflate, and thus to take measures tending to reduce P_t. It should be remembered, however, that this pressure to deflate could always be met by reducing the MIT parity of a national currency. If, in particular, prices had risen so much as to cause a very large short fall in aggregate reserves and thereby to impose excessive deflationary pressure, some or all countries could agree to a simultaneous devaluation of their currencies in relation to the MIT. This would preserve the purchasing power of the MIT while avoiding disruptive domestic deflationary pressures.

Variations of clause 6 are possible and might be desirable. In particular, it could be decided that P_t should rise at some pre-agreed rate, say 1 per cent per year, to allow for the usual downward bias of most price indices through failure to reflect quality improvements. In this case, the amount of reserve credit granted to each country would be given by $T_t / \left[\frac{P_t}{(1.01)^t}\right]$.

As countries might try to avoid the obligation to make adjustments by bilateral borrowing or lending of currencies against MIT's, the following clause would seem appropriate:

7. Any loan from one central bank to another shall be treated as part of the reserve of the lender and will be deducted from the reserve of the borrower, for the purpose of calculating the imbalance index I_t.

It should be apparent from the description of the plan that the basic function of the target reserve is to determine the range within which a country may allow its reserves to fluctuate, without incurring a mandatory obligation to take corrective steps. It follows that this range, and correspondingly, the target for a given country should be determined primarily by the extent to which a country's reserves may be expected to fluctuate because of random disturbances that do not reflect a " fundamental disequilibrium " and are likely to reverse themselves automatically or with minor corrective action. For this reason, the target should be based primarily on the variability of a country's actual reserve, as recorded in historical experience. Thus, it might be based initially on some multiple of the standard deviation of actual reserves over, say, the previous decade; or better yet, on a standard deviation in which the observations are weighted, with larger weights given to the recent observations. Once the plan is in force, the deviations might be computed not from the mean of actual reserves but from the target. The formula determining a country's target will also have to recognize special factors affecting that country. If, for example, the dollar and the pound are still used as " vehicle " currencies — and we would expect this to be so — this fact will have to be recognized in the formulae for the United States and the United Kingdom.

In any case, our suggestions regarding the formula for computing T_i are meant to be tentative. We believe that they are on the right track, as there is some evidence that central banks are already making policy with implicit reserve targets in mind and that these targets have been related to short-run variability in the balance of payments (1). But the final adoption of a formula will require extensive technical studies; and in the final analysis, will involve international bargaining, with unavoidable political overtones. We wish only to stress that the problems involved are by no means insoluble, and are indeed of the same general nature and complexity as those which have already been faced and solved in setting IMF quotas.

II. Modifications of the System to Permit the Continued Use of Gold As a Reserve Instrument

The ideal version of the plan outlined above clearly implies the demonetization of gold (and of official dollar and sterling balances). Present gold stocks and reserve-currency balances could be retained

(1) Cf., for instance, KENEN, P. B. and YUDIN, E. B., " The Demand for International Reserves ", *The Review of Economics and Statistics*, August 1965, pp. 242-50.

by the participating countries as contingent reserves which would be remonetized if, for some reason, it was decided to liquidate the new plan and return to the *status quo ante*.

We believe that this ideal version of our plan is the most desirable and effective one, provided the world is ready to implement its repeated pious statements about international cooperation. But out of respect for a tradition sacred to some and in order to ease the transition, we indicate below how the various clauses of our plan could be modified to allow the continued use of gold, together with the MIT, as a reserve medium.

In order to segregate the functioning of the system from the transitional problems arising in the liquidation of past arrangements, we shall here assume that, at the start of the new plan, gold holdings are distributed among countries in proportion to their initial targets, or else that countries with disproportionate gold holdings agree to receive a commensurately smaller amount of credit from the MIT bank (and that, if any country's holdings actually exceed its target, it will agree to sterilize the surplus gold for the duration of the plan).

In clause 2, the first sentence can then be replaced by the following:

2′. At the start of the plan, the MIT bank shall announce a buying price for gold in terms of MIT (which will not be changed thereafter, unless a qualified majority of members concur) and shall commit itself to buy (but not sell) gold for MIT's at that price. At the start of the plan, the MIT bank shall credit each member country with a demand deposit such that the sum of this deposit and the gold holdings of the country shall equal the initial target.

Clause 3 (a) can be modified as follows:

3 (a)′. Participating countries shall agree to use gold and MIT's as the sole and equivalent instruments to settle balances arising from international transactions (except as noted under 3 (b) below). Specifically, each country's central bank shall agree to buy from, and sell to, other central banks, on demand, its national currency against gold or MIT's at a rate of exchange established by that central bank. The bank paying out reserves shall have the option of paying in gold or MIT's. Participating banks shall also agree to report all transfers

of gold to and from other central banks. They shall further agree to sell gold only to each other or the MIT bank.

In clause 4, the first sentence can be modified as follows:

4′. The reserve of each country, to which reference is made in clauses 4 to 6, shall be deemed to consist of its deposit balances with the MIT bank plus its registered gold reserve. The registered gold reserve shall consist of gold held at the start of the plan plus *net* gold purchases from other central banks, as reported to the MIT bank, less gold sales to the MIT bank.

This clause, together with 3′, implies that gold can continue to perform its monetary function, but excludes the possibility of monetizing additional gold from privately held stocks or from new production. If further monetization of gold were desired — an aim which, in our view, has little merit — the following could be added to clause 4′:

4″. A central bank wishing to acquire gold from parties other than participating central banks, and wishing to include such acquisitions in its reserve, shall be allowed to do so by reporting such purchases to the MIT bank and agreeing that the MIT value of such purchases will be deducted from its deposit with the bank.

This clause insures that, at any date, the aggregate reserves of member countries, valued in MIT's, will precisely equal the intended amount described in clause 6. (Note that individual countries could be allowed to hold small stocks of gold for the purpose of buying and selling their own currency from their nationals and from non-participating countries. These balances, however, would not be included in the computation of reserves for the purpose of the plan.)

III. Some Remarks and Suggestions on the Problems of Transition

As noted in the Preamble, the problems of transition to the new system are fundamentally political, and are common to those raised by most other plans for improving the international monetary mechanism. In consequence, we shall not presume to provide solutions but will, rather, limit ourselves to outlining the basic alternatives from which countries will finally have to choose.

Alternative A: *The " Ideal Solution "*

Under this approach, countries would agree to try out the " ideal version " of the plan for some stated period, say five years. For the duration of the trial period, they would retain their present holdings of gold and reserve currencies, but would *not* include them in their reserves, which would then consist entirely of MIT's. The IMF would be liquidated and provisions would be made for amortizing credit-tranche drawings. Member countries would acquire their initial deposits at the MIT bank (and subsequent increases) by subscribing entirely in national currency. If the plan were liquidated on or before the termination of the trial period, each country would remonetize its pre-plan reserves of gold, dollars and sterling — on which the United States and United Kingdom would have given an MIT and/or gold guarantee in the interim. A member's balance with the MIT bank not exceeding the target would be liquidated in the country's own currency. The remaining reserves would be liquidated by distribution of the bank's remaining currency holdings (those of countries below target at the terminal date) in proportion to each country's remaining MIT claim. The disposition of these currencies, after their distribution, would have to be negotiated. There are, however, ample precedents, as in the liquidation provisions of the EPU. If, on the other hand, a qualified majority agreed to continue the plan beyond the trial period, a set of provisions would go into force providing for the gradual amortization of reserve-currency balances (presumably in gold).

This method of transition would be equally applicable to the alternate version of the plan described in II above; countries would then have the option of including in their reserves any gold in their possession after their subscriptions, on condition that the deposit initially received from the MIT bank would then be reduced by a corresponding amount.

Alternative B: *Redistribution of Existing Gold Reserves by Mutual Lending and Borrowing*

The essential feature of Alternative A is that a country whose present reserve holdings are large relative to its target would not benefit from its past accumulations for the duration of the plan. Alternative B provides for a limited reflection of pre-plan payments experience. Each country would make a gold subscription to the MIT bank amounting to a portion of its target equal to the ratio of all member countries' gold reserves to all members' targets, the remaining subscription being paid for in the country's own currency. Thus all gold would be transferred to the MIT bank. Countries having insufficient gold to make this gold subscription could purchase the required gold from the United States and the United Kingdom in exchange for dollars or sterling, respectively (although this might require transitional assistance to the United Kingdom). If some countries still had a deficiency of gold, and therefore other countries had exactly offsetting surpluses, the MIT bank could arrange to borrow the surplus and lend it to the deficit countries, at some agreed interest, and with provisions for gradual amortization of principal and interest in MIT's. Provisions would also be made for the payment of interest on any remaining dollar and sterling balances and for their gradual amortization in MIT's. Once again, amortization of the principal could be delayed until the end of a trial period.

Clearly, alternative B could also be adapted to the continued use of gold along with MIT's, as under version II of the plan, by allowing member banks to buy back gold from the MIT bank, against their MIT deposit, up to an amount not exceeding their gold subscription (minus any debt arising from the borrowing described in the previous paragraph).

Alternative C: *Version II of the Plan with Initial Conditions Reflecting the Full Legacy of the Past*

Once the initial target has been set in the specified fashion, each country would receive a proportion of its target in MIT's equal to the excess of aggregate targets over aggregate pre-plan reserves, divided by aggregate targets. Pre-plan reserves are here defined to include gold and reserve currencies, plus gold-tranche and super gold-tranche positions in the IMF.

At the start of the plan, then, the reserves of each country would consist of this initial MIT balance plus pre-plan reserves less debts to the IMF (credit tranche drawings). At this point, reserve-currency balances would be turned over to the MIT bank in exchange for an equivalent MIT deposit, while gold reserves could either be kept or exchanged for MIT's. As a result, a country might enter the plan with reserves different from its target, i.e., with an inherited imbalance, positive or negative, which could be outside the normal range in many instances. Such a country would have then to take immediate remedial action. This beginning might be deemed undesirable and inequitable. In order to spread out the adjustments required of such a country, it would therefore be agreed that a country with reserves different from its target would be assigned an interim target for the purpose of computing the measure of imbalance. Its interim target would be equal to its actual MIT *plus* gold reserve at the starting point, and would be changed by equal annual increments over a transition period of, say, five years, so that at the end of the transition period the interim target would come to coincide with the formula, or true, target. The United States and the United Kingdom would pay interest on currency balances transferred to the MIT bank and these balances might be retired gradually.

IV. Concluding Remarks

The several variants of our basic plan, outlined above, have much in common with other schemes which have been proposed to ensure an " adequate " supply of international reserves. In fact, formulation II of the plan is but an expanded version of the so-called " composite reserve unit " proposal in which *all* member countries would share in the creation of the reserve unit *in proportion to their targets*. The essential *new* features of our proposal, which could be readily grafted onto most other schemes, can be summarized as follows:

1. It provides a way of establishing the appropriate amount of total international reserves outstanding at any date, and the contribution of member countries to their creation, which is both fair and sound, being directly and operationally linked to the adjustment process.

2. The plan places the burden of adjustment evenly on the deficit and surplus countries, thus avoiding either inflationary or deflationary biases.

3. The rules for determining targets and credits granted ensure that the new MIT will tend to keep a constant purchasing power in terms of a broad spectrum of internationally traded commodities.

16

The existence of a stable unit, in turn, should make it easier for countries to change their parities, for contracts could be made directly in MIT. Indeed, one can foresee the time when prices in international trade would be directly quoted in MIT, although executed in a specific currency. Forward contracts could be directly denominated in MIT's. More generally, the MIT would become the natural medium for denominating international (and possibly even national) fixed money contracts, such as long term loans and bonds. Indeed, participating countries might be required not to outlaw the " MIT clause ", at least in international contracts, because such contracts might be very attractive.

At the same time, adoption of the plan, at least in version II, requires very little institutional change over and beyond what most countries seem already willing to entertain. The only additional demand it makes on member countries is that they be willing to codify and abide by certain norms of international monetary cooperation to which they have, for a long time, claimed to subscribe. Basic among these is the principle that the reserve position ought not be a tool of international politics.

FRANCO MODIGLIANI and PETER KENEN

Massachusetts Institute of Technology,
Columbia University

THE REFORM OF THE INTERNATIONAL PAYMENTS SYSTEM

The system of international settlement and liquidity presently in force and centering on the International Monetary Fund has served us, on the whole, rather well for a couple of decades. Under this system, there has been an unprecedented increase in international movement of goods and capital which has, by and large, benefited all participants. Unfortunately, with the passage of time, shortcomings have begun to be apparent in this system and they have become gradually more evident as economic and political crises have succeeded one another with increased frequency and severity. By now there is a general feeling that the system is no longer viable in its present form; yet no alternative design has been proposed that has sufficient economic cogency and political appeal to command the widespread support necessary for its implementation.

Our purpose here is to propose a set of reforms that would retain the major advantage of the present system, to wit the relative stability of exchange rates associated with a system of parities, while eliminating its major drawbacks, such as the need for occasional discontinuous large changes and attendant speculative upheavals, the severe constraint on the ability of countries to pursue independent domestic policies, the lack of an adequate mechanism for creating the "appropriate" amount of international liquidity or even of a criterion for judging what is "appropriate," and the uncertainty as to the desirability of the dollar as an international store of value. In addition, our reform would provide the world with a facility that has never existed before, namely, an international numéraire and store of value having a stable purchasing power. All this would be accomplished through a set of modifications of the present system which are institutionally and economically quite simple, although, no doubt, they presume a strong commitment to work for the common good, at the cost of some compromise.

In the conviction that our reforms are practical, we wish to address ourselves to a wide audience. Accordingly, before presenting our proposal, we devote respectively Sections I and II to a survey of the present system and to a review of its drawbacks and why these have become more acute with the passage of time. Then, in Section III we outline the basic ingredients of our reform, and, finally, in Section IV we analyze the properties and operating characteristics of the reformed system. The expert, who is thoroughly familiar with the present system and its ills, may wish to proceed directly to Section III.

I. A SURVEY OF THE PRESENT SYSTEM

The present international payments system for countries that are members of the International Monetary Fund can be characterized by the following set of rules and institutions.

1. Reserve Assets and Factors Controlling their Quantities
   (a) Monetized Gold: fixed in quantity, basically at the historical level determined by the gold reserves of member countries at the time of the adoption of the two-tier system. (That is, the understanding among the monetary authorities of major countries not to buy or sell gold except from one another.)
   (b) Special Drawing Rights or SDRs ("paper gold"): an intangible asset issued through the International Monetary Fund, having a fixed parity to gold; quantity changeable by a rather complex procedure requiring the agreement of a qualified majority of members.
   (c) Short-term Claims on the United States held by Foreign Official Holders (basically, Monetary Authorities): changed through payments deficits of the United States and redistribution of the outstanding stock of claims on the United States between official holders and other holders (commercial banks, nonbank public). Such redistribution results, in part, from foreign central-bank policy and, in part, from market forces. *De jure*, the rate of exchange between dollars and gold (and hence SDRs) is fixed by the United States and can be changed by the United States with the approval of the Fund; *de facto*, that parity is unshakable in that the United States is not, at present, willing to entertain the notion of changing it.

2. Permanently Fixed Parities

Each country fixes a "permanent" parity with SDR-gold which determines a permanently fixed parity with every other currency. The parities are subject only to discontinuous changes to a new "permanent" level. In practice, such changes have occurred only when the inappropriateness of the previous parity has become so glaring as to require a major change.

3. Narrow Allowable Bands of Fluctuation around Parity

Each participating country assumes the obligation to contain market fluctuations in exchange rates within a narrow band of parity. This obligation is enforced through each central bank (other than that of the United States) intervening in its country's dollar market to maintain the market price within a band which is, *de jure*, one per cent on either side of parity (hence, of a total width of 2 per cent), but *de facto* has been mostly maintained within ¾ of 1 per cent on either side of parity (hence, of a total width of 1½ per cent). The actual market rate of exchange with the dollar establishes all actual cross-rates.

4. *De Jure* Convertibility of Currencies into Gold and SDRs, and Conversely

Each monetary authority has the obligation to buy back its currency from, or to sell it to, other monetary authorities in exchange for gold and SDRs, with some special provisions with respect to the use of SDRs.

5. *De Facto* Semi-Inconvertibility of the Dollar

The United States has, for some time, been using its "power of persuasion" to discourage foreign monetary authorities from exchanging the dollars that they have acquired through interventions in the foreign-exchange market (3 above) for the other two reserve assets. Thus, *de facto, the convertibility of the dollar is limited and uncertain.* This is critical, because, with the obligation to remain within the band enforced by operation on the dollar market only, any country running a reserve surplus initially acquires just dollars. Thus, the United States is the only country that could be asked to exchange its currency for other reserve assets. Other central banks, as it were, are automatically re-acquiring any surplus of their currency flowing out when they support their exchange; and they are re-acquiring it for dollars. (If they run out of dollars, they can acquire more by selling other reserve assets for dollars to the United States or to some other official holder of dollars.)

6. Limitations on the Use of SDRs

When SDRs were introduced, some complex limitations were established on their use. In particular, the average SDR balance of a country over a five-year period may not be less than 30 per cent of its cumulative allotment. This restriction was a concession to the view, held by some countries, that the role of SDRs should be that of a transient reciprocal-credit arrangement.

II. DRAWBACKS OF THE PRESENT SYSTEM

The present system has at least four major drawbacks, which have become gradually more acute. These will be first listed and then examined in some detail.

5

1. As the underlying circumstances of various countries change in time, the initially fixed parities become inappropriate. As this happens, first tensions accumulate and, eventually, substantial discrete changes are forced on the system. The anticipation of these changes produces deeply disturbing speculative capital movements, and the execution is costly to the country making the adjustment. Thus, in the end, parities really do change, but in the worst possible way. Particularly disturbing (and still unresolved) problems arise when the country whose exchange rate has become inappropriate is the reserve-currency country (that is, at present, the United States).

2. Narrow bands have limited the ability of countries to carry out monetary policy suited for domestic stabilization; and, with increasing sensitivity of investors to intercountry differentials in short-term interest rates, this limitation has become gradually more stringent. Because of the size of the United States and its special role as provider of the reserve currency, this has meant, in practice, that other countries are increasingly forced to accept an interest policy imposed by American choice.

3. There is no adequate way of regulating the aggregate supply of international reserves; their creation through American deficits, not settled through other reserve assets, is haphazard. At the moment, it is generally deemed excessive, but there is no satisfactory mechanism for reducing it. And the creation of reserves through SDRs is a cumbersome process, hampered by lack of objective criteria for determining the appropriate amount.

4. With the short-term dollar claims convertible *de jure* but almost inconvertible *de facto*, every significant addition to the reserves of a major third country sends waves of tremors through the international financial community, besides giving rise to a chorus of acrimonious rebukes to the United States for running an uncontrolled deficit. There is, in fact, a well-grounded fear that if large conversions were forced on the United States there would be, at the very least, the danger of an unwarranted contraction in world liquidity and, at worst, the possibility that the United States might become "bankrupt," in the sense of being unable to carry out its obligations. Furthermore, the occasion for such crisis is increased by the fact that the surplus of any one country bears but an indirect relation to the American deficit, certainly far less direct than the layman is led to believe. A third country could experience a large surplus even if the United States were not running a deficit, or, indeed, even if it were running a huge surplus. This is because, under

the arrangement described in 3, any country experiencing a surplus on an official-transaction basis will initially acquire dollars which may well come from the deficit of other countries than the United States. Furthermore, ever since foreign central banks have started investing their dollar reserves in the Eurodollar market, it is not even true that the sum of all surpluses on an official-reserve basis equals the American deficit on that basis.

Comment on Items 1 and 4

With parities fixed, there is, in principle, a unique relation of the domestic price level (and interest rates) to the price level (and interest rates) in the rest of the world that is consistent with basic-balance equilibrium. Since price levels do not automatically respond promptly to imbalance, and countries are understandably unwilling to undergo the painful process of raising unemployment to reduce relative prices or of fostering inflation to increase relative prices, the fixed parities are bound to drift out of equilibrium. This drift, helped by the increasing liberalization of capital movements, has gradually occurred. Thus, eventually, discontinuous changes in parity have been forced on the system; and, because changes have been long delayed, and hence are large in size, they have produced deeply disturbing speculative movements. They have also been costly to the countries concerned, as speculators have gained at the expense of the monetary authorities.

The problem takes on a special dimension in the case of the United States. Since its official liabilities are a component of reserves, strictly speaking the equilibrium level of relative prices for the United States is that level which generates a deficit, on an official basis, equal to the "appropriate" growth in world reserves, less the "appropriate" growth in other reserves. Since gold does not grow, by present rules of the system, the growth in other reserves means growth of SDRs. Unfortunately, there is, at present, no objectively accepted criterion for what is the "appropriate" growth of total reserves; and the growth of SDRs is a very cumbersome process requiring the political agreement of an appropriate majority of the Fund members.

We have already noted that, with fixed parities, there is no effective mechanism to insure promptly that the American price level relative to the rest of the world will be such as to generate the "appropriate" growth of dollar reserves. We now see that there is also no way of agreeing what the "appropriate" level is. Hence, there must be, unavoidably, a continuous wrangle as to whether the deficit of the United States is excessive, too little, or just right. This is indeed an issue which has divided deeply both economic experts and political leaders.

7

At the present time, there seems to be growing agreement that, at least in recent years, the rate of deficit has been excessive. It is, therefore, also fairly generally agreed that, at current parities, the American price level is out of line with the rest of the world, although there is far less agreement as to just how far out of line it is. There is indeed even a "minority" that believes that the gap is small enough to be safely disregarded. The "minority" view is held, in part, by American experts claiming that the deficit is not excessive or can be handled by means other than a realignment of American prices; and, in part, in certain European circles holding that the excessive deficit does not reflect too low a trade surplus but only excessive capital exports. Hence, the cure would lie not in reducing the relative American price level in order to increase its export surplus, but instead in the United States taking measures aimed at curbing capital exports through which it is "buying up" Europe.

Whatever one's view on the extent of overvaluation, it is apparent to all concerned that the United States is not willing—or even realistically able—to bring about a rapid downward adjustment of its price level relative to the rest of the world. Under these conditions what would be called for is a one-time reduction of its parity *vis-à-vis other major currencies*. There are obviously two possible ways this could be accomplished:

(a) by devaluing the dollar relative to SDRs and monetized gold, while the other currencies retain the old parity, or
(b) by revaluing the other currencies relative to SDRs and gold, while the United States retains the old parity.

A substantial body of American opinion holding that a change in parity is appropriate refuses to consider alternative (a) on the grounds that the major important effects are really the same for all concerned under either alternative, while many "minor" considerations point to alternative (b) as economically and technically preferable. These "minor" considerations include such propositions as

(i) a revaluation of monetized gold relative to the dollar could threaten the continuation of the two-tier system;
(ii) a devaluation of the dollar relative to SDRs and gold could shake confidence in the dollar as a reserve currency, causing a collapse of the present system;
(iii) if the rest of the world feels that their currencies are undervalued relative to the dollar, why do not *they* raise their parity relative to the dollar? This, of course, would imply that their

currencies would be revalued relative to SDR and gold; but why should anyone care, since the only parity that affects the American deficit is that with the dollar.

(iv) the present parity with the dollar is enforced by foreign central banks supporting their parities by operating on the dollar market; hence, it is only *they* that can change this support level. There is, indeed, under the present set-up, no operational way in which the United States could reduce the market rates of exchange of foreign currencies with the dollar.

We shall have occasion to deal with all these arguments at various points below, and will only note at this point that argument (iii) can be used quite symmetrically to support alternative (a) over (b). However, what needs to be examined first is the argument that, in terms of major substantive effects, alternatives (a) and (b) should be regarded as equivalent by all "rational men." This argument deserves close scrutiny, because it is widely held (at least in the United States), while, in our view, it is untenable in at least one major respect.

There is, first, one essentially institutional reason why foreign central banks prefer devaluation by the United States over revaluation by themselves. Central banks hate to appreciate, because they then have to write down a portion of their assets, which creates complications in their own accounting and/or that of the government. However, we suggest that there is a far more fundamental economic argument to justify their preference for option (a).

Suppose that, under option (b), the currencies of other countries appreciate relative to the complex dollar-gold-SDR; then the reserves held by the rest of the world retain an *unchanged* purchasing power in terms of dollars, and have a *reduced* purchasing power with respect to all other currencies. On balance, their purchasing power is *reduced.* If, on the other hand, under option (a), the dollar is devalued, that portion of reserves consisting of dollar claims fares exactly the same as under option (b). But that portion consisting of gold and net SDRs (that is, the excess of SDR holding over SDRs allotted) has a higher purchasing power with respect to dollars and an *unchanged* one with respect to all other currencies. On balance, the purchasing power of total reserves *rises.* Hence, option (a) is distinctly preferable for the rest of the world.

Actually, the advantage of option (a) for the rest of the world (and its disadvantage for the United States) is, in reality, likely to be even greater. For, if the United States were to devalue, there would also be a "redistributional effect" among third countries. The gain to any country would be greater, the larger the share of their reserves held in gold

9

and SDRs, and the smaller the share in dollars. In short, there would be a relative loss for those countries which, in the past, have shown willingness to cooperate with the United States by holding their reserves in dollars instead of converting them into other reserve assets. It follows that under option (a) there would be an important loss of face and prestige on the part of the United States, to the advantage of countries and of political forces less sympathetic to the American position. Or, more likely, the United States would feel it necessary to show that it does not let its friends down by agreeing to compensate foreign countries for any loss on their net dollar-denominated claims on the United States (with proper allowance for the interest they have earned on their dollar reserves). This could be accomplished by issuing to them additional dollar claims as needed. With this further action, *all* the reserves of third countries would have increased purchasing power in terms of dollars, regardless of composition.

To summarize, the differences between the two options are not purely formal but, indeed, very substantial. The other countries are better off under option (a) than (b) (because their reserves are worth more), while the United States is either worse off in prestige, or worse off financially, or both. These considerations do not establish *per se* that one option is better than the other; but they do establish that the rest of the world is quite rational in preferring option (a) to (b), while the United States stands to gain financially, as well as politically, from option (b) versus (a).

There is, however, one further consideration which suggests that there is a case, on grounds of equity, in favor of option (a) over (b), particularly if we think of these options as relevant for the future. Assume that the overvaluation of the dollar relative to other currencies had resulted from American prices rising while other prices remained constant (or rose less rapidly), thus contributing to the rise in world prices. As long as all reserve assets bear a fixed parity to the dollar, this means that the American price behavior had caused a gradual erosion in the purchasing power of the rest of the world's reserves. A revaluation of other currencies is, in a way, a formal recognition of this relative loss of purchasing power. On the other hand, a devaluation of the dollar relative to other reserves would go in the direction of maintaining the purchasing power of reserves other than dollars. And, if accompanied by a compensation to the holders of dollar claims, it would maintain the purchasing power of all reserves and, in particular, the real value of dollar claims against the United States (that is, of the American debt). Since the assumption stated at the outset clearly has factual validity, we have established our equity case for option (a), accompanied by compensation to the holders of dollar reserves for the net loss sustained, not covered by interest earned. More generally, thinking about the future rather than about the past, *if* the United States (the reserve-currency country) were to take the position that its parity with other reserve assets is *never* to be changed and, therefore, all reserves are, in fact, denominated in dollars, then all other countries have a very definite stake and vested interest in the maintenance of a stable American price level. A policy of "benign neglect" is thus not consistent with the United States retaining the role of reserve-currency country. There is, in this sense, a good deal of truth to a recent statement of French President Georges Pompidou that "We cannot keep a monetary standard which continuously loses value as a result of American Internal Policy." (As quoted by the Paris Edition of the *Herald Tribune* on May 26, 1971.)

Comment on Items 2 and 3

A country's ability to stimulate domestic activity by an expansionary monetary policy, and concomitant reduction of short-term interest rates, is constrained by the fact that the fall in interest rates creates an incentive for capital to flow out of the country, motivated by the favorable differential between domestic and foreign rates. It is well known that if the monetary authority has the obligation of preventing the market rate of exchange from falling outside some agreed band, then, as the differential gets large enough, the authority is forced to intervene in the exchange market and reserves begin to flow out of the country. This outflow, in turn, limits the achievable differential in two ways: (i) because it reduces the domestic money supply—that is, a portion of the intended expansion of the money supply "leaks out" in the form of reserve outflow; and (ii) because it drains the country's limited stock of reserves. Furthermore, the outflow of reserves tends to increase the money supply of the recipient countries, thus reducing their interest rates. While this helps the first country, by reducing the interest differential, it will tend to interfere with the desired monetary policy of the other countries.

It can be readily established that the maximum differential between the domestic rate of interest and the rate in other countries that can be achieved before reserves begin to flow out depends primarily on four factors:

(a) the permissible band of fluctuations of the exchange rate;
(b) the responsiveness of the basic balance to variations in the rate of exchange;
(c) the responsiveness of the capital outflow to the so-called covered

11

differential spread; that is, the differential in the interest rates adjusted by the cost of hedging (by transactions in the forward market) against adverse movements in the rate of exchange at the time the lender wants to repatriate his capital;

(d) the risk premium required by speculators in the forward market, who provide the cover.

Item (b) reflects certain basic characteristics of the economy, such as the elasticity of its exports and imports with respect to variations in the relation between domestic and foreign prices. For the present argument, this characteristic can be taken as given. It can then be shown that the maximum differential between domestic and foreign rates that can be maintained before reserves begin to flow can be expressed approximately as the sum of two components, as follows:

(1) The first component can be written as B/t, where B is the total width of the band, and t is the maturity (measured in years) of the instrument whose yield we are comparing. (Thus, if the market rate of exchange is to be kept within ½ per cent of parity, B is 1 per cent. Then, for the three-month rate, the term B/t equals $1/(1/4) = 4$ or 400 basis points. For the six-month rate, the term comes to 200 basis points, and so on.)

(2) The second component of the maximum differential is more complex, but for present purposes, what matters is that it is positive; it grows large as the response coefficient under (c) above, call it R, gets low, and tends toward zero as that coefficient increases. It also tends to increase with the size of the risk premium.

We have seen under item 3, that, under present practice, B is somewhere between 1½ and 2 per cent. However, in the early postwar period the responsiveness, R, tended to be small for many reasons. These include (i) outright restrictions on, and encumbrances to, capital movements; (ii) diffidence toward foreign investments, lack of familiarity with foreign instruments, and lack of information about their probable yields; and (iii) lack of an organizational network such as had existed in part in the predepression period but had died out during the 30's and the war years. In addition, the risk premium required by speculators was probably higher. As a result, in the early years of the system, central banks retained substantial freedom of domestic monetary policy. As the postwar period unfolded, each of the above factors gradually developed in the direction of increased responsiveness. In addition, a new important institution began to develop and flourish, namely the multinational corporation. This new organization, because of its ubiquitous nature, and the resulting familiarity with institutions in different countries, and because of its concern with the efficient management of its liquid assets, has generated a very large pool of funds highly responsive to differential opportunities.

The result of these developments has been that, with the passage of time, the ability of each country to pursue an independent monetary policy has been gradually shrinking; and attempts at pursuing such a policy have frequently resulted in massive and disruptive flows of reserves. This has been especially true when the incentive to capital flows has been reinforced by processes generated by speculation on anticipated changes in parity, as witnessed in the recent experience of the German mark.

As is the case with other problems discussed earlier, the purely economic drawbacks of a narrow band have been reinforced and complicated by political considerations. It can be readily seen that the ability of a country to pursue an independent monetary policy depends on its relative size and on its ability to run a sustained loss of reserves. If a country is very large and is willing and able to stand a great deal of loss, then this country can pursue a policy of low interest rates and, as a result, spread this policy to other smaller countries. Now it happens that (i) the United States is the financial giant of the world, and (ii) it is able to disregard largely the loss of reserves. Indeed, in its case, the loss of reserves simply means an increase in the semi-inconvertible dollar claims held by the rest of the world. It is for this reason that the United States can blithely pursue a policy of "benign neglect" while other countries find themselves forced, in large measure, to dance to a tune called by the United States. The resulting and growing resentfulness and gripes of the rest of the world are then not so unjustified or hard to understand. Sacrificing independence to a common course of action is always irksome; but it is obviously more irksome when one feels that one has little to say about what that common policy shall be. And, for some at least, it is still more irksome if the party making unilateral decisions is called the United States and, further, influential voices in that country advocate a policy of "benign neglect" (or, in other words, a policy dictated entirely by domestic considerations).

These serious and growing shortcomings of the present system lead to the unavoidable, and generally accepted, conclusion that this system has but a short lease on life. However, no solution has yet been offered that appears economically and politically acceptable. In the next section we outline some proposed reforms, and in the concluding section we indicate how these reforms would help to handle the shortcomings of the present system.

III. OUTLINE OF PROPOSED REFORMS

1. Broaden the Band of Permissible Fluctuations around Parity

The maximum permissible deviations of market exchange rates from parity before the central banks are required to intervene will be increased significantly above the present 1 per cent up and down of parity *de jure* and ¾ per cent *de facto*. The total width of the band—now 2 per cent *de jure* and 1½ per cent *de facto*—should be increased to at least 4 per cent of parity, although a somewhat broader band deserves consideration.

2. Generalized Crawling Parities

(a) The official parity in terms of SDRs of each currency will be determined, indirectly, by the official parity of that currency with the dollar and the parity of the dollar with SDRs.

(b) The rate of exchange between the SDRs and monetized gold will remain fixed indefinitely (presumably, although not necessarily, at the current level).

(c) The official parity of each currency with the dollar will be an average of the market rates prevailing over a stated number of previous trading days; the specific number of days will be determined simultaneously with the permissible band in order to insure that the maximum annual rate of change of the parity to the dollar does not exceed x per cent per year. (The number x will have to be an object of negotiation, but we would favor a value of not less than 2 per cent—see below.)

(d) The parity of the dollar to the SDR (the price of SDRs in terms of dollars or dollars per SDR) will change if and when there is a change in an appropriately constructed index of the dollar price of internationally traded commodities. The dollar price of the SDR will increase continuously (daily) at an agreed maximum rate per year as long as it is less, relative to the price in the base period, than the current level of the price index relative to the same base period. The price will fall continuously as long as it is higher (relative to the base) than the price index (relative to the base).

3. Option of Foreign Official Holders to Denominate their Dollar Reserves in SDRs.

At the option of foreign official holders, the United States will have the obligation to denominate in SDRs any portion of the official reserves of a participating country having the form of short-term dollar claims.

Dollar reserves so denominated will take the form of a claim against the United States Treasury-Federal Reserve and will earn a rate of interest equal to that paid by the Fund on SDR balances. That portion of dollar reserves which is not so denominated will be managed, as under the present system, by the official holders and invested as they see fit, in earning assets in the United States, but *not* in Eurodollars or equivalent dollar-denominated assets.

4. *De Jure* Inconvertibility of the Dollar

The obligation of the United States to buy from, or sell to, foreign monetary authorities dollars in exchange for gold or SDRs shall be terminated *de jure.*

5. Use of "SDR Clause"

Participating countries will agree to make it legal, for their citizens entering into long-term international lending agreements, to denominate the loan in units of SDRs, no matter what currency may be elected for execution.

6. Acceptance by the United States of the Obligation to Reduce Its Deficit when "Excessive" and to Increase It when "Insufficient"

(a) A state of "excess American deficit" will be declared to exist if and when (i) the currencies of one or more countries remain at the upper limit of the permissible band for some stated interval of time; (ii) the aggregate increase in reserves of the countries whose currencies are at the upper limit, and which are gaining reserves, exceeds by some stated threshold value, the aggregate decrease experienced by countries whose currencies are at the lower limit, and which are losing reserves; and (iii) the United States is contemporaneously running a deficit on the official basis. While this state persists, the United States will have the obligation to take explicit measures to curb its deficit, through appropriate economic incentives.

(b) A state of "insufficient American deficit" will be declared to exist if and when (i) the currencies of one or more countries remain at the lower limit of the permissible band for some stated interval of time; (ii) the aggregate decrease of reserves of the countries whose currencies are at the lower limit, and which are losing reserves, exceeds, by some stated threshold value, the aggregate increase experienced by countries whose currencies are at the upper limit, and which are gaining reserves. While this state persists, the United States will have the obligation to take measures to increase its current deficit (or decrease its surplus) on an official-reserve basis.

15

7. Issuing SDRs

The issuance of SDRs will be regulated to achieve, on the average, a stipulated relation between the portion of reserves taking the form of SDRs and gold and the portion taking the form of claims on the United States. For example, suppose that at the end of a given "period" the stock of SDRs and gold represented a smaller proportion of total reserves than the agreed-upon target. Then, in the next "period" the issue of SDRs should be stepped up, and conversely.

8. Retention of Other Features of the Present System

Any feature of the present system that is not explicitly modified stays the same. In particular, this means the retention of the two-tier system. Possibly this system could be strengthened by eliminating *any* form of fresh gold purchase.

IV. PROPERTIES AND OPERATING CHARACTERISTICS OF THE PROPOSED REFORM

For the benefit of the expert who is interested in the "essence" and is used to technical jargon, the system resulting from our reforms can be characterized as follows:

1. Managed, limited float of the dollar with the power of management entrusted to foreign central banks.
2. Because the float is limited, all participating countries, including the United States, are committed to pursuing policies such that, in the long run, the equilibrium rate of exchange remains within the limit of the moving band. In the short run, however, the existence of reserves permits transient deviations from this requirement, and gives each country time to carry out the longer-run adjustment that may be required.
3. The management of exchange rates and the obligation to intervene at the limits of the band require, or make it desirable, to retain an international "money," for market intervention and settlement between monetary authorities. In the present system the dollar performs, *de facto* if not *de jure*, each of the three classical functions of money: numéraire, medium of exchange, and store of value, with the SDR and gold sharing in the role of store of value and, to a limited extent, in the role of medium of exchange. In the reformed system, the SDR and gold (though the latter could eventually be eliminated) become the numéraire, which is endowed with the valuable property of retaining a stable purchasing power. The dollar remains the principal medium of exchange, with the other two assets continuing to share this func-

16

tion to a limited extent, and the store-of-value function continues to be shared by the three reserve assets.

4. Through the management of exchange rates, the rest of the world is enabled to control the creation of reserves in the form of dollars and to provide an objective criterion for the creation of SDRs.
5. The availability of a numéraire with a stable purchasing power minimizes the possible unfavorable consequences of floating rates on the international movement of long-term debt capital.

Any *one* of the above features could probably be achieved by means other than our plan. But our plan achieves them all simultaneously, in the most convenient fashion. For instance, a stable purchasing power for the SDR could be insured through all member countries agreeing to change, simultaneously, the parity of their currencies with respect to SDRs in accordance with the price index of internationally traded commodities. Our proposal achieves this same end, far more conveniently, by changing explicitly only the parity of the dollar to the SDR, while tying the other currencies to the dollar.

We can now proceed to discuss in more detail, and in less technical language, what has been summarized above.

The key novel element of the plan is clause (2d). The purpose and effect of this clause is that the portion of reserves consisting of gold and SDRs will tend to have a stable purchasing power in terms of the broad collection of commodities that enter into international trade. Furthermore, when combined with clause (3), it gives to the rest of the world the option to hold the entirety of their reserves in a form which has constant purchasing power. Of course, a country opting not to denominate its dollar claims in SDRs will assume the risk of loss (or gain) of purchasing power if international prices rise and the dollar depreciates; but presumably, it will choose this option only when it expects that the yield obtainable in the American market is sufficiently high to exceed the expected depreciation plus the interest obtainable on reserves denominated in SDRs.

The other important effect of clause (2d) is that it eliminates the perpetual wrangling as to whether the dollar should be revalued with respect to SDR-gold, and by how much. This issue would be controlled by a mechanical rule, and one that makes sound economic sense.

Details as to the precise nature of the price index to be used need not detain us here, except for suggesting that it should be as broad as possible, preferably including major services as well as commodities. There are, no doubt, technical problems involved in the construction of the index, but they are not qualitatively different from those arising in

17

the widely used cost-of-living indices. Similarly, details as to how and when the option as to denomination of dollar claims can be exercised can be left for negotiation. For the sake of illustration, one might suggest that the price index be computed and published once a month on a stated date, at which date the dollar price of SDRs would change, and that the option for the next month be exercised within a few days of that publication. To minimize the incentive to massive shifts in the portion of reserves denominated in SDRs, we suggest that the index might well be a twelve-month moving average of monthly values and that the maximum change in the dollar price of SDRs in any one month be limited to a pre-established ceiling. It is relevant to point out in this connection that, according to the price index presently computed by the Fund, the change in the index from one year to the next has never been more than 3 per cent.

The other key clause, inseparable from (2d) and (3), is clause (4). By establishing *de jure* what is, at present, an uncertain *de facto* situation, this clause eliminates a major component of uncertainty and anxiety in the present system and bans forever the risk of a "run on the bank." Is there any reason why acceptance of this clause should be regarded as "onerous" to the rest of the world? We believe that, if we leave aside petty considerations of jealousy and prestige, the answer is clearly negative. First, accepting *de jure* what is nearly true *de facto*, cannot be very onerous, especially since the *de facto* situation arises, in part, from the fact that the United States could not, at present, convert all the dollar claims in official reserves into other reserve assets. But, in fact, the rest of the world would be better off, for, once the uncertainty about the status of the dollar is removed, it will be more freely accepted by all central banks in exchange for other reserves. Indeed, in view of the option of clause (3), dollar reserves should, rationally, be deemed at least as desirable and generally more desirable than other forms of reserves, as their expected return can be no lower than that of SDRs, and may be higher. (For this reason there may, at times, be a scramble to invest reserves in the form of dollars; and, since the supply is limited, some allocation rule may be needed. This point will be taken up again below.)

The purpose of clause (1), which simply incorporates in our reform earlier proposals of many other experts, is to increase the scope for an independent monetary policy. It is, by now, generally agreed that this increase in the ability of central banks to choose the monetary policy best suited for domestic stabilization is desirable; and that it can be achieved by broadening the band. Indeed, there are strong indications that many countries are already prepared to support this simple reform.

In terms of the analysis of Section III, a 2 per cent band would permit differences at least as large as 800 basis points in the three-month rate and 400 basis points in the six-month rate. Even though that analysis is not strictly valid once parities crawl, we believe that a band of the order of 2 per cent is adequate at least for a trial period, while still leaving the possible range of fluctuations sufficiently narrow to preserve much of the advantage of fixed parities—namely, to prevent expectations of large forthcoming changes in the market rate leading, through speculation, to large fluctuations in the actual market rate. Wider bands will tend to reduce the flow of short-term capital. But it is generally agreed that this is a desirable development, as short-term capital flows have primarily the disruptive effect of preventing countries from pursuing an appropriate domestic policy, while contributing little, if any, to the channeling of long-term capital to where it has larger social returns.

Proposal (2c) is also not original, although it is a good deal more controversial. All the relevant ideas in this regard are discussed in the *Bürgenstock Papers* (Princeton University Press, 1970). The purpose of (2c) is to allow parities to drift gradually in time, if, and as, differential developments in the economies of participating countries makes this desirable. With this proposal, over a period of years, parities would be allowed to change by very substantial amounts. At the same time, holding the maximum annual rate of change within modest limits provides little incentive to the massive flows that are generated by the expectation of a discontinuous, large change. In our proposed system, the maximum rate of change of the parity is controlled by the relation between the maximum allowable band and the length of the averaging period used in computing the current parity. Specifically, it can be readily established that the following formula holds:

> The maximum per cent annual rate of change of parity equals the total width of the band, measured as a percentage of parity, divided by the length of the averaging period, measured in years.

(For instance, if the band had a width of 4 per cent and the averaging period were two years, the maximum rate of change of parity would be 2 per cent per year; if the averaging period were six quarters (1½ years), the maximum rate of change of parity would be 2 2/3 per cent per year.) Thus, once a decision has been reached on the allowable band, the maximum rate of change of parity can be limited by an appropriate choice of the length of the averaging period.

The considerations relevant in choosing the maximum rate of crawl are, essentially, that it should be as small as possible, but large enough to take care of the foreseeable maximum rate at which parities may drift out of alignment. The postwar experience suggests that a maximum rate of change of 2-3 per cent would have been adequate to take care of all major needed adjustments. It should be stressed, however, that the rate at which parities may need to be changed is not an objective "economic fact"; it depends on the extent to which a country is prepared to rely on the whole set of tools of economic policy to control variations in its domestic price level. The smaller the maximum rate of crawl, the greater the chance for a country to have to take painful measures to keep price behavior under control for purely external reasons. But, at the same time, the smaller the maximum rate of crawl, the smaller the possible disturbances to the system from speculation. In a very real sense, in setting a limit to the maximum rate of crawl, countries are notifying the world—and hence speculators—that they intend to pursue policies which will not require rapid changes in parity. The more willing countries are to make this commitment, the less scope there will be for disturbing and, therefore, undesirable speculative fluctuations in the market rate.

The conclusion, then, is that the decision about the appropriate maximum rate of crawl is finally a "political" decision that involves trading between short-run fluctuations in the exchange rate and minimizing the need to implement unsavory domestic policies in order to adjust to the requirements of the foreign balance. Since this trade-off may well be different for different countries, we can see no reason why each country should not be free to choose a *different* averaging period and thus a *different maximum rate of crawl.* If no limitations were placed on this freedom, a country could, in practice, even opt for a freely floating rate, by making the averaging period short enough. Similarly, there is also no reason why a group of countries could not agree among themselves to limit the band of fluctuations relative to one another. This could be accomplished, for example, along the lines that the members of the European Economic Community are presently preparing to follow.

While the many advantages of crawling versus "permanently" fixed parities are increasingly being recognized, there continues to remain one very serious objection to moving parities, in terms of their unfavorable effect on the international movement of long-term capital. With respect to long-term capital flows, in fact, greater possible short-term movements of exchange rates resulting from a wider band are of little consequence; even a 4 per cent change in the market rate will have little effect on the yield of an investment whose length is measured in decades. But crawling parities pose a potentially serious threat: the parity might move continually in one direction at the maximum rate of crawl. If that rate were, for instance, as large as 3 per cent per year, a contract calling for, say, a 5 per cent yield to the lender (and cost to the borrower) could end up yielding (and costing) as little as 2 or as much as 8 per cent. In other words, crawling parities tend to increase substantially the risk of long-term capital movement—at least for debt capital. (In the case of equity capital, on the other hand, the situation may well be reversed, since the relative movements of the exchange rates would presumably tend to offset corresponding movements in relative prices, and would tend to stabilize the real rate of return.) But this potential hindrance to long-term debt-capital movements is eliminated by our proposed reform, thanks to clause (5). This clause will make it possible for the contracting parties, if they wish to avoid the exchange risk, to denominate the contract in SDRs. Because clause (3) has the effect of tending to insure that SDRs will have a stable purchasing power, by contracting in SDRs, they will be able to insure for themselves a stable outcome in "real terms." In this sense, SDR denomination bears close similarity to the traditional "gold clause"; but it clearly is potentially superior. Even under a pure gold-standard system there was nothing to insure a constant purchasing power for gold. In the present system, the purchasing power of gold is as uncertain and unstable as the purchasing power of the dollar—not terribly unstable but not notably stable!

The remaining major novel feature of the reform is that it provides an automatic mechanism for creating the "appropriate" amount of international liquidity. To lay bare the workings of this mechanism we must distinguish between normal and pathological conditions. We shall first discuss the normal working of the system and then the possible pathological cases which might arise if and when the American deficit were declared excessive or insufficient and clause (6) were to apply.

We first note that, as long as a central bank chooses to keep the rate of exchange of its currency within the maximum permissible band, one could justifiably infer that what was happening to the reserves of the country was considered desirable by its government, regardless of whether it was acquiring reserves, losing them, or neither. Suppose, for example, that the country's reserves were rising. This would mean that it was intervening in the market, acquiring dollars, and selling its own currency, in order to prevent its currency from appreciating. If it did not want to accumulate dollars (possibly to be exchanged for other reserves), or at least not at the current rate, then all it would need to do would be to stop buying them, or reduce the rate of purchase. Similarly, if it were losing reserves at a rate that it did not deem appropriate, all it would need to do would be to stop, or reduce, its selling of dollars to support the exchange value of its currency. To be sure, the country might, in the first place, be buying dollars for fear that an appreciation

21

of its currency would hurt its exports and expose domestic producers to greater pressure of foreign competition. But, in that case, the acquisition of reserves must still be regarded as wanted, in the sense of being the means for securing the desired condition of maintaining, or increasing, the export surplus. Similar considerations apply in the case of a loss.

This inference, that whatever was happening to a country's reserves was operationally "wanted," would cease to hold only at the limit of the band. Thus, if the exchange rate had reached the upper limit and the country was still accumulating reserves, this behavior could not be interpreted as necessarily reflecting a desire to hold more reserves. In fact, the country would then have no choice but to acquire dollars to keep the exchange rate within the required limits. Similar considerations apply, *mutatis mutandis*, if the exchange rate of its currency had reached the lower limit and the country was still losing reserves.

Suppose now that over some period of time we had observed that every currency had remained within the band. Suppose further that in the same period the total dollar reserves of the rest of the world had increased. This increase would be equal to the current American deficit on an official-reserve base. We would then be justified in inferring that the observed overall increase reflected a desire for larger reserves. Furthermore, the desired increase could be equated with the observed increase, that is, with the sum of the American deficit plus the period allotment of SDRs. This means, in the first place, that there could be no justifiable complaint about the American deficit, or the increase in world liquidity, being too large (or too small). At the same time, the experience of the period could be used to provide evidence about the adequacy of the allotment of SDRs. Specifically, suppose the agreed ratio of dollars to total reserves was 50 per cent, and this ratio had existed at the beginning of the period. If in the period, the allotment of SDRs had been, say, 3 per cent of the initial stock, while the growth of dollar reserves had been, say, 7 per cent, implying a growth of total reserves of 5 per cent, then we could infer that the SDR allotment had been insufficient. This information would provide the basis for the next "period" allotment. For instance, one might establish that SDRs should then grow by 7 per cent, in the expectation that, if the desired growth of total reserves remained 5 per cent, then the increase in dollars would tend to be around 3 per cent, reestablishing the desired ratio. Of course, the specific numbers used above are purely illustrative, and one could imagine more complex formulas taking into account circumstances other than the latest growth of total reserves and the initial composition. However, what has been said should be sufficient to indicate how the plan would help provide the basis for a rational decision about the rate of growth of SDRs.

We may now proceed to possible pathological situations in which clause (6) might apply. We need to examine both what circumstances would justify invoking this clause and what measures might be appropriate while this clause was in operation.

With respect to the first issue, one can readily describe circumstances in which our plan would bring to light an excessive American deficit. Suppose that, over some period, no currency was at the lower limit of the band while all or most other countries' currencies were at the upper limit, and that those countries were none the less accumulating dollars. There would then be a prima facie case for holding that the accumulation of these countries was unwanted, and was forced on them by an excessive American deficit. Furthermore, to a first approximation, the size of the excess deficit could be identified with the accumulation of reserves of these countries (over and above any increase due to SDR allotment), or with the American deficit, whichever was smaller.

At the other extreme, suppose that no currency was at the upper limit, and the currencies of all, or most, other countries were at the lower limit, and the countries were still losing reserves. One could then say that the loss was unwanted and forced by an insufficient deficit of the United States (or an excessive surplus), and the insufficiency could be deemed to be at least as large as the loss by these countries. (Note the asymmetry in these two cases. The reason for this asymmetry will be discussed later.)

Generalizing from these limiting cases, one might say that a "probable excess deficit" existed when the aggregate accumulation by countries whose currencies were at the upper limit, and which were gaining reserves, exceeded the aggregate decumulation of countries whose currencies were at the lower limit, and losing reserves; and that a "probable insufficient deficit" existed when the aggregate accumulation of the first group was less than the aggregate decumulation of the second group. Furthermore, the size of the net difference could be used to provide an indication of the size of the excess or deficit.

The considerations above provide the basis for our specification of clauses (6a) and (6b), to which the reader may wish to refer. Note that clause (6b) omits the counterpart (iii) of clause (6a). This omission implies that clause (6b) would be invoked regardless of whether the United States were running a deficit or surplus. On the other hand, clause (6a) would not be invoked unless the United States was running a deficit, since we do not propose that, under any circumstances, the United States should be required to run a surplus or, even less, to increase it. But we suggest

23

that if condition (6a), (i) and (ii), were verified, but not (iii), the rate of issue of SDRs should become zero or even negative. Finally, while we suggest that clause (6a) should automatically apply when the stated conditions have been verified, one could allow for its suspension by agreement of all countries having currencies at the upper limit. Similar conditions apply to suspension of clause (6b).

Once clause (6a) has been invoked and while it remains in force, the United States would be obligated to embark on a set of policies designed to reduce its deficit. There is little point in detailing here what these measures should be, for clearly the appropriate measures would depend on the particular circumstances. To begin with, we believe that there would be really little likelihood that clause (6a) would have to be invoked, provided at the time our proposal was put into effect the rate of exchange between the dollar and other major currencies had already been adequately realigned. An adequate realignment would imply, to begin with, that there would be some movement before the American deficit could become excessive; and if a situation of incipient excess surplus was developing, with the currencies of major countries close to, or at, the upper limit, then their exchange would be appreciating relative to the dollar, tending to correct the situation. Indeed, much of our proposal is predicated on the notion that crawling parities, together with responsible domestic policies with respect to price developments, provide enough flexibility to prevent pathological situations from developing.

None the less, one cannot exclude the possibility of pathological situations developing, the most likely source of this being large variations in the relatively volatile component represented by capital movements. If this turned out to be, in fact, the source of an "excessive deficit," then the appropriate set of remedies would revolve around measures aimed at discouraging American investments abroad. This could presumably be accomplished by economic incentives such as interest-equalization taxes, taxes on the profits from foreign equity investments, shifts in the mix of monetary and fiscal policies, and generally by policies showing "benign concern," while avoiding direct regulations such as quotas and discriminatory measures. In particular, in some instances, it might be appropriate to strive for an explicit coordination of monetary policies. It would also seem appropriate to require of countries with currencies at the upper limit of the band, and gaining reserves, to contribute to the elimination of the surplus, by removing or reducing impediments to capital outflows as well as to imports. Finally, while clause (6a) was in force, and assuming that all parties were absolving their duties, it would seem appropriate to reduce or suspend fresh allotments of SDRs.

In the light of recent experience, the likelihood of clause (6b), relating to an "insufficient American deficit," having to be invoked would seem even more remote, though we would hesitate to extrapolate that experience. In any event, the nature of measures that would be appropriate in this situation should be apparent enough from what has been said above. In particular, it would seem appropriate, while this clause was in force, to increase the allotment of SDRs.

Having raised the rather explosive issue of "excessive American capital exports," we should like to develop a few further considerations. These considerations are dictated, in part, by the awareness, kindled by exchanges with some European leaders, that this issue is paramount in the eyes of many influential Europeans and, therefore, any proposed reform has to face this issue squarely.

In the past, a substantial body of European public opinion has complained that (i) the United States, through its investments abroad, was acquiring valuable high-yielding assets as well as increasing economic dominance in their countries, and (ii) that it was paying with dollars which their central banks were forced to acquire, under the obligation to maintain their currencies at the fixed parity, and which could, at best, be invested in low-yielding, short-term American securities.

How does our proposed reform handle this problem? Under this system, if American investments were to continue more or less unabated, other countries would, of course, have the option of letting their currencies appreciate vis-à-vis the dollar, at least gradually, and this appreciation would increase the American net trade export and decrease theirs. In this way, American acquisitions would tend to be financed by a real transfer of resources, rather than by an increase in their dollar claims. But this solution might appear to them equally distasteful, if not more so. For, if there is one thing that they dislike even more than our continuing acquisition of assets and expansion of economic power in their country, it is to witness an increase in our net exports at the expense of theirs. This dislike, no doubt, reflects, in part, an inveterate mercantilistic tradition.

We have, in this paper, taken great pains in pointing out, and developing as forcefully as we could, the valid rationale of many European positions. Let us then take a look at what, if any, is sound and deserving in this position.

We submit that there are basically two grounds on which a country could, reasonably, object to American foreign investments. First, if it does not wish the United States to acquire assets and influence inside it.

25

And, second, if it does not wish to acquire additional reserves, least of all additional dollar balances.

The first objection is understandable, as a nationalistic sentiment, whether or not it is economically rational. But the answer to this problem very clearly lies in the country's using the power it generally already has (or can easily secure) explicitly to limit, discipline or prohibit American expansion—by way of acquisition, mergers, or direct investment in new productive facilities—within its borders. To some extent, this prohibition will make its balance of payments less favorable, thereby reducing either the acquisition of reserves or the need to let its exchange appreciate to avoid an increase in reserves.

Is there then any "rational" ground for a country to complain about American investments in other countries? Only if these investments were to cause that country to accumulate unwanted reserves. This could happen if the third countries, receiving American investments, were to utilize the resulting inflows of funds to increase, directly, or through triangular relations, their imports from the country in question. Such a development, however, should be regarded as favorable to a "mercantilist" mind; and if the country did not welcome an increase in its reserves, it could always let its currency appreciate. The outcome would then be a smaller increase in exports matched by some increase in imports, which could hardly be objectionable, especially since, presumably, it would be accompanied by an improvement in the terms of trade.

A problem could arise *only* if the required appreciation of the currency were larger than consistent with the obligation to maintain its exchange rate within the upper limit. For, once it had hit the upper limit, the country would be forced to let its reserves increase. The unwanted increase in reserves could then be traced to the American "excess" investment, and the country might even hold, with some reason, that through this increase it was helping to finance American expansionism. At this point, however, our clause (6a) becomes relevant. For if the country was acquiring reserves while some other countries were losing reserves even faster with the exchange rates of their currencies already at their lower limits, then the problem could not be reasonably laid at the American doorstep. While, if other countries were not losing sufficiently large amounts, then we would be in the circumstance in which the American deficit was indeed excessive and clause (6a) would apply. The invoking of this clause would then require the United States to take steps to curb its capital movements.

We, therefore, submit that our plan does protect the legitimate interest that any country might have in limiting American investment abroad.

Another point warrants brief consideration, though it borders on the kind of detail that is best settled at the level of concrete negotiations. If our reform is applied and is successful, one can anticipate that a sort of pecking order will tend to prevail between the three alternative forms of reserves. We would anticipate that, eventually, gold would be regarded as the least desirable of the three, because it yields no return. We would further anticipate that dollars would, at least some of the time, be preferred to SDRs, because they might yield a higher return, even after account is taken of the risk of devaluation. Any difficulties arising from this preference ordering could be resolved by the very simple principle that no country would have the right to hold SDRs and dollars in proportions significantly different from the composition of total reserves of the rest of the world. Thus, a country holding less than the average share of these two instruments would be entitled to acquire SDRs and dollars for gold, or dollars for SDRs, from a country having significantly more than the average share. In the longer run, if countries manifested a clear preference for SDRs over gold, one could conceive of a simple arrangement to change the overall composition, by allowing countries to sell some or part of their gold to the Fund against credit to its SDR account. The Fund could then sell this gold to the private market and use the proceeds to acquire earning assets whose return would be used to cover the interest payable on SDR balances. This arrangement would, however, run into difficulties if the free-market price of gold were to be significantly smaller than the monetized value of gold.

Another interesting issue for negotiation relates to the target composition of reserves between gold and SDRs, on the one hand, and dollars, on the other. We shall merely note in this connection that it is entirely conceivable that, at least at some later date, the target amount of dollars could be an absolute constant instead of a constant *proportion* of reserves; or it might be a proportion, or amount, decreasing in time, though, in our view, there are good reasons for keeping dollars as a substantial component of total reserves.

One could also readily amplify the scope of our reform by requiring countries to accept explicitly certain further obligations intended to insure a smoother working of the system. To illustrate, a country whose reserve had dipped below some stated level in relation to its Fund quota, could be required not to intervene in the market to support its currency, unless its exchange rate had actually reached the lower limit of the band. This would prevent a country from dissipating its reserves in an effort to manipulate its exchange market, at the risk of not having enough reserves left to perform its obligation. On the other hand, a country that was supporting its exchange rate at the lower limit, could be transiently accommodated with additional reserves if it had abided by the rules of the game and was enforcing a set of policies deemed adequate to restore equilibrium. Similarly, a country whose reserves exceeded some stated level in relation to its quota could be required not to intervene to hold down its exchange rate, unless it had reached the upper limit; and if it had reached the upper limit it could be required to embark on policies aimed at reducing the surplus. These rules, by curbing accumulation of reserves by countries already having a strong reserve position, would help other countries running a deficit. While we feel that there is much to be said for such rules, they clearly go well beyond the general framework that has existed heretofore, and, in view of the resistance they can evoke, we do not intend to propose them as an integral and necessary part of our reform.

One more question that cannot fail to be asked is: how much does the United States stand to gain from the proposed arrangement? We do not propose to go deep into this question but would like to offer two considerations. From a strictly economic point of view, we regard this reform as less advantageous—or more onerous—for the United States than the current system, in view of clauses (3) and (6). But, this is, in our view, a small price for the United States to pay to have the moral right to a greater independence in monetary policy and the management of the price level, and to have the advantage of a stable, livable system that minimizes the scope for political conflicts. As for the balance of absolute advantages and disadvantages (in contrast with a comparison with the past) we can see some advantages in being in part the "banker of the world," entitled to create a portion of the world's "money supply"—but it should be recognized that this banker pays interest on his "deposit liabilities" at the rate equal to the going market rate, and also that he gives his depositors the option of denominating their deposit claims in real terms. On the other hand, there are significant costs. In particular, the exchange rate of the dollar with the currencies of the rest of the world is now largely in the hands of these countries, which can manipulate it to serve their interests. Thus, the fortunes of American exports and imports are somewhat at the mercy of the rest of the world. However, the United States is in a uniquely good position to bear this cost, because it is so large, because it can count on some randomness and cancellation on the behavior of the countries that constitute the rest of the world, and, finally, because its foreign trade, though a very large share of the world's total, is but a small fraction of its Gross National Product. It is, therefore, doubtful that one could, at present, find any other country, or consortium of countries, that could substitute for the United States in the role of reserve-currency country.

Errata

Page 24, paragraph 2, line 12: ''excess surplus was developing'' should read ''excess deficit was developing.''

CHAPTER 14

International Capital Movements, Fixed Parities, and Monetary and Fiscal Policies

F. MODIGLIANI

I INTRODUCTION

There is a broad measure of agreement among professional economists on the proposition that the free movement of long-term international capital, just like the free movement of commodities, is highly desirable since it contributes to a more efficient use of resources, besides its likely contribution to a closer knit and a more peaceful world. There is, however, far less agreement as to what kind of international settlement system and what type of domestic policies are best suited to foster the international movement of capital.

One widely-held view is that the goal can best be served by retaining and strengthening the present system of permanently fixed official parities and forsaking any form of 'interference' with capital movements. Such interferences include not only direct controls but also the use of tax measures aimed at influencing the incentive to private capital movement by modifying the relation between the net private yield from, and the net private cost of, domestic versus foreign uses and sources of funds. The support of fixed parities rests on the consideration that variations in the rate of exchange between currencies increase the risk and, hence, have the effect of discouraging long-term capital movements. The opposition to any form of interference rests on the seemingly obvious proposition that it would prevent or reduce the flow of capital from where its productivity is lower to where it is higher. Since one of the most forceful and articulate expounders of this point of view in recent years has been C. P. Kindleberger, we find it convenient to refer to what follows as the 'CPK position', without necessarily implying that Kindleberger himself would endorse all that we ascribe to that position.

The basic purpose of this paper is to argue that the CPK position, despite its apparent cogency and attractive simplicity, suffers in reality from a number of fatal flaws and, as a result, its policy recommendations are inconsistent with the basic purpose they are supposed to serve.

The major conclusion of our analysis can be summarized in the following propositions:

1. Under a system of fixed and rigid parities, once proper allowance is made for widespread wage–price rigidities, complete freedom of capital movement may not only fail to achieve significant movements of real capital, but, in addition, tends to be inconsistent with domestic stability.

2. The above inconsistency can be eliminated through a 'co-ordinated monetary and fiscal policy approach'. It is shown, however, that under this approach fiscal policy is used not to *facilitate* the transfer of real capital, but rather to *eliminate the need* for a real transfer by removing the incentive for private investors to avail themselves of the freedom to move capital. Thus, the modern supporters of freedom of capital movements together with fixed and rigid parities are sacrificing the end to the mean: instead of wanting an open door so that capital can flow through it they want to remove the incentive for capital to flow so that the door can be kept open.

3. If freedom of capital movements is to achieve the intended purpose of bringing about a flow of real capital to those areas where its productivity is highest, then fixed and rigid parities must give way to a fuller and more systematic use of changes in parities.

4. Even with greater flexibility in exchange rates, it may be appropriate on occasions to modify the private incentive to the movement of capital. This result may be achieved through the use of conventional fiscal policy tools. It is argued, however, that contrary to the position taken by the CPK school, the use of tax incentives and related devices, aimed at modifying the relative cost and return of domestic versus foreign uses and sources of funds, provides an alternative approach which is preferable in most, if not all, relevant dimensions.

II FOUNDATIONS OF THE CPK POSITION AND THEIR SHORT-COMINGS

As indicated in Section I, the support of the CPK position for a system of fixed and rigid parities, free of any interference with private capital movements, rests on the ground that such a system maximizes the response of private capital flows to differentials between domestic and foreign private yields. But in order to conclude that such a response is 'socially' desirable it must be assumed that the movement of private capital in search for the highest private yield (or the cheapest source of funds) will redistribute the flow of *real investment*, without reducing its volume, towards those areas where its productivity is highest. We suggest that this assumption is subject to question on at least three major counts:

1. It presumes that differentials in private yields imply similar differentials in net social returns.
2. It presupposes that differentials in yields, with freedom of private capital movements, will lead to flows or transfers of *real* resources, as distinguished from international reserves, in predictably short order.
3. It neglects the possibility that under fixed and rigid parities, the transfer of real resources, if and when it occurs, may be achieved at significant economic and social costs, including reductions in output and in the overall flow of investment, through a fall in the rate of utilization of resources.

Let us examine each of these points more closely.

i. Private versus social returns. As has been pointed out by many authors, in a world in which net yields to private investors are affected in very large measure and in very complex ways by the entire fiscal system of the country as well as by direct controls, and in which the structure of capital markets and the intermediaries operating therein exhibit vast differences, there is not even a *prima facie* case for the proposition that differences in private yields can be taken as meaningful indicators of differences in social returns. On the contrary, the relation between private and social yields could be estimated only by a painstaking comparative analysis of fiscal and capital market structures, country by country. Thus, until such time as fiscal and capital market structures have been made reasonably uniform, there is no sound basis for arguing that freedom of capital to move where the private yield is greatest necessarily contributes to an improved allocation of world resources.

ii. Movements of private capital and transfer of real resources under fixed parities. It is generally agreed that, in a system of fixed exchanges, a movement of private capital from, say, country A to B, in response to an emerging difference in private yields will, in the first place, generate transfers of international reserves. But will these movements in turn soon give rise to corresponding transfers of real resources? For this to happen, there must eventually occur an increase in the current account balance of country A and a shrinkage in that of country B equal to the flow of capital to be transferred. These changes in turn will generally require a rise in the price level of B and a fall in the price level A – at least if we assume away the possible but unlikely case of perverse elasticities.

This change in relative price levels is precisely what is expected to happen under the idealized textbook version of the gold standard, through the working of two well-known mechanisms: a) the commitment of the monetary authorities of each country to respond promptly to changes in its international reserves with roughly proportional (or more than proportional) changes in its monetary base; plus the assumption that a change in the monetary base will, in short order, produce corresponding changes in the actual money supply; b) a high degree of flexibility, both upward and downward, in the entire structure of wages and prices. Under these idealized conditions the initial flow of reserves from A to B would cause first a contraction of money supply in A and an expansion in B, which, in turn would give rise to movements in the opposite direction in the interest rates in each country, tending to wipe out the differential and to put an end to the movement of reserves. The rise in interest rates in A, in turn, reduces investment (and possibly consumption), and hence aggregate demand, tending to create an excess supply of labour. However, because of the assumed flexibility, the excess supply promptly results in a fall in wages and prices. Meanwhile, the same sequence is occurring in B, with 'sign reversed'. Finally, the change in relative prices expands net exports of A and reduces those of B, bringing back aggregate demand to the initial level, so that price levels stop changing. In the new equilibrium, the rate of investment has fallen in A and has risen in B to the point where the yields are equal in the two countries, and a portion of the unchanged saving flow in A, no longer needed to finance the lower investment, finances the larger investment in B, through the rise in net exports. (The equalization of yields need not actually occur in the context of growing economies. It is conceivable that some yield differential and, corresponding to it, some flow or real capital, may persist for a long time, even indefinitely.)

So much for the textbook version of the gold standard. Consider now what would actually tend to happen under the present kind of managed gold exchange system, and with marked wage and price rigidities, at least in the downward direction. As long as there are no interferences with movements of private capital, the first step – that is, the transfer of international reserves – will still tend to occur. But what effects this will have on the money supply and aggregate demand in country A and B are now a matter of the response that the central banks choose to adopt. If country B does not like inflation, and especially if it does not welcome the foreign investments, it can offset the larger demand for domestic assets by foreigners by selling some of the assets it owns, leaving the monetary base, the money supply and the structure of interest rates largely unchanged. It will replace in its balance sheets the original income-yielding assets with international reserves, which, if kept in the form of gold, will yield nothing, and even if invested in eligible market instruments of country A will have a relatively 'low' yield since, by assumption, yields in A are lower than in B. By following this course, the central bank of B will also prevent the operation of any mechanism tending to reduce the incentive to the capital flow, and thus may keep accumulating reserves. (If country A happens to be the reserve currency country, B may also complain that that country is, in effect, buying up profitable assets in B and financing the purchase with 'forced' cheap credit from the central bank of B.) If, on the other hand, the receiving country B permits an expansion of the money supply – whether because it is consciously and willingly playing according to the rules of the game or because of inaction or lack of adequate institutions to offset the inflow of reserves – it will create some inflation at home, though very likely complaining that A is 'exporting inflation' through its deficit in the balance of payments.

Similarly country A may, at least initially, react to the loss of reserves by offsetting it in order to avoid domestic deflation. This will again tend to hinder the transfer of real resources, for any given policy of country B, by hindering accommodating changes in interest rates and in the balance on current accounts, thus contributing to the continuing flow of international reserves.

Suppose, on the other hand, country A did undertake a policy of monetary restraint either because it was following the rules of the game, or, more likely, because it was forced to do so to stem the continuing loss of reserves. How far would this really help? It is very likely that, initially, interest rates would tend to rise in A and this would help by reducing the incentives to capital exports. In addition, as in the idealized version, the contraction in money supply and rise in interest rates would reduce aggregate demand and, hence, the demand for labour. But because of rigidities, wages and prices would fail to respond promptly and thus generate a rise in net exports to offset the fall in domestic demand. Instead there would be a tendency for employment and output to fall – unless monetary restraint is adequately offset by expansionary fiscal policy, a possibility which will be considered separately below. In this process some improvement in the net exports of A and, hence, some real transfer may take place but not so much through the probably sluggish relative decline in prices as through the fact that the depressed level of income and employment would tend to reduce imports and possibly somewhat expand exports. In any event, the fall in investment in A will be offset only very partially by a rise in net exports and instead will mostly result in a fall in saving through the fall in income. Furthermore, the fall in economic activity in A, by generating excess capacity and depressing profits, is likely, in short order, to put downward pressure on market interest rates, unless the central bank is sanguine enough to keep contracting the money supply even faster than income and the demand for money is falling. It is, therefore, entirely possible that after an initial rise, the entire level of interest rates may sag even below the starting level, rekindling the inducement to capital exports.

The upshot of all this is that under the present system of fixed and rigid parities and widespread wage–price rigidities, there is no reliable mechanism that ensures the prompt transfer of real resources to match the movement of private capital. Furthermore, in so far as the transfer occurs, this comes about through a mechanism which interferes with the domestic goal of maintaining price stability and full employment. Under these conditions, complete freedom of capital movements may not only fail to achieve significant movement of real capital, but in addition, tends to be inconsistent with domestic stability.

III FISCAL POLICY AS THE CURE FOR ALL

Quite recently it has been suggested that the apparent inconsistency between freedom of private capital movements and domestic stability can be eliminated through a 'co-ordinated monetary and fiscal policy approach'. The goal of balance of payments equilibrium with complete freedom of capital movements, it is asserted, is not inconsistent with the goal of price stability and full employment because the *two* goals can be reconciled by the appropriate use of *two* tools, namely the monetary tool and the fiscal tool. Indeed, by suitably combining an 'expansionary' or 'contractionary' fiscal policy with a 'tight' or 'loose' monetary policy, it should, in principle, be possible to make full employment and price stability consistent with any desired level of interest rates – at least within sufficiently wide limits.

This possibility opens up new vistas. Clearly, under complete freedom of capital movements, interest rates must tend to be the 'same' in all countries (up to appropriate risk and liquidity differentials) or can differ at most by very moderate differentials accompanying a flow of real resources between countries. But this requirement of uniform interest rates at a somehow determined world level can be made consistent with the maintenance of full employment even in the face of inter-country differences in the propensity to accumulate and in the domestic 'marginal yield' that would correspond to a given flow of saving. In essence, this result would be achieved by varying government expenditure and by manipulating consumption, through taxation, so that the sum of expenditure and consumption fills the gap between full employment income and the level of domestic investment consistent with the given world level of interest rates. An alternative, and for present purposes, more enlightening formulation is to say that fiscal policy should aim at making full employment net domestic saving – the sum of private saving and government surplus – equal to the rate of domestic investment consistent with the uniform yield across countries (plus the historically given current account surplus). Monetary policy can then be relied upon to supply the quantity of money needed to transact a full employment income with a level of interest rates consistent with the 'world level'. This same concept is sometimes expressed by saying that monetary policy must be aimed at balance of payments equilibrium and fiscal policy at the maintenance of full employment. This formulation is somewhat misleading since, in reality, both monetary and fiscal policy must be determined simultaneously in view of both goals. It is true, however, that with perfect international mobility of capital, monetary policy loses much of its power to control interest rates; any attempt at maintaining rates to a level inconsistent with the world level would tend to create offsetting capital flows and surplus or deficits in the balance of payments of such dimensions as to make the goal an unrealistic one.

We have no significant disagreement with the above analysis and its implications for the consistency of domestic full employment and price stability with balance of payments equilibrium, in the presence of complete freedom of capital movements. We would only point out that two important changes in present institutions would be required:

1. We would need far greater short-run flexibility in fiscal policy than is consistent with the present institutions, at least in the US. Hence, if our policy-makers are inclined to opt for a mechanism of this type they ought to be much more active than they now seem to be in educating Congress and the public in the necessity of delegating discretionary power to the administration and also in the necessity of shaping US fiscal (and not just monetary) policy to accommodate the rest of the world.

2. Mechanisms and procedures would need to be set up for the main countries to agree on just what the level of interest rates should be for the world as a whole. For, in the last analysis, the world level would be determined by the average overall degree of fiscal tightness or looseness through its effects on the average world level of resources available for capital formation. This aspect of the problem is generally referred to as the necessity for all countries to adopt a co-ordinated monetary-fiscal policy mix. In the absence of explicit co-ordination, as has been pointed out repeatedly, for example, by Tobin, there would be a continuous danger of interest rate escalation with the overall level being swayed in the direction of levels prevailing in those countries opting for the highest level of interest rates. This situation is well illustrated by the experience of the 1960s when the US was pushed towards a high-interest-rate full-employment regime by the behaviour of its European partners.

IV A VITAL SHORTCOMING OF THE CPK POSITION

While we are prepared to concede that the above system could conceivably be made to work tolerably well, we see very little ground for arguing that such a system would be very desirable or economically efficient Quite the contrary, we suggest that it would be inferior in all major relevant respects to a system allowing at least some flexibility in exchange rates and relying on specific tax measures to control private incentive to the movement of capital.

Freedom of capital movement basically implies equality of yields across countries Now, as far as one can see, the only sound economic argument in favour of freedom of capital movement is that the equality of yields is brought about by a transfer of real capital from where its yields would otherwise be lower to where it would be higher. The transfer of real capital, in turn, requires surplus and deficit in the current account balance through which countries with 'surplus saving' – that is, saving in excess of the rate of domestic investment called for by the common yield – finance the excess of investment over saving of the countries 'short of saving'. Under the pure gold standards, the required rate of net exports is achieved primarily through changes in the relative price levels.

The obvious alternative mechanism to bring about transfer, without sacrificing price stability and full employment, would be recourse to suitable adjustments in the rate of exchange. Such adjustments, in fact, permit changing the relation between domestic and foreign price levels without requiring changes in either domestic or foreign price levels measured in terms of the domestic currency. The CPK school rejects this approach on the ground that changes in parities increase the risk incurred by investing or borrowing abroad and, hence, would sap the incentive to the movement of private capital. They advocate instead relying on co-ordinated fiscal policy to make changes in parity unnecessary to maintain equilibrium in the balance of payments, while retaining freedom of capital movements. But, paradoxically enough, by embracing this approach they are, in effect, *sacrificing the very feature that makes the freedom of capital worth having*. For, the purpose of the fiscal policy they recommend is not that of providing an alternative mechanism to *achieve the transfer* of the difference between domestic saving and investment at the common yield, but quite the contrary that of forcing saving into equality with domestic investment, thus *eliminating the need for the transfer*. Looked at from the point of view of private investors, this policy *removes* the incentive to take advantage of the freedom to move capital. Thus, the modern supporters of freedom of capital movement together with fixed and rigid parities are in effect sacrificing the end to the mean: instead of wanting an open door so that capital will flow through it, they want to remove the incentive for capital to flow so the door can be kept open!

V THE RELATIVE MERITS OF GENERAL FISCAL POLICY VERSUS SPECIFIC INSTRUMENTS AS DEVICES FOR REMOVING THE INCENTIVE TO CAPITAL FLOWS

Once it is clearly realized that the purpose to be achieved through the so-called 'co-ordination' of monetary and fiscal policies is that of controlling the incentive for capital to move, it is but natural to ask whether there are any other methods that will achieve the same purpose and how the available alternatives compare in terms of other effects.

Clearly, an alternative way of removing or controlling the incentive for private capital to move between A and B, consists in offsetting the difference between the private yields prevailing in A and B by fiscal devices aimed at a) equalizing the *private* returns a national of A can obtain from domestic and foreign investments and b) equalizing the private cost a national of B has to incur by raising funds in A as compared with B. The most obvious examples of such devices are the so-called 'interest equalization taxes' and the differential taxation of domestic versus foreign corporate profits. Both devices are presently being used to some extent in the USA, the first to reduce and the second to *enhance* the incentive to capital exports.

In our view, a strong case can be made to support the contention that the 'equalization of private returns' approach is preferable to the 'co-ordination of fiscal policies' in most, if not all, relevant respects: a) easiness of application, b) required degree of international agreement, c) dislocation of existing economic structures, and last but not least, d) the freedom it leaves to each country to pursue policies of more or less rapid expansion of the domestic stock of productive physical capital.

Of these various claims, the easiest to demonstrate is the last one. Obviously, under the 'co-ordination' approach a country loses the freedom to use fiscal policy to restrain or stimulate consumption (private and public) and thus to stimulate or restrain national saving and capital formation. It must instead use fiscal policy to enforce a level of national saving consistent with exogenously determined investment. In particular, it might be forced to thwart the thrift of its population by running a budget deficit on current account, thus 'artificially' increasing private disposable income and consumption, and satisfying the accumulation propensity of the community with government bonds instead of income producing addition to the stock of physical capital. This loss of freedom to manage the rate of capital formation, which can be clearly avoided through the equalization approach, seems particularly objectionable since it is hard to see how or why its use could significantly harm any other country.

Claim a) seems also fairly straightforward, though it involves, in part, considerations of a 'political' nature But, at least to a naïve observer, it would appear that it is generally easier to secure modifications of specific tax measures affecting a relatively minor sector of the economy–as required under the 'incentive equalization' approach–than to secure changes in broad-based levies as required under the 'fiscal co-ordination' approach We also suspect that, in the case of specific tax measures, it might be easier to institute fiscal devices involving some degree of automaticity, or delegation to the executive to vary the rate of taxation, within some limits.

As for claim b), while the 'co-ordination' approach, by its very nature, requires an appreciable measure of explicit international agreement, at least among the major financial powers, the 'equalization' approach would not seem to require much agreement, though undoubtedly co-ordination would help to make it work more smoothly and would avoid the possible danger of retaliatory measures. But we suggest that the danger of hostile retaliation is not really too serious, for the initiative for taking specific measures would normally fall on a country which was losing reserves because of excessive capital outflows not matched by corresponding surplus on current account – witness the instance of the USA. It is hard to see why other countries would want to go out of their way to pass legislation designed to thwart the effort of the losing country to re-establish equilibrium in its international accounts. It might be optimistic to expect other countries to pass legislation or regulations that will *help* the country in difficulty, but to suppose that a significant number of countries would go out of their way to *hinder* the adjustment process seems to be unwarrantedly pessimistic. In short, then, the 'co-ordination' approach requires *active co-operation*, whereas the 'equalization' approach can get by as long as we can count on the absence of *active obstructionism* – though co-operation would, no doubt, improve its workings.

Claim c) is probably the hardest to substantiate, especially since it involves two distinct aspects: dislocations of the domestic economy and dislocations imposed on foreign partners. In so far as the domestic effects are concerned, the claim can be defended at least with respect to one typical cause of difficulty. Suppose that, for a given country, the international accounts are initially balanced and now, for some reason, the returns to investments and, hence, the demand for funds, tend to shift markedly down (or up) without a similar shift occurring in the 'rest of the world'. In a closed economy, the natural response to this situation would be to pursue an easy monetary policy with a view to reducing market rates of interest in line with the reduced anticipated profitability of investment. Such a policy aims at maintaining aggregate demand and employment while, at the same time, also largely maintaining the distribution of output between consumption and capital formation. But with an open economy, if there is freedom of capital movements, the attempt at easing credit and lowering interest rates will tend to result in large outflows of capital, without even succeeding in reducing interest rates as much as desirable. The 'equalization' approach would handle the difficulty by fiscal devices aimed at reducing the *private* return from *foreign* investments to a level commensurate with the reduction desired in domestic rates, thus making it possible, by and large, to pursue the domestic monetary-fiscal policy mix that would have been available to a closed economy. By contrast, the 'co-ordination' approach would require stimulating consumption and reducing full employment saving to match the decreased flow of investment expenditure consistent with the maintenance of the initial level of domestic interest rates required by the unchanged level of world rates. But this approach, if successful in maintaining the aggregate level of output, still implies that the composition of output tends to change from investment goods towards consumption goods, causing a dislocation which can be avoided by the equalization approach. To be sure, if the initial shift in country A were due to a downward shift in the propensity to consume, the implications of the two approaches would be reversed. Now the composition of output would change if full employment were maintained by an easing of monetary policy, while the change would be avoided by relying on fiscal stimuli to consumption. But, in the first place, it is generally agreed that disturbances to equilibrium are much more likely to originate in shifts in the investment schedule than in the consumption function; and, in the second place, under the equalization approach the country would have the option to respond differently to different sources of disturbances so as to minimize dislocation, using, for example, fiscal policy to respond to disturbances originating in consumption and monetary policy to counteract changes originating in the investment sector. Under the co-ordination approach, by contrast, the country would have no choice but to respond primarily with fiscal stimuli, whether or not this would produce dislocations.

The comparative dislocation effects on foreign partners are more difficult to assess. To a first approximation, it would appear that the two approaches would have similar effects since they both endeavour to prevent changes in flow of capital or to contain them within the limits of concurrent changes in the current account balance. But admittedly, this aspect of the problem requires further exploration, both to understand the comparative implications and to see how disturbing dislocations might be minimized.

VI CONCLUSIONS: THE ALTERNATIVE TO FIXED AND RIGID PARITIES AND CO-ORDINATION OF FISCAL POLICIES

In summary, the 'CPK approach' suffers from a basic flaw: for the sake of achieving the purely formal goal of freedom of capital movement, it advocates a system which, paradoxically enough, tends, in effect, to stifle the flow of real capital – the only real justification for advocating freedom of capital movements. In addition, it also requires individual countries to give up the freedom of managing the rate of capital formation.

We have shown that, in so far as one wishes to influence the incentive to private capital movements, this result can be achieved at least as effectively, and generally more effectively, by relying on the equalization of yields rather than on the co-ordinated fiscal policy. However, both approaches are designed to minimize the need to transfer resources by removing the incentive for private investors to take advantage of the freedom to move capital. Clearly a yet better approach would be to adopt mechanisms to permit the flow of capital by facilitating the matching transfer of real resources, whenever differences in private yield were an indication of corresponding differences in social returns. As already noted, the obvious mechanism is that of changes in the exchange rates which result in changes in relative prices and thus in current account balances without relying on the costly and unreliable device of actual changes in price levels.

The adoption of greater exchange rate flexibility would also reduce, but not necessarily eliminate, the desirability, at least occasionally, to modify the incentive to private capital movements. Aside from the fact that differences in private yield may not be a reliable measure of differences in social yields, one must also remember that changes in net exports to accommodate the transfer of real capital are not costless, since they involve internal reallocation of resources. A good case can therefore be made for limiting the speed with which changes in parities are allowed to occur, and the case is further reinforced by the consideration that rapid changes in parities may give rise to disturbing speculative movements. Whether such limitations are best handled by crawling pegs or other devices is for present purposes a mere detail. The important point is that, with such limitations, there may arise a need, at least in the short run, for holding private capital movements in line with the achievable transfer of real capital. To achieve this goal, without outright limitations on the freedom of capital movements, countries could rely on general fiscal policy as one of the possible devices for influencing incentive to capital movements. But they should also be allowed to opt, just as freely, for the alternative approach relying on specific tax and related incentives, which, we have argued, is likely to be superior under most circumstances. Under this alternative, specific tax measures would be used by a country to control the relation between the return obtainable by its nationals from domestic and foreign investments and the cost incurred by foreigners by raising funds in its market as compared with other markets.

It is possible that greater reliance on changes in parities as a method of controlling balance of payments disequilibria might increase the uncertainty of return or costs from international lending or borrowing, and this result, in turn, might give rise to a somewhat smaller flow of funds for any given differential between foreign and domestic rates. But we suspect that the CPK position greatly exaggerates the significance and undesirability of this phenomenon. Without entering into lengthy details, it might be pointed out that, for short-term lending, the parties could always hedge through forward markets. If a system of gradual changes in parities were accompanied by a sufficiently broad band of permissible fluctuations around the parity, one might expect that the incentive to short-term capital movements, in response to transient changes in short-term rates, might be largely eliminated through movements in the spot and forward rates. But it is generally agreed that this is a desirable development as such movements contribute little, if anything, to the channelling of long-term capital to where it has larger social returns, while their elimination allows countries greater freedom to use monetary policy for short-term stabilization.

For long-term capital movements, on the other hand, the size of changes in parities required to accommodate the transfer of real capital may be expected to be small enough to have but a minor effect on the return or cost from long-term investments, especially when compared with the many other sources of risk associated with foreign operations. Note also that under the alternative of fixed parities, in so far as the capital movements had not been stifled by the use of general fiscal policy or specific tax measures, the transfer would require changes in the price level of each country; but this means that the reduction in the risk of foreign lending and borrowing would be achieved at the expense of a commensurate increase in the risk of real returns from *domestic* lending and borrowing operations, which are presumably much larger in volume than the international operations.

To be sure, changes in parities may come also from differential rates of price movements in different countries. But under these conditions, even the CPK school would have to accept the inevitability of changes in parities. Furthermore, with differential rates of inflation, offsetting changes in parities might well reduce the risk of the *real* return, if the contract were denominated in the currency with greater price stability. Quite generally, the real risk from both price level movements and variations in exchange rates could be minimized by denominating contracts in some numeraire having stable purchasing power; while no such numeraire exists at present, it could be created by escalator clauses or by appropriate reforms of the international payments system which we have suggested elsewhere.[1]

Last, but not least, it is by no means obvious that the moderate increase in risk from foreign lending that might arise under the proposed alternative might not, on the whole, have a salutary effect, like any other device that blunts the *incentive* to movement of capital without curtailing the *freedom* of movement. Indeed, why is this particular method of reducing the incentive to capital movement any less desirable than the 'co-ordinated fiscal policy' approach advocated by the CPK position? On the contrary, just like the use of specific fiscal instruments, it contributes to allow greater freedom to individual countries to pursue somewhat different interest rate and capital formation policies without curtailing the freedom of capital movements.

[1] Two alternative reforms which would result in an international numeraire with stable purchasing power have been suggested in Modigliani and Kennen, 'A Suggestion for Solving the International Liquidity Problem', *Banca Nazionale del Lavoro, Quarterly Review* (March 1966), and Modigliani and Askari, 'The Reform of the International Payments System', *Essays in International Finance* (Princeton, New Jersey, September 1971), no. 89.

Errata

Page 242, 5 lines from the bottom: "some flow or real capital" should read "some flow of real capital."

Page 253, footnote 1, line 2: "Kennen" should read "Kenen."

The International Transfer of Capital and the Propagation of Domestic Disturbances Under Alternative Payment Systems*

1. Introduction

In July of 1971, shortly before President Nixon's dramatic move of August 15, the authors outlined a new system of international payments (Modigliani and Askari, 1971). In this plan, we rejected both the then existing regime of fixed and rigid parities and a system of floating rates in favor of a system based on official parities; but we proposed, as have many other economists before us (Williamson, 1965), that these parities be allowed to change gradually in time, subject to limitations on the maximum rate of change over time. Why recommend a " Complicated " plan with sliding parities; is it not simpler and more efficient to adopt floating rates? With floating rates, we need no rules or reserves and free market forces will determine the correct rate of exchange between currencies. The usual reason for eliminating floating exchanges from practical consideration is that, whatever the economic claims for it, it is unachievable politically, because governments insist on some sort of fixed parities. Especially, countries for which trade is a large portion of GNP are not ready to abandon the right to control the exchange rate because floating rates would leave them at the mercy of market forces and " destabilizing speculation ". As a result, it has been argued that sliding parities is the maximum concession towards floating that one may hope to negotiate.

In this paper, we would like to develop briefly a different argument in favor of sliding pegs as compared to either extremes. The arguments rest on three propositions.

(*) The authors are respectively, Institute Professor at M.I.T. and Associate Professor of Economics at Wayne State University. They are very grateful to Profs. WILLIAM BRANSON, GEORGE HALM, CHARLES KINDLEBERGER and NIELS THYGESEN for some very helpful comments.

First, the international movement of capital benefits the world in so far as it tends to equalize social yields through the transfer of real resources from " surplus " countries, whose full employment national savings exceeds profitable domestic investment at the common yield to " deficit " countries, whose full employment national savings falls short of profitable domestic investment. Therefore, we would want an international payment system in which a differential in social yields across countries would lead to a transfer of *real* resources. However, we argue that with widespread wage and price rigidities, if countries are to retain the ability to pursue domestic stabilization goals, the required transfer of real capital from surplus to deficit countries cannot be achieved merely through a high mobility of private capital but it also requires appropriate adjustments in exchange rates. These considerations lead us to reject fixed rates in favor of at least gradual adjustments of exchange rates to achieve the transfer.

Second, given high mobility of private capital and assuming at first that no stabilization measures are taken, we show that cyclical disturbances in domestic demand resulting from transient changes in the propensity to invest or consume, that is from transient changes in " surplus ", will lead to a larger change in aggregate demand of the rest of the world (ROW) under floating rates than under fixed rates. This is because fixed rates impose on the country in which the disturbance originates a behavior pattern which dampens its impact on the rest of the world. In other words, fixed rates tend to dampen the international propagation of cyclical disturbances.

Third, we argue that, under fixed rates, the disturbing country has the incentive to respond to the initial disturbance by using policies which are stabilizing both for *itself and* for the ROW; whereas, with floating rates, the disturbing country has more to gain by adopting policies which further destabilize the ROW.

We are thus led to the conclusion that a system of sliding pegs combines the advantages of short-run fixity in mitigating propagation of cyclical disturbances with long-run or structural changes in surplus or deficit.[1]

---

[1] It has been argued that, because of the added exchange risk resulting from floating rates, a given differential in interest rates would lead to a smaller flow of capital under floating than under fixed rates. It is shown in 2 below that this argument has very little merit, at least with respect to movements of long term capital.

4

Needless to say, we recognize that the argument set out below is not sufficient to establish conclusively the superiority of some system of sliding parities. But we feel that our paper has at least the merit of calling attention to a set of issues that need to be thoroughly explored and understood in order to arrive at a balanced assessment of the merits and shortcomings of alternative payment systems.[2]

2. Capital Transfer and Domestic Stability under Alternative Payment Systems

In this section, we conclude that only with flexibility in exchange rates can the benefits of international mobility of private capital movements be reaped, without wastefully sacrificing the freedom of pursuing domestic stabilization goals.

Freedom of private capital movements benefits the world in so far as it tends to equalize social yields by transferring resources from surplus to deficit countries. This requires that two conditions be fulfilled. First, the social rate of return must equal, or at least be proportional to, the private rate. And second, the flow of financial capital must also lead to the transfer of real resources. However, for the transfer to occur, the current account balance (B) must equal the surplus or deficit to be transferred. Under the textbook version of the gold standard, hereafter the "ideal gold standard", the current account balance was supposed to adjust to the desired inflow and outflow of capital, despite the fixed parity, through the well-known mechanism of the fixed relation between a country's money supply and its gold reserves, coupled with a high degree of wage-price flexibility. For example, if the desired flow of capital from country A to country B increased, initially, this would result in a flow of reserves from A to B. However, this would lead to the contraction of the money supply in A and an expansion in B; and this in turn would result in a decrease in A's domestic

2 To illustrate this point, we note that, in interpreting our analysis as supporting a system of sliding parities, we are *implicitly* making the value judgment that international propagation of domestic disturbances is undesirable. Yet, as William Branson has pointed out to us, shifting a part of the burden of domestic disturbances to the rest of the world may actually be desirable, as it tends to dilute the impact of disturbances. While this is a plausible value judgment in making a choice between alternative payment systems, it is still essential to understand their implications with respect to the incidence of disturbances.

price level and an increase in B's, without any significant change in employment and real output, and thus finally to an increased current account surplus of A and deficit of B. Thus, the initial flow of reserves would, in short order, give rise to a transfer of real resources.

Under floating rates, exactly the same effect can be achieved, despite price rigidities and without interfering with any desired price and employment policy, because the increased desire of A's nationals to move capital to B, increases the price of B's currency in terms of A's; that is, it leads to a depreciation in A's exchange rate, which in turn makes A's goods cheaper for B's nationals and B's goods more expensive to A's nationals. This leads, under normal conditions, to an increase in A's current account surplus and a fall in B's and thus to the desired real transfer.

But if the exchange rate is fixed and wages and prices are rigid, at least downward, there is no method by which the current account balance can be changed except through domestic policies, consciously aiming at either unemployment or inflation, both of which are clearly inconsistent with the goal of domestic stability. Indeed, the current balance could be made *more* favorable only by an initial reduction in income and employment, decreasing imports, and could be *less* favorable only through an expansion of aggregate demand raising employment and income and/or prices. It is easy to see that under these conditions, if there were no capital movement, domestic full employment and price stability and balance of payment equilibrium could generally not be reconciled under a regime of fixed parities. For there would be a "unique" level of income and employment that would make imports equal exports and this level would not coincide with full employment at the current price level except by pure chance. This is the basis on which many economists today would advocate floating rates.

More recently, it has been shown, notably through the work of Mundell (1963), that, once we allow for the movement of private capital, in response to interest rate differentials, balance of payments (BP) equilibrium and domestic stability goals can be reconciled with each other, even in the presence of fixed parities. The argument is as follows:

(i) it is true that, given a target level of income, $\hat{Y}$, there

6

will be associated with it a unique current account balance, $\hat{B}$;

(ii) but balance of payments equilibrium no longer requires $B = O$. It requires only that $\hat{B}$ be offset by an equal inflow of capital if negative, or outflow of capital if positive. But the net outflow of capital, FL, depends on the relation between domestic and foreign rates, r and r_f respectively. Hence, given r_f and $\hat{B}$, there will exist some level of r, say $\hat{r}$, for which $FL = B$ and hence, BP is zero; given $\hat{Y}$, this level can be achieved by an appropriate money supply.

(iii) A given r will uniquely determine the level of domestic investment, K. But this level can be reconciled with $\hat{Y}$, independently of the private propensity to save, through an appropriate fiscal policy — including taxation (T) and expenditure (E).

Formally, we have the standard identity:

$$Y = C(T,Y) + E + K(r) + B(Y)$$

where: C(T,Y) denotes consumption, a function of taxes and income. More conveniently: Let $S_p = Y—C—T$ and $S_g = T—E$, then,

$$Y—C—T = S_p(T,Y) = E—T + K(r) + B(Y) = —S_g + K + B$$

Given a target $\hat{Y}$, and the consequent $\hat{r}$ needed to make $BP = O$, we can achieve that $\hat{Y}$ through any fiscal policy program which satisfies $S_p\ (T,\hat{Y}) = E—T + K(\hat{r}) + \hat{B}$. Thus, we have one equation in the two variables, T and E, which can be readily satisfied by choice of an appropriate combination of E and T.

All this is true. However, it hides one fatal flaw. Under this system, *one loses all the benefits that were supposed to result from the free movement of private capital.* Indeed, the given $\hat{B}$, resulting from the historically received price levels and fixed parities, now determines the amount of capital to be moved rather than B being determined by the flow of real capital that needs to be transferred in order to equate returns across countries, as would be true under the textbook version of the gold standard or floating exchanges.

Furthermore, in order to maintain full employment, fiscal policies must be used to *force* domestic saving, $S_p + S_g$, into *matching* $K(\hat{r})$, the rate of domestic investment which is profitable at the world rate $\hat{r}$, plus the given $\hat{B}$. This task is to be accomplished by increasing or reducing consumption through taxes and by varying the extent to which savings is offset by the government deficit. Under this system, it is again true that the rate of return will tend to be equalized across countries, but basically by each country forcing saving to match the rate of investment that is profitable at the (somehow given) common rate $\hat{r}$, rather than through the transfer of real capital from " surplus " to " deficit " countries, as defined earlier.

As is apparent from the previous paragraph, under the Mundell system, the three conventional tools of stabilization policy are to be used to achieve three targets: full employment $\hat{Y}$, balance of payment equilibrium ($BP = O$), and desired distribution of domestic resources between the public sector, E and the private sector. It is, however, impossible to choose and achieve a *target* level of domestic saving, as would be possible either in a closed system — where BP is not a target — or under floating rates — where BP always and automatically takes care of itself through the rate of exchange seeking the level which clears the foreign exchange market. (The same is true for the ideal gold standard, where prices adjust automatically to a level consistent with full employment and no transfer of reserves).

Even in the fixed parity, rigid price system, it is possible to pursue an independent target for domestic saving but only by recourse to additional tools. These tools include direct control of capital movements (though such controls are likely to be more effective in preventing capital outflows than in forcing capital inflows); devices for opening a wedge between foreign and domestic rates — interest equalization taxes, differential fiscal incentive to borrowing abroad; and devices affecting the relation between the cost of capital and domestic market rates — such as the investment tax credit and loans at subsidized reduced rates.

Another device that has been increasingly used to insulate the domestic from the international capital markets and to insure that capital movements match the trade balance B, is that of a " dual "

8

exchange system, with a fixed parity for "commercial" transactions and a floating rate for "financial" transactions (sometimes coupled with exchange controls designed to limit domestic and/or foreign transactor's access to the financial market). In so far as the authorities succeed in insulating completely the two markets, it is possible, with this device, to insure that capital movements precisely match and offset B, independently of domestic monetary policy. This only requires that the monetary authority sell (or buy) on the financial market an amount of foreign exchange equal to the surplus (or deficit) on the commercial account.[3] But even with these devices, it still remains true that with fixed parities we lose the benefit of international capital movements in that such movements are determined by B instead of B being determined by desirable movements of capital.

We must conclude, therefore, that under fixed exchange rates the mobility of private capital is desirable in that it permits the achievement of high employment and price stability even when these are inconsistent with current account balance; but it is not helpful in bringing about a transfer of real resources from would-be surplus to would-be deficit countries. This transfer can be achieved only if the mobility of private capital is accompanied by enough long-run exchange flexibility to permit the current account balance to accommodate, at least gradually, the needed real flows.

In light of the above it is paradoxical that fixed rates have been advocated in part by those who have stressed the desirability of international capital movements as a device for achieving an optimum allocation of capital across countries. They have recommended fixed rates on the grounds that certainty of exchange rates enhances capital movements by reducing the risk, and thus increasing the responsiveness of investors to differential rates of return. We have already shown that under fixed rates, the movement of capital is entirely determined by whatever happens to be the surplus or deficit in the current account balance and therefore cannot, in fact, be enhanced by the alleged reduction of risk entailed by fixed exchange rates.

But beyond that, the conclusion that fixed exchange rates

[3] In so far as the two markets cannot be totally insulated, the movement of rates on the financial market will tend to cause partial movements, in the same direction, in the *effective* commercial rate, causing this rate to float within some limits, around the official commercial rate.

reduce the risk of long term foreign borrowing and lending is open to serious question, once we take into account that (i) under floating rates, the average annual rate of change of the exchange rate between two countries is approximated by the difference in the average rate of change of the price level in the two countries, and (ii) that even under formally fixed parities, exchange rates can, in practice, be kept fixed only if price levels move roughly parallel. If the price levels move at significantly different rates, then the parity will have to be adjusted. This adjustment, even if discontinuous, will have to be roughly of the same size as the movement that would occur through market forces under floating rates.

It follows that if the price levels of the borrower and lender country move roughly parallel, the rate of exchange will tend to remain constant under floating as well as under a fixed exchange regime. In this case, under either regime, the risk of the return to the lender and the cost to the borrower, measured in real terms (the only relevant measure), will be the same as in the case of a domestic transaction and will be given by the uncertainty of changes in the common price level, with (unanticipated) increases benefitting the borrower at the expense of the lender. If, on the other hand, the price levels in the long-run move at different rates, then the outcome, under either regime, will depend on the denomination agreed upon by the parties. If the contract is denominated in the currency of the lender, then the risk to the lender is the same as in the case of domestic lending (i.e. determined by the uncertainty of the domestic price level); on the other hand, the borrower stands to reap a gain (or loss) equal to the average rate of inflation of the domestic price level minus the average rate of depreciation of his currency relative to the lender's currency. But, as just noted, in the long-run, this rate of depreciation must tend to equal the excess of the rate of inflation in the borrower's country, say $\dot{p}_b$, over the rate of inflation in the lender's country, say $\dot{p}_l$; hence the borrower's gain can be approximated by $\dot{p}_b—(\dot{p}_b—\dot{p}_l)=\dot{p}_l$. In other words, under either regime, in the long-run the risk to both parties is given by the uncertainty of the lender's price level. Similarly, one can establish that, if denomination is in the borrower's currency, the risk to both parties is given by the uncertainty of the borrower's price level. We can conclude, therefore, that under either regime, there is risk in international lending and borrowing just as there is in the corresponding domestic transaction. This risk can be minimized by denominating the contract in the currency of the country whose price level is expected to remain stable (strictly speaking, more predictable) which need not be either the lender's or the borrower's; and by doing so, the risk of international borrowing and lending can be made equal or smaller than that of a purely domestic transaction.

The proposition that fixed exchanges reduce the risk of long term international lending and borrowing could still be true to the extent that fixed parities reduce the uncertainty of price level movements in the more stable countries. This proposition would not be very easy to establish empirically and certainly does not command much a priori plausibility, at least if one is to judge from the experience under the fixed parity regime of the postwar period. Furthermore, proper account would have to be taken of the costs of more stable prices and parities as they affect the levels of employment and interfere with international flows of commodities and capital. Last but not least, if one holds that uncertainty in real returns is a major deterrent to capital movements, the most promising approach toward eliminating, or at least minimizing, the risk to lenders *and* borrowers from both exchange rates *and* price level changes is to create an appropriate international unit of account with constant purchasing power in terms of internationally traded commodities, as we have explicitly proposed elsewhere.[4]

In summary, for international capital movements to contribute most effectively to the optimum international allocation of capital, without interfering with domestic stabilization policies, we need a set of institutions (including possibly an international stable purchasing power numéraire) which make desired capital movements highly sensitive to differences in international real rates of return, and enough long-run exchange rate flexibility to permit the current account balance to accommodate at least gradually these desired movements.

---

4 An operational scheme for achieving this goal, in the context of a symmetrical international payment system in which the international medium of exchange and store of value is an intangible like the SDR, was set forth in Modigliani and Kenen (1966). This scheme could be readily incorporated in the proposal, which follows closely the basic line set forth in the above mentioned paper, recently put before the Group of Twenty by the United States. In a more recent joint paper (Modigliani and Askari, 1971), we have proposed an alternative scheme suitable for an asymmetric international payments system in which the dollar would be *de jure* inconvertible.

3. Implications of Alternative Payment Systems for the Propagation of Disturbances[5]

Let country A have a transient change in surplus, arising from variations in national saving or in the rate of domestic investment. For the sake of concreteness, let us assume a cyclical or transient decline investment (K) in country A. We want to examine to what extent the disturbance is propagated to the rest of the world under alternative payment systems. Initially, we will assume that the country does not take any discretionary measure designed to counteract the effect of the disturbance on income.

Under a system of fixed exchange rates, the first effect is a fall in income and a propagation effect through a decline in imports. In addition, because of the fall in income, if M were unchanged, the interest rate (r) would have to fall. The fall in imports improves the current account balance (B); but the fall in r increases FL; and if FL is sufficiently responsive, it will increase more than the fall in imports, so that the balance of payment (BP) will deteriorate. This will force country A to raise r by reducing the money supply. And clearly, the burden on country A and on the ROW will be greater the larger FL′,[6] because the larger FL′, the more one has to bring r back toward its original level; but this needed upward movement in r will lead to a further fall in investment and income beyond that resulting from the original disturbance. In the limiting case when $FL' = \infty$, r has to be restored to its original level, and therefore, in terms of the usual Hicksian IS—LM analysis, Y will fall by the full shift of the IS curve.

Under a system of floating rates, on the other hand, the money supply can be left unchanged, since changes in the exchange rate will always insure balance of payment equilibrium. The impact

---

5 RICHARD CAVES (1962) has also looked, from a different perspective, at the propagation of disturbances. Also EGON SOHMEN (1969) has, using the same framework, analyzed the behavior of income and employment under flexible exchange rates.

6 In this paper, we look at capital movement purely as flow. But in modern analysis, economists view capital movements as flows that adjust stocks (function of relative interest rates) to the desired levels. However, in our analysis we are looking at the short-run and as such FL′ is essentially a flow that is generated by the desired stock adjustment. This implies that FL′ will not, in general, be constant overtime but for our purpose, it can be considered as given at a point in time; thus, FL′ represents the *initial* flow response to the differential.

effect of the fall in investment is again a fall in income which reduces imports, improving the current balance, and a decline in interest rates, increasing capital exports to an extent depending on FL′, and thus deteriorating the balance on the capital account. If FL′ is high so that the increase in FL exceeds the improvement in the current account balance, there will occur a depreciation of A's currency. This will improve A's net exports in domestic currency and thus support its income; and, provided the Marshall-Lerner conditions hold, it will reduce further the net exports of the ROW.

Now what can we say about the relative impact effect of the transient disturbance under a system of fixed versus floating exchanges? Assume the exchange rate and the money supply to be constant. There will be some FL′ for which BP = O, that is, such that the additional lending due to the fall in the interest rate will be just enough to offset exactly the improvement in the current account balance. In this case, the propagation of cyclical disturbances will be exactly the same under the regime of fixed and floating exchanges; we will call this value of FL′ the "critical" value and denote it by $\widehat{FL}'$.[7] If, however, $FL' > \widehat{FL}'$, the resulting effect will be a deterioration in the balance; under a system of fixed exchanges, the money supply would have to be reduced in order to raise the domestic interest rate; however, under a regime of floating rates with M constant, the exchange rate falls and this will improve A's current account balance and thus support its income; as mentioned above, this will be at the expense of the ROW, reducing its exports. The reason for this is that under floating rates, the country originating the disturbance will end up with

[7] In a simple, Keynesian, open economy model with capital flows, the value of FL′ will depend on the feedbacks that are allowed. In the simplest case, total absence of any feedbacks, that is feedback's from changes in income and interest rate of the ROW;

$$\widehat{FL}' = \frac{sx + i}{\frac{r}{Y\varepsilon}(1 - x)} - xk' \quad \text{where}$$

s = the marginal propensity to save
x = the marginal propensity to import investment goods
i = the marginal propensity to import consumption goods
ε = the interest elasticity of demand for money
Y = domestic income
r = domestic interest rate
k′ = derivative of investment with respect to the interest rate

a larger money supply and a lower exchange rate; as a result, it will enjoy a larger net export and hence a smaller contraction in income. On the other hand, the ROW will have a smaller net export and a larger contraction in income. As a result, if FL′ is above the critical value (this being the interesting case, as we would want a high FL′ to insure the long-run transfer of capital), the originating country will suffer a smaller contraction of income under floating than under fixed rates. And under the same conditions, the ROW will lose more.[8] Note that for a small country, in the limiting case of $FL' = \infty$, the money supply is unchanged so that income is also unchanged; the entire disturbance is transferred outside.

The conclusion reached in this section, on the relative impact effect of a transient domestic disturbance is the opposite of the conventional view that flexible exchange rates shield the domestic economy from disturbances in the ROW. The reason for this apparent paradox is that in standard textbooks, the analysis assumes away the existence of capital flows; with this restrictive assumption, under flexible exchanges, the exchange rate will rise, preventing a fall in imports, and causing a fall in exports and the disturbing country ends up absorbing the entire disturbance internally. However, when we allow for international capital flows, *and* we postulate

[8] It may be objected that since FL′ is the derivative of capital exports with respect to the domestic interest rate r, this quantity cannot be assumed to have the same value under fixed as under floating rates. In fact, capital movements should be expected to respond to the "covered spread" between domestic and foreign rates. Under the strictest form of fixed parity, with no band, the increase in this spread may be identified with the fall in the domestic rate. But under floating rates, we must also take into account the likely appreciation of the forward rate relative to the spot rate, resulting from the increased capital exports, especially if the interest differential is seen as transient (or, equivalently, it is most pronounced at the short end of the maturity spectrum). If the investors cannot or do not hedge then one must allow for the risk of adverse exchange rate movements. In either case, if we interpret FL′ as the responsiveness of capital exports to a difference in the covered spread, then, for any given positive differential between foreign and domestic rates, the demand for foreign exchange to invest abroad is likely to be smaller under floating than under fixed rates. (We are indebted to C.P. Kindleberger for bringing this point to our attention). This implies that the "critical" value of FL′ may be larger than $\widehat{FL'}$ as defined in the text. Indeed for $FL' = \widehat{FL'}$ capital exports could fall short of the current account surplus, leading to some appreciation and a lower burden for the ROW than under fixed rates. Nonetheless, the conclusion reached in the text, that under floating rates the exchange will depreciate, increasing the burden on the ROW should tend to remain valid for values of FL′ sufficiently higher than FL′ (though admittedly this result does not necessarily hold).

a high FL′ (as needed to insure the desirable transfer of long term capital for allocative purposes) so that the increase in FL exceeds the improvement in the current account balance, then the conclusion is reversed.

4. Implications for Policy Measures

Let us allow for stabilization policies aimed at offsetting the decline in income. We want to show that floating rates encourage the use of stabilization measures which are destabilizing to the ROW, while fixed parities encourage the use of tools which minimize the impact on the ROW. Consider the possible policy responses of the country where the disturbance originated, taking first the case of fixed exchange rates. Clearly, the country cannot have recourse to a policy of lower interest rates through monetary expansion, as this would encourage capital exports leading to an unfavorable balance of payments. However, the fiscal policy devices, the wedge approach and the dual exchange system, singly or in combination, could still be useful, as short-run tools, if changes in parity were limited in the short-run (for example, as in a system of sliding parities with limitations on the maximum permissible rate of slide). These devices could, in fact, be relied upon to contain FL within the B that could be achieved at any point in time, within the restriction imposed by the limited slide, and without sacrificing other domestic goals. Its only choice, if no use is made of the above devices, is expansionary fiscal policy; while this will increase imports, it will not create a balance of payment problem, at least as long as income does not rise above the initial level, since the rise in imports only offsets the initial decline. It should be clear that such measures, in addition to helping the originating country, will also help the rest of the world; indeed, if fiscal policy succeeds in offsetting fully the decline in investment, then the ROW is unaffected by the disturbance which is entirely handled domestically.

Consider next the case of floating exchanges. Especially when FL′ is large, there will be little incentive for the originating country to take *ad hoc* measures, as the burden largely falls on the rest of the world. If, nonetheless, it were to take measures it could choose either monetary or fiscal measures. Monetary expansion may be quite effective if capital exports are very sensitive — for the resulting downward pressure in interest rates will encourage the export of capital which will put downward pressure on the exchange rate, thus raising net exports. But much of the improvement will clearly be at the further expense of the ROW. On the other hand, under the same assumption, fiscal policy will be ineffective for the country itself, but will mostly help the ROW — for it will put upward pressure on interest rates giving an incentive to capital imports which puts upward pressure on the exchange rate, decreasing net exports. This last effect will, of course, help the ROW. In fact, this beneficial effect to the ROW will be larger the less the country itself is helped.

Thus, under fixed parities, the country has an incentive to take measures and these are also helpful to the ROW. Under the floating rates, on the other hand, there is less of an incentive to take action since much of the burden is automatically shifted to the ROW, and even less to choose actions which relieve the burden of the ROW, over measures which increase it further.

5. Conclusion

The conclusion to be drawn from the above analysis, is that with respect to response to cyclical fluctuations in investment, fixed parities seem to have some advantages over floating rates. At first sight, this result may seem to contradict our earlier conclusions pointing to the serious shortcomings of the system of official parities. But, in reality, there is no contradiction. What we have established in both cases is that under a system of floating rates variations in the potential "surplus" or deficit of a country — whether due to variations in national saving or in the rate of domestic investment — tend to be accommodated by corresponding variations in capital exports and real transfer of resources through the current account surplus. Under fixed rates on the other hand, the current account surplus, at the target level of $\hat{Y}$, is a given, B(Y), and hence the only way to maintain Y is to use fiscal policy to make savings at $\hat{Y}$ equal to $K(\hat{r}) + B(\hat{Y})$. The reason for changing the ranking of the two alternative systems is that we have implicitly taken a very different view as to which was the desirable response to a change in surplus. In the first case, we were dealing with

16

variations in "potential" surplus of a long-run, "permanent" nature, and concluded that these should be accommodated by variations in capital movement through appropriate adjustment of exchange rates. In the second case, we were dealing with variations of a transient cyclical nature, and not surprisingly, concluded that these would best be absorbed domestically, through fiscal policies. This approach would avoid the need for the transient transfer of resources in and out of the sector exposed to foreign competition as well as reduce fluctuations in ROW output, while the adjustment is being made. On the other hand, this shift of resources is clearly desirable when structural changes have occurred. Kindleberger (1966), noted this argument about flexible rates, "clearly it (shift of resources) is desirable when significantly large structural changes occur".

We conclude that the ideal system of international payments would be one that would allow the transfer of permanent changes in surplus and would prevent or limit the transfer of cyclical or transient changes in surplus. This situation cannot be achieved under either fixed rates (which allow for no change in transfer) or under floating rates (which allow the transfer of both permanent and transient changes). Nor could one rely on a system that permitted selective transfer of one kind of change but not of the other because it would be hard to establish whether any given change would be transient or permanent.[9]

These considerations suggest that sliding parities may be preferable to either pure floating rates or permanently fixed parities. Under sliding parities, in fact, gradual changes in potential surplus — as well as other gradual changes tending to impinge on the trade balance such as sustained differences in the rate of infla-

---

9 These conclusions need to be modified to recognize that, under floating rates, the operation of private markets could be relied upon, to some extent, to contain the transfer of resources between the domestic and the foreign sector when the disturbance, and, hence, the interest rate differential, were generally recognized to be but transient in nature. In this case, in fact, one could expect the spot and the forward rate to move in opposite directions, reducing the change of the spot rate and the transfer of real capital generated by a given differential between domestic and foreign rates. Clearly these same conclusions would apply to some extent to a system of sliding parities, provided the system allowed a band of permissible fluctuations around parity. It is, in fact, precisely for this reason that an adequate band should be provided for. However, under sliding parities, if the spot rate, nonetheless, hits the lower limit of the band, the Monetary Authority would be required to intervene, and the argument in the text leads us to the conclusion that this would be appropriate.

tion — could be absorbed through gradual changes in parity.[10] On the other hand, limitations on the rate of slide would prevent a country from requiring the ROW to absorb significant short-run changes in imports and exports forced on it by rapidly, unconstrained, changes in exchange rates. Furthermore, this limitation on the rate of slide would encourage the originating country to take anticyclical policy measures which are stabilizing for both itself and for the rest of the world.

Franco Modigliani - Hossein Askari

Cambridge, Mass.

REFERENCES

Richard Caves, "Conditions of International Monetary Equilibrium, Flexible Exchange Rates", *American Economic Association Papers and Proceedings,* pp. 120-29, 1962.

George Halm and Fritz Machlup (editors), *Burgenstock papers,* Princeton University Press, 1970.

Charles Kindleberger, "Flexible Exchange Rates", in *Europe and the Dollar,* p. 122, 1966.

Franco Modigliani and Peter Kenen, "A suggestion for Solving the International Liquidity Problem", in this *Review,* No. 76, March 1966, pp. 3-17.

Franco Modigliani and Hossein Askari, "The Reform of the International Payments System", *Essays in International Finance,* No. 89, September 1971, Princeton University, Princeton, New Jersey.

Franco Modigliani, "International Capital Movements, Fixed Parities, and Monetary Policies" in *Development and Planning,* Essays in honor of Paul Rosenstein-Rodan, edited by Bhagwati, Eckaus, and Chakravarty, Allen and Unwin, London, 1973.

Robert Mundell, "Capital Mobility and Stabilization Policy under Fixed and Flexible Exchange Rates", *Canadian Journal of Economics and Political Science,* Vol. XXIX, No. 4 (November, 1963), pp. 475-85.

Egon Sohmen, *Flexible Exchange Rates,* second edition, University of Chicago Press. 1969.

John Williamson, "The Crawling Peg", *Essays in International Finance,* No. 50, December, 1965, Princeton University, Princeton, New Jersey.

---

10 It should be recognized that even with a system of sliding pegs, one may need some occasional, discontinuous large change in parity if a sudden "permanent" shock of large proportion occurs. In such cases, the appropriate policy measure is to float the exchange rate for a short period until a new maintainable level has been established.

Errata

Page 12, line 4: "decline investment" should read "decline of investment."

Page 13, footnote 7: equation should read "$\hat{F}L' = \dfrac{i(1-s)}{\dfrac{r}{\epsilon Y}\eta_Y} - xk'$," where the new symbol η_Y is the elasticity of money demand with respect to income.

Page 14, footnote 8, last line "higher than FL'" should read "higher than $\hat{F}l'$."

Page 16, 6 lines from the bottom: "$B(Y)$" should read "$B(\hat{Y})$."

PREPARED STATEMENT OF FRANCO MODIGLIANI

BALANCE OF PAYMENTS IMPLICATIONS OF THE OIL CRISIS AND HOW TO HANDLE THEM THROUGH INTERNATIONAL COOPERATION [1]

Despite the bland and tranquilizing reaction of U.S. officials such as Secretary Schultz and Representative Reuss, Sunday's (Jan. 20) decision of the French government to float the franc strikes me as potentially very destructive as well as terribly irksome. It is irksome in that it mirrors the narrow egotism as well as incredible myopia that has been the trademark of foreign policy of the Pompidou regime for some time and especially in recent months, as well as the hypocrisy of the pious recommendations that France never ceases to address to others about the duty of sacrifice in the superior interest of the European community or of the international community (whenever that interest happens to coincide with France's own). Examples of similar actions abound in recent months: for instance, the French decision to explode nuclear devices in the Pacific; the leading role that France (unfortunately with the support of England) has taken in rejecting a common policy toward the energy crisis for the economic community of Europe with respect to supporting Holland; the unilateral French dealings with the Arab countries in order to insure her oil needs.

As for her double standard, it might be sufficient to recall the outrage with which France has condemned the decision of Italy to remain outside of the European snake, and also the fact that France was among the signers of the communique of the group of twenty, released in Rome the previous Friday, which explicitly recognized the desirability for close *collaboration* and the need to avoid *unilateral* actions and competitive *devaluations*. Two days after this communique, France unilaterally let the franc float with the obvious intention to let it devalue and in this way unload on others a part of the difficulties in her balance of payment.

The immediate and ostensible purpose of the French move is obvious enough: to avert the danger that, in order to support the franc in the face of a sizable deficit on current account and a possible capital flight, she might have to encroach on her foreign reserves (even though still sizable), and above all the danger of having to liquidate even a single ounce of gold. One may well say that, with this latest move, France has confirmed what many have suspected for a long time: namely that for the France of Pompidou and of the "Grand Patrie" to lose its gold is incomparably worse than to lose its soul.

One may well suspect that the true final purpose of the move was that of letting the franc devalue, as has actually happened in the first days of the float, during which the franc lost some 5%, in the hope that this devaluation would help improve her balance on current account. It is more difficult to foresee the intended effect on capital of movement since France has already for some time established a double exchange system with two separate markets, one for the commercial and the other for the financial franc. Since in any event the float of the franc, both of the financial and of the commercial one, will

[1] This article is a fairly liberal translation of two articles of mine which have appeared in the column "Osservatorio" of the *Corriere della Sera* on Jan. 24 and 26, 1974.

certainly be a "dirty" float, that is, one in which the French monetary authorities will intervene in the market, it is hard to tell whether France will endeavor to maneuver the value of the franc on the two markets toward encouraging or discouraging capital imports.

In any event, through the devaluation of the commercial franc, France intended clearly to reduce, or perhaps even to eliminate, the deficit on current account resulting from the increased cost of oil. But obviously this improvement could only be obtained at the cost of increasing correspondingly the deficit of other countries producing goods competing with the French ones; this means, in the last analysis, the deficit of the other industrial countries, whose current account balance are already in serious difficulties, frequently in fact more serious than those of France itself. It is in this sense that the French initiative may be labelled as narrowly egotistic. The reason for characterizing it also as incredibly myopic is that it is naive to think that the other countries, will passively accept a further deterioration resulting from a French devaluation. It is much more likely that these countries would have an irresistible temptation to imitate the French behavior responding to the French devaluation with a devaluation of their currencies. Indeed, this is precisely what has happened in the case of Italy, whose currency has followed closely the French franc. Should other currencies follow this lead, where would it all end?

If all the industrialized countries endeavor to eliminate or reduce markedly their deficit through devaluations relative to the dollar, one has to raise first the question as to whether the United States would be ready to accept passively this behavior and its implications. Let us suppose for a moment that the U.S. were to accept it. In this case one could certainly count on three outcomes. First, a large part of the potential gain that France or Italy expected from their devaluation would be lost in as much as the franc would not have lost value relative to the lira or relative to any other currency which had followed the French devaluation. Consequently, a sizable improvement would require repeated and huge devaluations. In the last analysis, the only country whose imports would increase and exports decrease would be the United States and the countries which would maintain their exchange rate with the dollar, such as, presumably, Canada. Second, the countries which devalue would be subject to further inflationary pressures as a result of the increased cost of oil and of other raw materials and goods coming from the countries which had not devalued. Third, the oil producing countries would really welcome this rush to devalue relative to the dollar, since a barrel of oil whose price had been fixed at, let us say, $7, would end up by acquiring even more of the goods produced by France, or Italy, or any other devaluing countries, than they had hoped to acquire when they increased their price to $7. In other words, devaluation would only deteriorate further to terms of trade between the industrial countries and the oil producing countries.

But while these devaluations would clearly increase the purchasing power of the oil producing countries, it is extremely unlikely that these countries, at least those of the Persian Gulf, would be induced to increase significantly their net imports since already in the current situation their revenue are larger than they know how to use for the acquisition of goods and services, at least for some time to come. Consequently, their dollar revenue would remain largely unchanged, except for a possible modest reduction in the quantity of oil sold, modest because the demand for oil, at least in the short run, is notoriously very inelastic. It follows that their largely unchanged surplus would have to be mainly compensated, in the last analysis, by an increase in the deficit of the American block, partly through on increase in their imports from the countries devaluing, and in part through a decrease in their exports both to the devaluing countries and to the other countries. It has been estimated, even if with a large margin of error, that the increase in the deficit of the industrialized countries outside of North America resulting from the increase in the price of oil might reach 40-60 billion dollars. Even if we suppose that this figure might be somewhat reduced because of the decrease in demand, and supposing that the countries which devalue aimed at shifting to the United States 2/3 of their increased deficit resulting from the increase in the price of oil, we would have to conclude that the final result of the general rush to devaluation, even if accepted by the United States, would be a worsening in the current account balance of the United States in the order of 30-40 billion dollars. In other words, the current account balance of the United States would have to shift from the current rate of around 8 billion surplus to a deficit in the order of 25-30 billion. To appreciate the magnitude of these figures, it will suffice to note that the U.S. deficit at its peak in 1972 was around 6 billion, a figure which caused deep concern on the part of the entire financial world. It should be recognized, however, that at least initially this deficit would not create a balance of payment problem for the United States since it would be automatically financed by the acquisition of dollars on the part of the Arab countries.

At this point we need to raise two questions. First, is it possible that the United States would accept such a deficit passively? Secondly, even if this were the case, would this provide a sensible and rational solution to the oil crisis?

The answer to the first question seems to me to be a decided no. In the first place, an increase in the deficit of the order of 30 billion would have extremely serious deflationary effect in the United States and would threaten unemployment on large scale. These effects could of course, in principle, be compensated by careful expansionary fiscal and monetary policies leading to a corresponding increase in the domestic demand for consumption and investment, both private and public. But, even supposing that the government were capable of instituting promptly such a policy, this solution would still require massive shifts of internal resources from the production of internationally traded goods to other commodities. This would unavoidably lead to huge losses and widespread bankruptcies for many enterprises and massive lay-offs even if accompanied by a demand for labor in other activities. Such developments would unavoidably lead U.S. public opinion to demand effective countermeasures. One can readily visualize at this point quite a variety scenarios, such as massive interventions by the U.S. monetary authority in the foreign exchange market colliding frontally with the intervention of other countries, or the enactment of huge custom duties and import quotas. In other words, the unavoidable result would be international chaos and a new wave of nationalism and xenophobia on a world wide scale. All this may be to the liking of the Pompidous of this world, but it is doubtful that it would please anybody else. One must therefore conclude that unilateral actions and competitive devaluations are but a blind alley, moving the world to the brink of disaster.

The answer to the second question seems to be equally negative. That is, even if the United States were ready to absorb in an orderly fashion the increase in its deficit, offsetting it with refined anticyclical policies, the solution would not be a desirable one. This conclusion rests on the consideration that the transfer of internal resources from internationally traded commodities to other activities, both inside the United States and inside the devaluing countries, is an operation which is economically very costly and socially very painful. Such a massive shift might perhaps be justified if it could occur slowly, and if, once it had occurred, it promised to have some permanence. But a gradual transfer could not satisfy the immediate necessities of the balance of payments of the industrial countries. In addition, and this is the main point, there is no reason to suppose that the transfer would be a permanent or even a lasting one. In my view, in fact, the huge deficit which is confronting at this time the industrial countries outside of North America is certainly of a transitory nature. It is destined to shrink very rapidly even in the absence of competitive devaluations. In the first place, the majority of the producing countries, outside of those of the Persian Gulf, such as Iran, Indonesia, Venezuela, will tend rapidly, if not immediately, to use their increased revenues to increase their acquisition of goods and services, thus compensating their increased exports with larger imports which automatically would tend to eliminate the imbalance in current accounts. In addition, as I have indicated in previous articles in this column as early as late December, I regard it as highly improbable that oil prices can be maintained at the current level (in real terms) for any appreciable length of time. Some reductions may well come in the near future as seems to be suggested by recent reports of price behavior in some markets. But even if the price could initially be maintained I suggest that, as time goes by, the demand for oil will tend to diminish, both through techniques aiming at reducing oil consumption, and through substitutions with other sources of energy. There are also convincing reasons to suppose that the increase in price will soon give rise to a significant increase in production outside the cartel and that this in turn will reduce the demand for oil directed to the members of the oil cartel. At this point it would become very difficult to hold up the cartel price, or if the price could be maintained, this could probably happen only if the Persian Gulf countries were ready to reduce their market share, by absorbing both the reduction in the total demand directed toward the cartel and the probable increases in production on the part of other members of the cartel.

The willingness of the Gulf oil states to reduce their share is certainly credible, since at the moment they end up by using a good share of their receipts for financial investment; they might well decide that the best investment they can make is in oil underground. But, even in this case, one has to conclude that with high probability, the revenues of these states—who are the source of problems because they do not automatically use their larger revenues to buy commodities—would diminish rapidly. If so, the problem of the deficit for the industrial countries would rapidly shrink from the current 40 billion dollars (which is probably already an overestimate) down to relatively modest figures.

If this analysis of mine is valid, as I hope for the peace of the world, and consequently the problem of the balance of payments of the industrial countries is only a tranchent one, the rational solution is not that of competitive devaluation. What is called for instead is a tranchent remedy, which can only consist, fundamentally, in the acquiescence on the part of the industrial countries to a deficit, initially of large proportions, but rapidly shrinking in time. If the relevant countries are ready to move toward this rational solution, then the only problem is the technical one of finding a way by which the producing countries can be induced to finance the deficit of the deficit countries either directly or through a variety of indirect ways. For instance, it is entirely conceivable that the Arab countries might wish to employ their surplus in financial or real investment in the U.S.A., and that in turn the U.S.A. might provide through private, public or semi--public channels financing for the other countries, in part perhaps through the Eurodollar market. It would be particularly desirable to find a way to provide financing for the countries of the third world, either directly from the Arabs or indirectly, for instance through loans by the Arab countries to the International Bank and by the International Bank to the underdeveloped countries. In so far as this solution is adopted, one could largely eliminate the very deficit since the less developed countries would be rapidly acquiring goods produced in the industrial countries. It is not necessary to enter here in the details of how financing of the investment of certain countries and of the deficit of others could be arranged. Any international financial expert would be able to put together in a short time a reasonable plan. In fact it is my understanding that the International Monetary Fund has already been working on just such a plan (See the report on the Rome mid January meeting of the Committee of Twenty in the Economist of Jan. 26). Chances of success could be greatly enhanced if the would-be borrowers were prepared to guarantee the lenders a reasonable "real" rate of return by devices of the type outlined below. What is essential however is that the industrialized country accept the principle and immediately put an end to the trend toward competitive devaluations.

It should be noted that this suggestion does not mean that no country should be allowed to modify its exchange rate. It is conceivable for instance that certain countries like Italy, which already had large deficit in their balance of payment before the oil crisis, should be allowed to devalue moderately relative to the majority of other currencies, or that most of the European currencies should be allowed to devalue modestly with respect to the dollar in order to shift part of the deficit to the United Sttaes. But what is implied is that such changes should occur only through international consultation and agreement. These agreements should establish a reasonable initial set of parities values, subject to gradual change in time [but with limitations to the maximum permissible rate of change] and a reasonable band of permissible fluctuations around the parity established at any point of time. Finally, the commitment to maintain the market rate within the limits allowed by the agreement should be guaranteed and made credible through a solid understanding among central banks committing them, in case of speculative attacks, to support each other *essentially without limits*, either directly or through appropriate devices developed in the international monetary fund. Only the certainty on the part of international speculators that we have brought to an end the era in which every speculative attack, provided it was pressed hard enough, would reap large profits for the speculators, can put an end to the chaos which has greeted every attempt at reestablishing official parities, even if with broad band.

The conclusion then is that we have to start out with a moratorium on unilateral devaluations initiated by France, and promptly convene at international conference of the interested states, including the producing countries, in order to replace the threatening chaos with an orderly and rational system. Italy could substantially contribute to reestablishing order and calm by offering immediately to the countries which have remained in the snake, and have not followed the French devaluation, to enter the common market snake. In so doing she could demand appropriate guarantees of mutual assistance of the type which she had justifiably requested since the inception of the snake as a condition for entering it (and which the Germans were prepared to offer to France). I certainly do share the views expressed by many Italian leaders that the Werner plan and the common market snake, as initially designed under the inspiration of France, was not a viable creature. Before attempting to establish and maintain rigid parities, it is necessary to unify the institution of the various countries: taxation, the regulation of financial market and financial intermediaries, the policies of trade unions, and so on. But at this point, Italy, having had the satisfaction of demonstrating to France that she was right in not entering the snake, could take a step which would help to reestablish confidence, by moving against the tide. At the same time, if Italy takes this step, would it not perhaps be appropriate to suspend temporarily France from the economic community until such time as French political forces, more farsighted than the current regime, forces which we all know exist and flourish in France, are ready to take over in that country?

Some considerations may finally be appropriate concerning the implications of the current oil crisis for the long-term reform of the international payment system. Over the last two years, the major emphasis in any scheme to revamp the international monetary mechanism has been on the notion of *perfect symmetry*. In the system of the future, every country should have exactly the same rights and obligations, notably with respect to convertibility. As has been pointed out repeatedly, this implies among other things the symmetric right for the United States to control its rate of exchange with other currencies.

The latest move initiated by France toward unilateral devaluation vis a vis the dollar suggests however that the time may have come for second thoughts about the desirability of perfect symmetry, and that it may be advantageous for the rest of the world to preserve its right to fix its exchange rate with respect to the dollar, and thus control the U.S. balance on current account. But, under this condition, as was pointed out in the joint essay with Hossein Askari ["The Reform of the International Payment System" (Essays in International Finance, No. 89, September 1971)] it is no longer reasonable for the rest of the world to expect the United States to accept the responsibility of conversion. If, for instance, under the present circumstances, the United States should accept a certain amount of deficit in order to accommodate the rest of the world, it cannot then be expected to convert into some other asset the dollar balances which will have been accumulated in the process by other countries.

All this suggests that it may be time for those responsible for revamping the international monetary system to take a fresh look at the proposal set forth in the above mentioned essay. Under this proposal, the rest of the world would be responsible for setting up and managing, by market intervention, a system of crawling parities with the dollar. Since the rest of the world would thus have the responsibility and power to set the exchange rate with the dollar, and hence control the U.S. balance of payments, the United States would not be required to convert dollar reserves accumulated by other countries into the other international reserve asset, which would consist of an international intangible medium of exchange created by the International Monetary Fund, similar in nature to the present SDR.

Under the plan the United States monetary authority would hold no international reserves having no use for them, while the monetary authorities of other countries would hold two kinds of international reserves, namely SDR's and inconvertible dollars balances. The parity of the SDR with the dollar (and hence with every other currency in the system), would be periodically adjusted on the basis of an index of prices, expressed in dollars, of a suitable basket of internationally traded commodities and services. Specifically, any change in this price index would give rise to an equal percent change in the price of the SDR in terms of dollars. Through this device, the SDR would have *a constant purchasing power in terms of the stated basket of internationally traded commodities.* Foreign countries holding inconvertible dollar balances would be given an opportunity to secure protection against changes of the parity between the dollar and the SDR by turning any portion of their reserves over to the U.S. monetary authority, obtaining in exchange a claim against the U.S. denominated in SDR's and earning a moderate interest rate commensurate to that paid by the International Monetary Fund on SDR balances. By this device, all the rest of the world would have the opportunity to shed the risk associated with holding inconvertible dollar balances.

The fact that the SDR would, under this scheme, have a guaranteed constant purchasing power would make it a suitable numeraire for denominating international loans. In particular, the surplus oil producing countries, by making loans denominated in SDR to the deficit countries (directly or through an IMF facility) could shed not only the risk of exchange rate variations but also the risk of price level changes. Note also that with loans denominated in SDR's, there would be no danger, even in the case of direct lending, of creditor countries making massive shifts from one currency to another.

It would appear that this type of scheme could contribute substantially to the solution of a good many of the problems that have been created by the current oil crisis. Furthermore it could be put into effect quite rapidly even under the present unsettled conditions, a claim that no one could seriously make for any alternative system involving effective unconditional convertibility of the dollar.

Errata

Page 650, 4 lines from the bottom: ''capital of movement'' should read ''movement of capital.''

Page 651, paragraph 3, line 21: ''to terms of trade'' should read ''the terms of trade.''

Page 653, paragraph 3, line 3: ''tranchent'' should read ''transient.''

Page 654, line 2: ''convene at international'' should read ''convene an international.''

PART IV

The Role of Expectations and Plans in Economic Behavior

PRODUCTION PLANNING OVER TIME AND THE NATURE OF THE EXPECTATION AND PLANNING HORIZON[1]

By Franco Modigliani and Franz E. Hohn

Given the amounts required of a certain commodity in each of T future periods of time, we examine the problem of how production should be scheduled over time in order to satisfy these requirements at the lowest possible cost. A general solution to this problem is exhibited under certain "reasonable" assumptions concerning the nature of production and storage costs, and a convenient graphical method of securing the solution is outlined. One significant aspect of the solution is that under certain conditions (and especially if the cost of carrying inventories is "large" relative to the marginal cost of production), the optimal plan consists of a *sequence* of plans covering successive intervals of the entire horizon and having the following property: the production schedule for each interval is identical with the optimum plan for the corresponding interval *considered separately*; it depends, in other words, on requirements within the interval itself, but is essentially independent of requirements for earlier or later periods. It is shown that these results have significant implications concerning the length of the expectation and planning horizon relevant to current production decisions and that they throw some light on the rationale of certain observed business practices.

1. STATEMENT OF THE PROBLEM

We consider the problem of scheduling the production of a given commodity x over T equal, successive periods of time in such a way as (1) to meet initially known requirements $s_1, s_2, \cdots, s_T$ in these periods while (2) incurring the lowest possible cost.

Denote by x_j the production of the jth period. Any production plan with nonnegative components $x_1, x_2, \cdots, x_T$ which meets condition (1) will be called *feasible*. Any feasible plan which also meets condition (2) will be called *optimal* and will be denoted by $\tilde{x}_1, \tilde{x}_2, \cdots, \tilde{x}_T$.

Let h_0 denote beginning inventory and let h_k denote inventory at the end of period k. The relation between h_k, production, and requirements (or sales) is expressed by the equation

$$(1.1) \qquad h_k = h_0 + X_k - S_k, \qquad (k = 1, 2, \cdots, T)$$

where $X_k = \sum_{t=1}^{k} x_t$ and $S_k = \sum_{t=1}^{k} s_t$ denote cumulated production and requirements respectively.

In terms of the notation just introduced, the requirement of feasibility implies that inventory must always be nonnegative, that is, that

$$(1.2) \qquad h_k = h_0 + X_k - S_k \geqslant 0, \qquad (k = 1, 2, \cdots, T).$$

In order to make the problem determinate, we assume that a certain terminal inventory is required. Since its specific value does not affect the method of solution, we take this value to be zero, so that

[1] This paper was prepared as part of the research project on "Expectations and Business Fluctuations," financed by a grant of the Merrill Foundation for the Advancement of Financial Knowledge.

(1.3) $$h_T = h_0 + X_T - S_T = 0.$$

Conditions (1.2) and (1.3) constitute the *inventory constraints*. We have also the *production constraints*:

(1.4) $$x_k \geqslant 0, \qquad (k = 1, 2, \cdots, T).$$

Finally, we assume that

(1.5) $$h_0 < S_T$$

since, otherwise, there is no problem of planning production.

Let C denote the total cost of carrying out any given production plan. We shall regard C as consisting of the sum of the cost C_p of producing the given program, the cost C_s of carrying the resulting inventories, and a constant C_0 independent of the production schedule adopted.

We shall assume that the cost of production is the same function F of production in each period, so that

$$C_p = \sum_1^T F(x_t).$$

We further assume that the "marginal cost function"

(1.6) $$f(x) = \frac{dF(x)}{dx}, \qquad (x \geqslant 0)$$

is nonnegative, monotone increasing, and continuous. Equation (1.6) defines $f(x)$ only for $x \geqslant 0$ since $F(x)$ has no meaning for $x < 0$. For solving the problem, however, we find it convenient to assign values to $f(x)$ also for $x < 0$. This can be done in any convenient manner inasmuch as the nature of $f(x)$ for $x < 0$ does not affect the final result. We therefore define $f(x)$ as any function of x which is monotone increasing and continuous *everywhere* and which satisfies (1.6).

As for storage costs, we assume that the cost of storing a unit product is proportional to the length of time during which it is stored, and we denote by α the cost of storing one unit for one period. If we make the further assumption, reasonable as a convenient approximation, that production and sales take place at an even rate within each period, then the change of inventory $h_k - h_{k-1}$ within each period k, will itself occur at a constant rate and the average inventory held for the period will be $(h_k + h_{k-1})/2$. It follows that the total cost of storage, taking (1.3) into account, will be given by

$$C_s = \alpha\left[\frac{h_0}{2} + \sum_{t=1}^{T-1} h_t\right].$$

The total cost of the program can therefore be expressed as

(1.7) $$C = \sum_{t=1}^{T} F(x_t) + \alpha\left[\frac{h_0}{2} + \sum_{t=1}^{T-1} h_t\right] + C_0.$$

The problem is then to minimize (1.7) subject to the constraints (1.2), (1.3), and (1.4).

2. THE CASE OF CONSTANT MARGINAL COST

The simplest case in which the assumptions on $f(x)$ are met is that in which $f(x) = a =$ constant. In this case the cost C to be minimized reduces to

$$C = a\sum_{t=1}^{T} x_t + \alpha\left[\frac{h_0}{2} + \sum_{t=1}^{T-1} h_t\right] + C_0, \tag{2.1}$$

the constraints being the same as before. Using (1.3), we have

$$C = a(S_T - h_0) + \alpha\left[\frac{h_0}{2} + \sum_{t=1}^{T-1} h_t\right] + C_0 \tag{2.2}$$

in which only the total cost of storage varies with the plan adopted. Suppose $S_k \leqslant h_0 < S_{k+1}$. Then, since no h may be negative, $\sum h_t$ and hence C is minimized for

$$\begin{aligned} \tilde{x}_t &= 0, & (t = 1, 2, \cdots, k) \\ \tilde{x}_{k+1} &= S_{k+1} - h_0 \\ \tilde{x}_t &= s_t, & (t = k+2, \cdots, k). \end{aligned} \tag{2.3}$$

That is, in this case, nothing is produced until the initial inventory is used up, and thereafter production in each period is just enough to meet the corresponding requirement. It will be noted that under these conditions, no information beyond s_1 is required for making an optimal decision, $\tilde{x}_1$, on current production.

3. INCREASING MARGINAL COST; THE FUNDAMENTAL SOLUTION

Proceeding to the case in which marginal cost is a strictly increasing function of production, we first solve the problem when the constraints (1.2) and (1.4) involving inequalities are neglected but the equality (1.3) constraining the terminal inventory is retained. We call the solution of this restricted problem a *fundamental solution* and shall show later that the optimal plan for a T-period problem is made up of a sequence of fundamental solutions over successive blocks of periods. The fundamental solution is obtained, according to Lagrange's method of undetermined multipliers, by equating to zero the derivatives with respect to x_t, $t = 1, 2, \cdots, T$, of the function

$$C^* = \sum_{t=1}^{T} F(x_t) + \alpha\sum_{t=1}^{T-1}[h_0 + X_t - S_t] + \alpha\frac{h_0}{2} + C_0 + \lambda(h_0 + X_T - S_T). \tag{3.1}$$

This yields the system of equations:

$$\frac{\partial C^*}{\partial x_t} = f(x_t) + \lambda + (T - t)\alpha = 0, \qquad (t = 1, 2, \cdots, T) \tag{3.2}$$

which imply

$$(3.3)\qquad f(x_{t+j}) = f(x_t) + j\alpha, \qquad (2 \leqslant t + j \leqslant T).$$

(A simple economic interpretation of equations (3.3), which play a central role in establishing our results, appears at the end of this section.)

By means of equations (3.3) we can readily show how to compute the "fundamental solution" of the problem. From (3.3) we have, in fact:

$$(3.4)\qquad f(x_t) = f(x_1) + (t - 1)\alpha,$$

from which

$$(3.5)\qquad x_t = f^{-1}[f(x_1) + (t - 1)\alpha], \qquad (t = 2, 3, \cdots, T),$$

since the conditions imposed on $f(x)$ insure the existence of a unique inverse. Substituting into (1.3) and rearranging terms we obtain

$$(3.6)\qquad \sum_{t=1}^{T} f^{-1}[f(x_1) + (t - 1)\alpha] = S_T - h_0 .$$

Since the function f is strictly increasing, the left member of (3.6) is itself strictly increasing so that this equation will admit of a single solution, say $x_1 = \xi_1$. The fundamental solution is then completed by substituting for x_1 in (3.5):

$$(3.7)\qquad \xi_t = f^{-1}[f(\xi_1) + (t - 1)\alpha], \qquad (t = 1, 2, \cdots, T).$$

This fundamental solution will represent the *optimal* program for our T-period problem if and only if it is feasible, i.e., if it satisfies the constraints (1.2) and (1.4). From the monotonic nature of f and from (3.7) it follows that $\xi_t \geqslant \xi_1$, $t = 2, 3, \cdots, T$. Hence conditions (1.4) will be satisfied if $\xi_1 \geqslant 0$. This in turn is true if and only if

$$(3.8)\qquad \sum_{t=1}^{T} f^{-1}[f(0) + (t - 1)\alpha] \leqslant S_T - h_0 ,$$

since this is the necessary and sufficient condition for the unique solution of (3.6) to be nonnegative. For the conditions (1.2) to be satisfied by the fundamental solution we must have

$$(3.9)\qquad \sum_{t=1}^{k} \xi_t = \sum_{t=1}^{k} f^{-1}[f(\xi_1) + (t - 1)\alpha] \geqslant S_k - h_0 , \qquad (k = 1, 2, \cdots, T - 1).$$

The inequalities (3.8) and (3.9) are thus necessary and sufficient conditions for the fundamental solution to be the optimal solution of the T-period problem.

We are now in a position to point out the economic interpretation of equations (3.3) and to consider what happens to them when the inventory constraints are taken into account. In (3.3), $f(x_{t+j})$ is the cost of making available an additional unit in period $t + j$ by producing it in period $t + j$. On the other hand, $f(x_t) + j\alpha$ may be thought of as the cost of making an additional unit available in period $t + j$ by producing it in period t and storing it for j periods, thus incurring a storage cost $j\alpha$. If for any proposed plan $x_1, x_2, \cdots, x_T$ the right member of (3.3) were less than the left member, costs would be reduced by increasing x_t and decreasing x_{t+j}. Similarly, if the left member of (3.3) were less than the right member, we could, to the extent that the constraints (1.2) and (1.4) were not violated, improve on the proposed plan by decreasing x_t and increasing x_{t+j}. Because of the operation of these constraints, however, it may not be feasible to decrease x_t, for such a decrease might make it impossible to meet demand in the first $t + j - 1$ periods. Thus the optimal plan may not satisfy the conditions (3.3), but it will always satisfy the inequalities

$$f(x_{t+j}) \leqslant f(x_t) + j\alpha. \tag{3.10}$$

That is, one condition for minimum costs is that the cost of producing one additional unit in any period should not be larger than the cost of producing an extra unit in any earlier period and storing it until the given period.

4. AN EXAMPLE OF THE FUNDAMENTAL SOLUTION

To illustrate the results of the preceding section, we consider as an example the simplest case of increasing marginal cost, namely that in which $F(x)$ is quadratic and therefore $f(x)$ is linear. Let us write in this case

$$f(x) = ax + b, \qquad (a > 0, b > 0)$$

so that

$$f^{-1}(x) = \frac{x - b}{a}.$$

Then equation (3.5) becomes

$$x_t = x_1 + (t - 1)\frac{\alpha}{a}. \tag{4.1}$$

The solution of (3.6) yields

$$\xi_1 = \frac{S_T - h_0}{T} - \frac{T - 1}{2} \cdot \frac{\alpha}{a} \tag{4.2}$$

whence, substituting ξ_1 for x_1 in (4.1), we have the entire fundamental solution:

$$\xi_t = \left(\frac{S_T - h_0}{T} - \frac{T + 1}{2} \cdot \frac{\alpha}{a}\right) + t\frac{\alpha}{a}, \qquad (t = 1, 2, \cdots, T). \tag{4.3}$$

The condition $\xi_1 \geqslant 0$, that is, (3.8), becomes

$$S_T \geqslant h_0 + \frac{T(T - 1)}{2} \cdot \frac{\alpha}{a} \tag{4.4}$$

and conditions (3.9) become

$$\frac{S_k - h_0}{k} \leqslant \frac{S_T - h_0}{T} - \frac{T-k}{2} \cdot \frac{\alpha}{a}, \quad (k = 1, 2, \cdots, T-1). \tag{4.5}$$

If the given requirements $s_1, \cdots, s_T$ happen to satisfy these constraints, then the fundamental solution (4.3) is also optimal.

5. INCREASING MARGINAL COST; THE CONSTRAINED SOLUTION

In this section, we describe how we may construct the optimal plan in the event that the fundamental solution $\xi_1, \xi_2, \cdots, \xi_T$ obtained in Section 3 does not satisfy all the constraints (3.8) and (3.9). In phrasing this description, we find it desirable at several points to make use of the fundamental solution of the shorter problem based on, say, the first q of the T periods initially considered. For this problem, the requirements $s_1, s_2, \cdots, s_q$ and the initial inventory h_0 are the same as before, but now h_q is to be zero. We refer to this as the fundamental solution of "the q-period problem."

Inasmuch as, by hypothesis, the fundamental solution of the T-period problem is not feasible, we construct a feasible plan as follows. First of all, by considering successively the fundamental solution for the $(T - 1)$-period problem, then for the $(T - 2)$-period problem, and so on as far as is necessary, we determine the (largest) integer k, if such exists, with the following properties: (a) the fundamental solution of the k-period problem satisfies the constraints of the k-period problem; and (b) for $q > k$, the fundamental solution for the q-period problem does *not* satisfy all the constraints of the q-period problem.

If such an integer k exists, this procedure yields a feasible plan for a first *interval* consisting of the first k periods. Suppose, on the other hand, that no such integer exists; this means that even the fundamental solution of the 1-period problem is not feasible. Clearly, this solution is $\xi_1 = s_1 - h_0$, which can fail to be feasible only because $\xi_1 < 0$, that is, $h_0 > s_1$. In this case it is feasible to plan x_1 as 0, *which in fact we do.*

We now have a feasible plan for a first interval consisting of at least the first period, and possibly of more (if k exists and is greater than 1). The remainder of our feasible plan may be constructed by repeating the above procedure for the still remaining periods, until all T periods have been accounted for. At each stage, the initial inventory is determined uniquely by the part of the plan which has already been constructed. For instance, for the second interval, the initial inventory is $h_1 = h_0 - s_1$ if the integer k discussed above does not exist (and therefore first period production is zero), and is $h_k = 0$ otherwise.

The application of this procedure will yield first a sequence of say k_0 periods $(0 \leqslant k_0 < T)$ in which production is planned as zero because no fundamental solution is feasible. Since $h_0 < S_T$, some production will eventually be necessary, i.e., there must be at least one interval for which the fundamental solution is feasible. Let k_1 denote the number of periods in the first such interval. (If the integer k mentioned above exists, it is k_1 for the problem in question, and k_0 is 0). If $T > k_0 + k_1$, then at the end of this interval we have necessarily $h_{k_0+k_1} = 0$, so that there must follow a second interval of, say, k_2 periods for which the fundamental solution is feasible, etc.

We are thus led to a finite sequence of, say, $p + 1$ intervals containing respectively k_0, k_1, $\cdots$, k_p periods and a corresponding feasible plan. Since all T periods are accounted for, we have

$$\sum_{j=0}^{p} k_j = T.$$

Let ξ_j^i denote the jth component of the fundamental solution for interval i ($j = 1, 2, \cdots, k_i$; $i = 1, 2, \cdots, p$). Then the feasible plan may be expressed as follows:

$$(5.1)\qquad \begin{cases} x_1 = x_2 = \cdots = x_{k_0} = 0; \\ x_{k_0+1} = \xi_1^1, \cdots, x_{k_0+k_1} = \xi_{k_1}^1; \\ x_{k_0+k_1+1} = \xi_1^2, \cdots, x_{k_0+k_1+k_2} = \xi_{k_2}^2; \\ \cdots\cdots\cdots\cdots\cdots\cdots\cdots\cdots \\ x_{T-k_p+1} = \xi_1^p, \cdots, x_T = \xi_{k_p}^p. \end{cases}$$

The plan (5.1) is feasible by construction. We show in the next section that it is in fact the optimal plan. The proof is somewhat tedious, and the reader who is not interested in its details may proceed directly to Section 7, where we give an example of the construction of the optimal plan.

6. PROOF OF THE OPTIMALITY OF THE PRECEDING PLAN

Because of the constraint (1.3), any feasible plan can be obtained from (5.1) by a reallocation of production, i.e., by increasing production in some periods and by reducing it correspondingly elsewhere. In order to prove that (5.1) is optimal, it is therefore sufficient to prove that any such feasible reallocation will increase costs.

Consider first any feasible reallocation of production which alters the plan (5.1) only *within* one of the intervals $1, 2, \cdots, p$. Such a reallocation must increase costs since the plan for each interval is optimal for that interval by the manner in which (5.1) was constructed. A reallocation calling for a net decrease in production in any interval (or intervals), to be offset by increased production later, is not feasible since total production in each interval is either zero (in the opening interval) or is such as to make it possible to meet the total demand of that interval *exactly*. It therefore remains only to show that costs are increased by increasing production in any interval or intervals in order to reduce production later.

For use in the proof, we need to establish a preliminary relation. Let ξ_t^j, $t = 1, 2, \cdots, k_j$, have the meaning defined for (5.1). Then ξ_1^j denotes the plan for period $k_0 + k_1 + \cdots + k_{j-1} + 1$. Now let ξ_s denote the fundamental solution for this same period in a q-period problem which includes all k_j periods of the above interval and which has $q > k_j$. (It will become apparent that for this q-period problem initial inventory and demands are arbitrary.) Since a fundamental solution satisfies equations (3.3), we must have

$$f(\xi_{t+s}) = f(\xi_s) + t\alpha, \qquad (t + s \leqslant q),$$

and

$$f(\xi^j_{t+1}) = f(\xi^j_1) + t\alpha, \qquad (t + 1 \leqslant k_j).$$

From these equations we conclude

$$f(\xi_{t+s}) - f(\xi^j_{t+1}) = f(\xi_s) - f(\xi^j_1), \qquad (t = 0, 1, \cdots, k_j - 1).$$

Hence, in view of the monotonic character of f, we must have

$$\xi_{t+s} \gtreqless \xi^j_{t+1} \qquad (t = 0, 1, \cdots, k_j - 1) \tag{6.1a}$$

respectively, according as

$$\xi_s \gtreqless \xi^j_1 . \tag{6.1b}$$

In other words, the ξ^j's are simultaneously all less than, all equal to, or all greater than the corresponding ξ's.

We begin the proof of the principal result by demonstrating that it is not profitable to increase production in the first period of the first interval of non-zero production in order to carry the additional output over to the first period of the next interval, for the purpose of reducing production there. In order to establish this it will suffice to show that

$$f(\xi^1_1) + k_1\alpha > f(\xi^2_1), \tag{6.2}$$

in view of the interpretation of equation (3.3).

We note first that, by the definition of k_1, the fundamental solution of the $(k_1 + k_2)$-period problem starting with period $k_0 + 1$ does not satisfy all the constraints of this problem. Denote this fundamental solution by $\xi_1, \cdots, \xi_{k_1+k_2}$. Then we must have, for some integer m, where $1 \leqslant m \leqslant k_1 + k_2 - 1$, an inequality

$$\sum_{t=1}^{m} \xi_t < S_{k_0+m} - h_0 .$$

Suppose first $m \leqslant k_1$. Then, since the solution $\xi^1_1, \cdots, \xi^1_{k_1}$ satisfies the constraints (1.2), we must have

$$\sum_{t=1}^{m} \xi^1_t \geqslant S_{k_0+m} - h_0 .$$

Hence

$$\sum_{t=1}^{m} (\xi^1_t - \xi_t) > 0 \tag{6.3}$$

so that from (6.1) we conclude that, in fact,

$$\xi_t^1 > \xi_t, \qquad (t = 1, 2, \cdots, k_1). \tag{6.4a}$$

Next, since a fundamental solution leaves us with zero terminal inventory, we have

$$\sum_{t=1}^{k_1} \xi_t^1 + \sum_{t=1}^{k_2} \xi_t^2 = \sum_{t=1}^{k_1+k_2} \xi_t = S_{k_0+k_1+k_2} - h_0.$$

From this we conclude with the aid of (6.3) that

$$\sum_{t=1}^{k_2} (\xi_t^2 - \xi_{k_1+t}) < 0$$

so that we have, again with the aid of (6.1),

$$\xi_t^2 < \xi_{t+k_1}, \qquad (t = 1, 2, \cdots, k_2). \tag{6.4b}$$

If $m > k_1$, a similar computation yields the same conclusions, so that (6.4a, b) hold in either case. Then from (6.4a) and the monotonic character of f we have

$$f(\xi_1^1) > f(\xi_1),$$

and therefore, using (3.3) and (6.4b), it follows that

$$f(\xi_1^1) + k_1\alpha > f(\xi_1) + k_1\alpha = f(\xi_{k_1+1}) > f(\xi_1^2),$$

which establishes (6.2).

Similar reasoning shows that we have in fact

$$f(\xi_1^j) + k_j\alpha > f(\xi_1^{j+1}), \qquad (j = 1, 2, \cdots, p-1) \tag{6.5}$$

that is, costs are increased by increasing production in the first period of any interval (except possibly the first) in order to reduce it in the first period of the following interval.

Next, using relationships of the type

$$f(\xi_t^j) = f(\xi_1^j) + (t-1)\alpha, \tag{6.6}$$

we can show that cost will also be increased by a reallocation which involves increasing production in *any* period of a given interval (except possibly the first) in order to reduce it in *any* period of the next interval. In fact, from (6.6) we have the relations

$$f(\xi_1^j) = f(\xi_{t_1}^j) - (t_1 - 1)\alpha$$

$$f(\xi_1^{j+1}) = f(\xi_{t_2}^{j+1}) - (t_2 - 1)\alpha$$

which in combination with (6.5) yield the inequality

$$f(\xi_{t_1}^j) + (k_j - t_1 + t_2)\alpha > f(\xi_{t_2}^{j+1}) \tag{6.7}$$

so that the contention is proved. Combining relationships of the form (6.5) and (6.7) we obtain finally

$$f(\xi_{t_1}^{j}) + (k_j + k_{j+1} + \cdots + k_{j+r} - t_1 + t_2)\alpha > f(\xi_{t_2}^{j+r+1}).$$

Thus it increases costs to produce and store in any period of any interval (except possibly the first) more than is called for by the plan (5.1).

It remains only to show that a reallocation calling for positive production anywhere in the first interval, where (5.1) calls for zero production, will increase costs. For this purpose, it will suffice to show that

$$f(0) + \alpha > f(\xi_1^1).$$

In the $(k_1 + 1)$-period problem defined by the demands $s_{k_0}, s_{k_0+1}, \cdots, s_{k_0+k^1}$ and the initial inventory $h_0 - S_{k_0-1}$, the fundamental solution *does not* satisfy all the constraints, by hypothesis. Let us denote this solution by $\xi_1, \xi_2, \cdots, \xi_{k_1+1}$. Now recalling that in the k_1-period problem with initial inventory $h_0 - S_{k_0}$ and demands $s_{k_0+1}, \cdots, s_{k_0+k_1}$, the fundamental solution $\xi_1^1, \cdots, \xi_{k_1}^1$ *does* satisfy the constraints, we may show in a manner similar to that used above that

$$\xi_1 < 0$$

and

$$\xi_{q+1} > \xi_q^1 .$$

From these last two results we have then

$$f(0) + \alpha > f(\xi_1) + \alpha = f(\xi_2) > f(\xi_1^1)$$

and the fact that the stated plan is optimal is now completely proved.

7. AN EXAMPLE OF THE OPTIMAL PLAN

We shall illustrate the results of the last two sections by constructing the optimal solution for the case in which storage costs may be considered negligible. In this case, since $\alpha = 0$, equations (3.5) and (3.6) become, respectively,

$$\begin{aligned} x_t &= x_1 \\ Tx_1 &= S_T - h_0 \end{aligned} \qquad (t = 2, 3, \cdots, T)$$

so that the fundamental solution of the problem is

$$\xi_t = \frac{S_T - h_0}{T}, \qquad (t = 1, 2, \cdots, T). \tag{7.1}$$

This solution calls for production at a constant rate equal to the average net requirements per period, the fluctuations in requirements being absorbed by the accumulation or reduction of inventories. This production plan satisfies the constraint (1.3) and because of (1.5) it also satisfies the constraints (1.4). Hence, if it satisfies the conditions (1.2) it will actually represent the optimal plan.

A simple circumstance in which conditions (1.2) are satisfied is that in which

$$S_k/k < S_T/T, \qquad (k = 1, 2, \cdots, T) \tag{7.2}$$

that is, in which the *terminal average demand* is maximal. We have then, in fact

$$\frac{S_k - h_0}{k} < \frac{S_T - h_0}{T}, \qquad (k = 1, 2, \cdots, T)$$

so that using (7.1) we have

$$h_k = h_0 + \sum_1^k x_t - S_k = h_0 + k\left(\frac{S_T - h_0}{T}\right) - S_k > h_0 + k\left(\frac{S_k - h_0}{k}\right) - S_k = 0,$$
$$(k = 1, 2, \cdots, T - 1)$$

and the constraints are indeed satisfied. A special case of (7.2) is the case of nondecreasing demands:

$$s_1 \leqslant s_2 \leqslant \cdots \leqslant s_T .$$

In case the constraints (1.2) are not all satisfied by (7.1), then the process of Section 5 requires first that we seek the largest integer k_1, $1 \leqslant k_1 \leqslant T - 1$, such that the fundamental solution of the k_1-period problem, namely

$$\xi_t = \frac{S_{k_1} - h_0}{k_1}, \qquad (t = 1, 2, \cdots, k_1) \tag{7.3}$$

satisfies all the constraints of that problem. These constraints are

$$\sum_1^k \xi_t \geqslant S_k - h_0, \qquad (k = 1, 2, \cdots, k_1)$$

or, using (7.3),

$$\frac{S_{k_1} - h_0}{k_1} \geqslant \frac{S_k - h_0}{k}, \qquad (k = 1, 2, \cdots, k_1),$$

and

$$\xi_t = \frac{S_{k_1} - h_0}{k_1} \geqslant 0.$$

It may now be verified that this integer k_1 *is actually the largest integer such that the preceding inequalities hold for all* k *from* 1 *to* T, *that is, for which*

$$\frac{S_{k_1} - h_0}{k_1} \geqslant \frac{S_k - h_0}{k}, \qquad (k = 1, 2, \cdots, T). \tag{7.4}$$

Since such an integer k_1 always exists, we will never begin by planning production at the zero level. The plan for the first k_1 periods is given by (7.3) above.

After the first k_1 periods, the initial inventory is exhausted. Hence we next need to determine the largest integer k_2, $1 \leqslant k_2 \leqslant T - k_1$, such that, analogously to (7.4):

$$\frac{S_{k_1+k_2} - S_{k_1}}{k_2} \geqslant \frac{S_{k_1+k} - S_{k_1}}{k}, \qquad (k = 1, 2, \cdots, T - k_1). \tag{7.5}$$

We then use the left member of (7.5) as the plan in each of the periods $k_1 + 1, \cdots, k_1 + k_2$.

Proceeding in this manner we obtain a succession of say p similarly determined integers $k_1, k_2, \cdots, k_p$ such that $\sum k_j = T$ and such that the optimal plan is given by

$$\left\{\begin{array}{l} \tilde{x}_1 = \tilde{x}_2 = \cdots = \tilde{x}_{k_1} = \dfrac{S_{k_1} - h_0}{k_1} \\[2ex] \tilde{x}_{k_1+1} = \cdots = \tilde{x}_{k_1+k_2} = \dfrac{S_{k_1+k_2} - S_{k_1}}{k_2} \\[2ex] \cdots\cdots\cdots\cdots\cdots\cdots\cdots\cdots\cdots\cdots\cdots\cdots \\[2ex] \tilde{x}_{k_1+\cdots+k_{p-1}+1} = \cdots = \tilde{x}_T = \dfrac{S_T - S_{k_1+\cdots+k_{p-1}}}{k_p}. \end{array}\right. \tag{7.6}$$

Thus the horizon is divided into blocks of periods in each of which we produce *at an even rate.*

It is interesting to note that *the solution in the case of no storage costs is independent of the exact form of the cost function F.*

8. MARGINAL COST STRICTLY INCREASING; ALTERNATIVE METHOD OF SOLUTION

The solution outlined in Section 5 is a backward-looking one, so to speak, starting as it does with the T-period problem and working towards the present until at least a part of the solution has been determined. We may transform it, however, into an alternative, forward-looking procedure, which has significant implications for the planning process.

For the purposes of this section, we find it useful to introduce quantities ζ_t^q, related to the fundamental solution of the "q-period problem" (Section 5) as follows:

$$\text{If } \xi_1 \geqslant 0, f(\zeta_t^q) = f(\xi_1) + (t - 1)\alpha, \qquad (t = 1, 2, \cdots, T). \tag{8.1a}$$

$$\text{If } \xi_1 < 0, \zeta_1^q = 0, f(\zeta_t^q) = f(0) + (t - 1)\alpha = f(\zeta_1^q) + (t - 1)\alpha, \qquad (t = 1, 2, \cdots, T). \tag{8.1b}$$

If $\xi_1 \geqslant 0$, then ζ_t^q is the same as ξ_t for $t \leqslant q$, while for $t > q$, it represents the result of "extrapolating" the fundamental solution of the q-period problem beyond q periods. It is useful to note in particular that since for the 1-period problem $\xi_1 = s_1 - h_0$, $\zeta_1^1 = \max(s_1 - h_0, 0)$.

Using this notation, the steps involved in constructing a solution may be outlined as follows:

(a) In the first period, production must be at least $\zeta_1^1 = \max(s_1 - h_0, 0)$. If in addition

$$h_0 + \sum_{t=1}^{k} \zeta_t^1 - S_k > 0, \qquad (k = 2, \cdots, T), \tag{8.2}$$

then in fact $\zeta_1^1 = \bar{x}_1$.

For suppose $\zeta_1^1 \neq \bar{x}_1$. Then, since $\bar{x}_1$, being feasible, cannot be less than ζ_1^1, we must have $\bar{x}_1 > \zeta_1^1$. But then $\bar{x}_1$ is positive and hence, by Section 5, it must be ξ_1^1. From the monotonic character of f we have next

$$\xi_t^1 > \zeta_t^1, \qquad (t = 1, 2, \cdots, k_1)$$

so that

$$\sum_{t=1}^{k_1} \xi_t^1 > \sum_{t=1}^{k_1} \zeta_t^1. \tag{8.3}$$

From (8.2) and (8.3) we now have

$$h_0 + \sum_{t=1}^{k_1} \xi_t^1 - S_{k_1} > 0$$

whereas the values ξ_t^1 satisfy the constraint

$$h_0 + \sum_{t=1}^{k_1} \xi_t^1 - S_{k_1} = 0.$$

The contradiction shows that in fact $\bar{x}_1 = \zeta_1^1$. Hence, if (8.2) holds, the optimum plan for the first period has been established.

(b) If $\bar{x}_1 = \zeta_1^1$, we next seek to determine $\bar{x}_2$ in the same manner, using an initial inventory equal to $\max(h_0 - s_1, 0)$. The sequence of zero productions of the solution described in Section 5 will be found first of all by this process. The determination of $\bar{x}_2$ may, however, involve using the methods to be outlined in (c), (d), (e) below.

(c) Suppose that (8.2) is not satisfied. Then let t_1 denote the smallest value of t for which (8.2) fails to hold, so that

$$\begin{cases} h_0 + \sum_{t=1}^{k} \zeta_t^1 - S_k > 0, & (1 < k < t_1) \\ \text{but} & \\ h_0 + \sum_{t=1}^{t_1} \zeta_t^1 - S_{t_1} \leqslant 0. & \end{cases} \tag{8.4}$$

We then compute the fundamental solution, $\xi_1, \xi_2, \cdots, \xi_{t_1}$, of the t_1-period problem. This solution satisfies the condition

$$h_0 + \sum_{t=1}^{t_1} \xi_t - S_{t_1} = 0. \tag{8.5a}$$

Also, from (8.5a) and (8.4) and from the monotonicity of f, we have

$$\xi_t \geqslant \zeta_t^1, \qquad (t = 1, 2, \cdots, t_1),$$

and therefore

$$h_0 + \sum_{t=1}^{k} \xi_t - S_k \geqslant 0, \qquad (k = 1, 2, \cdots, t_1 - 1). \tag{8.5b}$$

From (8.5a) and (8.5b) we see that the plan $\xi_1, \cdots, \xi_{t_1}$ satisfies all the constraints of the t_1-period problem and is therefore the optimal plan for this problem *considered separately*. This same plan will in fact be optimal for these t_1 periods *in the entire T-period problem*, if the "extrapolation" of this plan exceeds requirements for the remaining periods. That is, we will have

$$\bar{x}_t = \xi_t = \zeta_t^{t_1}, \qquad (t = 1, 2, \cdots, t_1),$$

if

$$\sum_{t=t_1+1}^{k} \zeta_t^{t_1} > S_k - S_{t_1}, \qquad (k = t_1 + 1, \cdots, T). \tag{8.6}$$

To prove this last claim, we will show that the assumption that $\bar{x}_t \neq \zeta_t^{t_1}, t \leqslant t_1$, leads to a contradiction.

First, if $\bar{x}_t$ were less than $\zeta_t^{t_1}$ for some values of $t \leqslant t_1$, then it would have to be larger for other values since the optimal plan is necessarily feasible and hence

$$\sum_{t=1}^{t_1} \bar{x}_t \geqslant \sum_{t=1}^{t_1} \zeta_t^{t_1} = S_{t_1} - h_0.$$

But then costs could be reduced by increasing production above $\bar{x}_t$ for the first-mentioned values of t and decreasing it below $\bar{x}_t$ for the last-mentioned values since (3.3) would thereby be more nearly satisfied. This, of course, contradicts the assumption that $\bar{x}_t$ is optimal. Thus $\bar{x}_t \geqslant \zeta_t^{t_1}$ for $t \leqslant t_1$.

Next, in a manner analogous to that used in step (a), we can show that assuming that $x_t > \zeta_t^{t_1}$ for any such t also leads to a contradiction. This establishes that if (8.6) holds, we have

$$\bar{x}_t = \zeta_t^{t_1}, \qquad (t = 1, 2, \cdots, t_1).$$

(d) If the condition (8.6) is *not* satisfied, and if t_2 is the smallest value of k for which it does not hold, then we repeat the process by computing $\zeta_t^{t_2}$ and verifying whether (8.6) holds after t_1 is replaced by t_2 everywhere. Proceeding in this manner, we eventually locate an integer $k_1^* \leqslant T$ such that (8.6) holds with t_1 replaced by k_1^*. Then $\tilde{x}_t = \zeta_t^{k_1^*}$, $t = 1, 2, \cdots, k_1^*$. By making use of the uniqueness of the optimal solution and of the maximal character of both k_1^* and the k_1 of Section 5, it can be shown that in fact $k_1^* = k_1$.

(e) After thus finding k_1, we can handle by the same method the problem for the remaining $T - k_1$ periods with initial inventory zero and requirements $s_{k_1+1}, \cdots, s_T$.

By repeatedly using steps (a), $\cdots$, (e) above, we can determine the entire sequence of k's defined in Section 5.

9. A GRAPHICAL METHOD OF SOLUTION AND ITS APPLICATION TO A QUADRATIC COST FUNCTION

In order to develop the graphical implications of the alternative method of solution just outlined, let us suppose for the moment that $\tilde{x}_1 > 0$ so that the k_1 of the preceding section is not less than 1. Then the following conditions are all satisfied:

$$\sum_{t=1}^{k} \xi_t = \sum_{t=1}^{k} \zeta_t^{k_1} \geqslant S_k - h_0, \quad (k = 1, 2 \cdots, k_1 - 1), \tag{9.1}$$

$$\sum_{t=1}^{k_1} \xi_t = \sum_{t=1}^{k_1} \zeta_t^{k_1} = S_{k_1} - h_0, \tag{9.2}$$

and, in view of (8.6),

$$\sum_{t=k_1+1}^{k} \zeta_t^{k_1} > S_k - S_{k_1}, \quad (k = k_1 + 1, \cdots, T). \tag{9.3}$$

From (9.2) and (9.3), we have the additional conditions

$$\sum_{t=1}^{k} \zeta_t^{k_1} > S_k - h_0, \quad (k = k_1 + 1, \cdots, T), \tag{9.4}$$

which serve to complement the conditions (9.1) and (9.2). This set of conditions has a simple graphical interpretation.

Let us graph the time series of "cumulated requirements" $R(t) = S_t - h_0$, by plotting the point with ordinate $R(t)$ at the end of period t and joining the points with straight lines. Let us further define the "cumulated output" function $P(x, t)$ as follows:

$$P(x, t) = \sum_{j=1}^{t} f^{-1}[f(x) + (j - 1)\alpha].$$

For a fixed x, $P(x, t)$ may be interpreted as a cumulated fundamental solution, and may be graphed in the same way as $R(t)$. In particular, by the definition of $\zeta_j^{k_1}$, we have

$$P(\tilde{x}_1, t) = \sum_{j=1}^{t} f^{-1}[f(\tilde{x}_1) + (j - 1)\alpha] = \sum_{j=1}^{t} \zeta_j^{k_1}.$$

Conditions (9.1), (9.2), and (9.4) now tell us that $\bar{x}_1$, the optimum production program for the first period, is that value of x_1 for which the graph of the time series $P(\bar{x}_1, t)$ has the following properties:

(a) to the left of k_1 it is nowhere below $R(t)$, (condition (9.1));

(b) at the end of period k_1 it "touches" the graph of $R(t)$ (condition (9.2));

(c) between the end of period k_1 and the end of period T it is consistently above $R(t)$ (condition (9.4)). Since $P(x, t)$ is a monotonically increasing function of x, for $x > \bar{x}_1$, $P(x, t)$ is everywhere above $R(t)$, while for $x < \bar{x}_1$, $P(x, t)$ must intersect $R(t)$ or lie everywhere below it. We can therefore locate $\bar{x}_1$ graphically by plotting $P(x, t)$ for various values of x, until we determine a value of x and incidentally an integer k_1 for which the conditions (a), (b), and (c) above hold. The value of x so determined is $\bar{x}_1$. The values of $\bar{x}_2, \cdots, \bar{x}_{k_1}$ can then be read off the graph of $P(\bar{x}_1, t)$ or computed from $\bar{x}_j = f^{-1}[f(\bar{x}_1) + (j - 1)\alpha]$.

The above process was developed under the tentative assumption that $\bar{x}_1 > 0$. However, the procedure can be used in any event, for if $\bar{x}_1 = 0$ (but not otherwise) the value of x satisfying conditions (a), (b), (c) will be either zero or negative. Hence, when the above graphical procedure yields a solution $x \leqslant 0$, we put $\bar{x}_1 = 0$ and then proceed to determine $\bar{x}_2$, using the initial inventory $h_0 - s_1$ and beginning with period 2.

This graphical method of solution is illustrated in Figure 1, for the case of a quadratic cost function, first discussed in Section 4. Hypothetical requirements for each of the twelve periods of the horizon are shown in panel B. These requirements are assumed to have a roughly periodic pattern reflecting seasonal variation in demand. (If the seasonal variation has a periodicity of one year then each period in our example would cover two months.) The dashed "curve" in panel A represents the time series $R(t)$, i.e., cumulated demand less initial inventories, h_0, which are assumed to have a value of 2.0. Clearly, the value of h_0 does not affect the shape of $R(t)$ but only its height; a larger value of h_0 would merely shift $R(t)$ downwards, parallel to itself.

From the results of Section 4 we can immediately deduce the general form of $P(x, t)$, namely:

$$P(x, t) = tx + \frac{t(t-1)}{2}\frac{\alpha}{a}; \tag{9.5}$$

for any given value of x, this expression is a quadratic function of t and its second derivative depends only on the parameter α/a, which in our illustration is assumed to have a value of 0.2. The curve in the lower part of panel A represents $P(0, t) = t(t - 1)\alpha/2a = 0.1\, t(t - 1)$. If $R(t)$ were to lie everywhere below $P(0, t)$, or at most touch it, then $\bar{x}_1$ would be zero. With the assumed sale pattern this would require a value of $h_0 \geqslant 17.0$. The solid curve represents the cumulated optimum production program, $\bar{x}_t$; in our example this program consists of a sequence of three fundamental solutions, covering respectively periods 1 to 6 (first interval), periods 7 to 11 (second interval), and period 12 (third interval). The cumulated solution for the first interval is $P(1.75, t)$ which, as shown in the graph, meets $R(t)$ at the end of the sixth period, and is above $R(t)$ everywhere else. Hence, $\bar{x}_1 = 1.75$ and, from (4.1), $\bar{x}_j = 1.75 + .2(j - 1)$, $j = 2, \cdots, 6$.

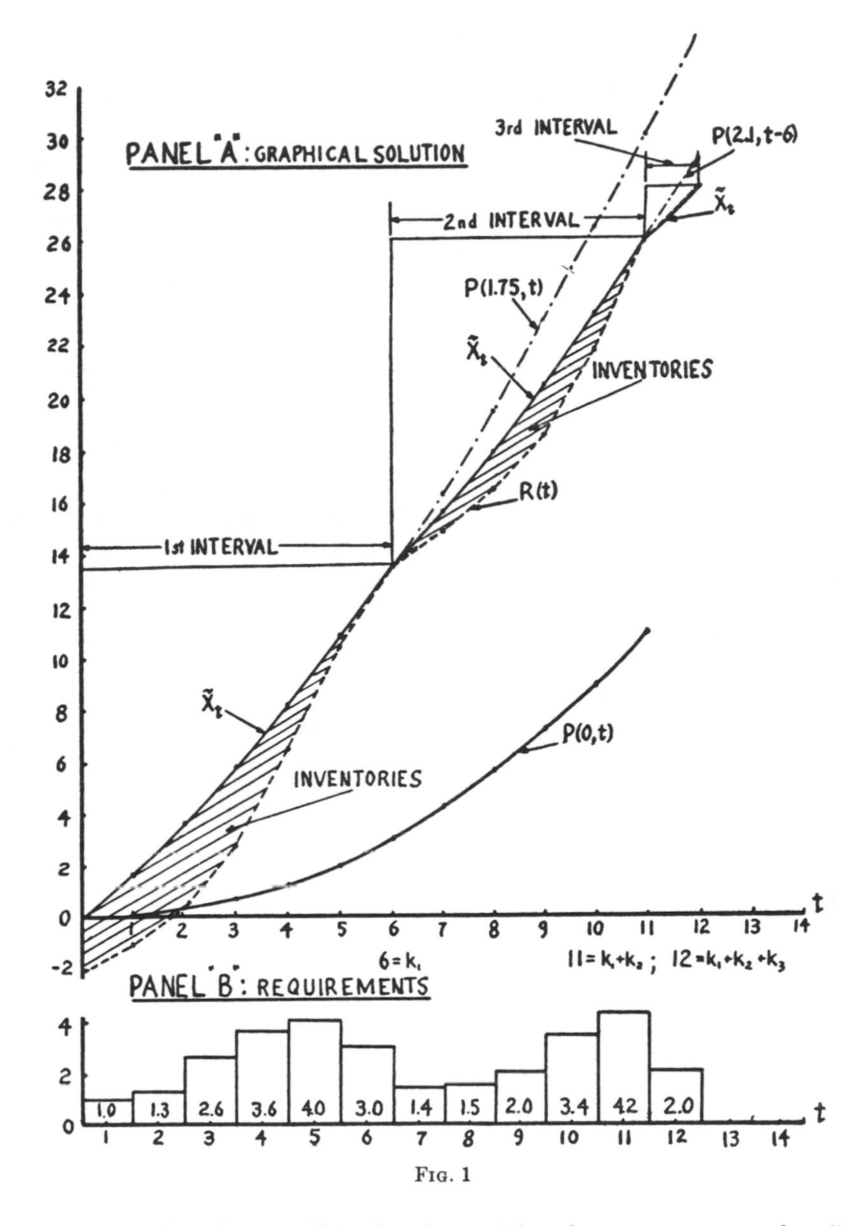

FIG. 1

The above value of $\tilde{x}_1$ could be found by trial and error as suggested earlier. However, in the case of a quadratic cost function it is possible to make use of a more systematic procedure. We seek a value of x, such that $tx + t(t - 1)\alpha/2a$ equals $R(t)$ for some t and is above $R(t)$ everywhere else; but this is equivalent to seeking a value of x such that the graph of tx, which is a straight line of slope

x through the origin, touches the graph of $R^*(t) = R(t) - t(t-1)\alpha/2a$ for some t, and is above $R^*(t)$ for any other value of t. But $t(t-1)\alpha/2a$ is precisely $P(0, t)$. Hence, the required value of x can be found as follows: (a) graph $R^*(t)$ by subtracting $P(0, t)$ from $R(t)$; (b) find a straight line through the origin which touches $R^*(t)$ at one point and is everywhere else above it. The value of t at which the curves touch is k_1 and the slope of the straight line is precisely $\tilde{x}_1$.[2]

In order to find the continuation of the optimum plan, covering the second interval, we simply repeat the above procedure but start now from a new origin with coordinates $[k_1, R(k_1)]$. In our particular illustration, one finds thus: $\tilde{x}_{6+j} = 2.1 + .2(j-1)$, $j = 1, \cdots, 5$; $\tilde{x}_{12} = 2.0$.

There are three significant aspects of the solution, which are clearly brought out by our graph and to which we should like to call attention for later reference.

(1) Every fundamental solution is represented in our case by a parabola; more generally, it follows from (3.7) that, if marginal cost is a strictly increasing function of output and inventory cost is positive, then every cumulated fundamental solution must be represented by a "curve" convex to the time axis. Now suppose that requirements have a fairly regular seasonal pattern; then, as is clearly illustrated by our graph, a fundamental solution will generally not cover more than (at most) one full seasonal cycle (or "year"), unless sales have a marked *over-all rising trend*, i.e., unless aggregate sales in each successive cycle are substantially above aggregate sales in the previous cycle. From our figure we see for instance, by following the curve $P(1.75, t)$ beyond period 6, that in order for the first fundamental solution to cover, say, two full cycles, $R(12)$ would have to be at least as large as 34.2, (or $R(11)$ as large as 30.25), as against a value 13.5 for $R(6)$; since sales over the first full cycle amount to 15.5, sales over the second cycle have to be in the order of 30% larger than in the first cycle.

(2) A large initial level of inventories tends to extend the interval covered by the first fundamental solution (unless it becomes so large that $\tilde{x}_1 = 0$). With the help of the graphical method outlined above, the reader can readily verify that if the initial inventories, h_0, were as large as 7.1 (instead of only 2.0 as assumed in our graph) then the first fundamental solution would cover the first 11 periods instead of only 6.

(3) An increase in storage costs, α, by raising the ratio α/a would have the effect of increasing the curvature of the graph of the cumulated fundamental solution and would thereby tend to shorten the length of the interval covered by any one fundamental solution.

The economic implications of these aspects of the solution will be brought out in the next section.

[2] The straight line tx may touch $R^*(t)$ at several points or even coincide with it for a stretch, but clearly this does not affect the uniqueness of $\tilde{x}_1$ or the method for locating it; by our definition k_1 corresponds in this case to the abscissa of the last point of contact.

If the line tx with the above properties has a negative slope, so that x is negative, then $\tilde{x}_1$ is zero; this can happen only if $R^*(t)$ is negative everywhere, i.e., if $R(t)$ is everywhere below $P(0, t)$, as indicated earlier.

10. SOME ECONOMIC IMPLICATIONS—THE "RELEVANT" EXPECTATION AND PLANNING HORIZON

The results of the previous sections have some very significant implications concerning the length of the expectation and planning horizon relevant to optimum decision making. In previous contributions ([**3**], [**4**]) it has been argued that *the* decision problem confronting the firm at any point of time is not that of determining the best possible plan for the entire future, as suggested by much of the existing theory of the firm (e.g., [**1**], p. 193), but rather that of choosing and implementing the *"best possible"* course of action for the immediate future—such as our first period. By the "best possible" course of action we mean that course which together with the appropriate course in later periods maximizes (or minimizes) whatever factor the agent is interested in. It has been further argued that, in order to determine the "best" first move, it is frequently sufficient to have information, and to make plans, for only a subinterval, possibly a small subinterval, of the entire economic horizon.

Our solution to the production scheduling problem illustrates and lends support to the above contentions. The goal of the agent in our problem is that of minimizing the cost of meeting the given requirements over the entire horizon of T periods; his decision problem is that of determining how much to produce in the first period so that this decision, together with later production decisions, will actually result in the lowest possible cost. Now, as we have just seen, in order to determine the optimum production for the first period, namely $\bar{x}_1$, it is sufficient to have information about requirements in the first k_1 periods—our first interval. This follows from the fact that *the optimum value of* x_1 *over a* T*-period horizon is identical with the optimum value of* x_1 *over the* k_1*-period horizon*; and, unless requirements have a rapidly rising over-all trend, or storage costs are negligible, k_1 will tend to be small relative to T. It is true that in order to determine k_1 we must have some knowledge of requirements beyond the first k_1 periods. But the only information actually needed is that sales beyond k_1 satisfy (roughly) the inequality represented by equation (8.6) (i.e., that $R(t)$ is less than $P(\bar{x}_1, t)$ for all t larger than k_1); and this very limited information may frequently be secured without extensive and detailed forecasting. In particular, when demand is subject to pronounced seasonal variation, a situation which is indeed very common, then, as we have shown in the last section, the first interval—and therefore the relevant horizon—is unlikely to extend beyond the period of seasonally high sales of the current seasonal cycle. Beyond this point, condition (8.6) will generally tend to be satisfied, unless sales over the next seasonal cycle will be substantially higher than in the current one. (The likelihood that periods beyond the next cycle will be relevant is, clearly, much smaller yet.)

We thus conclude that, with respect to production decisions of the type discussed in this paper, the relevant expectation and planning horizon will tend to cover a full seasonal cycle (or a shorter interval yet if storage costs are high) but is not likely to extend beyond this cycle except in the presence of a rapidly rising over-all trend. Furthermore, if the relevant horizon extends beyond the current cycle, this extension is likely to proceed by whole cycles. Finally, to the extent that new information will make it necessary to replan in the course of a seasonal cycle, the revised plan itself will tend to cover the balance of the given cycle (plus, possibly one, but seldom more than one, later cycle[3]). This conclusion finds empirical support in the planning practices of many firms[4] and in turn throws light on the rationale of such practices.

In concluding, it may be useful to single out the factors that tend to limit the size of the relevant planning and expectation horizon in connection with the problem on hand.[5]

As is clearly brought out by our fundamental equation (3.3), it is the inventory variable which provides the link between current and future production decisions. There are two major factors that tend to produce a break in this link in the context of our problem. One such factor is the non-negativity constraint on inventories. In the fundamental solution, in which this constraint is ignored, the optimum level of production and inventories at every point of time depends indeed on sales over the entire T-periods horizon. But when the non-negativity constraint is taken into account, the link breaks whenever the optimum plan calls for zero inventories; since the optimum level of inventories cannot be less than zero, at each one of these breaking points the optimum level of inventories remains zero regardless of the specific pattern of sales beyond this point.

The second factor that tends to make the distant future irrelevant is the cost of carrying inventories; if this cost is significant—and in this connection it should be remembered that storage costs include such things as deterioration, shrinkage, obsolescence, etc.—it becomes unprofitable to undertake any production *now* with a view to satisfying distant demands, and information on distant demand becomes irrelevant for current decisions. Thus, as storage costs increase relative to other costs the relevant expectation horizon must tend to shrink even in the absence of the non-negativity constraint.[6]

Carnegie Institute of Technology and *University of Illinois*

[3] If the replanning occurs as a result of a downward revision of expected demand, then the next cycle may well become relevant. Disregarding the next cycle, production would have to be reduced to the level that would insure liquidation of inventories by the end of the current cycle. But consideration of the following cycle may indicate that production should be kept above this level. This result illustrates one of the points to which attention was drawn in the previous section, to wit, that a large level on initial inventories generally tends to increase the length of the relevant horizon.

[4] This statement is based partly on a number of case studies of business planning conducted in the course of the project on "Expectations and Business Fluctuations" referred to in footnote 1.

[5] The relevant expectation and the relevant planning horizon turn out to coincide for the specific problem of this paper. But clearly, this coincidence need not hold. Thus, if in our problem we were to introduce a substantial lag between inputs and resulting outputs, the relevant expectation horizon would become longer than the relevant (input) planning horizon.

[6] This last statement cannot be developed further here. It is, however, fully supported by research currently in process at Carnegie Institute of Technology under a grant of the

REFERENCES

[1] HICKS, J. R., *Value and Capital*, First Edition.

[2] HOLT, CHARLES H., "Superposition Decision Rules for Production and Inventory Control," *O.N.R. Research Memorandum No. 3*, Graduate School of Industrial Administration, Carnegie Institute of Technology. (Duplicated)

[3] MODIGLIANI, FRANCO, "The Measurement of Expectations," Abstract of paper presented at the Boston Meetings, December, 1952, ECONOMETRICA, Vol. 20, No. 3, July, 1952.

[4] ———, "Some Considerations on the Expectation and Planning Horizon Relevant to Entrepreneurial Decisions," *Cowles Commission Discussion Paper: Economics 2038.* (Duplicated)

[5] ———, "A Method for Inverting the Matrix Arising from a Quadratic Decision Criterion," *O.N.R. Research Memorandum No. 15*, Graduate School of Industrial Administration, Carnegie Institute of Technology. (Duplicated)

[6] SIMON, HERBERT A., "Decision Rules for Production and Inventory Controls with Probability Forecasts of Sales," *O.N.R. Research Memorandum No. 8*, Graduate School of Industrial Administration, Carnegie Institute of Technology. (Duplicated)

Office of Naval Research. (See especially [1], [5], [6].) In the course of this research some attention has been given to one aspect of costs which was not considered in the present paper, namely the cost of changing the rate of production. This cost, which may be significant in certain concrete situations, has been neglected here because we did not find it possible to formulate some general and yet reasonable assumptions about the behavior of such costs, as we were able to do for other cost components. We may point out, however, that under conditions of increasing marginal costs the optimum production plan may generally be expected to be relatively "smooth," even if the "rate of change" cost is not explicitly taken into account; and this expectation is clearly confirmed by the results of this paper.

Errata

Page 55, line 10: last term in sequence "$s^1_{k_o+k}$" should read "$s_{k_o+k_1}$."

STUDIES IN BUSINESS EXPECTATIONS
AND PLANNING

THE ROLE OF ANTICIPATIONS AND PLANS IN ECONOMIC BEHAVIOR AND THEIR USE IN ECONOMIC ANALYSIS AND FORECASTING

BY

FRANCO MODIGLIANI
Professor of Economics
Northwestern University

and

KALMAN J. COHEN
Assistant Professor of Economics and Industrial Administration
Carnegie Institute of Technology

PUBLISHED BY THE UNIVERSITY OF ILLINOIS, URBANA
1961

INTRODUCTION

A. Purpose and Organization

This paper is an exposition of the theoretical structure developed in connection with the Project on Business Expectations and Planning, financed by a grant from the Merrill Foundation for the Advancement of Financial Knowledge[1] and originally established at the University of Illinois under the direction of one of the authors.

One of the major goals of this project has been a systematic exploration of the possible uses of statistical data bearing on anticipations and plans of firms both for the purpose of increasing our understanding of economic behavior in general and of decision-making by firms in particular and for the purpose of increasing our ability to forecast general economic activity or components thereof.

In pursuing this goal, we were led to do a good deal of basic rethinking concerning the role of expectations in the behavior of economic agents, especially business firms. This rethinking led to and was in turn supported by lengthy personal interviews with a number of firms in different industries, in the course of which we endeavored to explore the nature, purposes, and methods of their forward planning and the relations between anticipations, plans, and actual behavior.

The results of this rethinking are presented in Part I, where we discuss the problem of decision-making in a changing or dynamic world. Instead of developing a completely general theory of this subject, however, we focus our attention on a certain aspect of the problem which has largely been neglected in other approaches, namely, the role of anticipations and plans in the behavior of firms.[2] This aspect is singled out for two major reasons: (a) it helps to explain certain empirical regularities which are difficult to account for in terms of

[1] A highly abbreviated exposition of the ideas presented here can be found in Franco Modigliani and Kalman J. Cohen, "The Significance and Uses of Ex Ante Data," *Expectations, Uncertainty, and Business Behavior,* Mary Jean Bowman, ed. (New York: Social Science Research Council, 1958), pp. 151-64.

[2] Of the existing literature on the function of anticipations and plans in the theory of the firm, we especially recommend Albert G. Hart, *Anticipations, Uncertainty, and Dynamic Planning* (Chicago: The University of Chicago Press, 1940). Several of the ideas developed in this paper have been inspired by Hart's monograph, although we make no attempt at supplying further specific references.

other existing theories and speculation on the subject, regularities which are matters of commonplace observation and also have been confirmed by our interviews; (b) this aspect is helpful in developing a framework for formulating and testing hypotheses concerning the use of anticipatory data in economic analysis and forecasting.

Point (b) is elaborated in Part II, where we utilize the model developed in Part I to study possible and promising uses of data on anticipations and plans of economic units, especially firms. The purpose of this part is to develop a systematic framework for the exploitation of *ex ante* data in economic analysis and forecasting. This framework has actually guided a large part of the research completed and being carried on by the Project on Business Expectations and Planning. The concepts and approaches developed here are illustrated by passing references to a number of empirical investigations in the concluding Section II.D, although no systematic attempt is made to review the pertinent literature.

With respect to point (a), we make no attempt to report here in any systematic fashion the information that was gathered in the course of the interviews. First, much of this information has already been reported and analyzed elsewhere.[3] Second, the information gathered was not intended to and did not provide data of a kind that could be used for statistical testing in the modern sense of the word. The interviews were essentially case studies aimed much more at suggesting than at testing hypotheses. Nonetheless, these studies did reveal certain interesting regularities, some of which are worth reporting at this point.

Most firms were found to engage in a considerable amount of planning with respect to various parts of their operations, notably in the areas of production, sales, and capital outlays. Both plans and current decisions were generally based on more or less explicitly formulated anticipations of future demand, supply, and production conditions. However, the extent of overt planning was far smaller than one might expect on the basis of such theories as, say, Hicks's model of entrepreneurial decision-making over time.

Furthermore, reported plans generally were single-valued rather than "strategies," i.e., rules for choosing future actions in response to

[3] See Robert Eisner, *Determinants of Capital Expenditures — An Interview Study,* Studies in Business Expectations and Planning, Number 2 (Urbana: University of Illinois, Bureau of Economic and Business Research, 1956); and Robert Eisner, "Interview and Other Survey Techniques and the Study of Investment," *Problems of Capital Formation,* Studies in Income and Wealth, Vol. 19, National Bureau of Economic Research (Princeton, New Jersey: Princeton University Press, 1957), pp. 513-601.

later information. At the same time, it was frequently stressed by the respondents that plans did not represent decisions as to the actual levels of future activities; the respondents frequently emphasized that plans had almost no binding effects on future operations.

Finally, one phenomenon that was found to occur somewhat frequently is that the length of the horizon, for at least certain types of anticipations and plans, is a periodic function of time. It is longest at a certain point (or points) of the year (in one of the industries, for instance, it reached a length of approximately 16 months at this point). Thereafter, the terminal date of the horizon remains unchanged, so that the length of the horizon gradually shrinks to a minimum (about 4 months in the above instance). When the minimum length of the horizon is reached, the terminal date stretches back again, suddenly, to its maximum distance into the future (16 months in our example). The occurrence of this behavior appears to be associated with seasonality in the demand for the output or in the supply of some essential input. In fact, when sales exhibit several peaks, there tend to be the same number of points during a year when the length of the horizon suddenly expands.

The preceding three paragraphs illustrate some of the phenomena that our model of Part I purports to explain within the framework of a theory of rational decision-making.

A complete and rigorous exposition of the ideas presented in this paper requires the use of a considerable amount of technical terminology and formal symbolism. However, as an aid to the reader, we have provided in Section I.A a non-technical summary of Part I and in Section II.A a similar summary of the more formal sections of Part II, namely Sections II.B and II.C. These summary sections have a double purpose. First, they serve to provide an overview of the line of analysis and the main conclusions. In addition, they are designed to enable the non-technical or casual reader to acquire a general understanding of the ideas we are expounding by reading, after this Introduction, only Sections I.A, II.A, and II.D. The last-mentioned section, as indicated earlier, discusses the implications of our ideas for the use of anticipatory data in economic forecasting and analysis and examines the limited empirical results obtained to date. The reader who is primarily interested in the potential forecasting and analytical uses of *ex ante* data may skip the detailed development of the model of entrepreneurial decision-making contained in Part I, reading instead only the introduction and non-technical summary of this model which is presented in Section I.A before proceeding to Part II.

I. THE ROLE OF ANTICIPATIONS AND PLANS IN ENTREPRENEURIAL DECISION-MAKING AND THE NATURE OF THE "RELEVANT" HORIZON

A. Introduction and Non-Technical Summary

1. A Critical Review of Some Earlier Approaches and the Basic Assumptions of Our Model

a. *Static Analysis.* As indicated in the Introduction, our purpose in Part I is to analyze the role of anticipations and plans in economic decision-making, focusing on those aspects which appear most relevant to an understanding of how information on *ex ante* variables can be of use in economic analysis and forecasting.

The traditional static theory of the firm cannot be of much assistance to us in our undertaking. Anticipations and plans play no role in this model which endeavors to explain behavior at any point of time exclusively in terms of the "the present." This is accomplished by assuming either that there is no future or — which operationally comes to the same thing — that every future period is an exact replica of the current period regardless of the present course of action taken by the firm.

The problem of the firm is typically visualized as that of choosing a single course of action from an available set of alternatives. A course of action is determined by specifying a particular value for each of a number of variables. Not just any set of values may be chosen, however, because the variables are subject to certain constraints which may be broadly classified as demand constraints, supply constraints, and transformation or production-function constraints. The specific form of these constraints is determined by both the physical and the social environment, including the behavior of other units. Among the alternatives open, the firm is supposed to choose the one most conducive to the achievement of its goal. This goal is generally assumed to be the maximization of profit, which is regarded as a known single-valued function of the chosen set of values.

The assumptions underlying this model are obviously highly unrealistic. This unrealism is not an important objection per se, since

14

the relevant test of the model is its usefulness in explaining the behavior for which we wish to account. The static model is, in fact, sufficient for rationalizing a wide range of phenomena. It is, however, quite inadequate as an explanation of anticipatory and planning activity and many other features of observed behavior, including such disparate phenomena as the holding of terminal inventories of goods or money, the existence of debt, and the expenditure of resources to create "good will." In order to understand such phenomena, economists have been led to develop "dynamic models" of economic behavior. The starting point of such models is the recognition that decision-makers act with the realization that their interests extend beyond the current period, and that they are aware that their present actions may both influence the conditions which will confront them in the future and limit their future freedom of action.

b. *The Future and the Problem of Uncertainty.* In reality, the current actions of firms are influenced both by the fact that the future is relevant and by the fact that the future is uncertain. Nevertheless, it is possible to examine separately the implications of each of these considerations. Thus, the effects of uncertainty on behavior can be studied even in the context of a static model by recognizing that at least some of the constraints facing the decision-maker may be of a "stochastic" nature, where to a given chosen course of action may correspond not a single outcome but a set of mutually exclusive outcomes with varying degrees of likelihood. This recognition may help to explain *some* important aspects of economic behavior which cannot be accounted for by the "static certainty" model.

Similarly, the effect of the future per se may be analyzed by assuming that the future is known with certainty. Such an analysis shows *other* important aspects of behavior explainable in terms of a dynamic certainty model.[4] Thus, whether or not uncertainty has to be introduced explicitly into the analysis depends on the kinds of behavior we are interested in explaining. If the behavior in question can be understood without the complications of uncertainty, so much the better; although the model utilized may be less "realistic," to the extent that it is simpler, it is preferable. In what follows, we shall try to show that within the basic framework of a certainty model, we can go a long way towards explaining many aspects of anticipatory and planning behavior.

c. *The Dynamic Certainty Model of Hicks and Others.* In *Value and Capital,* J. R. Hicks developed a well-known dynamic model of

[4] See Section B.4.c.

entrepreneurial decision-making under certainty[5] which has later been elaborated by Mosak,[6] Lange,[7] and many others. This model, which in essence is a straightforward generalization of the static model, represents a convenient point of departure for much of our own analysis.

Just as in the static theory, the firm is viewed by these authors as choosing from among alternative available courses of action the one that is most conducive to the achievement of its goal. This goal is regarded as the maximization of a certain function, e.g., the present value of the stream of future profits, whose arguments include both the future and the current actions of the firm.

It is convenient to divide the prospective history of a firm into discrete time periods, say T in number. Since the life span of a corporate firm is potentially unlimited, T may be an indefinitely large number. To preserve in a clear fashion the useful distinction between present and future, we regard only the first of the T time intervals as "the present," while the remaining periods comprise "the future." We refer to T as the *horizon* at date zero, where "date zero" denotes the beginning of the first period.

During each of the T intervals, the firm decides on some course of action. This decision corresponds to assigning numerical values to a set of variables, which we call the firm's "decision variables" for that period. We call the action carried out by the firm in any period its *move* in that period.[8] The implementation of the firm's decision consists in making effective the numerical values assigned by the firm to all of its decision variables for that period.

In reality, the number of aspects of a firm's behavior may be extremely large if the firm is analyzed down to its ultimate details. We are interested, however, in only those aspects that form the object of decision-making by the "decision-maker," i.e., by whoever (whether it be one or more persons) controls the firm. We can call these aspects

---

[5] J. R. Hicks, *Value and Capital* (2nd Edition; London: Oxford University Press, 1946), especially Chs. IX and XV. We follow Hicks in our use of the term *dynamics:* "I call Economic Statics those parts of economic theory where we do not trouble about dating; Economic Dynamics those parts where every quantity must be dated." (p. 115) The dynamic model which we develop in Part I is a theory of behavior in a changing world, not a theory of how the world changes.

[6] J. Mosak, *General Equilibrium Theory in International Trade,* Cowles Commission Monograph No. 7 (Bloomington, Indiana: Principia Press, 1944), Ch. VII.

[7] O. Lange, *Price Flexibility and Employment,* Cowles Commission Monograph No. 8 (Bloomington, Indiana: Principia Press, 1944).

[8] We use the symbol $X(t)$ to denote the firm's move in period t, and the vector $X = [X(1), \ldots, X(T)]$ to denote the firm's collection of moves over its entire prospective lifetime.

of the firm's action the *major components* or, simply, the *components* of each move.[9] The components of a move are related to the remaining aspects of the firm's behavior, which we can call the *minor components,* by some sort of aggregation procedure. Implementing the decision requires the assignment of values to the minor components which will achieve the chosen values for the major components.[10]

There are a large number of different courses of action which the firm can choose over the horizon, and the firm is not indifferent about the consequences of choosing different paths. Our model assumes that the firm has a well-defined set of goals in terms of which it is able to decide when it prefers the results which follow from one course of action to the consequences resulting from another pattern of behavior. This set of goals is summarized in terms of the firm's "pay-off function." The value of the pay-off function depends upon the particular moves chosen by the firm during each time period comprising the horizon,[11] and our model says that the firm behaves as though it were trying to make the value of its pay-off function as large as possible, i.e., to maximize its pay-off function.

In the Hicksian model, the pay-off function reduces to the sum of discounted net receipts over the horizon. For our present purposes, such a narrow specification is not necessary. All we need to assume is that the decision-maker is able to rank consistently, in order of preference, all possible life histories.[12] Just what causes one life history to be preferred to another, whether it be profit or other considerations, is at the moment of little consequence.

As in the static analysis, the firm's decision variables are subject to demand, supply, and transformation constraints. In the Hicksian

[9] Each period's move is a vector, $X(t) = [x^1(t), \ldots, x^{K(t)}(t)]$; each $x^k(t)$ is a component of the *t*th move, and $K(t)$ is the total number of components in the *t*th move. $K = \sum_{t=1}^{T} K(t)$ is the total number of decision variables over the firm's entire prospective lifetime.

[10] To illustrate the distinction between major and minor components, a major component might be the volume of production, and the minor components, the aggregation of which determines volume of production, might be the quantity and type of raw materials and labor employed, the assignment of workers to specific machines, the scheduling of work through particular processes, and so forth. At our level of analysis, it is sufficient to consider only major components, e.g., volume of production.

[11] We let G denote the pay-off function. The arguments of G are the components of the vector X, i.e., the moves $X(1), X(2), \ldots, X(T)$. Hence, we can write the value of the pay-off function as either $G(X)$ or $G[X(1), \ldots, X(T)]$.

[12] For most of what follows, the pay-off function G needs to be defined only *ordinally,* i.e., up to a monotonic transformation. However, when we consider the possibilities of decision-making under uncertainty in Section E, we must assume that G is a *cardinally* defined utility function.

formulation, which is basically built on assumptions of perfect competition, the demand and supply constraints merely state that the purchase or selling price of each commodity is equal to some constant entirely outside the firm's control, i.e., completely determined by the environment. The transformation conditions take the form of a *single* constraint relating the inputs and outputs of every period — a formulation which is open to some rather serious objections (see Section B.1.b). These very special assumptions can be considerably broadened without affecting the essence of the problem. The basic points to keep in mind are that the decision variables are subject to various constraints, and that the constraints relating to the variables of *future* periods are largely determined by the *future* behavior of the environment.

d. *Anticipations and Plans in the Hicksian Analysis.* From this formulation, and by exact analogy to the static case, Professor Hicks draws the conclusion that the decision problem confronting the firm at any given point of time is the selection of the entire best course of action over the horizon. "Just as the static problem of the enterprise is the selection of a certain set of quantities of factors and products, so *the dynamic problem is the selection of a certain production plan* from the alternatives that are open";[13] and again, "...the decision which confronts any particular entrepreneur at any date...may be regarded as the establishment of a *production plan.*"[14] In other words, at the beginning of each interval the firm is supposed to face the entire maximization problem and to select the values of all the components of all the moves over the entire horizon which jointly maximize the pay-off function subject to the constraints. Clearly, to solve this maximization problem over the entire horizon would require forming definite anticipations about the specific form of every future constraint. The firm then proceeds to implement its selection with respect to the components of the first move. The remaining part of the solution, the values assigned to the components of later moves, represents the *plan* for future operations.

Thus, on the basis of the Hicksian analysis, we should expect to find that firms at all times have explicit plans — formal or informal — covering at least the major aspects of their operations over some definite horizon, and that underlying these plans are definite estimates of the parameters of all future constraints over the horizon. As we have already indicated in the Introduction, these implications are definitely not supported by our case studies. This is not surprising, for even

[13] Hicks, *op. cit.*, p. 194 (italics ours).
[14] *Ibid.*, p. 193.

introspection and casual observations suggest that economic agents do not generally behave in the way implied by the Hicksian analysis.

One possible explanation for the discrepancy between the conclusion of this analysis and observed behavior is that these observations relate to a world of uncertainty, and the existence of uncertainty tends to shorten considerably the horizon over which it is useful to form anticipations and to formulate plans. While this explanation may have some validity, it is far from complete. It may be pointed out, for instance, that plans and anticipations seldom cover every aspect of operations even for the very near future, whereas, with respect to some aspects of operations, they may extend fairly far into the future, being supported by definite anticipations about future conditions. Similarly, uncertainty per se appears inadequate to account for various other observed aspects of the planning and anticipation horizon which we have described in the Introduction. Another possible explanation is that actual behavior cannot adequately be accounted for in terms of a model which assumes rational behavior on the part of business firms, as does the Hicksian model.

We propose to show that many important aspects of anticipatory and planning behavior can, in fact, be adequately understood and analyzed within the basic framework of the Hicksian model of rational decision-making under certainty; all that is required are some relatively minor modifications of the basic assumptions in the direction of greater "realism" and a major change of viewpoint.

e. *Modifications of the Hicksian Assumptions — The Decision Problem of the Firm as the Selection of the "Best" First Move.* The assumption of certainty usually involves, explicitly or implicitly, the notion that information about the future is single-valued, is known to be correct, and is "inborn" in the agent or can be acquired and exploited by him without significant cost or effort. We propose to modify this assumption in three major directions. (1) While we continue to regard anticipations as single-valued, we assume that the agent recognizes that his single-valued expectations are not entirely reliable, i.e., may turn out to be wrong. (2) We further recognize that at a particular date, more reliable information about the future can be acquired only at the cost of devoting scarce resources to this task, while the cost of acquiring this information decreases as the future draws nearer. (3) Finally, we take into account the fact that problem-solving, decision-making, and planning are all costly activities, in that they absorb scarce resources, and are therefore to be avoided unless the return from such activities promises to exceed their cost.

Let us next consider the suggested change of viewpoint. We must first note that in the Hicksian analysis, the analogy between the dynamic and the static problems is carried one step too far. While it is perfectly true that in terms of the pay-off function the single current move of the static model is replaced by the entire set of moves over the horizon, it does not necessarily follow that, as in the static model, the firm must choose now its entire course of action. The only choice that *must* be made at a given point of time (such as date zero) and which *cannot* be postponed is the choice of the first move.[15] We suggest, therefore, that the decision problem confronting the entrepreneur at a given point of time is most usefully regarded not as that of selecting the best possible plan of operations over the horizon, but rather, as that of *selecting the best possible first move only*. By "best possible" we mean, of course, the move that is best, not merely with reference to the first period, as though it were the only period, but with reference to the entire maximization problem over the horizon. We suggest that the entrepreneur's proper concern is the determination and the enforcement of the first move components belonging to the optimal course of action over the firm's entire prospective history.

It is evident that our way of looking at the firm's decision problem is operationally feasible, since the first move is the only one that *must* be and that can be enforced right now. We further propose to show, in the rest of Part I, that once we adopt this point of view, regarding forecasting and planning as activities in which a firm must engage only for the purpose of selecting its first move, then we can readily account for many facets of observed behavior for which the Hicksian analysis proved inadequate. Through most of the analysis — Sections B, C, and D — we shall find it possible to proceed under our modified certainty assumptions. However, in the concluding Section E, we shall examine in summary fashion the need for relaxing these assumptions and the type and extent of systematic biases that may be present in the inferences drawn from our certainty model.

A non-technical summary of our argument in Part I will be provided by the following section.

2. Non-Technical Summary of Part I

a. *Section B — The Nature of the Dynamic Constraints — Relevant and Irrelevant Anticipations.* Although we regard the firm's decision problem as that of selecting only the first or current move, in order to choose it optimally, the firm may have to gaze some distance into the

[15] Note that our concept of "move," introduced earlier in Section c, is broad enough to include any failure to act as itself being part of the move that is made.

future. To see this point clearly, it is desirable to look at the nature of the constraints limiting the possible courses of action that the firm can choose over the horizon.

A course of action is specified by a sequence of moves, one for each period. Consider the constraints limiting the choice of the move for period t, say. As seen at the beginning of period t, these constraints reflect both given initial conditions — size and location of plants, state of productive facilities, established connections in buying and selling markets, inventories in the hands of customers, and so forth — and the behavior of the environment during the course of the period — general business conditions, competitors' behavior, and other developments affecting the position of demand and supply schedules, and so forth. The initial conditions, in turn, are largely the result of past history, and this past history may, to a considerable extent, consist of the firm's own moves in previous periods. Thus, when the constraints of period t are regarded from the vantage point of a period earlier than t, such as date zero, they are seen to depend, at least in part, upon moves made by the firm up through period $t - 1$; the latter are, of course, variables as of date zero. One of these moves is the first move, which must be decided currently.

These considerations help us to understand why a firm may have to form anticipations about some aspects of the future in order to make an optimal choice of the first move. If some components of the first move enter directly or indirectly into some future constraint, and thus affect the opportunities open at that time, then the optimum value of the first move may depend on the specific form of that constraint, or, as we shall say hereafter, upon the parameters of that constraint. When this is the case, we can say that these parameters are *relevant* as of date zero.

We can also see, however, why at date zero it may not be necessary to worry about many aspects of the future. Suppose, for example, that the components of the first move, whatever values they might take, do not affect the freedom of choice with respect to some components of, say, the *tth* move. Then any constraint involving only these later components is of no relevance for deciding the first move — that is, the constraints and the parameters therof can be said to be *irrelevant* as of date zero.

The concepts of relevance and irrelevance introduced in the above two paragraphs can be usefully formalized as follows: An "aspect of the future" — or more specifically, a future constraint or a parameter thereof — is irrelevant as of date zero, if the optimum value of the first move is the same, no matter what might be the specific form of the constraint (or the specific value of the parameter). Anticipations relating to irrelevant constraints or parameters are called irrelevant anticipations. We say that a parameter is *totally* irrelevant if it is irrelevant no matter what its value might turn out to be; that it is *conditionally* irrelevant when it is irrelevant provided its value falls within some stated range.

It follows from our formulation of the decision problem that the firm *need not* estimate totally irrelevant parameters at date zero. From our assumption that the cost of obtaining information about conditions in a future time period decreases as that period draws near, it further follows that at date zero the firm *should not* devote scarce resources to this task. If a parameter is conditionally irrelevant, then no more effort should be devoted to estimating it than is required to ascertain that the conditions for irrelevance are satisfied. The common sense of these conclusions can be summed up in the maxim: "Don't devote resources to estimate particular aspects of the future if, no matter what you might find out (with due consideration to what you might conceivably find out), you would not be led to act differently from the way you would act without finding out."

In order to illustrate the selective nature of relevant anticipations, a number of examples are provided in which aspects of the future which are obviously relevant to the choice of some moves are still irrelevant as of date zero, since they do not affect the *first* move. We shall only summarize here some of the major features and implications of these examples.

A very obvious situation in which the relevant horizon does not extend beyond the current period is where the pay-off is of the Hicksian type and the nature of the constraints is such that actions in one period in no way restrict the choices open in other periods. A reasonable approximation to this type of situation might be represented by a firm dealing in a non-storable commodity which must be produced (or purchased) and disposed of within the same period in a relatively perfect market and employing very little fixed capital. For such a firm, if the pay-off function is of the Hicksian type (cf. Section 1.c), decisions within each period would tend to depend exclusively on actual and anticipated conditions within that period. Knowledge about conditions in future periods would be of little value, since such knowledge would not lead to current decisions different from those taken in its absence.

Situations in which commodities cannot be stored at all are, of course, exceptional with present-day technology, and it would seem that once storage is possible, the first-period decision must affect later opportunities. But, while it is true that storage does tend to provide a link between present and future, it is found that in many important instances even this link breaks down, both because it is expensive, and because it can work only in one direction, it generally being possible to produce now to deliver later but not to deliver now and produce later.

This point is illustrated by a simple example involving a two-period problem. We consider a firm producing a single product, total cost being a linear function of the output of each period, though the (constant) marginal cost need not be the same in the two periods. In each period, the quantity salable depends on the price charged in the period and on that price alone, but the form of the demand curve can again be different in each period. Now suppose that the product can be carried over from the first period to the next at a constant cost per unit. It can readily be seen that as long as the second-period marginal cost is no larger than the first-period marginal cost plus the storage cost, then the optimum course of action will be to produce no more in the first period than can be profitably sold in this period — *regardless* of the demand conditions of the second period. Hence, the parameters of the second-period demand curve are irrelevant, and no more needs to be known about the second-period costs except that the previously mentioned inequality will in fact hold.

That this result is not due to the artificially short horizon that was assumed is shown by a third illustration in which we deal with a T-period horizon, where T can be indefinitely large. The problem considered here is that of scheduling the production of a commodity in such a way that the delivery requirements in each of the T periods are met at the lowest possible total cost over the horizon. It is shown that even if storage were costless, unless delivery requirements are expected to exhibit forever a steadily increasing trend, there will be some date t such that the actual course of requirements beyond t is irrelevant. The presence of storage costs tends to shrink the relevant horizon very much further. In particular, if sales are subject to seasonal variation, it is found that at any point within a given seasonal cycle, the relevant planning and anticipations horizons will tend to extend up to the peak of the given cycle or shortly beyond it; all further seasonal cycles normally tend to be irrelevant, especially when storage costs (including deterioration, obsolescence, and so forth) are significant. This result checks with certain characteristics of observed planning and anticipations horizons noted in the Introduction; e.g., the length of the horizon is a periodic function of time, linked with the seasonal cycle.

In general, the length of the relevant horizon may itself depend on certain strategic parameters. In particular, a number of considerations are pointed out which suggest that the relevant horizon may tend to grow when economic activity is high and expected to rise.

It is possible to establish certain general conditions under which parameters of future constraints are irrelevant with respect to the first move. Two formal theorems stating sufficient conditions for irrelevance are proved. The first theorem can be paraphrased roughly as follows:

Consider a set of components of future moves, and let p be a parameter of a constraint that effectively binds only these components. For any value of p (all the other data of the problem being given), there will be a best possible course of action, including specific values for the components under consideration. Now consider the relation between the stated components and the first move. If, in advance of selecting the first move, we were given some arbitrarily specified values for these components, we could determine what would then be the best first move. Suppose now that the best first move so computed turns out to be the same for a whole set of different values of these components. If this set of values includes the best possible value of the stated components corresponding to every admissible value of p, then p is totally irrelevant. If the last-mentioned condition is satisfied only for values of p falling within a stated range, then p is conditionally irrelevant.

The second theorem applies when the total outcome or pay-off can be expressed in terms of two sub-outcomes, the first of which depends on the first-period move, and possibly on components of later moves, while the second depends only on components of later moves. Such a decomposition is valid, for instance, for the Hicksian type of pay-off function. The assertion of the theorem can be summarized as follows: Suppose we choose a feasible first move so as to maximize the first sub-outcome. Now consider a set of components of later moves which are relevant only to the second sub-outcome. If, having chosen the first move as indicated, we find that we are still in a position to choose for the stated set of components those values which correspond to the best possible course of action over the horizon, then we say that the best values for these components are "still available." The theorem states that a parameter p, binding only the stated components, is irrelevant if for every admissible value of p, the best values corresponding to the stated value of p are still available.

b. *Section C — The Nature of Planning Activity.* In Section B we have been concerned with the concepts of relevance and irrelevance as they apply to parameters of constraints and the anticipations thereof. We now consider how these concepts may be extended from parameters to moves.

The irrelevance of parameters is generally connected with the existence of components of future moves such that no matter what their optimum values turn out to be, the best first move is precisely the same. It is natural to call such components of future moves irrelevant components as of date zero and to call plans relating to such components irrelevant plans at date zero. The firm would not devote scarce resources to making irrelevant plans, for knowledge of the best values of such components is of no help to the firm in deciding its optimal first move. We say that all the remaining components of moves are relevant as of date zero.

What does relevance of a component imply with respect to the advisability of planning, i.e., selecting a value for the component at date zero? Our fundamental proposition that the problem of the firm is that of selecting the best first move might appear to carry the implication that no components of future moves are worth planning, even if the components are relevant. Actually, there are a number of considerations which suggest that this conclusion is not warranted and which help us to understand why relevant components will frequently — although not necessarily — be worth explicit planning. In essence, relevant components are intimately tied up with the components of the current move, in the sense that the optimal values of these various components depend on each other. Stated in more formal terms, the maximization problem that needs to be solved in selecting the first move involves, in a logical sense, finding the solution to a system of simultaneous relations. Relevant components — in contrast to irrelevant ones — appear as variables in this system of simultaneous relations. It follows, in the first place, that all the information required to solve for the relevant future components is already available at no extra cost, since it is required in the solution for the first move. Furthermore, once a system has been solved for some of its unknowns, the remaining ones can frequently be computed at a low marginal cost. Finally — and this is probably the most important consideration from the empirical point of view — the most economical or "natural" way of solving for the first move may well involve solving first for certain components of future moves. Indeed, the promulgation of a plan may be a convenient way of providing information to various parts of an organization as to what actions they are expected to take in the current period. This idea is closely related to the organization theorists' concept of "the coordinating function of a plan."

We may conclude, therefore, that relevant components of future moves may be worth explicit planning as a by-product of the most convenient way of solving the first-period decision problem and/or because the marginal cost of making such plans is not large and although part of the plan may eventually be discarded, the value of the rest of the plan may still be greater than the cost of making it explicit. We must remember, however, that plans are not decisions about the future course of action. Decisions refer to planned moves not subject to replanning, and therefore only to components of the current or first move. Plans should preferably be regarded as representing the best forecast that can be made by the firm at date zero as to the values that certain components of future moves will eventually take; this forecast is made for the purpose of deciding the *first* move, *not* for the purpose of deciding *later* moves.

c. *Section D — The Effects of Costs of Obtaining and Exploiting Information — Practical Irrelevance.* The analysis so far has focused on parameters and components of moves which do not affect *at all* the optimal first move and are therefore strictly irrelevant. These parameters are not worth estimating and these components are not worth planning even if the costs of gathering information and problem-solving are negligible. However, once we take into account the existence of such costs we find that strictly irrelevant parameters are not the only ones which are not worth estimating. To determine whether information-gathering costs are worth incurring the question to be asked is not "Does the parameter affect the first move?" but rather "How much can be gained by knowing the value of the parameter before reaching a decision?" It is then readily apparent that among relevant parameters there may be some which are "practically irrelevant" in the sense that "they are not worth bothering about." We point out three sources of practical irrelevance.

First, there are limits on the accuracy with which decisions may be implemented; in particular, adding a few more decimal places to a component of a decision may make no difference in the behavior of the agent whose job it is to implement that component. Accordingly, a parameter is practically irrelevant if letting it range over all values which are admissible on the basis of the initial information affects each component of the optimal first move by less than some appropriately small amount.

Second, even if accurate execution of decisions is possible, a parameter may be practically irrelevant because the most that can be gained from knowing it is negligible. This type of irrelevance we call epsilon irrelevance.

The significance of irrelevance arising from these two sources is illustrated by drawing on recent development in "management science." In the course of research dealing with optimal inventory policy, it has been shown that epsilon irrelevance will arise under a fairly weak set of conditions. The solution to an important class of problems in the area of production and employment scheduling illustrates situations where a large class of parameters are irrelevant because of either or both of these two reasons. Often, as in the examples referred to, practical irrelevance is closely connected with "the fading of the horizon": parameters of future constraints tend to have a decreasing effect on the current decision as their date lengthens into the future and thus they gradually fade into irrelevance.

A third and probably very important source of practical irrelevance arises from the problem-solving cost of exploiting information about relevant parameters, i.e., of establishing the way in which the optimal first move is affected by the values of the parameters. Suppose the cost of exploiting the information about a parameter exceeds the most that can be gained from this information. Such a parameter is practically irrevelant, for information about it is not worth exploiting even if it were available and hence is certainly not worth gathering.

A limiting case of prohibitive costs of exploiting information is where the problem is so complex relative to the state of the arts that we are not able even to establish just how the information could be utilized. One may well speculate that, as the recent major advances in computing techniques through digital and analog computers and in management science become increasingly exploited by firms, the anticipations and planning horizon will tend to lengthen and grow in the detail encompassed. Fewer relevant plans may be made explicit, however, for better problem-solving methods may make it preferable to solve directly for the current move instead of indirectly through the use of plans for the future.

d. *Section E — The Effects of Costs of Obtaining and Exploiting Information — Practically Relevant Parameters Not Worth Estimating.* Our modified certainty model has now been pushed as far as it will stretch, and there remains the problem of taking a quick look at its limitations. A convenient link between certainty and uncertainty models is provided by the following consideration: even when a parameter is relevant, and even if by incurring an appropriate cost the decision-maker could ascertain its value with (subjective) certainty, the value of the parameter may still not be worth ascertaining if the cost is sufficiently high. It turns out that even to analyze the problem of whether or not the exact value of a relevant parameter is worth estimating, we need a theory of decision-making under uncertainty. For, clearly, what is gained by having information about a parameter is the difference in the pay-offs corresponding to the best course that the agent can take with and without the information, respectively. But, if the agent acts without acquiring the information, he is, in fact, making choices under conditions of uncertainty: to any decision he reaches correspond two or more mutually exclusive outcomes with different degrees of likelihood or subjective probability. Hence, we need a theory of how he will choose under uncertainty and how he will value an uncertain pay-off (which valuation, in turn, is an essential element of a theory of choice under uncertainty). We shall do no more than take a passing and superficial look at this problem, partly because of its complexity and partly because we do not possess as yet a generally accepted model of decision-making under uncertainty. Probably the best available tool at this stage is the so-called "expected utility" theory which, after a long history, has recently been elaborated and developed by many authors, among them Savage, whose formulation we follow here.

Starting from some basic postulates of rational behavior, this theory shows: (a) that the information available to the agent concerning an uncertain event — such as the value of an unknown parameter — can be represented by a "subjective" probability distribution, and (b) that there exists a (cardinal) utility function such that the agent acts as though he were endeavoring to maximize the *expected value* of his utility.

To illustrate the working of this model as well as the complexity of the problems of choice under uncertainty, we shall analyze the issue raised at the beginning of this section: whether it is worthwhile to pay the cost to acquire certainty about a relevant parameter. The problem at issue can also be looked at as that of determining the (economic) value of information; for once this value has been established, the decision merely involves a comparison of value and cost.

If we regard the pay-off function as a cardinal measure of utility, then we can suppose that when uncertain about the value of one or more practically relevant parameters, the decision-maker will choose the course of action that maximizes the *expected value* of the pay-off. At this stage, it is necessary to include in the pay-off function the cost of obtaining information. We shall consider first the problem of whether the information should be acquired now or not at all.

What the pay-off will be if the agent incurs the cost of obtaining information on the parameter depends, of course, upon the *true* value of that parameter. In advance of actually acquiring the information, the agent does not know this true value, but he does have a subjective probability distribution relating to it; hence he can compute an *expected* pay-off were he to incur the cost of estimating the value of the parameter and act optimally under certainty on the basis of the information acquired. He then compares this with the *expected* pay-off if he does not estimate the value of the parameter and acts under uncertainty. The parameter p is then either worth estimating or not according to which of these quantities is larger.

The problem becomes far more complex when we recognize that there is also the alternative of acquiring the information at various future points of time, the cost of the information depending itself on when the information would be acquired. The nature of the solution to this problem is exhibited though it is too complex to be summarized here.

These sample problems provide the basis for some considerations presented in the concluding sub-section concerning the kind and extent of systematic biases that may arise in Part II from relying on our modified certainty model. These considerations may be summarized as follows. Because of information costs, rational behavior may dictate not acquiring certainty about all relevant parameters. The agent must then act under conditions of uncertainty. In this case, anticipations and plans will not be single-valued. Anticipations may have to be represented by subjective (joint) probability distributions, or analogous devices; and plans may have to be represented by strategies, or schedules, expressing future actions as functions of later information.

Our modified certainty model makes only partial allowance for these phenomena; it assumes that many relevant aspects of anticipatory and planning activity may be described as though anticipations and overt plans could be characterized by single representative numbers. However, it makes the proviso that single-valued anticipations are not regarded by the agent as subjectively certain and that the agent recognizes that single-valued plans may have to be discarded in the light of future information. An explicit single-valued plan can be considered as the one point of a strategy which arises as an almost costless by-product of deciding on the optimal first move.

Although our entire analysis is built within the framework of a model of rational decision-making, the last considerations pave the way for a few remarks concerning anticipatory and planning activity in practice. There can be little question that firms in general are deeply aware of the fact that their constant and pressing decision problem is to determine what to do right here and now. For this reason, we might expect that, in many cases, current decisions tend to be made on the basis of too short-run a view of the situation and without worrying about many aspects of the future that are, in fact, relevant. Lack of know-how and disinclination to handle complex problems are likely to contribute to this tendency. On the other hand, there probably also are cases where lack of an adequate understanding of the operational role of anticipatory and planning activity leads to the formulation of irrelevant anticipations and irrelevant plans.

In Part II we shall continue to rely basically on the modified certainty model, but we shall make occasional use of the analysis of Section E to indicate where and in what directions our results may have to be qualified because of the empirical limitations of our model.

B. The Nature of the Dynamic Constraints — Relevant and Irrelevant Anticipations

1. A Re-examination of the Nature of the Dynamic Constraints

a. *Representation of the Constraints.* Even though we regard the decision problem facing the firm as that of selecting only the current or first move, since this move must be the best move in the context of the entire course of actions over the horizon, in order to choose it optimally it may be necessary to gaze into the future. In order to see this point clearly, we must consider the nature of the constraints which restrict the possible courses of action which the firm can choose over the horizon.

In the static analysis, the constraints limit the possible values that the firm may select for its decision variables. For instance, for any given product the firm cannot implement any price and quantity it may like. If it deals in a perfect market, the price is entirely outside its control; if it deals in an imperfect market, it can choose only combinations of prices and quantities which lie on, or to the left of, the market demand function.

In the dynamic model, there are also constraints which restrict the firm's freedom to select values for its decision variables. There may be a large number of these constraints, each of which involves only some particular set of decision variables and specifies a relation which these variables must satisfy. For example, the t*th* period's terminal inventory constraint might specify that the t*th* period's terminal inventory must equal the $(t - 1)$*th* period's terminal inventory plus the t*th* period's production minus the t*th* period's sales.

The most general way of representing constraints is as point sets — that is to say, a constraint on certain variables defines a set of admissible values in the space of these variables. In general, each constraint can be written as a relation among particular variables, $R[x^k(t), \ldots, x^j(\tau)]$. For purposes of exposition, however, we frequently find it convenient to assume that the constraints can be represented in parametric form, so that the specific nature of a constraint is fully determined by the values of its parameters. In most parametric representations in which we are interested, the constraining relations can be written in the form of equalities or inequalities. Constraints expressed as inequalities are commonplace, as, for example, the conditions that sales in a given period cannot exceed production plus initial inventory and that production cannot be negative. Such inequalities play an important role in part of our argument.

b. *Dating the Constraints.* A distinction which is very important for our purpose is whether or not a specific variable effectively enters a particular constraint. One "intuitively obvious" way of drawing this distinction would be to say that a specific variable $x^i(\theta)$ does or does not effectively enter a particular constraint $R[x^k(t), \ldots, x^j(\tau)]$ according as $x^i(\theta)$ is or is not one of the variables $x^k(t), \ldots, x^j(\tau)$. However, this "intuitively obvious" distinction fails to deal adequately with a problem which arises from the generality of mathematical notation, for a variable can be written as an argument of a function or a relation even though the function or relation in no way depends on that variable.[16] The distinction which we *wish* to draw as to whether or not a specific variable effectively enters a particular constraint can properly be conveyed by the following definition.

We say that a variable y_i does not effectively enter the constraint

$$R(y_1, \ldots, y_i, \ldots, y_n)$$

if and only if the set of values of the variables $y_1, \ldots, y_{i-1}, y_{i+1}, \ldots, y_n$ which satisfy the relation

$$R(y_1, \ldots, y_{i-1}, y_i, y_{i+1}, \ldots, y_n)$$

is the same for all conceivable values of the variable y_i.

We can now define the date of a constraint as the latest date of any variable which effectively enters that constraint, i.e., as the largest value of t corresponding to any variable $x^k(t)$ which effectively enters that constraint. Each constraint is thus uniquely dated.

We can define the first-period constraint set, S_1, as the set of points $X(1)$ which satisfy all constraints of date 1. The constraints of the first period are entirely analogous to those of the static model;

[16] For example, the relation $R(x, y, z)$ might actually be the property

$$x^2 + y^2 > 0$$

which in no way depends on z.

they involve the first-period variables, and their specific form is determined by initial conditions and by the behavior of the environment in the course of the period. Furthermore, these first-period restrictions cannot possibly involve the future behavior of the environment or variables of a later date, for the obvious reason that things which have not yet happened cannot possibly limit what is currently achievable.

Consider now the constraints of the second period as they appear to the decision-maker at date zero; they clearly involve the second-period variables $x^k(2)$ and certain parameters whose values depend on initial conditions and on the behavior of the environment in the first and second periods. In addition, however, they may well involve at least some of the components $x^k(1)$ of the first move. For, generally, the specific limitations within which the $x^k(2)$ can be chosen will depend on moves made (or not made) in the first period. For example, the form of the Marshallian demand schedules for the second period might depend, among other things, on prices charged in the first period and first-period advertising outlays. Similarly, the conditions under which second-period inputs can be transformed into output might depend on such first-period actions as changes in production facilities and the production of parts. Therefore, the second-period constraints can, in general, be written in the form

$$X(2) \epsilon S_2[X(1)],$$

where $S_2[X(1)]$ is the set of points $X(2)$ which satisfy all the constraints of date 2 corresponding to a given first-period move, $X(1)$.

Generalizing, we may conclude that the constraints on the components of any period t, as they appear at date zero, will involve not only variables dated t but also components of earlier moves from 1 to $t - 1$. As time passes and successive moves are completed, the components of these moves are no longer variables but stated constants. In fact, by the time the *tth* period has become "the present," all the components of earlier moves will have become past history, and therefore they will be constants which are embodied in the initial conditions of date $t - 1$. Similarly, what appear as initial conditions at date zero are largely the results of earlier moves of the agent. We can therefore represent the constraints of the *tth* period, as seen at date zero, as $X(t) \epsilon S_t[X(1), \ldots, X(t-1)]$, where $S_t[X(1), \ldots, X(t-1)]$ is the set of points $X(t)$ which satisfy all the constraints of date t corresponding to a given preceding sequence of moves, $X(1), \ldots, X(t-1)$.

We note in passing that the Hicksian formulation, according to which all the limitations on inputs and outputs are expressed by a single production function, is equivalent to the rather awkward assumption that there is a single constraint of date T. It is indeed difficult to see how the Hicksian production function could relate to any period except the last, for it is hard to imagine how, say, the output of some earlier period could be affected by inputs of later dates. Assuming a single constraint relating to the terminal period implies, of course, that all earlier inputs and outputs can be chosen subject to no constraints — an assumption somewhat hard to defend, to say the least.[17]

The over-all constraint set, S, can be defined as the set of points X which satisfy all the constraints. More specifically, denoting by $X = [X(1), \ldots, X(T)]$ a "plan" or "strategy" consisting of a specification of moves over the whole planning horizon, we can define S as the set of feasible plans, i.e., S is the set of points X for which

$$\begin{array}{l} X(1) \epsilon S_1 \\ X(2) \epsilon S_2[X(1)] \\ \cdot \\ \cdot \\ \cdot \\ \cdot \\ X(T) \epsilon S_T[X(1), \ldots, X(T-1)]. \end{array}$$

2. The Two Views of the Firm's Decision Problem Contrasted

The fresh look we have taken at the nature of the dynamic constraints enables us to state in more formal terms the major difference between the Hicksian formulation of the problem of the firm — the establishment of a plan of operations over the entire horizon — and our own formulation of the problem — the selection of the best first move. In both of these formulations, the firm is viewed as endeavoring to choose an $X \epsilon S$ which maximizes $G(X)$. Now, because of the way in which the over-all constraint set S is related to the dated constraint sets S_t, we can write

$$\max_{X \epsilon S} G(X) = \max_{X(1) \epsilon S_1} \max_{X(2) \epsilon S_2[X(1)]} \cdots \max_{X(T) \epsilon S_T[X(1), \ldots, X(T-1)]} G[X(1), X(2), \ldots, X(T)].$$

Let us now suppose that a first move X(1) has somehow been chosen, and let us consider the problem of choosing the remaining moves X(2), X(3), . . . , X(T), to maximize the value of the pay-off

[17] It must be recognized that Hicks tries to cover himself against this type of criticism by brief footnotes (*op. cit.*, pp. 85-86, n. 2, and p. 194, n. 1) in which, however, he merely suggests that the objection is unimportant.

function G subject to the constraint set S, given the chosen value for X(1). The resulting outcome, i.e., the highest achievable value of the pay-off function which can be achieved subject to the stated conditions, will then be a function of X(1); we call this outcome $\hat{H}[X(1)]$. Note that this outcome is not a function of any later moves X(2), X(3), . . . , X(T), for these have all been "maximized out." Thus, we can write

$$\text{(B1)} \quad \hat{H}[X(1)] = \max_{X(2)\epsilon S_2[X(1)]} \cdots \max_{X(T)\epsilon S_T[X(1),\ldots,X(T-1)]} G[X(1), X(2), \ldots, X(T)].$$

Hence,

$$\text{(B2)} \quad \max_{X\epsilon S} G(X) = \max_{X(1)\epsilon S_1} \hat{H}[X(1)].$$

Equation (B2) embodies the two different ways of looking at the firm's problem. Considering the problem in the form of choosing $X\epsilon S$ which maximizes G(X) is the classical approach of Hicks and others. At date zero the firm is supposed to reach a "decision" not only with respect to its first move, but also with respect to every component of every future move over the horizon, although only the first of these moves can be implemented currently. In order to reach this "decision," it must have expectations about the parameters of every future constraint.

In our formulation, on the other hand, the problem of the firm is visualized as that of choosing the best first move $\tilde{X}(1)$; this move is best in that it is the first move component of the optimal solution $\tilde{X}$. As equation (B2) shows, this problem can be stated formally in terms of the function $\hat{H}[X(1)]$ as that of choosing an $\bar{X}(1)\epsilon S_1$ such that $\hat{H}[\bar{X}(1)] \geq \hat{H}[X(1)]$ for every $X(1)\epsilon S_1$. From the definition of the function $\hat{H}[X(1)]$, it is readily seen that $\bar{X}(1) = \tilde{X}(1)$.[18]

3. The Concept of Irrelevance

Our formulation of the problem of the firm paves the way for introducing the concept of *irrelevance*. We say that "an aspect of the future"—more specifically, a future constraint or a parameter

[18] This tacitly assumes both the existence and the uniqueness of the $X\epsilon S$ which maximizes G(X). The uniqueness assumption could, in fact, be relaxed. Allowing multiple maximizing values means that we have to speak of *"the set of* X which maximize," instead of speaking of *"the* X which maximizes," and this makes the statements and proofs which we give below considerably less compact. Since the essential nature of the discussion remains unaltered, we shall assume the uniqueness of $X\epsilon S$ maximizing G(X); the modifications necessary to allow for multiple maximizing values are quite clear.

thereof—is irrelevant at date zero if *the optimum value of the first-period move can be determined without knowledge of the specific form of the constraint (or of the parameter).* There is undoubtedly some vagueness in the italicized portion of this definition. For this reason, we have been led to give a more formal definition of the concept of irrelevance.

As a preliminary to this definition, let us recall that we have defined $\tilde{X} = [\tilde{X}(1), \tilde{X}(2), \ldots, \tilde{X}(T)]$ as the best sequence of moves the firm can choose, i.e., $\tilde{X} \epsilon S$ and $G(\tilde{X}) \geq G(X)$ for all $X \epsilon S$. Consider now any parameter p which appears in at least one of the constraints which determine S. We can write $S = S(p)$ to indicate that the over-all constraint set S in general depends upon the value of the parameter p. Hence $S(p')$ is the over-all constraint set which is determined when the parameter p assumes the specific value p'. Since the optimal sequence of moves $\tilde{X}$ is generally a function of the over-all constraint set S, which in turn depends upon the value of the parameter p, we can write $\tilde{X}(p) = [\tilde{X}(1; p), \tilde{X}(2; p), \ldots, \tilde{X}(T; p)]$, which is, of course, defined by $\tilde{X}(p) \epsilon S(p)$ and $G[\tilde{X}(p)] \geq G(X)$ for all $X \epsilon S(p)$.

We can now formally define the concept of irrelevance by the following necessary and sufficient conditions. A parameter p of a given future constraint is *conditionally irrelevant* within some stated collection of values P if and only if the optimum value of every component of the first move is the same no matter what value p might have within the stated collection of values, i.e., if and only if $\tilde{X}(1; p') = \tilde{X}(1; p'')$ for all p', p'' such that $p', p'' \epsilon P$. A parameter p is *totally irrelevant* if and only if it is conditionally irrelevant in the collection of all a priori admissible values.[19]

We shall speak hereafter of a parameter as *irrelevant* if it is at least conditionally irrelevant for some non-trivial collection of values.[20] A constraint is irrelevant provided every parameter of that constraint is irrelevant. Anticipations relating to irrelevant parameters or constraints are called irrelevant anticipations. The earliest date after which all future constraints are irrelevant is called the *relevant anticipations horizon.*

It follows from our formulation of the decision problem that the

[19] By a priori admissible values we mean those values which are consistent with physical and institutional limitations, such as the laws of gravity or the fact that certain prices cannot be negative.

[20] As a little exercise in semantics, we could say that a parameter which is conditionally irrelevant is also conditionally relevant, while if p is not irrelevant (either conditionally or totally), then it is totally relevant. (Strictly speaking, a continuous parameter p is totally relevant if it is irrelevant at most over a set of measure zero.)

firm *need not* estimate totally irrelevant parameters at date zero. From our assumption that the cost of obtaining information about conditions in a future time period decreases as that period draws near, it further follows that at date zero the firm *should not* devote scarce resources to this task. If a parameter is conditionally irrelevant, then no more effort should be devoted to estimating it than is required to ascertain that the conditions for irrelevance are satisfied.

The concept of irrelevance developed so far applies directly only to future constraints or parameters and anticipations thereof. In Section C.1 we shall show, however, that the concept of irrelevance can be usefully extended, with appropriate modifications, to apply to components of future moves and to the planning thereof.

It remains to be seen whether the concept of irrelevance has sufficient empirical content to be useful. This we propose to consider, first by presenting in the next section some examples of situations in which large classes of parameters are irrelevant. Then in Section 5 we shall establish some general conditions under which parameters of future constraints are irrelevant.

4. Some Illustrations of Irrelevant Parameters

a. *Example 1.* Our very simple example will be stated in analytical form and then given economic content. Suppose the following conditions are satisfied:

(a) The pay-off function can be written in the form

$$G = F[Q(1), Q(2), \ldots, Q(T)],$$

where $Q(t)$ is a function of the components of the t*th* move only, say,

$$Q(t) = Q_t[x^1(t), \ldots, x^{K(t)}(t)],$$

and the form of F is such that G increases whenever any one $Q(t)$ increases, regardless of the value of the other Q's.

(b) Only variables dated t effectively enter the constraints S_t.

Condition (a) implies that the entire outcome of the firm's activity can be regarded as a function of the outcome for each period, which is not unrealistic in many economic problems. For instance, the Hicksian pay-off function satisfies this condition, $Q(t)$ being defined as net receipts in period t. In this case, in fact, F is linear, and the coefficients of the Q's are simply appropriate discount factors. Condition (b) implies that actions in one period in no way restrict or modify the choices open in other periods.

It is clear that, under these conditions, the problem of maximizing G subject to the constraints can be reduced to T disjoint maximization problems, one for each of the T periods. That is, let $\bar{X}(t)$ denote the values of the *tth* move which maximize Q(t) subject to the constraints S_t (more precisely, let $\bar{X}(t)\epsilon S_t$ be such that $Q_t[\bar{X}(t)] \geq Q_t[X(t)]$, for every $X(t)\epsilon S_t$); then, clearly, $\tilde{X}(t)=\bar{X}(t)$, $t=1, 2, \ldots, T$. This implies, in particular, that $\tilde{X}(1)$ can be found by maximizing Q(1) subject only to the first period constraints, S_1. The solution is, therefore, entirely independent of the form of any later constraint S_t, $t>1$, and these later constraints (and their parameters) are irrelevant at date zero. It is also readily seen that for this conclusion to hold, an assumption much weaker than condition (b) would be sufficient. In fact, it is only required that no variable dated 1 effectively enters any constraint dated later than 1.

It is probably impossible to find an exact economic counterpart to this analytical example. A reasonable approximation might, however, be found in the case of a firm dealing in a non-storable commodity which must be produced (or purchased) and disposed of within the same period and employing very little fixed capital. For such a firm, if the pay-off function is of the Hicksian type, decisions within each period would tend to depend exclusively on actual and anticipated conditions within that period. Knowledge about conditions in future periods would be of little value, since such knowledge would not lead to current decisions different from those taken in its absence. To be sure, the anticipation of drastic changes might call for some special actions now and make it worthwhile to devote resources to increase whatever rudimentary knowledge about future periods might already be available. But, generally, the relevant anticipations horizon would tend to be very short.

This example may be regarded as having limited empirical content, at least with present-day technology. Situations in which commodities cannot be stored at all are exceptional. Once storage is possible, first-period decisions, e.g., production decisions, must affect opportunities of later periods, at least through inventory carry-over. The next two examples are designed to show that while storage does, in principle, provide a link between present and future, in many important instances this link will break down both because it is expensive and because it can work only in one direction, since it is generally possible to produce now to deliver later but not to deliver now and produce later.

b. *Example 2.* Our second illustration consists of a two-period horizon problem which, while rather artificial, nonetheless throws light on some important aspects of more realistic situations.

Let u_1, u_2, q_1, q_2 denote, respectively, production and sales in each of two periods, and let the demand conditions in each period be described by the demand functions:

$$p_1 = p_1(q_1); \quad p_2 = p_2(q_2).$$

Suppose that production occurs at constant marginal cost, though the marginal cost may be different in the two periods. Then the total cost of any program u_1, u_2 can be described by:

$$C(u_1, u_2) = C_1u_1 + C_2u_2 + a.$$

We let h_t denote the inventory at the end of period t, and we assume that h_o, the initial inventory at the start of the first period, is zero. Suppose that storage costs per period are proportional to the terminal inventory, H being the proportionality factor. We assume that the firm seeks to maximize the profit function,

$$G = q_1p_1 + q_2p_2 - C_1u_1 - C_2u_2 - a - Hh_1 - Hh_2,$$

subject to the previously mentioned demand functions, to the inventory identities,

$$u_1 - q_1 = h_1, \quad u_2 + h_1 - q_2 = h_2,$$

and to the non-negativity constraints,

$$q_1, q_2, u_1, u_2, h_1, h_2 \geq 0.$$

The solution is considerably different depending on the relation between the first-period and second-period (marginal) costs of production.

Suppose first that the second-period cost C_2 is lower than (or equal to) the first-period cost C_1 plus the storage cost H. Then the solution can be stated:

$$\text{(B3)} \qquad q_1 = \tilde{q}_1,$$

where $\tilde{q}_1$ is the root of the equation $\frac{d}{dq_1}[q_1p_1(q_1)] = C_1$;

$$\text{(B4)} \qquad \tilde{u}_1 = \tilde{q}_1; \quad \tilde{h}_1 = 0; \quad \tilde{p}_1 = p_1(\tilde{q}_1); \quad q_2 = \tilde{q}_2,$$

where $\tilde{q}_2$ is the root of the equation $\frac{d}{dq_2}[q_2p_2(q_2)] = C_2$;

$$\tilde{u}_2 = \tilde{q}_2; \quad \tilde{h}_2 = 0; \quad \tilde{p}_2 = p_2(\tilde{q}_2).$$

Equation (B3) essentially states that in period 1, price should be set at the level that equates marginal revenue to first-period marginal cost. Equations (B4) state that the first-period production should be just equal to first-period demand at this price, the optimum amount of terminal inventory being zero, *regardless* of second-period demand conditions. These demand conditions are only relevant for the second-period move, the second-period optimum price being such as to equate marginal revenue to second-period marginal cost, and second-period production being such as to satisfy the second-period demand at this price.

Thus, even though the commodity can be stored, the optimum first-period move can be chosen without any knowledge of the second-period demand function, which is, therefore, totally irrelevant. Note that the second-period cost parameter C_2 is irrelevant, but only conditionally; no precise knowledge of its value is required besides the information that it will not exceed the first-period cost C_1 by more than H.

However, if the latter condition is not satisfied, i.e., if C_2 is expected to exceed C_1 by more than H, then the second-period conditions become relevant at date zero. In this case, in fact, the best course of action is to manufacture in the first period the entire output required to satisfy both the first-period and the second-period demand, i.e.,

$$\text{(B5)} \qquad \tilde{u}_1 = \tilde{q}_1 + \tilde{q}_2.$$

The value of $\tilde{q}_1$ and $\tilde{p}_1$ is again given by equation (B3); as for $\tilde{p}_2$ and $\tilde{q}_2$, they should again be such as to equate second-period marginal revenue to marginal cost. But, since the production occurs entirely in the first period and is then stored for sale in the second period, the relevant marginal cost is not C_2 but rather $C_1 + H$. Hence, $\tilde{q}_2$ is now the root of the equation:

$$\text{(B6)} \qquad \frac{d}{dq_2}\,[q_2 p_2(q_2)] = C_1 + H.$$

It is clear from (B5) and (B6) that, in this case, optimum first-period production cannot be determined without knowledge of the second-period demand equation, which is, therefore, relevant.

An important point brought out by Example 2 is that the irrelevance of certain parameters may itself depend on the values of certain other *crucial* parameters. As long as the second-period cost is expected to be roughly the same as that of the first period, which we may well regard as the normal situation, the parameters of the second-period demand functions are (totally) irrelevant. However, the expectation of rising costs may be sufficient to make a greater part of the future relevant to the first-period decision.

c. *Example 3.* In Example 2, the irrelevance of (part of) the future may be thought of as resulting from the expensiveness of the inventory link; in other situations, irrelevance may be brought about by the fact that inventories can provide only a one-directional link. An example of such a situation is represented by a production-scheduling problem which has received considerable attention in the literature,[21] namely the problem of scheduling the production of a particular commodity in each period over a T-period horizon in such a way that the delivery requirements in each period are fulfilled at the lowest possible over-all cost. In this problem, the parameters of future constraints are the quantities to be delivered in each future period, which are considered as given constants, and the parameters of the cost function.

Here we can only indicate certain features of the solution to this problem which are particularly relevant to our present subject.[22] This solution is valid as long as the marginal cost in each period is an increasing function of the rate of output in that period.

Suppose first that storage costs are negligible. In this case, if there is any date within the horizon, say t′, beyond which average sales are expected to be no larger than average sales up to t′, then t′ is the relevant sales anticipations horizon. The precise course of sales in each of the periods following t′ is (conditionally) irrelevant.

Consideration of storage costs tends to shrink the relevant anticipations horizon very much further. The results, by and large, indicate that distant sales can be relevant only if they are expected to exceed

[21] Franco Modigliani and Franz E. Hohn, "Production Planning Over Time and the Nature of the Expectation and Planning Horizon," *Econometrica,* Vol. 23 (1955), pp. 46-66; A. Charnes, W. W. Cooper, and B. Mellon, "A Model for Optimizing Production by Reference to Cost Surrogates," *Econometrica,* Vol. 23 (1955), pp. 307-23; A. Charnes and W. W. Cooper, "Optimization in New Item Production," *Minutes of the Third Annual Logistics Conference* (Washington, D. C.: Office of Naval Research, May, 1952); Francois Morin, "Note on an Inventory Problem Discussed by Modigliani and Hohn," *Econometrica,* Vol. 23 (1955), pp. 447-52; A. J. Hoffman and Walter Jacobs, "Smooth Patterns of Production," *Management Science,* Vol. 1 (1954), pp. 86-91; H. Antosiewicz and A. J. Hoffman, "A Remark on the Smoothing Problem," *Management Science,* Vol. 1 (1954), pp. 92-95; Richard Bellman, "Dynamic Programming and the Smoothing Problem," *Management Science,* Vol. 3 (1956), pp. 111-13; G. Dantzig and S. Johnson, "A Production Smoothing Problem," *Proceedings of the Second Symposium on Linear Programming,* Vol. 1 (Washington, D. C.: National Bureau of Standards, U. S. Department of Commerce, 1955), pp. 151-76; Alan S. Manne, "A Note on the Modigliani-Hohn Production Smoothing Model," *Management Science,* Vol. 3 (1957), pp. 371-79; S. M. Johnson, "Sequential Production Planning Over Time at Minimum Cost," *Management Science,* Vol. 3 (1957), pp. 435-37; Kenneth J. Arrow, Samuel Karlin, and Herbert Scarf, *Studies in the Mathematical Theory of Inventory and Production* (Stanford, California: Stanford University Press, 1958), Chs. 4-6; and William Karush, "On a Class of Minimum-Cost Problems," *Management Science,* Vol. 4 (1958), pp. 136-53.

[22] For the details, see Modigliani and Hohn, *op. cit.*

substantially sales in the near future; the further away the sales, the greater must be this excess. Thus, the presence of significant storage costs tends to cut down the length of the relevant anticipations horizon.

In particular, if sales are subject to seasonal variation, it is found that at any point within a given seasonal cycle, the relevant planning and anticipations horizons will tend to extend up to the peak of the given cycle or shortly beyond it; all further seasonal cycles normally tend to be irrelevant, especially when storage costs (including deterioration, obsolescence, and so forth) are significant. This result checks with certain characteristics of observed planning and anticipations horizons noted in the Introduction; e.g., the length of the horizon is a periodic function of time, linked with the seasonal cycle.

We may note, once more, that while the relevant production planning horizon may terminate with the end of the current season, the length of the relevant anticipations horizon may itself depend on certain strategic expectations. Suppose that anticipated requirements for the current season are such that direct costs could be reduced by expanding or improving productive capacity. In order to reach an optimal decision on the appropriateness of such a course of action, it may be necessary to estimate demand and technological conditions over a much longer horizon (although this estimate may require much less detail than would be necessary for planning production). If, on the other hand, current expectations do not warrant any action with respect to changing productive facilities, then the horizon of relevant anticipations may not extend beyond the current season.

These last considerations suggest that the relevant anticipations horizon may tend to grow when economic activity is high and expected to rise. There are, indeed, several other reflections that point in this direction. For instance, when activity is low and there is plenty of excess capacity, it may be feasible and profitable to "live from hand to mouth," producing in each period just enough to meet current demand and arranging procurement along similar lines. When the level of activity is high (relative to capacity), however, there may not be sufficient capacity on hand to meet seasonal peaks out of current production, and it would then become desirable to increase production in some earlier periods to satisfy the demand expected in later periods. Similarly, lengthening delivery periods may require procurement further in advance of actual production. Finally, anticipations of rising costs, which are likely to occur in a period of high and rising activity, may also tend to lengthen the relevant expectation horizon, a conclusion suggested by Example 2 and supported by many other considerations.

Further examples of irrelevance are presented in Section C, in connection with the problem of irrelevant moves and plans. First, however, in Section 5 we attempt to characterize in formal terms certain types of situations in which the conditions for irrelevance are satisfied, i.e., in which the optimum value of the first move is independent of some future constraints or parameters thereof.

II. THE ROLE OF ANTICIPATORY DATA IN ECONOMIC ANALYSIS AND FORECASTING

A. Introduction and Non-Technical Summary

1. General Remarks

a. *Purpose and Nature of the Approach.* In Part I we have developed a model of entrepreneurial decision-making in a changing world, focusing our attention on the role of anticipations and on the nature of decisions and plans.[60] Although this model could profitably be elaborated further in many directions, we have gone far enough to provide the basis for the inquiry which is our concern in Part II. As explained in the Introduction, our purpose in this Part will be to examine the uses of statistical information on anticipatory variables in economics.

It is helpful to draw a distinction between two different ways in which anticipatory data may prove useful, namely, by improving our ability to forecast economic activity and by improving our understanding (or analysis) of economic behavior. We shall refer to these two functions as forecasting and analytical uses, respectively. We propose to explore the issues involved with the view of developing a comprehensive framework to guide in the collection and exploitation of *ex ante* data. Some of the approaches suggested by our inquiry will be illustrated with reference to empirical investigations which have been completed or are still in process, although we shall make no attempt to present a systematic and complete picture of the empirical work which has thus far been carried out in this area.

b. *Conditional and Unconditional Forecasts and the Relation Between Analysis and Forecasting.* An "unconditional forecast" of some variable X is generally considered to be a categorical statement made at some date t concerning the value of the variable X at some point of time T later than t. In contrast, a "conditional forecast" is a statement made at date t about the value of X at time T which is conditional upon, or stated in terms of, the values of some other variables (ob-

[60] As indicated in Section I.C.2, decisions are choices relating to the components of the current move, while plans are choices relating to later moves which are, in principle, always subject to revision or "replanning."

servable at least in principle) at dates preceding or coinciding with T. Thus, from the formal point of view, a conditional forecast states a functional relation between X and some other contemporary or earlier "independent" variables (although the function may be defined only for some stated set of values of the independent variables and may not even be single-valued).[61] Conversely, an asserted functional relation between X and some other simultaneous or preceding variables can always be considered as representing a conditional forecast of X.

For our purposes, it is convenient to modify slightly the above terminology. We shall use the term "economic forecast" to include unconditional forecasts of economic variables as well as forecasts of economic variables which are conditional upon noneconomic variables (e.g., weather, politics, and so forth) or upon policy variables controlled by the government. By a "conditional forecast" we shall usually mean a forecast of economic variables which is conditional upon other economic variables (except for the above-mentioned policy variables).

A conditional forecasting function which is defined for all a priori admissible values of the (economic) "independent variables" will be called a "forecasting equation." Clearly, one can derive an unconditional forecast from a forecasting equation if and only if it is possible to specify the values of all the relevant "independent variables."

Economic forecasting equations may be usefully divided into two classes. Suppose first that every one of the independent variables leads the dependent variable X, in the sense that its date precedes the date of X. Clearly, such forecasting equations can in principle be utilized to make unconditional forecasts up to θ time units ahead, where θ is the minimum lead time of all the independent variables. Such equations can accordingly be labeled "unconditional forecasting equations." If, on the other hand, at least one of the independent variables is contemporaneous with the dependent variable, the equation will be called a "conditional forecasting equation."

A conditional forecasting equation taken in isolation is of relatively little use in forecasting, for it can provide a forecast only if one has available unconditional forecasts of all the relevant non-leading (i.e., simultaneous) independent variables. It is important to note, however, that a *set* of conditional forecasting equations *can* be used to generate unconditional forecasts. This possibility exists whenever the set forms a "closed system," in the sense that the number of such equations equals the number of contemporaneous variables appearing in the equations

[61] E.g., a conditional forecast might take the form: "Barring a war, GNP in 1968 will not exceed $450 billion," or "Consumption in any future year t will be between 93 percent and 95 percent of disposable personal income in the year t."

(and the equations are consistent and independent of each other). The contemporaneous variables appearing in the system are usually referred to as the "jointly dependent variables," and the unconditional forecast generated by this system is represented, of course, by the values of the jointly dependent variables which satisfy simultaneously all the equations.[62] The possibility of using conditional forecasting equations to generate unconditional forecasts, a procedure which is familiar to economists through the general equilibrium approach, will play a central role in much of the following discussion.

The above considerations are helpful in clarifying the relation between economic analysis — or positive economics[63] — and economic forecasting. Broadly speaking, positive economics is concerned with explaining the behavior of economic variables, these explanations generally taking the form of testable hypotheses or laws concerning the relations between economic variables. Such laws clearly represent conditional forecasts; in fact, they generally take the form of (or at least can be cast into the form of) forecasting equations in the sense of our earlier definition, and the major criterion for assessing their validity or acceptability is their success in forecasting.

It does not follow, however, that these laws represent an effective and useful device for economic forecasting. In the first place, they may take the form of conditional forecasting equations, which, as we have already noted, may not per se be particularly useful in making unconditional forecasts. Second, even if these conditional forecasting equations can be imbedded in a closed system, their forecasting usefulness will be limited by the empirical validity of the remaining relations of the system. Finally, even if the remaining relations are sufficiently reliable, or if the law takes the form of an unconditional forecasting equation so that it could be utilized in principle to generate unconditional forecasts, it may in practice still not represent an efficient device for economic forecasting. It is quite conceivable, for instance, that the collection of the information required and/or the computational work involved in utilizing the known relations might be so expensive or so time consuming as to make them useless for the purpose of forecasting, or at least to make them more expensive or less useful than some alternative method.

On the other hand, it may be quite possible to generate satisfactory forecasts on the basis of some observed empirical regularity without

[62] The set of equations must clearly have at least one solution if the individual equations represent an adequate description of the "real world." If more than one solution exists, then the unconditional forecast is not single-valued.

[63] See Milton Friedman, *Essays in Positive Economics* (Chicago: University of Chicago Press, 1953), Part I.

understanding or explaining the reason for this regularity. To give an example from the natural sciences, having observed a systematic regularity between the state of the weather and the height of a certain mercury column at some earlier point of time, it is possible to use the height of the column of mercury to forecast the weather. This is forecasting without understanding or explaining, for we do not assert that the fall in the mercury column is the *cause* of the rain. Presumably underlying the use of such an observed regularity to forecast the weather is a notion that both the rain and the height of the mercury column are simultaneously "caused" by some unknown mechanism. "Explaining" or "understanding" would consist of formulating some testable hypothesis about the nature of this mechanism. Constructing and testing such an hypothesis may increase our confidence in using the observed regularity as a forecasting device and may also indicate the conditions under which the forecasts will be erroneous. However, it is important to note that the observed regularity may be extremely useful in forecasting even if we do not have a satisfactory theory which explains the underlying mechanisms.

An important example in the economics of forecasting without theory is the use of expectations as direct forecasts of the future (see Section C.3). Specifically, this may involve (1) using the reported planned future course of action as a forecast of the agent's future course of action, and (2) using the reported anticipations concerning the future environmental behavior as a forecast of the future behavior of the environment. Both (1) and (2) hypothesize a relation between some variable at a given point of time and an expectation reported at an *earlier* point of time, and thus they represent unconditional forecasting equations. These equations might very well turn out to be empirically valid, and hence provide satisfactory forecasts. But, clearly, these forecasts are forecasts without explanation, for except in very special cases, we do not believe that the agent behaves as he does *because* of his reported plans. Rather, we believe that both the stated plan and the actual later behavior are caused by some common mechanism. This proposition holds with even greater force for the relation between anticipations and the behavior of the environment. The observed regularity does not per se throw any light on the nature of this underlying common mechanism. Nonetheless, as long as our interest is in forecasting rather than in explanation, we would be fully justified in using plans and anticipations as forecasting devices, provided only that they yield good forecasts. In what follows, such forecasts without explanation will be referred to as "non-causal forecasts."

c. *The Homogeneous Decision Period Model and Its Function.* In order to explore systematically the possible analytical and forecasting uses of *ex ante* data, we find it useful to examine first the issues involved in the context of a formal model which we label "the homogeneous decision period model." In this model time is divided into discrete, nonoverlapping periods quite analogous to the "weeks" which Hicks uses as the basis for his dynamic analysis in *Value and Capital*.[64] For this reason we shall frequently refer to our homogeneous periods as "Hicksian weeks." We shall also assume — unless otherwise noted — that entrepreneurial behavior can be described in terms of the modified certainty model of Part I.

In the Hicksian week, there is only a brief time (called "Monday") at the beginning of the period during which anticipations are formed and decisions and plans are made. During the rest of the week the decisions made on Monday are carried out; e.g., goods are sold, production plans are implemented, and so forth. However, no new decisions and plans are made until the following Monday.

> During the time which must elapse between the plan-making dates, the last plan is carried out more or less as laid down, though some power will generally be delegated to subordinates to make minor changes. When the next plan-making date arrives, the whole position is reconsidered in the light of new information, and a plan drawn up. . . . Let us then assume that firms (and private persons) draw up or revise their plans on Mondays in the light of the market situation which is disclosing itself. . .[65]

The homogeneous decision period model will play a useful role in our analysis by allowing us to formulate precise propositions and to derive their implications. To take full advantage of this, the arguments set forth in Sections B and C will be of necessity somewhat technical and formal. We shall provide, however, a non-technical summary of these sections in Section 2. The analysis of Sections B and C will provide the basis for the concluding Section D, in which we shall examine the uses of anticipatory data in the "real world" and review briefly some of the empirical work to date.

2. Non-Technical Summary of Sections B and C

a. *Section B — A Formal Model of the Economy Under the Assumption of Homogeneous Decision Periods.* The purpose of this section will be to examine the role of anticipations and plans in the mechanism which determines the activity of each economic unit, and hence of the economy as a whole, in each successive period. In carrying out this task we shall rely basically on the classical approach of

[64] Hicks, *op. cit.*, pp. 122-24.
[65] *Ibid.*, p. 124.

general equilibrium analysis integrated with the model of decision-making developed in Part I.

At the beginning of any given period, we can visualize each firm as reaching a decision concerning its current move. According to the model of Part I, the chosen move may be thought of as the solution of a constrained maximization problem. Since the over-all relevant constraints on the choice of a course of action can be regarded as determined by the initial conditions of the period and the anticipated relevant behavior of the environment, the same must be true of the chosen move. We shall use the term *decision function* to refer to the relation which determines the chosen current move in terms of the initial conditions and the anticipated environmental behavior.

Our primary interest, however, is to be focused on the move actually made, not on the decided move. These may not coincide, because the chosen move is restricted only by the *anticipated* constraints, which depend upon the *anticipated* environmental behavior, while the actual move must conform to the *actual* constraints, which depend on the *actual* behavior of the environment. Hence, if the anticipations are erroneous, the chosen move may not be feasible in terms of the actual constraints, and in this case the firm generally cannot simultaneously enforce *all* components of its chosen move.

Since we have specified that no replanning occurs within the period, we must assume that if the move is not feasible in its entirety as laid down in the decision, some of its components will be adjusted in a routine fashion to make it consistent with the actual behavior of the environment. Thus, in the final analysis the actual move must depend on — or be a function of — (1) the decided move, (2) the actual behavior of the environment over the current period in relation to (3) the anticipated one and, possibly, (4) some initial conditions. This last factor may have to be taken into account because the nature of the adjustment when the move is not enforceable may depend to some extent on the initial conditions of the period. The relation between the actual move and the four factors listed above we shall call the *enforcement function.* Note that this relation must have the property that the actual move must coincide with the decided move whenever the latter is feasible. This coincidence must hold in particular when the behavior of the environment in the current period coincides with the anticipated one.

In this formulation, the actual move is seen to depend partly on *ex post* variables — initial conditions and the actual behavior of the environment — and partly on *ex ante* variables — the decided move and the anticipated environmental behavior. It is also possible, however, to conceive of the actual move as entirely determined by *ex post* variables. This is because the *ex ante* variables may be regarded as "intervening variables" which can themselves be expressed in terms of *ex post* variables. Consider first the anticipations. Provided we conceive of initial conditions in a broad enough way to include past history, it would seem that we can think of anticipations as being entirely generated by initial conditions, although the mechanism of generation may, of course, be a very complex one. Similar considerations apply to the other *ex ante* variable, the decided move. Let us recall, in fact, that the decided move can be regarded as depending on initial conditions and anticipations which, as we have just argued, depend themselves on initial conditions.

If we eliminate the intervening *ex ante* variables from the enforcement function, we obtain a relation which expresses the actual move — an *ex post* variable — entirely in terms of other *ex post* variables, namely, initial conditions and the actual behavior of the environment in the period. This relation, which we shall call hereafter the *general behavior function,* corresponds to the type of formulation customarily used in economic analysis, at least at an empirical level.

If now in the general behavior function we replace the initial conditions by their actual value at the beginning of a given period, say the *t*th period, the results express the activity of the firm in that period as a *dated* function of only the relevant environmental behavior in the period. We call this function the *specific behavior function for the* tth *period.* This specific behavior function may be thought of as a schedule expressing the response of the agent to the behavior of the environment in period t. We say it is dated because the form of this schedule will, in principle, change from period to period depending on the actual initial conditions of the period.

We are now ready to look at the behavior of the economy as a whole in any one period as resulting from the interaction of all the economic units. Let us first note that although we have hitherto generally been focusing our attention on firms when discussing the role of anticipations and plans in this monograph, nothing that we have said is specific to firms as such instead of to economic units in general. Therefore, the word "firm" can be regarded as a convenient abbreviation for the expression, "decision-making unit in the economy."

For each unit there is a specific behavior function expressing its activity in the period in terms of environmental behavior. For a particular unit, the relevant environmental behavior may be regarded as consisting of (or resulting from) two components: (a) the activities of the other economic units in the system, which activities we are trying also to forecast, and (b) all other relevant environmental behavior. We shall call the activities of the other economic units in the system the *endogenous environmental behavior,* and all other relevant environmental behavior we shall call the *exogenous environmental behavior.* The set of specific behavior functions represents a system of simultaneous equations in which the left-hand sides contain only variables relating to a single unit, while the right-hand sides contain variables relating to other units (the endogenous environmental behavior) and the exogenous environmental behavior. The simultaneous solution of this system (for the given value of the exogenous environmental behavior) determines the t*th* period activity of each unit.

The argument just presented can be extended sequentially to later periods. For, clearly, the initial conditions at the beginning of the t*th* period, the activities of each unit during the t*th* period, and the exogenous environmental behavior during the t*th* period together determine the initial conditions at the beginning of the (t + 1)*th* period. When these initial conditions are inserted in the general behavior function for each unit we obtain a new system of simultaneous specific behavior functions for period t + 1, whose solution determines the activity of that period. Similar considerations apply to all later periods.

The mechanism we have discussed and its relation to the various functions we have introduced is illustrated by a simple example based on the kind of economy which is implied in the well-known inventory cycle models of Metzler.

b. *Section C — Implications of the Model Concerning Forecasting and Analytical Uses of* Ex Ante *Data.* Supposing that the functioning of the economy could be adequately described by the model of Section B, what can we infer about possible forecasting and analytical uses of *ex ante* data? This is the question that Section C is designed to answer.

It follows from the analysis of Section B that in principle one could forecast the future course of economic activity by first estimating for each period all of the specific behavior functions for each economic unit, and then solving this just-determined system of simultaneous relations. The question under consideration might therefore be rephrased more specifically as follows: In what ways and to what extent can the availability of information on anticipations and plans be of help in securing estimates of the specific behavior equations entering the system?

In order to gain a proper perspective, let us suppose, for a moment, that we possessed accurate and reliable knowledge of all the decision, anticipations, and enforcement functions, and hence, by implication, of the general behavior functions. Under these conditions would knowledge of anticipatory data be of any significant value? Clearly such data would not be required for forecasting since, from knowledge of the general behavior functions, we could, at least in principle, secure short-term forecasts and build up sequentially long-run forecasts, limited only by the possibility of adequate prediction of the exogenous environmental behavior. And if we were interested in such data per se, we could "compute" them from our assumed knowledge of the appropriate functions.

The above considerations serve to highlight the point that the usefulness of information on *ex ante* variables largely reflects and stems from the inadequate knowledge we have, at least at present, of the causal mechanisms underlying the general behavior functions. This conclusion, however, needs to be modified in one respect. It must be recognized that even if we had all the required knowledge, *ex ante* data might still provide a useful computational short cut. First, even if we know the anticipations and decision functions, at least for short-term forecasting it might be cheaper and faster to determine decisions and anticipations through surveys rather than to compute them from the known functions, especially since in order to compute them we might require all sorts of information on initial conditions that might be of very little interest per se. The survey approach is tantamount to using the respondents as computing machines providing us with the values that these functions actually assume at the given point of time. (The survey method could, of course, be useful only as far as relevant anticipations and plans extend.) The information could then be inserted directly in the enforcement function to secure specific behavior functions for the forthcoming period, as is shown in more detail later in this section. Second, causal forecasting might be computationally so expensive or so time consuming that it might be more practical to rely on some of the non-causal or semi-causal forecasting procedures, based on anticipatory data, to be discussed presently.

In reality, of course, we have a very inadequate knowledge of the basic functions or of the general behavior function, at least with respect to many important variables. We shall proceed, therefore, to examine the implications of our model concerning the forecasting and analytical uses of *ex ante* data under these conditions.

An important part of a firm's anticipations of the relevant future environmental behavior refer to other economic units in the system. Hence these anticipations might be used as direct forecasts of the behavior of certain variables in the system. Similarly, as we have suggested in Section I.C.2, a plan may be regarded as the best judgment that the decision-maker can formulate at the planning date as to the future value of a move or a component of a move. We may therefore use the plan as a direct forecast of the future value of a planned component. As has been pointed out earlier, such forecasts are of the non-causal type. But insofar as our goal is forecasting, this fact is of no particular concern, the only relevant test being whether the method "works." In some cases it may be found that a forecast based on anticipatory data can be improved by some adjustment of the data. If, for instance, anticipations or plans appeared to generate systematically biased forecasts, even though we had no causal explanation for the bias, we could improve the accuracy of the forecast by basing it on some empirically established function of the *ex ante* data. It should be noted, however, that the direct forecasting value of anticipatory data must be judged in relation to the performance of alternative available methods of estimating specific behavior functions, performance being gauged both in terms of comparative costs and relative accuracy.

Insofar as non-causal methods "work," they can be used to secure unconditional forecasts of the corresponding *ex post* data. Furthermore, these unconditional forecasts could also be used in place of the corresponding specific behavior functions in the system of simultaneous relations determining the value of the variables in each period.

Another way of exploiting *ex ante* data for forecasting which, in our view, is more promising consists in the simultaneous use of anticipations and/or plans with *ex post* data in what we may call the *semi-causal* approach to the estimation of specific behavior functions. We have seen in Section B that the specific behavior function for a given period is the function obtained from the general behavior function by replacing the initial conditions with their actual values at the beginning of the period. A strictly causal derivation of specific behavior functions requires, therefore, a knowledge of the corresponding general behavior functions. The semi-causal approach is in essence a device for securing specific behavior functions without prior knowledge of the general behavior functions. We refer to it as "semi-causal" because it relies partly on the causal mechanism laid out in Section B and partly on the use of information on *ex ante* data to make up for our inadequate knowledge of other parts of the mechanism. This approach will be illustrated with special reference to what we shall call the *realization function* method, which is based on the simultaneous use of information on decisions or plans *and* on the anticipations on which the plans are based.

The following summary of the realization function approach is meant to be suggestive rather than rigorous, for it glosses over many fine points and blurs some important distinctions. Unfortunately, a rigorous development of the argument without the use of mathematical symbols would be both too lengthy and too opaque to find a place in this non-technical summary of Section C. Therefore, the reader interested in the precise formulation must be referred to Section C.4.

Suppose that we know both the decisions for the current period and the plans for the further future. The non-causal approach already discussed would consist of using these decisions and plans as direct forecasts of the corresponding actual moves. The analysis of Section B indicates that this forecast could be expected to prove entirely correct only if the actual behavior of the environment during the coming period agrees in fact with the anticipated behavior, for it is only under these conditions that the actual move will necessarily coincide with the decision. Furthermore, the analysis of Section I.C.2 indicates that plans are not enforced decisions about future moves but, rather, the best forecasts that can currently be made by the firm as to the moves that should later be carried out if, in the interim, no changes are perceived in the constrained maximization problem the firm is facing. In particular, the absence of perceived changes implies that from the date when the plan was made until the date when the move was implemented, no significant discrepancies have occurred between the initially anticipated behavior of the environment and both the actual behavior and the anticipations for the relevant further future behavior. It appears, therefore, that plans should tend to provide accurate forecasts of actual actions when the anticipations underlying the plan are not disappointed. But when these anticipations turn out to be erroneous, we would expect to find differences emerging between the initially planned and the actual course of action — i.e., discrepancies between plans and the realization thereof. The relation between this divergence on the one hand and the error of anticipations or forecasts on the other, we have labeled the *realization function.*

It should be noted that the error of forecast need not be the only factor accounting for the discrepancy, i.e., the only argument of the realization function. The extent to which errors of anticipations will cause deviations from the planned course of action may well depend on some initial conditions of the period and on initially held anticipations, especially anticipations pertaining to the further future. In brief, the same type of considerations apply here as were presented in connection with the enforcement function; as a matter of fact, the realization function is closely related to the enforcement function. The exact nature of this relation need not detain us here, but is exhibited explicitly, both analytically and graphically, in Section C.4.

Let us now suppose that we have a reliable estimate of the realization functions. It can then readily be shown that this estimate, together with appropriate information on decisions or plans and underlying anticipations, could be used to derive specific behavior functions of the type needed in the simultaneous equations approach to forecasting. To see this point, let us recall first that the specific behavior function can be regarded as a schedule expressing the actual course of the agent in a period in response to the behavior of the environment in the same period. The realization function, on the other hand, can be looked on as a relation between the actual course of action, the planned course, the anticipated and actual behavior of the environment, and, possibly, certain initial conditions. If this relation is known, and if we assign to plans and anticipations their known values, and do the same with the initial conditions, we are left with a known relation or schedule between the actual course of action and the actual behavior of the environment. Such a relation is precisely the specific behavior function we are seeking.

It appears, therefore, that knowledge of the realization functions, together with information on anticipations and plans, enables us to derive specific behavior functions of the type required in the simultaneous equations approach even though we lack adequate knowledge of the general behavior functions. To be sure, this method of deriving the specific behavior function still requires a usable estimate of the realization function. The important point, however, is that the realization function should be far easier to approximate than the general behavior function.

First, there are cogent reasons to suppose that the general realization function actually depends upon fewer variables than does the general behavior function. A great many components of the initial conditions may appear as arguments of the general behavior function because they affect the formation of decisions or anticipations and yet have no influence on the extent to which decisions, once made, are realized. Hence, while actual behavior may be very significantly shaped by some of the initial conditions, these components may have no bearing on the extent to which plans fail to be realized as a result of disappointments of expectations. Such components of the initial conditions would not appear as arguments of the general realization function, for their effects are already taken into account by the decisions and anticipations.

Second, the functional form of the general realization function should be considerably simpler than that of the general behavior function. The general realization function has to reflect only the effects of errors in anticipations on the extent to which decisions are implemented. In contrast, the general behavior function must account not only for those aspects of the firm's behavior already encompassed in the general realization function but also for the role of initial conditions on the *formation* of decisions and anticipations.

In summary, the availability of simultaneous information on plans and underlying anticipations and its systematic exploitation through the realization function model might simplify considerably the task of deriving specific behavior functions of the type required in the simultaneous equations approach to forecasting. It would enable us to bypass the problem of estimating general behavior functions, replacing it with the presumably much easier task of estimating realization functions, that is, determining the extent to which errors of anticipations cause the actual course of action to deviate from decisions and plans.

It may be useful at this point to illustrate both non-causal and semi-causal forecasting uses of anticipatory data in terms of a very simple two-sector Keynesian-type model. Let $Y(t)$ = income, $C(t)$ = consumption, $I(t)$ = investment, all in period t. We then have the following definitional relation:

$$Y(t) = C(t) + I(t). \tag{A1}$$

Let us suppose next that the behavior of consumers can be described by the "consumption function" as:

$$C(t) = C[Y(t)]; \tag{A2}$$

for the sake of illustration, we assume that this "specific behavior function" for the consumers' sector can be adequately estimated at the beginning of period t from a general behavior function, without recourse to anticipatory data.

We now have two equations in three unknowns. To close the system, we need an investment function, i.e., a specific behavior function for investment. Let us suppose that this function cannot be usefully derived from a general behavior function because our knowledge of this function is entirely inadequate. One possible way of proceeding would then be to secure information on investment plans and to use this information as a direct non-causal forecast of investment. Denoting by $I_{t-1}(t)$ the investment expenditure for period t planned at the beginning of the period, we would then have:

$$I(t) = I_{t-1}(t). \tag{A3a}$$

Equation (A3a) represents an unconditional forecast of investment;

but, it can also be regarded as a "specific behavior function" for investment in period t and used in conjunction with equations (A1) and (A2) to close the system and thus to derive also a forecast for the remaining variables C(t) and Y(t).

The alternative semi-causal approach would involve instead securing also information on the anticipations underlying the investment plans and using this information to derive a specific behavior function for investment from an investment realization function. To keep the illustration as simple as possible, we shall suppose that the deviation of investment from initial plans depends only on the difference between anticipated and actual income and is proportional to this difference, so that the realization function takes the simple form

$$\text{(A4)} \qquad I(t) - I_{t-1}(t) = k[Y(t) - Y_{t-1}(t)],$$

where k is a known constant.[66] From equation (A4), making use of information on aggregate planned investment, $I_{t-1}(t)$, and aggregate anticipated value added, $Y_{t-1}(t)$, secured at the beginning of the period, we derive immediately the specific behavior function for investment in period t:

$$\text{(A3b)} \qquad I(t) = I_{t-1}(t) + k[Y(t) - Y_{t-1}(t)].$$

Equation (A3b), unlike (A3a), does not, per se, yield a direct forecast of investments, because the right-hand side involves the "simultaneous" and hence unknown variable Y(t). However, by adjoining (A3b) to equations (A1) and (A2), we have a determinate system which can be solved for the unknowns, including I(t). The value of I(t) so determined will be different from the planned value $I_{t-1}(t)$ except in the limiting case where the income generated by the investment plans happens to coincide with the expectation $Y_{t-1}(t)$.

The realization function approach as set out in the previous paragraphs can be directly exploited only if we have adequate information covering both decisions and plans and the underlying anticipations. However, we can readily see, on the basis of the model of Section B, how this approach can be modified if we have available only partial information on *ex ante* variables. Thus, if we have only information on decisions and plans, we can use this information as a substitute for knowledge of the decision function. To derive a specific behavior function we shall generally need, in addition to the enforcement func-

[66] One may think of this equation as being obtained by aggregating over all firms, assuming that for each firm the deviation from plans is proportional to the difference between anticipated and realized "net value added." Since the sum of the net value added is precisely income, if the proportionality factor is (roughly) the same, the aggregation will yield equation (A4).

tion, some information on the underlying anticipations. This information must now be derived (explicitly or implicitly) from an estimate of the anticipations function and the initial conditions (unless it can be inferred from knowledge of plans). Similarly, if we have only knowledge of relevant anticipations, we can use this information in place of the anticipations function while the missing information on decisions and plans would have to be derived (explicitly or implicitly) from an estimate of the decision function and from relevant initial conditions. Note that in these approaches, anticipations are used as a building block in forecasting the agent's course of action, not as a direct forecast of the behavior of the environment to which the anticipations refer. More generally, the uses of anticipatory data thus sketched out also come under the heading of semi-causal forecasting; the *ex ante* data are used as non-causal proxies for part of the causal mechanism underlying the specific behavior function.

Aside from the forecasting uses that we have been reviewing, anticipatory data also have important potential uses for analytical purposes — that is, for improving our understanding of the causal mechanisms underlying the courses of action adopted by economic agents. The implications of the model of Section B in this respect should be readily apparent and require little comment.

We have already seen how anticipatory variables can be used in the study of the enforcement function, one of the causal mechanisms specified in the model. The availability of information on the actual course of anticipations might also be expected to prove helpful — if not essential — in the study of the anticipations function, that is, in the study of how anticipations for the future are related to initial conditions and previous history. Similarly, information on anticipations, together with information on the associated decisions and plans, can be exploited in the study of the decision function.

There are several reasons why it may be useful to analyze separately the various links in the process that relates certain *ex post* variables — initial conditions and environmental behavior — to the course of action finally adopted by the agent, a process which is subsumed in the general behavior function. First, this may facilitate appreciably the task of developing adequate general behavior functions, by enabling us to study separately various parts of the complex mechanism underlying this function. If we are able to work through the structural relations of the model, we can derive from them the general behavior functions as reduced form relations. But even when we are able directly to estimate reliable general behavior functions without specifying and studying separately the various intervening mechanisms, the understanding of these links, if achievable, would clearly provide a deep and valuable insight into the causal structure underlying the general behavior function.

BIBLIOGRAPHY

This Bibliography is, with only a few exceptions, restricted to those publications and oral papers actually cited in this monograph. The numbers in square brackets following an item indicate the pages in this monograph where references to that item are made. An asterisk preceding an item indicates that it is a direct outgrowth of the Project on Business Expectations and Planning.

"An Appraisal of Data and Research on Businessmen's Expectations about Outlook and Operating Variables," *Report of the Consultant Committee on General Business Expectations.* Board of Governors of the Federal Reserve System, September, 1955. [138, 140, 146]

ANDERSON, O., JR., BAUER, R. K., and FELS, E. "On the Accuracy of Short-Term Entrepreneurial Expectations," *Proceedings of the Business and Economic Statistics Section,* 114th Annual Meeting of the American Statistical Association, Montreal, Canada, September, 1954, pp. 124-50. [145]

———, BAUER, R. K., FUHRER, H., PETERSEN, J. P., and WOLFSTEINER, M. "Short-Term Entrepreneurial Reaction Patterns." Paper presented to the Econometric Society, Kiel, Germany, September, 1955 (abstract and discussion in *Econometrica,* Vol. 24 [1956], pp. 313-17). [145, 150]

———, FURST, H., and SCHULTE, W. "Zur Analyse der unternehmerischen Reaktionsweise," *Ifo-Studien,* Heft 2, 1956. [150]

ANTOSIEWICZ, H., and HOFFMAN, A. J. "A Remark on the Smoothing Problem," *Management Science,* Vol. 1 (1954), pp. 92-95. [40]

ARROW, KENNETH J., KARLIN, SAMUEL, and SCRAF, HERBERT. *Studies in the Mathematical Theory of Inventory and Production.* Stanford, California: Stanford University Press, 1958. [40]

BALDERSTON, F. E. *See* Modigliani, Franco.

BASSIE, V LEWIS. *Economic Forecasting.* New York: McGraw-Hill Book Company, 1958. [137]

———. "Recent Developments in Short-Term Forecasting," *Short-Term Economic Forecasting,* Studies in Income and Wealth, Vol. 17. National Bureau of Economic Research. Princeton, New Jersey: Princeton University Press, 1955, pp. 7-52. [137]

BAUER, R. K. *See* Anderson, O., Jr.

BELLMAN, RICHARD. "Dynamic Programming and the Smoothing Problem," *Management Science,* Vol. 3 (1956), pp. 111-13. [40]

*Bossons, John, and Modigliani, Franco. "The Source of Regressiveness in Surveys of Businessmen's Short-Run Expectations," *The Quality and Economic Significance of Anticipations Data.* Universities–National Bureau Committee for Economic Research. Princeton, New Jersey: Princeton University Press, 1960, pp. 239-62. [146, 151]

Bratt, Elmer Clark. *Business Cycles and Forecasting.* 4th Edition; Homewood, Illinois: Richard D. Irwin, Inc., 1953. [137]

Bronfenbrenner, Jean. *See* Friend, Irwin.

Business Forecasting in Japan. Business Forecasting Study Team, Japan Productivity Center and International Cooperation Administration, April, 1959. [140]

Charnes, A., and Cooper, W. W. "Optimization in New Item Production," *Minutes of the Third Annual Logistics Conference.* Washington, D. C.: Office of Naval Research, May, 1952. [40]

——————, Cooper, W. W., and Mellon, B. "A Model for Optimizing Production by Reference to Cost Surrogates," *Econometrica,* Vol. 23 (1955), pp. 307-23. [40]

Cohen, Kalman J. *See* Modigliani, Franco.

Cohen, Morris. "The National Industrial Conference Board Survey of Capital Appropriations," *The Quality and Economic Significance of Anticipations Data.* Universities–National Bureau Committee for Economic Research. Princeton, New Jersey: Princeton University Press, 1960, pp. 299-324. [138, 144]

"Consumer Survey Statistics," *Report of the Consultant Committee on Consumer Survey Statistics.* Board of Governors of the Federal Reserve System, July, 1955. [138]

Cooper, W. W. *See* Charnes, A.

Daly, Donald J. "Seasonal Variations and Business Expectations," *The Journal of Business,* Vol. 32 (1959), pp. 258-71. [152]

Dantzig, G., and Johnson, S. "A Production Smoothing Problem," *Proceedings of the Second Symposium on Linear Programming,* Vol. 1. Washington, D. C.: National Bureau of Standards, U. S. Department of Commerce, 1955, pp. 151-76. [40]

Darcovich, William. "Evaluation of Some Naive Expectation Models for Agricultural Yields and Prices," *Expectations, Uncertainty, and Business Behavior,* Mary Jean Bowman, ed. New York: Social Science Research Council, 1958, pp. 199-202. [152]

Di Cani, John. "Anticipatory Investment Information as an Exogenous Variable." Paper presented to the Econometric Society, Cambridge, Massachusetts, August, 1958 (reported by title in *Econometrica,* Vol. 27 [1959], p. 280). [150]

Dvoretzky, A., Kiefer, J., and Wolfowitz, J. "The Inventory Problem: I. Case of Known Distributions of Demand; II. Case of Unknown Distributions of Demand," *Econometrica,* Vol. 20 (1952), pp. 187-222 and pp. 450-66. [63]

*Eisner, Robert. "A Distributed Lag Investment Function," *Econometrica,* Vol. 28 (1960), pp. 1-29.

*EISNER, ROBERT. *Determinants of Capital Expenditures — An Interview Study,* Studies in Business Expectations and Planning, Number 2. Urbana: University of Illinois, Bureau of Economic and Business Research, 1956. [10, 151]

*————. "Expectations, Plans, and Capital Expenditures: A Synthesis of Ex Post and Ex Ante Data," *Expectations, Uncertainty, and Business Behavior,* Mary Jean Bowman, ed. New York: Social Science Research Council, 1958, pp. 165-88. [144, 146, 147, 149, 151]

*————. "Interview and Other Survey Techniques and the Study of Investment," *Problems of Capital Formation,* Studies in Income and Wealth, Vol. 19. National Bureau of Economic Research. Princeton, New Jersey: Princeton University Press, 1957, pp. 513-601. [10, 151]

FELS, E. *See* Anderson, O., Jr.

*FERBER, ROBERT. *Employers' Forecasts of Manpower Requirements: A Case Study,* Studies in Business Expectations and Planning, Number 3. Urbana: University of Illinois, Bureau of Economic and Business Research, 1958. [143, 145, 151]

*————. "Measuring the Accuracy and Structure of Businessmen's Expectations," *Journal of the American Statistical Association,* Vol. 48 (1953), pp. 385-413.

————. "On the Stability of Consumer Expectations," *Review of Economics and Statistics,* Vol. 37 (1955), pp. 256-66. [151]

*————. "The Accuracy and Structure of Industry Expectations in Relation to Those of Individual Firms," *Journal of the American Statistical Association,* Vol. 53 (1958), pp. 317-36.

*————. *The Railroad Shippers' Forecasts,* Studies in Business Expectations and Planning, Urbana: University of Illinois, Bureau of Economic and Business Research, 1953. [146, 151]

*————. "The Railroad Shippers' Forecasts and the Illinois Employers' Labor Force Anticipations: A Study in Comparative Experience," *The Quality and Economic Significance of Anticipations Data.* Universities–National Bureau Committee for Economic Research. Princeton, New Jersey: Princeton University Press, 1960, pp. 181-203. [145, 151]

FESTINGER, LEON, and KATZ, DANIEL. *Research Methods in the Behavioral Sciences.* New York: The Dryden Press, 1953. [141]

FIRESTONE, O. J. "Investment Forecasting in Canada," *Short-Term Economic Forecasting,* Studies in Income and Wealth, Vol. 17. National Bureau of Economic Research. Princeton, New Jersey: Princeton University Press, 1955, pp. 113-260. [140, 144]

FOSS, MURRAY F., and NATRELLA, VITO. "Investment Plans and Realization," *Survey of Current Business,* Vol. 37, No. 6 (June, 1957), pp. 12-18. [149]

————. "Ten Years' Experience with Business Investment Anticipations," *Survey of Current Business,* Vol. 37, No. 1 (January, 1957), pp. 16-24. [144]

————. "The Structure and Realization of Business Investment Anticipations," *The Quality and Economic Significance of Anticipations Data.* Universities–National Bureau Committee for Economic Research. Princeton, New Jersey: Princeton University Press, 1960, pp. 387-405. [145, 149]

FRIEDMAN, MILTON. *Essays in Positive Economics.* Chicago: University of Chicago Press, 1953. [83]

FRIEND, IRWIN. "Critical Evaluation of Surveys of Expectations, Plans and Investment Behavior," *Expectations, Uncertainty, and Business Behavior,* Mary Jean Bowman, ed. New York: Social Science Research Council, 1958, pp. 189-98. [144]

*———— and BRONFENBRENNER, JEAN. "Business Investment Programs and Their Realization," *Survey of Current Business,* Vol. 30, No. 12 (December, 1950), pp. 11-22. [144, 150]

*————. "Plant and Equipment Programs and Their Realization," *Short-Term Economic Forecasting,* Studies in Income and Wealth, Vol. 17. National Bureau of Economic Research. Princeton, New Jersey: Princeton University Press, 1955, pp. 53-111. [144, 149]

FUHRER, H. *See* Anderson, O., Jr.

FURST, H. *See* Anderson, O., Jr.

GOLDBERGER, A. S. *See* Klein, L. R.

GORDON, ROBERT AARON. *Business Fluctuations.* New York: Harper and Brothers Publishers, 1952. [137]

GREENWALD, DOUGLAS. *See* Keezer, Dexter M.

*GRUNBERG, EMILE, and MODIGLIANI, FRANCO. "The Predictability of Social Events," *The Journal of Political Economy,* Vol. 62 (1954), pp. 465-78. [108]

HART, ALBERT G. *Anticipations, Uncertainty, and Dynamic Planning.* Chicago: The University of Chicago Press, 1940. [9]

————. "Quantitative Evidence for the Interwar Period on the Course of Business Expectations: A Revaluation of the Railroad Shippers' Forecast," *The Quality and Economic Significance of Anticipations Data.* Universities–National Bureau Committee for Economic Research. Princeton, New Jersey: Princeton University Press, 1960, pp. 205-38. [146, 152]

————. "Risk, Uncertainty, and the Unprofitability of Compounding Probabilities," *Studies in Mathematical Economics and Econometrics — In Memory of Henry Schultz,* O. Lange, F. McIntyre, and T. Yntema, eds. Chicago: The University of Chicago Press, 1942. [71]

HARTLE, DOUGLAS. "Predictions Derived from the Employment Forecast Survey," *The Canadian Journal of Economics and Political Science,* Vol. 24 (1958), pp. 373-90. [140, 144, 145]

HASTAY, MILLARD. "The Dun and Bradstreet Surveys of Businessmen's Expectations." *Proceedings of the Business and Economic Statistics Section,* 114th Annual Meeting of the American Statistical Association, Montreal, Canada, September, 1954, pp. 93-123. [146]

————. "The Formation of Business Expectations About Operating Variables." *The Quality and Economic Significance of Anticipations Data,* Universities–National Bureau Committee for Economic Research. Princeton, New Jersey: Princeton University Press, 1960, pp. 91-148. [152]

HICKS, J. R. *Value and Capital.* 2nd Edition; London: Oxford University Press, 1946. [15, 16, 18, 33, 85, 98]

HOFFMAN, A. J., and JACOBS, WALTER. "Smooth Patterns of Production," *Management Science,* Vol. I (1954), pp. 86-91. [40]

————. *See also* Antosiewicz, H.

HOHN, FRANZ E. *See* Modigliani, Franco.

HOLT, CHARLES C. "Forecasting Requirements from the Business Standpoint," *The Quality and Economic Significance of Anticipations Data.* Universities–National Bureau Committee for Economic Research. Princeton, New Jersey: Princeton University Press, 1960, pp. 9-27. [67]

————, MODIGLIANI, FRANCO, and MUTH, JOHN F. "Derivation of a Linear Decision Rule for Production and Employment Scheduling," *Management Science,* Vol. 2 (1956), pp. 159-77. Reprinted in Edward H. Bowman and Robert B. Fetter, eds., *Analyses of Industrial Operations,* Homewood, Illinois: Richard D. Irwin, Inc., 1959, pp. 200-18. [57, 58, 60]

————, MODIGLIANI, FRANCO, and SIMON, HERBERT A. "A Linear Decision Rule for Production and Employment Scheduling," *Management Science,* Vol. 2 (1955), pp. 1-30. Reprinted in Edward H. Bowman and Robert B. Fetter, eds., *Analyses of Industrial Operations,* Homewood, Illinois: Richard D. Irwin, Inc., 1959, pp. 169-99. [57]

HULTGREN, THOR. "Forecasts of Railway Traffic," *Short-Term Economic Forecasting,* Studies in Income and Wealth, Vol. 17. National Bureau of Economic Research. Princeton, New Jersey: Princeton University Press, 1955, pp. 363-80. [146]

JACOBS, WALTER. *See* Hoffman, A. J.

JOHNSON, S. M. "Sequential Production Planning Over Time at Minimum Cost," *Management Science,* Vol. 3 (1957), pp. 435-37. [40]

————. *See* Dantzig, G.

JUSTER, F. THOMAS. *Consumer Expectations, Plans, and Purchases: A Progress Report.* Occasional Paper 70. New York: National Bureau of Economic Research, Inc., 1959. [139, 140, 145, 152]

————. "The Predictive Value of Consumers Union Spending Intentions Data," *The Quality and Economic Significance of Anticipations Data.* Universities–National Bureau Committee for Economic Research. Princeton, New Jersey: Princeton University Press, 1960, pp. 263-97. [139]

KARLIN, SAMUEL. *See* Arrow, Kenneth J.

KARUSH, WILLIAM. "On a Class of Minimum-Cost Problems," *Management Science,* Vol. 4 (1958), pp. 136-53. [40]

KATONA, GEORGE. "Business Expectations in the Framework of Psychological Economics (Towards a Theory of Expectations)," *Expectations, Uncertainty, and Business Behavior,* Mary Jean Bowman, ed. New York: Social Science Research Council, 1958, pp. 59-73. [151]

———. "Changes in Consumer Expectations and Their Origin," *The Quality and Economic Significance of Anticipations Data.* Universities–National Bureau Committee for Economic Research. Princeton, New Jersey: Princeton University Press, 1960, pp. 53-89. [152]

———. "Federal Reserve Board Committee Reports on Consumer Expectations and Saving Statistics," *The Review of Economics and Statistics,* Vol. 39 (1957), pp. 40-45.

——— and MUELLER, EVA L. *Consumer Expectations.* Ann Arbor, Michigan: Survey Research Center, 1953. [151]

KATZ, DANIEL. *See* Festinger, Leon.

KEEZER, DEXTER M., ULIN, ROBERT P., GREENWALD, DOUGLAS, and MATULIS, MARGARET. "Observations on the Predictive Quality of McGraw-Hill Surveys of Business Plans for New Plants and Equipment," *The Quality and Economic Significance of Anticipations Data.* Universities–National Bureau Committee for Economic Research. Princeton, New Jersey: Princeton University Press, 1960, pp. 369-86. [145]

KIEFER, J. *See* Dvoretzky, A.

*KISSELGOFF, AVRAM, and MODIGLIANI, FRANCO. "Private Investment in the Electric Power Industry and the Acceleration Principle," *The Review of Economics and Statistics,* Vol. 39 (1957), pp. 363-79.

KLEIN, LAWRENCE R. "Applications of Survey Methods and Data to the Analysis of Economic Fluctuations," *Contributions of Survey Methods to Economics,* Lawrence R. Klein, ed. New York: Columbia University Press, 1954, pp. 241-60. [150]

———. *Economic Fluctuations in the United States, 1921-1941.* Cowles Commission Monograph, No. 11. New York: John Wiley and Sons, Inc.; and London: Chapman and Hall, Ltd., 1950. [136]

——— and GOLDBERGER, A. S. *An Econometric Model of the United States, 1929-1952.* Amsterdam: North-Holland Publishing Company, 1955. [136]

——— and LANSING, J. B. "Decisions to Purchase Consumer Durable Goods," *Journal of Marketing,* Vol. 20 (1955), pp. 109-32. [145, 147, 150]

LANGE, O. *Price Flexibility and Employment,* Cowles Commission Monograph No. 8. Bloomington, Indiana: Principia Press, 1944. [16]

LANSING, J. B., and WITHEY, S. B. "Consumer Anticipations: Their Use in Forecasting Consumer Behavior." *Short-Term Economic Forecasting,* Studies in Income and Wealth, Vol. 17. National Bureau of Economic Research. Princeton, New Jersey: Princeton University Press, 1955, pp. 381-453. [145, 147, 150]

———. *See also* Klein, L. R.

LEVINE, ROBERT A. "Capital Expenditures Forecasts by Individual Firms," *The Quality and Economic Significance of Anticipations Data.* Universities–National Bureau Committee for Economic Research. Princeton, New Jersey: Princeton University Press, 1960, pp. 351-68. [144]

LEVINE, ROBERT A. "Plant and Equipment Expenditures Surveys: Intentions and Fulfillment." Cowles Foundation Discussion Paper No. 17, October, 1956. [144]

MANNE, ALAN S. "A Note on the Modigliani-Hohn Production Smoothing Model," *Management Science,* Vol. 3 (1957), pp. 371-79. [40]

MARCH, JAMES G., and SIMON, HERBERT A. *Organizations.* New York: John Wiley and Sons, Inc.; and London: Chapman and Hall, Ltd., 1958. [55]

MARSCHAK, J. "Economic Measurements for Policy and Prediction," *Studies in Econometric Method,* W. Hood and T. Koopmans, eds. Cowles Commission Monograph No. 14. New York: John Wiley and Sons, Inc.; and London: Chapman and Hall, Ltd., 1953, Ch. 1. [129]

———. "Probability in the Social Sciences," *Mathematical Thinking in the Social Sciences,* Paul F. Lazersfeld, ed. Glencoe, Illinois: The Free Press, 1954. pp. 166-215. [68]

———. "Towards an Economic Theory of Organization and Information," *Decision Processes,* R. M. Thrall, C. H. Coombs, and R. L. Davis, eds. New York: John Wiley and Sons, Inc.; and London: Chapman and Hall, Ltd., 1954, pp. 187-220. [69, 72, 73, 77]

MATULIS, MARGARET. *See* Keezer, Dexter M.

MELLON, B. *See* Charnes, A.

METZLER, LLOYD. "Business Cycles and the Modern Theory of Employment," *American Economic Review,* Vol. 36 (1946), pp. 278-91. [104]

———. "Factors Governing the Length of Inventory Cycles," *Review of Economic Statistics,* Vol. 29 (1947), pp. 1-5. [104]

———. "The Nature and Stability of Inventory Cycles," *Review of Economic Statistics,* Vol. 23 (1941), pp. 113-30. [104]

MODIGLIANI, FRANCO. "An Alternative Method for Inverting the Matrix Arising from a Quadratic Decision Criterion," *ONR Research Memorandum No. 22,* Pittsburgh: Carnegie Institute of Technology, Graduate School of Industrial Administration, August, 1954. [58]

*———. "The Measurement of Expectations." Abstract in *Econometrica,* Vol. 20 (1952), pp. 481-83.

*——— and BALDERSTON, F. E. "Economic Analysis and Forecasting: Recent Developments in the Use of Panel and Other Survey Techniques," *American Voting Behavior,* Eugene Burdick and Arthur J. Brodbeck, eds. Glencoe, Illinois: The Free Press, 1959, pp. 372-98.

*——— and COHEN, KALMAN J. "The Significance and Uses of Ex Ante Data," *Expectations, Uncertainty, and Business Behavior,* Mary Jean Bowman, ed. New York: Social Science Research Council, 1958, pp. 151-64. [9]

*——— and HOHN, FRANZ E. "Production Planning Over Time and the Nature of the Expectation and Planning Horizon," *Econometrica,* Vol. 23 (1955), pp. 46-66. [40]

*———— and SAUERLENDER, OWEN, H. "Economic Expectations and Plans of Firms in Relation to Short-Term Forecasting," *Short-Term Economic Forecasting,* Studies in Income and Wealth, Vol. 17. National Bureau of Economic Research. Princeton, New Jersey: Princeton University Press, 1955, pp. 261-361. [143, 146, 150, 151]

*———— and WEINGARTNER, H. M. "Forecasting Uses of Anticipatory Data on Investment and Sales," *Quarterly Journal of Economics,* Vol. 72 (1958), pp. 23-54; a "Comment" and a "Reply" are in *ibid.,* Vol. 73 (1959), pp. 169-72. [144, 146, 149, 151]

*———— and ZEMAN, MORTON. "The Effect of the Availability of Funds and the Terms Thereof on Business Investment," *Conference on Research in Business Finance.* Universities–National Bureau Committee for Economic Research, New York: National Bureau of Economic Research, 1952, pp. 263-309.

————. *See also* Bossons, John; Grunberg, Emile; Holt, Charles C.; and Kisselgoff, Avram.

MORIN, FRANCOIS. "Note on an Inventory Problem Discussed by Modigliani and Hohn," *Econometrica,* Vol. 23 (1955), pp. 447-52. [40]

MOSAK, J. *General Equilibrium Theory in International Trade.* Cowles Commission Monograph No. 7. Bloomington, Indiana: Principia Press, 1944. [16]

MUELLER, EVA L. "Consumer Attitudes: Their Influence and Forecasting Value," *The Quality and Economic Significance of Anticipations Data.* Universities–National Bureau Committee for Economic Research. Princeton, New Jersey: Princeton University Press, 1960, pp. 149-79.

————. "The Effects of Consumer Attitudes on Purchases," *American Economic Review,* Vol. 47 (1957), pp. 946-65. [147]

————. *See* Katona, George.

MUTH, JOHN F. *See* Holt, Charles C.

NATRELLA, VITO. *See* Foss, Murray F.

NILSSON, K. G. "Den Svenska Industriens Kapitalinvesteringar Aren 1937 Och 1938," *Kommersiella Meddelanden,* Vol. 25 (1938), pp. 705-15. [138]

OKUN, ARTHUR M. "The Value of Anticipations Data in Forecasting National Product," *The Quality and Economic Significance of Anticipations Data.* Universities–National Bureau Committee for Economic Research. Princeton, New Jersey: Princeton University Press, 1960, pp. 407-60. [143, 145, 150]

PETERSEN, J. P. *See* Anderson, O., Jr.

SAUERLENDER, OWEN H. *Level of Aspiration and Classical Utility Analysis.* Unpublished Ph.D. thesis, Department of Economics, University of Minnesota, 1959. [69]

————. *See also* Modigliani, Franco.

SAVAGE, LEONARD J. *The Foundations of Statistics.* New York: John Wiley and Sons, Inc.; and London: Chapman and Hall, Ltd., 1954. [68]

SCARF, HERBERT. *See* Arrow, Kenneth J.

SCHILD, A. "On Inventory, Production and Employment Scheduling," *Management Science,* Vol. 5 (1959), pp. 157-68. [57]

SCHULTE, W. *See* Anderson, O., Jr.

SCHWEIGER, IRVING. "The Contribution of Consumer Anticipations in Forecasting Consumer Demand," *Short-Term Economic Forecasting,* Studies in Income and Wealth, Vol. 17. National Bureau of Economic Research. Princeton, New Jersey: Princeton University Press, 1955, pp. 455-83. [145]

SIMON, HERBERT A. "Bandwagon and Underdog Effects and the Possibility of Election Predictions," *Public Opinion Quarterly,* Vol. 18 (1954), pp. 245-53. [108]

————. "Causal Ordering and Identifiability," *Studies in Econometric Methods,* W. Hood and T. Koopmans, eds. Cowles Commission Monograph No. 14. New York: John Wiley and Sons, Inc.; and London: Chapman and Hall, Ltd., 1953, pp. 49-74. Reprinted in Herbert A. Simon, *Models of Man,* New York: John Wiley and Sons, Inc., 1957, pp. 10-36. [43]

————. "Dynamic Programming Under Uncertainty with a Quadratic Criterion Function," *Econometrica,* Vol. 24 (1956), pp. 74-81. [62]

————. *See also* Holt, Charles C., and March, James G.

"Statistics on Business Plant and Equipment Expenditure Expectations," *Report of the Consultant Committee on Business Plant and Equipment Expenditure Expectations,* Board of Governors of the Federal Reserve System, July, 1955. [138, 144]

THEIL, H. *Economic Forecasts and Policy.* Amsterdam: North-Holland Publishing Company, 1958. [140, 144, 146, 150, 152]

————. *Linear Aggregation of Economic Relations.* Amsterdam: North-Holland Publishing Company, 1954. [136]

————. "Recent Experiences with the Munich Business Test," *Econometrica,* Vol. 23 (1955), pp. 184-92.

TINBERGEN, J. *Statistical Testing of Business Cycle Theories.* Vol. II: *Business Cycles in the United States of America, 1919-1932.* Geneva: League of Nations, 1939. [136]

TOBIN, JAMES. "On the Predictive Value of Consumer Intentions and Attitudes," *The Review of Economics and Statistics,* Vol. 41 (1959), pp. 1-11. [145, 150]

ULIN, ROBERT P. *See* Keezer, Dexter M.

WEINGARTNER, H. M. *See* Modigliani, Franco.

WITHEY, S. B. *See* Lansing, J. B.

WOLFSTEINER, M. *See* Anderson, O., Jr.

WOLFOWITZ, J. *See* Dvoretzky, A.

ZEMAN, MORTON. *See* Modigliani, Franco.

FORECASTING USES OF ANTICIPATORY DATA ON INVESTMENT AND SALES*

By F. Modigliani and H. M. Weingartner

I. Introduction, 23; purpose of the analysis, 23; nature of the data, 25. — II. Direct forecasting value of the anticipatory data, 26; capital outlay plans, 26; sales anticipations, 34. — III. Errors of sales anticipations and the realization of investment plans — an example of the realization function approach, 36; statement of the problem, 36; formulation of the model, 39; empirical results, 43; some analytical implications, 47; some forecasting implications, 50. — Appendix, 53.

I. Introduction

A. Purpose of the Analysis

The systematic collection of data on expectations and plans of firms dates back almost two decades and has grown in importance since the end of World War II.[1] The purpose of the present paper is to explore the usefulness of survey data on capital outlay plans and sales expectations in economic forecasting. Of the three main series on investment plans which are currently being compiled in the United States, this paper focuses on only one, namely, the "Annual Survey of Business Anticipations of Plant and Equipment Expenditures" collected by the Securities and Exchange Commission and the Department of Commerce.[2]

Several previous investigations of this and other surveys have concentrated on cross-section analyses, i.e., on the relation between

* The present paper is an outgrowth of the project "Expectations and Economic Fluctuations" financed by a grant from the Merrill Foundation for the Advancement of Financial Knowledge, and carried out at the University of Illinois under the direction of the senior author. The research reported herein was supported in part by a research grant from the Graduate School of Industrial Administration, Carnegie Institute of Technology. The paper was completed at Carnegie Institute of Technology in May, 1957.

1. Probably the earliest efforts in this area are represented by the survey of capital outlay plans carried out in Sweden since 1930. Since that time the collection of similar data has been imitated in many other countries, including the United States. In the postwar period surveys have also been conducted on a number of other anticipatory variables, such as prices, profits, sales, and employment. Notable examples of such surveys are those conducted by Dun and Bradstreet in the United States, and by the IFO-Institute in Germany.

2. The other surveys are the McGraw-Hill Publishing Company's Department of Economic Surveys, "Business' Plans for New Plants and Equipment"; and the "Quarterly Survey of Capital Appropriations of the 1000 Largest Manufacturing Firms," conducted by the National Industrial Conference Board and published in *The Conference Board Record.*

anticipations and realizations of individual firms. The present paper, on the other hand, while it has benefited from these earlier studies, notably those of Friend and Bronfenbrenner and of Eisner,[3] is concerned exclusively with the time-series analysis of the data, that is, with assessing the usefulness of aggregate investment plans and sales anticipations in forecasting broad aggregates. Such a time-series analysis is the most relevant one in so far as one is interested in forecasting aggregates; cross-section analyses are of only indirect value in this respect.

However, up to this date a series of sufficient length for time-series analysis has not been available. At this writing the annual SEC-Commerce Survey provides data covering both investment plans and sales expectations for a period of nine years. This is a body of data which is by now worth exploring, even though conclusions derived from it must be regarded as somewhat tentative.

Section II of this paper is devoted to an analysis of the record of the anticipatory data as direct forecasts. Simple comparisons between anticipated and actual investment have been made previously by a number of authors, especially in the *Survey of Current Business*.[4] The analysis presented in Section IIA differs from these earlier studies in that it attempts to evaluate systematically the predictive ability of investment plans by developing various relevant standards of comparison. Furthermore, the desirability of making certain adjustments to the data, notably adjustments for changes in price level, is examined and tested. In Section IIB a similar analysis is applied to the sales anticipations reported by the Survey, a body of data which, so far, has received little attention.

Section III analyzes possible uses of the anticipatory data other than in direct forecasts. Here primary reliance is placed on the "Realization Function Approach," a theoretical framework which relates the realization of investment plans to the realization of sales and other anticipations. A brief outline of this framework is provided

3. I. Friend, and J. Bronfenbrenner, "Business Investment Programs and Their Realization," *Survey of Current Business*, Dec. 1950, and "Plant and Equipment Programs and Their Realization," *Short-Term Economic Forecasting* (*Studies in Income and Wealth*, XVII, National Bureau of Economic Research, Princeton, 1955), pp. 53–111; and R. Eisner, "Expectations, Plans and Capital Expenditures; A Synthesis of *Ex Post* and *Ex Ante* Data (Based on the McGraw-Hill Data)," *Proceedings of the Conference on Expectations, Uncertainty, and Business Behavior*, Social Science Research Council, October 27–29, 1955, forthcoming.

4. Cf. also "Statistics on Business Plant and Equipment Expenditure Expectations," *Report of the Consultant Committee on Business Plant and Equipment Expenditure Expectations*, organized by the Board of Governors of the Federal Reserve System at the request of the Sub-Committee on Economic Statistics of the Joint Committee on the Economic Report, Washington, D.C., July 1955, especially p. 32.

in Section IIIA. This is followed in Section IIIB by the formulation of a simple model which demonstrates this approach, and which is capable of empirical testing with the data at hand. The empirical results of the tests, which were generally quite satisfactory, are reported in Section IIIC, while additional consequences of the model are discussed in the following section. Finally, some forecasting implications of this approach are presented in Section IIIE.

B. Nature of the Data

The Commerce-SEC data used in the analysis are estimates of national aggregates of plant and equipment expenditures of the previous year, and anticipated expenditures for the current year, based on questionnaires returned by a sample of firms in each of the industrial categories. Because the anticipations and actual expenditures are reported in different years, problems of comparability arise on several levels. First, at the level of the firm, because of personnel turnover and other reasons, changes in interpretation and reporting methods may occur between the time the anticipation is filed and the time the actual expenditures are reported. Second, the sample of respondents also changes somewhat from year to year, as does the universe of firms in the various industries. These changes must be recognized in the method of "blowing up" the sample to obtain an estimate of the aggregate statistic. The method used has actually been altered several times since the series was begun in 1947. In fact, in several instances the procedure employed in estimating anticipated expenditures from the sample at the beginning of the year was different from that used in estimating actual expenditures at the end of the year.

For these reasons published figures on anticipated expenditures are not directly comparable with the latest and presumably most reliable figures for actual expenditures. As a result the data on anticipated expenditures presented in the table below involve certain adjustments and do not necessarily agree with the latest published figures.[5] The purpose of these adjustments is to make the series as far as possible comparable with the latest Commerce-SEC series on actual outlays.[6]

5. The figures on revised anticipated capital outlays can, however, be reconstructed from the table of percentage changes in anticipated and realized investment given in M. Foss and V. Natrella, "Ten Years' Experience With Business Investment Anticipations," *Survey of Current Business*, Jan. 1957, p. 17. Unrounded figures were made available to the authors through the co-operation of Mr. Larry Bridge of the Department of Commerce.

6. It should be noted in this connection that what one would really like to test is whether the anticipations accurately forecast *actual* investment. Operationally, however, the only thing it is possible to test is how well they forecast the Commerce-SEC *estimates* of actual investment.

II. Direct Forecasting Value of the Anticipatory Data

A. *Capital Outlay Plans*

The first three columns of Table I present for each year actual expenditures, I_t, expenditures anticipated at the beginning of the year, $I_t(t - 1)$ and the forecast error as a percentage of actual expenditure. Part A of the table relates to manufacturing and Part B to the aggregate of all industries included in the survey. As an indication of over-all forecasting accuracy of the anticipatory data, the average absolute error of forecast is presented in row a(i) of column (3). This measure is the average error computed by disregarding signs, so that errors of opposite sign do not offset each other.

The average error, as well as the errors for individual years, appears to be relatively small with the single exception of 1950. The large error in this year is not surprising, however, because the beginning of the Korean War occurred in the middle of that year and its consequent effects on investment activity could hardly have been anticipated at the beginning of the year. It appears therefore that the omission of the year 1950 may serve to provide a more reliable indication of the performance of the anticipatory data. Accordingly all measures of accuracy presented in the table have been computed including and excluding 1950. The significance of the figures of column (3) is difficult to evaluate in the absence of an appropriate yardstick. One useful standard which has been frequently utilized in recent years in assessing the quality of forecasts is represented by the error resulting from the so-called "naive model": "next year will be like this year." Denoting by I_t the level of investment expenditure in any year t, the naive model forecast for the year t is simply I_{t-1} and the error of such a forecast is given by the formula $\frac{I_{t-1} - I_t}{I_t}$, which has been used in computing the entries of column (4).

There are two distinct, though closely related, senses in which the naive model error of column (4) can be regarded as a yardstick for the forecast error of column (3).[7] In the first place, a naive model forecast is the cheapest and simplest method of forecasting one can conceive of. It represents therefore a sort of minimal standard, a zero point, from which to measure the performance of any alternative forecasting procedure. Unless the alternative method can perform at least as well, it is essentially worthless. Alternatively, one may

7. Cf. F. Modigliani and O. H. Sauerlander, "Economic Expectations and Plans of Firms in Relation to Short-Term Forecasting," *Short-Term Economic Forecasting*, XVII, *op. cit.*

note that the naive model error for any given year is, by definition, identical with the yearly movement of the series — except for sign. Hence the average absolute error, shown in rows *a*(i) and (ii) of column (4), represents the average year to year variation and may be regarded as a measure of the difficulty inherent in forecasting the variable under consideration.

It appears from column (4) that, in spite of the stability of the postwar period, investment expenditure has been subject to considerable yearly fluctuations. When this variability is taken into account, the forecasting record of the anticipatory data appears quite favorable, as can be seen by comparing columns (3) and (4). In particular, if 1950 is omitted, the naive model error turns out to be nearly five times higher than that of the anticipatory data in the case of manufacturing, and nearly three times higher for the aggregate of all industries covered by the survey.[8] This same result can be usefully expressed in terms of the "coefficient of relative accuracy" computed by subtracting the average forecast error of column (3) from the average error of the naive model in column (4), and expressing the difference as a percentage of the naive model error. This coefficient, shown in rows *b*(i) and (ii) of the table, measures the proportion of the variability of the series which has been correctly forecasted. It has a maximum value of 100 if the forecast is perfect throughout, a value of zero when the forecast is on the average no better than a naive forecast, and a negative value when it is worse.

It may be noted that while in terms of the average absolute error the forecasting performance of the manufacturing sector appears somewhat poorer than that of all industries, the difference very nearly vanishes in terms of the coefficient of relative accuracy. The larger absolute error of the manufacturing sector appears to be accounted for by the greater short-run variability, which in turn is likely to reflect, at least in part, the general tendency for individual components to fluctuate more than broad aggregates.

A test based on the naive model which has been used so far may be regarded as too lenient. Since the investment series is available on a quarterly basis, one could base the naive model forecast on the latest (seasonally adjusted) quarterly rate, rather than on the average rate of the last four quarters as is done in the test of column (4).

The result of using the fourth quarter of a year to forecast the following year's expenditure on plant and equipment is shown as

8. The figures of column (4) probably tend to overestimate the success of naive model forecasts since they are based on the latest revised figures rather than on the preliminary estimates actually available at the relevant points of time.

TABLE I

Planned and Actual Capital Outlays, and Selected Measures of Forecast Accuracy

A — Manufacturing

Year	Actual Expenditure (I_t) ($ Million) (1)	Planned Expenditure ($I_t(t-1)$) ($ Million) (2)	Forecast Error (%) Raw Data: Investment Plans[1] (3)	Raw Data: Naive Model I[2] (4)	Raw Data: Naive Model II[3] (5)	After Adjustment for Changes in Prices: Naive Model I'[4] (6)	After Adjustment: Naive Model II'[5] (7)	After Adjustment: Investment Plans[6] (8)
1 — 1947	8,703							
2 — 1948	9,134	8,499	−7.0	−4.7	−1.4	3.9	4.0	−1.9
3 — 1949	7,149	7,139	−0.1	27.8	24.2	32.3	23.3	−0.8
4 — 1950	7,491	6,143	−18.0	−4.6	−14.8	−2.6	−12.5	−15.7
5 — 1951	10,852	10,863	0.1	−31.0	−17.8	−25.0	−13.9	4.9
6 — 1952	11,632	11,769	1.2	−6.7	0.5	−5.6	1.2	1.9
7 — 1953	11,908	11,675	−2.0	−2.3	−1.5	−0.2	0.2	−4.6
8 — 1954	11,038	11,068	0.3	7.9	7.2	8.4	6.9	0
9 — 1955	11,439	10.704	−6.5	−3.5	−7.5	−1.9	−5.8	−0.3
Summary Measures of Forecast Accuracy								
a — Average Absolute Error								
(i) All years			4.4	11.1	9.4	1.00	8.5	3.8
(ii) Excluding 1950			2.5	12.0	8.6	11.0	7.9	2.1
b — Coefficient of Relative Accuracy								
(i) All years				60[7]	53[7]	62[9]	55[9]	
(ii) Excluding 1950				79[8]	71[8]	81[10]	73[1]	
c — Arithmetic Mean Error								
(i) All years			−4.0	−2.1	−1.4	1.2	0.4	−2.1
(ii) Excluding 1950			−2.0	−1.8	0.5	1.7	2.3	−0.1

For footnotes, see Table B.

B — ALL INDUSTRIES

Year	Actual Expenditure (I_t) ($ Million) (1)	Planned Expenditure ($I_t(t-1)$) ($ Million) (2)	Forecast Error (%) Raw Data: Investment Plans[1] (3)	Raw Data: Naive Model I[2] (4)	Raw Data: Naive Model II[3] (5)	After Adjustment for Changes in Prices: Naive Model I′[4] (6)	After Adjustment for Changes in Prices: Naive Model II′[5] (7)	After Adjustment for Changes in Prices: Investment Plans[6] (8)
1 — 1947	20,612							
2 — 1948	22,079	21,470	−2.7	−6.6	−3.4	1.8	1.8	2.5
3 — 1949	19,285	19,487	1.0	14.5	15.4	18.6	14.6	0.3
4 — 1950	20,605	17,863	−13.3	−6.4	−13.6	−4.5	−11.2	−10.9
5 — 1951	25,644	26,114	1.8	−19.6	−9.1	−12.7	−4.8	6.7
6 — 1952	26,493	26,519	0.1	−3.2	0.3	−2.0	1.0	0.8
7 — 1953	28,322	27,051	−4.5	−6.5	−5.7	−4.5	−4.0	−2.8
8 — 1954	26,827	27,180	1.3	5.6	6.3	6.1	6.1	1.1
9 — 1955	28,701	27,063	−5.7	−6.5	−8.9	−4.9	−7.1	−4.0
Summary Measures of Forecast Accuracy								
a — Average Absolute Error								
(i) All years			3.8	8.6	7.8	6.9	6.3	3.6
(ii) Excluding 1950			2.4	8.9	7.0	7.2	5.6	2.6
b — Coefficient of Relative Accuracy								
(i) All years				56[7]	51[7]	48[9]	43[9]	
(ii) Excluding 1950				73[8]	66[8]	64[10]	54[10]	
c — Arithmetic Mean Error								
(i) All years			−2.8	−3.6	−2.3	−0.3	−0.5	−0.8
(ii) Excluding 1950			−1.2	−3.2	−0.7	0.3	1.1	0.7

1. $\dfrac{I_t(t-1) - I_t}{I_t} \times 100.$ 2. $\dfrac{I_{t-1} - I_t}{I_t} \times 100.$ 3. $\dfrac{I^{IV}_{t-1} - I_t}{I_t} \times 100.$ 4. $\dfrac{I_{t-1}\dfrac{P_t}{P_{t-1}} - I_t}{I_t} \times 100.$ 5. $\dfrac{I^{IV}_{t-1}\dfrac{P_t}{P'_{t-1}} - I_t}{I_t} \times 100.$ 6. $\dfrac{I_t(t-1)\dfrac{P_t}{P'_{t-1}} - I_t}{I_t} \times 100.$

7. Difference between naive model error (row a (i)) and error of anticipations (Col. (3), row a (i)), expressed as percentage of naive model error.
8. Same as in note 7, but with row a (i) replaced by row a (ii).
9. Difference between naive model error (row a (i)) and error of anticipations adjusted for price changes (Col. (8), row a (i)), expressed as percentage of naive model error.
10. Same as in note 9, but with row a (i) replaced by row a (ii).

Naive Model II in column (5). The outcome represents an improvement over Naive Model I, but a relatively small one. The coefficient of relative accuracy in column (5) shows that the record of the anticipatory data is quite good even in terms of this more stringent test.[9]

An additional question frequently raised in assessing forecasts is how well they perform in predicting the direction of change, especially at turning points. By this criterion, obviously, naive model forecasts are very poor. The anticipatory data, on the other hand, appear to have done reasonably well also in this respect. In the course of the eight years covered by the series, which included four turning points, the anticipations for all industries correctly predicted the direction of change in all but one instance, namely the increase of 1950 associated with the Korean War. The manufacturing series missed one additional turn in 1955.

There remains one further refinement of the naive model which is worth considering here. Over the period covered by the investment series there occurred substantial changes in prices and at least part of the fluctuations in the level of investment resulted from such price changes rather than from changes in the physical volume of investment. It is therefore useful to examine the following variant of the naive model test, "Next year's level of investment, valued at current prices, will be the same as the current year's level" (or "the same as the rate of the last quarter of the current year"). Denoting by P an appropriate price index for investment expenditure, the naive model error becomes

$$\frac{I_{t-1} - I_t \dfrac{P_{t-1}}{P_t}}{I_t \dfrac{P_{t-1}}{P_t}} = \frac{I_{t-1} \dfrac{P_t}{P_{t-1}} - I_t}{I_t} .$$

If, instead of extrapolating the current yearly rate it is desired to extrapolate the rate of the last quarter of the year, I_{t-1}^{IV}, the above formula needs only to be modified by replacing the term $I_{t-1}\left(\frac{P_t}{P_{t-1}}\right)$

9. Even Naive Model II may be slightly biased in favor of the anticipatory data because investment plans are reported toward the middle rather than at the very beginning of the first quarter. A test based on projections of the first quarter rate would be biased, however, in the opposite direction, especially when account is taken of the unavoidable lag in the availability of information about past performance. In any event, rough calculations based on projections of the first quarter rate suggest that the conclusions would not be substantially altered.

by $I_{t-1}^{IV}\left(\frac{P_t}{P'_{t-1}}\right)$, where P'_{t-1} is the price level of the last quarter of the year $t - 1$. The results of such tests, based respectively on the latest year (Model I') and on the last quarter of the latest year (Model II'), are shown in columns (6) and (7).[1]

It is apparent that these naive models perform better than the earlier ones, especially when the extrapolation is based on the last quarter. None the less the forecast error remains substantially higher than that of the anticipatory data, two to three times as high when 1950 is omitted. Furthermore, once a price adjustment is introduced in the naive model, it appears proper to inquire whether a similar adjustment could and should also be performed on the anticipatory data. Presumably, what the respondents to the survey are reporting are certain plans for physical investment valued at some level of prices anticipated or assumed.[2] If this is so, part of the error of the anticipatory data may reflect a failure to anticipate correctly changes in prices rather than a failure to anticipate the correct volume of investment. It would therefore be desirable to try to establish how well the anticipatory data perform in predicting the volume of investments.

To carry out such a test properly it would be necessary to know what assumptions about the future level of prices of investment goods were utilized by the respondents in submitting their investment anticipations. Unfortunately no precise information is available on this point. The question was actually raised in 1956 by the agencies responsible for this survey, and the results of this inquiry have been partly reported in the March 1956 *Survey of Current Business* (p. 20). They show that about one-third of the firms supplying information expected prices to rise, one-third expected prices to remain the same, and one-third did not consider price changes. This information is, unfortunately, of very limited value as it relates to a single year and does not provide any indication of the size of the expected change in prices or the base period to which the change relates.

The authors of the above quoted article seem to consider the base

1. The index P_t for the entire year, and the index P_t' for the final quarter of the year, were constructed from separate deflators for construction and producers' durable goods. The base year for the index is the year 1947. A more detailed description and the actual values of the indexes may be found in the Appendix.

2. This statement controverts one by Messrs. Foss and Natrella in the January 1957 *Survey of Current Business* (p. 18), in which they speculate that some investment plans represent expenditure of the year's depreciation allowance for existing assets.

period to be the time at which the questionnaires are actually filled out, which is the beginning of the year. It seems much more reasonable to suppose, however, that the relevant base period is the planning period, and planning takes place much earlier as it involves making engineering estimates, letting contracts, cash budgeting and arranging for other financing. Hence, if the prices utilized in reporting investment plans were those of the planning period, either because no change in prices was assumed, or because the possibility of changes in prices was disregarded, one might reasonably guess that the price level implicit in the plans is that of the last half of the year. From the information collected in 1956 we know, however, that a sizeable proportion of the respondents takes expected price changes into consideration. It may not be unreasonable to suppose that expected price changes will tend to represent an extrapolation of recent trends. Hence, lacking any precise information, it has been assumed, as a very crude compromise, that the average prices implicit in the reported investment plans are those of the last quarter of the year.[3] Needless to say, this is an extremely crude solution. It is used here only for exploratory purposes, pending the availability of better information.

Column (8) of Table I shows the yearly errors of the price-adjusted investment plans. For manufacturing the price adjustment decidedly increases the average forecasting accuracy. The results are less conclusive in the case of all industries. While the average error is reduced somewhat when all years are included, it rises slightly if 1950 is omitted. A comparison of columns (3) and (8) for individual years shows that the price correction almost uniformly reduces the error with one notable exception, namely 1951. In this year the error is increased from 1.8 per cent to 6.7 per cent for all industries, and even for manufacturing it rises from 0 to about 5 per cent. One may well suspect that the poor results for this year reflect the unsatisfactory nature of this price adjustment. In view of the unparalleled increase in prices which occurred throughout most of 1950 it is not unreasonable to suppose that the level of prices implicit in plans for 1951 was above that of the fourth quarter of the year. In this case the price adjustment would overestimate the anticipated level of investment in volume terms, explaining the sizeable overestimate of the price-adjusted anticipatory data. Indeed, if the year 1951 is omitted the average absolute error for all industries falls from 2.6 per cent for the

3. Second half deflators were also tried, but the results were less successful. Another possibility, not attempted, is to use one-half the change between the second half and the following year.

unadjusted anticipatory data to 1.9 per cent for the price-adjusted data. For manufacturing the corresponding decrease is from 2.9 per cent to 1.6 per cent. Finally, it may be noted that the price-adjusted anticipatory data for both manufacturing and all industries predicted the direction of change correctly in every year except 1950.

On the whole, the evidence suggests that if one is interested in forecasting the volume of investment, as is usually the case, one could usefully base such a forecast on the planned *volume* of investment. The planned volume of investment, in turn, could be determined by requesting information from the respondents as to the level of prices implicit in their plans. In the absence of such information, there seems to be some ground for assuming that, on the average, investment anticipations represent the planned volume of investment stated roughly at the level of prices of the last quarter of the year. This assumption will be utilized in the analysis of Section III.

Before closing this section, it is of some interest to inquire whether the anticipatory data exhibit any systematic tendency either to overestimate or to underestimate the level of investment. An answer to this question is provided by the arithmetic mean error of forecast shown in rows *c*(i) and (ii). A positive figure would indicate a tendency for the anticipatory data to overestimate investment, while a negative figure would indicate the opposite tendency. It appears from column (3) that over the years covered by this series, the anticipatory data have systematically tended to underestimate the level of investment. The error is again somewhat greater for manufacturing than for all industries, although if 1950 is omitted it is quite small in both cases. If one could count on a continuation of this tendency, it would be possible to obtain a better forecast from the anticipatory data by adjusting them upward by an appropriate correction factor. However, one should be careful in drawing inferences about systematic biases from the data presented. It must be remembered that, over the period of observation, prices have on the whole tended to rise. The underestimate therefore may merely reflect the failure of the respondents to anticipate this price rise properly. As a matter of fact, if we look at the behavior of the price-adjusted anticipatory data shown in column (8), it is found that, once 1950 is omitted, the mean error is approximately zero for manufacturing and slightly positive for all industries. We may therefore tentatively conclude that the underestimate observed in column (1) reflects primarily the failure to anticipate the rising price trend of the postwar period, rather than any systematic tendency to underestimate the volume of investments.

B. Sales Anticipations

In addition to their investment plans the respondents to the Commerce-SEC survey are also asked to report sales expectations, though not in actual dollars but rather in terms of percentage changes over the previous year. These expectations are analyzed in Table II, which, however, covers only manufacturing inasmuch as for other sectors a continuous series has not been made available by the collecting agencies on the ground that the respondents were too few and hence the estimates unreliable.

The actual level of (monthly average) sales reported in column (1) is taken from the *Survey of Current Business;* the anticipated level of sales in column (2) is computed by applying the anticipated percentage change in sales to the actual level of sales of the previous year. The remaining columns are obtained by an exact repetition of the procedure used in Table I. In order to adjust the sales expectations for price changes one should ideally have information as to the level of prices implicit in the sales forecast. Lacking such information use was again made of the plausible, though not directly verifiable, assumption that, on the average, sales forecasts are stated in terms of prices prevailing in the last quarter of the year. The yearly index of manufactured goods prices is denoted hereafter by π, and the index for the last quarter by π'.[4]

The conclusions suggested by Table II may be summarized as follows:

(a) The average forecast error of sales anticipations is somewhat higher than the error of investment plans, in spite of the smaller variability of the series, as measured by the average error of Naive Model I. Accordingly the coefficient of relative accuracy in terms of this naive model is well below that obtained for investments, though it is still fairly high.

(b) Extrapolation of the fourth quarter rate yields a considerably smaller error, so that, when Naive Model II is used as a yardstick, the coefficient of relative accuracy is reduced further.

(c) Adjustment for price changes diminishes markedly the error of forecast of both naive models but it reduces the error of sales anticipations even more. Accordingly, the coefficient of relative accuracy for the price adjusted anticipations turns out to be fairly impressive, even in terms of Naive Model II.

(d) Sales anticipations appear to have predicted correctly the direction of change in sales in every one of the eight years, which included four turning points. The price-adjusted anticipations were

4. For further details on these indexes, see the Appendix.

TABLE II

ANTICIPATED AND REALIZED SALES AND SELECTED MEASURES OF FORECAST ACCURACY (MANUFACTURING)

Year	Actual Sales (S_t) (Monthly Average) ($ Million)	Anticipated Sales ($S_t(t-1)$) (Monthly Average) ($ Million)	Forecast Error (%): Raw Data			Forecast Error (%): After Adjustment for Changes in Prices		
			Sales Expectations[1]	Naive Model I[2]	Naive Model II[3]	Naive Model I'[4]	Naive Model II'[5]	Sales Expectations[6]
	(1)	(2)	(3)	(4)	(5)	(6)	(7)	(8)
1 — 1947	15,917							
2 — 1948	17,630	16,713	−5.2	−9.7	−4.6	−2.0	−0.5	−1.1
3 — 1949	16,416	17,454	6.3	7.4	8.5	5.2	4.2	2.2
4 — 1950	19,285	16,744	−13.2	−17.4	−18.5	−11.8	−14.5	−8.9
5 — 1951	22,309	21,406	−4.0	−13.6	−4.5	−4.6	−1.0	−0.6
6 — 1952	22,850	23,424	2.5	−2.4	−2.5	−4.6	−3.8	1.3
7 — 1953	24,869	24,450	−1.7	−8.1	−2.1	−7.5	−1.2	−0.7
8 — 1954	23,396	24,123	3.1	6.3	2.3	6.8	2.2	3.0
9 — 1955	26,415	24,771	−6.2	−11.4	−11.0	−8.7	−9.2	−4.3
Summary Measures of Forecast Accuracy								
a — Average Absolute Error								
(i) All years			5.3	9.5	6.8	6.4	4.6	2.7
(ii) Excluding 1950			4.1	8.4	5.1	5.6	3.2	1.9
b — Coefficient of Relative Accuracy								
(i) All years				44[7]	22[7]	58[9]	41[9]	
(ii) Excluding 1950				51[8]	20[8]	66[10]	41[10]	
c — Arithmetic Mean Error								
(i) All years			−2.3	−6.1	−4.1	−3.4	−3.0	−1.1
(ii) Excluding 1950			−0.7	−4.5	−2.0	−2.2	−1.3	−0.0

1. $\frac{S_t(t-1) - S_t}{S_t} \times 100.$ 2. $\frac{S_{t-1} - S_t}{S_t} \times 100.$ 3. $\frac{S^{IV}_{t-1} - S_t}{S_t} \times 100.$ 4. $\frac{S_{t-1} \frac{\pi_t}{\pi_{t-1}} - S_t}{S_t} \times 100.$ 5. $\frac{S^{IV}_{t-1} \frac{\pi_t}{\pi'_{t-1}} - S_t}{S_t} \times 100.$ 6. $\frac{S_{t(t-1)} \frac{\pi_t}{\pi'_{t-1}} - S_t}{S_t}$

7, 8, 9, 10: see Table I, notes 7, 8, 9, and 10.

equally successful in predicting the direction of change in the volume of sales. At the same time, both the adjusted and the unadjusted anticipations have tended consistently to underestimate the *extent* of change, with the single exception of the year 1952. This tendency confirms the findings of the previous studies of sales forecasts.[5]

(e) Sales anticipations have on the whole tended to underestimate sales, as indicated by a negative arithmetic mean error. But, once more, this result may reflect primarily the failure to anticipate fully the rising trend of prices. Indeed, for the price-adjusted anticipations the average error is rather small, and it vanishes altogether if 1950 is omitted.

In general, then, over the period of observation the forecasting record of sales expectations appears rather good. This conclusion takes on added interest from the fact that previous analyses of sales forecasts collected by other surveys have generally revealed rather poor forecasting performances.[5] While the present evidence is far too short and limited in coverage to permit firm conclusions, it does suggest that yearly sales anticipations hold some promise as a direct forecasting device.

III. Errors of Sales Anticipations and the Realization of Investment Plans — An Example of the Realization Function Approach

A. *Statement of the Problem*

The present section is concerned with examining whether, and to what extent, the difference between anticipated and actual investments — which in the previous section has been called the error of forecast of investment plans — is affected by the discrepancy between sales expectations and the actual course of sales which is, of course, the error of forecast of sales.

This question is of considerable interest for several reasons. In the first place, both users and analysts of the anticipatory data have suspected that the remarkably good record of these data in forecast-

5. Cf. Modigliani and Sauerlander, *op. cit.*, and R. Ferber, *The Railroad Shippers' Forecasts* (University of Illinois, Bureau of Economic and Business Research, 1953). It should be acknowledged that a recent analysis of Dun and Bradstreet data by M. Hastay, "The Dun and Bradstreet Survey of Businessmen's Expectations," *Proceedings of the Business and Economic Statistics Section* (14th Annual Meeting of the American Statistical Association, Montreal, Sept. 10–13, 1954), pp. 93–123, has attempted to rehabilitate the forecasting record of these data. A forthcoming paper by the authors, however, will cast considerable doubt on Hastay's conclusions.

ing the actual course of capital outlays may have been due to the considerable stability in general business conditions during the period covered by the series. Although the data suggest that, by and large, investment plans have been carried out in the aggregate, one may have doubts as to whether this would continue to be true in the presence of an unanticipated marked business contraction.

It should be possible to throw some light on this question by the kind of analysis suggested above. Although sales were relatively stable over the postwar period, it was shown in Section IIB that there have been repeated, even if moderate, errors in sales expectations, at least for the manufacturing sector, where the information is available. One can therefore examine whether such errors have had a systematic effect on the realization of investment plans. If a stable relation were uncovered between the two variables, this would throw further valuable light on the reliability of investment plans as direct forecasts of investment. Furthermore the stated relation could be of help in improving our ability to forecast general economic conditions, as will be shown in more detail in Section IIIE.

The effect of the disappointment of sales expectations on the realization of investment plans has already been repeatedly and fairly extensively studied at the cross-section level, especially by Bronfenbrenner and Friend and by Eisner.[6] By and large, these studies have indicated that there exists a positive correlation between the error of sales expectations (actual sales minus expected sales) and the error of investment plans (actual investment minus investment plans). The correlation, however, is not very pronounced and is mostly confined to a certain class of firms which the above authors have referred to as expansionary.[7] At the time when these tests were carried out, cross-section analysis was the only practicable tool because the anticipatory data covered a very short span of years. With observations now available for eight years it is possible to attempt to carry out a similar analysis at the time-series level even though inferences based on a sample of only eight observations must be regarded as very tentative.

The relation between the actual and planned behavior of the firm on the one hand and the error of expectations on the other has been referred to as "the realization function" in previous studies resulting from the project on "Expectations and Economic Fluctuations."

6. *Op. cit.*

7. Expansionary firms may be roughly characterized as firms whose investments were largely for purposes of expansion, the classification between expansionary and nonexpansionary firms being, of course, based on criteria other than the responsiveness to the error of forecast.

The nature of this function has been examined at some length elsewhere[8] and therefore will be discussed only briefly here. It has been shown that there are good a priori reasons for expecting that the discrepancies between actual and planned behavior should largely be accounted for by the discrepancy between the behavior of the environment as anticipated at the time the plan was made and the actual behavior of the environment over the period to which the plan refers. By "environment behavior" is meant, in this connection, the behavior of all variables which are outside the direct control of the firm, as, for instance, the behavior of demand for the firm's product, prices to be paid for factors of production, the cost of securing capital, etc.

The asserted relation between the realization of plans and the error of expectations is supported by the consideration that a plan does not represent a decision by the firm as to what it will do at various future points of time. Decisions, in this sense, are made only at the time when they are to be carried out. A plan should rather be regarded as the best guess that the firm can now make as to what future course it will adopt *if* the expectations held at the time of planning have not changed significantly. Such plans are made not for the purpose of deciding *future* actions, but rather for the purpose of deciding the best *current* course of action. Thus a plan should be regarded as a conditional statement of what the firm will do, *if* the expectations are not revised in subsequent periods. The actual course of action, however, will eventually depend on the behavior of the environment over the planning period. If the behavior of the environment departs from expectations, the actual behavior of the firm will also tend to depart from plans. Thus, by and large, the discrepancy between actual and planned behavior should be a function of the discrepancy between the actual behavior of the environment and the anticipated behavior — the discrepancy tending to be smaller in absolute value, the smaller the error of expectations.

In principle, the realization function should include all variables that may exert a significant influence on the actual behavior of the firm and which are capable of significant unanticipated variation over the interval covered by the plan. In general, however, it need not include variables which may be expected to exert an influence on the behavior of the firm if these are not capable of variation within the

8. F. Modigliani and K. J. Cohen, "The Significance and Uses of *Ex Ante* Data — A Summary View," *Proceedings of the Conference on Expectations, Uncertainty, and Business Behavior*, Social Science Research Council, Oct. 27–29, 1955, forthcoming, and *The Role of Anticipations and Plans in the Economy of the Firm, and Their Use in Economic Analysis and Forecasting*, Bureau of Economic and Business Research, University of Illinois, Part II.

interval. That is, it need not include initial conditions. This is because the initial conditions are fully reflected in the plan itself, as well as in the anticipations underlying the plan.

In the present case the only information available on relevant expectations refers to sales. A priori considerations, as well as the results of the cross-section studies referred to above, suggest that these are not the only relevant variables. It would seem, nevertheless, that sales are a sufficiently important variable to justify formulating and fitting a realization function for investment involving this anticipatory variable alone.

There remains the problem of determining the exact form of the relation to be tested, which is taken up in the next section.

B. Formulation of the Model

In view of the limited information available and the shortness of the series, the model about to be presented has been kept to a maximum of simplicity, leading also to simple empirical tests.

The point of departure is a well-known variant of the acceleration hypothesis.[9] Specifically, the level of investment planned at the end of year $t - 1$ for the year t is taken to be a fraction of the difference between the desired stock of capital, as seen at the planning date, and the existing stock adjusted for wear and tear in the course of the year. This hypothesis can be stated formally as follows:

$$I_t(t-1) = \gamma\,[K_t^d(t-1) - (1-\delta)K_{t-1}] \quad . \tag{1}$$

The three variables appearing in this equation, $I_t(t-1)$, $K_t^d(t-1)$ and K_{t-1} represent, respectively, planned investments for the year t, the desirable stock of capital and the actual stock of capital, as of the planning date, all regarded as measured in "real" terms, i.e., at prices of some chosen base year. The parameter δ denotes the fraction of the initial stock expected to be worn out in the course of the year t and γ is a coefficient measuring the speed with which firms, on the average, endeavor to adjust the stock of capital. Both δ and γ, as well as the remaining coefficients about to be introduced, will be regarded as approximately constant over the period of time relevant for the analysis.

In line with the notion of the acceleration principle, the optimum stock of capital as seen at the planning date can be expressed as

9. For a more detailed discussion of the basic model underlying equations (1) and (2) below, see F. Modigliani, "Comment on 'Capacity, Capacity Utilization, and the Acceleration Principle' by B. C. Hickman" in *Problems of Capital Formation* (*Studies in Income and Wealth*, XIX, National Bureau of Economic Research, Princeton, 1957).

$$K_t^d(t-1) = \alpha S(t-1) \tag{2}$$

where $S(t-1)$ denotes the rate of sales which the firm should be geared to meet, as anticipated at the planning point, and α is the so-called capital coefficient (or acceleration coefficient).[1] Substituting from (2) into (1) yields

$$I_t(t-1) = \gamma[\alpha S(t-1) - (1-\delta)K_{t-1}]. \tag{3}$$

By analogous reasoning, the optimum stock of capital, as seen in the light of conditions actually prevailing in the year t — the *ex post* optimum as we may call it — will be

$$K_t^d = \alpha S(t)$$

where $S(t)$ represents the revised anticipated rate of sales. Therefore the "*ex post* desirable" level of investment, say I_t^*, can be expressed as

$$I_t^* = \gamma[\alpha S(t) - (1-\delta)K_{t-1}]. \tag{4}$$

The actual level of investment in the year t can then be expected to represent a weighted average of the initially planned investment and the *ex post* desirable investment, i.e.,

$$I_t = \beta I_t^* + (1-\beta)I_t(t-1) = I_t(t-1) + \beta[I_t^* - I_t(t-1)] \tag{5}$$

where β may be regarded as a measure of the speed with which initial plans for the given year are modified within the year itself in the light of information accruing in the course of the year. Now, making use of (3) and (4), the quantity in brackets in (5) can be reduced to

$$I_t^* - I_t(t-1) = \gamma[\alpha S(t) - (1-\delta)K_{t-1}] - \gamma[\alpha S(t-1) - (1-\delta)K_{t-1}] = \gamma\alpha[S(t) - S(t-1)].$$

Substituting this result into (5) yields

$$I_t = I_t(t-1) + \beta\gamma\alpha[S(t) - S(t-1)]. \tag{6}$$

No direct information is available on the variables $S(t)$ and $S(t-1)$ appearing in the above equation. We do, however, have information on the level of sales anticipated for the near future, $S_t(t-1)$ and we may conjecture that the change in the relevant long-run sales expectations will largely depend on the extent to which

1. The coefficient α is, in general, not determined exclusively by technical considerations. It may include, for instance, appropriate allowances for a *normal* margin of spare capacity related to the short-run variability and the long-run growth trend of sales. See on this point the reference cited in the preceding note and also H. B. Chenery, "Overcapacity and the Acceleration Principle," *Econometrica*, Vol. 20 (Jan. 1952), and A. Kisselgoff and F. Modigliani, "Private Investments in the Electric Power Industry and the Acceleration Principle," *Review of Economics and Statistics*, XXXIX (Nov. 1957).

these shorter-run anticipations have been confirmed, or have failed to be confirmed, by the actual course of sales. We propose, therefore, to approximate the quantity $S(t) - S(t-1)$ in terms of observables as fc llows:

$$S(t) - S(t-1) = \mu[S_t - S_t(t-1)], \tag{7}$$

where the proportionality factor μ is akin to the Hicksian elasticity of expectations. From (7) and (6) we now derive

$$I_t = I_t(t-1) + b[S_t - S_t(t-1)], \qquad b = \mu\beta\gamma\alpha, \tag{8}$$

which represents the desired realization function, expressing investment as a function of investment plans and the sales forecast error. It will be noted that in this equation the initial stock of capital, K_{t-1}, no longer appears. This variable, in spite of its obvious influence on investment (which is recognized explicitly in equations (3) and (4)), is an initial condition, and therefore does not appear explicitly in the realization function. Its influence on investment is exerted entirely through planned investment, which depends, of course, on the initial stock of capital, as well as on other initial conditions.[2]

Equation (8) is not yet in a form entirely suited for empirical testing because all the variables are measured in prices of some base year, whereas the survey data to be utilized in the tests are measured in current prices. However, equation (8) can readily be expressed in terms of current prices. Denote respectively by P_t and π_t the average value of the price index of investment goods and of finished products in the year t relative to the base year. Similarly denote by P'_{t-1} and π'_{t-1} the average level of prices relative to the base year implicit in

2. For the sake of simplicity the reasoning leading up to the realization function, equation (8), has glossed over a number of technical details necessary for a more rigorous and general formulation. The desired stock of capital is presumably affected by initial conditions other than the initial stock of capital, e.g., by balance sheet variables, and by anticipatory variables other than sales expectations, e.g., the availability and cost of funds. If these variables appeared in equations (2) and (4) in additive form, the initial conditions would again drop out in the realization function, although additional terms expressing disappointment of other expectations would appear. (Some of these disappointment terms may represent the difference between initially held expectations and expectations held at a later point of time that relate to the more distant future.) Initial conditions not entering in linear form, by contrast, may appear as parameters in the realization function. Such refinements do not appear warranted for the present analysis in view of the nature of the data available at the present time.

Finally, it must be recognized that the various hypotheses stated in the text are of a stochastic nature, and accordingly each of the corresponding equations should have contained a random term. This is especially true since, in the formulation given, many relevant variables have been omitted; their effect must be regarded as subsumed in the random term. These random terms have been omitted in the text for brevity.

the investment plans and in the sales forecast for the year t. Then equation (8) can be rewritten as

$$(9) \qquad \frac{I_t}{P_t} = \frac{I_t(t-1)}{P'_{t-1}} + b\left[\frac{S_t}{\pi_t} - \frac{S_t(t-1)}{\pi'_{t-1}}\right]$$

where I_t and S_t again represent investment and sales in current prices and similarly for the corresponding anticipations. If we now multiply both sides of this equation by P_t, and for brevity let

$$X_t = I_t(t-1)\frac{P_t}{P'_{t-1}}, \qquad E_t = \left[S_t - S_t(t-1)\frac{\pi_t}{\pi'_{t-1}}\right]\frac{P_t}{\pi_t},$$

hypothesis (9) can be conveniently rewritten as

$$(10) \qquad I_t = X_t + bE_t,$$

which can be generalized to

$$(10') \qquad I_t = aX_t + bE_t + c$$

to allow for the possibility of systematic biases in investment plans, as discussed below. Hypothesis (10′) can be tested directly from available Commerce-SEC data, if one is willing to approximate P'_{t-1} and π'_{t-1} by the corresponding price indexes for the last quarter of the previous year, as suggested in Section II.

In addition to the hypothesis just developed an alternative formulation will also be tested in the next section. The reason for formulating a variant of the hypothesis, which is given in equation (12′) below, is that estimates of the parameters of equation (10′) obtained by the method of least squares may be subject to some bias because of the sizable range of the dependent variable.[3] This danger can be reduced by dividing all terms by a suitable scale factor. In previous analyses of data of this type at the cross-section level the value of fixed assets has been commonly used as the divisor.[4] Unfortunately this method cannot be utilized here because reliable information on aggregate fixed assets is not readily available. Hence the following alternative procedure has been adopted. One can first transpose the planned investment term of equation (9), obtaining

$$(11) \qquad \frac{I_t}{P_t} - \frac{I_t(t-1)}{P'_{t-1}} = b\left[\frac{S_t}{\pi_t} - \frac{S_t(t-1)}{\pi'_{t-1}}\right].$$

3. It cannot be assumed that the data have the property of homoscedasticity, or constant variance, throughout the range. It seems far more likely that the variance is proportional to the expected value of the dependent variable.

4. Friend and Bronfenbrenner, *op. cit.*, and Eisner, *op. cit.*

Now it is possible to divide each side by either variable found there, to wit, I_t/P_t or $I_t(t-1)/P'_{t-1}$ on the left, and S_t/π_t or $S_t(t-1)/\pi'_{t-1}$ on the right. In particular, selecting the anticipatory variables for the divisors, one obtains[5]

$$(12)\quad \frac{(I_t/P_t) - (I_t(t-1)/P'_{t-1})}{I_t(t-1)/P'_{t-1}} = b'\left[\frac{(S_t/\pi_t) - (S_t(t-1)/\pi'_{t-1})}{S_t(t-1)/\pi'_{t-1}}\right].$$

In this equation the left-hand side expression (multiplied by 100) represents the percentage error of investment plans, denoted hereafter for brevity by I'_t, while the expression in brackets on the right hand (multiplied by 100) is the corresponding percentage error of sales expectations, denoted hereafter by E'_t. Hypothesis (12) can again be broadened to

$$(12')\quad I'_t = b'E'_t + c'$$

and a positive (negative) value of the constant term can readily be interpreted as indicating a systematic downward (upward) percentage bias of investment plans.

While equation (12′) has certain statistical advantages over (10′), it also has certain drawbacks in that there is no clear analytical justification for dividing the two sides of (11) by two different quantities. None the less, hypothesis (12′) is clearly a sensible one and has the further advantage, as compared with that of equation (9), that it involves only two variables whose relation can be exhibited graphically on a scatter diagram.

C. *Empirical Results*

Proceeding to the empirical test of the hypotheses, the following results are obtained for equation (10′):

$$(13)\quad I_t = \underset{(\pm 0.05)}{0.91X_t} + \underset{(\pm 0.011)}{0.031E_t} + 0.98, \qquad R = 0.989^6$$

(all variables measured in billions of dollars).[7]

5. The choice of the anticipatory variable for the divisor is dictated by considerations of convenience for forecasting purposes. While the left side of (12) does not directly yield a forecast of investment, as is true for equation (9), a forecast can be obtained very simply by first multiplying both sides of equation (12) by $I_t(t-1)/P'_{t-1}$ which is known in advance, and then adding this same quantity to the result. This manipulation immediately yields the forecast of the volume of investment, I_t/P_t. This volume forecast can then be expressed in terms of any desired price level by multiplying by the corresponding price index. In particular, one can obtain a forecast of the value of investment in the following year by multiplying by the forecasted level of prices.

6. Adjusted for degrees of freedom.

7. It should be noted that, in the computation of the variable E_t, S_t and $S_t(t-1)$ were measured in terms of yearly sales rather than average monthly

In terms of standard statistical criteria these results are rather favorable to the hypothesis presented. Focusing on the critical variable for this test, namely E, it is found that its regression coefficient "passes" the customary test of significance at the 5 per cent level. In other words, the error of sales expectations appears to exert a significant effect on the relation between investment plans and actual investment. Another view of these results can be gained from Table III which presents actual investments together with the value calculated from (13) and the corresponding hypothetical percentage

TABLE III

	I_t^c	I_t	$\frac{I_t^c - I_t}{I_t} \times 100$
	(1)	(2)	(3)
1948	9,176	9,134	0.5
1949	7,260	7,149	1.6
1950	7,401	7,491	−1.2
1951	11,351	10,852	4.6
1952	11,605	11,632	−0.2
1953	11,821	11,908	−0.7
1954	10,694	11,038	−3.1
1955	11,338	11,439	−0.9
Average Absolute Error			1.6

error of forecast. It appears that (13) provides a remarkably accurate "explanation" of investment for most years, including 1950. The most noticeable exception is the year 1951 when, as noted earlier, the error may have resulted from an overcorrection for price changes; presumably more direct information on prices implicit in the anticipations would reduce such errors. A comparison of column (3) with column (8) of Table IA indicates that, with the help of (13), one can account for nearly 60 per cent of the average discrepancy of 3.8 per cent between actual investments and the price-adjusted investment plans.

A further bit of evidence for the usefulness of this approach is provided by the results of extrapolating this equation to the year 1956, which was not included in estimating the regression coefficients.

sales, as in Section IIB. Also, in estimating (13) the year 1950 was not excluded for its omission does not seem appropriate here, even though it was appropriate in the analysis of Section II. The point is that, in the present section, the error in sales anticipations is taken into account and it is not apparent that the effect of a forecast error resulting from an unanticipated military emergency is necessarily qualitatively different from the effect of errors arising from other unanticipated events.

In this year manufacturers' investment plans, adjusted for price changes, amounted to $15.7 billion, an overestimate of 4.9 per cent over actual outlays of the year, which came to $15.0 billion. However, sales expectations overestimated actual sales by 3.9 per cent (after adjustment for price changes), or by $12.9 billion out of $321 billion. Utilizing these values in equation (13) yields a computed investment of $14.8 billion, which represents an error of only 1.2 per cent.

The numerical estimates of the coefficients of (13) also deserve some comments. The coefficient of X_t is seen to fall short of unity, and fairly significantly so, when account is taken of its standard error. This finding, per se, would imply that investment plans tend systematically to overestimate investment by approximately 9 per cent, even when there is no error of sales expectations. This apparent tendency is, however, largely offset by the constant term which implies an underestimation also roughly on the order of 10 per cent. This combination of a relatively low coefficient of X_t offset by a relatively high constant term indicates that plans do not, on the average, tend to over- or underestimate the *level* of investment — as was already suggested by the analysis of Section II — but that they *do* tend to overestimate systematically the extent of year to year *change*.[8] This tendency is diametrically opposite to that noted for sales anticipations.

Proceeding to the test of the alternative hypothesis (12′), one obtains the following results

$$I'_t = 1.51E'_t + 0.54 \qquad r = 0.85 \tag{14}$$
$$(\pm 0.34)$$

which can again be regarded as quite satisfactory, the correlation coefficient being significant, by standard criteria, at the 1 per cent level. The relation between I' and E' is also exhibited in the scatter diagram of Figure I, together with the regression line. The positive estimate for the constant term indicates that plans have a systematic downward bias, but the indicated bias is negligibly small — about one half of 1 per cent — which is in line with previous results. Also, according to the regression coefficient, a 1 per cent error in sales

8. This tendency can be detected even by a direct comparison of actual with anticipated investment corrected for price changes, and can be inferred from Table IA by comparing the figures of column (8) with those of column (6). It will be seen that in the five years in which investment rose by more than 3 per cent the anticipated change was even larger (or at least as large). The same phenomenon appears to have been repeated in 1956. For the unadjusted data of column (2) this phenomenon is not readily apparent because it is hidden by the prevailing underestimation of price changes.

expectations tends to generate an excess of investment over plans by roughly 1.5 per cent. As the scatter shows, these results are heavily influenced by the extreme observation of 1950. It does not seem, however, that they are entirely due to this extreme observation. Indeed, if one is willing to discount the observation for the

FIGURE I

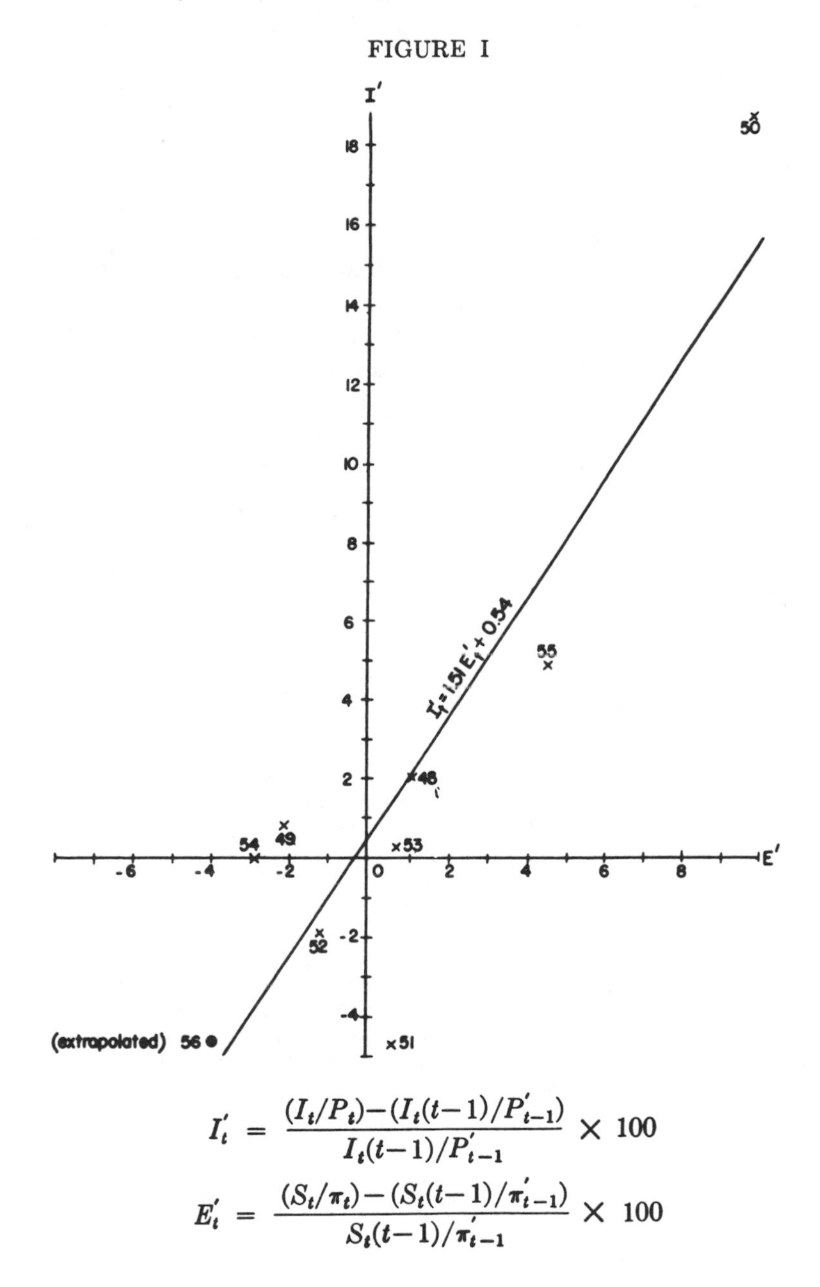

$$I'_t = \frac{(I_t/P_t) - (I_t(t-1)/P'_{t-1})}{I_t(t-1)/P'_{t-1}} \times 100$$

$$E'_t = \frac{(S_t/\pi_t) - (S_t(t-1)/\pi'_{t-1})}{S_t(t-1)/\pi'_{t-1}} \times 100$$

year 1951 for the reasons repeatedly mentioned, the remaining points are seen to fall roughly into a line with the year 1950. Furthermore, the observation for the year 1956, again not utilized in the regression, falls almost exactly on the regression line.[9]

D. Some Analytical Implications

The empirical results of the previous section provide some interesting though tentative insights into the influence of current business conditions on investment. In the first place, these results indicate that realization of plans, and hence the actual level of investments during a given year, is indeed influenced by the course of economic activity in the same year, at least to the extent that this course affects the behavior of current sales. (Current developments may, of course, influence the realization of plans through other links, though this possibility cannot be analyzed at present, lacking anticipatory data other than those on sales.) Specifically, equation (9) is seen to imply that the real volume of investment in a given year, I_t/P_t, is a linear function of the volume of sales in the same year, S_t/π_t, since the remaining two variables, investment plans and sales expectations, are given as of the beginning of the year, and therefore are not subject to change during the course of the year. By comparing equation (9) with equations (10) and (13), it is seen that a quantitative estimate of the effects of current sales on investment is provided precisely by the coefficient of the variable E in (13), namely, 0.031. Since both investment and sales are measured in billions of dollars at 1947 prices, this coefficient implies that a change of $1 in current yearly sales tends to change current investment by about 3 cents in the same direction.[1]

9. Similar tests were also carried out for the data without adjustment for price changes. The equation corresponding to equation (13) in the text is

$$(13') \qquad \underset{(\pm 0.04)}{I_t = 0.91\, I_t(t-1)} + \underset{(\pm 0.005)}{0.026\,(S_t - S_t(t-1)} + 1.02. \qquad R = 0.995$$

The multiple correlation coefficient, as well as the standard errors of the regression coefficients, would seem to indicate that the unadjusted data yield "better" results. However, for the reasons cited in the text, there are strong a priori reasons for regarding the price-adjusted model as more meaningful, and hence more reliable in the long run. Actually, for 1956 the predicted value of investment computed from equation (13′) is $14.64 billion, which represents an error of 2.1 per cent, considerably poorer than the error of 1.2 per cent obtained from the extrapolation of equation (13). The counterpart to equation (14) which omits the price adjustments is

$$(14') \qquad I_t'' = \underset{(\pm 0.21)}{1.03}\, E_t'' + 1.79. \qquad r = 0.88$$

Comments similar to the above apply here also.

1. This statement applies strictly only for the volume of investment and sales measured in base year prices, i.e., in the present instance, 1947 prices.

This estimate can be compared with the results obtained for the alternative formulation of equation (14). According to this equation, a 1 per cent error in sales forecasts tends to alter investment by 1.5 per cent of the planned figure. To convert this relation between per cent errors to a relation between actual investment and actual sales, one needs to multiply this 1.5 per cent by the ratio of investment to sales.[2] While this ratio has, of course, varied from year to year, it is of the order of 1/25, indicating that a change of $1 in current sales has tended to affect investment by 1.5/25 = 0.06, or 6 cents per dollar. This estimate is somewhat larger than that provided by equation (13), but it is not inconsistent with that estimate when account is taken of the effect on both estimates of sampling fluctuations, as shown by the standard errors.

These results suggest that although current sales have a systematic effect on current investment, this effect is quantitatively rather small, especially as compared with what one might expect from the acceleration principle in its original strict formulation. According to this formulation, the stock of capital adjusts instantaneously to the *rate* of sales so that investment is proportional to the *rate of change* of sales. The factor of proportionality is the capital coefficient, the α of equation (2), which represents the ratio of the optimum stock of capital to yearly sales. If this model were correct, an increase in the yearly rate of sales above the expected rate should lead to an increase in investment over plans equal to the unexpected increase in the rate of sales times the capital coefficient. In other words, the coefficient of the variable E in equation (13) would be equal to the capital coefficient α.

There is very little statistical information on the size of the capital coefficient for manufacturing industries. All the information that is available, however, indicates that it is a great deal larger than the coefficient of 0.03 of equation (13) or even the larger estimate of 0.06 derived from equation (14). For example, the actual ratio of the book value of fixed assets to the value of annual sales in recent

However, it can be seen from equation (10) and the definition of E_t, that this relation is approximately valid also in terms of current prices inasmuch as the ratio P_t/π_t is generally close to unity, prices of investment goods and finished products generally tending to move closely together.

2. The regression coefficient of equation (14), say b', measures essentially the elasticity of investment with respect to sales, i.e., $\frac{\Delta I}{I}/\frac{\Delta S}{S} = \frac{\Delta I}{\Delta S} \times \frac{S}{I}\cdot$ Therefore the desired estimate of $\frac{\Delta I}{\Delta S}$ is given by $b'\frac{I}{S}\cdot$

years has been of the order of 45 cents per dollar of yearly sales.[3] Furthermore, this figure undoubtedly underestimates the capital coefficient substantially in that in a period of rising prices, book value (the only measure available) is considerably below replacement cost, which is the relevant measure.[4]

The finding that the effect of a change in current sales on investment is very much smaller than any reasonable estimate of the capital coefficient is, of course, fully consistent with our model according to which the coefficient of the variable E is not simply α but represents instead the product of α and three other coefficients. Each of these coefficients may be expected to be well below unity: γ, because the adjustment in the stock of capital will be planned to occur but gradually over time; μ, because current sales may be expected to have but a limited influence on the longer-run sales outlook which controls the stock of capital that is eventually to be secured; β, because of the difficulty of revising plans in the short run, even when expectations have been revised in the light of current events.

Unfortunately the analysis does not per se provide a direct numerical estimate of the individual coefficients. It can be used, however, to shed at least some light on the possible value of the critical product $\mu\beta$ which measures the effect of current sales experience on the current rate of investment. Clearly this product must be larger than zero, for, if it were zero — as would happen if plans were absolutely rigid one year ahead or the behavior of current sales had no effect at all on longer-run anticipations — then the coefficient of E would itself be zero. But to draw more specific inferences would require quantitative information not only about α but also about γ. Unfortunately, very little is known at present about γ. Some very fragmentary evidence relating to specific manufacturing industries suggests that it might be on the order of one-third to one-fifth.[5] If then the value of α is estimated at between .5 and 1, which is probably still a conservative estimate, it would appear that the value of $\mu\beta$ is not likely to be larger than .5, and it is probably considerably lower, possibly on the order of .1 or even less.

3. Based on *Quarterly Financial Reports, United States Manufacturing Corporations*, Federal Trade Commission and Securities and Exchange Commission.

4. Some information on capital coefficients is being provided by the so-called interindustry studies or input-output analyses. This information cannot be utilized for present purposes because of obvious aggregation problems. However, Harold J. Barnett, in his comment to Hickman, *op. cit.*, p. 465, suggests that the capital coefficient might be closer to 2.

5. See F. Modigliani, "Comment on 'Capacity, Capacity Utilization, and the Acceleration Principle,' " *op. cit.*

In summary, the evidence available at present suggests that, on the average, both investment plans and long-run expectations tend to be fairly rigid in the short run, with the result that the effect of current sales on current investment, though not entirely absent, is rather minor. Furthermore, the results of Table III suggest that the effect of current events other than sales is also not likely to be very pronounced.[6] These conclusions must, of course, be regarded as extremely tentative. In the first place, they are based on very few observations and on very uncertain estimates of α and γ. Second, and more important, over the period of observation there is but a single instance in which sales were significantly above expectations — namely the year 1950 which can hardly be regarded as representative — and no single instance in which sales fell significantly short of expectations. It is quite conceivable that in the presence of a substantial disappointment of sales expectations there would be considerably more readiness to adjust plans downward than is suggested by the observations presently available.

On the other hand, if the apparent short-run unresponsiveness of investment is confirmed by further analysis, this finding would have rather far-reaching analytical and policy implications. From an analytical point of view, for instance, it would imply that the level of investment over intervals on the order of a year or less can be explained fairly closely in terms of lagged variables alone. From the policy point of view it would strengthen the case of those who doubt the short-run effectiveness of monetary and credit policies in controlling the rate of investment in fixed capital.[7]

E. Some Forecasting Implications

A few remarks are still needed concerning possible forecasting applications of realization functions of the type represented by equa-

6. It may be suggested that this unresponsiveness of investment to current events merely reflects the fact that commitments involved in investment in plant and equipment must be made with long lead times, and that plans simply report these commitments. It would follow, if this were the case, that all one would need for accurate forecasts of investment is information on commitments. While this point could never be refuted by a time-series analysis, it is a type of problem on which cross-section evidence can shed much light. The analysis of this evidence (see references in note 3, p. 24) would seem to cast considerable doubt on this proposition. In any event, the recently initiated survey of capital appropriations by the National Industrial Conference Board should soon provide further evidence on this point.

7. Note that even if this conclusion is valid, it does not imply that monetary policy is altogether ineffective in influencing the level of investments. It merely indicates that the effectiveness of such policies is not very significant in the short run, i.e., for spans on the order of a year. However, monetary and credit policy may still have a significant lagged effect by affecting investments for later periods.

tions (13) and (14). As indicated earlier these equations do not directly yield a forecast of investment in the coming year. While two of the variables appearing in the equations, namely $I_t(t-1)$ and $S_t(t-1)$, are known at the beginning of the year, to make a forecast one still needs to know the level of sales for the year, S_t.[8] Under these circumstances it would appear as though these equations are of little help in forecasting, for they require a prior forecast of S_t, while generally the main purpose of forecasting I_t is precisely that of arriving at a forecast of the level of activity, of which S_t is itself a good measure.

In spite of this circularity, realization functions of the type of equations (13) and (14) can be effectively exploited for forecasting purposes by *imbedding them in broader models which explicitly or implicitly take into account the interdependent nature of economic variables.* Such models may either take the form of a closed econometric system of simultaneous equations of the type made familiar by the work of Tinbergen, Klein and others,[9] or they may take a less formal structure as those underlying many variants of the extensively used Gross National Product approach.[1]

The way in which a relation of the type of equation (13) can be utilized in either of these approaches can be sketched out by taking a very simple illustration. One may begin with equation (13) (although what follows is just as applicable if one used equation (14) as an alternative) by assuming tentatively that the level of sales will be exactly the level anticipated. Since E is then equal to zero, the tentative forecast of investment can be computed, utilizing only known information on plans. From this computed investment, and certain other relations such as the relation between consumption and income, i.e., a consumption function, one can then compute the level of income (and of consumption) which would correspond to the given level of investment. From the known level of income one can project the

8. For the purpose of the present discussion the assumption is made that prices remain at the level of the previous year, or, equivalently, that consideration is limited to forecasting the volume of investment. In order to forecast the value of investment it would be necessary in addition to be able to forecast changes in the price level. In what follows, therefore, the symbol I_t is used to denote the volume of investment, i.e., in notation used previously, I_t/P_t, and similarly for the remaining symbols.

9. Cf. J. Tinbergen, *Statistical Testing of Business Cycle Theories*, Volume 2, "Business Cycles in the United States of America, 1919–1932," League of Nations, Economic Intelligence Service (Geneva, 1939); L. Klein, *Economic Fluctuations in the United States*, Cowles Commission Monograph No. 11 (New York, 1950).

1. See, for instance, E. C. Bratt, *Business Cycles and Forecasting* (Homewood, Ill., 1953), especially chaps. 17 and 18, and the references cited therein.

level of sales which would be generated by this level of income.[2] One can then compare this computed level with sales anticipations. If the value of computed sales agrees with the forecast of sales, the value of E will be zero, indicating that the tentative forecast of investment is consistent with the sales implications of this investment plan and that, therefore, the initial forecast need not be adjusted further. The final forecast has then been reached. If, on the other hand, E is different from zero, a second estimate of investment can be made by utilizing equation (13) again. From this estimate a new estimate of income and of sales, and a new value for E may be obtained, which can again be compared with its initial value. This procedure can be repeated until one finds a value of E such that the level of investment corresponding to it generates a level of sales equal to that implicit in the initial value of E.

This iterative procedure is, of course, not necessarily the computational method one would apply. The actual process utilized would depend on the specific nature of the over-all model, which in practice would be considerably more complex than that described above. In the special case in which all the relevant relations can be expressed in terms of equations, the iterative process can be replaced by simultaneous solution of the system, equation (13) (or (14) appearing as one of the equations of the system.

At the present time the possibility of utilizing the approach just illustrated is limited by the nature of the published information. The availability of data on other expectations and on other sectors of the economy, should make it possible to refine the analysis and extend it to such other sectors, increasing the range of practical applicability of the realization function approach.

In summary, in the short span of years for which the information is available, yearly investment plans and sales expectations have had a very favorable record as direct forecasts, especially after making allowances for the effect of changes in the general level of prices. This result is especially significant in the case of investment plans since alternative approaches have not proved very successful in forecasting investment in fixed capital, which is, in turn, a key variable in short-run forecasting of economic activity. The usefulness of these anticipatory data may be further enhanced by the simultaneous use of expectations and plans in the realization function. This approach enables us to exploit anticipatory data without losing sight of the

2. The level of sales will most likely be some multiple of income, since sales is a gross concept, involving a great deal of double counting.

interdependent nature of economic variables and holds some promise as a useful addition to the tool kit of the short-run forecaster.

APPENDIX

The price indexes used to deflate plant and equipment expenditures were derived from the *Survey of Current Business*, and from the *National Income Supplement* to the *Survey of Current Business*. The annual index for all but the last year represents a weighted average, in the ratio of two to one, of the "Producers' Durable Equipment" Deflator and "Other New Construction" Deflator of Gross National Product. This ratio represents the approximate relation between the value of equipment purchases and plant construction during this period.

The fourth quarter index for this series was constructed by interpolating the annual index with the aid of the wholesale price index of "Total Machinery and Motive Products," and the E. H. Boeckh Associates index of construction costs for commercial and factory buildings — brick and steel — from the *Survey of Current Business*. A similar procedure was used to estimate the annual index for 1956.

The deflator for sales of the manufacturing sector which was used is the wholesale index of "Commodities Other than Farm Products and Foods" from the *Survey of Current Business*.

The values of the indexes are given in the table below.

TABLE IV

PRICE DEFLATORS FOR INVESTMENT AND SALES

	Investment Deflators 1947 = 100 Annual (P_t)	Sales Deflators 1947–49 = 100 Annual (π_t)
1947	100.0	95.3
1948	109.0	103.4
1949	112.9	101.3
1950	115.2	105.0
1951	125.1	115.9
1952	126.6	113.2
1953	129.3	114.0
1954	129.9	114.5
1955	132.1	117.0
1956	140.9	122.2

	4th Quarter (P'_t)	4th Quarter (π'_t)
1947	103.4	99.1
1948	113.7	105.4
1949	112.1	100.1
1950	119.4	111.9
1951	125.7	114.6
1952	127.1	112.9
1953	130.2	114.6
1954	129.7	114.7
1955	135.2	119.4

F. Modigliani.

Harvard University
(On leave from Carnegie Institute of Technology)

H. M. Weingartner.

University of Chicago

Errata

Page 42, paragraph 2, line 5: ''may be subject to some bias'' should read ''may be inefficient.''
Page 52, paragraph 2, line 7: ''(or (14'' should read ''(or (14)).''

PART V
Miscellaneus

THE JOURNAL OF POLITICAL ECONOMY

Volume LXII DECEMBER 1954 Number 6

THE PREDICTABILITY OF SOCIAL EVENTS[1]

EMILE GRUNBERG AND FRANCO MODIGLIANI[2]

Carnegie Institute of Technology

I. THE PROBLEM

THE fact that human beings react to the expectations of future events seems to create difficulties for the social sciences unknown to the physical sciences: it has been claimed that, in reacting to the published prediction of a future event, individuals influence the course of events and thereby falsify the prediction.[3] The purpose of this paper is to investigate the validity of this claim. Since it is specifically concerned with the problem raised by the agents' reaction to a published prediction and not with the broader problem of the prediction of social events in general, the argument will proceed under the assumption that prediction, *if not divulged*, is possible.

The assumption that *private* (not published) prediction is possible implies that the forecaster has a complete[4] predictive model and also knows the initial values of the variables appearing in the model.[5]

[1] We benefited from the criticism and advice of several colleagues who kindly read various drafts of this paper. We are especially indebted to Professor Herbert Simon, who patiently read and painstakingly criticized all drafts of the present paper—of which there were many. His contributions to our argument are too numerous to be listed; in particular, he suggested the use of Brouwer's Fixed Point Theorem. However, the responsibility for the final form in which this argument is now presented and, especially, for any errors of commission or omission is entirely ours.

[2] My contribution to this paper is an outgrowth of the research on "Expectations and Business Fluctuations" financed by a grant of the Merrill Foundation for the Advancement of Financial Knowledge.

[3] Professor Carl Christ, for example, seems to argue that the reaction of observed individuals always falsifies predictions in which they are involved as dramatis personae and counteracts policies based on such predictions (*American Economic Review*, May, 1953, p. 274). Cf. also F. H. Knight, *Freedom and Reform* (New York, 1947), p. 38; and R. Vining, "Methodological Issues in Quantitative Economics," *American Economic Review*, June, 1950, *passim.*

[4] Cf. p. 467, n. 12.

[5] In symbolic language this may be stated in the following way: let there be a system consisting of a number of variables. Prediction in such a system requires:

(i) A set, O, of observation statements ascribing (initial) values to the variables of the system. These statements are of the form: $x_i = o_i$.

(ii) A set, L, of general empirical laws stipulating the transformation of the observed values of the

Since the agents remain unaware of the prediction, it cannot affect their behavior. The problem of invalidation of a public prediction arises because the public prediction may affect the agents' expectations and thus become a determinant of their behavior.[6] Under these conditions the public prediction becomes itself one of the factors which determine the future course of events: *because* a public prediction has been made, the event which occurs at the specified time is different from the one which has been predicted and which would actually have occurred if the prediction had remained private.[7]

It must be noted at once that the difficulty encountered here is not merely that of establishing the concrete form of the agents' reaction to a public prediction. As a matter of fact, once private prediction is assumed to be possible, the agents' reaction to a public prediction must also be regarded as knowable. For the assumption that private prediction is possible implies that it is possible to ascertain (*a*) how the agents' expectations are formed and change as a result of given information and (*b*) how the agents act in response to given expectations.[8] Since the public prediction is information available to the agents, its effect on expectations (and hence also on behavior) must be knowable. Furthermore, the forecaster knows, of course, the content of his own prediction; thus he can know how the course of events will be altered as a result of its publication.[9]

---

variables into specified other values, about which a new set, O', of observation statements can be made. Usually a statement about the duration of the transformation process is included, giving the time which must elapse until O' is to be observed after O has been observed. This statement appears generally in the form of dating O and O'.

Prediction statements now have the general form:

$$O(t) \,.\, L. \supset . \,O'(t)\,, \qquad (1.1)$$

where L has the general form

$$(t) \,.\, O(t) \,. \supset . \,O'(t)\,.$$

The use of the universal quantifier t for "time" has interesting implications. It points out the omnitemporal nature of the statements in which it appears and thus seems to be in conflict with the claim of predicting historical (unique) events. Discussion of this point transcends the scope of the present notes. It can only be briefly noted that all predictive statements arrived at on the basis of observation statements and empirical laws (which are all omnitemporal) must be omnitemporal. What makes them historical is the composition of O and L, which is unique in each case. Cf. E. Grunberg, "Notes on Historical Events and General Laws," *Canadian Journal of Economics and Political Science*, November, 1953.

[6] If the public prediction does not affect the agents' expectation, publication of the prediction will have no effect on the course of events: public and private prediction are identical.

[7] This means that the prediction itself becomes a variable of the system about which a statement is made in O; thus, to the set O is added a new element $o_k = V\{O'\}$, where $V\{O'\}$ denotes the statement made *now* that some O' will be observed at a specified future date. ($V\{O'\}$ may be either in the complete form [1.1] or in the abridged form represented by the right side of [1.1].) At the same time, in L a new empirical law is added which states the effect of the inclusion of o_k on the predicted values of all other variables in the system. Let O^* be O augmented by o_k, and L^* be L augmented by the new empirical law. Then:

$$O^*(t) \,.\, L^*. \supset . \,O'^*(t) \qquad (1.2)$$

and

$$O'^* \neq O'\,.$$

The prediction $V\{O'\}$ would have been correct if not divulged; once it has been made known to the agents, it changes O' into O'^* and is therefore falsified. Note that, as a rule, individuals do not react to the entire set O', but rather to one or a few of the variables only. Their reaction, however, affects the values of all variables in O' (cf. Sec. II and n. 20).

[8] Cf. Sec. III, especially pp. 471–72. For a brief discussion of the methodological problem involved in predicting the agents' expectations, given certain observations, see pp. 470–71 at the end of Sec. II.

[9] The assumption that private prediction is possible implies the forecaster's knowledge of the sets O and L, enabling him to make a correct private

But this knowledge is not sufficient to overcome the difficulty created by the agents' reaction to public prediction. Let the forecaster be able to predict the agents' reaction to a predictive statement and adjust his prediction accordingly. Upon publication of this adjusted prediction, the agents will act differently from the way they would have acted if the adjusted prediction had not been made public; and so on and on.[10] In short, the public prediction of social events seems to carry within itself the seeds of its own destruction.

In what follows we propose to show that—under very general conditions—the difficulty outlined above can be resolved and correct public prediction *is* possible.[11]

The possibility of correct public prediction in the face of the agents' reaction is formally proved by exhibiting only one case in which such prediction is possible. This, however, would not satisfy the social scientist's needs and aspirations. It is desirable to show that correct public prediction is at least *normally* (i.e., in most cases) possible.[12] This requires (1) the proof that there exist conditions in which at least one correct public prediction is possible in the face of effective reaction by the agents; (2) evidence that these conditions are actually fulfilled in the normal case of public prediction of social events, so that cases where these conditions are not fulfilled are, at worst, rare exceptions. While the first step is formal, the second is empirical.

prediction of the form (1.1). Once it is assumed that L can be known, L^* is also assumed to be knowable. This is so because L and L^* differ only as a result of an empirical law. Similarly, the assumption that private prediction is possible also implies that the forecaster can know the set O^*, which differs from the set O only by the element $V\{O'\}$, the forecaster's own prediction. Thus the forecaster can know what effect his prediction will have on the course of events.

[10] If the forecaster knows L^* and adjusts his prediction from $V\{O'\}$ to $V\{O'^*\}$, he will thereby generate further reaction, changing O'^* to O'^{**}, and so on apparently *ad infinitum*.

[11] Formally expressed, this means that there exists under these conditions at least one set of values for the variables in the predictive system such that if $V\{O'^*\}$ is publicly predicted, O'^* will actually be observed.

It is useful to distinguish between two types of prediction: (i) the unconditional prediction or prophecy and (ii) the conditional prediction.

(i) Is of the form: event E, will occur at time t, no matter what. It is falsified if E fails to occur at t.

(ii) Is of the form: $E_1, E_2, \ldots, E_n$, will occur alternatively and mutually exclusively at time t according to whether conditions $C_1, C_2, \ldots, C_n$, are fulfilled. No assertion is made as to which, if any, of the C_i's will actually be fulfilled. It is falsified if, and only if, one of the C_i's occurs and the corresponding E_i does not occur. If none of the C_i's occurs, failure of any E_i to occur does not imply falsification but only unverifiability of the prediction.

The case where the reaction of the agent prevents the occurrence of any of the conditions listed in the prediction belongs in this group of unverifiable, but not falsified, predictions. Since in this case the reaction of the agents may prevent any of the E_i's from occurring, it is frequently, but erroneously, regarded as one of falsification.

Both conditional and unconditional prediction occur in the domain of the social sciences. The difference between them is often blurred and sometimes simply a matter of emphasis and intention. Conditional predictions are made especially as a basis for policy decisions where alternative events and the corresponding conditions (here alternative courses of action) are considered and a choice is made. The argument in the text deals only with the unconditional public prediction; it can, however, be shown to hold also for the conditional prediction (cf. also n. 12).

[12] Within the realm of the social sciences, prediction is limited. The system within which the prediction is made is not closed: the number of variables that can affect the course of events is indefinitely large. Predictive models normally include (for technical reasons) only a small number of variables and are subject to the *ceteris paribus* clause. Conceptually, the number of variables in a theoretical model can be increased indefinitely. However, the probability that excluded variables will affect the events always remains significantly greater than zero. These issues, connected with the problem of explaining "unique events," transcend the scope of the present argument.

In Section II a single case is examined in which correct public prediction is possible, even though agents react effectively to the publication of the prediction. In Sections III and IV the argument is generalized, proceeding from the one-variable case to the public prediction of n variables. Section V deals with a special case, and Section VI raises the problem of the welfare effect of public prediction.

II. A SIMPLE EXAMPLE

Suppose that at time t it is desired to predict publicly for some commodity the price that will prevail at time $t + 1$ and, since price and quantity are functionally related, the amount supplied at that time. Let

p_t be the actual market price at time t;

q_t be the quantity sold at time t;

p_e be the price expected at time t to rule at time $t + 1$ (suppliers' expectation);

P be the publicly predicted price for time $t+1$.

By hypothesis, private prediction is possible; hence the following relevant information is assumed known to the forecaster:

The price prevailing in the market at $t + 1$ is determined by the demand; thus

$$p_{t+1} = D(q_{t+1}) . \qquad (2.1)$$

The quantity supplied at $t + 1$ is assumed to be irrevocably determined by decisions made at time t in the light of the price expected to hold at $t + 1$; thus

$$q_{t+1} = S(p_e) . \qquad (2.2)$$

Price expectations are assumed to be determined only by the current price and the public prediction (if such a prediction is made); thus

$$p_e = E(p_t, P) . \qquad (2.3)$$

When no public prediction is made, the expectation function will be written as

$$p_e = E(p_t, -) . \qquad (2.3a)$$

On the other hand, the symbol $E(p_t, 0)$ denotes the expectation when a price of zero is publicly predicted.

Consider, first, the problem of making a correct private prediction. Since p_t can be directly observed by the forecaster and the variable P does not exist in this case, the system consisting of the three equations (2.1), (2.2), and (2.3*a*) in three unknowns—p_{t+1}, q_{t+1}, and p_e—can be solved simultaneously. First, from (2.3*a*) the price p_e^*, expected to hold at time $t + 1$, can be directly obtained. Next, substituting this value in (2.2) yields the solution for q_{t+1}, say q^*, i.e., the quantity which, under these conditions, suppliers will bring to market at $t + 1$. Finally, substitution of the value q^* in the demand function (2.1) gives the solution for p_{t+1}, say p^*, i.e., the price that will actually rule if the quantity q^* is marketed. Note that p^* need not, and in general will not, coincide with p_e^*.[13] In economic terms this means that suppliers hold an unwarranted expectation and, acting upon it, bring to market a supply that results in a price different from the expected price.

Publication of the correct private prediction leads in general to its falsification. It is clear from (2.3) that, as a result of the public prediction, $P = p^*$, the price expected by the agents becomes

$$p_e^{**} = E(p_t, p^*) \neq p_e^* = E(p_t, -) .$$

Accordingly, the quantity supplied by the agents becomes

$$q^{**} = S(p_e^{**}) ;$$

[13] This discrepancy between p^* and p_e^* is familiar from the well-known cobweb situation.

and the market price becomes

$$P^{**} = D(q^{**}) \neq P = p^* = D(q^*) .$$

So far it has been shown that the correct private prediction may be—as in the present example—the wrong public prediction. But it does not follow that correct public prediction is impossible. In fact, it will be shown that correct public prediction is normally possible under the conditions of our example.

The publication of the prediction introduces an additional variable, P, into equations (2.1)–(2.3). We now have an undetermined system of three equations in four unknowns. However, the requirement that the public prediction is to be correct yields an additional *requirement* equation:

$$P = p_{t+1} . \qquad (2.4)$$

Thus the system is again determined, and correct public prediction is possible, provided that this system has at least one (meaningful) solution. The conditions under which at least one such solution exists can be found by reference to Figure 1. Let q_{t+1} be measured on the ordinate, and both p_{t+1} and the publicly predicted price, P, on the abscissa.

If the suppliers fully believe the public prediction, the expectation function is

$$p_e = E(p_t, P) = P .$$

Substituting for p_e in (2.2) gives q_{t+1} as a function of the publicly predicted price P:

$$q_{t+1} = S(P) . \qquad (2.2')$$

The graph of this function is represented in Figure 1 by the S-curve; the demand function (2.1) is represented by the D-curve.

For every public prediction P, the quantity that will be supplied is read from the supply curve; once this quantity is known, the price that will rule at $t+1$ is read from the demand curve. If, for example, the forecaster were to predict p^* (the correct private prediction), the quantity supplied would turn out to be q^{**}. According to the figure, the corresponding price is p^{**}, which is much higher than the predicted price p^*. Correct public prediction requires that a value for P be predicted, say $\bar{P}$, such that the quantity supplied

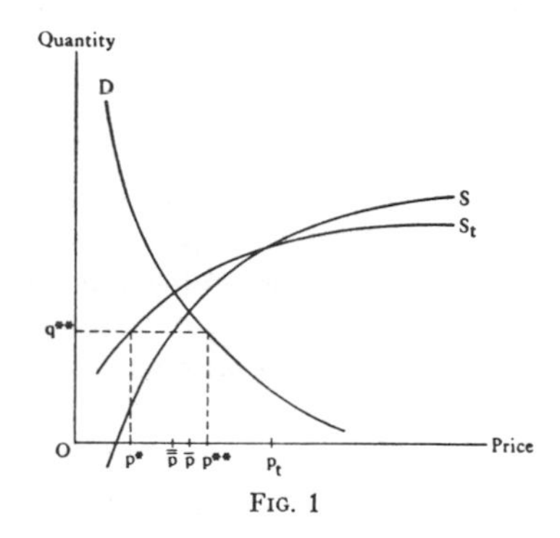

FIG. 1

at this particular price will also be cleared from the market and therefore

$$p_{t+1} = \bar{P} .$$

In Figure 1 there is one and only one such value for P, namely, the abscissa of the point of intersection of the D- and S-curves. There exists, then, at least one correct public prediction, provided that the supply and the demand curves intersect once in the positive quadrant. Note that in our example public prediction prevents possible error of expectation on the part of the suppliers. As suppliers fully accept the public prediction—which turns out to be correct—they act on the basis of warranted expectation.

If the suppliers do not fully believe the public prediction, the S-curve in Figure 1 can no longer be the supply curve. Now, from (2.3) it is seen that, with p_t known, p_e depends only on P;

hence the quantity supplied can be expressed in terms of P only, thus:

$$q_{t+1} = S[E(p_t, P)] = S_t(P). \quad (2.2'')$$

Function (2.2″) may be called a *fictitious* supply function.[14] A corresponding curve can be drawn in our figure whose relationship to the S-curve depends exclusively on the specific form of the expectation function, i.e., on the *degree of belief* in the public predictive statement.

The S_t-curve in Figure 1 is drawn on the assumption that, in the absence of a public prediction, suppliers expect the current price to continue, while after a public prediction has been made, the expected price is a weighted average of p_t and P.

The expectation function then takes the form

$$\begin{aligned} p_e &= aP + (1-a)p_t \\ &= P + (1-a)(p_t - P), \end{aligned} \quad (2.3')$$

where the *weight* is a measure of the extent to which the suppliers believe the prediction. The fictitious supply function then becomes

$$S_t = S[P + (1-a)(p_t - P)].$$

The S_t-curve must intersect the original supply curve at $P = p_t$. The quantity q_{t+1}, corresponding to any other P, is found as the ordinate of a point on the original S-curve, whose abscissa is the publicly predicted price, P, plus $(1 - a)$ per cent of the distance from there to the current price p_t. If a approaches unity, the S_t-curve coincides with the S-curve: perfect belief in the prediction. If a approaches zero, the S_t-curve becomes a line parallel to the P-axis through the point on the S-curve at p_t: complete disregard of the prediction.[15]

As in the previously examined case of perfect belief in the public prediction, there exists at least one correct public prediction, provided that the fictitious supply curve and the demand curve intersect once in the positive quadrant. In Figure 1 this correct public prediction is $\bar{P}$. Note that, since the public prediction (even though it is correct) is here not fully believed by the suppliers, they act (again) upon unwarranted expectations, and therefore the values obtained for p_{t+1} and q_{t+1} are different from those that would establish a stable market equilibrium.[16]

Finally, it is reasonable to anticipate that as consistently correct public predictions are made, "learning" occurs, so that the expectation function will, over time, undergo continuous or, more likely, discontinuous change until it takes the form $p_e = P$. Agents will then act upon warranted expectations and will no longer be (agreeably or disagreeably) disappointed.[17]

The expectation function, rather blithely assumed to be known along with the other functions of the system, offers particular methodological difficulties and is actually different from the other functions encountered in economic theory. *Expectations are themselves pre-*

[14] Function (2.2″) is called "fictitious" because it relates the quantity supplied not to expected price but to predicted price. Its shape is determined by the structure of the expectation function (in addition to cost conditions).

[15] If $a = 0$, then the correct public prediction is the same as the correct private prediction.

[16] As long as $a > 0$, the suppliers' expectation will deviate from the actually observed value by less than in the case of no public prediction, considered at the beginning of this section.

[17] Since (2.1) leaves no room for the reaction on the part of the buyers, the possibility of such a reaction has here been neglected. But the argument of the text can easily be extended so as to take into account the reactions of buyers, or, in general, of all individuals in any way affected by a public prediction.

dictions, ranging from the elaborate scientific forecast of the large business enterprise to primitive guesses and dark hunches. While the other economic laws assert what people will do, given (1) motivational postulates and (2) certain expectations, the expectation function asserts what people will *predict*, given certain past and current observations. In the predictive model it predicts what the agents will predict. The familiar motivational postulates of economics are here of no use. Thus for some time to come the expectation function will, at best, appear in the form of broad statistical generalizations. This, however, is not a difficulty of public prediction in particular, but rather of social theory and prediction in general.

III. CORRECT PUBLIC PREDICTION OF A SINGLE VARIABLE

In the preceding section one case has been considered in which correct public prediction is possible in spite of the agents' reactions. In the present section the general conditions assuring the existence of at least one correct public prediction of a single variable will be set forth. The predictive system of the social forecaster must generally contain more than one unknown and consequently more than one equation.[18] Unlike the experimenter, the forecaster of social events is normally unable to manipulate, deliberately and systematically, any of the variables in his predictive systems. He is rather called upon to predict the action of those—the agents—who do manipulate some of the variables. In the predictive system these variables directly manipulated by the agents are not independent variables, as are the variables manipulated by the experimenter, but are unknowns for which values must be found. Predicting publicly the values of a single variable in the context of social events then means announcing only one out of the several variables of the system.

In the example of the last section it was shown that the existence of a correct public prediction is equivalent to the existence of at least one solution to a determined system of simultaneous equations. If only one variable—for instance, the price—is to be predicted, this system can be reduced to one of two simultaneous equations in two unknowns. The first of these equations relates the market price p_{t+1} to the predicted price P. It is obtained by expressing q_{t+1} in terms of P (substituting from [2.3] in [2.2]) and next substituting for q_{t+1} in (2.1). Thereby, an equation of the form

$$p_{t+1} = R(P)$$

is obtained. Relations of this form between the variable to be predicted and the prediction will be called *reaction functions*. It must be emphasized that, in general, this function expresses the result of the interaction of more elementary behavior laws.[19] It also expresses the fact that whenever the agent reacts to the public prediction, the forecaster becomes—however unintentionally—a *manipulator*, since his pronouncement affects the operations performed by the agent upon some variables.

[18] In the laboratory situation the predictive system may consist of only one equation: the experimenter manipulates the independent variable of his experiment and predicts the resulting effect on the dependent variable. For each value arbitrarily assigned to the independent variable, x, of the experiment, the system must contain an observation statement of the form $x = x^*$. Actually, our system (2.1)–(2.3) is also supplemented by such an observation statement, giving the forecaster in each case the required information about the market price ruling at time t.

[19] The reaction function expresses a verifiable assertion about the real world (i.e., a law statement).

The second equation is the requirement equation expressing the condition that the price observed at the specified time must be equal to the publicly predicted price:

$$p_{t+1} = P$$

Generally, correct public prediction of a single variable pertaining to a social event can always be reduced to the form just described. Let, generally, p denote the variable to be predicted, and P the public prediction. Then p must be a function of P, or else the reaction problem does not arise.[20] Moreover, since, by assumption, correct private prediction is possible, any deviation of the observed value of p at time $t + 1$ from the correct private prediction must be due only to the public prediction. Thus we have the reaction function:

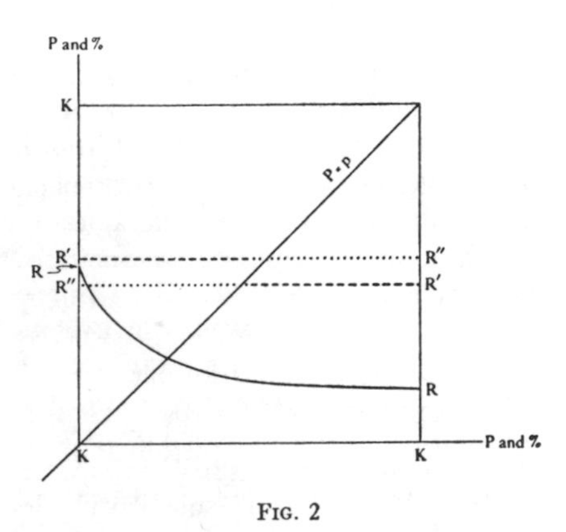

FIG. 2

$$p = R(P) . \qquad (3.1)$$

With the addition of the requirement function:

$$p = P , \qquad (3.2)$$

we have a determined system of two equations in two unknowns. Does it also have one or more solutions? The *sufficient* conditions for the existence of at least one solution of a system such as that represented by (3.1) and (3.2) follow from a theorem of topology, Brouwer's Fixed Point Theorem. They are: (*a*) the variable p must possess a lower bound k and an upper bound K, where k and K are real and finite; (*b*) the function $R(P)$ must be continuous over the interval $k \leq P \leq K$.[21]

The plausibility of this theorem can be verified with the aid of Figure 2. Let P be measured on the X-axis and p on the Y-axis. Since, by condition *a*, p can take no value greater than K or smaller than k, no value of P outside these limits will be predicted. Therefore, if we measure the distances Ok and OK on both axes and form a square with corners (k, k), (K, k), (K, K), and (k, K), the relevant portion of the reaction function $R(P)$ lies entirely within this square.[22] The diagonal joining the points (k, k) and (K, K) is a segment of the 45° line through the origin. It is the graph of the relevant portion of the requirement equation (3.2). Every intersection of the

[20] If p is not a function of P, correct public prediction coincides with the private prediction. Note that it is not immaterial which variable in the system is selected for public prediction. If in the example of Sec. II the quantity supplied alone, instead of the price, is publicly predicted, the agents do not react, and correct public prediction coincides with correct private prediction.

[21] If any n-dimensional simply connected and bounded set is subjected to any transformation, which leaves it simply connected (does not "tear" it), but not necessarily of the same dimensionality, then there exists at least one point which is fixed, i.e., whose transformation vectors are zero. Cf. Courant and Robins, *What Is Mathematics?* (New York, 1942), pp. 251 ff.; also J. von Neumann, "A Model of General Economic Equilibrium," *Review of Economic Studies*, XIII (1945–46), 1–9. Neumann applies the theorem to the solution of a saddle-point problem.

[22] For the sake of convenience, $k = 0$ in Fig. 2; but the argument in the text would not be affected if any other positive or negative value had been chosen.

reaction curve with this diagonal represents a solution of the system (3.1) and (3.2). The X-co-ordinate of such a point represents the correct public prediction.

Since there must be one p-value for every P-value, it follows from condition b that the graph of the reaction function is a continuous curve beginning on the left side of the square, (k, k)–(k, K), which in Figure 2 coincides with the Y-axis, and ending on the right side, (k, K)–(K, K), as, e.g., the R-curve in the figure.[23] It is immediately obvious that such a continuous curve must either intersect the diagonal or have a point in common with it at either corner.[24] There could exist several points of intersection between the diagonal and the reaction curve, each of which is a solution of the system.

Correct public prediction may, however, be impossible if the reaction function is not continuous over the relevant range. An illustration may be helpful in clarifying the situation. Suppose the outcome of an election with the two candidates A and B is to be predicted. Let the forecaster possess the following information: 47 per cent of the voters will vote for A, while 45 per cent of the voters will vote for B; finally, 8 per cent of the voters will vote for the candidate expected to lose (the underdog effect). Voters fully believe whatever prediction is published, with the exception of a predicted tie. In this last case voters expect candidate A to win. If, now, a prediction is made that A will poll less than 50 per cent of the votes, he will actually receive 55 per cent of the votes. If, on the other hand, it is predicted that he will receive 50 per cent or more, he will wind up with only 47 per cent of the votes. In Figure 2, let $k = 0$ per cent and $K = 100$ per cent. The reaction curve is then represented by the broken line R', indicating that, for every $P < 50$ per cent, $p = 55$ per cent; and for every $P \geq 50$ per cent, $p = 47$ per cent. At $P = 50$ per cent, the R'-curve has a point of discontinuity, and no correct public prediction is possible.[25]

The conditions of continuity and boundedness are, however, sufficient but not necessary. A solution may exist even if the variables are not bounded.[26] Similarly, the reaction curve, even if discontinuous, may intersect the diagonal. Thus suppose that in our example 8 per cent of the voters will vote for the winner instead of for the candidate expected to lose (the bandwagon effect). The reaction curve (R'' in Fig. 2) still shows a discontinuity at $P = 50$ per cent; nonetheless, it intersects the diagonal twice, at $P = 47$ per cent and at $P = 55$ per cent, so that there are two possible correct predictions.

IV. THE GENERAL CASE: CORRECT PUBLIC PREDICTION OF n VARIABLES

The result of the previous section may now be generalized. Let $x_1, x_2, \ldots, x_n$, denote the values of n variables at $t + 1$; and $X_1, X_2, \ldots, X_n$, denote their values publicly predicted at t. As before, correct private prediction— $x_1^*, x_2^*, \ldots,$

[23] This reaction curve is drawn on the basis of the fictitious supply curve, S_t, of Fig. 1. Note that condition b requires continuity, but not differentiability, of the reaction curve.

[24] The two curves might, of course, also overlap over some span. If the reaction curve meets the diagonal only at the corner (K, K), then the correct public prediction is the value of the upper bound K.

[25] If the predictor also knows that in the absence of any prediction the critical 8 per cent of the voters will vote for candidate B because they expect candidate A to win, he can make a correct private prediction, namely, $P = 47$ per cent.

[26] Although in the example of the preceding section price and quantity supplied do possess upper and lower bounds, the solution obtained there did not depend on this property.

x_n^*—is assumed to be possible. Any deviation of the values actually observed at $t+1$ from the correct private prediction at t must again be due only to the public prediction. This implies the existence of a set of reaction functions of the following form:

$$x_i = R_{i\,t}(X_1, X_2, \ldots, X_n) \qquad (i = 1, 2, \ldots, n). \tag{4.1}$$[27]

These equations are analogous to equation (3.1) and are based on more elementary behavior laws, such as those expressed in equations (2.1) and (2.2).[28]

In addition, we again have a set of equations analogous to (3.2), expressing the requirement that for each variable in the system the publicly predicted value be equal to the one observed at the specified time:

$$x_i = X_i \qquad (i = 1, 2, \ldots, n). \tag{4.2}$$

Since we have $2n$ equations in $2n$ unknowns, the system (4.1) and (4.2) is determined. Any solution is a correct public prediction. As in the one-variable case, the *sufficient* conditions for the existence of at least one solution follow directly from Brouwer's Fixed Point Theorem. Such a solution always exists if all variables possess an upper bound K_i and a lower bound k_i and if all reaction functions are continuous over the interval $k_i \leq X_i \leq K_i$.[29] Again, since these conditions are only sufficient but not necessary, solutions may exist (and in Sec. III have been shown to exist) even when the reaction functions are discontinuous and the variables unbounded. It is neither possible nor, in this context, required to formulate the necessary conditions of the existence of a solution.[30]

To complete the argument, it must be shown that the (sufficient) conditions for the possibility of correct public prediction derived from Brouwer's theorem are likely to be fulfilled in the real world in which social events occur.

(i) The variables of economic theory generally cannot increase or decrease without bounds. For example, (*a*) population and natural resources are fixed at any point in time; (*b*) individual incomes and their sum, aggregate income, are finite and likewise given at any point in time; (*c*) therefore, as increasing fractions of income are allocated to any specific use, the marginal rate of substitution between this use and all other uses of income decreases; (*d*) consumers may starve or go naked, but they cannot possibly do worse than reduce their consumption to zero;[31] (*e*) on the other hand, there exists a physical saturation point for (practically) every commodity; individuals can neither consume nor store indefinitely large supplies.

(ii) Normally the functions formulated in economic theory are conceived to be continuous.[32]

The argument is now complete, but it is important to keep in mind its precise and limited content. It is not a proof

[27] In any of the equations (4.1), only some of the X_i's may appear explicitly. In the limiting case no X_i appears; the particular equation then takes the form $x_i = x_i^*$. For this variable, private and correct public prediction coincide.

[28] The time subscript t here indicates that, according to their peculiar nature, these equations are subject to shift over time.

[29] If all variables have upper and lower bounds, we have a simply connected, n-dimensional set (convex) which takes the form of a hyperparallelepiped. If all R-functions are continuous, the set remains simply connected under transformation.

[30] Cf. H. Seifert and W. Threlfall, *Lehrbuch der Topologie* (Leipzig, 1934), paragraph 80, on "fixpointless" transformations.

[31] While there can be disinvestment, total existing investment cannot be reduced to less than zero.

[32] Owing to indivisibilities, this procedure represents an approximation which, in principle, imposes a limit to the obtainable accuracy.

that, in spite of the agents' reaction, public prediction is always possible. As was shown, there need not be a solution satisfying our system of equations. However, a solution exists under conditions *normally* fulfilled in the real world about which predictive propositions are to be formulated. It is false that the reaction of agents—where it occurs—necessarily or normally falsifies public prediction. In fact, since boundedness and continuity were found to be general properties of the variables in our predictive models, it may be asserted that if private prediction is possible, then in all but *exceptional* cases correct public prediction is also possible. The writers could construct only a few artificial examples in which public prediction is impossible even though private prediction is possible.[33]

V. THE CASE OF DELIBERATE ATTEMPTS AT FALSIFICATION

Brief mention must be made of a further possibility which, while formally interesting, does not seem to be empirically important. This is the case where individuals may find a *general climate of uncertainty* desirable and therefore set out to make prediction in general—rather than specific predictions only—impossible by systematic falsification. Certainly, this does not imply that every single public prediction must be falsified. It is sufficient to falsify just enough of them to maintain a general atmosphere of disbelief and uncertainty.[34] A speculator could, for instance, be thought of as adopting such a course of action and willing to incur costs in order to achieve uncertainty. Since there is, in principle, an indefinitely large number of actions by which any specific prediction can be falsified, no correct public prediction could be made in this case.[35]

The predictor, even though he knows of the agents' intentions, must publish his prediction, that is, commit himself, while the agents remain free to choose their own actions afterward in full knowledge of what event has been predicted. The situation here becomes that of a game of matching coins where, however, one player must show his coin before his opponent decides what move to make: correct public prediction is here impossible.

However, this is probably not a realistic situation. No individual could pursue such a strategy by himself. The collusive and rigidly concerted action of large numbers of individuals would be required. Abstracting even from such institutional obstacles as American antitrust legislation, collusion of this form would be difficult to achieve, and vastly more difficult to maintain for any length of time. Although not every single public prediction must be falsified and the collusive group could therefore choose its ground to *some extent* (subject to the requirement that a minimum number of predictions must be falsified), serious internal short-run conflicts of interests are very likely to break out.[36]

VI. THE WELFARE ASPECTS OF PUBLIC PREDICTION

There remains an intriguing, if forbidding, aspect of the problem of cor-

[33] Cf. the voting illustration above, p. 473.

[34] It must be remembered that it is not sufficient for the forecaster to achieve occasionally correct public prediction. In order to create an atmosphere of certainty, a sufficient number of his public predictions must turn out to be correct.

[35] The set L contains in these circumstances an empirical law asserting that the relation between a given $V\{O'\}$ and the reaction is one to indefinitely many.

[36] Even powerful monopolistic enterprises may not be able to follow such a strategy consistently without being forced, at times, into very heavy losses.

rect public prediction, namely, the question of the *effect* of such prediction on the course of events in those cases where public and private prediction are different. The first rather obvious and important consequence of this difference between private and public prediction is that the response of agents to the publication of a prediction may actually increase predictive ability. The forecaster may, for instance, have knowledge of how agents react to given expectations but little information on the determinants of these expectations. To the extent that expectations are determined by public prediction, such prediction then supplies the forecaster with the missing information.

More important, however, is the fact that in those cases where individuals react effectively to public prediction, the event which will actually occur is different from the one which would have occurred if no prediction or only a private one had been made. This poses a question of the value implications of public prediction. We shall cautiously restrict our attention to the economic effects of public prediction, i.e., those aspects which belong in the domain of welfare economics.

Only a few general remarks will be made here for the case in which the agents fully believe the public prediction.[37] These, at least, may throw some light on the problems with which a systematic analysis would have to deal. Note that the agents' full belief in the public prediction does not give the forecaster the power to regulate their actions at will. This would be true only if the system consisting of (4.1) and (4.2) had several solutions, among which the forecaster could, as it were, choose.[38] But normally there will exist only one solution, so that the forecaster cannot at the same time both manipulate people and make correct public predictions.

The simple example used in Section II may again be helpful in organizing ideas. In the absence of public prediction, suppliers were found to act on the basis of unwarranted price expectations, so that they bring to market a quantity which either falls short of or exceeds what can be sold at the expected price.[39] Consequently, there is a misallocation of resources. If the market price is higher than the expected price, not enough resources have been allocated to this particular industry (and too much to other industries) and conversely. If, on the other hand, correct public prediction is made, suppliers will make their decisions on the basis of warranted price expectations, and no misallocation of the resources used in the industry occurs. By making available to the suppliers relevant information previously unknown to them, the public prediction causes an improved allocation of the resources used in the economy.

This result suggests a first, though quite limited, conclusion about the welfare effects of correct public prediction. It has been shown that the general equilibrium of a perfectly competitive static system satisfies the conditions of a Pareto optimum (with a given income

[37] In this case the expectation function takes the form $x_i^e = X_i$. Even if, initially, public predictions are only partially believed, repeated experience with correct prediction is assumed to bring about *learning* (cf. p. 466). Since the agent thus sooner or later comes to believe fully what is publicly predicted, partial belief turns out to be a transitional phenomenon which therefore is neglected in the text.

[38] In terms of Fig. 2 this would mean several points of intersection between the reaction function and the diagonal.

[39] With the exception of the case where the agents expect the (equilibrium) price at which the market is cleared. Here their expectation coincides with the correct private prediction.

distribution).[40] Now the assumption of perfect competition includes that of perfect knowledge of all relevant variables.[41] If decisions are taken in the light of unwarranted expectations, misallocation of resources will result. The effect of correct public prediction is precisely that of removing unwarranted expectations by providing agents with the relevant information previously unknown to them. The correct public prediction coincides with the equilibrium position of the system.[42]

However, the foregoing is true only if perfectly competitive conditions prevail throughout the economy and if the public prediction includes all the variables appearing in the expectations of the agents. If either competition fails to be perfect or only part, but not all, of the relevant variables are covered by the prediction, the conclusion need no longer hold true. Enforcing perfectly competitive conditions in only some sectors of the economy and not in others may result in increased misallocation of resources rather than in a closer approximation to optimum allocation. Analogously, public prediction of some, but not all, of the relevant variables may push the system farther away from, rather than bring it closer to, its equilibrium position. We should generally expect that correct public prediction, like measures to eliminate market imperfections, will increase the economic welfare of the community. Yet we cannot be sure, unless perfect competition and perfect foresight are simultaneously achieved throughout the economy.[43]

Consider, for instance, the case where a certain decline of GNP and of the level of employment is publicly predicted. Because of the agents' (precautionary) action, the correctly predicted decline in economic activity may turn out to be greater than the decline that would occur if no prediction or only a private one were made. As a result, some individuals may actually be better off than they would have been otherwise: businessmen, for instance, may avoid loss of income by preventing inventory accumulation or by abandoning expansion projects which they would have started without the public prediction. Since, however, GNP is smaller than it would have been without the public prediction, the condition that somebody be better off and nobody worse off is not fulfilled and, furthermore, those who are better off cannot compensate those who are worse off.

Fortunately, complete ignorance of the future, on the one hand, and correct (and detailed) public prediction, on the other, are not the only alternatives. Depressions, unlike earthquakes and attacks of the common cold, do not hit suddenly. There are always signs and portents from which the economic agents

[40] For recent treatment cf. K. Boulding, "Welfare Economics," in *A Survey of Contemporary Economics*, II, ed. B. F. Healy (Homewood, 1952), 11–23; I. M. D. Little, *A Critique of Welfare Economics* (Oxford, 1950), chaps. viii and ix.

[41] F. H. Knight, *Risk, Uncertainty, and Profit* ("London School of Economics and Political Science Reprints," No. 16), pp. 20–21 and 76–80.

[42] This holds true also in an imperfectly competitive system. Under static conditions the position of general equilibrium of the system is usually considered to be uniquely determined. If several (equilibrium) solutions to the system exist, the one publicly predicted will materialize. Two possibilities exist here: (i) one of the equilibria is an *optimum optimorum* and will be chosen by the forecaster; (ii) all equilibria are welfare-indifferent. In this case the forecaster can choose between them only on the basis of some additional preference criteria, i.e., value-judgments. With regard to the problem of several optima and the *optimum optimorum*, cf. Boulding, *op. cit.*, pp. 27–28.

[43] Note that public prediction is not a prerequisite for the execution of policy which can be based on private prediction.

endeavor to read the shape of things to come. Thereby they may well overestimate the deflationary tendencies and—by acting according to their expectations—increase the severity of the downturn. By substituting knowledge for exaggerated fears, correct public prediction would, in this case, make the community better off than it would have been otherwise.

VII. CONCLUSION

It has been shown that, provided that correct private prediction is possible, correct public prediction is also conceptually possible. Two possibilities may be distinguished: (1) The public prediction does not affect the course of events because the agents are indifferent to or incapable of reacting to the public prediction.[44] In this case correct public prediction coincides with correct private prediction. (2) Agents react to public prediction, and their reaction alters the course of events. The reaction can conceptually be known and taken into account. It has been shown that the boundedness of the variables of the predictive system and the continuity over the relevant intervals of the functions relating the variables to each other are sufficient, though not necessary, conditions for the existence of correct public predictions. These conditions were found to be normally fulfilled in the world about which predictive statements are to be made.

The argument of this paper establishes the falsity of the proposition that the agents' reaction to public prediction necessarily falsifies all such prediction and that therefore social scientists may never hope to predict both publicly and correctly. But it demonstrates no more than that correct public prediction is possible if the possibility of correct private prediction is accepted. About the possibility of private prediction it has nothing to say. So, in the end, the major difficulties of predicting in the domain of social phenomena turn out to be those of private prediction.[45]

[44] This includes situations where the actions of individuals (can be known to) cancel out.

[45] The argument of this paper suggests that the agents' reaction may create difficulties for the formulation and execution of policy. The problems raised by this relationship between public prediction and policy do not belong within the scope of the present paper.

Errata

Page 469, column 1, line 2: "$P^{**} = D(q^{**})$" should read "$p^{**} = D(q^{**})$."

Page 469, figure 1: the point with abscissa p^* is incorrectly placed at the intersection of the S_t curve and the horizontal line at q^{**}. It should be placed at the intersection of the S curve and the horizontal line at q^{**}.

Page 470, column 1, 6 lines from the bottom: delete "per cent."

Page 472, figure 2: the label on the vertical axis "P and %" should read "p and %."

Page 472, figure 2: K in the lower left-hand corner should be lowercase and the others uppercase.

Page 473, column 1, line 1: "the right side $(k,K) - (K,K)$" should read "the right side $(K,k) - (K,K)$."

Page 477, column 1, footnote 40, line 3: "11-23" should read "1-36."

CONTENTS

Volume I Essays in Macroeconomics

Preface ix

Introduction xi

Part I. The Monetary Mechanism

1. "The Monetarist Controversy or, Should We Forsake Stabilization Policies?" *American Economic Review* 67 (March 1977): 1–19. 3
2. "Liquidity Preference and the Theory of Interest and Money," *Econometrica* 12 (January 1944): 45–88. Plus "Postscript" of the paper in *The Critics of Keynesian Economics,* edited by Henry Hazlitt, pp. 183–184. D. Van Nostrand Co., Inc., 1960. 23
3. "The Monetary Mechanism and Its Interaction with Real Phenomena," *Review of Economics and Statistics* 45 (February 1963):79–107. 69
4. "Liquidity Preference," *International Encyclopedia of the Social Sciences,"* edited by David L. Sills, vol. 9, pp. 394–409. Cromwell, Collier and McMillan, Inc., 1968. 98
5. "The Channels of Monetary Policy in the Federal Reserve-MIT-University of Pennsylvania Econometric Model of the United States," *Modelling the Economy,* based on papers presented at the Social Science Research Council's Conference on Economic Modelling, July 1972, edited by G. A. Renton, pp. 240–267. London: Heinemann Educational Books, 1975. 114
6. "Impacts of Fiscal Actions on Aggregate Income and the Monetarist Controversy: Theory and Evidence," (with Albert Ando, and with the assistance of J. Giangrande), *Monetarism,* edited by Jerome L. Stein, pp. 17–42. Studies in Monetary Economy, vol. 1. Amsterdam: North-Holland Pub. Co., 1976. 142

Part II. The Demand and Supply of Money and Other Deposits

7. "Central Bank Policy, the Money Supply, and the Short-Term Rate of Interest," (with Robert Rasche and J. Phillip Cooper), *Journal of Money, Credit, and Banking* 2 (1970): 166–218. 171

8. "The Dynamics of Portfolio Adjustment and the Flow of Savings Through Financial Intermediaries," *Savings Deposits, Mortgages, and Housing: Studies for the Federal Reserve-MIT-Penn Econometric Model,* edited by Edward M. Gramlich and Dwight M. Jaffee, pp. 63–102. Lexington Books, 1972. 224

Part III. The Term Structure of Interest Rates

9. "Innovations in Interest Rate Policy," (with Richard Sutch), *American Economic Review* 56 (May 1966): 178–197. Paper presented at the seventy-eighth annual meeting of the American Economics Association, Dec. 28–30, 1965. 267

10. "Debt Management and the Term Structure of Interest Rates: An Empirical Analysis," (with Richard Sutch), *Journal of Political Economy* 75, part 2 (August 1967): 569–589. Paper presented at the Conference of University Professors, The American Bankers Assoc., Sept. 19, 1966. 287

11. "Inflation, Rational Expectations and the Term Structure of Interest Rates," (with Robert J. Shiller), *Economica,* February 1973, pp. 12–43. 309

Part IV. The Determinants of Investment

12. "On the Role of Expectations of Price and Technological Change in an Investment Function," (with Albert K. Ando, Robert Rasche, and Stephen J. Turnovsky), *International Economic Review* 15 (June 1974): 384–414. 345

Part V. The Determinants of Wages and Prices

13. "A Generalization of the Phillips Curve for a Developing Country," (with Ezio Tarantelli), *Review of Economic Studies* 40 (April 1973): 203–223. 379

14. "New Development on the Oligopoly Front," *Journal of Political Economy* 66 (June 1958): 215–232. 400

15. "Targets for Monetary Policy in the Coming Year," (with Lucas Papademos), *Brookings Papers on Economic Activity* 1 (1975): 141–163. 419

Contents of Volumes 2 and 3 443

Acknowledgments 447

Name Index 449

CONTENTS

Volume 2 The Life Cycle Hypothesis of Saving

Preface ix

Introduction xi

Part I. Antecedent and Overview

1. "Fluctuations in the Saving-Income Ratio: A Problem in Economic Forecasting," *Studies in Income and Wealth*, vol. 11, pp. 371–402, 427–431. New York: National Bureau of Economic Research, 1949. Paper presented at Conference on Research in Income and Wealth. 3
2. "The Life Cycle Hypothesis of Saving Twenty Years Later," *Contemporary Issues in Economics*, edited by M. Parkin, pp. 2–36. Manchester University Press, 1975. 41

Part II. The Theory

3. "Utility Analysis and the Consumption Function: An Interpretation of Cross-Section Data," (with Richard Brumberg), *Post Keynesian Economics*, edited by Kenneth K. Kurihara, pp. 388–436. Rutgers University Press, 1954. 79
4. "Utility Analysis and Aggregate Consumption Functions: An Attempt at Integration," (with Richard Brumberg). MIT Press, 1979. 128
5. "Consumption Decisions Under Uncertainty," (with Jacques Drèze), *Journal of Economic Theory* 5 (December 1972): 308–335. 198

Part III. Empirical Verifications

6. "The 'Permanent Income' and the 'Life Cycle' Hypothesis of Saving Behavior: Comparison and Tests," (with Albert Ando), *Consumption and Saving*, vol. 2, pp. 74–108, 138–147. Wharton School of Finance and Commerce, University of Pennsylvania, 1960. 229

7. "The 'Life Cycle' Hypothesis of Saving: Aggregate Implications and Tests," (with Albert Ando), *American Economic Review* 53, part 1 (March 1963): 55–84. 275

8. "The Consumption Function in a Developing Economy and the Italian Experience," (with E. Tarantelli), *American Economic Review* 65 (December 1975): 825–842. 305

9. "The Life Cycle Hypothesis of Saving, the Demand for Wealth and the Supply of Capital," *Social Research* 33 (Summer 1966): 160–217. 323

10. "The Life Cycle Hypothesis of Saving and Intercountry Differences in the Saving Ratio," *Induction, Growth and Trade: Essays in Honour of Sir Roy Harrod,* edited by W. A. Eltis, M. FG. Scott, and J. N. Wolfe, pp. 197–225. Oxford: Clarendon Press, 1970. 382

Part IV. Policy Applications

11. "Long-run Implications of Alternative Fiscal Policies and the Burden of the National Debt," *Economic Journal* 71 (December 1961): 730–755. 415

12. "Monetary Policy and Consumption: Linkages via Interest Rate and Wealth Effects in the FMP Model," *Consumer Spending and Monetary Policy: The Linkages,* Conference Series No. 5, pp. 9–84. Federal Reserve Bank of Boston, June 1971. 442

Contents of Volumes 1 and 3 519

Acknowledgments 523

Name Index 525

ACKNOWLEDGMENTS

The author, editor, and The MIT Press wish to thank the publishers of the following essays for permission to reprint them here. The selections are arranged chronologically, with chapter numbers in brackets.

"The Predictability of Social Events," (with Emile Grunberg), *Journal of Political Economy* 62 (December 1954): 465–478. Copyright 1954 by the University of Chicago Press. [18]

"Production Planning over Time and the Nature of the Expectation and Planning Horizon," (with Franz E. Hohn), *Econometrica* 23 (January 1955): 46–66. Copyright 1955 by The Econometric Society. [15]

"Forecasting Uses of Anticipatory Data on Investment and Sales," (with H. M. Weingartner), *Quarterly Journal of Economics* 72 (February 1958): 23–54. Copyright 1958 by John Wiley & Sons, Inc. [17]

"The Cost of Capital, Corporation Finance and the Theory of Investment," (with Merton H. Miller), *American Economic Review* 48 (June 1958): 261–297. Copyright 1958 by the American Economic Association. [1]

The Role of Anticipations and Plans in Economic Behavior and Their Use in Economic Analysis and Forecasting, (with Kalman J. Cohen), Studies in Business Expectations and Planning, no. 4, pp. 9–11, 14–42, 81–96, 158–166. Bureau of Economic and Business Research, University of Illinois, January 1961. Copyright 1961 by the University of Illinois. [16]

"Dividend Policy, Growth and the Valuation of Shares," (with Merton H.

Miller), *Journal of Business* 34 (October 1961): 411–433. Copyright 1961 by The University of Chicago Press. [2]

"Corporate Income Taxes and the Cost of Capital: A Correction," (with Merton H. Miller), *American Economic Review* 53 (June 1963): 433–443. Copyright 1963 by the American Economic Association. [3]

"A Suggestion for Solving the International Liquidity Problem," (with Peter Kenen), *Banca Nazionale del Lavoro Quarterly Review,* no. 76 (March 1966): 3–17. Copyright 1966 by the Banca Nazionale del Lavoro. [10]

"Inflation, Balance of Payments Deficit and their Cure through Monetary Policy: The Italian Example," (with Giorgio LaMalfa), *Banca Nazionale del Lavoro Quarterly Review,* no. 80 (March 1967): 3–47. Copyright 1967 by the Banca Nazionale del Lavoro. [6]

"A Theory and Test of Credit Rationing," (with Dwight M. Jaffee), *American Economic Review* 59 (December 1969): 850–872. Copyright 1969 by the American Economic Association. [4]

Franco Modigliani and Hossein Askari, *The Reform of the International Payments System,* Essays in International Finance No. 89, September 1971. Copyright © 1971. Reprinted by permission of the International Finance Section of Princeton University. Pp. 3–28. [11]

"International Capital Movements, Fixed Parities, and Monetary and Fiscal Policies," *Development and Planning: Essays in Honor of Paul Rosenstein-Rodan,* edited by Jagdish Bhagwati and Richard S. Eckaus, pp. 239–253. Copyright 1972 by George Allen & Unwin, Ltd. [12]

"The International Transfer of Capital and the Propagation of Domestic Disturbances Under Alternative Payment Systems," (with Hossein Askari), *Banca Nazionale del Lavoro Quarterly Review,* no. 107 (December 1973): 3–18. Copyright 1973 by the Banca Nazionale del Lavoro. [13]

"Balance of Payments Implications of the Oil Crisis and How to Handle Them through International Cooperation," *1974 Economic Report of the President,* pp. 650–655. Washington, D. C.: U.S. Government Printing Office, 1974. Prepared statement for Hearings before the Joint Economic Committee, Congress of the United States, Ninety-third Congress, Second Session, Part 2, Feb. 19–22, 1974. [14]

"The 1974 Report of the President's Council of Economic Advisers: A Critique of Past and Prospective Policies," *American Economic Review* 64 (September 1974): 544–557. Copyright 1974 by the American Economic Association. [7]

"Some Economic Implications of the Indexing of Financial Assets with Special Reference to Mortgages," *The New Inflation and Monetary Policy* by Mario Monti, pp. 90–116. Copyright 1976 by Macmillan Publishing Co., Inc. [5]

"Monetary Policy for the Coming Quarters: The Conflicting Views," (with Lucas

Papademos), *New England Economic Review*, March/April, 1976, pp. 2–35. Copyright 1976 by the Federal Reserve Bank of Boston. [8]

Franco Modigliani and Tommaso Padoa-Schioppa, *The Management of an Open Economy with "100% Plus" Wage Indexation,* Essays in International Finance No. 130, December 1978. Copyright © 1978. Reprinted by permission of the International Finance Section of Princeton University. [9]

Name Index

Abel, Andrew, 221n
Ando, Albert K., 56n, 172n, 183n
Allen, F. B., 23, 24, 29n, 38
Anderson, O., Jr., 417
Andreatta, Nino, 221n
Antosiewicz, H., 398n, 417
Arrow, Kenneth J., 398n, 417
Askari, Hossein, 319n, 321–336, 329n, 336

Baffi, P., 100, 102, 123
Balderston, F. E., 417, 423
Barnett, Harold J., 452
Bassie, V. Lewis, 417
Bauer, R. K., 417
Bellman, Richard, 398n, 417
Bodenborn, Diran, 43n, 44n, 46n, 47n, 61
Bossons, John, 418
Boulding, Kenneth E., 473n
Bowman, Mary Jean, 369n
Branson, William, 321n, 323n
Bratt, Elmer Clark, 418, 454n
Bridge, Larry, 428
Bronfenbrenner, Jean, 418, 427, 440, 445n
Bruni, 150n
Burns, Arthur F., 187n, 211n, 217

Cagan, Phillip, 186n
Campalongo, A., 146n
Casarosa, C., 239n
Caves, Richard, 330n, 336
Charnes, A., 398n, 418
Chenery, Hollis B., 443
Christ, Carl F., 204n, 461n
Clendenin, John, 53n, 60n, 61, 62
Cohen, Kalman J., 368–416, 418, 423, 441n
Cohen, Morris, 418
Cooper, Richard, 177
Cooper, W. W., 398n, 418
Courant, Richard, 468n

Dale, Edwin, Jr., 217n
Daly, Donald J., 418
Dantzig, George, 398n, 418
Darcovitch, William, 418
Dean, Joel, 33n, 38
De Menil, George, 180n
Di Cani, John, 418
Dodd, David, 18n, 20n, 23n, 39, 53n, 61n, 62
Domar, Evsey, 3n
Donaldson, Gordon, 61n
Dornbusch, Rudiger, 186n, 221n
Dougall, H. E., 20n, 39
Drèze, J., 99, 123
Duesenberry, James S., 3n
Durand, David, 13n, 18n, 20–21, 21n, 22, 38, 47, 60n, 61n, 62, 64n
Dvoretzsky, A., 418

Eisner, Robert, 3n, 370n, 418–419, 427, 440, 445n

Eiteman, W. J., 19n, 38
Enzler, Jared, 180n, 185

Fels, E., 417
Ferber, Robert, 419, 439n
Festinger, Leon, 419
Firestone, O. J., 419
Fischer, Stanley, 109–110, 111–113, 123, 172n, 186n
Fisher, Franklin, 74n
Fisher, G. R., 61n, 62
Fitzgerald, William, 183n
Foss, Murray F., 419, 428n, 434
Freimer, Marshall, 74, 75n, 78n, 96
Friedman, Benjamin, 186n, 200n
Friedman, Milton, 216, 403n, 420
Friend, Irwin, 420, 427, 440, 445n
Fromm, G., 204n
Fuhrer, R. K., 417
Furst, H., 417

Goldfeld, Stephen M., 74n, 200n
Gordon, Myron, 33n, 38, 47n, 49n, 53–54, 61n, 62, 74, 75, 75n, 76n, 78, 78n, 96
Gordon, Robert J., 181n, 184, 185, 186n, 420
Graham, B., 18n, 20n, 23n, 39, 53n, 61, 62
Greenwald, Douglas, 422
Grunberg, Emile, 420, 461–474, 462n
Guthman, G., 20n, 39

Halm, George, 321n, 336
Hand, John, 90, 91, 96
Harkavy, Oscar, 55n, 61n, 62
Hart, Albert G., 369n, 420
Hartle, Douglas, 420
Hastay, Millard, 420, 439n
Healy, B. F., 473n
Hickman, B. C., 442, 452n
Hicks, J. R., 4n, 39, 230, 330, 373–376, 390–391, 395, 405, 421
Hirshleifer, Jack, 71n
Hodgman, Donald R., 74, 75n, 85, 96
Hoffman, A. J., 398n, 417, 421
Hohn, Franz, 347–367, 398n, 421, 423
Holt, Charles C., 421
Holt, Charles H., 367
Hultgren, Thor, 421
Hunt, Pearson, 5n, 39, 61n, 62

Izzo, Lucio, 221n

Jacobs, Walter, 398n, 421
Jaffee, Dwight M., 74–96, 76n
Johnson, L. R., 61n
Johnson, S. M., 398n, 418, 421
Juster, F. Thomas, 421

Kaldor, Nicholas, 134n
Kane, Edward J., 74n, 96
Karlin, Samuel, 398n, 417, 421
Karush, William, 398n, 421
Katona, George, 422
Katz, Daniel, 419
Kaufman, G. C., 107, 123
Keezer, Dexter M., 422
Kenen, Peter B., 263–277, 319n, 336
Keynes, John M., 8n, 39, 140, 144, 331n, 413
Kiefer, J., 418
Kindleberger, Charles P., 305–306, 321n, 332n, 335
Kisselgoff, Avram, 422, 443n
Klein, Lawrence R., 204n, 422, 454n
Knight, Frank H., 461n, 473n
Koopmans, Tjalling C., 56n
Kuh, Edwin, 146n

Labini, Sylos, 150n, 157n, 224–225
Lagrange, Joseph Louis, 349
La Malfa, Giorgio, 127–171
Lange, Oskar, 4n, 39, 374, 422
Lansing, J. B., 422
Lerner, Abba, 180, 185
Levine, Robert A., 422–423
Lintner, John, 3n, 35n, 39, 59n, 62
Little, I. M. D., 473n
Lutz, F., 4n, 39
Lutz, V., 4n, 39

Machlup, Fritz, 336
Malinvaud, Edmond, 90n, 96
Malkiel, Burton G., 74n, 85, 96
Manne, Alan S., 398n, 423
March, James G., 423
Markowitz, H., 111
Marschak, Jacob, 423
Matulis, Margaret, 422
Mellon, B., 398n
Merton, Robert C., 109–110, 111, 123, 172n
Metzler, Lloyd, 408, 423
Miller, Merton H., 3–38, 40–61, 59n, 62, 63–73, 73n, 74, 75n, 76n, 96
Modest, David, 186n
Modigliani, Andrea, 56n
Modigliani, Franco, 5n, 35n, 39, 43n, 59n, 62, 99, 123, 133n, 162n, 185n, 193n, 319n, 321n, 329n, 336, 398n, 418, 421, 422, 423–424, 424n, 441n, 443n
Moore, Geoffrey, 197n
Morin, Francois, 398n, 424
Morton, W. A., 13n, 21n, 39
Mosak, Jacob L., 374, 424
Mueller, Eva L., 424
Mundell, Robert, 324, 336
Muth, John F., 56n, 62, 421

Natrella, Vito, 419–420, 428n, 434n
Nilsson, K. G., 424

Nixon, Richard M., 321

Okun, Arthur M., 186n, 424
O'Meara, J., 61n, 62

Padoa-Schioppa, Tommaso, 220–259
Paladini, R., 239n
Papademos, Lucas, 186–219, 193n
Petersen, J. P., 417
Phelps, Edmund S., 186n, 213n
Phillips, A. W., 11, 146, 180, 188–189, 192, 202, 214n
Pogue, Gerald A., 74n
Pompidou, Georges, 286, 338
Poole, William, 100, 123, 186n, 210n

Robbins, Herbert, 468n
Robbins, S. M., 20n, 39
Roberts, Harry V., 33n, 39
Robinson, Joan, 180, 185
Roosa, Robert V., 74, 96

Sachs, Jeffrey, 221n
Samuelson, Paul, 172n
Sauerlender, Owen H., 424, 429n, 439n
Savage, Leonard J., 424
Scarf, Herbert, 398n, 417
Schild, A., 425
Scholtes, C., 109, 123
Schulte, W., 417
Schultz, George, 179, 338
Schwartz, Anna Jacobson, 216n
Schweiger, Irving, 425
Seifert, H., 470n
Shapiro, Eli, 33n, 39, 61n, 62
Simon, Herbert A., 367, 423, 425, 461n
Sitzia, Bruno, 221n
Smith, D. T., 37n, 39
Smith, Robert, 23, 24, 27n, 39
Sohmen, Egon, 330n, 336
Somers, H. M., 3n, 39

Tarantelli, Ezio, 99, 123
Theil, H., 425
Thompson, G. L., 56n
Threlfall, W., 470n
Thurow, Lester, 172n
Thygesen, Niels, 321n
Tinbergen, Jan, 425, 454n
Tobin, James, 111, 113, 425
Triffin, Robert, 263
Tucker, D. P., 102, 107, 123

Van Cleave, M., 53n, 62
Vining, R., 461n
Von Neumann, John, 468n

Wachter, M., 197n
Walter, James E., 46n, 47, 61n, 62
Weingartner, H. M., 424, 426–457
Williams, Charles, 61n, 62
Williams, John B., 13n, 39, 47n, 62
Williams, M., 5n, 39
Williamson, John, 321, 336
Willis, P., 94n
Withey, S. B., 422
Wolfowitz, J., 418
Wolfsteiner, M., 417

Yudin, E. B., 271n

Zeman, M., 5n, 35n, 39, 424